# The Rebel's Dilemma

*Economics, Cognition, and Society*

This series provides a forum for theoretical and empirical investigations of social phenomena. It promotes works that focus on the interactions among cognitive processes, individual behavior, and social outcomes. It is especially open to interdisciplinary books that are genuinely integrative.

Editor: Timur Kuran

Editorial Board: Ronald Heiner
Shelia Ryan Johansson

Advisory Board: James M. Buchanan
Albert O. Hirschman
Mancur Olson

*Titles in the Series*

Ulrich Witt, Editor. *Explaining Process and Change: Approaches to Evolutionary Economics*

Young Black Choi. *Paradigms and Conventions: Uncertainty, Decision Making, and Entrepreneurship*

Geoffrey M. Hodgson. *Economics and Evolution: Bringing Life Back into Economics*

Richard W. England, Editor. *Evolutionary Concepts in Contemporary Economics*

W. Brian Arthur. *Increasing Returns and Path Dependence in the Economy*

Janet Tai Landa. *Trust, Ethnicity, and Identity: Beyond the New Institutional Economics of Ethnic Trading Networks, Contract Law, and Gift-Exchange*

Mark Irving Lichbach. *The Rebel's Dilemma*

# The Rebel's Dilemma

Mark Irving Lichbach

*Ann Arbor*

THE UNIVERSITY OF MICHIGAN PRESS

1998   1997   1996   1995     4   3   2   1

*A CIP catalogue record for this book is available from the British Library.*

Lichbach, Mark Irving, 1951–
    The rebel's dilemma / Mark I. Lichbach.
       p.      cm. — (Economics, cognition, and society)
    Includes bibliographical references (p.      ) and indexes.
    ISBN 0-472-10532-9 (acid-free paper)
    1. Social action—Decision making. I. Title. II. Series.
HM281.L645  1994
302′.14—dc20                                      94-34624
                                                    CIP

*For Dad, who would have been proud*

"Although the rational behavior approach to revolutionary activity gives some insights into why revolutions occur, it does not generate a rich harvest of testable implications."

*Dennis C. Mueller*


"Gordon Tullock's (1971) economic theory of revolution is a good illustration of the limits of the purely economic approach when applied to group behavior in situations where there are incentives for free riding."

*Thrainn Eggertsson*


"In Olson's (1965) analysis of the problem of collective action many social scientists found a basis for reinterpreting social movements. Incorporation of this new perspective, however, has been unsystematic and mostly confined to generalities. Everyone assumes that collective action and social movements have a close relationship, but the nature of that relationship remains ill-defined."

*Gerald Marwell and Pamela Oliver*


"A version of rational choice theory — Olson's *The Logic of Collective Action* — . . . was particularly insensitive to politics."

*Sidney Tarrow*


"It is not clear that this is the best way of theorizing about either utopian or religious groups . . . Where nonrational or irrational behavior is the basis for a lobby, it would perhaps be better to turn to psychology or social psychology than to economics for a relevant theory."

*Mancur Olson*

# Preface

My book is about the interrelationship among three dilemmas: Hobbes's Dilemma, the Prisoner's Dilemma, and the Rebel's Dilemma.

## Hobbes's Dilemma

Thomas Hobbes, the seventeenth-century social philosopher and author of *Leviathan*, was the first great rational choice theorist. He assumed that human beings are motivated by self-interest, that men and women always pursue personal profit. The social consequence, accordingly, is that the natural state of human relations is one of perpetual war and strife, or in Hobbes's famous phrase, a state of "continuall feare, and danger of violent death; And the life of man, solitary, poore, nasty, brutish, and short" (Hobbes [1651] 1988, 186).

Why does this terrible social consequence, a war "of every man, against every man" (Hobbes [1651] 1988, 185), follow from the assumption of self-interest? People hold contradictory interests, so conflict appears inevitable. Yet different preferences can lead to mutually beneficial exchange. People have limited and unequal resources, so a struggle over resources seems unavoidable. Yet different endowments can lead to a mutually beneficial division of labor. Diverse interests and resources can thus lead rational actors to both cooperation and conflict, benign and malevolent interactions, the world of Adam Smith ([1776] 1976b) and the world of Thomas Hobbes ([1651] 1988). The assumption that "people have different interests and unequal resources" is insufficient to generate the conclusion that "rational actors are always at war."

The deduction lacks an important premise: "people use any means to pursue their interests." Such *realpolitik* includes force and fraud. As Parsons notes,

> In the absence of any restraining control men will adopt to this immediate end the most efficient available means. These means are found in the last analysis to be force and fraud. Hence a situation where every man is the enemy of every other, endeavoring to destroy or subdue him by

force or fraud or both. This is nothing but a state of war. (Parsons 1937, 90)

*Realpolitik* also includes power-seeking. Men and women seek power, because it allows one to command assistance in the pursuit of one's interests. Parsons again offers a classic formulation:

> Thus the concept of power comes to occupy a central position in the analysis of the problem of order. A purely utilitarian society is chaotic and unstable, because in the absence of limitations on the use of means, particularly force and fraud, it must, in the nature of the case, resolve itself into an unlimited struggle for power, and in the struggle for the immediate end, power, all prospect of attainment of the ultimate, what Hobbes called the diverse passions, is irreparably lost. (Parsons 1937, 93-94)

*Realpolitik* thus implies that human affairs are characterized by cleavage, conflict, chaos, and, ultimately, disintegration.

Hobbes thus raises two questions about the possibility for consensus, cooperation, stability, and, eventually, integration. First, how can a community, commonwealth, or state be created? Can voluntary cooperation through a social compact overcome anarchy and end the state of nature? Second, how can society, social order, and social organization be maintained? Must those who somehow escape anarchy inevitably return to the state of nature? In short, Hobbes wants to understand what binds the collectivity. *Leviathan* could have been entitled *Why People Don't Rebel*.

The theme of revolt against authority is an ancient one. Recall three biblical stories: Moses led the Hebrews in a slave revolt against the Egyptians; Korach and his followers then rebelled against Moses and Aaron; and finally, Moses never entered the Holy Land because he rebelled against the Lord.[1] Recall also that Machiavelli ([1514] 1961, 103), at least a century before Hobbes, instructed the Prince on how to prevent "internal subversion from his subjects." It is only after Hobbes, however, that Hobbes's Dilemma began to shape social philosophy and social science. In the eighteenth century, Adam Smith ([1759] 1976a) suggests a theory of moral sentiments and poses the question: "Given the division of labor, what holds society together?" In the nineteenth century, Hobbes's Dilemma became synonymous with the origin and growth of sociology. George Simmel (cited in Dahrendorf 1968, 133) asks "How is society possible?" Alexis De Tocqueville ([1856] 1955) wonders why the ancien régime fell. Max Weber ([1924] 1968, chap. 3) explores the legitimation of authority. Emile Durkheim ([1893] 1933) studies mechanical and organic solidarity. Karl Marx ([1895] 1964) examines class conflict and revolution. This line of thought culminated in the first half of the twentieth century with the great synthesis of Talcott Parsons (1937). His classic statement of Hobbes's Dilemma, as well as his solution to it, helped to define the discipline of sociology during the 1950s and 1960s.

After World War II interest in Hobbes's Dilemma produced an entire interdisciplinary field, conflict studies, an important goal of which is to study power seeking via force and fraud. A myriad of specific concerns evolved over the postwar period: workers' movements, fascism, communism, the U.S. civil rights movement, urban riots, student upheavals, military coups, national liberation struggles, guerrilla warfare, social revolution, and terrorism. Currently, new social movements and ethnic conflicts attract attention. Such negative cases to theories of social order are referred to here as *collective dissent*.

Many scholars have recognized the importance of Hobbes's Dilemma to social thought. Dahrendorf (1968, 133) points out that "it is easy to assert or assume that man is a social animal, but how social groups persist, and what holds them together, are questions that remain to be answered." Fireman and Gamson (1979, 36) note that "the existence of social order cannot be taken for granted. . . an explanation is required to account for the large numbers of people going about their daily lives in coordinated fashion." Hobbes's Dilemma, one might even argue, is not just *a big question* in social thought; it is *the big question*: "Surely there is no problem in the social sciences that is more important than that of explaining why people cooperate" (Elster 1985, 366).

## The Prisoner's Dilemma

The modern restatement of Hobbes's Dilemma is instructive. Men and women in a state of nature desire the public good (PG) of social order.[2] Peace is a blessing that all may enjoy. However, the collectivity finds itself in a Prisoner's Dilemma (PD). Everyone wants everyone else to voluntarily renounce the use of force and fraud. However, everyone also wants to unilaterally retain the force and fraud option. Free riding and PD behavior produce a war "of every man, against every man" that leaves everybody worse off.

Many have noted that Hobbes's "original situation of mankind" is a PG or PD problem (Barry 1965, 253; Rawls 1971, 269; Ullmann-Margalit 1977, 62-73). For example, Hechter (1988, 27) points out that "Parsons's (1937) famous discussion of the 'Hobbesian dilemma' reflects the fact that the social order is a common good constantly at risk of subversion by the action of free riders."

Hobbes's Dilemma shaped classical social thought. Similarly, the PG-PD scenario has shaped modern social thought. Mancur Olson (1965) was the pioneer. I will refer to his approach as the Collective Action (CA) research program.

## The Rebel's Dilemma

Given that Hobbes's Dilemma and the Prisoner's Dilemma are intimately connected, the first task of CA theories should be to explain collective dissent. The guiding questions of this study are therefore as follows: How is Hobbes's Dilemma of social order solved? How is society possible? How do states avoid endless rebellion against authority? In other words, how do rational people overcome their PD of a war "of every man, against every man" and achieve the PG of society?

To fashion an answer, suppose we take CA reasoning one step further and focus on the dissidents who wish to upset an existing social order. One solution to Hobbes's Dilemma then suggests itself: dissident groups have their own Hobbesian problem of order. They face a Rebel's Dilemma. Dissidents seek a PG of either capturing the state or forcing the existing authorities to redress their grievances. Rational dissidents will not voluntarily contribute to this PG. Unless free riding is overcome, however, the rebels are in a PD. No potential dissent will become an actual dissident; none will assist in either overturning the state or forcing the state to redress grievances.

If dissidents are unable to band together and press the state for a redress of grievances, social order results. If, however, dissidents are able to overcome the Rebel's Dilemma and mobilize as a collectivity, social disorder ensues. In Karl Deutsch's homey example (cited in Bell 1973, 90), "So long as the sailors on the *Bounty* could not coordinate their actions, Captain Bligh was irresistible. Once they managed to coordinate their efforts, Bligh was out of a job."

This approach to understanding collective dissent is suffused with paradox and irony. *Social order in a state results from social disorder in dissident groups. Social disorder in a state results from social order in dissident groups. Hence, to explain a state's social order, explain the social disorder of each of its dissident groups; and to explain cleavage and conflict between states and dissidents, explain consensus and cooperation among dissidents. The existence of conflict among social forces is therefore rooted in the existence of consensus within social forces. The absence of conflict among social forces is rooted in the existence of conflict within social forces.*

CA theories teach that the PG-PD problem is chronic. *When the Rebel's Dilemma is not solved, Hobbes's Dilemma does not arise.* CA theories also suggest many solutions to the PG-PD problem. *When the Rebel's Dilemma is solved, Hobbes's Dilemma quickly follows.* The CA approach thus uses the same framework to explain how both the state (i.e., cooperation) and dissident groups (i.e., conflict) arise.

## The Linkages

In sum: the CA approach to social theorizing emphasizes the PG and PD problems. The perspective directs us to study Hobbes's Dilemma, or collective dissent. This book seeks to solve Hobbes's Dilemma, "How is social order in a nation possible?", by raising a derivative question about the Rebel's Dilemma, "How is social order in a dissident group possible?" I answer this question by considering the Rebel's Dilemma as a Prisoner's Dilemma, a perspective that leads to an exploration of the solutions to the PD and PG problems offered by CA theories.

It is in this sense that I interrelate Hobbes's Dilemma, the Prisoner's Dilemma, and the Rebel's Dilemma. I also connect the CA research program and conflict studies, using the former to inform and illuminate the latter. Ideas about cooperation stimulate the development of ideas about conflict. A set of microassumptions about individuals, taken from the CA research program, are thus used to arrive at a set of macroconsequences about collective dissent, relevant to the substantive domain of conflict studies. Problem, theory, and application are thus bound together. CA theories illuminate conflict studies and in the process elucidate the Rebel's Dilemma. Conflict studies illuminate CA theories, and in the process elucidate the Prisoner's Dilemma. A fortuitous by-product of learning about the Rebel's Dilemma and the Prisoner's Dilemma is that we also learn about Hobbes's Dilemma.

## The Plan

The organization of this book is relatively straightforward. However, as is the case for this entire preface, some of the following terms and ideas are better appreciated after reading Chapter 1.

Part 1 elaborates on the themes introduced in this preface. Chapter 1 identifies the problems in the CA research program, and in conflict studies, with which this book wrestles. Chapter 2 discusses the book's approach to the problems.

Part 2 explores twenty-one sets of solutions to the Rebel's Dilemma. The solutions are divided into four categories. Chapter 3 examines Market solutions, which explore changes in the parameters of the canonical model of CA. The other three categories of solutions vary the context in which the baseline model is placed. Community solutions (chap. 4) focus on the way common belief systems solve Olson's Problem, Contractual solutions (chap. 5) focus on the way mutual agreement produces CA, and Hierarchy solutions (chap. 6) focus on how hierarchies structure CA.

Part 3 discusses the book's two principal themes. Chapter 7 explores the origins of various solutions to the Rebel's Dilemma and develops the theme that solutions are politics, or that regimes and oppositions struggle over CA solutions. Chapter 8 explores the outcomes of various solutions to the Rebel's Dilemma and develops the theme that solutions are pathologies, or that CA solutions bring both intended and unintended consequences.

I conclude my analysis in Part 4 with an appraisal of CA theories of collective dissent. Chapter 9 evaluates the contributions of CA theories to conflict studies and argues that solutions to the Rebel's Dilemma can answer some but not all questions about protests and rebellions. In short, CA theories have their limits. Chapter 10 offers some suggestions for improving CA theories of collective dissent by extending those boundaries. Some final thoughts appear in chapter 11.

This is a long book and readers might appreciate some suggestions about how to tackle it. The reader with the time and the interest can read the whole work. A reader who is rushed may get a sense of the argument by reading chapters 1, 2, 7-11, and a discussion of one solution (I suggest sect. 6.5.3, *Administer Selective Incentives*, which appeared as Lichbach 1994b). A reader who is even more pressed for time can read chapters 1 and 2, and the introductory and concluding paragraphs of chapters 3-11. An article length version appears as Lichbach (1994a). Those who want the executive summary should consult the first paragraph in chapter 2. Finally, those who want to scan the book should consult the analytical table of contents.

# Acknowledgments

When I started this book, I had hair. If I did not know so much about quasi-experimental design, I would attribute causal significance to my fateful decision to begin this project.

Some very fine people were kind enough to help me on my long journey. The political scientists who were interested enough to read all or part of *The Rebel's Dilemma* and/or its companion volume, *The Cooperator's Dilemma*, that considers Olson's Problem more generally, include Ted Gurr, Andrew S. McFarland, Michael D. McGinnis, Barry Rundquist, Peter C. Sederberg, Gerald Strom, Sidney Tarrow, John Williams, and Alan Zuckerman. The sociologists who provided important advice and encouragement include Jack A. Goldstone, Karl-Dieter Opp, James Rule, and Adam Seligman. The economists who offered valuable comments and suggestions include Timur Kuran, Mancur Olson, and Todd Sandler. I owe a special debt to Peter C. Sederberg (who read an early draft), Timur Kuran (who read a later version), and Alan Zuckerman (who read the penultimate manifestation) for their line-by-line critiques. My research assistants, Brad Abrahamson, Lisa Barre, David Lewis, Brian Sevier, and Sandy Straus, contributed helpful editorial assistance. My various editors and copy-editors, Ilene Cohen, Colin Day, Laurie Ham, and Christina Milton, helped whip the final version of the manuscript into shape. Diana Stahl helped prepare camera-ready copy. Needless to say, none of these people are responsible for any remaining flaws.

I also accumulated debts to two institutions. A sabbatical provided by the University of Illinois at Chicago during the 1987-88 academic year allowed me to begin this project. Research assistants provided by the University of Colorado during the 1991-94 academic years helped me to complete it.

Starting this book felt good, finishing it even better. Writing the book, however, required that I steal time from my wife, Faye, and from Sammi Jo, our baby girl. It was *their* time. I thank Faye and Sammi Jo for trying to remind me about the really important things in life. Faye's approach was to hug me and say, "Remember, X's and Y's don't love you like I do," or "Remember, your computer doesn't miss you when you're gone." Sammi Jo's approach was to run to daddy and shout "up-py." Their words often fell on deaf ears. I should have recalled *Ecclesiastes* (12:12): "Of making many books there is no end; and much study is a weariness of the flesh."

I dedicate this book to my father, Joseph Lichbach, who missed the *simcha* of Sammi Jo's birth. He now misses yet another *simcha*. My mother, my sister, and I miss him in ways that words cannot express. Sammi Jo will miss him in ways that she can never know.

# Contents

**Part 3  Themes**

# Exhibits

# Abbreviations

CA   Collective Action
DA   Deprived Actor
PD   Prisoner's Dilemma
PG   Public Good

# Part 1
# Introduction

CHAPTER 1

# The Problem Defined

This chapter defines the book's *problematique*. I offer an example of collective dissent (sect. 1.1) and show how the Deprived Actor (DA, sect. 1.2) research program tackles the problem. Attention then shifts to the Collective Action (CA, sect. 1.3) research program for a consideration of how applied theorists of conflict (sect. 1.4) and pure theorists of CA (sect. 1.5) have reacted to CA ideas.

## 1.1. An Example

To fix ideas, consider the following thought experiment. Jane Smith, an undergraduate at the University of Colorado, strongly supports the principle of diversity in employment. She also believes reports claiming that academic tenuring practices for minorities and women at the university have been discriminatory. Jane thus advocates a vigorous affirmative action program, one with quotas in various job categories for certain protected classes. The Cause, a campus civil rights organization, holds similar beliefs and advocates a similar program. Moreover, it has just announced that it plans to picket The Administration next Monday morning, starting at 9:00 A.M, and has called for volunteers. Question: will Jane join the demonstration, or will she wish the picketers well and stay home?

Students of conflict seek to explain Jane's (non)participation in the protest demonstration in terms of both general premises about participation in collective dissent and conditions unique to Jane's situation. In other words, students of conflict have studied such specific situations by posing a more general question: why do individuals participate in collective dissent? By *collective* is meant that individuals participate in some group activity. By *dissent* is meant that the individuals' objectives are to change government institutions, policies and/or personnel. Dissent also involves means that are somewhat unconventional. Participants go beyond voting and interest group activities; that is, they typically threaten and/or employ physical coercion and/or other illegal activities. The boundaries of this concept have always been ill defined (Zimmermann 1983, chap. 2; Taylor and Jodice 1983, chap. 2). The core political behaviors under scrutiny are clearer, however. They consist of the negative cases to theories of social order mentioned in the preface (page xi). [1]

*The purpose of this book is to explore the implications of the CA research program for the major puzzles and problems of the causes, courses, and consequences of collective dissent.* I also intend to evaluate, in both Lakatos's (1970) and Popper's (1968) senses, how well the CA research program explains these major riddles in conflict studies. The remainder of this chapter elaborates upon my purposes.

## 1.2. The Deprived Actor Research Program

The DA research program provides the traditional answer to the question of whether Jane will participate in the demonstration. This approach, whose foremost proponent is Ted Gurr (1970), maintains that deprivation produces discontent and that discontent, in turn, produces dissent. Collective dissent is therefore ultimately caused by people's preferences, beliefs, and attitudes towards personal deprivations.

DA theories have suggested many specific psychological processes (both cognitive and emotional) that turn deprivations, such as the discrimination perceived by Jane, into dissent. Hence, Jane may join the demonstration because she experiences any one or more of the following: frustration over wants and necessities which she cannot satisfy; a lack of just deserts, or a discrepancy between what she felt entitled to and what she actually got; a lack of equity and distributive justice because her inputs into the system have far exceeded her outputs from it; relative deprivation vis-a-vis more advantaged groups; alienation from government and a belief that the government is illegitimate because of policy dissatisfaction and lack of system responsiveness; lack of support for government due to political cynicism and the absence of political trust; class or racial consciousness; or radicalism and the identification with dissident groups that promise to end the deprivations (Zimmermann 1983, chap. 4). Whichever specific psychological processes are involved, DA theorists expect that deprivations generate grievances about patterns of authority; that grievances generate identification with similarly deprived actors; and that these deprivations, grievances, and identifications generate the anger that eventually produces behavioral dissent.

DA theorists such as Gurr (1970) therefore interpret the thought experiment posed earlier as follows: if the job discrimination is severe, Jane's grievances will be profound, her sympathies for The Cause and its concerns will be deep, and she will become angry enough to join the demonstration.

While one might question the specific psychological processes involved, the general perspective offered by the DA approach seems beyond dispute. It is obvious, is it not, that deprived people become frustrated, that frustrated people become angry, and that angry people often strike out at those responsible for their frustrations?

## 1.3. The Collective Action Research Program

The challenge to the truisms of DA theories was first formalized in Mancur Olson's (1965) seminal work, *The Logic of Collective Action*. The most widely cited application of Olson's argument to protest is Gordon Tullock's (1971a) "The Paradox of Revolution." Both works challenge the assumptions made by DA theories about a rebel's motivation, and consequently dispute the conclusion that individual deprivation eventually leads to collective dissent. I call this approach the CA research program.

To understand the CA alternative to DA theories, reconsider Jane's problem. Jane and all of The Cause's sympathizers may choose to Demonstrate (D) or to Stay Home (S). Suppose Jane ponders the possible outcomes of her two choices, given what she expects Everyone Else to do. Outcomes may be represented in the 2x2 matrix shown in Exhibit 1.

|  |  | Everyone Else's Choices | |
|---|---|---|---|
|  |  | Demonstrate | Stay Home |
|  | Demonstrate | Benefits = Diversity<br>Costs = Time Lost | Benefits = 0<br>Costs = Time Lost |
| Jane's Choices | Stay Home | Benefits = Diversity<br>Costs = 0 | Benefits = 0<br>Costs = 0 |

Exhibit 1. Jane's Dilemma

If $D$ represents "Demonstrate" and $S$ represents "Stay Home," the strategy combination "Jane chooses to Demonstrate ($D$) while Everyone Else chooses to Stay Home ($S$)" is denoted $(D,S)$.

The matrix indicates that Jane must weigh four logically possible outcomes.

*(D,D).* Jane chooses to Demonstrate and Everyone Else also chooses to Demonstrate. If all of its sympathizers choose to Demonstrate, The Cause will be politically powerful. Jane thus assumes that The Administration will end job discrimination, provide additional academic positions for minorities, and uphold the principle of diversity. However, Jane must bear a personal cost. She has spent her valuable time at the demonstration.

*(S,D).* Jane chooses to Stay Home but Everyone Else chooses to Demonstrate. If all of its sympathizers *except* Jane choose to Demonstrate, The Cause's loss of strength is imperceptible. Jane thus continues to assume that

The Administration will provide additional academic jobs for minorities and uphold the important principle of diversity. However, Jane now bears no personal cost.

(S,S). Jane chooses to Stay Home and Everyone Else also chooses to Stay Home. The Cause is now powerless. Jane thus assumes that The Administration will provide no additional jobs for minorities. However, Jane bears no personal cost.

(D,S). Jane chooses to Demonstrate but Everyone Else chooses to Stay Home. The Cause is now powerless *except* for Jane, who now assumes that The Administration will provide no additional jobs for minorities. Much to her dismay, moreover, Jane must bear a personal cost that arises from the time she has spent demonstrating. (The campus police will not react kindly to Jane's solo attempt to picket the dean's office; they are much kinder and gentler when hundreds of students block the office.)

Now the key question: given the assumptions made in the above model of CA, will rational Jane participate in the demonstration? The answer comes in two parts.

Consider a normative analysis of the situation. Jane and Everyone Else believe that they are better off if all Demonstrate rather than all Stay Home. Mutual cooperation is in the interest of every member of The Cause, including Jane.

Now consider a positive analysis of the situation. Everyone Else has two choices. First, suppose Everyone Else Demonstrates. Jane then prefers to Stay Home rather than to Demonstrate. The benefits of diversity will come regardless of whether she protests, and protest is, after all, costly. Second, suppose Everyone Else Stays Home. Jane still prefers to Stay Home, rather than to Demonstrate. The benefits of diversity are unavailable, regardless of whether she protests, and protest is, once again, costly. In sum, Jane's beliefs about Everyone Else's choice is irrelevant. She always chooses to Stay Home. Since a similar analysis holds for each of The Cause's sympathizers, all will Stay Home. No one will Demonstrate. The Administration is safe, and the dean can conduct business as usual.

Accordingly, rebels like Jane face what has been called a Prisoner's Dilemma (PD). The normative and positive analyses of their situation conflict. Mutual cooperation (i.e., all choose to Demonstrate) is better for Jane and Everyone Else than mutual noncooperation (i.e., all choose to Stay Home). However, individualistically rational behavior produces mutual noncooperation.

Jane's predicament has also been called a public goods (PG) problem. The costs of participation are high and involve time, money, and the risk of injury. The benefit of participation, if the group is successful, is a PG that can be enjoyed by anyone, regardless of his or her (non)participation.[2] Even if she does not protest, Jane benefits from ending job discrimination, the provision of additional academic jobs for minorities, and the principle of diversity. Hence, each of The Cause's sympathizers wants to free ride on the contributions of others; that is, everyone hopes that someone else will absorb the costs, yet everyone wishes to share in the benefits.

In sum, all of the cards seem stacked against large-scale protests and rebellions. On the benefit side: (1) a successful outcome to a revolt is a low-probability event, and hence, the revolt is a risky undertaking; (2) a successful outcome to a revolt is almost independent of any one individual's participation; (3) the benefits of a successful revolt are also independent of any one individual's participation. On the cost side: (1) rebels are typically interested in many social causes; (2) rebels have many personal demands on their time that have priority — their opportunity costs include, for example, forgone wages; (3) participation is often quite costly and dangerous since governments maim or murder their enemies. Thus, rebels confront possibly disastrous private costs and uncertain public benefits. Moreover, the benefits provide no incentive to act and the costs provide every incentive not to act. Rebels have everything to gain and nothing to lose by staying home. Unless this CA problem is somehow overcome, rational people will never rebel — rebellions, that is, require irrationality.[3] I call the general tragedy confronting all participants in CA the Cooperator's Dilemma (Lichbach forthcoming). I call the specific tragedy confronting dissidents the Rebel's Dilemma.

What has been the reaction to Olson's ideas? The next two sections position my study in the collective action and collective dissent literatures.

### 1.4. The Reaction to Olson: Applied Students of Collective Dissent

Students of conflict have been intrigued by Olson's reasoning and have attempted to wed CA ideas and conflict studies. The marriage brokers were sociologists, political scientists, and economists.

Sociologists and political scientists have utilized the general rational actor aspect of Olson's approach. Many (Zimmermann 1983, 603–4, fn. 47) define political violence in terms of rational action. Thus, some definitions of political violence emphasize its bargaining aspects: "*acts of disruption, destruction, injury whose purpose, choice of targets or victims, surrounding circumstances, implementation, and/or effects have political significance, that is, tend to modify the behavior of others in a bargaining situation that has consequences for the social system*" (Nieburg 1969, 13, emphasis in original). Such reasoning has also influenced explanations of rebel's motivations; nonelites, many argue, also calculate costs and benefits and pursue rational political action (Armstrong 1976, 394). Tarrow (1989, 8, 16), for one, suggests that people protest when other ways of achieving their interests and values are less productive or when the gains from protest outweigh the costs. Finally, rational actor reasoning has influenced general theories of conflict. Widely cited efforts by sociologists include Oberschall (1973), Zald and McCarthy (1990), Korpi (1974), Gamson (1990), Tilly (1978), and Blalock (1989).

Some sociologists and political scientists have also confronted CA theories more directly. Charles Tilly (1978), among others, rejects the core CA assumption of individual rationality (that is, a person participates in collective dissent when his or her individual benefits exceed the individual costs) and posits instead collective rationality. As Gamson (1990, 138) puts it, "The collective goals of political actors rather than the personal goals of members are assumed to be the relevant part of an explanation of political behavior." Tilly thus assumes that a person will participate in collective dissent when his or her group's benefits exceed the group's costs. Tilly's inquiry is therefore guided by the central Marxian question: "How and why do groups in society come into conflict over valued conditions and positions?" It is less influenced by the central CA question: "Why do rational people rebel?" Tilly, in short, does not explain how the Rebel's Dilemma is solved. Rather than using the CA research program, he develops an alternative to it. Tilly's model of group conflict thus combines rational actor theory and class theory, or perhaps as he would put it, Adam Smith and Karl Marx. Gamson (1990) and Zald and McCarthy (1990) proceed similarly, combining a rational actor perspective with organizational theory.

Thus, studies by sociologists and political scientists did acknowledge the rebel's PG–PD problem. But Tilly, Gamson, and others vigorously disputed the assumptions behind CA theories, and thus never took the Rebel's Dilemma seriously. They merely borrowed one or two of its key insights (e.g., selective incentives, entrepreneurs) and for inspiration looked elsewhere (e.g., Marxist theory, organizational theory).

With their half-hearted attitude toward the CA approach, the efforts by sociologists and political scientists had two negative consequences for conflict studies. First, the bulk of the ideas available in the CA research program were ignored. Sociologists and political scientists never fully exploited the potential of CA theories for explaining domestic political conflict. As Marwell and Oliver (1984, 3, emphasis in original) put it, "Although Olson's work has thus had a general impact on social movement theory, *most* of his analysis is only marginally considered in that literature." For example, no sociologist or political scientist has ever examined the full range of post-Olson solutions to the free-rider problem that have appeared in CA studies.

Second, the bulk of the implications of CA thought for collective dissent have been unexplored. Neither Gamson, Tilly, nor any of their followers ever made much heuristic use of the theory. Marwell and Oliver's (1984, 4) comments are, again, to the point:

Despite near universal recognition by this decade's scholars of social movements of the importance of collective action theory, little systematic work has been done to link collective action theory to social movements theory. Most social movements scholars simply cite Olson concerning the problematic of collective action. Only a few . . . have developed formal models for particular collective action situations and have discussed their implications for certain problems of mobilization.

In short, sociologists and political scientists have never systematically developed the implications of the CA approach for conflict studies. The contrast with Gurr's (1970) work is stark. Whereas he attempted to derive propositions from DA assumptions that integrated numerous middle-level hypotheses and stylized facts about domestic political conflict, Tilly never ventured that far into conflict studies.[4]

Where do the economists stand in these matters? Several economists and their followers in political science and sociology have offered models of collective dissent based on rational actor reasoning (Lichbach 1992, 345–47). Some have argued and/or modeled how externalities and PGs (Olson 1969), positional or status goods (Shubik 1971), and the zero-sum tradeoff along a contract curve (Hirshleifer 1987) produce conflict. There are utility maximization models of the decision calculus of regimes (Lichbach 1984; Wintrobe 1990) and of oppositions (Lichbach 1987). And some have proposed game theoretic models of conflict over economic inequality (Lichbach 1990), the interaction between states and oppositions (Sandler, Tschirhart, and Cauley 1983), and the emergence of consociational institutions to contain ethnic conflict (Tsebelis 1990, chap. 6). None of these efforts confront Olson's Problem, however. Rational choice models, though they are, they do not address the Rebel's Dilemma.

Some economists and their followers in political science and sociology have offered models to capture Olson's insights (Lichbach 1992, 345–47). Some expected utility models formulate a dissident's choice as a binary one: people choose dissent over nondissident activities when the expected utility of the former is greater than the expected utility of the latter. This framework has been applied to rebellion by Tullock (1971a), DeNardo (1985, 52–54), Muller and Opp (1986), and Opp (1989). Other expected utility models formulate a dissident's choice as a continuous one: rebels choose a continuous level of contributions (e.g., time spent) so as to maximize their expected utility. This framework has been applied to international terrorism (Sandler and Scott 1987), hijacking of U.S. aircraft (Landes 1978), riots (Chalmers and Shelton 1975; Coleman 1978; Mason 1984), government violence (Frohlich and Oppenheimer 1973), and revolution (Mueller 1989, 173–75). PD models (e.g., Buchanan 1979) also exist.

Unlike the previously cited studies, these works by economists and their followers do take the rebel's PG–PD problem seriously.[5] Unless the free rider problem is overcome (e.g., by selective incentives), they suggest that a rational person will ordinarily not rebel. Despite these strengths, however, such studies still manifest some of the limitations found in the sociological studies cited above. First, most ideas from CA theories have not been explored — no economist has ever examined the full range of post-Olson solutions to the free rider problem. Second, many of these authors were either unfamiliar with or unconcerned about the substantive and theoretical work done in the field of conflict studies. Economists have generally made no attempt to address the major puzzles and problems in that field. The bulk of the implications of the CA research program for collective dissent, again, went unexplored.

In sum, most sociologists, political scientists, and economists who have studied conflict have ignored much of Olson and his follower's work, preferring instead to examine general rational actor arguments, rather than the specific Rebel's Dilemma. Those who apply Olson's insights do so in limited ways: they neither use all that much of the theory nor explore all that much of the application. Thus, sociologists and political scientists have mostly ignored the CA research program (the theory), while economists have mostly ignored conflict studies (the substance).

The marriage between the CA research program and conflict studies, in short, has largely failed. Two sympathetic sociologists, Marwell and Oliver (1984, 2) comment that

> in Olson's (1965) analysis of the problem of collective action many social scientists found a basis for reinterpreting social movements. Incorporation of this new perspective, however, has been unsystematic and mostly confined to generalities. Everyone assumes that collective action and social movements have a close relationship, but the nature of that relationship remains ill-defined.

Economists generally agree with such skeptical appraisals of what their theories have brought to the field of conflict studies. A presumably sympathetic economist, Mueller (1989, 175), observes that "although the rational behavior approach to revolutionary activity gives some insights into why revolutions occur, it does not generate a rich harvest of testable implications." Another sympathetically inclined economist, Eggertsson (1990, 73–74), suggests that Gordon Tullock's (1971) economic theory of revolution is a good illustration of the limits of the purely economic approach when applied to group behavior in situations where there are incentives for free riding."

Even Olson (1965, 161–62), alas, apparently believes that participation in "mass movements" is better explained by social psychological theories and collective behavior theories than by his own approach. But he waffles on the point. On the one hand, he is confident about the scope of his theory. He refers (1965, 162) to mass movements "which, incidentally, are usually not very massive," and maintains (1965, 162, fn. 97) that his theory fits the amoral familism culture discovered by Banfield (1958). He (1965, 161, fn. 94) goes so far as to suggest that his theory could explain utopian mass movements: "Even large groups that work for a utopia could have a reason for acting as a group, even in terms of the theory offered here . . . If the benefit that would come from establishing a utopia is infinite, it could be rational even for the member of a large group to contribute voluntarily to the achievement of the group goal (the utopia)." However, he is clearly uncomfortable in pushing this last point: "It is not clear that this is the best way of theorizing about either utopian or religious groups" (Olson 1965, 162, fn. 94). He is, ironically, quick to express confidence that an alternative approach to collective dissent, the one that I have called DA theories, would work where his own approach fails:

> Where nonrational or irrational behavior is the basis for a lobby, it would perhaps be better to turn to psychology or social psychology than to economics for a relevant theory . . . The adherents of "mass movements" are usually explained in terms of their "alienation" from society. This alienation produces a psychological disturbance or disequilibrium. The support for "mass movements" can accordingly be explained mainly in psychological terms, though the psychological disturbances are in turn related to various characteristics of the social structure. A fanatic devotion to an ideology or leader is common in mass movements, and many of these movements are often said to be on the "lunatic fringe." This sort of lobby is more common in periods of revolution and upheaval, and in unstable countries, than it is for stable, well-ordered, and apathetic societies that have seen the "end of ideology." (Olson 1965, 161–62)

Olson (1990, 1991a,1991b,1991c, 1991d) subsequently regained confidence in his theory and produced a series of analyses of protest and rebellion that make very imaginative use of his seminal insights.[6]

### 1.5. The Reaction to Olson: Pure Theorists of Collective Action

While students of conflict were meeting Olson's ideas with disinterest, disappointment, and disillusion, CA theorists were busily elaborating Olson's basic argument. It is to this happier story that I now turn.

The obvious challenge to Olson is that he is simply wrong: people quite often rebel, sometimes in very large numbers. CA theorists tackle this problem by considering the two logically possible categories of people. There are, first, those with grievances who do not rebel. By far the larger category, this group represents at least ninety-five percent of aggrieved people, at least ninety-five percent of the time, in at least ninety-five percent of the places. In short, potential rebels mostly do not rebel, even when it would be in every rebel's interest to do so. This category, which critics tend to ignore, is consistent with Olson's ideas. There are, second, those who do rebel. While this is by far the smaller category, one cannot ignore the fact that some people at some times in some places are able to overcome the Rebel's Dilemma and rebel. This is referred to as the *paradox* or *puzzle* of CA.

Thus, the canonical conclusion drawn from the prototypical case must be taken seriously. The central CA question is, How *is* the Rebel's Dilemma solved? Put otherwise, under what circumstances will cooperation emerge? What induces an individual to make a sacrifice to obtain a PG? And not only CA theorists but also many other researchers in conflict studies raise a similar question. From their various theoretical and practical perspectives, DA theorists,[7] Marxists,[8] Weberians,[9] and agenda setters[10] all seek the causes of political unity. All want to determine what factors influence the ability of different groups to form and people to come together in defense of their common economic, social, and political interests.

CA theorists of course proceed in their own distinctive way to solve the Rebel's Dilemma, that is, to explain deviations from Olson's General Law of Collective Inaction. Their analysis rests on four assumptions. (1) Individuals are utility maximizers; given the alternative states of their environment, they evaluate the outcomes of their various possible actions. (2) Political demands are typically for a PG; if job discrimination is ended, for example, people can enjoy the principle of diversity regardless of whether they participate in the demonstration. (3) The group of potential sympathizers is very large; there may be thousands of individuals interested in the principles espoused by a dissident group. (4) Large groups have the power to affect government policy; however, each person's individual participation has no discernible impact on the group's success at winning adoption of its policy.

For CA to occur, the Rebel's Dilemma must be solved by revising one or more of these and other assumptions. Thus, one can make the assumptions more realistic or complicated by considering the potential dissident's choice among more than two tactics (e.g., staying home, voting, lobbying, and demonstrating), given more than two expectations about the behavior of others (i.e., the *number* of other participants), and given some uncertainty about the outcome of the actions he or she takes. Most CA theorists, accordingly, have attempted to modify the CA research program by proposing solutions to the free rider problem. To explain why *rational* people might participate in CA, they modify the assumptions behind the basic PG–PD game (Lichbach forthcoming, chap. 2). There are presently more than two dozen distinct solutions to Olson's Problem.

It should now be clear that DA and CA theorists face opposite tasks. Given the ubiquity of grievances, for Gurr (1970) the *problematique* is to explain why people do not rebel. He thus elaborates a set of structural conditions that must be present before anger can be turned into rebellion. Given the ubiquity of free riding, Olson's (1965) *problematique* is to explain why people do rebel. He thus elaborates the selective incentives and federal group solutions to the CA problem.

In sum, students of conflict found the marriage of theories of CA with problems of collective dissent to be a failure, because few CA ideas were actually used and few substantive issues actually studied. This deficiency is ironic because pure theorists of CA have elaborated Olson's basic insight into more than two dozen different solutions to the PG–PD game. The purpose of this book is to remedy this sad state of affairs and bring the richness of the CA research program to bear on conflict studies. The next chapter outlines the approach.

## CHAPTER 2

# The Approach Adopted

While Olson's Problem teaches that extensive collective dissent is improbable, the many solutions to the CA problem, and reality, teach that some collective dissent is probable. Solutions to the Rebel's Dilemma are thus the principal focus of *The Rebel's Dilemma*. These solutions are divided into Market, Community, Contract, and Hierarchy approaches. I am interested in why and what if a solution is adopted. *Why* questions revolve around the conditions under which one or more combinations or sets of solutions are adopted. They involve us in the politics of collective dissent, or in the struggle over the Rebel's Dilemma. *What if* questions revolve around the conditions under which solutions produce intended and unintended consequences. They lead us to the pathologies of collective dissent, or the organizational repercussions of group mobilization and group success. In short, this book explores where and when solutions to the Rebel's Dilemma are ignored or adopted, and effective or counterproductive. *Why* and *What if* questions are important because CA solutions are major features of collective dissent. The probability of winning, risk taking behavior, dissident self-government, dissident entrepreneurship, and dissident organizational structures, for example, are some of the significant conflict issues that both rational actor and deprived actor theorists believe require explanation. The focus on CA processes, in particular, establishes the microfoundations of the rational actor, or resource mobilization, approach to conflict studies, because CA processes are the *modus operandi* or mechanisms through which dissident groups act. While the potential of the approach is great, there is an analytical flaw: each solution to the Rebel's Dilemma offers a logically incomplete explanation of collective dissent. There is also an empirical flaw: CA theories do not produce a general theoretical statement of the etiology of conflict that one may use to predict protest and rebellion.

Five principal themes underlie this approach: the improbability of extensive collective dissent, the probability of some collective dissent, CA solutions as politics, CA solutions as pathologies, and the appraisal of CA theories of collective dissent.

## 2.1. The Improbability of Extensive Collective Dissent:
## The Rebel's Dilemma

The conventional wisdom, based on DA theories, is that "people who 'really care' about an issue can . . . overcome all difficulties" (Nagel 1987, 50) and participate in groups dedicated to solving the problem. In short, deprivations and grievances are necessary and sufficient for collective dissent.

CA theories challenge this idea. The benefits derived from changing unpopular policies or regimes rebound to all members of a dissident group, including those who have not participated in the group's activities. The costs of participation, however, are paid only by those who participate. Some costs (e.g., wages forgone at an income-producing job) could be minimal. Other costs (e.g., jail, injury, or even death) are maximal. The level of costs depends on an unknown: the regime's response strategy. But if the individual receives the benefits regardless of whether he or she participates, why participate and pay *any* costs? This reasoning holds even when all rebels benefit if all contribute. The consequence is clear: no invisible hand moves dissidents to remedy their grievances. Unpopular policies remain in force and unpopular governments remain in power.

In short, "rationality *requires* inaction" (Buchanan 1979, 66, emphasis in original). Those with a reason to make a revolution do not always make their revolution. Most rebels do not actually rebel. As Olson (1990, 13) puts it, "If most human beings would really rather be dead than red, then no society would be red. But in the real world most individuals care much more about their own welfare and survival than about public policy or the ideology of the society." Extensive collective dissent, therefore, is improbable.[1] Moreover, academics are not the only ones who understand this. Rebels themselves are quite aware of the collective inaction problem. Thomas Jefferson,[2] Saul Alinsky,[3] and Karl Marx[4] each articulated ideas that are strikingly similar to Olson's.

The CA research program thus teaches us that private vice does not necessarily beget public virtue. The improbability of extensive collective dissent is manifested in four important ways. First, in spite of the common interests of its potential members, a dissident group does not readily, naturally, and automatically coalesce. Many potential dissident groups never form; potentially common resources remain unpooled. Second, even if a dissident group does form, many potential supporters do not join. With self-exclusion from politics, or political apathy, passivity, and inertia the norm, most dissident groups fail to move beyond a narrow core of supporters. Their major problem is that dissidents try to free ride and let others do the dirty work of rebelling. Third, even if a dissident group does form, those who join participate in few activities. Most neither attend the group's meetings, nor join its marches, nor pay their membership dues (e.g., see Schwartz 1976, 121–25, on the Southern Farmers' Alliance). Finally, even if a dissident group does form, even if potential dissidents do join, and even if members do participate in the group's activities, low-cost and short-lived activities predominate. CA, if relatively costless, may indeed occur; CA that is costly does not (sect. 3.2). CA, if undertaken on a short-term basis, may indeed occur; CA that requires long periods of time does not. Thus, Tarrow (1991, 15) refers to "the exhaustion of mass political involvement" and Ross and Gurr (1989, 414) refer to political "burnout." Given that most people's commitments to particular causes face inevitable decline, most dissident groups are ephemeral, most dissident campaigns brief. Information on terrorist campaigns collected by Gurr (1979, 30, table 3) confirms this expectation.

Following from these four propositions, one may distinguish five levels of involvement in a dissident group:

> The *constituents* (target community or social base) are those members of the nation's population whom the group claims to represent by its activities. *Sympathizers* are those constituents who support the dissident group's cause because they believe they will benefit from the PG sought. In addition to having the same grievances as the group, they also typically accept the principal strategies and tactics of the group. *Members* are those sympathizers who formally join the organizational apparatus of the dissident group; they usually support the group in some material fashion. *Activists* are those members who are actually involved in the dissident group. They participate in at least some of the group's activities at least some of the time. *Militants* are those activists who are full-time employees of the group or who are totally involved in it. They are to be distinguished from the part-timers, or those who devote most of their working hours to activities outside the group. Militants include full-time workers (troops and administrators), leaders, and operations people.

CA theorists expect that in any dissident group, one will find many more constituents than sympathizers, sympathizers than members, members than activists, and activists than militants.[5] In short, many more people will express their support for a dissident group in polls than will contribute resources to the group. *Checking member/sympathizer, activist/sympathizer, and militant/sympathizer ratios is thus the first step in studying the Rebel's Dilemma.[6] The prediction is that the five percent rule holds* (sect. 1.5; Lichbach forthcoming, chap. 1).[7]

These five aspects of the first CA problem have clear consequences: dissident movements attract a very small percentage of the total population.[8]

Most people who theorists and activists think *should* and *will* participate in collective dissent do not join dissident groups. Movements in countries where the overwhelming majority of the people detest the ruling elite are not exceptions. Movements that turn out to be successful also do not deviate from the rule.[9]

In sum, protests lack protesters, rebellions lack rebels, and revolutions lack revolutionaries. Active dissidents are a small minority in *all* types of collective dissent. The evidence is overwhelming that the five percent rule holds for neighborhood organizations,[10] community conflicts,[11] urban rebellions,[12] student revolts,[13] trade unions,[14] guerrilla wars,[15] and rural populist movements.[16] Rebels, moreover, are a small minority in *all* major instances of collective dissent. The rule also holds for the American,[17] Russian,[18] Algerian,[19] and Cuban[20] revolutions, and several fascist revolutions.[21]

The evidence confirming the existence of the first CA problem, at least with respect to individual participation in collective dissent, is therefore overwhelming. Since the percentage of people mobilized into collective dissent is almost always small, the study of collective dissent involves the study of minorities and not the majority, exceptions and not the rule.

This first CA problem also has an impact at the organizational level: cooperation among factions of a single dissident group and among separate dissident organizations is rare. Consider a single dissident group. It is difficult to get suborganizations to voluntarily participate in the activities of the larger organization. Olson's model thus explains why local groups often participate in supralocal or national demonstrations at only a feeble level: "What incentives do local groups have to participate in the larger event? They know that some collective good (a Civil Rights Act) will have to be obtained at the federal government level, even though local collective goods (the desegregation of a local public facility) can be gotten with local action. Since obtaining local changes is going to be easier if the national legislation is passed, it is in their interest to participate in national action" but at a less than optimal rate (Oberschall 1980, 51). Decentralized dissident groups thus have many local chapters that fail to participate in national campaigns. The *Create a Federal Structure* solution to the Rebel's Dilemma (sect. 6.3.3) confronts a major stumbling block.

Now consider a set of related dissident groups. It is also difficult to get separate dissident organizations to cooperate; they in fact face a more severe CA problem than do individuals. In Wilson's words,

> The "logic of collective action" of which Mancur Olson writes may be more applicable to coalitions of organizations than to those of individuals. Individuals will often contribute to large organizations without receiving any specific material benefit from it; organizations rarely will.

And when organizations do form coalitions, the largest or richest members of it tend to pay a disproportionate share of the cost. (Wilson 1973, 277)

In short, competition, not cooperation, is the norm among dissident organizations (sect. 6.4).

One may consequently posit a certain pattern in relations among dissident groups. (1) United or popular fronts among dissident groups may be proclaimed, but only infrequently are successful. (2) Temporary and ad hoc alliances of dissident groups may form, but long-lived coalitions are rare. (3) Protest events may be endorsed by umbrella protest organizations, but the activities of the various component protest organizations are difficult to coordinate. (4) Joint operations by several dissident groups may often appear to be appropriate, but most protest incidents are the work of a single group of dissidents. (5) Minor forms of cooperation among dissident groups (e.g., the exchange of information, meetings) are possibilities, but major forms of cooperation (e.g., sharing of patrons' support, coordinating operations) are impossibilities.

In sum, there is little doubt that the Rebel's CA problem, the improbability of extensive collective dissent, is quite severe. The five percent rule holds for individuals, for factions within a dissident organization, and for independent dissident organizations. Dissidents often do not join dissident groups to battle regimes; dissident factions and dissident groups often do not join together to fight states.

## 2.2. The Probability of Some Collective Dissent: Solutions to the Rebel's Dilemma

As I indicated in chapter 1, CA theorists wish to account for both the presence and the absence of protests and rebellions. Since the theory easily accounts for the ninety-five percent who do not rebel, most CA theorists concentrate on the flip side, the five percent, by proposing solutions to the Rebel's Dilemma.

These solutions vary along two dimensions (Lichbach forthcoming, chap. 1). The first dimension is deliberative. People involved in a CA problem may or may not discuss their situation and, ultimately, forge a resolution. Solutions to the CA problem may thus result in either unplanned or planned order. The second dimension is ontological. One might believe that the entities involved in a CA problem are individuals only; alternatively, one might believe that institutions, structures, and/or relationships preexist individuals, and that they help impose order. Solutions to the CA problem may thus result in either spontaneous or contingent order. Combining dimensions produces the classic distinctions of social thought: Market, Community, Contract, and Hierarchy.

*riots* - *Market* approaches to social order and CA assume only individuals who engage in no social planning. They therefore feature unplanned and sponta-neous order, the idea being that anarchy, or a state of nature, exists among rebels. Market approaches then seek processes representing the "invisible hand" that lead rebels to the voluntary provision of the PG they seek. Unco-ordinated exchange relations among dissidents thus serve as the basis for cooperation in the political market just as they do in the economic market. The following Market solutions to the Rebel's Dilemma will be examined in part 2: increasing benefits, lowering costs, increasing resources, improving the productivity of tactics, reducing the supply of the PG, increasing the probability of winning, increasing the probability of making a difference, using incomplete information, increasing risk taking, increasing team com-petition among enemies, restricting exit, and changing the type of PG.

*Community* approaches assume that communal institutions exist, and that they are so effective as to render social planning unnecessary. Commu-nity approaches thus feature unplanned, but contingent, order. This is *civil rights movement* *Gemeinschaft*, or the creation of a common belief system. These primary groups and mechanistic patterns of solidarity are the basis for cooperation among dissidents. Thus, social relationships among rebels facilitate their political relationships. The following Community solutions to the Rebel's Dilemma will be examined in part 2: using common knowledge to overcome mutual ignorance and using common values to overcome pecuniary self-interest.

*Contract* approaches assume individuals, but individuals who collec-tively plan their society. They feature planned, but spontaneous, order, with rebels engaging in a face-to-face encounter during which they bargain about the type of institutions to create to solve their CA problem. This is *Gesell-schaft*, or the forging of contract or agreement, with secondary groups and organic solidarity constituting the basis for cooperation. Associational rela-tionships among rebels thus facilitate their political relationships. The fol-lowing Contract solutions to the Rebel's Dilemma will be examined in part 2: self-government, Tit-For-Tat agreements, and mutual exchange agreements.

*Hierarchy* approaches assume the existence of institutions that are cre-ated to manage society. These approaches thus feature planned and contin-gent order, the idea being that a deliberate attempt to solve the dissidents' CA problem is made by some preexisting organization of dissidents. Hierarchy solutions thus seek visible hand processes that coerce contributions to the PG. Collective dissent comes about, therefore, because some collectivity has sufficient power to bring it about. The following Hierarchy solutions to the Rebel's Dilemma will be considered in part 2: locating entrepreneurs, locating patrons, reorganizing, increasing team competition among allies, and imposing, monitoring, and enforcing agreements.

In sum, there are two approaches to unplanned order, Market and Community, and two approaches to planned order, Contract and Hierarchy. There are also two spontaneous approaches to social order, Market and Contract, and two contingent approaches to social order, Community and Hierarchy. The four possible solutions to the CA problem are displayed in Exhibit 2.

|  |  | Deliberation | |
|---|---|---|---|
|  |  | Unplanned Order | Planned Order |
| Ontology | Spontaneous Order | Market | Contract |
|  | Contingent Order | Community | Hierarchy |

Exhibit 2.  Solutions to the CA Problem

Of these four possibilities, Market approaches to social order and CA may be thought of as the baseline; they operate by changing the parameters of the canonical model of CA. The other three sets of solutions vary the context in which the baseline model is placed. Community solutions explore how common belief systems solve Olson's Problem, Contractual solutions study the ways in which mutual agreements produce CA, and Hierarchy solutions examine how hierarchies structure CA.

These four categories offer alternative research programs for ordering theory and practice and may be used to construct several instructive comparisons. Many claim that the state of nature (Market) can never produce CA, but must be supplemented by civil society (Community), a constitution (Contract), or state (Hierarchy). Private interests, in short, must be subordinated to social ends by tradition (Community), reason (Contract), or force (Hierarchy). Rational choice and liberal-individualistic approaches usually maintain that reason (choices with constraints, i.e., Market) and Reason (choices to shape constraints, i.e., Contract) are sufficient for CA. Those who oppose liberal solutions advocate either communitarian (Community) or statist (Hierarchy) approaches. Those who advocate a vanguard party to lead a revolution are pitting Market, Community, and Contract against Hierarchy. These debates about the virtues of no leadership (Market), elders (Community), judges (Contract), and kings (Hierarchy) are central to social thought. The distinctions structure this study of challenges to social order.

## 2.3. Solutions as Politics: The Origins of Collective Action

Dissidents know that the Rebel's Dilemma is solvable, so the question they must answer is, "What kind of appeal is most effective in getting people to contribute to an organization seeking a public good" (Kaplowitz and Fisher 1985, 48). The Rebel's Dilemma, therefore, is the origin of dissidents' mobilization drives. Regimes also recognize that a dissident group's CA problem can be solved. They seek to intensify the problem. The Rebel's Dilemma, therefore, is also the origin of regimes' demobilization efforts. In short, only the most naive rebel leaders believe that they have the correct answer to popular grievances, *and* that their proposals, if clearly presented, will find immediate and universal acceptance. Rebel leaders know that they must overcome their followers' CA problem. Regime leaders know it, too. They are not so naive as to believe that rebel leaders can appear before dissidents and immediately command a following. They too are aware that rebel leaders must overcome the dissidents' CA problem.

Thus, both the regime and the dissidents must respond to the PG–PD situation. Oppositions know that they are kept from power because of their CA problem; regimes know that they stay in power because of their opponents' CA problem. Whereas dissidents try to solve their CA problem by implementing solutions to the Rebel's Dilemma, the regime tries to intensify that problem by impeding those solutions. The regime has its own CA problem — the State's Dilemma (sect. 7.2.2) — that also generates political conflict. This struggle over solutions to the CA problems of the dissidents (the Rebel's Dilemma) and the authorities (the State's Dilemma) *is* the fundamental political struggle between regimes and oppositions. Almost every section in part 2 contains examples of this struggle. Consider several.

- *Increase Benefits* (sect. 3.1). Dissident leaders try to create zealots by promoting an ethos, vision of the future, or a moral code that endorses a PG. Regime leaders, on the other hand, try to stave off zealotry by promoting an alternative ethos that disparages that PG.
- *Lower Costs* (sect. 3.2). Dissident leaders try to minimize the costs of collective dissent (sect. 3.2.6). They try, for example, to reduce travel costs by holding meetings at a convenient place and time (sect. 3.2.2). They also try to reduce the costs of government repression, and thereby shield dissidents from government reprisals. Finally, dissident leaders attempt to minimize organizational costs, or the costs of creating and maintaining a dissident organization. One key organizational cost is search costs, the entrepreneur's costs of finding aggrieved dissidents. Dissident groups thus use cost-effective methods of recruitment, for example, by recruiting at public gatherings. They also search for dissidents with favorable preferences and

endowments. Regimes respond by trying to maximize the costs of collective dissent. For example, they repress dissidents by outlawing dissident organizations.

- *Increase Resources* (sect. 3.3). Dissident groups take action to increase their resources. They place a high priority on the theft of government and private resources, holding and controlling territory and people, and seeking domestic and foreign supporters. Governments, in turn, take action to reduce dissidents' resources, concentrating their attacks on the dissidents' inputs, or their sources of supplies.
- *Improve the Productivity of Tactics* (sect. 3.4). Dissidents make efficient use of their tactics. Regimes respond by attacking the dissidents' production function, or the mechanism that converts dissident inputs into PG outputs. Dissident entrepreneurs, moreover, try to invent new technologies of collective dissent (sect. 3.4.2). Such innovations ultimately diffuse to other dissident groups. Regimes attempt to counter the spread of new technologies of dissent by developing new technologies of repression.
- *Increase the Probability of Winning* (sect. 3.6). Dissident entrepreneurs attempt to justify sacrifice and sustain hope by convincing people that the regime is a "colossus with clay feet," that "history is on our side," and that "defeat is temporary, victory inevitable." They wage a war of words that claims widespread, enduring, and intense support, and predicts eventual victory. They also fight a war of deeds, taking action only when they think they can win, sequencing their actions to show progress, trying to capture important symbols of government authority, fighting indirectly when outgunned, and seizing control over space (people plus territory). The state, too, conducts a war of words, making identical claims and predictions for its side. The state also fights a war of deeds, making public displays of its power, via pomp and ceremony, making prominent and conspicuous use of its repressive apparatus, and labelling dissidents as "deviants," and as a small minority of "outside agitators." The regime and the dissidents thus compete over the probability-of-winning issue. Each side tries to convince citizens that it will win. Each side tries to show that it is a tower of strength. Each side claims that the other is a paper tiger. And each subverts the other's displays of power. Claims and counterclaims fly, as both sides make different assessments of the dissidents' past success, current support, and prospects for future success.
- *Increase the Probability of Making a Difference* (sect. 3.7). Dissident groups try to create an illusion of individual efficacy. They attempt to convince sympathizers that *with* their help they *can* win. Regimes respond by trying to convince dissidents that the regime is all-power-

ful, and hence that an individual dissident cannot possibly make a difference to the outcome.

- *Use Incomplete Information* (sect. 3.8). Dissidents seek information about all of the variables in the PG–PD model (e.g., the success possible, the resources available, the selective incentives obtainable). Thus, regimes and oppositions both have an interest in controlling the flow of information, and engage in an ongoing battle over communication. The strategy of a regime (or dissident group) is to disseminate information about a dissident group (or regime) that works to its own benefit. The dissidents use publicity, illusions, ideology, and symbols to intensify and focus grievances, thereby overcoming the Rebel's Dilemma. The regime uses publicity, illusions, ideology, and symbols to conceal the existence of grievances, thereby intensifying the Rebel's Dilemma. Moreover, a regime (or dissident group) tries to limit the communication between a dissident group (or regime) and potential dissidents. And, finally, a regime (or dissident group) gathers information about a dissident group (or regime).
- *Increase Team Competition between Regimes and Oppositions* (sect. 3.10.1.2). Regimes try to portray dissidents as an irredeemable enemy. Dissidents, on the other hand, try to identify the regime as an all-pervasive evil.
- *Restrict Exit* (sect. 3.11). The state, recognizing a dissident's exit/ voice option, uses accommodative and repressive response strategies to control the dissident's choice. One tactic is to exile dissidents and create refugees, expatriots, and emigrants. Another is to restrict the mobility of property rights but permit the mobility of people.
- *Overcome Mutual Ignorance* (sect. 4.1). Dissidents exchange information about their willingness to act. This leads to the temporal and spatial diffusion of collective dissent. Regimes limit the flow of information about the willingness of dissidents to act together, trying thereby to cut off bandwagons of collective dissent.
- *Overcome Pecuniary Self-Interest* (sect. 4.2). Dissident entrepreneurs provide doctrinal and ideological symbols (e.g., flags) and rituals (e.g., oaths) to increase group identification and common grievances, and a sense of common fate and like-mindedness (sect. 4.2.2). Governments try in the same way to bring about identification with their own interests.
- *Use Tit-For-Tat* (sect. 5.1.2). Dissident entrepreneurs appeal to the investment value of a dissident's participation in collective dissent. Regimes disparage such investments. They appeal to the consumption value of a dissident's nonparticipation in collective dissent (sect. 5.2.1). Dissident entrepreneurs recognize that preexisting social ties

reduce the transaction costs of the *Use Tit-For-Tat* solution to the Rebel's Dilemma. Consequently, they exploit preexisting formal and informal organizations in the dissident community. If such organizations are weak or do not exist, dissident entrepreneurs try to create a community of dissidents to compensate for the lack of preexisting organizations. Regimes, aware of these strategies on the part of dissident entrepreneurs, act accordingly. They try to disrupt preexisting social ties, for example, by resetting dissidents internally. Both the regime and the opposition, then, work through the dissidents' social structure, competing to control the formal and informal organizations in the dissident community (sect. 5.2.3). Finally, dissidents try to gain autonomy from regimes by isolating themselves (sect. 5.2.4). They set up sanctuaries, massing, for example, in locations remote from the locus of the regime's coercive strength. This accounts for base areas. Regimes, however, are wise to dangers base areas pose to them; counterinsurgency theorists are well aware that dissident isolation operates to the advantage of the dissidents. Consequently, states work hard to prevent dissidents from being isolated from the regime.

- *Locate Agents or Entrepreneurs* (sect. 6.1). Regimes and dissidents battle over leadership and organization, aiming to out-organize each other. As Brinton (1965, 39) asks, "Does the disorganization of the government find a counterpart in the organization of its opponents?" Dissident and regime entrepreneurs also compete more directly. As Pettee ([1938] 1971, 144) suggests, "Where there is a Bismarck, instead of a Lenin, there is no revolution."

- *Locate Principals or Patrons* (sect. 6.2). Both regimes and dissidents are aware of the potential impact that a domestic military establishment can have on protest and rebellion. Thus, they battle over the military's patronage of collective dissent. Since dissidents seek out the regime's military as perhaps their most valuable ally, the government recognizes the potential threat represented by its own military establishment. To prevent coups, dictators typically try to create a division of labor, a balance of power, and competing factions within their armed forces. The dictator, in short, organizes his or her military apparatus so as to increase its CA problem (sect. 6.2.3.1). Both regimes and dissidents are also aware of the impact that foreign support can have on protest and rebellion. Hence, they also battle over foreign patronage of collective dissent. Both are concerned with the international connections among like-minded regimes and dissidents. Dissidents (or the state) thus often claim that the state (or dissidents) is part of an international conspiracy and thus they, too, need external support. As dissidents try to locate external supporters, regimes, of course, try to cut them off (sect. 6.2.4). The competition between regimes and dissidents is thus reciprocally related to the competition between the regime's patrons and the dissidents' patrons.

- *Administer Selective Incentives and Disincentives* (sect. 6.5.3). Regimes and dissidents battle over the selective incentives offered to rebels by dissidents and to nonactivists by government. They also battle over the selective disincentives offered to nonactivists by dissidents and to rebels by government.

In sum, the fundamental competition between the regime and the dissidents is over solutions to the Rebel's Dilemma. Dissidents try to promote collective dissent by overcoming the Rebel's Dilemma; regimes try to prevent collective dissent by reinforcing the Rebel's Dilemma.[22]

The real competition among dissident groups is also over solutions to the Rebel's Dilemma. Another mechanism behind the choice of CA solutions is therefore the political struggle among dissident groups. Efficient solutions to the Rebel's Dilemma drive out inefficient ones; only efficient solutions survive. The argument works as follows. Some groups adopt one set of solutions to the Rebel's Dilemma, other groups adopt another set of solutions. Competition for members occurs among dissident groups, for example, in the same dissident movement (sect. 6.4). Dissident groups that adopt inefficient solutions to the Rebel's Dilemma eventually disappear. Only those dissident groups that efficiently solve their Rebel's Dilemma survive. It is possible that none will be successful and all will eventually disappear. Assuming no restrictions on competition, if the existing dissident groups fail, new dissident groups will rise to fill the gap. Competition among the dissident groups in a dissident movement thus explains how dissidents are led to select institutions that ultimately survive. Dissident groups experiment and adapt solutions to the Rebel's Dilemma until either they are successful or until they die out. Researchers should therefore study the political competition among dissident groups in the same dissident movement, each of which might solve their CA problem in a different way.[23]

This focus on the politics of CA is part of a larger question: under which conditions is a CA solution (or set of solutions) adopted? For example, where and when are material selective incentives, rather than nonmaterial altruistic appeals, emphasized? This is an important question because CA solutions are important features of collective dissent. The probability of winning, risk taking, dissident self-government, dissident entrepreneurship, and dissident organizational structures, for instance, are some of the key aspects of conflict that require explanation.

The explanation must be sought, as indicated above, in the political struggle between regimes and oppositions, and among oppositions. The use of any particular solution is, in part, a function of what dissident groups and the regime do respectively to encourage and discourage various solutions. Different dissident groups, with different CA problems, facing different regimes, thereby adopt different solutions. Moreover, the explanation must also be sought in the political situation in which regimes and dissidents find themselves. Group mobilization and success are, thus, contingent upon political maneuverings and political situations. My focus on the politics of the Rebel's Dilemma thus reinforces the idea that choice and contingency matter as much to CA as compulsion and constraint do.

However, some *solutions* (e.g., fungibility of costs and benefits, mutual expectations) are relatively unalterable. They simply vary across CA situations, existing or not existing, happening or not happening. Hence, are they not better described as *explanations* of outcomes rather than as *solutions* to the relevant actors' CA problems?

Given the politics involved in the etiology of CA solutions, the difference between *explaining* and *solving* a CA problem blurs. It is true that dissidents cannot always *choose* to *implement* a CA solution in some direct manner. It is also true that regimes cannot always *decide* to oppose a CA solution in some simple way. For example, zealotry, entrepreneurship, and mutual expectations are affected by opportunities and constraints that vary with the particular CA situation. They are not *solutions* to CA problems in the sense that one or more of the parties involved can *choose* to *implement* them. However, solutions are not all merely structurally determined by deep rooted historical forces. Regimes and oppositions are not simply passive subjects of their environment. Rather, they actively work to increase or decrease things like zealotry, the availability of benevolent despots, and mutual expectations. Hence, *opportunities/constraints* plus *strategies* produce *solutions* to the CA problem. In this sense, *solutions* are like any other *outcome* in a rational choice problem.

Studying CA processes thus raises important questions about why certain opportunities and constraints vary across CA situations, and what rational actors do to create opportunities and intensify constraints. The origins of selective incentives, zealotry, entrepreneurship, and mutual expectations, for example, take center stage in my analysis of collective dissent. Hence, one challenge is to determine under what circumstances the emphasis is placed on material selective incentives, rather than nonmaterial altruistic appeals (sect. 6.5.3.3).

No one in the CA literature has looked at CA solutions in this manner. Such solutions have not been seen as important outcomes or features that must be explained politically. Tarrow (1988, 426) thus criticizes Olson's formulation as constituting "a version of rational choice theory . . . that was particularly insensitive to politics." But just as Riker (1982) is able to detect the politics in Arrow's seemingly apolitical theory of collective choice, politics lies at the center of my reconstruction of Olson's seemingly apolitical theory of collective action.

Nor has anyone in the rational actor or resource mobilization approach to conflict studies (Costain 1993, 6-11) looked at CA solutions in this manner. The approach used here, however, provides a key link between CA and resource mobilization ideas, both of which examine how the contention among political forces affects CA. My focus on the politics of CA solutions thus provides a microfoundation for the struggle over resource mobilization.

## 2.4. Solutions as Pathologies: The Outcomes of Collective Action

Each solution to Olson's Problem no doubt expresses part of the truth. Examples can easily be found of patrons proving crucial to collective dissent. Counterexamples, however, can just as easily be found, where patrons were irrelevant to protest and rebellion. The key challenge is to discover where and when the solutions work. What are the conditions under which altruism actually does mitigate the Rebel's Dilemma? Where will entrepreneurship achieve the PG sought? When will Tit-For-Tat bring victory? Why do some groups achieve success with a federal group solution? Why do other groups achieve success by pooling particularly risk prone individuals?

Again, the answers must be sought, at least in part, in the political struggle between regimes and oppositions. Some types of struggles might render material selective incentives more effective than altruistic appeals, outside entrepreneurship more productive than dissident self-government, or the probability of winning more important than the probability of making a difference. Once again, structural and institutional factors in state and society will affect the answers.

CA solutions have a second type of consequence. A solution might be effective at mobilizing supporters and achieving a PG, but counterproductive in other ways. Wills (1970, 337) makes a very interesting observation about revolutionary thought. He points out that the Old Left's problem is how to start the revolution. Given that society shapes (wo)man, how does one find a group of (wo)men not ruined by society? In short, how can (wo)man reshape society? The New Left's problem, in contrast, is how to end the revolution. Given that revolutions start personally and every day, how does (wo)man fix the revolution in new social arrangements that do not pervert its original lofty aims? In short, how does one institutionalize a revolution?

One important new social arrangement is the dissident group, itself. The dissidents' organization, once it comes into being, often perverts the dissidents' purposes. While a dissident's goals may be noble, the same cannot often be said of the dissident institution. What would Marx have thought of the party created by Lenin, or Engels of the party created by Mao? Moreover, dissident groups that become regimes often produce ethically unappealing societies. While the day of the revolution may be glorious and liberating, the same cannot often be said of the morning after. What would Lenin have thought of Brezhnev, Bolivar of Peron, or Washington of Nixon? Walton (1984, 184) thus remarks that "the more fundamental question that still haunts is whether revolutions make a difference and, indeed, a difference for the better." Both academics[24] and dissidents[25] have pondered just such questions.

More specifically, an organization's incentive system for bringing about participation (Clark and Wilson 1961) can have many unexpected impacts on the organization's structure and dynamics. Patrons, for example, might provide needed resources, but only at the cost of coopting the dissident group into a reformist strategy. Self-serving leaders, opportunistic followers, authoritarian organizations, and compromised goals are often the unintended consequences of solving the Rebel's Dilemma. It is not just power that corrupts — seeking power also corrupts. Dissidents, in short, face as many problems from themselves as from their enemies.

The CA research program offers a deeper understanding of the flaws in revolutionary groups and postrevolutionary societies than have either the theorists or the practitioners of revolution. Accordingly, CA theorists are not surprised when dissident groups that fight for power turn out to be corrupt, or when dissident entrepreneurs that capture power turn out to be rent seekers. In many ways, CA solutions are self-defeating because they lead to numerous pathologies of collective dissent. Several unintended and unwanted consequences follow from the dissident group's attempts to overcome their CA problem. After all, "politics," as Hardin (1982, 12) remarks, "is more interesting than the problem of collective action."

Here, then, is another theme of this book: CA solutions might be effective at mobilizing supporters and achieving a PG, but counterproductive in other ways. Solutions to the Rebel's Dilemma can beget a thorny Organizational Dilemma, because paradoxes and ironies are built into CA processes.

These unintended, unwanted, and unexpected consequences of CA processes are more important to explore than either the causes of CA processes or their intended impact on CA. This is because structuralists tell us that deep-rooted forces drive CA processes toward outcomes in a mechanistic way. Hence, the processes can be traced back and ultimately reduced to certain structural causes. The implication is that CA processes are themselves trivial epiphenomena. To rebut this argument, CA theorists must show that CA processes have independent repercussions on state and society. By uncovering the ironies, tragedies, and comedies of collective dissent, CA theories demonstrate that one cannot ignore CA processes.

## 2.5. Appraising Collective Action Theories of Collective Dissent

One fundamental question haunts students of conflict who look longingly at the many varieties of CA theories: how useful is this approach for explaining someone's (non)participation in protest or rebellion? Is looking at collective dissent in this manner fruitful, or, is the CA perspective a fool's gold?

The issue of theory evaluation is important for all approaches in the social sciences. It is particularly relevant to CA theories, because the CA research program has generated the problem of explaining two interrelated puzzles: why dissident groups form and why a dissident group's members are "rational." But any of the two dozen or so aforementioned solutions to the Rebel's Dilemma is a reason why someone's participation in collective dissent is "rational" and, hence, why dissident groups form. It is thus difficult to argue that group formation and individual rationality still present puzzles to CA theorists. If the CA problem can be solved in some two dozen different ways, it surely does not pose an insurmountable hurdle for dissidents — the Rebel's Dilemma, that is, cannot be all that much of a dilemma.

But how much of an accomplishment is this? Have we not merely redescribed (non)participation in what some would consider an intellectually pleasing way? Is a primer or minimanual, "How Dissidents Overcome the CA Problem," sufficient? I offer several standards by which CA theories of collective dissent may be evaluated.

An analytical criterion is logical completeness: which types of CA solutions, if any, offer a logically complete explanation of protest and rebellion? Market solutions reduce the structures, institutions, and contexts within which one lives to certain variables that affect the decision to rebel. For example, one's community might earn rebels high benefits, the social contracts that he or she has entered might yield rebels low costs, and the hierarchical institutions (e.g., the dissident group) to which he or she is subject might eliminate rebels' exit option. The approach's theoretical reduction means that Market solutions offer no overall perspective on the decision-making environment, itself. Given that they must be supplemented by other types of CA solutions, Market solutions are logically incomplete. The search for a more complete solution to the Rebel's Dilemma points to Community, Contract, and Hierarchy solutions, but each of these approaches also offers an incomplete approach to the Rebel's Dilemma. Hence, each type of CA solution offers a logically incomplete explanation of collective dissent.

An empirical standard for evaluation is the predictability of particular outbreaks and aggregate levels of collective dissent. CA theories, it turns out, do not yield a general theoretical statement of the etiology of conflict. They cannot be used to forecast protest and rebellion.

CA theories of collective dissent thus fall short on the analytical criterion of logical completeness and the empirical criterion of predictability. CA theories fare better, however, on two empirical criteria based on Lakatos and Popper. Lakatos (1970) would argue that the CA research program must go beyond merely asserting that "rational people, at least under the right circumstances, do (not) rebel"; it must account for some *additional* and *true* observations about protest. Popper (1968) would argue that it must explain these observations *differently* and *better* than competing theories.

Consider the criteria of *additional* and *true*. This book will demonstrate that CA solutions, as politics and as (un)intended consequences, offer a rich perspective from which to understand protest and rebellion. CA theories have rich implications because they pose *why* and *what if* questions about CA solutions. The questions dissect dissident groups in that they focus attention on a group's actions (e.g., rhetoric, deeds), internal organization (e.g., membership characteristics, entrepreneurs), and external relations (e.g., competition with the regime, patronage). In short, each CA solution leads to a series of ideas about collective dissent. Taken together, these ideas offer consistent themes and messages about the politics and pathologies of collective dissent.

Now consider the criteria of *different* and *better*. Given that truth emerges from the confrontation of ideas, CA models must be tested against their competitors. The principal competitor to rational actor theories in conflict studies is Gurr's (1970) DA theory, *Why Men Rebel*. Are rebels frustrated or rational? DA theories tend toward the former view, CA theories toward the latter. Are CA theorists too cynical, or DA theorists too naive? This great debate in conflict studies has raged for over twenty years (Snyder 1978). This book contributes to that debate by determining just how far cynicism about the motives of protesters can usefully be pushed. It demonstrates that, by establishing the microfoundations of the rational actor or resource mobilization approach to conflict studies, the CA research program offers a different and better approach than either traditional DA theory or traditional resource mobilization theory.

To rebel or not to rebel, that is the question. It would be foolish to pretend that CA theories offer the master key to this issue. The Rebel's Dilemma is no Philosopher's stone or Rosetta stone. CA theories neither resolve all fundamental problems, nor clarify all obscure puzzles, nor settle all outstanding controversies in conflict studies. Science (but not pseudoscience) seeks to establish boundaries. It is only when we can "limit, specify, focus and contain" (Geertz 1973, 4) CA theories of collective dissent that we can begin to appreciate their true value. They can explain a great deal, though clearly not all, about collective dissent. I suspect that their successes will come as a pleasant surprise to those sociologists, political scientists, and economists who have been disappointed by the contributions of the CA research program to conflict studies. I know that their shortcomings will come as no surprise to critics.[26]

# Part 2
# Solutions

## CHAPTER 3

# Market

Part 2 discusses the four types of solutions to the Rebel's Dilemma. Recall from section 2.2 that Market solutions vary the parameters of the canonical PG-PD model, and that Community, Contract, and Hierarchy solutions place the baseline model in the context of those types of institutions. The idea, as argued in section 2.5, is to ask *why* and *what if* questions about each solution. I then try to determine whether a solution offers a logically complete explanation of protest and rebellion and how well it meets the predictability, Popperian, and Lakatosian standards. Consider, now, Market solutions to the CA problem.

Microeconomists employ a well-developed approach to the study of how the market for public or private goods operates (Cornes and Sandler 1986, chap. 2). They perform a *gedanken*, or a thought experiment, based on a comparative statics analysis between two time periods. The first period manifests the baseline PG-PD game, which involves a series of highly restrictive assumptions about the actors, their strategy sets, the states of nature, the possible outcomes, preferences, and decision rules. The result is an endogenous outcome, referred to as the CA problem, or noncontribution to the PG. To solve this problem, certain assumptions of the model are held constant while one particular assumption is varied. An exogenous shock is thus introduced in order to perturb the equilibrium of the game. The model is reexamined in the second time period in order to determine how the equilibrium outcome of participation has shifted.

The objective, then, is to discern how changes in exogenous variables create changes in endogenous variables, or the comparative statics from time $t$ to time $t+1$. The key question, of course, is whether or not CA has been induced. I am also interested in two broader questions: the origins of these shocks (i.e., the politics of collective dissent) and their second-order consequences (i.e., the pathologies of collective dissent).

Traditional microeconomic models vary only a few parameters, with price and income usually at center stage. CA theorists, however, have employed many different models of individual and group decision making (Lichbach forthcoming, chap. 2). Hence, many initial conditions of a dissident's decision-making situation, or many parameters in his or her environment, can be varied. This chapter examines what happens when we increase benefits (sect. 3.1), lower costs (sect. 3.2), increase resources (sect. 3.3), improve the productivity of tactics (sect. 3.4), reduce the supply of the PG (sect. 3.5), increase the probability of winning (sect. 3.6), increase the probability of making a difference (sect. 3.7), use incomplete information (sect. 3.8), increase risk taking (sect. 3.9), increase team competition between enemies (sect. 3.10), restrict exit (sect. 3.11), and change the type of PG (sect. 3.12).

### 3.1. Increase Benefits

While CA theories indicate that most rebels will not sacrifice much for their rebellion, and that heroism and dedication will be in short supply, they also demonstrate that CA will occur if there are zealots (Tilly 1978, 88). A zealot is someone who contributes towards the PG because the marginal benefits of his or her contribution are very large.[1] These marginal benefits are, in fact, large enough to exceed the marginal costs of the contribution. Intensity of demand for the PG can thus overcome the Rebel's Dilemma. A group with one or more zealots, especially ones with a great deal of resources (sect. 3.3), is considered "privileged" in Olson's (1965, 49–50) terms or to have a "hegemon" in Keohane's (1984, chap. 3 ) idiom.

This solution offers one explanation of why rational people rebel: the value a dissident attaches to the PG determines his or her involvement in protest and rebellion.[2] The greater the intensity of a dissident's demand for the PG, the greater his or her participation in collective dissent.[3] Political discontent, contra the "grievances are irrelevant" argument (sect. 9.2.2.1) does affect political action.

Besides explaining why rational people might rebel, the *Increase Benefits* solution yields several other implications about collective dissent. As with all solutions, these implications can be teased out by seeking the causes and consequences of the *Increase Benefits* idea.

Consider the sources of zealotry. The intensity proposition explains two intriguing observations that can, with some modifications, be applied to collective dissent. First, government workers have the highest voter turnout of any occupational group (Marsh 1967, 150; Schwartz 1987, 116). The reason is that government employees have an obvious interest in who governs. Following this line of reasoning, one also expects that they will be in the forefront of revolutionary and counterrevolutionary efforts. The second observation is differential lobbying: shoemakers, for instance, devote more resources to lobbying for tariff barriers to imported shoes than do consumers for lobbying for free trade in shoes. The reasons, as Downs (1957, 246, 254–57) notes, are that while concentrated and asymmetric benefits encourage rent-seeking, dispersed and symmetric benefits discourage such activities, and that most people receive more of their income from their contributions to factor markets than to product markets. Following this line of thought, one also expects that movements of protest and rebellion are more likely to arise out of grievances over production than out of grievances over consumption. Specifically, we would expect more protest about unemployment than about inflation, more protest from farmers about farm prices than from consumers about the general price level.

Direct personal experience is another source of intense demands that leads one to place great value on achieving a PG. For instance, people who lose a relative or friend in Vietnam become antiwar activists; people who experience racial discrimination become civil rights activists; people whose family members die from AIDS become AIDS activists; and women who are attacked by rapists become committed feminists. Truong Chinh (cited in Popkin 1978, 223–24) recognizes that personal experience leads one to value the PG sought by a dissident group, as he comments about the Viet Minh mobilization against the French: "How many able people still consider that the resistance war is the affair of the government and the army, and maintain the indifferent stand of 'doing nothing while your neighbor's house goes up in flames'?" Reactions to such intense emotional experiences are, however, inherently difficult to anticipate, one of the many explanations for the unpredictability of collective dissent (sect. 9.2).

Finally, both dissident entrepreneurs and regime elites understand the value of creating zealots. Both recognize it as a solution to the Rebel's Dilemma and act accordingly, the former to encourage zealotry and the latter to discourage it. Dissident leaders promote an ethos, a vision of the future, or a moral code to endorse the PG. Rebel entrepreneurs, especially great leaders like Martin Luther King Jr., typically try to convince their followers to "focus on the pleasures rather than the travails of their struggle" (Chong 1991, 87).[4] Regime leaders, for their part, try to discourage zealots by promoting an alternative ethos, one that disparages the PG. They focus on the travails, rather than the pleasures, of the dissidents' struggle. In short, leaders of dissident groups try to create zealots by disseminating an ideology to increase the value of the PG they seek. Simultaneously, leaders of the regime try to prevent zealots by disseminating an alternative ideology to decrease the value of the PG sought by the dissidents.

Other implications of the *Increase Benefits* solution can be derived by seeking the consequences of zealotry. The solution has two sets of unintended effects on dissident organization: zealotry strengthens the organization and shapes recruitment strategy.

First, given a small dissident group, the intensity proposition implies an obvious solution to the Rebel's Dilemma: locate a zealot. If this were the only solution to the Rebel's Dilemma, one would expect only fanatics and extremists to participate in collective dissent. But the *Increase Benefits* solution is not the only solution to the Rebel's Dilemma. Moreover, participation by zealots may increase the expected value of participation for others. Hence, one simply expects dissident movements to be particularly adept at pooling fanatics and extremists.

How does this group of fanatics and extremists react to their less-aggrieved fellow dissidents who remain outside the movement and do not carry their share of the burden? Zealots recognize that inequality in the intensity of demand leads to inequality in participation, which leads to inequality in burden sharing. One thus suspects that they will vehemently object to free riding by their less-intense colleagues. Zealots will demand cost-sharing arrangements that socialize the costs of collective dissent. They will also be interested in strengthening the group's organization so that contributions can be assessed and monitored, and rewards and sanctions imposed for (non)compliance (sect. 6.5). Such pressure is an important explanation of the form that dissident organizations take.

Second, a dissident organization's recruitment strategy often focuses on the zealot. Leaders look for members who have intense preferences for the PG (as well as those who are resource rich; sect. 3.3) because such dissidents are the most sympathetic and responsive to the group's cause and appeal, and thus are particularly easy to mobilize (sect. 5.2.6). For this reason, dissident groups conduct "get out the vote" campaigns and spend more time and effort activating zealots than either mobilizing those who are relatively indifferent or transforming enemies into allies. They fish, in other words, in troubled waters. Such a "get out the zealot" recruitment strategy, of course, influences the membership and hence the character of a dissident organization.

## 3.2. Lower Costs

Dissidents care about the cost of their participation in collective dissent (Rogowski 1985, 89). The rebel's PG-PD problem can be overcome if the costs of participation are either nonexistent (sect. 3.2.1) or low (sect. 3.2.2). Two of the key costs are the opportunity costs of engaging in other behaviors (sect. 3.2.3) and the fixed costs of starting a dissident organization (sect. 3.2.4). Both rank-and-file dissidents (sect. 3.2.5) and dissident entrepreneurs (sect. 3.2.6) seek to lower such costs.

### 3.2.1. No-Cost Collective Dissent

If collective dissent is costless (relative to benefits or income), rational people will rebel. Costs are negligible (Ireland 1967, 50), for one, when they are refundable if the PG is not obtained. Elster (1989, 42) describes the "money back" method as follows: "A promise to contribute will be enforced only if a sufficient number of others promise to do the same. The advantage of this method, which is frequently used in fund-raising campaigns, is that nobody risks being taken advantage of." While models that incorporate such a method work only under a restrictive set of conditions (Rapoport 1985, 149), McNall (1988, 232) does offers an example of the approach: organizers of a farmer's group encouraged people to join a local chapter, but concealed the actual number of subscribers. As soon as a critical mass was reached, they announced that there were enough subscribers to form the chapter.

The costs of participation also fall to negligible levels when almost all potential dissidents are actual dissidents. When enough people participate, dissidents no longer face the possibility of either repression or of a long and difficult struggle. Confronted by a united and active opposition, the regime is no longer able to repress its opponents and will be toppled shortly and easily. Hardin (1990, 372) points out the implications of such a situation: "Just as it would be odd for many Americans in communities in which voting is easy to balk at the minor cost in inconvenience, so it might seem odd for many workers or soldiers or others to balk at joining a crowd to march on the palace or the Bastille." It is, therefore, the costs imposed by the regime that make collective dissent a PD game rather than an Assurance or Stag Hunt game (Lichbach forthcoming, chap. 2). If the costs of participation were considerable, the individual would rather defect when all others cooperated; if the costs of participation were negligible, the individual might well prefer to cooperate when all others cooperated.

When participation is virtually costless, as in voting in an election (Feigenbaum, Karoly, and Levy 1988, 201) or joining a mob that police cannot control, benefits become more important than costs in influencing behavior. Participation thus can be expressive rather than consequentialist. Preferences, ideology, and grievances (contra sect. 9.2.2) matter. The CA model is thus less effective at explaining participation in situations of negligible costs than in high cost situations (Lichbach forthcoming, chap. 7).

### 3.2.2. Low-Cost Collective Dissent

A dissident, being a rational actor, does not maximize the level of his or her participation in collective dissent. Instead, rational rebels choose a level of participation that will maximize their returns from CA. Hence, *ceteris paribus*, individuals choose low-cost methods of participating in collective dissent.

By implication, then, any widespread form of collective dissent must be a low cost method. This is the rationale, for example, behind everyday forms of peasant resistance (Scott 1985). But what about those forms of collective dissent, such as terrorism, that seem to impose great personal costs — why do people participate in them? In fact, the costs of such methods are often more apparent than real: terrorism imposes far fewer personal costs on terrorists than people realize. Consider the following:

- Few terrorists become casualties. Gurr's (1979, 38, table 8) analysis of data from the 1960s shows that terrorists themselves were casualties in only 14 percent of all instances. This is a far lower figure than in rioting and guerrilla warfare, two alternative forms of political violence.
- Few terrorists are captured. A RAND Corporation study of ninety international hostage episodes from August 1968 to December 1975 reveals that there is a 77 percent chance that *all* the members of a kidnapping team will escape punishment or death, whether or not they successfully seize hostages (Jenkins, Johnson, and Ronfeldt 1978, 92). In the 127 terrorist attempts at aircraft hijacking between March 1968 and July 1974, there was less than a 10 percent chance that the hijackers would die or be imprisoned.
- Of the small number of terrorists who are captured, few are tried in courts of law. Many are ultimately released and sent to neutral or friendly countries.
- Of those few terrorists who are captured and tried, even fewer receive heavy sentences. Laqueur (1987, 92) points out that "no West European, North American, Japanese or Middle Eastern terrorist of the 1960s and 1970s has been executed (except in some cases by his comrades), and there is always a good chance that he will be released even before serving his term, his comrades having blackmailed the authorities into freeing him. Much of the risk has gone out of terrorism." Wilkinson (1979, 115) also cites a study that claims that for the small proportion of terrorists that are actually caught and tried, "the average sentence awarded to terrorists . . . was eighteen months."
- Of the small number of terrorists who are captured, tried, and receive heavy sentences, few actually serve out their full prison term. As Wilkinson (1979, 115) observes, "According to Robert A. Fearey, special assistant to the U.S. Secretary of State and Coordinator for Combatting Terrorism, between 1971 and 1975, less than 50 percent of captured international terrorists actually served out their prison sentences."

It seems that even terrorists have chosen a low-risk and, hence, low-cost method of collective dissent.

What are the factors that determine whether the methods of collective dissent cost little? Travel, for one — as travel costs (e.g., time and distance) to a collective dissent event increase, the dissident is less likely to participate in that event. Several examples may be offered. Most student protest occurs on campus, not at faraway government buildings or bodies. Most black rioting is concentrated in black neighborhoods, not white ones. During jacqueries, most peasants do not venture far from their homes. In the 1969 March on Washington, the number of participants from any given state was negatively related to the state's distance from Washington (Cicchetti, Freeman, Haveman, and Knetsch 1971, 722). A tax protest at the L.A. Coliseum was less than fully attended because "the Coliseum is located far from the interested areas, so that persons had to travel a long way through heavy traffic to attend" (Jackson, Peterson, Bull, Monsen, and Richmond 1960, 40). Rochon (1982, 23) offers a final example: "A train ride across [the Netherlands] lasts about three and a half hours and costs about $15. Thus for Dutch demonstrators to converge on the Hague is a far less complex and expensive undertaking than is mounting such a protest in Washington by their American counterparts."

Weather is yet another cost borne by dissidents. American revolutionaries complained about "sunshine patriots" and "fair-weather soldiers." The tsarina recognized that the February 1917 Revolution in Russia was aided by favorable weather conditions (Kuran forthcoming). Indeed, the problem persists today: as weather conditions worsen (e.g., cold, heat, rain), collective dissent decreases. One corollary is that more collective dissent occurs in the summer than in the winter. Most civil rights and student protests of the 1960s, for example, occurred during the summer months. Another corollary is that rain will prematurely terminate many collective dissent events. Oberschall (1980, 46-47) proposes an interesting bandwagon scenario that illustrates this phenomena (Lichbach forthcoming, chap. 4).

In choosing low-cost methods of participating in collective dissent, different individuals, with different endowments and skills, contribute different resources because the same contribution carries different costs to each: the choice is a function of each person's cost/benefit calculations. When the relative cost of one resource increases for a dissident, he or she will contribute another resource. As affluence increases, for example, the opportunity cost of time increases. Thus, a wealthier dissident contributes less time-intensive resources (e.g., money) and a poorer dissident contributes his or her time. In short, the wealthy litigate and lobby, rather than protest and riot, preferring, in effect, to pay others to demonstrate for them.[5]

A division of labor thus occurs naturally and voluntarily, as dissidents contribute differently according to their own preferences and endowments. In short, dissidents willingly adopt unequal and dissimilar forms of participation. For this reason dissident organizations are complex. Terrorist networks, for example, include training camps, hideouts, safe houses, diplomatic offices, business enterprises, and public relations bureaus. Some terrorists do political work; others do military work.

A second consequence of cost counting is that dissident groups can more easily mobilize collective dissent that imposes few personal costs than that which imposes great costs. Since dissidents pursue the path of least resistance — the low-cost alternative — the strategies of dissident groups are severely constrained by a tradeoff: as a form of collective dissent demands fewer resources, the extent of participation it can command increases (Nagel 1987, 54). In other words, as the resource commitment (e.g., time, energy, money) involved in a participatory act decreases, the percentage of people performing the act increases. Dissident groups must therefore locate themselves on an intensity/extensiveness curve: they can place many demands on their followers if they are prepared to manage with few followers; they can mobilize large numbers of followers if they are willing to place only modest demands on them.

Hence, there will be fewer formal members in a dissident group if formal membership entails attendance at meetings rather than only paying dues, and even fewer formal members if formal membership requires many group activities. Moreover, dissident organizations will be able to mobilize more voting than campaigning, more campaigning than lobbying, and more lobbying than protesting. In short, dissident groups are in the paradoxical position of being able to mobilize more legal (i.e., regime-accepted) than illegal (i.e., regime-denied) forms of participation. They can put together more collective participation than collective dissent, and more collective dissent than collective violence.[6]

### 3.2.3. The Opportunity Costs of Collective Dissent

Important costs of collective dissent are opportunity costs (Coleman 1990, 495); that is, a dissident's involvement in protest means that his or her efforts and energies are unavailable for use in alternative areas. The dissident must therefore forgo the benefits that would derive from those other activities. Hence, the CA approach implies a commonly offered and widely accepted rational actor-based explanation for why people do not rebel most of the time: it is economical to accept authority (Dahl 1970, 40–55). Yes, subordinates certainly recognize that superordinates are less than perfect, but they also know that nonaction conserves their attention, energy, resources, and so on.[7] In short, only people who have nothing to lose but their chains will rebel.

The particular opportunity costs of participating in collective dissent are revealing.[8] Consider forgone wages. Since most people spend their weekdays at work, more collective dissent will occur on the weekend than on weekdays. Since more wages will be lost if collective dissent occurred during the day, a great deal of collective dissent occurs at night. Hobsbawm and Rudé (1968, 239) indeed report that during Captain Swing, the English agricultural uprising of the 1830s, incendiaries were thrown and machines broken by "men who operated at dead of night."

More generally, the financial opportunity costs of protest and rebellion are related to the extent of the rebels' economic dependence on authorities. The greater the economic pressure that can be brought to bear on dissidents, the greater their opportunity costs and, hence, the less their dissent.[9]

Some people are relatively immune to the financial hardships that derive from time forgone at a job. Professionals are insulated from the possible negative financial consequences of political activism in many ways (Weber 1946, chap. 4; Lipset, Trow, and Coleman 1962, 241; also see Lipset 1971b, 35–36). They do not have to punch a time clock; their flexible schedule permits participation in dissident movements. Moreover, they often have some form of job security - the seniority or tenure that makes them immune to employer-imposed penalties. Finally, professionals can often leave their jobs for long periods of time. Rather than suffering the penalties of lost status or earning power, they can capitalize on their newfound skills to enhance their prestige and their income. Lawyers, journalists, and academics in every society thus provide a disproportionate number of dissidents.

A second group that does not suffer a financial hardship from time forgone at a job is students. The typical student, having fewer job responsibilities than the typical nonstudent, thus engages in a great deal of collective dissent (sect. 5.2.6). Nevertheless, students are subject to one pressure that keeps them at *their* job — competition for future employment and studying for exams. As Lipset (1964, 38) argues, "The greater the pressure placed on students to work hard to retain their position in the university or to obtain a good appointment after graduation, the less they will participate in politics of any kind." As the demands on the academic time of students increase, student participation in collective dissent decreases.[10] Hence, collective dissent is less likely in tough universities (i.e., those with high academic requirements) than in easy ones; in elitist institutions (i.e., those that admit few) than in mass universities; among those in more rigorous majors (e.g., natural sciences) than among those in more liberal majors; and among those in fields with definitive career paths (e.g., law, medicine, and dentistry) than among those lacking such paths. All of these predictions turn out to be true (Lipset 1964, 1967, 1971b).

The unemployed and underemployed constitute a third group that does not suffer financial hardship from participating in collective dissent due to the time forgone at a job. The unemployed, with no job responsibilities, have much free time; part-time employees, with few job responsibilities, have some free time. Of those who participate in collective dissent, one thus expects a higher percentage of the unemployed than of part-time employees, and a higher percentage of part-time employees than of those who are employed full time. As de la Hodde (cited in Laqueur 1978, 185-86) puts it, dissidents are to be found among "lawyers without clients, doctors without patients, writers without readers, merchants without customers."

There are also nonfinancial opportunity costs associated with participating in collective dissent; time forgone with family, for example. As family responsibilities increase, collective dissent decreases. One would expect, therefore, to find a higher percentage of single people than of married people engaged in revolutionary activities.

Forgone leisure is an opportunity cost that people are loath to pay. Hence, collective dissent decreases as the number of competing recreational events and activities increases. Consider student strikes: the U.S. student protests against the Cambodian incursion of 1970 began in April and ended just about the time that summer vacation began. Lipset (1964, 45) thus suggests that "participation in politics is an alternative to other forms of extracurricular activity . . . In the United States, organized sports were expressly introduced in colleges and universities to divert adolescent energy which in many college communities had grown into brawls and 'town and gown' riots." Hence, Lipset (1971b, 75) maintains that "many more [students] still fill the stadiums to cheer on their varsity eleven on fall Saturdays than take part in political rallies or demonstrations of any kind."

The very time spent protesting and rebelling is an opportunity cost that deradicalizes people. Since time is scarce, participation eventually decreases as the duration of a collective dissent event, episode, or campaign increases. After some high point of political involvement, political apathy and nonparticipation grow. The masses withdraw, leaving radicals to complain about the "depoliticization" of everyday life as people turn "their backs on high-blown ideological goals" and return "to the more prosaic pursuits of making a living and enjoying the simple pleasures of existence" (Hagopian 1974, 228). This process explains cycles of dissent (Tarrow 1989, 61): events are the triggers that produce peaks (sect. 4.1.1); opportunity costs are the dampers that produce valleys.

A demonstration is a good example. Given the diminishing marginal utility attached to spending time at a rally, crowds eventually shrink. Alinsky (1971, 160) thus complains that "after a while — and by 'a while' meaning 2-3 hours — the 8,000 would have dwindled to 800 or less." Revolution is another example. Brinton (1965, 152) writes that "there is also a good deal of evidence that as the revolution goes on, a very large number of people just drop out of active politics." A telling manifestation was that people stopped voting. There was a decline in the number of votes cast in Russia from June to September of 1917 and in France from 1789 to 1793. As Brinton (1965, 153) puts it, "The great numbers of qualified voters just don't vote; in Trotsky's compact phrase, they are politically nonexistent." The vast majority of participants in the French Revolution were thus only temporary activists. Richard Cobb concludes that

> the revolutionary . . . is only a provisional being, who does not resist time, wear and tear, lassitude — a creature of exceptional circumstances . . . Our men of 1793 were not . . . ideologues or professors in revolutionary theory. Just when they donned their slippers, this was the end of their career as political activists. With the passage of the great hopes and the great dangers, there was thus a return to the banality of everyday life. (cited in Hagopian 1974, 204)

In sum, dissidents try to minimize their opportunity costs - the fundamental unintended effect is that it is hard to radicalize people and easy to deradicalize them.[11]

### 3.2.4. The Fixed Costs of Collective Dissent

Dissidents must pay another cost as well. Start-up costs, fixed costs, or sunk costs are the initial investment in CA (Popkin 1979, 263). There are both truths and fallacies about the fixed costs of collective dissent.

First the truths. Early joiners often must bear the entire initial cost of creating a dissident organization. Many potential early joiners decide that these costs are too high. Hence, one truth about fixed costs is that as the set-up costs of dissident institutions increase, collective dissent is less forthcoming. Moreover, those who do join early try to minimize these costs. Thus, another truth is that early joiners create dissident organizations that start out as simple and uncomplicated bodies.

In certain situations, seed money is available, financing is obtainable, or payment is postponable - a fortuitous situation that can help overcome the stumbling block of fixed cost and allow participation to be more forthcoming. Popkin (1979, 263) offers an example from Vietnam: "When the Communists seized control of village government in much of Annam and Tonkin, many projects that increased production and repaid themselves many times over were possible because the Communists then had resources to finance projects and did not require the beneficiaries to pay in advance."

There is one final truth: as the initial (fixed) costs of a PG increase, participation becomes discontinuous. More specifically, participation in collective dissent comes later in the dissidents' campaign. The reason for this is that the existence of start-up costs implies that some PGs require a great deal of participation before any of the PG is provided at all. Very little of the PG will be provided initially because there is a big hurdle to get over. PGs with smooth supply functions will produce continuous CA, whereas those with rough supply functions will produce discontinuous CA.

Now to address the fallacy concerning fixed costs. Consider this formulation by Kanter (1972, 228): "The process of investment provides the person with a stake in the fate of the group. He commits his resources to it: time, energy, money, property, and reputation all become bound up with the movement." The suggestion seems to be that as an individual's investment in a dissident group increases, his or her participation in collective dissent increases. This is the fallacy of sunk costs: a dissident's investment will influence a dissident's behavior. Investment will not influence behavior, however, because as the sunk costs of a strategy increase, the marginal costs and benefits of participation are unaffected. Rational rebels let bygones be bygones and cut their losses. Their future participation in collective dissent will be unaffected by their past fixed costs.

### 3.2.5. Dissidents Minimize Costs

In general, dissidents attempt to minimize the private costs of participating in collective dissent. They especially want to minimize the cost of government repression.

One thus expects to see more dissident activities when it is safe to carry them out. Dissidents, for example, are much more likely to join spontaneous riots than planned protest campaigns. Tullock (1971b, 10) offers some interesting observations on this point:

> A spontaneous eruption of riots is, from the standpoint of the person participating in it, very much safer than is a conspiracy. It is far less likely that the government will be able to catch and punish him if the uprising is unsuccessful than if he enters into a conspiracy. Thus a person discontented with the government is unlikely to be motivated to join in any formal effort to overthrow it. If, however, he sees a mob coming down the street without much opposition and large enough for the chances to be good that if it gets beaten he will be able to withdraw and resume his life without the police even knowing he participated, he may well join.

One also expects that rioters will choose to riot in safe places, at safe times.

Once collective dissent is carried out, moreover, one expects dissidents to try to minimize the negative consequences. Few dissidents, including terrorists, are suicidal; most are unwilling to die for their cause. Those who commit deadly acts of violence that are expected to bring immediate police attention usually have elaborate escape plans. As the Task Force on Disorders and Terrorism (1976, 13) concludes, "Few terrorists have been willing to die rather than accept defeat."

Dissidents have other ways as well of minimizing the consequences of their actions. One is to appeal to government directly and demand amnesty. Students are notorious for including amnesty among their demands for ending their protests. A more forceful way of minimizing costs is to damage the regime's coercive capacity. Guerrillas often target the government's security apparatus. In the urban riots in the United States during the 1960s, for example, the police were among the principal targets. Another way to minimize postevent costs is to seek security from another government: hijackers often seek political asylum; terrorists often demand safe conduct to a neutral nation as the price for surrendering.

Finally, dissidents attempt to minimize their private costs by appealing to the leadership of their dissident group. First, rebels appeal for subsidies. As the dissident group reimburses dissidents for their participation, collective dissent increases. Thus, well-organized social movements often subsidize a dissident's costs of participation, in essence paying or bribing dissidents to dissent (sect. 6.5.3.2). Second, rebels appeal for compensation. Collective dissent increases when the dissident group provides funds for the injured and the survivors. Thus, the PLO operates as an insurance agency for widows and orphans. Third, rebels appeal for protection; as the dissident group uses its resources to prevent government reprisals against dissidents, rational people are more likely to rebel.

### 3.2.6. Entrepreneurs Minimize Costs

Dissident entrepreneurs, of course, recognize the *Lower Costs* solution to the Rebel's Dilemma. They therefore attempt to minimize the costs of collective dissent by minimizing organizational costs, or the costs of creating and maintaining a dissident organization.

Consider search costs, or the costs of finding aggrieved dissidents. To minimize these costs, dissident groups use cost-effective methods of recruitment. They recruit at existing public gatherings - parades, funerals, and public hearings. Given the travel costs problem (sect. 3.2.3), dissident leaders try to hold meetings at a convenient place and time: union or worker organizing occurs where people work; neighborhood or community organizing occurs where people live. Entrepreneurs are also careful not to waste their time attempting to recruit people who are hostile to the group and are thus not likely to join (sect. 3.1). A final recruitment device involves offering a commission to members of the group who recruit new members. In sum, the recruitment strategies, and hence composition, of dissident organizations are affected by the *Lower Costs* solution to the Rebel's Dilemma.

### 3.3. Increase Resources

Resources can be increased at the individual level, at the group level, and at both levels simultaneously. I will explore all three situations.

At the individual level, an increase in a dissident's resources allows him or her to buy more of both the private good and the PG. A high income elasticity of demand for the PG yields a high level of CA (Cornes and Sandler 1986, 84-91). Hence, the greater a dissident's resources, the greater his or her participation in collective dissent. In other words, expect active dissidents to be among the better-endowed members of an aggrieved group. But why is it that some dissidents, at certain times and places, have more resources than other dissidents?

One particular type of potential dissident - the soldier[12] - already has just the right resources for collective dissent. Trained in organized combat, demobilized soldiers are in high demand by dissident groups. Supply factors, in terms of low opportunity costs (sect. 3.2.3), also lead demobilized soldiers, decommissioned officers, and deserters to engage in collective dissent. Former soldiers tend to be unemployed in a job market that is weakened by the economic dislocations produced by war. They also tend to be young, without family responsibilities (sect. 3.2.3). Hence, factors related to both supply and demand lead former soldiers to participate in a great deal of collective dissent.[13] Francis Bacon (see Zagorin 1982a, 47), for example, thought disbanded soldiers responsible for much rebellion, a contention supported by a wealth of evidence.[14]

Next, consider an increase in resources at the group level. Most dissident groups have inadequate resources and high rates of resource depletion. Thus, the dissidents' production process (sect. 3.4.1) must ensure the flow of resources: "To survive in modern society, [social movement organizations] need financial resources if they are to pursue goals in more than a local context. Money is needed for personnel, transportation, office supplies, and the like" (Zald and McCarthy 1980, 4). Hence, as an organization's resources increase, it can engage in more collective dissent.[15] Dissident organizations with greater supplies of money, arms, equipment, and training facilities will therefore be able to sustain greater levels of protest and rebellion. As the availability of weapons increases, for example, political violence increases.[16]

There is, however, one important qualification to the group resources-group dissent proposition. A dissident group's resource requirements vary. As Freeman (1979, 172) argues:

> A major distinguishing factor between a social movement and an organizing interest group is the particular mix of resources each relies on. Interest groups tend to mobilize tangible resources, some of which are used to hire professional staff to translate the rest of the resources into political pressure. Social movements are low in tangible resources, especially money, but high in people resources.

Hence, at least in the short run, certain dissident groups may be able to operate with limited resources.

In spite of this difficulty, the group resources-group dissent proposition holds many consequences for collective dissent. It implies that governments will try to reduce dissident resources. Regimes will concentrate their attacks, as Leites and Wolf (1970, 76–78) argue, on the dissidents' supplies or input sources. Regimes will also attack the dissidents' production function, or the mechanism that converts inputs into outputs (sect. 3.4.1). The more successful such attacks, the less the collective dissent.

Another implication of the group resources-group dissent proposition is that dissident groups undertake actions against government in order to increase their resources. Gurr (1970, 269) thus suggests that dissident organizations seek to build their power: "Once armed conflict has begun, dissidents can increase their military capacity by concentrating attacks on barracks and armories or isolated patrols to obtain needed weapons." Stealing government and private resources, holding and controlling territory and people, and seeking domestic and foreign supporters (sect. 6.2) are therefore all high-priority activities of dissident groups.

A concluding implication of the group resources-group dissent proposition is that dissident groups act to preserve their scarce resources. This is particularly apparent in guerrilla warfare. Guerrillas are urged to be conservative in battle, to avoid squandering scarce resources on fights that they cannot win (Mao 1961).

Finally, consider an increase in resources at both the individual and the group levels. Recall that an increase in either a dissident's or a dissident group's resources can increase collective dissent. The latter may in fact reinforce and qualify the former. Verba, Nie, and Kim's (1978, chaps. 4, 5) cross-national study of participation shows that for each country they study, the level of individual resources is related to political participation. There is, however, much cross-national variation in that relationship. Their explanation is that organizations, such as political parties, can either weaken or reinforce the impact of individual resources on individual action. Group resources, in other words, qualify individual resources. As a dissident group's resources increase, a dissident's personal resources may have less of an impact on his or her participation in collective dissent. This is because a well-endowed dissident group can subsidize a dissident's costs (sect. 3.2.6) and thus permit even a poorly endowed dissident to join. This is one reason why the evidence concerning the influence of economic development upon collective dissent is mixed (Zimmermann 1983, 94–96).

## 3.4. Improve the Productivity of Tactics

The Rebel's Dilemma can be overcome if a dissident's time spent procuring the PG is relatively more productive than his or her time spent procuring private goods. Dissidents try to improve the productivity of their tactics by learning about their production function (sect. 3.4.1), introducing innovations into the technology of protest and rebellion (sect. 3.4.2), thoughtfully selecting targets (sect. 3.4.3) and tactics (sect. 3.4.4), and choosing carefully between violence and nonviolence (sect. 3.4.5).

### 3.4.1. The Production Function

Many have suggested that there is a technology of collective dissent.[17] The production function of a dissident group uses some production process to translate an input of the group's resources into an output of the PG. Hence, the production function measures the group's power — its ability to achieve its goals. To produce collective dissent might require expertise in survival, electronics, communications, map reading, chemistry, first aid, interrogation, intelligence work, cryptography, undercover procedures, propaganda, politics, networking, fund-raising, personnel management, negotiations, and foreign relations. The dissident group is therefore like a factory: it combines many diverse skills to manufacture a PG.

Dissident entrepreneurs try to learn about this production process and improve the productivity of their tactics. They then formalize their knowledge; as dissident groups age, they write training manuals (Alinsky 1946, 1971; Oppenheimer and Lakey 1964; Kahn 1982; Staples 1984; Adams 1991; Bobo, Kendall, and Max 1991) and establish training facilities. This is the institutionalization of protest.

### 3.4.2. Innovations in Technology

Dissident entrepreneurs know that rank-and-file dissidents are more likely to participate if the costs are low (sect. 3.2) and the benefits high (sect. 3.1). Leaders thus want to find the most efficient way to attain the group's PG

(Fireman and Gamson 1979, 33). They draw upon their own experience and that of others, they attempt to develop theoretical understanding of the concrete historical situation they face, and then they carefully plan group actions. Most important, entrepreneurs introduce technological innovation into the group's production process.

Prior to the nineteenth century, collective dissent was based on "traditional" forms of organization. Familial, clan, village, and patron-client ties mobilized dissidents. Collective dissent thus became the "politics of notables." Elite patrons mobilized their mass clients. Mass participation was thereby restricted. Elites made little effort to articulate and represent mass demands, nor to mobilize mass support. The consequence was that protests and rebellions tended to be spontaneous, undisciplined, unstable, anarchic, and decentralized. Tilly (1978, chap. 5) argues that collective dissent "modernized" during the nineteenth century. Specific political objectives came to be pursued by formal organizations that were continuous, hierarchical, and composed of a cadre of salaried professionals. The consequence was that mass participation in protests and rebellions was institutionalized. Organizations were populist and mass-mobilizing, political and ideological, and directing and controlling. Protests and rebellions tended to become more planned, disciplined, stable, ordered, and centralized. Specific examples of institutional innovations in collective dissent during the nineteenth century include unions, factory councils, workers' assemblies, and people's soviets.[18]

The invention and innovation of new technologies continues today. For example, in the United States, people have learned how to form public interest groups from individual contributions. Activists now understand the uses of seed grants, direct mail, advertising copy, and related financial planning. They know that newspaper ads or VHF television commercials are not usually cost effective. They have a good idea of which mailing lists contain a higher ratio of future contributors (McFarland 1991, 20). This technology is catelogued in training manuals.

All such innovations in the technology of collective dissent affect the level of collective dissent. As Dunn (1989, 232) argues, the implications of technological innovation are profound: "Revolutions may become possible in conditions in which they would previously had been quite inconceivable." A proposition immediately suggests itself: as the dissidents' production technology improves, collective dissent increases. Dissident groups that have exhausted their ideas are more likely to fail than are those that pursue novel approaches.[19]

Dissidents recognize this proposition and thus seek to copy the successes of others and invent new technologies of collective dissent. Therefore, innovations in the dissidents' production function ultimately diffuse and it is impossible to keep the genie of collective dissent in the bottle. Diffusion occurs more quickly in open democratic states than in autocratic states. But whatever the rate, successful innovations in the technology of collective dissent will be adopted by all dissident entrepreneurs (sect. 4.1.2). Moore (1966, xiii) thus refers to the "spread and reception of institutions that have been hammered out elsewhere." For example, after a new approach was introduced in the U.S. civil rights movement, copycat campaigns dominated the movement for several weeks (Chong 1991, 178).

Regimes also recognize this proposition. They do not stand passively by but try instead to invent new technologies of repression. Hence, Dunn (1989, 232) points out that it is also conceivable that "revolutions will become impossible in conditions in which previously they would have been comparatively simple to bring about." Thus, the U.S. government's response to the civil rights movement included expanded FBI surveillance and improved methods of riot control.

### 3.4.3. Targets

Targets refer to the audience for dissident tactics. As Marwell and Oliver (1984, 17) suggest, "Collective events rarely produce the collective goods of interest directly, but rather indirectly through persuading someone else to do something." This implies that dissidents who are trying to improve the productivity of their tactics must always keep their target in mind: "There must be an identifiable group or agency or firm which is capable of granting the end sought. There must, in a sense, be not only a specific goal but a specific *target*" (Wilson 1961, 294, emphasis in original). In general, dissident groups try to influence four target populations: governments, publics, dissidents, and victims.

First, dissidents target the government. The "state," of course, is too gross a target for all but the least discerning dissidents, so the political arena in which the dissidents confront the regime involves specific legislative, executive, and/or judicial actors. Dissidents try to influence governmental actors who are powerful enough to deliver the dissidents' PG yet vulnerable enough to be susceptible to the dissidents' influence.

The dissidents' second audience is the general public. They need to win over allies and patrons (sect. 6.2) from among both the bystanders at a dissident event and all those who might become aware of the event. Dissidents trying to improve the productivity of their tactics therefore choose targets with publicity value. Hence, as the publicity value of a target increases, collective dissent directed at that target increases. For example, more terrorism occurred in Western than in Eastern Europe during the 1970s, because Western democratic governments were more vulnerable to terrorist appeals than were the Communist governments.

Third, dissident groups target potential dissidents. Unlike the second group, they do not need to be converted to the cause; they just need to be activated. Hence, dissident entrepreneurs take their follower's reactions into account when deciding upon their strategy.

Appealing to these three targets often involves complex tradeoffs. Compromise on policy might be required in order to win government accommodation of demands (sect. 3.5) and external support from sympathizers (sect. 6.2), yet doctrinal purity might be required to produce adherents ready and willing to act. Deciding which of the three groups to target is therefore an important choice facing dissident entrepreneurs. It is the political (and thus more interesting) analogue of determining complements and substitutes in a production function (sect. 3.4.4).

A fourth target is the victims — the people and property that are the proximate objectives of dissident tactics. Dissidents trying to improve the productivity of their tactics will choose vulnerable targets. As the accessibility of a target increases, collective dissent directed against that target increases. Terrorism is a classic illustration. Terrorists attack targets that are less well guarded. Evidence on this point comes from a study of assassinations (Snitch 1982, 60-62). Moreover, as targets become better guarded, they are attacked less frequently. Laqueur (1987, 109) thus reports that car bombings have been limited by techniques ranging from "physical barriers to banning motor transport altogether in the vicinity of buildings believed to be possible targets." A second classic illustration comes from guerrilla warfare. Partisans choose vulnerable targets by matching their strategy and tactics to an opponent and the terrain. This occurred in the Rhodesian guerrilla war (Himes 1980, 178).

### 3.4.4. Tactics

Dissidents choose from a repertoire of possible tactics (Tilly 1978, 151-59), including legal rent seeking, extremist voting, emigration, banditry, strikes, demonstrations, and terrorism. Some tactics are individually effective and some collectively effective.

The *Improve the Productivity of Tactics* solution to the Rebel's Dilemma implies that dissidents seek the most individually efficacious tactics from among the set of possible tactics. They therefore are after the most favorable benefit/cost ratios. As Tilly (1978, 153) argues, dissidents consider "the relative appropriateness and efficiency of the means the group actually uses and the alternative means which are theoretically available." Alinsky (1971, 126) puts it even more simply: "Tactics mean doing what you can with what you have."

Dissident entrepreneurs looking to employ effective tactics must discover their group's demand functions for various tactics, including relative costs and benefits. Dissidents discover these demand functions by experimentation and adapt their tactics accordingly. Lack of success in one channel leads dissidents to try others. As the marginal benefits (costs) from using one tactic increase relative to the benefits (costs) from using another tactic, the probability that dissidents choose the first tactic increases (decreases). Examples of dissidents learning from their mistakes and changing their tactics in response to unsuccessful experiments include socialists,[20] terrorists,[21] and revolutionaries.[22]

Adaptation therefore generally works in the dissidents' favor. A corollary is that the more adaptable the dissident group, the greater the level and success of collective dissent. This proposition holds for at least four reasons. First, adaptable groups use a variety of tactics. As Gurr (1970, 305) argues, variety in tactics leads to a high volume of collective dissent: "Dissident institutional support varies strongly with the number and scope of means for anti-regime action provided by dissident-oriented organizations." Second, adaptable groups mix inputs to produce outputs more efficiently. Dogmatic, slow, and inflexible dissident groups are less successful because they do not use their resources effectively. Third, adaptable groups quickly adopt innovations that have been used successfully elsewhere (sect. 3.4.2). Finally, adaptable groups are less predictable. As the unpredictability of the dissidents increases, collective dissent increases, because the regime's ability to repress the rebels decreases (Gerlach 1971, 825–26). Terrorists and guerrillas thus often try to confuse and surprise the regime with essentially random tactics.[23]

Dissidents must also discover which of their tactics are collectively effective. Those that are complements will be positively related: as one increases, the other will increase. Those that are substitutes, will be negatively related: as one increases, the other will decrease. Several different rational actor models lead to competing expectations about such linkages among types of collective dissent.[24] The idea that forms of collective dissent are correlated has also led to many factor analytic and correlational studies, with equally mixed results.[25] Further theoretical work is needed in order to make predictions about complementarity and substitutability. Empirical work will then be needed to verify the predictions.

### 3.4.5. Tactics: Collective Violence and Nonviolence

Dissidents must choose whether to take the path of violence or that of nonviolence. The value of legal tactics often stunned Marx ([1895] 1964, 27): "The irony of world history turns everything upside down. We, the 'revolutionaries' — the 'rebels' — we are thriving far better on legal methods than on illegal methods and revolt. The parties of order, as they call themselves, are perishing under the legal conditions created by themselves." The choice is hotly debated in dissident circles; Lenin and Bernstein, for example, exchanged polemics over whether the revolution had to be violent. CA thinking can clarify both the confusion and the debate.

### 3.4.5.1. Why Collective Violence Is Used

Collective violence is used purposively. Tarrow (1989, 16) maintains that "people are induced to protest for the same reasons that they engage in conventional political activity, only less often: when they see it as being in their interest and when the opportunity presents itself to do so." Hobsbawm (1959, 111) writes that "the classical mob did not merely riot as a protest, but because it expected to achieve something by its riot."

What do dissidents expect to achieve by violence? For one, dissidents employ violence to seize power. Clausewitz maintains that "war is the continuation of politics by other means." In a similar vein, Mao (1961) suggests that "political power grows out of the barrel of a gun." For another, dissidents employ violence to influence power. As Stevens (1975, 373, emphasis in original) contends, collective violence is a form of political communication: "Participants in protest activities clearly intend to communicate with *somebody* about *something*." What dissidents often wish to communicate, Hobsbawm (1959, 116) observes, is their willingness to enter the give-and-take of reformist politics: "Provided the ruler did his duty, the populace was prepared to defend him with enthusiasm. But if he did not, it rioted until he did. This mechanism was perfectly understood by both sides." In short, collective violence is collective bargaining by another name. Hobsbawm (1952, 59) refers to "collective bargaining by riot" and Etzioni (1970, 18, emphasis in original) calls demonstrations an "*interim election tool.*" If dissident leaders believe that collective violence is a bargaining chip for gaining concessions, they will choose that tactic.[26]

Collective violence, then, is part of both the revolutionary and reformist political struggles between regimes and oppositions (chap. 7). For the dissident, it holds four potential strategic advantages: collective violence permits dissidents to enter conventional politics, disrupts the conventional politics from which they are excluded, lets them enter the struggle for resources, and allows them to sort out their friends and enemies. Let us now examine these advantages more closely.

First, where dissidents are by definition excluded from conventional politics, collective violence enables them to enter the political fray. It achieves this objective in several ways.

- Collective violence publicizes a dissident group's existence. As a dissident group's violent actions increase, so does its visibility. Given that the maxim, "Out of sight, out of mind," has a particularly acute meaning for the dissidents' cause, all dissident groups seek visibility.
- Collective violence advertises a dissident group's grievances. Collective violence is thus a warning or a demand for change that calls attention to conditions seen as unjust.[27]
- Collective violence announces a dissident group's programs and solutions. It trumpets the group's political message to the world and its demands to state authorities.[28]

Second, once dissidents are able to inform conventional politicians of their presence, they must disrupt the cozy world of establishment politics. Collective violence achieves this objective in several ways.

- Collective violence disrupts the status quo. Tarrow (1989, 93) offers some interesting examples of tactics designed to create chaos: "Truck drivers affected by slowdowns of customs officials could block traffic at the border; commuters delayed by railroad strikes could block platforms and tracks; medical patients affected by doctors' strikes could parade in wheelchairs. The government would have to intervene to force a settlement of the work-related issues when third parties intervened - which is precisely why they did intervene."
- Collective violence pierces the veil of legitimacy so prized by authorities. The technique forces government to take reprisals and thereby demonstrate that it rules by naked force. Many dissidents therefore find violence and counterviolence useful, because they believe that such a spiral can awaken a "brainwashed" people.
- Collective violence shocks people out of their complacency. Huntington (1968, 359) suggests that dissidents seek tactics that are new and different, unconventional and antiestablishment, because of their shock value:

  The effectiveness of violence and disorder in stimulating reform, however, does not lie in its inherent character. It is not violence per se but rather the shock and novelty involved in the employment of an unfamiliar or unusual political technique that serves to promote reform. It is the demonstrated willingness of a social group to go beyond the accepted patterns of action which gives impetus to its demands. In effect, such action involves the diversification of political technique and a threat to existing political organization and procedures.

This search for tactics that are expected to shake people out of their complacency accounts for the use of obscenity during protest demonstrations (Stewart, Smith, and Denton 1984, chap. 11).[29]

* Collective violence reveals a dissident group's potential for further collective violence. Dissidents use collective violence to demonstrate "their capacity to disrupt society if their demands are not satisfied" (Gurr 1970, 212). Collective violence at time $t$ therefore always carries an implicit threat of collective violence at time $t+1$. As Nieburg (1962, 865) notes, "The 'rational' goal of the threat of violence is an accommodation of interests . . . Similarly, the 'rational' goal of actual violence is demonstration of the will and capability of action, establishing a measure of the credibility of future threats." Regimes always take such threats of future disorder seriously because they fear that collective violence could trigger a bandwagon (sect. 4.1.2).

Third, once dissidents disrupt establishment politics, they can enter into the struggle for resources. Collective violence furthers this goal in several ways.

* Collective violence establishes a dissident group's resources (sect. 3.3). Dissidents must be reassured of their own strength, which increases their confidence that they will be successful (sect. 3.6). Regimes must also be convinced of the dissidents' strength. If a group does not have access to conventional political channels, its viewpoint will be dismissed unless it can somehow signal its strength. Only strong dissidents are credible threats to regimes. Furthermore, regimes are often patrons of collective dissent (sect. 6.2.3.2), seeking out and granting recognition and privileges to certain groups as the legitimate spokespeople for a grievance. Paradoxically, since this recognition is accorded only to groups known to have considerable resources, regimes provide dissidents with incentives to demonstrate their strength and power.
* Collective violence increases a dissident group's resources, facilitating the *Increase Resources* solution to the Rebel's Dilemma (sect. 3.3). Dissidents sometimes have few resources to use in bargaining with a regime. To gain those resources, they will therefore resort to collective violence. As Gurr (1970, 211) puts it, "The most direct utilitarian use of violence is to seize a desired value, as rioters do when they pillage warehouses and as conspirators do in a coup d'etat." Collective violence might also be used to gain third-party patrons (sect. 6.2) who are extremists.
* Collective violence enhances a dissident group's bargaining resources

in three ways. First, it establishes a group's irrationality. As Schelling (1966, 42) argues, it is sometimes in a bargainer's interest not to appear completely calm, calculating, and rational. And Chong (1991, 86) maintains that "'reckless' strategies that are pursued by individuals in the course of a conflict (like the freedom rides or the policy of jail-no-bail), which risk their lives and well-being, may also exact a significant cost from their adversaries — enough of a cost that they are more willing to negotiate." Second, collective violence enhances a group's reputation for toughness (Chong 1991, 179), and tough bargainers are more likely to get what they want. Third, collective violence enhances a group's ability to make credible threats (Schelling 1966, 36), which makes them more likely to gain concessions from the regime.

- Collective violence — guerrilla war, for instance — reduces a regime's resources and can fatally weaken it.
- Collective violence demonstrates a regime's weakness, for example that it is unable to protect even its own supporters. This reinforces the *Increase the Probability of Winning* solution to the Rebel's Dilemma (sect. 3.6), which can convert the uncommitted, and possibly even those committed to the regime, to the dissidents' side.

Finally, once dissidents are able to enter the struggle for power, they will use collective violence to try to divide the political world into new, and more favorable, alignments (Riker 1982). Collective violence accomplishes this goal in several ways.

- Collective violence polarizes a conflict by provoking reprisals by regimes. The deepening conflict shows neutrals that their position is untenable. It frightens nonvictims into thinking that they may one day become victims and that they therefore must choose sides. It convinces sympathizers that they need the dissident group for protection.
- Collective violence, in provoking reprisals, can generate a new issue - the government response itself - that may divide a regime's coalition (Riker 1982, chap. 9). Oberschall (1979, 47) thus writes that

> in addition to the original issue at stake in the conflict — the collective good sought by the challenger — the challenger's nonconventional tactics and the authorities' social control response in the confrontation create new issues . . . Did the police use rough tactics and unnecessary force against peaceful demonstrators? Were the demonstrators responsible for broken windows? Did the prose-

cuted lawbreakers get fair trials? Was the speech made by a leader an incitement of violence? And so on. Derivative issues will create conflict over the apportionment of responsibility, blame, penalties, and compensation for wrongs, damages, injuries, and deaths resulting from nonconventional means of waging conflict.

- Collective violence helps to build a dissident movement by attracting new members and arousing old ones, by increasing popular support and group solidarity. Thus, dissidents can mobilize their supporters by their choice of tactics, as well as by their choice of goals.
- Collective violence radicalizes a dissident group. Extremists often use violence and counterviolence to polarize the group and thereby outflank the moderates by forcing them either to fight or to yield leadership. Italian terrorists are a case in point: they set out to destroy the Communist Party (through provoking government reprisals) or to force it to assume the leadership of the revolution (Tarrow 1989).

In sum, collective violence can be a quite attractive strategy.

### 3.4.5.2. When Collective Violence Is Used

Dissidents seeking to improve the productivity of their tactics choose violent tactics when the relative returns to collective violence increase. Several factors influence these returns: the regime's tactics, the dissidents' demands, the length of the campaign, the levels of dissident violence and nonviolence, and dissident strength.

*Regime violence.* Reprisals by the regime require self-defense by the dissidents. Hence, as the use of violence by government increases, dissident tactics come increasingly to emphasize violence. All of this is part of the team competition between enemies (sect. 3.10.1.2).

*Dissident demands.* The more radical the demands, the more likely they are to be rejected by the regime, which makes it all the more likely that dissidents will try to overthrow the regime; and the more dissidents try to overthrow a regime, the greater the need to resort to more violent tactics. Hence, as dissident demands become radical, their tactics become violent. Nonviolence does not work for radicals for another reason: extremism marginalizes extremists. Since radicals cannot muster enough support to compete in the interest group or electoral arenas, and since their militant programs cannot attract a mass movement dedicated to social revolution, violence becomes their weapon of choice. It is the weapon of revolutionaries in a nonrevolutionary situation, the weapon of small minorities who cannot mobilize the great majority of people to their side. Expect terrorism, in short, when mass-based movements of nonviolent reform or social revolution fail. As Rubenstein (1987, 164) puts it, terrorism is the "dark twin" of reform in that both terrorism and reformism become attractive when mass social revolution is impossible.

*Length of the dissidents' campaign.* Lengthy campaigns tend to be associated with few concessions by government and a strong dissident group. Hence, as the struggle wears on, dissidents turn to more violent tactics.

*Existing level of collective violence.* The returns to collective violence are likely to be highly nonlinear throughout the range of violence. As Gurr (1989, 20) suggests, "Limited violence sometimes helped dramatize a cause and demonstrate the risks of resistance to reform. More extensive violence usually proved a liability for the group and cause with which it was associated." Hence, as the level of collective violence increases, dissident groups experience first increasing and then diminishing marginal returns.

*Existing level of collective nonviolence.* Collective violence and collective nonviolence may complement each other in the dissidents' production process. Especially when used in conjunction with nonviolence, collective violence may be a powerful impetus to reformist political change. The two strategies are often pursued by different members of the dissidents' coalition — radicals and reformists. Hence, the reformists, much to the regime's dismay, often do not disown the radicals: "Such violence, indeed, may well be encouraged by leaders who are completely committed to working within the existing system and who view the violence as a required stimulus for reforms within that system" (Huntington 1968, 357–58).[30]

*Strength of the dissidents.* The number of dissidents is critical to the dissident group's choice of tactics. There are, however, two competing views on how group strength influences group violence.

Some hold that collective violence is a resort of the powerful, not of the weak. Gamson (1990, chap. 6) maintains that only strong groups can afford to use collective violence because they have the resources to sustain that violence in the face of the government's likely violent response: "Violence grows from an impatience born of confidence and a sense of rising power. It occurs when the challenging group senses that the surrounding community will condone it, when hostility toward the *victim* renders it a relative safe strategy. In this sense, violence is as much a symptom of success as a cause" (Gamson 1974, 39). Hence, as a dissident group's resources increase (e.g., with external support), collective violence increases. Any factor that increases a dissident group's resources (e.g., external support) will therefore be associated with more collective violence by that group.

Others maintain that collective violence is a resort of the powerless, of those who lack domestic and foreign support. A weapon of the weak, violence allows dissidents with limited means to attempt to achieve unlimited goals. For example, terrorists are those who can neither organize a mass movement for a rebellion nor the military for a coup. Terrorism, in this view, is the weapon of those who have no mass following and face overwhelming government power.[31]

Tarrow suggests an interesting resolution to the group strength-group violence controversy. He argues on the basis of the Italian case that there are cycles of protest. On the upswing of collective dissent, when mobilization is increasing, dissidents estimate their probability of winning (sect. 3.6) on the high side. Since in this phase organization is not needed to solve the Rebel's Dilemma, dissidents tend to be loosely organized. By contrast, on the downswing, when demobilization is occurring, no serious prospect for revolution exists to encourage collective dissent. In this phase, organization becomes necessary in order to solve the Rebel's Dilemma. As Tarrow (1989) suggests, when mobilization is on the increase, movement leaders can either challenge or ignore the existing institutions. As mobilization declines, fewer new participants are available, and those who remain prefer to participate in institutions that provide more certain rewards. The result: "The heritage of protest was organization . . . organization is a product of the decline of mobilization; to survive in a period of quiescence it must retain the memory of the injustice that gave it birth" (Tarrow 1989, 319).

Moreover, on the downswing, unorganized collective dissent bifurcates into two forms of organization: organized collective violence (e.g., terrorist groups) and organized collective participation (e.g., leftist political parties): "As the cycle of mass mobilization in which it is born comes to an end, a social movement organization has only two choices: either to follow the route of 'an extremism — lacking a solid mass foundation' . . . or a shift towards institutional politics" (Tarrow 1989, 285–86). Only two types of dissident organizations are therefore possible: "Highly-structured ones with national programmes and memberships, on the one hand, and small cells of militants using street violence, industrial sabotage, and clandestine organizing, on the other" (Tarrow 1989, 320). Dissidents will thus become either alienated, radicalized, and violently antisystem (e.g., terrorist organizations) or institutionalized, reformist, and within-system (e.g., interest groups, community groups, political parties). According to Tarrow (1989, 325), "When mobilization declines [movement entrepreneurs] can only choose their roles from a limited repertoire — the agitator turned journalist, the interest group bureaucrat, the co-opted politician, the advocate of armed struggle."

In short, violence is a strategy of some of the strong who have become weak. As a dissident group weakens, it may factionalize (sect. 6.4) into one subgroup that uses *more* violence and another subgroup that uses *less* violence.

### 3.5. Reduce the Supply of the Public Good

When the PG is a normal good, if the level that is exogenously supplied decreases, more of it will be demanded. One solution to the Rebel's Dilemma is therefore to reduce the supply of the PG. Exogenous changes in the dissident's supply of the PG are primarily the result of the regime's policy of accommodating dissident demands. Hence, a simple prediction from CA theories is that when government makes concessions, collective dissent decreases.

Neither theory nor reality, however, are quite so simple. There are those who argue that government accommodation reduces collective dissent and those who argue the contrary, that accommodation increases collective dissent. Why is it that accommodation sometimes succeeds and sometimes fails? And why also do governments sometimes accommodate and sometimes repress their opponents?

There have been some speculations on these questions (Lichbach 1984). Nonetheless, they remain largely unanswered. We do not know much about the origins and consequences of government response strategies to collective dissent. The accommodation-dissent nexus, like the repression-dissident nexus, is a puzzle for conflict studies. Nor does the CA research program offer a simple resolution to such puzzles. I discuss the implications of these gaps in section 9.3.3.

### 3.6. Increase the Probability of Winning

Dissidents' beliefs and expectations about their potential successes and failures are crucial to collective dissent. As a dissident's estimate of the chances of victory increases, his or her participation in collective dissent also increases. Rational dissidents only participate in winning causes. Hence, protest movements begin when a group of dissidents is hopeful, optimistic, and indeed confident of achieving their objectives. Alternatively, as a dissident's estimate of the chances of victory decreases, his or her participation in collective dissent also decreases. Rational dissidents do not participate in losing causes. Hence, protest movements end when the group despairs of ever achieving its objectives.

The supporters of this idea are legion,[32] but there is a counterargument as well. There are four reasons why collective dissent often occurs when the prospects of victory are low.

First, although the prospects of success might well encourage dissidents, the prospects of failure often do not discourage them. A high probability of winning, in other words, is a sufficient but not a necessary condition for collective dissent. The reason is quite simple: successful collective dissent is often a long-shot (Chong 1991, 94). As Falcoff (1976, 38) observes, "All revolutionary regimes seem inevitable in power and impossible in defeat." Some dissidents, however, are evidently committed to lost causes — the probability of winning, at least in any immediate sense, being quite irrelevant. As Weber (1946, 128) puts it, "Certainly all historical experience confirms the truth — that man would not have attained the possible unless time and again he had reached out for the impossible." Or as stated in *Mr. Smith Goes to Washington*, "The only causes worth fighting for are lost causes." After the failure of the Huk rebellion, a Filipino rebel expressed such sentiments: "Even if we got nothing, that's not important. What's important is that we *had* to fight back. And we fought so well that the big people and the government will never forget us again . . . No strike, no demonstration, no rebellion fails. Protest against injustice always succeeds" (Walton 1984, 68-69). One should therefore not be surprised to find, as did Chorley ([1943] 1973, 42), that "insurrections have frequently broken out spontaneously in conditions where any chance of permanent success was impossible and have even occasionally been launched deliberately in the accepted knowledge that they could achieve no positive and direct success."

A second and related argument is that dissidents might be particularly risk-prone individuals (sect. 3.9). If rebels are convinced that they can beat the odds, they might rebel in spite of a low probability of success.[33] They might also ignore the probability of winning if they attach value to the means of protest, regardless of its ends (sect. 4.2.1).

Third, losses reinforce group identity. Lasswell and Kaplan (1950, 47) remark that "defeat may serve only to heighten group solidarity and consciousness. The defeat may itself provide common interests — in rehabilitation and revenge, for example — and increase awareness of what is *to* the group interest." Collective dissent that fails and is repressed reveals the regime's brutality and creates martyrs; troops are rallied and team competition between enemies increases (sect. 3.10).

Finally, collective dissent begets more collective dissent, much like a bandwagon (sect. 4.1.2), *regardless* of its immediate success. One reason for this is that *any* collective dissent shows that victory is at least possible, even if not at present. In other words, a defeat can lead a rational dissident to update, in a Bayesian sense, his or her estimate of the probability of victory. Debray (1967, 51–52) thus explains the use of violence in lost causes: "The physical force of the police and the army is considered unassailable [by the masses], and unassailability cannot be challenged by words but by showing that a soldier and a policeman are no more bullet-proof than anyone else . . . In order to destroy the idea of unassailability . . . there is nothing better than combat." Chorley ([1943] 1973, 42) argues similarly: "Regarding revolutionary strategy, by and large it does not necessarily follow that such insurrections [doomed to defeat] are always unjustifiable. Indirectly, they can sometimes alter the whole political situation so deeply that from a revolutionary standpoint they may be a valuable factor in long-term strategy, even though foredoomed to military failure." Such is often the reasoning behind terrorist actions.

This counterargument to the probability of winning solution has some validity, and is well worth exploring.[34] It is, nonetheless, possible to set it aside for the moment[35] and explore the many rich implications of the probability of winning solution. The solution tells about the calculus and actions of dissidents, dissident entrepreneurs, and states, and about the competition between state and opposition.

### 3.6.1. The Dissident's Calculus

The *Increase the Probability of Winning* solution to the Rebel's Dilemma reveals much about a rational dissident's decision calculus and hence about protest and rebellion: that a dissident's expectations matter a great deal; that a dissident's expectations, costs, and benefits interact to produce rational dissent; and that collective dissent is difficult to predict.

First, one would expect expectations to matter and that there to be a correlation between belief in the efficacy of protest and protest behavior. And, indeed, direct survey evidence[36] and indirect aggregate evidence[37] corroborates that point: as a dissident's belief in the efficacy of protest increases, his or her participation in collective dissent increases.

Second, interactions matter and affect how benefits influence collective dissent. Thus, some dissidents will value the benefits of their contribution to the PG (sect. 3.1) more than they will regret the cost of their contribution toward the PG (sect. 3.2), but will still not contribute. This is because the value of the PG minus the cost of the PG is less than the value of the PG times the probability of receiving the PG (Frohlich, Oppenheimer, and Young 1971, 23). If dissidents attach low probabilities to winning, they will usually not participate in collective dissent, even if they value the potential benefits of their contribution from the PG more than they deplore the costs of their individual contribution toward the PG.

Interactions matter in another way. As the probability of the government's eventual victory increases, the strength and immediacy of the reward to the dissidents must increase if they are to participate (Leites and Wolf 1970, 44). If dissidents attach low probabilities to winning, they will participate only if they value the private benefits of their contribution from the PG much more than they regret the costs of their individual contribution toward the PG.

Finally, there is one major unintended consequence of dissidents solving the Rebel's Dilemma by participating because victory is possible: collective dissent becomes volatile and hence unpredictable (sect. 9.2).[38] One reason for the volatility of collective dissent is that expectations are so erratic. Expectations of success are even more erratic than interests, or the probabilities are more volatile than utilities (Blalock 1989, 59). Sudden outbreaks of collective dissent are therefore better explained by updated estimates of the probability of success than by recalculations of utility.

This solution produces volatility in collective dissent for a second reason: dissidents switch sides (sect. 9.2.2.2), from the regime to the dissident group and back again, as they recalculate the probability of victory.[39] The regime's supporters, for example, will reconsider their loyalties if they discover that the dissidents have a broad base of support and the regime's capacity to enforce its claims is limited. Given the greater volatility of expectations than interests, changing sides in a conflict is more likely to be a function of a change in expectations than a change in interests: as their calculations of the probability of victory change, dissidents switch sides. Such recalculations, as both Tocqueville and Trotsky (Stinchcombe 1978, chap. 2) argue, are more common during turbulent times than during stable eras. Dissidents, therefore, will be consistent in their allegiance during nonrevolutionary periods and fickle during revolutions.

The third way that volatility results from this solution relates to timing. People flock to a dissident group that appears about to win. Many of these late arrivals are driven by preference falsification (Kuran 1987) because it is increasingly advantageous to switch sides. Edwards (1927, 190–91) writes that

> as soon as it becomes evident that the revolution is going to succeed, a vast number of "political careerists" crowd into the public service. A political careerist is a person without political convictions who desires to win fame and fortune in politics. As long as the future of the revolution is in doubt he keeps out of sight. As soon as its success is assured he outdoes all the old revolutionaries in his loyalty to revolutionary principle.

Consequently, as a dissident group approaches victory, the ratio of opportunists to ideologues increases. Wilson (1973, 107) suggests that "as a party comes close to power, it tends to be dominated by the officeseekers; once in power, it will tend to be controlled by its officeholders." Hence, those who join a dissident group first tend to be more committed than those who join last. Early joiners, since they assume more costs, will also probably demand more benefits, remain longer in the group, and seek greater influence over policy.

Moreover, after the dissident group has won power, additional dissidents will flock to it (sect. 9.2.2.2). When the probability of victory becomes a certainty, that is, potential dissidents become actual dissidents and gravitate toward the winning side. Coleman (1990, 498) argues that this explains the oft-cited observation that government legitimacy follows, rather than precedes, government effectiveness:

> The divesting of authority and revesting of authority may not take place among most of the populace until after a revolt has succeeded. In coups d'état, which occur quickly, the divesting and revesting of authority merely legitimate the transfer of power. The more general principle which this exemplifies is that the vesting of the right to control depends in part on the *existence* of control. If an actor holds effective power over others, the right to exercise that power is often forthcoming from them; if an actor is not able to exercise power, the right to do so is often withdrawn.

Hence, more individuals join a dissident group after it is successful than before. Most revolutionaries to arrive late to the revolution.

## 3.6.2. Estimating the Probability of Winning

Rational dissidents seek information (sect. 3.8.1) about their relative strength vis-à-vis the regime. As Edelman (1971, 131) indicates, "Far from being the resolute, monolithic 'dedicated' militants that are stock characters in the stylized scenarios of their political opponents, potential rioters are peculiarly anxious to respond to any information that will resolve their gnawing uncertainty about their support and the risks they run." Dissidents acquire this information during their various confrontations with the regime. Rule (1988, 75) argues that "forces realign in the process of militant confrontation." Hence, protests and rebellions are more than acts in an ongoing conflict; they also indicators of the political balance-of-power. Regimes and oppositions are therefore well known to one another before any single, final, dramatic confrontation. Rebels use the prelude to the final showdown to acquire information about the dissidents' victories and about the regime's weaknesses so that they can update their estimates of the probability of winning.

### 3.6.2.1. The Dissident Group's Victories
The dissidents' past successes and failures are key indicators of the probability of future victories and losses. "A highly publicized conspicuous failure"

(Jackson, Peterson, Bull, Monsen, and Richmond 1960, 40) can weaken confidence by increasing a sense of futility and frustration; a highly publicized conspicuous success can strengthen confidence by showing that the regime is vulnerable. In short, success breeds success; failure breeds failure. The empirical prediction is clear: collective dissent will increase after a dissident victory; collective dissent will decrease after a dissident defeat.[40]

Not all dissident victories are equal, however. Timing is a critical factor. First, major victories in the past tend to justify subsequent rebellion. As Gurr (1970, 222) suggests, "The dramatic successes of previous generations are likely to be enshrined in group traditions, more than losses or failures, and to be invoked to justify future rebellions decades and even centuries hence." Second, if a dissident group is not successful early, few will ever come to support the group. As Waterman (1981, 580, emphasis in original) argues, "*Early successes seem a nearly universal prerequisite of sustained and ultimately successful collective political activity of all kinds.*" The policy implication is clear: dissidents (and regimes) should "attempt to achieve successes to provide a display of power as early as possible in the revolt" (Coleman 1990, 500). This is the only way to overcome the "catch-22" of success: "People refrain from joining in the protests until they can see some tangible success, but any chance of success is ruled out unless people initially enlist in the campaign" (Chong 1991, 159). Third, while early victories are important, sheer perseverance has its own value. Potential dissidents discount flash-in-the-pan parties. Moreover, dissidents gain in strength by simply enduring — a sure sign of the regime's weakness is that it is unable to quash its opponents. Coleman (1990, 499) thus argues that "legitimacy may be withdrawn from the authorities not only before any organized revolt or at the end of a revolt (as acknowledgment of a fait accompli), but over the period of the revolt itself, as the authorities lose strength." Hence, the persistence of a dissident group enhances collective dissent: as the duration of a dissidents' campaign increases, the extent of collective dissent increases. Finally, periodic victories are important. As Gurr (1970, 222) puts it, "Value gains in the immediate past are probably recalled more clearly than more remote gains."

The dissident victory-collective dissent idea can be applied in two areas. Stinchcombe (1975, 573) argues that "the sudden conviction of a new party that it can win . . . can create radical (right or left) surges." This "sudden" conviction can come from a recent electoral success or a current membership drive. Hence, this proposition can be successfully applied to extremist party voting. The aggregate success of an extremist party among aggrieved and dominated groups is contingent upon its perceived probability of winning. For example, as the size of the total vote of a Communist party increases, the proportion of the vote it receives from the lower classes increases. Lipset's (1963, 177) evidence demonstrates where Communist parties are weak (i.e., not the largest party on the left), they win less support from the poorer workers.

The dissident victory-collective dissent proposition can also be successfully applied to guerrilla war. A story related by Bienen (1968, 61–62) makes this point quite effectively:

> Harry Villegas, a Cuban who operated with Guevara in Bolivia, was asked, on arrival in Chile, why the guerrillas were unable to gain the support of Bolivia's peasants. He was quoted as replying: "Because peasants are always with forces of power and strength. We did not reach the necessary phase of power. A guerrilla movement has three steps. The first is forming a people's army against the government. Next the guerrilla army becomes as powerful as the army. Finally the guerrillas become the power in the country. That is when the peasants support them. We lost our fight before reaching the second step."

Regis Debray (1967) thus suggests that a successful military operation is the best propaganda in guerrilla warfare.

### 3.6.2.2. The State's Weakness
The other major factor in a dissident's estimate of the probability of victory is the strength of the regime. As the state weakens, the likelihood of victory increases. Hence, weak states invite collective dissent and revolution.[41]

Judging how weak a state *really is* becomes complicated. Both dissidents and social scientists gauge state strength (Skocpol 1985) in many ways — as a function of government resources, government inefficiency and ineffectiveness, elite cooperation, succession fights, political crises, duration of the regime, external competition facing the regime, external examples, and external patronage.

*Government's resources.* This is the first factor that enters the calculations. The less the government's resources, the greater the dissidents' probability of success and, hence, the greater the collective dissent.

Financial problems are one manifestation of feeble government resources. Governmental financial crises appear to be a common precursor of revolution.[42] A disloyal military is another sign of weak government resources. Revolutions also often occurred after the regime's repressive apparatus disintegrated.[43] The repression argument is discussed in section 3.2 and the importance of the military as a patron is explored in section 6.2.3.1.

*Government inefficiency and ineffectiveness.* Dissidents are also alerted to a weak regime by its impotent and incompetent use of whatever resources it has. Thus, as government inefficiency and ineffectiveness increase, so does collective dissent.

Inflexibility is one indicator of government ineffectiveness. A regime that has resources, yet is dogmatic and slow in its policies, is incapable of governing. Many regimes were inflexible, for example, in the face of the challenges brought by modernization: "If *anciens régimes* had learned to cope with [modernization], they could master the problems of an industrial society with traditional strategies, up-dated. If not, they were usually already vulnerable and internally divided before the actual bourgeois or proletarian onslaught" (Mann 1987, 341). Crozier (1973) and Bonanate (1979a, 1979b) argue that a regime that is inflexible in the face of new challenges often produces a "blocked society" — a social order strong enough to preserve itself but resistant to innovation. This self-perpetuation yet immobility, they argue, is a recipe for collective dissent. A regime that is inflexible in the face of new challenges also often produces revolution. This is because an inflexible regime eventually begets an antiregime coalition (sect. 7.2.1). Stinchcombe (1975, 582) recognizes this point: "When a governing elite either does not see the challenge or is internally too rigid to do anything about it and incorporates developing forces too late, all the developing grievances and aspirations are forced into a single opposition movement, very often of a revolutionary character. Colonial regimes, absolutist monarchies, and military dictatorships are often inflexible in this way."

Irresponsible leaders are another factor in government ineffectiveness (Hagopian 1974, 158–62). Many have attributed revolution to ruling classes characterized by corruption, debauchery, idleness, luxury, frivolity, indolence, blundering, and stupidity. A political elite that no longer performs a productive function, one that is engaged exclusively in conspicuous and wasteful consumption, has often been considered a harbinger of revolution. This is a common theme in comparative studies of the Great Revolutions,[44] cyclical theories of dynastic decline in China,[45] and studies of ancient autocratic states.[46]

*Elite cooperation.* States have their own CA problem (sect. 7.2.2). The various members of the state do not always act in concert to support or oppose a dissident group; that is, a government may be divided against itself. Dissidents believe that disunity among elites increases their chances of victory so they try to exploit these divisions. When the competition for national political power (e.g., elections) is greatest, the state is therefore most vulnerable to collective dissent.[47] Elite disunity also encourages collective dissent by facilitating several additional solutions to the Rebel's Dilemma.

First, it provides patrons (sect. 6.2) for the dissidents. As Dobel (1978, 969) argues, collective dissent occurs because "a member of the elite or one of the dominant factions might try to provide the poor with leadership and mobilize them as a power base." Huntington (1965, 420–21) too argues that "if the elite divides against itself, its factions appeal to the masses for support." Protest, then, becomes a bargaining chip used by the competing factions of government. Elite-directed political mobilization thus begets collective dissent.

Second, conflicts within the ruling class open the way for placing new issues on the political agenda. Riker (1982, chap. 9; also see Schattschneider 1960, chap. 4) argues that this situation encourages political realignment, as coalitions form and reform. Entrepreneurs thus have new ways to shape an efficacious group (sect. 6.3.2).

Third, elite disunity, in revealing regime vulnerabilities, improves the dissidents' production function (sect. 3.4). Dissidents become aware of when and how to strike. As Tarrow (1989, 50) argues, "Temporary disequilibria in the balance of power can be exploited by groups whose social power under ordinary conditions would be minimal."

Finally, factionalism among the elite increases the CA problem of the regime when it attempts to mobilize its forces for its own defense. Goldstone (1988, 123) argues that "what is perhaps most striking in the fall of the Ming, and in the failures of restoration attempts, is the inability of gentry, officials, and commercial interests to find common ground on which to mobilize for defense. Support for the central government declined in favor of private mobilization to protect local areas, and by the mid-seventeenth century the integration of local gentry and state officials was nonexistent." Thus, the regime's power and resources, and hence ability to raise the costs of CA (e.g., repression), are undermined.

There is substantial evidence to support the elite disunity-collective dissent proposition. Where there is elite unity, there tends not to be violent collective dissent.[48] And where there is elite disunity, the polity tends to be prone to political violence.[49]

*Sucession fights.* Dissidents also consider fights over leadership succession when estimating the weakness of a regime. Regularized patterns of executive recruitment deter dissidents and hence lead to stability; indeterminate patterns engender protest and rebellion (Shin and Kim 1985). Thus, as leadership crises[50] increase, including failed attempts at taking power, protest and rebellion increase. Another reason that succession crises and unregulated executive recruitment lead to collective dissent is that they open up the polity to new groups with new grievances. When a king dies without heirs, for example, the survivors often fight over who rules and may try to mobilize previously quiescent groups (Avrich 1972, 13). Increased rent seeking, factions, and purges follow. Examples of succession crises leading to collective dissent are legion.[51]

*Political crises.* Dissidents also take account of political crises in gauging the weakness of a regime. Tarrow (1991, 16) suggests that "most successful social movements arise as part of general periods of political disorder."

This is because political alignments are up for grabs — old coalitions are deteriorating and new coalitions are emerging. Hence, dissidents realize that losers may become winners and winners may become even bigger winners.

Political crises also increase collective dissent because they offer everyone political opportunities (Tarrow 1991, 13–14). Dissident entrepreneurs have the chance to expand their power by building a new movement or rebuilding an old one. Regime entrepreneurs have the chance to extend their influence by attracting new supporters from outside of the polity. Finally, it is also an opportune time for rank-and-file dissidents, mobilized into CA by both these entrepreneurs (sect. 6.1) and by patrons (sect. 6.2). The potential benefits (sect. 3.1) from CA increase, because big issues, for example power relations, are being decided. The potential costs of CA (sect. 3.2) decrease, because the regime's coercive apparatus has collapsed. The probability of making a difference (sect. 3.7) increases, because individual dissidents believe they can legitimately and effectively make claims. And, the costs of collective inaction increase, because threats increase (sect. 3.12.1).

*Duration of the regime.* A dissident also looks at the duration of a regime in estimating weakness. Consider what happens after the collapse of the old regime and after the installation of a new order.

Revolutionary interregnums often occur after the fall of the old regime because many different dissident groups sense victory. The collapse of state power in the French, Russian, and Mexican revolutions, for example, led to a fight over state power. All social conflicts — among classes, between the center and the periphery, and between town and country — intensified. There are several reasons why revolutionary interregnums have such high levels of political violence. First, some revolutionaries will act only after they are certain that the old regime is gone. Second, revolutionary interregnums are often situations of dual sovereignty which invite conflict. Examples of dual sovereignty include the English Revolution (at first King versus Parliament, then Parliament versus the New Model Army), the French Revolution (at first King versus Parliament, then Parliament versus the Jacobin societies and the Paris commune), and the Russian Revolution (at first the Tsar versus the Duma, then the Duma versus the Bolsheviks and Soviets). Third, interregnums are often situations of multiple sovereignties, essentially a power vacuum that also invites violent conflict. Fourth, a collapse of the state signals the removal of both coercion (force) and consensus (legitimacy). As Pettee ([1938] 1971, 100) notes, "The revolution does not begin with the attack of a powerful new force upon the state. It begins simply with a sudden recognition by almost all the passive and active membership that the state no longer exists." Skocpol (1979, 47) thus argues that "the events of 1787-9 in France, of the first half of 1917 in Russia, and of 1911-16 in China . . . disorganized centrally coordinated administration and coercive controls over the potentially rebellious lower classes." Finally, revolutionary interregnums are particularly violent because as the political institutions of the old regime collapse, new groups are mobilized into politics. This is, of course, Huntington's "Western" type of revolution (1968, 266).

Even after the installation of the new order, dissidents do not give up on victory. In a postrevolutionary regime, another group of rebels may still be victorious. Many potential dissidents test the new regime's coercive capacity. In short, newly established regimes are particularly vulnerable to protest and rebellion.[52]

Three examples of how new regimes are challenged are instructive.[53] First, collective dissent often follows a sudden grant of independence. Conversely, as the number of years since independence increases, collective dissent decreases. There are numerous examples of protest and rebellion following the dissolution of colonial empires after World War II. As soon as the fight against the foreign enemy was won in the Congo and Angola, for example, rival guerrilla groups engaged in a free-for-all struggle for power that set former comrades-in-arms against one another. Communal strife and peasant uprising also followed the collapse of British authority in India (Moore 1966, 382). Military coups offer a second example. Potential coup makers will not give a newly installed postcoup regime the time to strengthen. Expect countercoups to follow coups, and expect them sooner rather than later. Radically different types of regimes offer a final example. Some types of postrevolutionary regimes are unprecedented (e.g., the French revolutionary state, the Soviet state). These present particular difficulties in estimating the opposition's probability of success. Many challenges, some half-baked, are to be expected.

*External competition facing the regime.* Dissidents also try to estimate the regime's foreign competition (Skocpol 1979, 20–21). War is the most important form of interstate competition.[54]

Defeat is taken as a sign of weakness; hence, it increases collective dissent. Edwards (1927, 48) argues that "defeat in foreign war hastens revolution." Chorley ([1943] 1973, chap. 6) argues that the defeat of the armed forces is the "supreme solvent" (p. 108) for their disintegration. Furthermore, defeat also weakens the coercive capacity of the regime (thereby reducing dissident costs, sect. 3.2). As put by Gurr (1970, 254), "Defeat in war . . . may signal the populace that the military is too weak to maintain internal order." Finally, defeat produces protest and rebellion by leading to resistance movements that unite many diverse interests in a nationalist appeal to "do something" about government's weakness (thereby increasing team competition, sect. 3.10). Illustrations of these arguments abound.[55]

In any event, regardless of victory or defeat, war increases collective dissent. Bianco (1967, 164) suggests that "war has no equal as a catalyst of revolution." Laqueur (1968, 501) stresses the same point: "War appears to have been the decisive factor in the emergence of revolutionary situations in modern times; most modern revolutions, both successful and abortive, have followed in the wake of war." A general relationship between internal and external war holds for a number of reasons. War, in the first instance, increases the financial burdens on a regime, burdens that are subsequently passed on to citizens in the form of taxes; this raises the possible benefits to be derived from CA (sect. 3.1). Tilly (1975b, 74) thus maintains that the preparation for war induces revolution because "the exaction of men, supplies and - especially - taxes for the conduct of war incites resistance from crucial elites or important masses." Examples include the French Revolution (Skocpol 1979) and the European revolutions of the seventeenth century (Brustein and Levi 1987). Second, war produces collective dissent because it diverts, depletes, and dilutes government resources. Most important, it diverts troops from internal repression to external adventures, which reduces the probability of repression and thus lowers the costs of participation in collective dissent (sect. 3.2). An example is the Russian Revolution. A third connection between internal and external wars relates to the postwar situation. Demobilized soldiers often find themselves unemployed, victims of the economic dislocations produced by war. Their skills are sought by dissident entrepreneurs, however. Factors of demand and supply thus bring them into dissident movements (sect. 3.3). Landsberger (1974, 52) neatly sums up these three arguments linking the causes, courses, and consequences of wars for the case of peasant rebellions: wars "impose additional burdens on the peasantry and they undermine the strength of the ruling class. But in addition, and of more relevance here, wars teach peasants to fight." This expectation of a general relationship between war and collective dissent also turns out to be true.[56]

*External Examples.* I have concentrated so far on the state within which dissidents are acting. Government resources, elite cooperativeness, succession fights, political crises, regime duration, and external competition all refer to the regime against which dissidents fight. But all of these phenomena may also describe *other* states. Such attributes of foreign states may change the way dissidents estimate the probability of victory within their own territory. The collapse of Communist regimes in Eastern Europe, for example, brought potential dissidents in the remaining Communist regimes to question the stability of their own regimes: they updated their estimates of the probability of winning. Such a mechanism may underlie bandwagons of collective dissent (sect. 4.1.2).

*External Patronage.* Dissidents take account of the probability of foreign support for the regime. For example, the success of the Iranian and Nicaraguan revolutions was partly a result of the withdrawal of American support to the Shah and Samoza, respectively. The question of external patronage is considered more fully in section 6.2.3.4.

In sum, many factors are behind the dissidents' expectations about the state's weakness. This complexity complicates the dissident group's and the state's strategies.

### 3.6.3. The Dissident Group's Strategy

Dissident entrepreneurs are keenly aware of the *Increase the Probability of Winning* solution to the Rebel's Dilemma. They therefore attempt to justify sacrifice and sustain hope by convincing people that the regime is a "colossus with clay feet" and that the dissidents have "the support of the masses." Examples of dissident entrepreneurs who realize the importance of this message are legion.[57]

One thus expects all dissident groups to wage their campaigns with an eye toward increasing their perceived probability of winning. Dissident entrepreneurs are more interested in building hope about the future (i.e., expectations of the probability of success) than creating despair about the past (i.e., grievances). They are, in addition, more concerned with convincing potential supporters that the group is strong than that the group is right, that their cause will succeed than that their cause is just. "It is less important that the empire is good or bad than that it is unavoidable," argues Wesson (1967, 192). Consequently, as Coleman (1990, 481) points out, the "revolutionaries' strategy should not be to win the support of the people, but to ensure that the people regard them as powerful." This was, he continues,

> the strategy of terrorists and guerrillas in Vietnam and elsewhere — not to win the support of the population but to immobilize it, to ensure through example that the population recognized that aid to the authorities would be swiftly and certainly punished. In such circumstances it seems unimportant whether the majority of the populace prefers the authorities or the revolutionaries; what is important is perceived power: what the people believe about the relative power of the two sides and about what will happen to them if they support one side or the other.

Both words and deeds matter for dissident entrepreneurs in their efforts to enhance estimates of their probability of winning.

Consider how they manipulate words. First, dissident groups strive to create the illusion of a large and fervently committed social base. Though such a claim is often very far from the truth, all dissident groups profess widespread, enduring, and intense support. Tilly (1985, 736) thus suggests that "the reality of the social movement hides behind a veil of mystification, shared by both sides of the conflict, that identifies the current actors with a broad base of support at the very moment when the self-styled spokespersons of the movement rush to create coalitions, eliminate rival leaders, solidify their own bases, avoid visible breaks, and organize public displays of unitary will."

Dissident leaders also make unqualified predictions of eventual victory. They inflate revolutionary expectations by maintaining that they have had victories, continue to win, and will eventually succeed. Calvert (cited in Laqueur 1978, 237) suggests that "revolutionaries aim to create an impression of power, invincibility and effectiveness, representing themselves as a force which must inevitably assume supremacy." Walt (1992, 337) indicates that "unless potential supporters believe their sacrifices will eventually bear fruit, a revolutionary movement will not get very far. Revolutionary ideologies are thus inherently optimistic: they invariably portray victory as inevitable despite what may appear to be overwhelming odds." These sentiments find their classic expression in the song of the U.S. civil rights movement, "We shall overcome someday."

Dissidents often invoke some sort of ironclad logic in support of their predictions that their struggle will inexorably produce success (Walt 1992, 337-39). In the case of Marxists and their followers in communist revolutions the irresistible force inheres in the "laws" of capitalist development. Khomeini and his followers in the Iranian Revolution invoked divine provenance. To bolster such predictions, dissidents try to portray the regime not only as dangerous (so as to increase team competition between enemies, sect. 3.10.1.2), but also as disorganized, unpopular, and vulnerable. Walt (1992, 338) offers some examples of dissidents arguing that their opponents' superiority is mere illusion:

> Mao Zedong argued . . . that "reactionaries" were "paper tigers" who "in appearance . . . are terrifying but in reality . . . are not so powerful," and Marshal Lin Biao asserted that "U.S. imperialism is stronger, but also more vulnerable, than any imperialism of the past." Lenin's assessment of imperialism was similar: as the "highest stage of capitalism," imperialism contained both the power to dominate the globe *and* the seeds of its inevitable destruction at the hands of the proletariat.

This approach is obviously designed to convince supporters to persevere in the face of a seemingly hopeless struggle.

As they predict eventual victory, however, dissident entrepreneurs take care to remind their followers that victory will not come easily, but only after a long and difficult struggle. After all, even the most die-hard supporters can be discouraged by the failure of the revolution to materialize. So dissident entrepreneurs are careful not to inflate revolutionary expectations and produce a string of unfulfilled promises. They are also careful to justify the inevitable setback and the temporary lack of progress, as well as heroic sacrifices and martyrdom (sect. 4.2.1). Thus, dissident entrepreneurs overestimate the probability of victory, while taking care not to underestimate the efforts required.[58]

Dissident entrepreneurs know, however, that their followers are not merely fools and dupes, that they must provide more than high-flown rhetoric and promises. They know that deeds are critical. Obviously, then, dissident leaders must organize collective dissent so as to increase expectations of the probability of victory. As Kuran (1989, 63-66) observes, dissident leaders are people with exceptional abilities to detect and expose a regime's vulnerabilities. Dissident leaders have numerous ways of organizing their struggle so as to increase their followers' estimates of their probability of winning.

First, the dissident group fights only when it thinks it can win. Otherwise, it retreats to fight another day. Guerrillas, for example, seek to maintain an image of inevitable victory. Mao (1961) argues that one should retreat when attacked. Che Guevara (cited in Scott et al. 1970, 91), too, warns against engaging in any battle, combat, or skirmish that cannot be won.

Second, the dissident group sequences its actions to show steady progress. At the beginning of the campaign "the basic strategy is to demonstrate influence by picking a target that offers promise of a quick success, thus showing potential constituents that the social movement actor is one to be reckoned with and that opportunities exist for collective action" (Fireman and Gamson 1979, 30). During the campaign the basic strategy is to choose a series of issues that can demonstrate gains to potential sympathizers. Given that "achievements are related inversely to aims" (Gauthier 1986, 4), dissidents will aim high but set achievable goals along the way. They thus select issues that are small, short-term, and specific, thereby reinforcing hope of an eventual, even if slow, victory. To raise 5000 pounds in "tuppenny subscriptions" (Thompson 1966, 699), for example, is an achievable goal.

Third, the dissident group tries to capture important symbols. Dissident entrepreneurs are well aware of the power of such symbols as the fall of the Bastille in France in 1789, Dublin Castle in Ireland in 1916, and the Winter Palace in Russia in 1917 (Chorley [1943] 1973, 32–33).

Fourth, the dissident group fights indirectly. If the dissident group's strength is considerably less than the government's, as is usually the case, it will not attack the regime's armies head-on. As Gurr (1970, 212) suggests, "A primary determinant of the directness and extent of tactical violence is the balance of force its strategists perceive between themselves and those they oppose. The greater the disparity, the more likely strategists are to emphasize the indirect and threatened use of violence." In the face of overwhelming odds, dissidents resort to unconventional and unpredictable tactics in order to harass, obstruct, disrupt, and hence damage the regime. They strike at the regime's weakest points, choosing specific and vulnerable targets, so as not to dilute their own strength. All dissident groups who face powerful regimes use such unconventional warfare, because these forms of combat create advantages for the dissidents and disadvantages for the regime. Examples include weapons of the weak (Scott 1985), terrorism, and guerrilla warfare.

Fifth, the dissident group tries to expose the genuine opposition to the status quo. For example, the procession at an ayatollah's funeral can be an occasion for showing that Iranians take religion much more seriously than does the Shah.

Finally, the dissident group occupies and controls public or private space — territory (e.g., a school, a factory) plus people (e.g., teachers, factory supervisors) — against the demand that the government take some action. Such occupation of space can involve asserting property rights (e.g., setting up housekeeping, running the factory) or simply taking people hostage and creating a highly visible blockage of the space. By this means, dissidents create a forum in which to state demands and to consolidate their bargaining position. This tactic is used in all forms of collective dissent. Protest organizations call general strikes to demonstrate their control over people. Rioters seize control of city blocks to demonstrate their control over property. Coup leaders seize television and radio stations to demonstrate their control over communications. Guerrilla bands create and administer de facto governments (bases) in liberated areas to demonstrate their control over both the people and the property normally associated with the regime (sect. 5.2.3). Terrorist groups kidnap people, especially prominent members of the government, to demonstrate that the government's claim to control space is under dispute. The presence of this same tactic in the repertoire of so many different types of dissidents is indeed remarkable (Tilly 1978).

The dissident group, in sum, has at least six ways to organize its struggle with the regime so as to increase expectations that it will emerge victorious. The group can fight only when it thinks it can win. It can sequence its actions to show progress. It can try to capture important symbols of governmental authority. It can fight indirectly when outgunned. It can attempt to expose the genuine opposition to the status quo. And lastly, it can seize control over space (people plus territory).

Suppose, however, that the dissident group's probability of winning is manifestly low. What alternatives does it have? It can, as Green (1982, 243) implies, emphasize the short-term consumption value of its actions rather than long-term investment value of the policies it seeks. That is, unsuccessful dissident groups emphasize means rather than goals (sect. 4.2.1). But such a strategy cannot continue indefinitely. As the saying goes, "You can fool some of the dissidents some of the time, but not all of the dissidents all of the time."

### 3.6.4. The State's Strategy

Rebels, in sum, attempt to signal (sect. 4.1) that they are strong. Arrow (1974, 72–73) notes that authorities, too, wish to signal their power:

> Authority is viable to the extent that it is the focus of convergent expectations. An individual obeys authority because he expects that others will obey it . . . It may therefore be important to make authority visible, so that it serves as a coordinating signal. This is perhaps why external symbols surround authority.

States are therefore also concerned with the dissidents' perceived probability of winning. They seek to deflate expectations of the dissidents' strength and inflate expectations of their own power.

One of the state's strategies parallels perfectly the dissidents' strategy: claiming widespread, enduring, and intense support. Government warns the populace that it will defeat the dissidents, hoping to convince people that the benefits of collective dissent will not be forthcoming and that the costs will be high. A further parallel strategy is that all regimes predict eventual victory. In fact, regimes are more interested in portraying dissenters as "losers" rather than as "deviants."

The second part of the regime's strategy emphasizes its deeds. Wesson (1967, 305) observes that in autocratic world empires "the autocracy makes a great display of splendor and wealth to evidence and glorify its power." In general, governments seek to create an aura of power and omnipotence: "The role of the sovereign, Hobbes tells us, is to inspire 'Awe' throughout the populace — that is, respect for power greater than one's own" (Rule 1988, 22). Regimes demonstrate that power by surrounding themselves with pomp and ceremony, parades and monuments, luxury and wealth. Such extravaganzas often emphasize public displays of the military on parade, because the military best conveys the idea of power and invincibility (Tullock 1987a, 117).

Several intriguing examples illustrate how regimes exploit symbolic displays of power. In ancient times, rulers posed as deities. In Roman times, the emperor Caligula had his horse elected consul (Wesson 1967, 60). In modern times, "Just to make its commanding position clear, each day at noon the occupying [Nazi] army marched a detachment of troops up to the Champs-Elysées to the Arc de Triomphe where they passed in review" (Tilly 1986, 331).

Governments also make it clear that they are prepared to use the repressive apparatus that they parade around. Coleman (1990, 502) points out that one lesson of the *Increase the Probability of Winning* solution to the Rebel's Dilemma is that authorities should "not let an internal challenge to authority go unmet. If unable to meet a challenge, divert attention through a compensatory use of power in another arena." For example, regimes often try to demonstrate their invincibility by hurting a few conspicuous and prominent dissidents. Governments also typically ban mass meetings and demonstrations because they fear that such protests will reveal the dissidents' strength.

Finally, in seeking to deflate dissidents' expectations of success, regimes, too, seek to control space; no government willingly cedes part of its territory to dissidents.

### 3.6.5. The Competition between State and Opposition

In sum, dissidents have their strategy and regimes have theirs. The competition between state and opposition has both subjective and objective aspects.

Regimes and dissidents compete to win the "probability of winning" issue. Each side tries to convince people that it will succeed: "The real point of the civil war is to convince people that one side or the other is going to win" (Tullock 1987b, 373). Each side tries to demonstrate that it is a tower of strength and that the other side is a paper tiger. Each side subverts the other side's displays of power. Wickham-Crowley (1989, 170) suggests that "both guerrillas and governments, then, commonly competed in both proposals and policies for the mass loyalties of the populace. Where governments refused to compete, in Cuba and Nicaragua, the dictators eventually fell."

Claims and counterclaims fly. Each side challenges the other's assertions of widespread support and eventual victory. Where dissident entrepreneurs overestimate their probability of winning, regime elites underestimate that probability. Both sides claim that many of their supporters are underground and hence represent the "silent majority." The loser, therefore, is able to claim that the winner was really in the minority because *they* had the support of the masses of people who never participated. In short, both sides offer different estimates of the dissidents' past success, current support, and prospects for future success. Moreover, both sides discourage independent polling to check such claims. Body counts in Vietnam and the size of U.S. civil rights demonstrations, for example, have been hotly debated. Hence, the CA research program teaches us that all appraisals of dissident group success, whether by the regime or the dissidents, are self-serving and biased, inflated or deflated, and most definitely hypocritical.

The competition between regime and opposition also has an objective aspect to it. The actual balance of forces influences the level and form of collective dissent. Gurr's two "balance" propositions, the "balance of institutional support"[59] and the "balance of coercive control,"[60] are the classic statements of this idea.

### 3.6.6. An Example: Military Coups

All aspects of a regime-opposition conflict are influenced by probability-of-winning calculations. Consider, for example, how the origin, order, and outcome of a military coup is affected.

Before attempting a coup potential coup makers calculate the probability of success.[61] As a coup approaches, there are discussions about the balance of power. The political resources of both sides are calculated. The political climate is judged. These assessments guide the coup makers' tactical decisions. Who should be won over by conceding programs? Who should be neutralized by isolation, exile, or elimination? The political struggle is intense. Coups have thus been likened to bargaining,[62] coalition formation,[63] and elections.[64] If the bargaining, coalition building, and electioneering go well, military coups are quite stylized, orderly, and predictable affairs.[65]

Several actors play an important part in the bargaining, coalition building, and electioneering that occur before a coup. Consider military forces, crucial middle-level officers, police and paramilitary forces, "swing men," and the populace.

*Military forces.* A coup maker must calculate where the various units of the military stand. The military units making the coup expect that other military units will acquiesce to a fait accompli. Coup makers thus assume that most of the  military will start out neutral and then join the winning side. Nordlinger (1977, 105) indicates that "a typical coup situation finds a small number of conspirators facing a large number of neutral, uncommitted officers and a significant number of loyalist officers." An important part of a coup maker's pre-coup calculations (Luttwak 1968, 62, emphasis in original) involves deciding which military forces to subvert and which to neutralize: "*The forces relevant to a coup are those whose locations and/or equipment enables them to intervene in its locale (usually the capital city) within the 12-24 hours time-span which precedes the establishment of its control over the machinery of government.*" Luttwak (1968, vii) also suggests that since the state is so strong, "the technique of the coup d'état is the technique of judo: the planners of the coup must use the power of the state against its political masters. This is done by a process of infiltration and subversion in which a small but critical part of the security forces are totally subverted, while much of the rest is temporarily neutralized."

*Crucial middle-level officers.* Nordlinger (1977, 102–3) suggests that "the active participation of strategically situated, middle-level troop commanders is crucial for the coup's success." Middle-level officers thus face the Rebel's Dilemma most acutely. Luttwak (1968, 64) offers several suggestions for building the coup coalition out of the key middle level members of the armed forces. For example, he suggests making general rather than specific appeals so as to avoid principled opposition (Luttwak 1968, 80).

*Police and paramilitary forces.* These are largely irrelevant, because their resources are usually less than the military's. This provides an answer to Luttwak's (1968, 95) interesting question as to why the police and paramilitary forces do not stage coups. With their more modest resources and organization, they are much less likely to succeed than the military. Who makes the coup is therefore also decided by probability-of-winning calculations.

*"Swing men."* A "swing man" is a well-respected general, popular with the public, yet conservative. He is put at the head of the coup in order to guard its general purpose of overthrowing the regime.

*Populace.* Nordlinger (1977, 64) argues that the military seeks popular, as well as military, support: "Despite the enormous power enjoyed by the military, there are several reasons why it is almost never used against civilian governments unless (or until) they have lost their legitimizing mantle. Legitimacy deflations are crucial in facilitating the transformation of interventionist motivations into coup attempts." The reason why coup makers are concerned with the people is clear: if the government is popular, then it will be supported by many military officers, and hence the probability of a successful coup is diminished. Finer (1976, 80–88) thus argues that civilians are part of the probability-of-success calculus. Examples where coups have failed due to civilian opposition include Germany in 1920 (Kapp Putsch), Japan in 1936 (February Mutiny), and France in 1961 (the April Rebellion).

Several aspects of how a coup is conducted are also contingent upon calculations about how to increase its probability of success. Coups are carefully planned in terms of numerous strategical and tactical considerations: "The coup is a consciously conceived and purposefully executed act. It is purposefully undertaken in order to achieve consciously formulated goals, with an awareness of the possible costs and risks involved" (Nordlinger 1977, 63).

The actual operations of capturing the mass media and other power centers affect the coup's probability of success. Coup leaders decide which key points of the modern state to seize — whether transportation (railroad, roads) and/or communications (TV, radio stations). They also decide which government figures to hold.

Things must move quickly. A quick success encourages others to join the bandwagon (sect. 4.1.2),[66] whereas protracted coups allow opposition (often on policy grounds) to grow: "If, in the operational phase of the coup, we are at any stage delayed, then our essential weakness will emerge: we shall probably acquire a definite political coloration, and this will in turn lead to a concentration of those forces which oppose the tendency we represent (or are thought to represent)" (Luttwak 1968, 49). Finer (1976, 142) reports that most military people wait out the coup; if it is successful, they jump on the bandwagon: "The uncommitted garrisons and units will stand aside at first, and then jump on the bandwagon if the movement looks like it is succeeding." The attempted coup against Gorbachev in 1991 is a case in point. His own defense minister reported "sick" for three days, until it became clear who had won.

Timing is also crucial. Anything that temporarily increases either the power of the military or civilian dependence on the military, such as external or internal war, also increases the probability of a successful coup, and thereby increases the chances of a coup. Nordlinger (1977, 91), citing evidence from Fossum (1967, 234–36) and Thompson (1973, 45), shows that disorder and protest stimulates coups: "When turbulence becomes endemic and violence escalates, the officers realize that the government has become critically dependent upon them. Without their support the government could easily collapse, thereby presenting them with an interventionist opportunity if motivated to take it." Another typical precipitant of a coup is the absence of leadership from the capital city (Luttwak 1968, 156).

Finally, coup makers remain concerned about calculations of the probability of winning even after a coup succeeds. Their concerns now shift to the possibility of some countercoup coalition taking action. Coup makers generally resist those who argue for immediate elections and a quick return to constitutional normality. They argue that the military must retain power for a while. After all, they face formidable tasks: to purge the sympathizers of the Old Regime and to restructure politics — in short, to end the threat that former power holders could return to power.

Coup makers thus hope to restore order and assert their legitimacy. Luttwak (1968, 175) suggests that the best way to accomplish these goals is to claim victory and demonstrate strength: "Our first objective will be achieved by conveying the reality and strength of the coup instead of trying to justify it; this will be done by listing the controls we have imposed, by emphasizing that law and order have been fully restored, and by stating that all resistance has ceased." Luttwak's (1968, 174) postcoup strategy is thus intended "to discourage resistance to us by emphasizing the strength of our position." The new regime therefore claims enduring support and predicts victory. The circle is complete.

### 3.7. Increase the Probability of Making a Difference

A dissident will rebel if he or she is convinced that his or her individual participation in rebellion will make a difference in achieving the PG that all dissidents seek (Tullock 1971a). This solution to the Rebel's Dilemma affects both the calculus of the individual dissident and the strategy of the dissident group.

### 3.7.1. The Dissident's Calculus

The *Increase the Probability of Making a Difference* solution focuses on a type of individual efficacy: the belief that individual action can make a difference in obtaining the PG. Both leaders of dissident groups of any size and rank-and-file members of small dissident groups might think that they can make a difference. Rank-and-file members of large dissident groups cannot possibly think that they can make a difference. This solution is therefore no solution: large-scale CA is still impossible.

Or so went the argument in early applications (e.g., Tullock 1971a) of CA thinking to collective dissent. More recent work, however, shows that an individual dissident could believe that he or she makes a difference. CA modelers have demonstrated that such a belief could arise for any number of reasons: because all dissidents are needed; because some subset of all dissidents are needed; because a single contribution is somehow unique; because a single contribution clearly adds something to the PG; or because a single contribution affects everyone else's contribution. Hence, as a rational dissident comes to believe that his or her contribution makes a difference in the likelihood that the PG will be obtained, his or her participation in collective dissent increases.[67] A basic corollary follows: participants in collective dissent will report higher expectations of their personal efficacy than nonparticipants.[68]

An examination of the substitution of terms in the dissident's contribution calculus reveals more about why rational people rebel. In the expected value formulation of the CA problem (Lichbach forthcoming, chap. 2), the "utility differential" and the "probability of making a difference" terms are multiplicative. Intensity of demand (zealotry, sect. 3.1) may therefore substitute for personal efficacy. Thus, the greater a rational dissident's intensity of demand for a PG, the smaller his or her "probability of making a difference" needs to be before he or she participates in collective dissent. Similarly, personal efficacy may substitute for intensity of demand. Thus, more powerful dissidents (i.e., those with a greater "probability of making a difference") require less of a utility differential to participate in collective dissent.

Now consider the origins of this solution to the Rebel's Dilemma. What sorts of dissidents calculate that they can make a difference? Under what conditions are dissidents more likely to believe that they can make a difference?

Several sorts of dissidents calculate that they matter. Quite ordinary people might think that they are personally influential and hence believe that their actions will have a non-negligible influence on the outcome (Muller, Dietz, and Finkel 1991). Those with high socioeconomic status (income, education, occupation) might believe that they can have an impact. Certain personality types, such as people with a high-degree of self-confidence, might also believe that they matter, as might people who think that they are particularly resourceful. Celebrities — Dick Gregory, for example — often take up social causes because they have a greater probability of making a difference, in part because they can often induce the participation of others (Chong 1991, 125). In fact, people of some renown may gain even more prominence and social prestige for their efforts (sect. 4.2.2). Moreover, under certain social and political conditions they are less likely to be repressed than others and hence pay a lower price for their participation (sect. 3.2).

One set of conditions is particularly likely to induce widespread perceptions that individual efforts matter: as the dissidents and the regime move closer to each other in strength, the probability of a single dissident making a difference in the conflict increases. Collective dissent thus becomes more likely.[69]

Regimes are almost always more powerful than dissidents, however. The reverse is rare. If the dissidents' strength approaches that of the regime, the regime usually falls. Hence, as dissidents strengthen and regimes weaken, the dissidents' estimates of the probability of making a difference increase. But recall from section 3.6.2 that as the closeness of the contest between the regime and the dissidents increases, dissidents update their calculations of the probability of winning. In the case of collective dissent, probability-of-making-a-difference calculations are thus highly correlated with probability-of-winning calculations: as the relative strength of the dissidents increase (due to any of the factors cited in sect. 3.6.2), dissidents update their calculations of both the probability of winning and the probability of making a difference. Collective dissent becomes *doubly* likely.

This helps to resolve a major puzzle in CA theories. The probability of winning is not supposed to matter to CA, yet the evidence that it does is overwhelming. The probability of making a difference is supposed to matter to CA, yet the evidence that it does is underwhelming. The two probabilities are derivative of the same real-world observations and hence are highly correlated. Neither statistically nor in people's minds can they be separated. Hence, both the probability of winning and the probability of making a difference influence collective dissent.

### 3.7.2. The Dissident Group's Strategy

A close election increases electoral turnout in part because a close election produces a "get out the vote" campaign by party elites. During a close campaign, party officials emphasize the importance of every vote. But what strategies do dissident entrepreneurs adopt in the more typical situations where a contest is not close?

The implication of the *Increase the Probability of Making a Difference* solution for the dissidents' strategy is clear: dissident entrepreneurs try to create an illusion of individual efficacy by trying to convince their followers that they cannot win without their help. Rothenberg (1988, 1143–44) thus argues that "group leaders have an incentive to foster the confusion between individual and associational efficacy. To the extent that they control the information contributors employ to update their cost-benefit calculi, the elites will add to the confusion by telling members that they make a difference by acting collectively." Dissident entrepreneurs, that is, will try to fool their followers into believing that (1) all $n$ dissidents are required, (2) $j$ particular dissidents are required, (3) each contribution is unique, (4) each contribution adds something, and/or (5) each contribution affects all other contributions.

Thus, fund-raising appeals mask the logic of free riding by making highly personalized requests for contributions. Consider this appeal from Julian Bond of Klanwatch (cited in Kaplowitz and Fisher 1985, 50): "You have been a valued part of our team in the ongoing fight against bigotry and injustice and we simply cannot afford to lose you as a member." Or consider this appeal from Ira Glasser of the ACLU (also cited in Kaplowitz and Fisher 1985, 50): "You are part of a small group that has made the difference between victory and defeat." Such appeals often work. Moe (1980a, 33-34) argues that people typically overestimate their individual efficacy.

Another strategy used by dissident entrepreneurs to increase a dissident's probability of making a difference is to disaggregate larger tasks into smaller ones and delegate these tasks to particular individuals. Popkin (1988, 21) observes that "effective leaders elicit contributions by breaking up a large goal into many steps with critical thresholds. If a larger goal can be broken into many small individual pieces, all of which are necessary to the larger goal, the free-rider problem can be overcome, for if each person has a monopoly on a necessary factor for the final goal, all contributions are essential." Successful dissident groups apply this strategy.

Dissident entrepreneurs also personalize tasks by linking one contributor to one beneficiary. To convince followers that they can make a difference, leaders point to particular individuals that *you* can cure (e.g., people in wheelchairs), animals *you* can save (e.g., baby seals), or families *you* can assist (e.g., houses to be built, children to feed).

As one suspects, regimes pursue the opposite strategy: they attempt to make dissidents underestimate their individual efficacy. Toward this end, they point out that assumptions (1) through (5) cited above are fallacious: (1)

all $n$ dissidents are not enough, (2) $j$ particular dissidents are insufficient, (3) each contribution is redundant, (4) each contribution adds nothing, and/or (5) each contribution has no affect on any other contribution. In short, regimes attempt to convince dissidents that the state is so powerful that individual rebels could not possibly make a difference in the outcome of protests and rebellions.

### 3.8. Use Incomplete Information

In general, as Moe (1980b, 594) argues, individuals are not "perfectly informed, e.g., about the costs and benefits of political success . . . when individuals base decisions on their subjective estimates of such quantities, the inducement-value of politics may be greater than Olson claims." Arguments about incomplete information have also been made with respect to many other parameters in the dissident's calculus. Kreps, Milgrom, Roberts, and Wilson (1982), for example, extend the incomplete information idea to Tit-For-Tat. Other applications include Frohlich and Oppenheimer (1970, 1978), Frohlich, Oppenheimer, and Young (1971), and Marsh (1976, 1978).

The information issue is significant because objective conditions influence the equilibrium outcome of the PG-PD game only indirectly. It is *beliefs* about objective conditions that directly influence dissidents' actions and induce various equilibrium outcomes. The information conditions of the Rebel's Dilemma thus have a very direct impact on CA. To know which equilibrium outcome will occur one must know the information available to the dissidents. The *Use Incomplete Information* solution to the Rebel's Dilemma therefore holds a wide-ranging set of implications for collective dissent. The following sections demonstrate the impact of incomplete information on dissidents (sect. 3.8.1), dissident groups (sect. 3.8.2), and states (sect. 3.8.3). I then discuss (sect. 3.8.4) the political battle over information.

### 3.8.1. The Dissident's Calculus

Information is costly to obtain. The benefits of information, moreover, are dispersed and the costs concentrated. Hence, dissidents do not always seek information and often prefer to remain rationally ignorant. This point is argued by Olson (1982, 25–26):

> Information and calculation about a collective good is often itself a collective good. Consider a typical member of a large organization who is deciding how much time to devote to studying the policies or leadership of the organization. The more time the member devotes to this matter,

the greater the likelihood that his or her voting or advocacy will favor effective policies and leadership for the organization. This typical member will, however, get only a small share of the gain from the more effective policies and leadership; in the aggregate the other members will get almost all the gains, so that the individual member does not have an incentive to devote nearly as much time to fact-finding and thinking about the organization as would be in the group interest.

Expect dissidents, in short, to remain rationally ignorant about policy - both policies pursued by the regime and alternatives advocated by the dissident group. Most will be relatively naive and operate with relatively little information about the costs and benefits of collective dissent.

There are, however, several situations in which rational dissidents seek information. First, information might itself be valued. If information is entertaining, for instance, dissidents seek it (sect. 4.2.1). And politics *is* often entertaining.

Second, information might be relatively cheap and easy to obtain. As the cost of information decreases, dissidents are more likely to seek it. They seek, for instance, cheap and readily obtainable information about each others' intentions toward collective dissent: they look for cues and precipitants of mutual action (sect. 4.1.1). Hence, dissidents often mill around at the start of a protest event, "collecting information about the likelihood that the other people will defect instead of sticking with the action; if much of the information reads 'defect', even determined veterans often call off the demonstration, raid, or occupation" (Tilly 1984, 32).

Third, information might be critical and might yield considerable benefits. Such is the case for dissident entrepreneurs. As dissent becomes a full-time "career," rather than a part-time "hobby," dissidents become more concerned with the costs and benefits of collective dissent. They then have a greater incentive to acquire information about cost-efficient modes of protest. Consequently, professional dissidents (i.e., entrepreneurs) are far more interested in acquiring information than are the nonprofessionals (i.e., the rank-and-file). Dissident leaders must acquire knowledge, for example, of the dissidents' production function (sect. 3.4.1). If the dissident group is to lobby the regime for benefits, it must learn the rules, procedures, and institutions of the government.[70]

Another such situation is that of intense team competition between regimes and oppositions (sect. 3.10.1.2). As the conflict between regime and opposition intensifies, dissidents may well have to choose sides. They will then attempt to acquire information, so as to make an informed choice. Hence, as the conflict between the regime and the dissidents increases, the amount of information sought by dissidents increases. Note that this implies that dissidents probably take longer to make critical decisions than to make less consequential ones.

In sum, while some dissidents under some circumstances remain rationally ignorant, other dissidents under other circumstances (e.g., when information is entertaining, cheap, or critical) become rationally informed. This explains why the young and the inexperienced join dissident movements in such large numbers: they are the ones most likely to be fooled. It also explains why dissident movements have such a high turnover: even fools eventually learn.

Operating with incomplete information has additional consequences. First, incomplete information produces failure, so collective dissent is often unsuccessful. For example, thirty percent of the coups between 1945 and 1967 were unsuccessful (Luttwak 1968, 204–7) and approximately fifty percent between 1945 and 1972 failed (Kennedy 1974, Appendix A).

Second, incomplete information produces surprises, so collective dissent is often unanticipated. Examples[71] of unsuccessful and unanticipated collective dissent suggest that dissidents lacked important information. Similarly, such examples indicate that social scientists lack important information and have equal difficulty predicting protest and rebellion (sect. 9.2).

Third, incomplete information about the probability of victory produces intransigence and prolongs collective dissent. One might even argue that if information were complete, there would be no need for conflict, no need for the parties to test one another; the winning side would present the losing side with its demands, and the conflict would be over. Realistic estimates of the probability of winning are thus associated with short-lived conflicts.[72]

### 3.8.2. The Dissident Group's Public Relations Calculus

The reason people are willing to operate with incomplete information, then, is that rational dissidents consider most information most of the time to be dull, costly, and mundane. But, as already indicated, rational dissidents realize that some information some of the time might be valuable. This reaction by rational dissidents has another major impact on collective dissent: there are opportunities for lobbyists who can provide interesting, cheap, and important information to potential dissidents. As Olson (1982, 26) explains, "The limited knowledge of public affairs is in turn necessary to explain the effectiveness of lobbying. If all citizens had obtained and digested all pertinent information, they could not then be swayed by advertising or other persuasion." These opportunities, in turn, allow people to specialize in providing information to potential dissidents. As Olson (1982, 26) again argues, "Individuals in a few special vocations can receive considerable rewards in private goods if they acquire exceptional knowledge of public goods. Politicians, lobbyists, journalists, and social scientists, for example, may earn more money, power, or prestige from knowledge of this or that public business."

How will such specialists in dissent present their information to nonspecialists? Here we learn of yet another important impact of incomplete information on collective dissent. Information offers power. It is therefore to be expected that dissident leaders try to use the relative ignorance, ambiguity, and confusion of their followers to their advantage. Entrepreneurs disseminate information that they find helpful and avoid disseminating information that they find harmful; that is, they manipulate information so as to present their story in the best light.[73]

In sum, specialists in information distort the information they provide their clients. Dissident entrepreneurs try to set up such a "smoke screen" for their rank-and-file followers by adopting several strategies, including manipulating publicity, illusions, ideology, and symbols.

### 3.8.2.1. Publicity

Potential dissidents, because of imperfect information, might not even know that a dissident group exists. Dissident groups need in the first instance to alert dissidents to the *possibility* of contributing to CA, a course of action that might never have occurred to them. Dissident groups also try to make dissidents aware of *how* to contribute to CA, by building the dissident's contribution skills. In short, dissident entrepreneurs seek to extend public awareness in hopes of facilitating the identification and mobilization of new dissidents.

Hence, all dissident groups try to publicize their existence (at least to supporters if not to government; sect. 3.4.5.1). As Olson (1982, 27) writes, "Extravagant statements, picturesque protests, and unruly demonstrations that offend much of the public they are designed to influence . . . make diverting news and thus call attention to interests and arguments that might otherwise be ignored. Even some isolated acts of terrorism described as 'senseless' can, from this perspective, be explained as effective means of obtaining the riveted attention of a public that would otherwise remain rationally ignorant." Terrorist groups are so interested in publicity that they often claim credit for one another's actions.

All dissident groups, moreover, try to publicize their demands. Dissident entrepreneurs thus typically assemble a list of grievances and notify the media of the group's existence.

Dissident groups also try to publicize their successes so as to enhance estimates of the group's probability of winning (sect. 3.6). Hence, they present the group's credentials — a résumé that details its accomplishments. Organizations, says Kahn (1982, 174), should celebrate their victories. Farhi (1990, 85) argues that memory of resistance and hope . . . chronicles actual or imagined instances of resistance and liberation. These accounts are a declaration of the possibility of change, and they are examined continuously in an attempt to understand what enables resistance in specific, historical situations. They are also generally reenacted in symbolic fashion through plays, sermons, religious ceremonies, and the like to sustain the revolutionary fervor.

The victories and accomplishments celebrated by a group need not even be their own. As Walt (1992, 338) points out, "Revolutionaries may also invoke the successes of earlier movements to sustain confidence in their own efforts; thus, the Sandinistas saw Castro's victory in Cuba as evidence that their own efforts in Nicaragua could succeed."

Another part of the group's résumé is a set of symbols detailing its present resources. For example, "New political movements may adopt paramilitary forms of organization even when, as in the case of the S.A. before Hitler's coming to power, their arsenals are empty or virtually non-existent" (Wrong 1988, 41).

Dissidents recognize, however, that people do not rationally seek information that is boring. Dissidents therefore seek to publicize their existence, demands, and successes in a particularly newsworthy and sensational manner: they appeal to human interest. Dissidents attempt to create news that emphasizes the more entertaining aspect of political life rather than the complexities of political give-and-take. Media editors who must sell their coverage to the public are quite willing to accommodate the dissidents' strategy. Hence, assassinations, bank robberies, and kidnappings always grab the headlines.

These last propositions suggest a corollary: as media coverage of collective dissent increases, collective dissent increases. Huntington (1974, 165) posits that as the mass media in a nation increases, the chances for collective dissent increase, because the media "multiply tremendously the impact of any one event throughout the society." Many have suggested, moreover, that new communications technologies, such as telephones and direct mail (McAdam, McCarthy, and Zald 1988, 722–23), have had a major impact on CA. This argument about the impact of mass media on collective dissent is most frequently made about terrorism (Stohl 1988b, 580–82), but it should not be forgotten that the Reformation coincided with the spread of the printing press (Bercé 1987, 12).

The mass media, of course, are not the only communications network that facilitates protest and rebellion. Dissident groups also have other ways to publicize their cause, for example with consciousness-raising sessions during which individual dissidents are supposed to discover shared experiences, aspirations, goals, and identities.

### 3.8.2.2. *Illusions*

Dissident groups, as indicated earlier, try to take advantage of incomplete information. Persuasion is even more important in politics than in economics.[74] Entrepreneurial leaders of dissident groups thus attempt to persuade dissidents of the value of all of the parameters in the PG-PD model (Lichbach forthcoming, chap. 2), efforts that foster many illusions about solving the CA problem. Several of the more prominent illusions bear discussion.

*Preference Illusion.* Leaders try to convince followers that the benefits of collective dissent (sect. 3.1) are higher than they really are. They attempt to create a benefit illusion by changing preferences or tastes and thereby increasing demand for the PG. Substantively, this implies that entrepreneurs try to radicalize dissidents and create zealots.

*Fiscal Illusion.* Authorities employ a variety of institutions to mask the tax burden, a topic often discussed in the literature on PGs. Buchanan (1987, 131-36) argues that rulers carefully organize the fiscal system so as to minimize taxpayer resistance for any given level of revenues. Those who actually bear the tax burden for a PG are therefore not necessarily the same set of people who think they bear the burden. Fiscal consciousness about collective dissent suffers a similar fate; leaders try to convince followers that the costs of collective dissent (sect. 3.2) are lower than they really are. All dissident entrepreneurs thus attempt to create fiscal illusion: they systematically underestimate the government's ability to engage in repression. They assert, following Marx and Engels ([1848]1968, 121), that "proletarians have nothing to lose but their chains," when, in fact, they are embarking on a personally dangerous course of action. The Sandinista leader, Humberto Ortega, is an excellent example of the dissident entrepreneur misinforming the rank-and-file: "Trying to tell the masses that the cost was very high and that they should seek another way would have meant the defeat of the revolutionary movement" (Borge, Fonseca, Ortega, Ortega, and Wheelock 1982, 71).

*Victory Illusion.* Leaders try to convince followers that the probability of winning is higher than it really is. They attempt to create a group efficacy illusion (sect. 3.6.3) by overestimating the government's willingness to be pressured into concessions and/or vulnerability to overthrow.

*Efficacy Illusion.* Leaders try to convince followers that the probability of making a difference is higher than it really is. They attempt to create an individual efficacy illusion (sect. 3.7.2) by convincing the rank-and-file that a single victory garden actually contributes to victory.

*Competition Illusion.* Leaders try to convince followers that the competition between regime and opposition (sect. 3.10.1.2) is more intense and polarized than it really is.[75] The consequence of trying to create such a competition illusion, as Brinton (1965, 194) observes of all of the Great Revolutions, is the intolerant dissident entrepreneur who holds that there is only one truth. Dissident entrepreneurs are thus always hostile to collective dissent against themselves. Revolutionaries typically attack moderation, reformism, pragmatism, and compromise in order to increase ideological purity (and prevent free riding).

*Community Illusion*. Leaders try to convince followers that they are part of an enduring community. This is the homogeneity illusion, discussed further in section 5.2.2.

*Exclusion Illusion*. Leaders try to convince followers that the PG is in part excludable and that selective incentives for participation are therefore possible. This is the exclusion illusion, discussed further in section 6.3.1.

In sum, dissident entrepreneurs try to create illusions about all solutions to the Rebel's Dilemma.

### 3.8.2.3. Ideology
An ideology, in the sense of Downs (1957, chap. 7), means a simple belief system outlining the sources and remedies for troubles. Ideologies define and redefine the dissident's world, thus manipulating an individual's interests in that world (Breton and Breton 1969, 202-3). Given incomplete information, dissident entrepreneurs try to create an ideology that influences a rank-and-file dissident's estimates of all of the parameters in the PG-PD model (Lichbach forthcoming, chap. 2). Incomplete information and the leaders' desires to overcome the free-rider problem therefore explains the existence of a dissident group's ethos, vision of the future, and moral code (North 1981, chap. 5). Dissident entrepreneurs thereby become specialists in ideology. If "the first duty of an iconoclast is to know his icons" (Poggi 1978, xi), his or her second duty is to create new icons.

In short, all dissident groups eventually flirt with developing an ideology.[76] Its manifestations during revolution, for example, include renaming everything, eschewing privacy, and emphasizing puritanism, virtue, and a life without the ordinary vices (Brinton 1965, 178–80).

Many argue, in fact, that an ideology is essential to the dissidents' success.[77] An ideology performs numerous "functions": it criticizes the existing social, economic, and political order; explains grievances; provides knowledge and understanding of an alternative and more desirable and legitimate order; assists in forming a collective identity; furnishes targets (scapegoats) for grievances; demonstrates that a better society is possible; and supplies the means to move from here to there. Dissident ideologies thus influence the totality of collective dissent including organization, strategy, and tactics. And differences in ideologies matter; they account for the fact that "reformist and revolutionary movements will naturally tend to behave differently, and to develop different organization, strategy, tactics, etc." (Hobsbawm 1959, 11).

Many also argue that while collective dissent without a real program, goal, purpose, or direction, may arise spontaneously, it cannot last in the long run. For collective dissent to endure, it must eventually link up with some ideology. As Stone (1972, 98) writes, "A true revolution needs ideas to fuel it — without them there is only a rebellion or a *coup d'état*." Tarrow (1989, 16, 24) points out the importance of master "*interpretative themes*" that provide meaning to dissidents: "In collective action, as in politics in general, people cannot for long sustain campaigns on behalf of their rights of benefits without identifying them with general values and reaching out to others through a framework of common understandings." Examples of cases in which the lack of ideology has led to rebellion rather than revolution abound.[78]

There are, of course, examples of conflict groups that are guided by explicit, fully formed, well-articulated, and coherent ideologies, for instance in the Russian and Chinese revolutions. But sometimes goals are unclear and develop only during a political struggle (Lichbach forthcoming, chap. 7). As Trotsky ([1932] 1974, xviii) argues, "The masses go into a revolution not with a prepared plan of social reconstruction, but with a sharp feeling that they cannot endure the old régime." Examples of successful conflicts that lacked explicit ideological guidance include the English and French revolutions. Given that dissidents have sometimes been driven by ideology, but sometimes not, there are those who argue that ideologies are not crucial to collective dissent. In the phrase of the Tupamaros (Laqueur 1987, 327), "Words divide us; actions unite us."

Finally, some argue that ideologies and actions are needed in combination. Laqueur (1987, 401) maintains that "no guerrilla movement has obtained its objectives solely through propaganda; equally none has succeeded by terrorism alone."

The degree to which ideologies are important to dissident success is, therefore, an empirical question. Laqueur (1987, 326) points out, for example, that some of the most successful guerrilla wars produced no doctrines, while "some guerrilla movements which barely functioned were very strong on doctrine." Eisenstadt (1978, chaps. 1, 2) thus ponders the extent of symbolization and articulation of heterodox ideologies of political change. In other words, strong ideologies are a sufficient but not necessary condition for collective dissent. As I argue in section 9.1, this is true for *all* the solutions offered here. Hence, dissident leaders manipulate dissident ideologies, even if those ideologies may not be all that well developed, because it is one route to overcoming the Rebel's Dilemma.

### *3.8.2.4. Symbols*
Incomplete information also explains the use of symbols by dissident groups. Rituals are symbols: the initiation ceremony indicating the rite of passage into the dissident group and the celebration associated with advances in rank are examples. Symbols also include banners and flags; handshakes and code

names; badges, salutes, insignias, and uniforms; marches and rallies; music and songs; history and stories; memorial days and periods; and public places, monuments, and statues (Lasswell and Kaplan 1950, 103).

One particularly effective symbol used by dissident groups is protest songs and music (Stewart, Smith, and Denton 1984, chap. 9). Chong (1991, 183) reports that "song was a particularly effective tonic in this [civil rights] campaign as in others, in part, I am sure, because it was an overt method by which people could reassure each other of their continued commitment to the movement." Another key symbol is the slogan (Stewart, Smith, and Denton 1984, chap. 10). Among the more memorable are "Wilks and Liberty," "No Popery and Woodenshoes," "Long Live the Third Estate," "For the Democratic and Socialist Republic," "Workers of the world unite," and "We must all hang together, or most assuredly we shall all hang separately" (Rudé 1964, 245). Dissident groups also use the loyalty oath, which they take to unite in the face of factionalism. The basis of CA is thus often a "sworn association, the *sacramental*, created in the peasant assemblies" (Hilton 1973, 121). Examples of oaths of mutual allegiance binding rebels may be found in the English Rising of 1381 (Hilton 1973, 219), the rebellions of the sixteenth century (Zagorin 1982a, 263), and the Mau Mau movement of the twentieth century (Carl G. Rosberg, cited in Gurr 1970, 291–92).

All dissident groups employ symbols of one type or another and Brinton (1965, 195–96) observes that all of the Great Revolutions had symbols and rituals associated with them. Symbols, in general, influence perceptions of the past, present, and future. They abstract, screen and condense, thereby creating and re-creating reality. They influence dissident behavior with illusion, misperception, myth, and distortion. Symbols also facilitate several solutions to the Rebel's Dilemma. By increasing collective unity, solidarity, and identity, symbols advance the *Overcome Pecuniary Self-Interest* solution to the Rebel's Dilemma (sect. 4.2). This group bonding function of symbols has been noted by several scholars.[79] Symbols also facilitate group secrecy, reducing the possibility of government repression, and thereby permitting the *Lower Costs* solution to the Rebel's Dilemma (sect. 3.2) to operate. Practical rituals, says Hobsbawm (1959, 152), "permit the members to carry out their functions effectively, such as secret and formal recognition signs." Symbols also separate the regime from the dissidents, facilitating the *Increase Team Competition between Regimes and Oppositions* solution to the Rebel's Dilemma (sect. 3.10.1.2). As Edwards (1927, 112–15) argues, shibboleths spring up in all revolutions to separate forces. Finally, symbols signify intentions, thereby facilitating the *Use Tit-For-Tat* solution to the Rebel's Dilemma (sect. 5.2). Bates (1988, 398) thus argues that "in the presence of uncertainty about true motives, it may pay to shape others' perceptions of one's preferences. Some insignia — such as the cross — proclaim the commitment of the bearer to play 'nice' strategies; others — such as the scepter — suggest that although nice strategies may be reciprocated, 'hostile' first moves will surely be punished; the first player to move may then calculate her own best strategy accordingly." Badges and uniforms thus enable like-minded dissidents to locate one another and cluster together.

### 3.8.3. The State's Public Relations Calculus

If the dissidents' strategy is to use publicity, illusions, ideology, and symbols to intensify and focus grievances, thereby overcoming the Rebel's Dilemma, the state's strategy is to use the very same techniques to conceal grievances and thereby intensify the Rebel's Dilemma. Both sides, in short, play the incomplete information game.

Three examples illustrate the point. First, all regimes use propaganda and "education" both to counter the idea that grievances are just and to transform grievances into socially accepted norms. Regimes, just like dissidents, rely on persuasion. To insure compliance, they support an ideology, attempt to socialize people into it, and thereby acquire legitimacy. Second, all regimes try to conceal people with grievances and to downplay the content of those grievances; hence, they often point a finger at "outside agitators." Third, all regimes try to channel the flow of information. The American Secret Service issues press releases describing its effectiveness. Television commentators discuss the information fed to them about massive security precautions at the 1976 Olympic Games in Montreal. The U. S. State Department describes developments in the fight against terrorism: behold our new electronic sensors and newly trained dogs that can sniff dynamite!

Fledgling regimes are weak and because they are vulnerable to collective dissent (sect. 3.6.2.2) are likely to rely on all three strategies. Lasswell and Kaplan (1950, 115) observe that "the early phases of a revolutionary regime always involve an enormous quantity of propaganda."

### 3.8.4. The State's and the Dissidents' Struggle to Control Information

Dissidents seek information about all of the variables in the PG-PD model: the probability of success, the resources available, the selective incentives offered, and so forth. The communications media facilitate or hinder outbreaks of collective dissent by controlling the flow of such information. As Taylor (1986, chap. 7) reports, media coverage of a dissident group shapes the members' perceptions of political alignments, public opinion, and the level of CA.

Since regimes and oppositions seek to control the flow of information, they always battle over communication networks. The Chartist press, for example, helped spread the British working class movement, keep it together, and give it focus. The government, for its part, tried to put it out of business (Thompson 1984, chap. 2). There is nowadays in the Western world almost always an establishment media associated with the government. There is also often an opposition media, including movement newspapers, journals, radio and TV stations, associated with the dissidents. Both the state and the opposition use their respective media to publicize their own incentives and disincentives, and to try to hide or distort those of their opponent. Both use their respective media to dispute the facts surrounding a grievance. On the gap between rich and poor, for example, they dispute whether it is growing and whether the cause is the industriousness of the rich or the laziness of the poor. Both sides also exaggerate the danger posed by the other side, leveling charges about atrocities, so as to raise the costs to its supporters of losing the conflict. Dissident misperception and miscalculation are thus reinforced by both regime and opposition.

Such media competition has two aspects. First, all regimes (dissident groups) shape information about dissident groups (regimes) to benefit themselves. Second, all regimes (dissident groups) try to limit the flow of communication from dissident groups (regimes) to potential dissidents. In this political struggle over the construction of news and information, the battle over language is important. The terms demonstrator/rioter, martyr/casualty, deaths/massacre, or terrorist/freedom fighter assume great importance.

Moreover, both regimes and dissidents conduct intelligence operations against the other. They establish information-gathering and espionage organizations to collect and assess information about relative capabilities, intentions, and plans.

Given these various efforts on both sides, it is hard for potential dissidents to separate chaff from wheat, data from noise, information from disinformation. Thus, dissidents do not always fully understand their situation. While the CA research program leads us to expect rational beliefs, or beliefs that are grounded in the available evidence, and to expect that dissidents will collect information in an optimal way, the nature of regime-opposition conflict makes it difficult to collect information to form rational expectations. Expect dissidents, in short, to have simultaneously a "true" consciousness and a "false" consciousness, "true" cognitions and "false" cognitions.

### 3.9. Increase Risk Taking

Collective endeavors are risky undertakings. Dissidents are those daring, bold, and heroic few who are willing to chance injury and death. Another solution to the Rebel's Dilemma is therefore to increase a dissident's propensity to take risks. It could be that "uncertainty may act at times as a discriminating monopolist as it extracts from each person with a 'taste' for a certain policy the *full* amount he would be willing to pay for that policy; this would happen if each individual becomes convinced that his contribution makes the difference between success and failure of the movement" (Hirschman 1974, 10). Or it could be that if people are uncertain about others' contributions, and if they are risk averse, they will contribute to CA (Austen-Smith 1980). In either event, the propensity to take risks leads to the propensity to join rebellions.

This solution implies that dissidents are on the average more accepting of risk than is the general population. Mueller (1989, 175) speculates that revolutionaries must be "risk takers with extreme optimism regarding their ability to beat the odds." As Brinton (1965, 202) puts it, revolutionaries "are reckless players, apt to play to the gallery."[80] This proposition explains why dissidents who believe that collective dissent will probably fail choose to participate anyway (sect. 3.6).

Evidence for this proposition is that many, if not all, dissident movements are launched with the odds against them. Kuran (1989, 43–45; 1991a, 7-13) provides a further clever piece of evidence on this point: most revolutionaries are surprised when they succeed. Additional evidence that dissidents are particularly risk prone comes from interviews with dissidents. Pye's (1956) interviews with Communist guerrillas in Malaya and Keniston's (1968) interviews with antiwar activists in the United States found dissidents to be particularly risk prone individuals.

In looking at risk-taking dissidents, one finds that three types of people have greater than average risk propensities toward collective dissent and thus have greater than average levels of participation: the wealthy, the independent, and the unsuccessful.

*The wealthy.* Scott (1976) argues that peasants are not profit maximizers. Their life situation (i.e., living close to the margins of subsistence) forces them to be concerned with survival and not profits. Hence, they avoid risks. Their "safety first" approach implies, for example, that they are reticent to adopt new technologies that could increase crop yields but could also fail to produce any crops at all. One can apply Scott's reasoning to the case of collective dissent. A dissident living at a subsistence level risks his or her life by supporting a dissident group. Survival is at issue because any action by the regime that disrupts the dissident's efforts at eking out a living may mean death. The poor are too concerned about their short-run survival to engage in CA to promote their long-run welfare; they are risk averse. The rich, by contrast, can afford to be more risk acceptant because their subsistence is not threatened. Risk taking behavior by elites thus leads to dissident entrepreneurship (sect. 6.1.2). The first group of potentially risk prone individuals are therefore the wealthy: as income decreases, risk-taking decreases and thus collective dissent decreases.[81]

*The independent.* The individual with an independent income also has greater than average risk propensities toward collective dissent. Oppenheimer and Lakey (1964, 19) suggest that "people with independent incomes... tend to be readier to act than those who depend on others and are insecure." Hence, free professionals (e.g., lawyers, journalists, artists, writers, professors, physicians, students, and intellectuals) have high participation rates in collective dissent. Those in more exposed occupations (e.g., lower civil servants, white collar employees, peasants, agricultural workers, tenants) have low participation rates (Oberschall 1973, 164–72; sect. 3.2.3).

*The unsuccessful.* Those who have little to lose by their actions comprise a third group of potentially risk prone people. If the probability of victory is low, such dissidents might well roll the dice anyway and engage in desperate acts. Small bands of terrorists who have no chance of overthrowing a regime may well undertake riskier operations than a large guerrilla organization about to topple a shaky government. In short, the chronically unsuccessful dissident is risk prone and hence dissent prone.

Risk-taking dissidents affect dissident institutions in three ways. First, risk-prone dissidents participate in more collective dissent than do risk-averse dissidents. Hence, dissident movements that are large and long-lasting are likely to be particularly adept at pooling risk-acceptant individuals. Dissident groups are therefore themselves likely to take chances — yet another reason why collective dissent is unpredictable (sect. 9.2).

Second, dissident groups attempt to transform uncertainty into risk. Uncertainty means that a dissident cannot estimate the probability of an event. A dissident in such a situation cannot figure out a way of insuring against the occurrence of the event. Risk means that a dissident can, in some actuarial sense, determine the likelihood of an event. A dissident in such a situation can indeed figure out a way of insuring against the occurrence of the event. Dissidents attempt to transform uncertainty into risk by gathering information (sect. 3.8.1) and learning about their production functions (sect. 3.4.1).

Third, dissident groups attempt to manage risk. Several sorts of dissident strategies and institutions spread risk. Dissidents take out insurance policies: some terrorist organizations, for example, offer pensions to survivors and life insurance policies to the widows of those who do not survive (sect. 6.5.3). Dissident groups also manage risk by choosing low-risk tactics. Thus, they may opt for terrorism over other methods of collective dissent because it is a relatively low-risk strategy. As Gurr (1979, 38) explains, "Political terrorism has been a relatively low-risk tactic for those who use it. Rioting and guerrilla warfare — two alternative violent political action — can be shown to cause disproportionally larger numbers of casualties among rioters and guerrillas by comparison with either the security forces or, usually, non-combatants." Finally, dissident groups manage risk by diversifying their portfolio with a mix of high- and low-risk actions. Dissident organizations thus reduce risk by investing simultaneously in several projects expected to yield uncorrelated income flows. Expect dissidents, in other words, to become professionals engaged in a variety of social causes. There is indeed evidence that terrorists rank their tactics according to risk/reward ratios (Mickolus 1980, xix-xxviii) and diversify their portfolio of actions so as to balance more and less risky activities (Sandler and Scott 1987, 38-41).

### 3.10. Increase Team Competition between Enemies

The idea behind this solution to the Rebel's Dilemma is that a mobilization-countermobilization dynamic, a Hatfield-McCoy type of struggle, produces collective dissent. The team competition idea is widely recognized,[82] especially among those who stress the positive functions of conflict[83] or the importance of external enemies.[84]

This section develops three themes. First, dissident groups have many potential enemies (sect. 3.10.1). Second, dissident entrepreneurs can create and fan intergroup tensions (sect. 3.10.2). Finally, the mobilization-countermobilization dynamic holds several consequences for protest and rebellion (sect. 3.10.3).

### 3.10.1. The Enemies

Many dissident groups beget other dissident groups: the pro-choice movement begets the pro-life movement and vice versa, Communists beget fascists and vice versa, Hindu activism begets Muslim activism and vice versa. One possible enemy of a dissident group is therefore another dissident group (sect. 3.10.1.1). In addition, the regime coalition begets the antiregime coalition: revolutionaries beget counterrevolutionaries and vice-versa, conservatives beget radicals and vice versa. Another possible enemy of a dissident group is therefore the state (sect. 3.10.1.2). Finally, a foreign state can be a potential enemy (sect. 3.10.1.3), and such enemies beget cross-class nationalist alliances.

#### *3.10.1.1. Other Dissident Groups*
Dissident groups often compete. They may even be enemies. The greater the contributions to one dissident group, the greater the contributions to a threatened counter-dissident group. The mobilization-countermobilization dialectic therefore offers a solution to the Rebel's Dilemma: intergroup conflict among dissident groups begets intragroup cooperation within dissident

groups. Protest by group $i$ that affects the interests of group $j$ begets counter-protest by group $j$. Dissident grievances spread; claim begets counterclaim. Dissident groups spread; opposition begets counteropposition, movement begets countermovement, and organization begets counterorganization. Dissident tactics spread; strategy begets counterstratcgy. Finally, dissident actions spread; mobilization begets countermobilization and collective action begets collective reaction. The mobilization-countermobilization dialectic therefore accounts for some common patterns: violence begets counterviolence, coups beget countercoups, demonstrations beget counterdemonstrations, revolutions beget counterrevolutions, terrorism beget counterterrorism, and so on.[85] Examples of a movement producing a backlash and a counter-movement are abundant.[86]

What is the origin of dissident-dissident clashes? Class struggle, ecological competition, and communal conflict bear examination.

*Class struggle.* Marx believes that individuals constitute a class only insofar as they are engaged in a common struggle against another class. Class struggle begets class formation and, subsequently, collective dissent. Otherwise, as Marx and Engels ([1846] 1970, 82) write, class members "are on hostile terms with each other as competitors." Marx's ([1895] 1964, 33) comments on Louis Bonaparte's coup illustrate this view: "Revolutionary advance made headway not by its immediate tragi-comic achievements, but on the contrary by the creation of a powerful, united counter-revolution, by the creation of an opponent, by fighting whom the party of revolt first ripened into a real revolutionary party." The working class thus forms a revolutionary consciousness only in opposition to the bourgeoisie class.[87] Since class division engenders class conflict, anything that reduces the team competition between bourgeoisie and proletariat reduces the possibility of revolution. Fraternizing with the enemy is thus a revolutionary's cardinal sin.[88] Finally, Marx held that the origin of conflict in capitalist society lies in the relations of production rather than in simple market position (sect. 10.2.1). This is because conflict over the relations of production increases team competition — and CA — much more than does conflict over market position. A person's relationship to the means of production is therefore a far more likely basis for their participation in CA than their position in, say, the market for factors of production.

*Ecological competition.* A second type of competition among enemy dissident groups occurs over scarce and fixed economic assets (Mack and Snyder 1957, 215, proposition 5). Under such circumstances, team competition becomes conflict along some contract curve. The only change possible is redistribution of existing resources; increasing efficiency, to make more resources available to all, is not an option. This sort of zero-sum competition leads groups to plunder their opponents. Emerson (1983, 433) thus argues, contra the *Seek Public Bads* solution (sect. 3.12.1), that less CA is defensive (i.e., a "protective coalition") than is offensive (i.e., a "predatory coalition").

Zero-sum ecological competition may result from a disputed territory. One finds that "ethnic competition for disputed territory brings mobilization of many neighborhood forces, as ethnic identity becomes activated in defense of a neighborhood turf, or in an attempt to expand that ethnic group's geography" (Olzak 1985, 69). Neighborhood gangs are one example. Zero-sum ecological competition may also result from limited growth (Ophuls 1977). Gurr (1985), for example, explores "the political consequences of scarcity and economic decline" in postindustrial society.

*Communal conflict.* A third type of competition among enemy dissident groups is communal competition over social position (Zimmermann 1983, 140–41). This form of competition is also zero-sum. Communal conflict may be based on ethnic, racial, linguistic, familial, or religious divisions. Differences are symbolic, a matter of principle, and often nonnegotiable. If there is to be a state religion, for example, there can be only one. Communal cleavages thus give rise to more collective dissent than economic cleavages. Indeed, economic conflict may be based on financial divisions, with differences a matter of degree. Since there is the possibility of splitting the differences, gains can be had by all contenders. Horizontal divisions (i.e., social differentiation) are thus more likely sources of conflict than vertical divisions (i.e., social stratification).

Ecological competition often mixes with communal conflict, as in the following pattern (Olzak 1985, 65, 71–74; Levi and Hechter 1985, 140). Certain social processes — migration, invasion, colonialization, urbanization, industrialization, modernization, population increases, demographic change, and state penetration — bring segregated ethnic groups into competition over the same economic resources (e.g., jobs). The increase in ecological competition upsets settled niches of production and disturbs previously quiescent ethnic boundaries. Ethnic identities become activated as groups compete for ethic dominance *and* jobs. In short, ecological competition fuels communal competition, and vice versa. Such commingled macrointeractions, rooted in a micro *Increase Team Competition between Enemies* process, accounts for much intergroup conflict in ethnically divided societies.

### 3.10.1.2. States

States and oppositions are enemies. Their competition may lead to conflict spirals, as Coleman (1990, 491) observes: "The social structure often changes over the course of a revolt; a number of the nonparticipants may come to actively support the opponents of the authorities, and in some cases others come to actively support the authorities." In general, intergroup conflict between regime and opposition begets intragroup cooperation, thereby solving the Rebel's Dilemma.

Implied in models of team competition between regimes and oppositions is a very important idea: with respect to its own supporters, the regime has a CA problem referred to here as the State's Dilemma (sect. 7.2.2).

### 3.10.1.3. Other States

An internal enemy, such as the regime or another dissident group, can unite dissidents behind a narrowly based group. A foreign enemy can go one better: it can unite a whole nation behind an opposition movement. Nationalism is a very potent way of overcoming the Rebel's Dilemma, because nationalism cuts across lines of cleavage. It can mobilize *everyone*, "peasant and landowner, industrialist and worker, businessman and intellectual, the religious faithful and the nonbelievers, rich and poor, and people in the villages and in the cities" (Greene 1990, 80). Nationalism may in fact be the only common denominator that unites otherwise contending dissidents. For this reason, dissident groups frequently exploit nationalist symbols (e.g., the tricolor, the hammer and sickle). Several scholars stress nationalism's importance to modern dissident movements.[89] Examples abound.[90]

### 3.10.2. The Origins of Countermobilization

Dissident entrepreneurs know that to succeed, their group must engage in confrontations with significant others, that intergroup struggle builds group consciousness and leads to mobilization. A group enemy offers one solution to the Rebel's Dilemma,[91] and to that end dissident entrepreneurs adopt passive, moderate, and active strategies.

The passive strategy consists of differentiating the group, or setting it apart from other groups. Moses mobilized Jews by stressing that they would be "separate" from other nations. New religions responded with their own forms of countermobilization. Weber (1991[1922], 71) speculates that Christianity chose Sunday and Islam Friday as days of rest to distinguish their faiths from Judaism which adopts Saturday as a Sabbath. The passive strategy also consists of identifying and publicizing an outside enemy. Hence, all dissident leaders remind their followers about their enemies. Many appeal to a national "united front" against an external enemy. For example, Communists have often tried to capture the leadership of a nationalist movement and use it for their own ends. They succeeded in China and Vietnam, but failed in Burma, the Philippines, Indonesia, and Malaya. American revolutionaries tried to do the same thing: "Washington had the greatest difficulty in recruiting his continental army for the general campaign; but in the face of immediate enemy invasion the farmer militiamen would rise with enthusiasm" (Chorley ([1943] 1973, 68).

The moderate strategy involves exaggerating the position of counterdissidents and regimes, fanning intergroup hostilities, politicizing a conflict, and framing the conflict in "we vs. them" terms. Edelman (1971, 114–15) sees the tactic of defining the adversaries as enemies as a way to mobilize one's forces. Examples once again abound.[92]

When all else fails, dissident entrepreneurs can adopt the active strategy and manufacture an outside enemy. Merkl (1986b, 28) observes that "juxtaposition does wonders for recruitment, motivation, and discipline of a group. If the WVO [Workers Viewpoint Organization] communists had not had the Klan and the American Nazis, they literally would have had to invent them. And, indeed, inventing a diabolic, virulent enemy is what most violent groups have done, in a manner of speaking, by inventing a believable monster that will galvanize normally lazy, unheroic, and uncooperative young people into coordinated action." Hitler is thought to have once remarked that he would not want to destroy the Jews because "then we would have to invent them. One needs a visible foe, not an invisible one" (cited in Jäckel 1982, 16). This active strategy explains why rumors of counterrevolutionary plots — papist plots in revolutionary England and aristocratic plots in revolutionary France — flourish during revolutionary times (Goldstone 1991, 427). It also explains why Communists (fascists) fake fascist (Communist) terrorist actions.

When dissident entrepreneurs identify, magnify, or create an outside enemy, they risk the possibility that the strategy may backfire. Recall that an increase in group $i$'s CA produces an increase in group $j$'s CA. Hence, solving the Rebel's Dilemma through the *Increase Team Competition between Regime and Opposition* solution may make the dissidents worse off.

This unintended consequence can occur in the class conflict between workers and the bourgeoisie. As Elster (1989, 18) points out, an organization of workers begets an organization of employers, which can leave workers worse off: "It is not obvious that the collective of workers facing a collective of employers will do better than individual workers facing individual employers in a competitive market." Wallerstein (1974, 352) points out that the bourgeoisie face similar unintended consequences vis-à-vis workers:

> But the bourgeoisie had another opponent, the workers. Whenever the workers became conscious of themselves as a class, which was not too frequently in the sixteenth century, they defined the situation as a polarized two-class situation. In such circumstances the bourgeoisie found

itself in a deep tactical dilemma. To the extent that they maintained their own *class*-consciousness, they abetted the factory workers' class-consciousness, and thereby risked undermining their own political position. To the extent that, in order to deal with this problem, they muted their class-consciousness, they risked weakening their position vis-à-vis the tenants of traditional high rank.

What bourgeoisie, however, has so successfuly solved its CA problem that it can deal with such subtle unintended consequences?

### 3.10.3. The Consequences of Countermobilization

Zald (1980, 62) remarks that "much of the mobilization potential of a movement, its tactics, and its ultimate fate stem from its battles with a countermovement." Among the consequences of the *Increase Team Competition between Enemies* solution to the Rebel's Dilemma are conflict spirals, diverse and ephemeral coalitions, negative ideologies, and authoritarian and radical dissident groups.

One net result of the mobilization-countermobilization syndrome is an overall increase in the level of conflict in a society. This dynamic produces a general politicization of society as all social forces come to defend their position. Huntington (1968, 194) calls this situation a "praetorian society" and observes that "all these specialized groups tend to become involved in politics dealing with general political issues: not just issues which affect their own particular institutional interest or groups, but issues which affect society as a whole." He thus suggests that "countries which have political armies also have political clergies, political universities, political bureaucracies, political labor unions, and political corporations" (Huntington 1968, 194).

Second, as the threat from an enemy (e.g., another dissident group, the regime, or a foreign regime) increases with countermobilization, the diversity of the opposition group increases. Revolution involves strange bedfellows, as Wallerstein (1984, 82–83) suggests. This is especially so in predatory regimes, such as the widely despised Cuba of Batista, Nicaragua of Samoza, Iran of the Shah, and the Philippines of Marcos. Civil war, too, often produces diverse revolutionary coalitions. For example, Catholic Basques, bourgeois anticlericals, communists, and anarchists were all on the same side during the Spanish Revolution (Hagopian 1974, 220).

These negative coalitions tend to be short-term phenomena, however, that tend to disintegrate as the external threat recedes. For example, an elite-level ethic of nationalist cooperation of nationalist movements often merely papers over fundamental cleavages that reemerge once independence is achieved (Rabushka and Shepsle 1971, 467). Hence, independence movements typically fragment upon taking over from a colonial power. Many African states thus experienced a series of coups and countercoups after achieving independence.

Dissident groups try to deal with the problem of ephemeral coalitions, but their approach is often negative and defensive rather than positive and offensive. Their ideologies and programs stress what dissidents oppose and ignore what they support. The reason is clear: enemies *always* unite dissidents, programs *sometimes* divide them.

Countermobilization also begets authoritarianism within dissident groups. Dissident groups become intolerant of internal opposition. Coser (1956, 95–104) suggests that as a conflict grows more violent or intense, suppression of internal dissent increases. Intense competition with a regime may thus lead to restricted liberty for dissidents within their own group.

A final unintended consequence of this approach to the Rebel's Dilemma is the radicalization of protest. Revolutionary struggles radicalize revolutions. Hence, "Revolutionary ideology . . . often tends to an aggressive, intolerant nationalism" (Goldstone 1991, 427). For example, during the English and French revolutions the king's opponents became more radical out of fear of counterrevolution rather than out of socioeconomic or ideological conviction (Goldstone 1991, 432).

## 3.11. Restrict Exit

Dissidents sometimes have another alternative: they may simply abandon their efforts to get the state to redress their grievances and leave in search of an equivalent PG elsewhere. Three PG–PD models capture this argument. In Hirschman's (1970a) terms, dissidents have the option of "exit" rather than "voice." Tiebout (1956) suggests that people vote with their feet in choosing PGs. The ideas of both form the basis of a literature on local PGs (Atkinson and Stiglitz 1980, lecture 17).

All three models imply that if a rational dissident's exit option is cut off, his or her voice option — protest and rebellion — looks relatively more attractive. Without the safety valve of exit, voice is the only resort left for changing one's situation. Voice will thus be wielded by those with literally no place else to go. Moreover, as the possibility of exit increases, the best and the brightest (i.e., the most motivated and best able) leave, taking the clearest voices out of the picture (Barry 1974, 107). For example, revolutionaries who are out of town are unavailable for revolution at home — unless, like Lenin, Trotsky, and Stalin after the February Revolution in Russia, they make a fast retreat back.

Exit takes three forms: withdrawal, secession, and emigration. Each may occur as individual exit (a private refuge) and as collective exit (a "Mayflower Compact" with its associated PG–PD problems).

*Withdrawal.* Dissidents can sometimes bypass the government and obtain the PG they seek through private, rather than public, sources. They essentially retreat to a domestic refuge.[93] Many utopian communities and millenarian movements, for example, begin as an internal emigration. In such a movement, a dissident group attempts to cut itself off from the larger state and form an isolated, self-contained community. This was the thinking behind many rural communes in the United States in the 1960s. New social movements offer a contemporary example: "An important characteristic of the new social movements is that *they are not focused on the political system.* Essentially they are not oriented toward the conquest of political power or of the state apparatus, but rather toward the control of a field of autonomy or of independence vis-à-vis the system" (Melucci 1980, 220, emphasis in original). Urban migration, too, can be a form of exit, as per Huntington (1968, 299): "Urban migration is, in some measure, a substitute for rural revolution," and hence "the susceptibility of a country to revolution may vary inversely with its rate of urbanization." The *Restrict Exit* solution to the Rebel's Dilemma thus implies that both rural communes and urban migration reduce collective dissent.

*Secession.* Dissidents often seek federalism or autonomy within a state or separation from the state. Hirschman (1978, 93) refers to "fissiparous politics" and "geographic separation" and invokes several examples from the anthropological literature of in- and out-migration in stateless societies. Autonomy and secessionist movements are also common in the contemporary world (e.g., Quebec, Northern Ireland). Their success would by definition eliminate the problem of domestic political conflict.[94]

*Emigration.* The classic sense of exit is, of course, emigration from a state unable to supply the PG to another state than can supply it. It generates two very interesting propositions about collective dissent. First, there is a tradeoff between staying and exiting: as the relative benefits (costs) of emigration increase, collective dissent decreases (increases). In the words of Edwards (1927, 33), "Emigration is a preventative of revolution."[95] And second there is the inverse: as the relative benefits (costs) of collective dissent increase, emigration decreases (increases). Hence, revolution prevents emigration.[96] The anecdotal evidence in support of these ideas is overwhelming.[97]

Who chooses exit over voice? What factors, in other words, increase the possibility of exit?[98] As Niskanen (1971, 19, fn. 2) argues, "The most important differences among all types of organizations probably involve the cost and procedures for the transfer of an individual's property rights among organizations." Hence, the mobility of property, or whether dissidents can take their property with them when they leave, affects the exit/voice choice (Hirschman 1978, 96–101). Where property is transportable, exit becomes feasible. Dissidents who hold property in the form of land and buildings rather than cash, jewelry, and human capital are less likely to choose exit over voice. Thus, aggrieved workers protest and aggrieved capitalists move, as Hall and Ikenberry (1989, 44) conclude: "There is here something of an asymmetry in class relations: workers are much more clearly caught inside their nations than are capitalists."

The exit/voice choice is also affected by family considerations. Moving an entire family is obviously more difficult than moving a single individual. Such factors prevented many Jews from emigrating before and during the Holocaust (Goldscheider and Zuckerman 1984, 147–48).

A final determinant of the exit/voice choice is the state. Sometimes governments encourage exit as a tactic to reduce collective dissent. This "forced exit" creates refugees, expatriots, and emigrants. For example, Lenin and many other Bolshevik leaders fled the tsar's repression and lived as émigrés in Western Europe; Israel has deported many Palestinians from the occupied territories. Sometimes governments discourage exit; they may restrict the mobility of property and thereby restrict the mobility of people. Of course, governments that discourage exit only intensify their conflict management problem by keeping potential troublemakers at home. Regimes, however, might be willing to retain potential dissidents for many reasons. For example, the former Soviet government at one time restricted the emigration of Jews for three reasons: many Jews were skilled and educated and hence valuable to the regime, a bandwagon of émigrés from other groups was a possibility, and there was in place a sufficiently repressive apparatus to minimize Jewish protest.

### 3.12. Change the Type of Public Good

This solution has two parts. The first, considered in section 3.12.1, is to *Seek Public Bads*. People are often more sensitive to losses than to gains (Quattrone and Tversky 1988, 724–27). They suffer, in other words, from task framing and hysteresis (Hardin 1982, 82–83). Rebels who confront public bads are thus more likely to be able to overcome their Rebel's Dilemma than are rebels who seek public goods. The second solution, considered in section 3.12.2, is to *Seek Nonrival Public Goods*. This contrasts with rival benefits where the gain from one's contribution is diminished by everyone else's membership in the group. Rivalness therefore damages CA, because it dilutes the benefits of successful CA.

### 3.12.1. Seek Public Bads

Rational dissidents, as suggested above, may devote more energy to preventing something bad from occurring than to assuring that something good happens. As Hardin (1982, 83) argues, "If hysteresis is important, we should expend more collective action to prevent a quality deterioration than we would have expended to achieve a quality improvement over exactly the same range. We should expect that in some sense individual responses to impending public bads will be more intense than to potential collective goods." One should therefore expect more CA aimed at reducing costs than increasing benefits (Mitchell 1979, 112), especially when public bads offer no possibility of exit (sect. 3.11). Three expectations follow.

First, one would anticipate more collective dissent in opposition to government-imposed evils than in support of government-provided benefits. Most collective dissent should therefore be defensive, in response to declining capabilities, rather than to rising expectations. In Tilly's (1975a, 506–7; 1978, 144) terms, there should be more violence that is reactive (i.e., aimed at preventing a public bad) than is proactive (i.e., aimed at obtaining a public good).[99]

Second, there should be more collective dissent in opposition to a PG being removed than occurred initially in favor of obtaining the PG. Such a proposition bears investigation.

Third, it should be easier to mobilize declining social forces than rising ones. Rising social forces, such as British workers in the nineteenth century, seek to achieve the PG of incorporation into a state. Declining social forces, such as petit bourgeoisie shopkeepers in pre-Nazi Germany, seek to avoid the public bad of loss of position in the state. Huntington (1974, 179) suggests that rising groups are harder to mobilize than declining ones:

> A decline in the relative numbers, status, and position of a group does not necessarily lead to a decline in political power . . . Declining social forces, indeed, are often galvanized into political action precisely because they are declining. Threatened by the apparent flow of events, they are stimulated to greater unity, better organization, and more vigorous action to protect their interests, entrenching themselves behind political and legal barricades, using the power of the state to preserve a privileged position.

I again have a sense that this proposition is true and that Huntington and Hardin are right. Nevertheless, there is no real evidence on this point.

## 3.12.2. Seek Nonrival Public Goods

As suggested above, another solution to the Rebel's Dilemma is to seek nonrival PGs — goods whose benefits do not diminish as they are consumed by everyone else. Rivalness is best avoided because it hurts the prospects for CA (even successful CA, after all, results in fewer benefits for all) and because it leads dissidents to limit the size of the dissident group (White 1988, 40; also see the *Become Clubbish* solution, sect. 6.3.1).[100]

A dissident group's types of preferences and goals should therefore influence the number of its contributors. For example, one expects that unemployment among blacks will not lead to CA because of crowding effects: one person's gain of a job reduces the possibility that someone else will get that job (Mason 1984). Unemployment thus produces competition and hence is conducive to individual action (e.g., crime, job training). Discrimination, however, should increase CA among blacks, because there are no crowding effects: one person's gain from antidiscrimination laws does not reduce another person's gains. Measures that generate a stratified or segmented workforce thus generate CA, because extending advantages to the disadvantaged group is not subject to crowding effects. Unemployment and discrimination have indeed generated the predicted patterns of black mobilization (Mason 1984).

This chapter has examined a variety of Market solutions to the Rebel's Dilemma. We saw what happens to collective dissent when we increase benefits (sect. 3.1), lower costs (sect. 3.2), increase resources (sect. 3.3), improve the productivity of tactics (sect. 3.4), reduce the supply of the PG (sect. 3.5), increase the probability of winning (sect. 3.6), increase the probability of making a difference (sect. 3.7), use incomplete information (sect. 3.8), increase risk taking (sect. 3.9), increase competition (sect. 3.10), restrict exit (sect. 3.11), and change the type of PG (sect. 3.12). The key characteristic of all of these solutions is that they examine the parameters of a dissident's decision-making situation. Market approaches thus reduce the structures, institutions, and contexts of a person's life to certain variables that affect his or her decision to rebel. For example, one's community might raise benefits, one's social contracts might lower costs, and the hierarchical institutions (e.g., the state) to which one is subject might eliminate the exit option.

This approach provides many insights into protest and rebellion. Market solutions appear to be reductionist, acontextual, and ahistorical, however, offering no overall perspective on the decision making environment itself. They also appear to be eclectic, offering an incomplete explanation of CA. They are indeed all of these things (sect. 9.1).

It is useful, therefore, to regain a sense of the context within which a dissident dwells. Attention now moves one step farther back in the dissident's decision calculus. Community, Contract, and Hierarchy solutions place the baseline model in the context of communal, contractual, and hierarchical institutions. I will explore these structures within which the individual decides whether or not to rebel.

CHAPTER 4

# Community


Market solutions imply that dissidents are isolated atoms in an impersonal market for a PG. Dissidents, however, are often members of a shared community. Communal groups, characterized by strong social institutions, hold common beliefs and eventually engage in common behavior. In short, communal relationships beget communal understandings, which beget communal action.

CA solutions based on Community focus on the intermediate step of communal beliefs. Part of these belief systems is common knowledge that overcomes mutual ignorance (sect. 4.1). Dissidents might share a common understanding that they will act together, out of a mutual expectation of either simultaneous (e.g., crowds, riots; sect. 4.1.1) or sequential (i.e., temporal and spatial bandwagons; sect. 4.1.2) action. Communal belief systems also include common values that overcome pecuniary self-interest (sect. 4.2). Dissidents might share a process orientation (sect. 4.2.1) or other-regardingness (sect. 4.2.2).

## 4.1. Common Knowledge: Overcome Mutual Ignorance

The members of a rebel community can be involved in either simultaneous interactions or sequential interactions. Each type of "game" gives rise to problems of common knowledge.

### 4.1.1. Simultaneous Choice: Increase Mutual Expectations

Potential protesters do not make their decisions in a social vacuum. Their decisions are strategic in a game theoretic sense: the optimal choice is the optimal reply to everyone else's decisions. One example is club-type calculations (sect. 6.3.1): as the number of protesters increases, the marginal benefits (receiving the good) and the marginal costs (probability of repression) both decrease. Another example is an Assurance Game (Lichbach forthcoming, chap. 2). If the underlying CA game is Assurance, as Chong (1991, chap. 6) argues was the case for the U.S. civil rights movement, rebels must coordinate their efforts on one of two equilibria. If the underlying CA game is a PD, and if players do not use dominant strategy analysis, but rather a type of expected utility calculation, models of convergent and mutual expectations (Jeffrey 1983; Guttman 1978; Aumann 1974) are relevant.

These simultaneous choice models imply that rebels who see things similarly are more likely to rebel together. Many students of conflict recognize the importance of mutual expectations of acting together for the dissidents' actual ability to act together.[1] In addition to the experimental evidence about the importance of preplay communication (Bornstein and Rapoport 1988; Rapoport and Bornstein 1989), there is also some real-world evidence.[2]

Anything that increases the perception that others will protest is therefore likely to bring about protest. Four factors in the dissidents' community can increase the dissidents' beliefs that they will act in unison: mutually understood signals, places and times, causal mechanisms, and communications.

First, mutually understood signals or cues can indicate to rebels that there is a general readiness for mutual action. Schelling (1960, 90) presents the clearest discussion of this idea:

> It is usually the essence of mob formation that the potential members have to know not only where and when to meet but just when to act so that they act in concert. Overt leadership solves the problem; but leadership can be identified and eliminated by the authority trying to prevent mob action. In this case the mob's problem is to act in unison without overt leadership, to find some common signal that makes everyone confident that, if he acts on it, he will not be acting alone. The role of "incidents" can thus be seen as a coordinating role; it is a substitute for overt leadership and communication. Without something like an incident, it may be difficult to get action at all, since immunity requires that all know when to act together.

Signals may be as overt as a police incident or as subtle as O'Donnell and Schmitter's (1986, 49) "gestures by exemplary individuals." Such cues serve, whether implicitly or explicitly, as highly visible coordinating mechanisms that generate "rational expectations" about the actions of others. As mutually understood signals that collective dissent is imminent increase, collective dissent becomes more likely.

There is much evidence in support of this hypothesis. Signals are certainly important in riots. Many have felt that if only an *initial* blow could be struck at some prominent place or against some prominent people, then surely all members of the community would rise up and rebel against their oppressors. Some events, such as white policemen assaulting a black citizen, are known by a community to be "calls to action" — incidents perceived by all as obvious signals. A crisis involving a widely publicized and visible event can also act as a stimulus: the decision to build a nuclear plant can trigger the environmentalist community; the decision to deploy U.S. Pershing missiles in Europe can trigger the peace community. Terrorists, too, like to think that cues are important. Some believe that an initial blow struck by a small elite will set off an alarm for mass action. Much irrationality is attributed to terrorism because in fact the signal often does not have its intended effects. The "community," in other words, has been misunderstood by the terrorists.

Prominence, which relates to mutually understood places and times, is a second basis of rebels' beliefs that they will act together. Consider place. The location of a riot (e.g., a major intersection, a major store) is often known by all community members and can thus serve as a rallying point. Hence, riots often occur at central and conspicuous places.[3] If it were known, for example, that everyone will meet at a particular fountain during a campus demonstration, the prospects for a successful demonstration is enhanced. The Place de Grève during the French Revolution and its successor, the Hôtel de Ville during the nineteenth century, served as rallying points (Tilly 1986, 54-56). Chong (1991, 120-21) points out that "Leipzig's long and fabled tradition for opposing authority, for example, dating from the Protestant Revolution may help to explain why the mass protests that toppled the Communist Party in East Germany started in that city before spreading elsewhere." Even more telling is the fact that demonstrations started in a church frequented by dissidents. One also expects, by way of contrast, that areas without central meeting places will have fewer riots and more frequently aborted riots.

Now consider time. The hour set for some action (e.g., high noon) is also often known by all community members. Moreover, a prominent and convenient time can also serve as a rallying point; demonstrations are often set for at an obvious and unmistakable time, which can increase their size and effectiveness. Common knowledge, of course, is often about both place and time — riots in a certain community tend to occur at the same time and place as in the past. History thus helps create common or communal knowledge about CA.

The third basis for rebels' beliefs that they will act together is a mutually understood causal mechanism. Members of a community know that they are not alone and that their choices are mutually interdependent. This implies that one's actions have consequences for others' actions and that one's choices about whether to contribute influences the choices made by others. Hence, as dissident $i$'s beliefs that his or her contribution will make a positive difference in dissident $j$'s contribution increase, $i$'s participation in collective dissent increases. Such causal understandings underlie Guttman's matching

behavior, Cornes and Sandler's nonzero-conjectural variations, and Stackle-
burg behavior (Lichbach forthcoming, chap. 4).

Mutually understood communication is the final basis for a rebel community's belief that its members will act together. When there is a great deal
of communication among dissidents, expectations of mutual action converge.
Such preplay communication also increases collective dissent because it
facilitates several other solutions to the Rebel's Dilemma. It facilitates the
*Shape an Efficacious Group* solution (sect. 6.3.2) by which a prior agreement
is reached as to who constitutes the members of a Minimum Contribution
Set. This agreement renders each contributor critical; hence, all carry
through with the agreement. Since everyone knows that no one will renege,
everyone agrees to agree. Rapoport and Bornstein (1989, 463) thus suggest
that "when permitted to discuss the dilemma, groups achieve structural solutions requiring coordinated activity that is difficult or even impossible to
achieve under conditions that deny within-group communication." Preplay
communication also allows the *Overcome Pecuniary Self-Interest* solution
(sect. 4.2) to operate. As Rapoport and Bornstein (1989, 463) suggest,
"Group discussion also serves to promote a sense of social duty and 'group
regardingness' among group members." Preplay communication also facilitates the formation of formal or informal social contracts (chap. 5).[4]

In sum, mutual expectations of common action among a community of
dissidents can arise because preplay communication has emphasized that a
mutually understood signal will activate either a mutually understood time
and place or a causal mechanism. However groups manage to achieve such
convergent expectations of mutual action, two consequences are clear. First,
small events can have huge consequences. Seemingly insignificant occur-
rences can produce major political upheavals. Second, as signals change, CA
changes. Political ferment follows political apathy and political apathy follows political ferment when the political signs change. A third consequence
follows from these first two consequences: given that no one can predict
when a small event is the appropriate cue or signal that activates just the right
time and place or causal mechanism, collective dissent is unpredictable.
Indeed, one is hard-pressed to come up with a major political eruption that
was generally predicted. The problem of the unpredictability of collective
dissent is discussed more fully in section 9.2.

### 4.1.2. Sequential Choice: Build a Bandwagon

Perhaps simultaneous choice is a poor assumption to make about a dissident's decision-making situation. If we allow the individual a choice of when
to contribute, he or she may adopt a "wait-and-see" attitude. Hence, his or
her contribution may depend on previous (non)contributors. Those who

arrive early to collective dissent influence the latecomers. Suppose, for example, that the most committed join at time *t*; this both raises the probability of success (benefits) and lowers the probability of repression (costs) at time *t+1*. The less committed join at *t+1*; this, in turn, encourages those even less committed to join at *t+2*, and so on. Hence, it is theoretically possible for one person to join at time *1*, a second person to join at time *2*, a third person to join at time *3*, and so on. Such models are often called bandwagon models, threshold models, or models of critical mass (Granovetter 1978; Oberschall 1980, 48–51; Salert 1982), the idea being that successful CA becomes a self-fulfilling prophecy that leads to more CA and that unsuccessful CA becomes a self-denying prophecy that leads to less CA.

The common knowledge among members of a community that a bandwagon is either about to begin or is in the process of unfolding can be a powerful inducement to collective dissent. After all, everyone likes to jump on a bandwagon and no one likes to be left behind. This idea of collective dissent as a ripple effect passing through a community has several implications.

First, there will be people who have wanted to participate in protest for a long time, but only participated after they saw others participating. In short, bandwagons again demonstrate that preferences alone are not enough to generate collective dissent (sect. 9.2.2.1).

Second, heterogeneity promotes collective dissent. Heterogeneity within and among dissident communities facilitates protest and rebellion. Suppose, for a within-group example, that each member of a dissident community has a different threshold, and that subsequent rebels use earlier rebels as a signal. The more risk-acceptant members of a community thus will spur their more risk-averse colleagues to rebel (sect. 3.9). Suppose, for a between-group example, that each of several potentially dissident groups has a different threshold and that earlier groups signal subsequent groups. Student protest might then beget worker protest which might beget lower-middle-class protest.

Third, zealots (sect. 3.1), entrepreneurs (sect. 6.1), or patrons (sect. 6.2) solve the "who moves first" problem. They are the ones willing to pay the often-considerable start-up costs (sect. 3.2.4) of collective dissent. Bandwagons are another reason why such community leaders are important to protest and rebellion.

Fourth, it is easy to destroy a bandwagon. Chong (1991, 132) points to "the difficulty of resurrecting large scale collective action after it has collapsed . . . when collective action comes unglued, it cannot be reconstituted wholesale." That is, bandwagon models are fragile, based as they are on a knife-edge result: small variations in precipitants greatly influence outcomes. If the person with a 0 threshold is absent, there will be no collective dissent at all; if the personal with a threshold of *x*, where $0 < x < 100$, is absent, collective dissent will stop at *x-1*. Authorities may therefore stop a bandwagon by removing critically placed participants, or critical participants may be absent due to chance factors. In either event, collective dissent is hard to predict (sect. 9.2).

There are two other major consequences of bandwagon models: conflict will be temporally diffused among members of a single dissident community and spatially diffused among dissident groups that are part of some larger community.

### 4.1.2.1. The Temporal Diffusion of Collective Dissent

One important consequence of bandwagons of collective dissent is that the success of a tactic at time *t* increases the use of that tactic at time *t+1*. Hence, if dissident group *j* with tactic *i* succeeds at time *t*, dissident group *j* will employ tactic *i* at time *t+1*. I refer to this argument as the success-breeds-dissent proposition. Others have suggested variations on this hypothesis.[5] Examples of the temporal diffusion of successful collective dissent among members of a dissident community may be found in peasant uprisings,[6] postwar insurrections,[7] and military coups.[8]

The success-breeds-dissent proposition has two important corollaries. First, there will be temporal clusters of collective dissent. As Tarrow (1991, 13) argues, "Social movements tend to cluster in distinct historical periods — what Hirschman has called periods of increased public involvements (1982) and I have elsewhere called 'cycles of protest.'" Examples of eras of revolution include the mid seventeenth century (Spain, France, and England), the late eighteenth century (France, Belgium, and the United States), 1848 (Germany, France, and Italy), 1917–20 (Russia, Turkey, Mexico, and China), 1945–48 and 1989 (Eastern Europe). Examples of temporal clusters of riots within the United States include 1899–1908, 1915–21, 1935–43, and 1964–70.

A second corollary of the success-breeds-dissent proposition is that there will be temporal reaction functions and hence cycles of collective dissent.[9] The reasoning is as follows. Dissident success breeds dissident success, but this pattern cannot last forever. Regimes adopt response strategies and those that are successful generate further successful response strategies. Hence, both regimes and dissidents adopt successful challenges and responses. Cycles of collective dissent result from team competition between regimes and oppositions (sect. 3.10.1.2). The following is a typical pattern: a successful action by a dissident group is imitated; a successful countermeasure by the government is eventually developed and also imitated; just as collective dissent reaches a nadir, dissidents develop a new and successful tactic, which eventually diffuses; the government responds with a new countermeasure; and the cycle continues. In short, positive diffusion occurs because successful collective dissent breeds more successful collective dissent; negative diffusion occurs because successful collective dissent eventually breeds counteractions by government (as well as counterdissent by opponents, sect. 3.10.1.1). Gunning (1972, 35) thus argues that violence perpetrated at time *t* to influence government to act at time *t+1* can lead to government violence at time *t+2*, or a sequential game. This interaction between regimes and dissidents accounts for the cyclical nature of collective dissent. Cycles in terrorism, for example, may well be due to such an interactive process between regimes and dissidents.[10]

In spite of the persuasive arguments, solid evidence, important corollaries, and intriguing extensions of the success-breeds-dissent proposition, many have argued a contrary proposition — that successful collective dissent at time *t* does not necessarily lead to more collective dissent at time *t+1*. Two reasons have been offered. The first is that successful dissidents will eventually achieve their goals and return to private pursuits. Gurr (1970, 304) thus asks, "But what are the consequences of value gains achieved through hostile demands? They are highly likely to increase the degree of dissident institutional support; they also are likely under some circumstances to decrease the intensity of dissident commitment to violent opposition." The second reason that successful protest may not lead to temporal diffusion is that successful collective dissent may act as a safety valve (Coser 1956, 39–47). Hence, protest may prevent revolution. The premise here is that periodic outbursts enable newly emerging groups to challenge established hierarchies; that repeatedly challenged authorities often institutionalize procedures for conflict resolution; and that conflict resolution procedures can minimize conflict.[11] Present collective dissent may thus serve as a surrogate or substitute for more violent future collective dissent, rather than as an incubator or precursor.

Many have also advanced a second contrary proposition: unsuccessful collective dissent at time *t* does not necessarily lead to less collective dissent at time *t+1*. One reason is the lack of success itself: "The failure of instrumental means should not necessarily be expected to weaken the organization. Lack of success in obtaining demanded values is more likely to intensify than to reduce dissident opposition, because initial hostility not only persists, it is intensified by the effort expended in what was thought to be value-enhancing action" (Gurr 1970, 304). Another reason is sheer persistence. As has been remarked, unsuccessful revolutionaries often try again, which can only be explained by Samuel Johnson's comment on a man who remarried: "It was the triumph of hope over experience."

In spite of these qualifications, some researchers have suggested an even stronger argument about the temporal diffusion of collective dissent than the success-breeds-dissent proposition. They have proposed that it is not only the success, but also the level, of collective dissent that diffuses. Hence, as the extent of collective dissent at time *t* increases, the extent of collective dissent at time $t+1$ increases. Welch (1980, 74), for example, suggests that "the spread of support for violence probably follows previously established patterns of collective action."

What is the reasoning behind the dissent-breeds-dissent proposition? As past collective dissent increases, future collective dissent increases, because the weakness of government has been demonstrated, hence facilitating the *Lower Costs* (sect. 3.2) and *Increase the Probability of Winning* (sect. 3.6) solutions to the Rebel's Dilemma. Even unsuccessful collective dissent may produce organizations (sect. 5.1) that can be activated later. Finally, because of the allocation of resources over time, as in a capital goods model, collective dissent by group $i$ at $t+1$ will be a function of collective dissent by group $i$ at time $t$; protest and rebellion, that is, will be correlated over time.

There is a great deal of evidence behind the dissent-breeds-dissent proposition.[12] Communal traditions of conflict appear to exist at all levels of analysis, national,[13] group,[14] and individual.[15] Hence, the level of collective dissent does appear to diffuse temporally, regardless of whether it is successful.

Note that the "any dissent breeds dissent" proposition implies the "successful dissent breeds dissent" proposition, but the inverse is not necessarily true. Proponents of the latter proposition would argue that the extent to which a dissident group's tactic is used is relevant to the group's subsequent actions; but familiarity without success is useless, because only useful innovations are imitated and diffused. Only utilitarian calculations about violence, then, should figure in collective dissent. The difference between the two propositions can serve as a critical test of DA and CA theories (sect. 9.3.2.2).

### 4.1.2.2. The Spatial Diffusion of Collective Dissent

The idea that collective dissent can be explained as a ripple effect passing through a community has one other principal implication: the spatial diffusion of conflict among dissident groups who are members of some larger community. The success of a tactic at time $t$ increases the use of that tactic and other related tactics at time $t+1$ by some other group. Hence, as dissident group $m$ with tactic $i$ succeeds at time $t$, dissident group $n$ will employ tactic $i$ and related tactic $j$ at time $t+1$. In this reaction function, one successful dissident group politicizes, organizes, and radicalizes other groups, as protest by group $m$ correlates with protest by group $n$. To a regime, these groups look like a set of dominoes ready to fall, with one dissident group the instigator for even more widespread collective dissent by other dissident groups.[16]

How does the spatial diffusion of collective dissent actually operate? The first issue to consider is how contacts among dissident groups are established. Several mechanisms are important. Publicity through the mass media is obviously relevant. Moreover, early collective dissent might occur at a key focal point (e.g., a capital city, like Paris), from which information is readily dispersed. This facilitates the *Increase Mutual Expectations* solution (sect. 4.1.1). Contacts can also be established through travel. Exposure to revolutionary ideas while living and traveling abroad can produce revolutionary behavior (Greene 1990, 47-48). Hence "travel increases unrest" because of demonstration effects (Edwards 1927, 23–27). Finally, there are personal contacts. Tarrow (1989, 10) suggests that protest spreads because of proselytizing by the "'earlier risers.'" Walton (1984) argues that these personal ties are themselves the result of communal structures and in turn facilitate the spatial diffusion of protest from urban to rural areas:

> These alliances did not rise from the astute designs of political organizers but were guaranteed by institutional mechanisms — built into the organizational arrangements for managing underdevelopment. This fundamental fact is best illustrated in Kenya and the Philippines with the practices of officially combining rural and urban labor matters, the system of labor registration, absentee landlords, and interregional trading networks. All of this "proto-urbanization" brought the peasantry into closer contact with urban political influences" (1984, 149–50).

Once contacts among a community of dissident groups are established in these various ways, success by one dissident group diffuses to other dissident groups via mechanisms that activate solutions to the Rebel's Dilemma. In the first instance, successful dissident groups facilitate the *Lower Costs* (sect. 3.2) solution for other dissident groups. The reason is that the successful group has diverted resources that the regime might otherwise use to repress a second group.[17]

Second, successful dissident groups facilitate the *Improve the Productivity of Tactics* (sect. 3.4) solution for other dissident groups by offering workable ideas for leadership, coalitions, ideologies, tactics, and so on. Two strategies often diffuse. An important strategy that diffuses among dissident groups is the technique for gaining governmental accommodation to dissident demands. A dissident group in endeavoring to improve the productivity of its tactics (sect. 3.4) substitutes between dissident tactics $i$ and $j$ as well as between $i$ and $j$ and various legal tactics $k$ and $l$. Hence, as past and current levels of accommodation of tactic $i$ used by group $m$ increase, future use of tactic $i$ by group $n$ increases while future use of tactic $j$ by group $n$ decreases. In other words, if group $m$ with tactic $i$ succeeds at time $t$, group $n$ will employ tactic $i$ at time $t+1$. Dissident groups update their production technologies to take account of new information about other groups' successes. A second important strategy that diffuses to dissident groups is the technique for avoiding governmental repression of dissident demands. The dynamics that were described above for accommodation also work in the case of repression. As past and current levels of repression of tactic $i$ used by group $m$ increase, future use of tactic $i$ by group $n$ decreases and future use of tactic $j$ by group $n$ increases. In other words, as group $m$ with tactic $i$ fails at time $t$, group $n$ will not employ tactic $i$ at time $t+1$. Dissident groups also update their production technologies to take into account new information about other groups' failures.

Third, dissident groups that are successful facilitate the *Increase the Probability of Winning* (sect. 3.6) solution for other dissident groups. The success of a dissident group at time $t$ increases other dissident groups' estimates of their probabilities of victory at time $t+1$.[18]

Finally, dissident groups that are successful facilitate the *Locate Principals or Patrons* (sect. 6.2) solution for other dissident groups. Successful dissident groups can provide material support to subsequent dissident groups, acting as their patrons.

In sum, success diffuses among a community of dissident groups because one group's solutions to its Rebel's Dilemma facilitate another group's solutions to its Rebel's Dilemma. One group's success activates another group's *Lower Costs, Improve the Productivity of Tactics, Increase the Probability of Winning*, and *Locate Principals or Patrons* solutions to its CA problem.

There is strong evidence for these ideas. The classic examples come from the Great Revolutions, all of which sought to spread their gospel. Proselytizers, universalist in aspiration, attempted to export revolutionary ideas. Successful revolutions thus became "meccas" for foreign revolutionaries (Walt 1992, 346–47) as dissident entrepreneurs flocked to their capitals to learn new tactics and win patrons.[19] Hence, the English,[20] French,[21] Cuban,[22] and Eastern European revolutions[23] had important demonstration effects. There are as well many other less dramatic examples of the phenomenon.[24] There are also many examples where the failure of one dissident group at one time has bred failure in another dissident group at a subsequent time.[25]

In sum, protest and rebellion diffuse among a community of dissident groups, because subsequent groups learn about the successful (i.e., accommodated) and unsuccessful (i.e., repressed) tactics of prior groups. As Tilly (1978, 158) notes, "When a particular form of riot or demonstration spreads rapidly, what diffuses is not the model of behavior itself, but the information — correct or not — that the costs and benefits associated with the action have suddenly changed."[26]

## 4.2. Common Values: Overcome Pecuniary Self-Interest

Another part of communal belief systems is common values that overcome the pecuniary self-interest calculations characteristic of Market solutions to the Rebel's Dilemma. Potential dissidents will participate in CA if they share a process orientation (sect. 4.2.1) or other-regardingness (sect. 4.2.2).

### 4.2.1. Process Orientation

If one had a process, rather than a pecuniary, orientation to a protest or rebellion, he or she could be a willing participant. Communal norms might lead the individual to value protest as a self-actualizing political experience (Nagel 1987), attach an entertainment value to participation (Tullock 1971a), seek to bring his or her actions into conformity with the actions of fellow rebels (Riker and Ordeshook 1968), see the means of protest as an end in themselves (Sorel 1950), and/or think of the costs of participation as benefits (Hirschman 1982a, chap. 5).

*Self-actualizing political experience.* Looking at dissent as a self-actualizing political experience is one aspect of process orientation. Dissent is a political statement that defines the dissident; rebels do not make rebellion so much as rebellion makes the rebel. As Chong (1991, 74) suggests, dissidents seek to "affirm their efficacy." Participation in new social movements[27] and political violence[28] are often thought to provide such self-actualizing political experiences.

Dissident entrepreneurs are keenly aware that many of their followers are trying to find themselves. Kahn (1982, 7), for instance, argues that

> through organizing, people learn something new about themselves. They find dignity in place of mistreatment. They find self-respect instead of a lack of self-confidence. They begin to use more fully the skills and abilities that they possess: to work with other people, to influence, to speak up, to fight back. Through organizing, people begin to rediscover themselves. They find out who they are, where they come from, their background, their history, their roots, their culture. They rediscover the things in their family, their gender, their ethnic or language group, their race that give them strength. They rediscover their own history of struggle and resistance.

Vactar Havel's books, for example, promote the idea that rebels gain self-respect by stopping the *lie*.[29]

*Entertainment value.* Another aspect of process orientation is its entertainment value: protests and rebellions can be an enjoyable communal experiences. Many have suggested that people participate in collective dissent because it is fun and exciting.[30] The implication is that idleness, restlessness, boredom, and emptiness contribute to collective dissent.[31] Examples where the entertainment value of collective dissent inspired activism are legion.[32]

Most dissident entrepreneurs again recognize this solution to the Rebel's Dilemma. Alinsky (1971, 128, emphasis in original) writes that "*a good tactic is one that your people enjoy.*" Kahn (1982, 196, emphasis in original) asserts in a similar vein that "*a good tactic is fun.* It's enjoyable. It provides people with a good time. It has humor and spirit." Dissident entrepreneurs who fail to grasp this point pay the consequences: parties that offer few parties have a hard time surviving. Chong (1991, 37, citing Harvey Klehr) recounts the fate of one dissident community that took itself too seriously: "Endless meetings and speeches, esoteric terminology, burdensome and excessive party chores and duties, constant dues collections, exploitation of new Party members, and other disincentives weakened the commitment of individual members and discouraged many Communist sympathizers from joining the [American Communist] Party."

*Conformism/rebellion in actions*. Some people, it is often believed, are "natural" rebels who always oppose the established hierarchy in their community and to that end participate in collective dissent. Other people, it is also believed, are "natural" conformists who always go along with the majority in their community. The desire to conform leads to crowd behavior and hence also promotes participation in collective dissent.

*Means are ends*. Dissidents may hold a process orientation toward collective dissent because they glorify one particular form of dissent. Their attitudes toward dissent may "range from Gandhian doctrines of nonviolence to Sorelian glorification of violence per se" (Gurr 1970, 193). Some communities of dissidents, thus, solve their Rebel's Dilemma by treating means as ends[33] and advocating violent means. Laqueur (1987, 255) argues that "the real inspiration underlying terrorism is a free-floating activism." Jenkins (1982, 15) maintains that the terrorist personality is "action-prone." Russell, Banker, and Miller (1979, 36) argue that terrorism can become an end in itself: "As terrorism loses its tactical status in favor of a strategic and/or philosophical one, it tends toward elevation to an 'ism' among existing ideologies." Other dissident communities manifest a strong preference for nonviolence. Such a commitment can also sustain CA. The commitment to nonviolence of Dr. Martin Luther King Jr. and his followers, for example, sustained the U.S. civil rights movement in the 1950s and early 1960s. To the extent that such "normative justifications" are central to a dissident community's ideologies and doctrines (Gurr 1970, 157), particular forms of CA are encouraged.

For other dissident communities any means are valuable. Action is always preferred to inaction, as nothing dissipates a movement so much as doing nothing. As Chong (1991, 89) argues, "Whereas direct action involves many, negotiations are necessarily conducted by a few, so the ability to claim credit for a successful outcome is significantly reduced if it is achieved peacefully rather than through a protracted conflict. Moreover, courage, fortitude, bravery, and dependability are more easily demonstrated on the streets than in the bargaining room; therefore even the leaders of the negotiating team for the activists may prefer to achieve a victory through their leadership on the battlefield." Dissident entrepreneurs thus often escalate conflict for "expressive" rather than "instrumental" reasons. Action builds the movement for the long term, so leaders sometimes prefer "action" over "talk" even when activism brings fewer immediate benefits. Chorley ([1943] 1973, 238) observes that fascist private armies "were kept alert and closely knit in the units by continual calls to action of one sort and another." A contrary view on the implications of overactivism has also been expressed (sect. 5.2.1).

*Costs are benefits*. A final aspect of a process orientation to collective dissent is that members of a dissident community treat costs as benefits. Both culture and entrepreneurship can be at work here.

White (1988) argues that Japanese culture imbued Japanese dissidents with values that defined the costs of protest as benefits. He (1988, 58) writes that "a considerable body of literature suggests that there is a cultural strain of romantic, death-defying (or even death-seeking), self-sacrificing, expressive radicalism in Japan. Rationality pales in this sphere; the deed becomes all; means that contradict the ostensible end become common; going down in flames becomes an end in itself."

Dissident entrepreneurs may encourage their community to frame costs as benefits. Rebel entrepreneurs may glorify rather than hide their members' sacrifices and suffering. As Bittner (1963, 938, emphasis in original) argues, "Since disappointments, reversals and failure are commonplace in the lives of radicals, *suffering must be made an integral part of the conception of the progress of the movement* in order to minimize its effect on the morale of the members." Dissident entrepreneurs therefore exploit martyrs, extol martyrdom, and exalt communal heroes and heroines. Dissident entrepreneurs, in fact, may deliberately choose particularly costly courses of action, as in Chong's (1991, 88) example from the U.S. civil rights movement: "Alabama was an oft-chosen site of demonstrations and marches because that state constituted perhaps the greatest obstacle to the movement. Similarly, members of the more radical civil rights groups — especially SNCC — went out of their way to tackle difficult projects that required tremendous courage and dedication." The particularly difficult challenge — and the hard-won victory — yields the greatest payoffs. Chong (1991, 86) offers another civil rights example:

> Civil rights activists, we should note, often behaved (for strategic reasons) *as if* the punishments threatened by the authorities for engaging in protest and demonstrations were a benefit rather than a cost. When the

jail-no-bail tactic was initiated, for example, southern authorities were shocked to discover that protesters *chose* prison over an opportunity to pay a small fine and be free. The confusion showed by the authorities was understandable, since the threat of imprisonment had historically been the strongest deterrent again political activism. When the protesters turned around and revealed a preference for being jailed, this erased the most effective penalty possessed by local officials.

Of course, such cultural values or entrepreneurial strategies may backfire. One downside of framing costs as benefits is to reduce the probability of winning (sect. 3.6): "An intransigent and difficult opponent will also foster disillusion and frustration in the movement" (Chong 1991, 88). Another downside is to increase costs (sect. 3.2): "When the opposition is strong, all but the most eager activists will be deterred from participation until there is some safety and security in numbers" (Chong 1991, 88). Self-sacrifice is thus a self-limiting approach to CA. You cannot fool all of the members of a dissident community all of the time. Nowhere can the costs-are-benefits approach long endure.

### 4.2.2. Other-Regardingness

A person just might care about someone besides himself or herself, the other members of the community, for instance. If the individual were other-regarding, he or she would be a willing participant in the community's protests and rebellions. One's enlightened self-interest, or move "beyond self-interest" (Mansbridge 1990), could include altruism (Jasay 1989, 197), the desire to express an ethical preference (Taylor 1988, 88), Kantian ethics (Ullmann-Margalit 1977, 53), fairness (Elster 1989, 187), communal consciousness (Alinsky 1946), and/or social incentives (Olson 1965, 60–64).

*Altruism.* A dissident's self-interest can be overcome through altruism. Lefebvre (1947, 50) argues that "there is no true revolutionary spirit without the idealism which alone inspires sacrifice." He (1947, 50) offers the example of bourgeois revolutionaries: "Undoubtedly the interest of the bourgeoisie, which was the first to profit from the new order, can easily be detected beneath the philosophy of the eighteenth century. But the bourgeoisie believed sincerely that it worked for the good of humanity . . . the men who rose on the 'great days' of the Revolution, who fought at Valmy, Jemappes, and Fleurus, would not have risked their lives had they been thinking only of themselves."

*Express an ethical preference.* Chong (1991, 74) suggests that dissidents seek "to voice their convictions." Hence, a dissident might be a moral being who is very concerned with issues of right and wrong. Entrepreneurs try to reinforce such beliefs by stressing the importance of doing the right thing and living up to the community's moral code. Leaders like Gandhi thus try to increase their followers' sense of moral outrage. Often this is done by demonstrating that the regime transgresses the values — democracy, human rights, justice, equity, fairness — that it claims to represent. Hence, the vices of the old regime are contrasted to the virtues of the new regime. Dissident politics therefore has two rules of thumb: bang on the table to state your demands *and* point out the justice of your cause.

*Kantian ethics.* Chong (1991, 74) also suggests that dissidents seek "to fulfill their obligations." Hence, a dissident might believe that it is the duty of every member of the community to contribute to a PG. Much evidence supports the idea that feelings of obligation are important to political participation (Opp 1986; 1989, 65, 68; Riker and Ordeshook 1968, 38; Chong 1991, 93-100).

*Fairness.* Dissidents might be motivated by a desire to provide their "fair share" contribution to a dissident group. One who believes that every member of the community, or at least a significant number of other members, is going to cooperate, might also cooperate. Dissident entrepreneurs work hard to instill in their followers this particular ethical norm of conditional cooperation (sect. 5.1.2).

*Communal consciousness.* Communal consciousness is another important aspect of other-regardingness. Alinsky (1946, 100, emphasis in original) argues that collective dissent is likely when people learn that "*the other guy's welfare means their own welfare.*" Organizers thus often complain that a "bourgeois mentality" of individual profit seeking is the root explanation of the absence of CA. If only potential dissidents were more concerned with communal needs and less concerned with private goals, entrepreneurs charge, the Rebel's Dilemma could be easily overcome. Hence, all dissident groups try to reinforce a sense of community; they use doctrinal and ideological symbols (e.g., flags) and rituals (e.g., oaths) to induce common identification, fate, and like-mindedness (sect. 3.8.2.4). Governments, of course, try to bring about the opposite identification with their own interests.

Academics often stress the importance of communal consciousness to collective dissent.[34] Considerable evidence in fact exists to support the idea that communal consciousness increases collective dissent. The search for individual identity through identification with some community has played a major part in fascist,[35] terrorist,[36] peasant,[37] youth,[38] and millenarian[39] movements, as well as the new social movements.[40]

*Social incentives.* Social incentives are the final part of other-regardingness. Communities bestow prestige on those who concern themselves with communal needs. As one's desire for this prestige increases, one's participation in collective dissent increases. Considerable survey evidence[41] and numerous examples[42] may be used to drive home this point.

Dissident entrepreneurs, who of course recognize this solution to the Rebel's Dilemma, use various techniques to bestow social incentives on supporters: passwords, hand grips, and recognitions signs are used with fellow dissidents. Uniforms are available to members of the group. Titles and informal leadership positions are bestowed upon major contributors. Dissident groups also have several techniques to bestow social disincentives on nonsupporters: they publicize the names of noncontributors; in unions, noncontributors are labeled "scabs" and ostracized. More generally, dissidents refer to noncontributors as "traitors" and "Uncle Toms."

States, it should be noted, also recognize this solution to the CA problem. It is the idea behind hsiao tsu groups in China and accounts for the value that communist regimes in China, Cuba, and the former Soviet Union attach to Stakhanovites.

This chapter has examined what happens to the Rebel's Dilemma when dissidents are members of a community. Dissidents who share common knowledge (sect. 4.1) can overcome the mutual ignorance characteristic of Market solutions. Dissidents who share common values (sect. 4.2) can overcome the pecuniary self-interest characteristic of such solutions. Common cognitions and values are therefore the basic components of a system of norms that allows dissidents to overcome their CA problem. Parsons (cited in Hardin 1990, 359) thus maintains that "the famous problem of order . . . cannot be solved without a common normative system."

This approach yields many insights into protest and rebellion. The existence of common norms, however, has one fatal flaw as an explanation for CA: such theories presume that rebels are socialized into common norms. However, this presumes that there are common norms into which rebels can be socialized. This, in turn, presumes that some social order among dissidents already exists that can encourage commitment to its underlying cognitions and values. But where do these common norms and the preexisting social order come from? Ellis (1971, 692) concludes that "the normative solution has consistently avoided a direct confrontation with the Hobbesian problem of order. Whereas Hobbes was primarily interested in transforming a society characterized by civil war into one characterized by civil peace, normative theorists are primarily interested in identifying the sources of social integration in social systems in which the problem of order has been solved [or norms already exist]." The Community approach to the dissident's CA problem is therefore fundamentally incomplete, because it assumes that dissident norms exist but that a dissident social order does not - yet the latter is clearly a precondition for the former. One therefore infers that community alone is never sufficient to solve the dissidents' CA problem. A community of norms must ultimately be created either by long-term exchange (a contract) or by long-term coercion (a hierarchy). The consequence is that Community solutions to the Rebel's Dilemma offer as incomplete an explanation of CA as Market solutions did, an issue that requires elaboration (sect. 9.1).

Let us now turn to the two other institutions within which a dissident dwells. Given that communal institutions are rooted in contractual and hierarchical structures, perhaps these later contexts will offer a more complete solution to the Rebel's Dilemma.

CHAPTER 5

# Contract

Contractual institutions provide yet another context for Market solutions to
the Rebel's Dilemma. Social contract theorists emphasize *Gesellschaft*, the
forging of more or less formal agreements. The idea is that the agents (i.e.,
members) of society find their current arrangements unsatisfactory: some are
benefiting at the expense of others, no one can reach his or her personal
goals, and/or the cooperation that would benefit all is missing. Concluding,
therefore, that it is in everyone's best interest to specify rights and obligations, the agents set about negotiating the type of institutions under which all
will live.

Rebels, in other words, recognize the deficiency of Market solutions to
the Rebel's Dilemma. Such solutions cannot achieve a PG, based as they are
on the narrow rationality of material self-interest that is reconciled through
an invisible hand process. Rebels believe that a larger Reason, or more conscious cooperation, can achieve that PG.

Dissidents thus attempt to alter the parameters of the canonical PG–PD
game to their advantage by creating a set of institutions that serve as the context in which the game operates. I consider first (sect. 5.1) the types of contracts that dissidents can establish and then (sect. 5.2) the social origins of
social contracts.

## 5.1. Types of Social Contracts

Dissidents forge three types of social contracts: self-governing institutions
(sect. 5.1.1), Tit-For-Tat arrangements (sect. 5.1.2), and mutual exchange
agreements (sect. 5.1.3).

### 5.1.1. Self-Government

New forms of dissident organization often emerge spontaneously during
periods of collective dissent. Soviets, communes, base areas, revolutionary
committees, revolutionary parties, factory councils, socialist cooperatives,
intentional communities, gangs, patron-client arrangements, provisional governments, constituent assemblies, national conventions, and constitutional

conventions have all been created *after* collective dissent was already under way. Spontaneous collective dissent often begets spontaneous dissident self-government.[1] Two extended examples, one from medieval peasant rebellions and the other from contemporary peasant revolutions, demonstrates that dissident self-government can become quite complex.

The French peasant rebellions of the fourteenth and fifteenth centuries provide an interesting example of peasant disturbances that started out spontaneously and eventually acquired organization. As Mousnier (1970, 59) puts it, after peasants started a rebellion in France, "they then proceeded to perfect their organization." This is how their self-governing arrangements worked.

- Peasants held assemblies at which actions were debated, votes recorded, and decisions taken. For example, Mousnier (1970, 78) reports that peasants "held a great assembly at the pond of La Vernède, near Bordes, in the commune of Grun and the canton of Vergt. A huge crowd of peasants came from all parts of the district. They resolved to arm themselves, take control of the province, and put an end to the doings of the *gabeleurs*." Zagorin (1982a, 220) reports on the convening of these representative assemblies:

    > Typically, insurrection started with the surge of rumors, the flare-up of resentment of some new excess of fiscality, an act of resistance to soldiers or tax gatherers, and the angry talk of country people in taverns, markets, and fairs. Church bells summoned the parish, whose inhabitants came together in arms. Letters and emissaries were sent around, distant parishes roused, and joint meetings of parishes appointed on a Sunday or a feast day. As the revolt widened, the parishes elected captains; the men marched to meetings with other parishes in military order, perhaps accompanied by their priests. Very soon assemblies of scores of parishes, with thousands of people present, were being held. Thus appeared the "commune," meaning the union or association of parishes, as the widest degree of organization achieved by the revolt.

    The commune was therefore an assembly of dissident communities, with its members formal representatives of the peasants from each village within a particular district or province.
- Peasants issued a formal statement of their goals and demands. Mousnier (1970, 59) reports that "their assembly at Blanzac drew up an ordinance for these parishes, and elected deputies to seek out the king, beg for his mercy, and convey to him the conditions on which they would agree to submit."

- Peasants elected leaders (Mousnier 1970, 78) who were invested with very definite powers:

    > The general had "complete power to command" and to convene assemblies, to decide on measures to be taken and on the use of force against property and persons. The general "in his council" would judge all the "persons hostile to the people's liberty who had agreed to the general over-taxation and extraordinary and unauthorized taxes," these persons to be deliver to him by the captains of the communities. The captains would oblige their men to take an oath to serve them . . . By virtue of these decisions, La Mothe La Forest, "general of the Commune of Périgord . . ." issued orders, directed the communes to arm, gave safe-conducts to merchants... and invited the noblemen of Périgord to join the commune. (Mousnier 1970, 81)

- Peasants sought out allies among the nobility. As Mousnier (1970, 60) writes, "Thus we see a rural commune and an army of rural commoners, with a sort of peasant dictatorship, forcing those having the technical ability to command and negotiate to carry out the will of the peasants."
- Peasants ordered that recruits (especially soldiers) be found. Formal agitators, mobilizers, and organizers were designated.
- Peasants established a rudimentary military organization. Mousnier (1970, 66) reports that "they erected four barricades on the four main roads leading to La Couronne, and posted three hundred men to guard each one. In the meadow they formed themselves into four battalions."
- Specific rules for distributing the tax burden were enacted (Mousnier 1970, 63–64).
- Peasants organized the social services in the areas under their control. According to Mousnier (1970, 59), "The totality of the parishes affected was constituted a 'commune'" which functioned as a sort of local government.
- After they agreed to surrender, the rebels designated negotiators who presented a list of grievances to the king and conducted formal negotiations (Mousnier 1970, 68–71).[2]

Another classic case of complex dissident self-government, this time one formed with a good deal of outside entrepreneurship (sect. 5.1), is the base area. A basic assumption of theorists of guerrilla warfare is that dissidents must organize their mass base (Mao 1961). If rebels can use a territory that is under their control as a base of operations, they can rearrange communal life to facilitate the operation of Tit-For-Tat and mutual exchange agreements. Base areas are also important to rural guerrilla warfare because they facilitate three other solutions to the dissidents' PG–PD game. First, dissident entrepreneurs establish a base area in order to demonstrate that "the revolutionary infrastructure will *outadminister* the government's bureaucracy" (Hagopian 1974, 372, emphasis in original). If the guerrillas can win control of space (i.e., territory and people), the *Increase the Probability of Winning* solution (sect. 3.6) is facilitated. Second, base areas provide the infrastructure to enforce agreements by offering selective incentives (sect. 6.5.3). Finally, base areas provide food, refuge, weapons manufacturing sites, training facilities, and a magnet for recruits. This allows dissidents to increase their resources, facilitating the *Increase Resources* solution (sect. 3.3). In sum, base areas are an important part of the regime-opposition struggle (sect. 7.2.2) that allows guerrillas to compete with governments.

The classic case of the base area comes from China during the 1930s.[3] The Vietnamese Communists also developed an elaborate base area during their revolutionary war.[4] Despite the spectacular successes of base areas in the Chinese and Vietnamese revolutions, a counterargument asserts that they are not terribly effective. The criticisms raises strategic considerations. Debray (1967, 27–46) maintains that fixed base areas are vulnerable to regimes with preponderant power. Moreover, they produce a defensive mentality. Such arguments imply that efforts to improve the productivity of dissident tactics (sect. 3.4) may work at cross-purposes with efforts to forge a social contract. The interrelationship among solutions to the Rebel's Dilemma is considered in Lichbach (forthcoming, chap. 7).

Debray relies instead on mobile guerrilla forces that are less vulnerable to regimes and have a more offensive orientation. He has in mind small groups of intellectuals (e.g., students and workers) who wage war against the central government from the countryside, where they try to convert the peasants and use them as a source of food, shelter, and protection from the regime's forces. Hence, "The main differences between the rural guerrilla *foco* and the Maoist People's war lies in the rather scanty numbers in guerrilla bands, the absence . . . of a strong, revolutionary party or of close relationships to professedly revolutionary parties, and the reluctance to build up a political-administrative structure going beyond the immediate logistical needs of the military effort" (Hagopian 1974, 373). *Focos*, in other words, lack ties to community organizations. They are likely therefore to be less successful in using a social contract approach to overcome the Rebel's Dilemma. It is often alleged that Che Guevara failed in his revolutionary efforts because the *focos* he attempted to create lacked an adequate revolutionary infrastructure of self-government.

## 5.1.2. Tit-For-Tat

Tit-For-Tat or contingent cooperation (Taylor 1976; Axelrod 1984) is another social contract approach to the CA problem. Dissidents who feel certain that their participation will be reciprocated by others will participate. The implication for the Rebel's Dilemma is clear: contractarians, or Tit-For-Taters, engage in more collective dissent than noncontractarians, or non-Tit-For-Taters. For Tit-For-Tat to work, then, conditional reward must be bestowed and conditional punishment must be exacted. It rests on a bedrock of mutual monitoring and enforcement (Lichbach forthcoming, chap. 5).

Dissidents need to find out if the contract is violated and to measure the extent of the violations. They thus monitor each other's contributions to collective dissent. Indeed, there is much evidence to support the idea that dissidents often overcome their CA problem by reaching a priori agreements about visible and monitorable contributions. Brinton (1965, 181–82), for example, reports that dissidents watch each others' affairs closely during revolutions. There is much prying, spying, and informing. And Moore (1966, 206) reports that under the *pao-chia* system of mutual surveillance in China, individual members are responsible for reporting the conduct of other members of the group. The Chinese Communists turned such procedures to their advantage. One also expects dissidents to punish deviants — those dissidents who refuse to participate in collective dissent. Indeed, that too is documented. Social incentives (sect. 4.2.2) and selective disincentives (sect. 6.5.4) are used to enforce norms about contributions to CA.

## 5.1.3. Mutual Exchange

Can trade somehow solve the rebel's PG–PD problem? Rational dissidents do enter into mutual exchange agreements, realizing as they do that specialization and the division of labor serve everyone's interests.

Taking account of this possibility are numerous models of bargaining (Davis and Whinston 1967), side payments (Forst and Lucianovic 1977), threat strategies (Shubik 1982, 259–60), redistribution of property rights (Coase 1960), and logrolling over several PG's at one point in time (Riker and Brams 1973) or over several PGs at several points in time (McGinnis 1986). One type of mutual exchange agreement involves redefining property rights and letting bargaining proceed. Well-defined property rights, in other words, can be exchanged to produce a Pareto-optimal outcome (Coase 1960).

Mutual exchange agreements are also effective in solving the CA problem because two other solutions to the Rebel's Dilemma are made operative. First, explicit social contracts may lead to implicit social contracts because common knowledge of the propensity to conform leads to a convention, increasing mutual expectations (sect. 4.1.1). Lewis (1969, 84) suggests that a contract's "major effect is transmitted through a growing causal chain of expectations, actions, expectations of actions, and so on. The direct influence fades away in days, years, or lifetimes. We forget our agreement." Second, specific obligations to reciprocate can evolve into a generalized obligation to reciprocate. Specific contributions to mutual assistance can lead to a general exchange of favors. Explicit social contracts, that is, may become general exchange relationships that become part of preexisting organizations (sect. 5.2.3). Dissidents involved in social exchange relationships (Blau 1964) are thus likely to be able to sustain protest and rebellion: they are interconnected with one another, rather than isolated; they have relations with one another that are many-sided rather than narrowly specialized in one area; and they have direct relations with one another rather than those mediated by representatives, leaders, bureaucrats, institutions, and so on. In short, rebels who regularly engage in mutually beneficial exchange are likely to be able to coordinate their efforts on the particular issues behind collective dissent.

## 5.2. The Social Origins of Social Contracts

Social contracts, such as self-governing arrangements, Tit-For-Tat deals, and mutual exchange agreements, have transaction costs, principally those involved in bargaining a contract, monitoring compliance to the agreement, and punishing violators. Transaction costs arise from the dissidents' attempt to acquire information about their contract partners. The more costly the information, the higher the transaction costs of dissident social contracts. Transaction costs also arrive from mistrust. Amoral familism (Banfield 1958), for example, implies that a great deal of resources must be devoted to monitoring and enforcing agreements. The less the trust, the higher the transaction costs of dissident social contracts. Finally, transaction costs arise from the absence of social norms. Such norms reduce the need for particular agreements, and the need to monitor and enforce them. Weak social norms imply high transaction costs of dissident social contracts.

Hence, the higher the transaction costs of bargaining, monitoring, and enforcing social contracts, the less likely it is that a social contract can solve the Rebel's Dilemma. Anything that increases information, trust, and norms reduces those costs and thereby helps rebels.

This argument holds for all three forms of social contract. Consider self-government — institutions to decide policy, administer decisions, and adjudicate differences. Anything that reduces the transaction costs of self-governing institutions helps solve the Rebel's Dilemma and increase collective dissent. Now consider Tit-For-Tat. As I indicate elsewhere (Lichbach forthcoming, chap. 5), Tit-For-Tat is *not* a dominant strategy, just a Nash equilibrium. It is also not a unique outcome, just one of many possible outcomes. Hence, a dissident will not adopt Tit-For-Tat unless he or she is certain that the others will also adopt Tit-For-Tat. If the *Use Tit-For-Tat* solution to the Rebel's Dilemma is to work, dissidents must be able to coordinate their mutual expectations (sect. 4.1.1) and arrive at the belief that everyone will choose Tit-For-Tat. They must possess sufficient information about others' Tit-For-Tat behavior, they must be able trust each other, and they must develop norms of conditional cooperation. Anything that reduces the transaction costs of bargaining, monitoring, and enforcing a Tit-For-Tat agreement helps solve the Rebel's Dilemma and increases collective dissent. Consider, finally, mutual exchange agreements. By lowering the transaction costs per exchange, dissidents can exchange cooperation for cooperation and thus realize the potential gains from trade. Here too, as the transaction costs of exchange among dissidents decrease, collective dissent increases.

Clearly, then, the key to understanding when the contractarian solution will be implemented is knowing when transaction costs will be low. What factors reduce those costs?

First, specific aspects of a contract can reduce transaction costs. For example, rules of thumb for establishing cost-sharing arrangements, monitoring those arrangements, and punishing defectors may exist (sect. 6.5).

Second, certain forms of the culture shared by dissidents can reduce transaction costs. For example, norms of reciprocity developed by peasants (Scott, 1976) can be generalized and become the basis of the Tit-For-Tat approach.

Finally, structural aspects of the community of dissidents can reduce transaction costs. The transaction costs of organizing groups thus also relate to the communication structure among potential members of the group, or to the social structure supporting social interaction (Coleman 1990, 189–94, 278). Certain social structures bring people into face-to-face contact, while in other social structures, the probability of future contact with the same individual is low. In general, "The more numerous the recollected interactions with the same players and the greater the degree of 'closure', that is, the nonpermeability of a social structure to outsiders, the more likely is the emergence of norms that promote cooperation . . . a universe of freely associating individuals provides the poorest social structure for generating effective norms of cooperation" (Levi, Cook, O'Brien, and Faye 1990, 10). Hence, any factor that strengthens the dissidents' community increases information, allows trust to develop, and permits social norms to emerge. Bargaining, monitoring, and enforcement costs are therefore affected by several structural aspects of the dissidents' community: communities which are long-lived, homogeneous, have preexisting organizations, and are autonomous, stable, and concentrated will be able to forge social contracts. The following sections explore these social origins of social contracts.[5]

### 5.2.1. Longevity

A long-lived dissident community is one that has persisted for generations. Why should such a community be able to spawn much protest and rebellion?

Consider a dissident's discount rate, that is, the marginal rate of time preference for the present over the future. The more patient the dissident, the less he or she discounts the future. The more willing a dissident is to wait for his or her benefits, the lower his or her discount rate. Dissidents who can wait for benefits are more likely to forge social contracts and participate in collective dissent.

The longevity of a community obviously influences the members' discount rates. A future orientation means believing that the likelihood of subsequent encounters with one's partners is high. The greater the belief that a common future is shared, the greater the ability to adopt contractarian solutions. Thus, a long-lived community contributes to low discount rates. Discount rates and community, moreover, are mutually reinforcing. People who do not discount the future very much will be able to establish a set of social institutions that strengthen their community. Popkin (1979, 47) reports that "the extent of such village-wide [insurance] schemes depends on . . . whether cooperation is expected to continue in the future, so that a peasant can be certain that his specific need will be recognized when he makes his claim." These social institutions are really preexisting organizations that can serve as the basis of collective dissent (sect. 5.2.3). High discount rates thus do double damage to collective dissent by weakening both direct and indirect contractarian solutions to the Rebel's Dilemma. Dissidents who greatly discount the future are unable to forge either the communal institutions that assist collective dissent or dissident institutions themselves.

Several other factors affect dissidents' marginal rate of time preference and hence the viability of Contract solutions to the Rebel's Dilemma. Consider the impact of dissident groups, grievances, dissident characteristics, and politics.

Dissident groups are themselves a type of "community." Dissidents in long-lived groups are more likely than are dissidents in recently formed groups to believe that their encounters with other dissidents will continue. Hence, age breeds success in dissident groups. Long-lived dissident groups manifest greater levels of participation than short-lived ones.[6]

The nature of grievances also influences discount rates. If grievances are to terminate by a known and fixed date, collective dissent will be harder to organize than if the grievances extend indefinitely. For example, government action that will be completed once and for all by December 31, 1999 (e.g., completion of a controversial airport runway) will produce less collective dissent than government action that will extend indefinitely into the future (e.g., apartheid legislation). More generally, some political cultures and some dissident ideologies are particularly future-oriented. One expects such belief systems to inspire dissidents to be interested in future interactions, long-range planning, and communal investments, and hence to manifest high levels of collective dissent. Hoffmann (1979) argues that the heightened sense of the future during the 1960s partially accounts for the era's high level of collective dissent.

Some types of dissidents are likely to have high discount rates, for example, the poor living on the margins of subsistence. This phenomenon is discussed as part of the *Increase Risk Taking* solution to the Rebel's Dilemma (sect. 3.9).

Other types of dissidents are likely to have low discount rates, the young, for example, who expect to receive more long-term gains from CA than the old. Benefits will be compounded and costs discounted over a longer life span. Hence, as dissidents age, they participate in less CA.[7] Two other factors lead young people to protest and rebellion. One is low opportunity costs (sect. 3.2.3). Since many youths are students, they do not suffer the opportunity costs of forgone wages. The young also have few family obligations. As Mason and Krane (1989, 184) observe, young people have not yet established their own families and hence do not have spouses and children who are dependent upon them.[8] Another catalyst is geographic concentration (sect. 5.2.6). As Eckert and Willems (1986, 147) put it, "Young people are increasingly held together in groups of the same age." Students experience particularly high levels of geographic concentration and are likely to have contact with preexisting student organizations (sect. 5.2.3). University settings are therefore highly conducive to collective dissent.[9] College-age students in college thus engage in more collective dissent than do college-age students in the workplace.

The facts bear this out.[10] Indeed, "the revolutionary of yesterday is the conservative of tomorrow" (Crozier 1960, 16). Youths have a disproportionate place in dissident movements and collective dissent is largely a "children's crusade." Goldstone (1991, 137) draws the demographic implications: "Small changes in the age distribution of a population can have a marked effect on popular mobilization."

There are, finally, the politics of discount rates. Both states and oppositions have a stake in influencing how dissidents discount the future: whereas dissident entrepreneurs appeal to the investment value of a dissident's participation in collective dissent, regimes disparage such investments and appeal to the consumption value of a dissident's nonparticipation. Appeals and counterappeals are made along these lines.

The most obvious implication of solving the Rebel's Dilemma through a social contract based on a community of dissidents with low discount rates is that dissident groups pool community members who can wait. Such groups believe that *putchism*, or ultra-activism, is harmful to the cause of revolution (sect. 4.2.1). They argue against exploiting the political opportunities of the moment if such exploitation damages the political possibilities for the future. As Elster (1989, 46) points out,

> Successful collective action often requires the ability to wait — to delay action rather than seize upon any reason to act. The self-defeating character of activism, or left-wing opportunism, is a well-known theme in the history of social movements. Activism may appeal to a highly motivated form of cooperation, but in a temporal perspective it can well represent a noncooperative strategy.

The classic application of this advice is, of course, to the working class: "A mature working class, that is, should be capable of *waiting*" (Elster 1985, 348, emphasis in original), of saying "no" to ostensibly favorable opportunities.

A second consequence of solving the Rebel's Dilemma through a social contract based on a community of dissidents with low discount rates is to create a CA problem among the community's generations. Some dissident groups, such as the IRA, have fought governments for decades and are thus composed of many generations of supporters. While the persistence of such groups is in many ways remarkable, the social contract approach alerts us to a potential problem: members of the present generation of dissidents with high discount rates will be opportunistic with respect to their long-term interests, and hence may well sacrifice the interests of future generations of dissidents.

## 5.2.2. Homogeneity

A homogeneous dissident community is one whose members are identical in social background and interchangeable in life situation. By definition, such a community does not suffer from cleavages or distinct subgroups, stratification or inequality, factions or conflicts of interest (sect. 6.4). Its members share similar patterns of education, recruitment, and training; have similar outlooks, interests, and preferences; and possess similar cost functions and resource endowments.

The transaction costs of arranging cooperation among dissidents through a social contract is affected by homogeneity. Members of a heterogeneous group of dissidents have different interests. These differences about the PG will lead members to debate the terms of a social contract, hence maximizing the collective choice problem (Riker 1982). By contrast, a like-minded community of dissidents has clear interests and thus concurs about the nature of the PG and how to achieve it. Members have an easier time agreeing on the terms of a social contract and the collective choice problem is minimized. Homogeneity, moreover, facilitates the development of information, trust, and norms, and hence reduces the bargaining, monitoring, and enforcement costs of social contracts. Finally, homogeneity facilitates a group consciousness that is crucial to the *Overcome Pecuniary Self-Interest* solution to the Rebel's Dilemma (sect. 4.2). In sum, as the homogeneity of dissidents increases, collective dissent increases.[11]

Students of conflict offer three important corollaries to the homogeneity proposition. Taylor (1982, 95) focuses on the degree of economic equality among dissidents: "Community in turn clearly requires a measure of economic equality — a rough equality of basic material conditions — for as the gap increases between rich and poor, so their values diverge, relations between them are likely to become less direct and many-sided, and the sense of interdependence which supports a system of (generalised and near generalised) reciprocity is weakened." Hence, economic equality permits homogeneity; homogeneity promotes community; community facilitates contract; contract produces collective dissent. Ergo, as economic inequality among dissidents increases, collective dissent decreases.

A second corollary of the homogeneity proposition is the division of labor hypothesis. Too extensive a division of labor among dissidents increases heterogeneity and discourages CA. Calhoun (1982, 121–22) recounts the hurdles faced by early factory workers:

> Unlike artisans, whose various tasks were essentially similar and who produced whole products, the factory workers were engaged in different tasks and each produced only a part of a product. This meant that any attempt to organize could not proceed simply by accretion of members. That is, if each tailor could produce a whole garment, then a cooperative of tailors could have any number of members. If each factory worker labored on only a part of the process, then a cooperative would have to have a complete set and could not add or subtract members at will.

Thus, the factory's division of labor is one of the classic explanations of why the newly emerging working class found organizing so difficult.

A third corollary of the homogeneity proposition is the overlapping cleavages hypothesis, which is widespread in conflict studies.[12] If a nation has reinforcing social cleavages, such that position on one cleavage dimension is highly correlated with position on other cleavage dimensions, dissident groups are likely to form homogeneous dissident communities. Hence, as the social cleavages in a nation overlap, collective dissent increases.

Another factor contributes to homogeneity among dissidents. Authorities often unintentionally promote homogeneity. Colonial powers, for example, in teaching a common language (e.g., English or French) in order to overcome local dialects, made nationalist movements possible. Stinchcombe offers two further examples of how regime elites unwittingly fostered homogeneity and consequently protest and rebellion. Concerning the interaction of workers and firms, he (1990, 277, emphasis in original) argues that the "bureaucratization of the wage contract" facilitated CA by workers:

> This means that *within the firm* it seems unfair to make individual and different arrangements with each worker, and the social basis of the *individualization of contracts* between workers and employers disappears. The employer then makes the contracts of employment for categories of workers uniform and subjects the workers to uniform standards of work (e.g., uniform output criteria); the category of workers becomes a "collective worker." Consequently, the labor market wage rate becomes a social and psychological reality to the workers, because it is an explicit part of the incentive system.

Stinchcombe also points to working-class suffrage, suggesting that "legal uniformity of suffrage is an important political precondition for working-class consciousness, since it makes the political demands of different groups of workers in different parts of the country uniform" (Stinchcombe 1990, 278).

There are many illustrations of the homogeneity proposition and its three corollaries. The success of student demonstrations,[13] ghetto riots in the United States,[14] revolutions,[15] and worker movements[16] is attributed to homogeneity, and the failure of peasant struggles,[17] society-wide movements in caste-based societies,[18] and worker movements[19] is attributed to heterogeneity.

Some analysts remain unswayed, however, and put forth the counterargument: as homogeneity increases, CA decreases. Rather than likes attract likes, they hold, more often politics makes strange bedfellows. First, they would say, homogeneous groups are homogeneous in preferences, so that they lack relatively more intense potential providers of the PG (sect. 3.1). Homogeneous groups are, moreover, homogeneous in resources, which means that they also lack a relatively more wealthy patron (sect. 6.2) or an efficacious subgroup (sect. 6.3.2). Third, the members of homogeneous groups are interchangeable. Why, therefore, should anyone, particularly in a large group, think that he or she has a high probability of making a difference (sect. 3.7)? Fourth, homogeneity cannot produce the division of labor which allows dissidents to increase the productivity of their tactics (sect. 3.4). As Nielsen (1985, 145) argues, "A composition of the potential membership that reflects more closely the distribution of roles, occupations, and talents in the system as a whole enhances the organizational potential of the group. Organization is easier when the group can tap individuals already trained to fulfill a variety of specialized functions that are necessary for collective action." Hence, dissident groups are successful when they persuade people with different skills to work under a single umbrella. A division of labor, moreover, permits a group to achieve its goals, facilitating the *Increase the Probability of Winning* solution to the Rebel's Dilemma (sect. 3.6). Fifth, homogeneity reduces the gains from trade and therefore makes mutual exchange (sect. 5.1.3) less valuable. Sixth, heterogeneity allows dissidents to take advantage of partially overlapping networks of preexisting organizations (sect. 5.2.3). As Granovetter (1978) puts it, mobilization is facilitated where networks are neither completely identical nor completely isolated, but rather have "weak ties." For example, if workers spend all their free time with each other less information will flow than if they have friends at their workplace and friends from other firms (Opp and Gern 1993, 673). Finally, homogeneity does not allow for leaders and followers, eliminating an entire class of solutions to the Rebel's Dilemma: Hierarchy (chap. 6). In sum, the counterargument (Nielsen 1985, 145) is that internally differentiated groups are better integrated and thus have higher levels of collective dissent.[20]

The homogeneity-dissent argument is thus context specific: in certain contexts, homogeneity facilitates certain solutions to the Rebel's Dilemma, whereas in other contexts, heterogeneity facilitates other solutions.[21] While a heterogeneous group might have a zealot or a patron, a homogeneous group can arrange self-government and Tit-For-Tat. Given the conflicting arguments and evidence, dissident entrepreneurs probably face a tradeoff in deciding whether to encourage homogeneity or heterogeneity among their followers.[22]

## 5.2.3. Preexisting Organization

A community is also characterized by networks — familial, social, economic, and religious — of mutual interdependence (Calhoun 1988, 148–50). A strong community has interactions that are extensive (i.e., they include a number of different concerns), dense (i.e., they involve a large number of contacts per concern), enduring (i.e., they are long-run), exclusive (i.e., they bar outsiders), and mutually reinforcing (i.e., they overlap). This notion of community has implications for protests and rebellions at both the individual and group levels.

At the individual level, one expects that rebels will participate in collective dissent as members of local communities, bound by preexisting solidarities, networks, institutions, and organizations. As the dependence of an individual on his or her community increases; as a person's life problems are increasingly solved by the institutions associated with a dissident group; and as an individual's involvement in the internal relations of a dissident group increases, his or her chances of participating in collective dissent increase.

Dissidents therefore are not likely to be rootless social isolates. Homeless people and transients pose little threat to the state. Given that rebels hold strong formal and informal ties to their communities, one expects a strong individual-level correlation between social characteristics and collective dissent. This is because a random social network yields a weak correlation between social background and political behavior (i.e., anyone may rebel) while a distinct social network yields a strong correlation (i.e., only certain types of people will rebel). For example, surveys in a nation with strong communities should indicate that religious affiliation and participation in collective dissent are highly correlated. Given that the stronger the community, the greater the correlation, one also suspects that the stronger the individual level correlation between social characteristics and collective dissent, the higher the aggregate level of collective dissent. Coleman (1990, 292) thus suggests that within-nation correlations found in surveys should predict between-nation differences in aggregate CA.[23]

Turning to the group level, one expects that protests and rebellions will occur where extensive, intense, durable, mutual reinforcing, and exclusive preexisting political, economic, and social ties among dissidents are found. Protest groups thus build upon the infrastructure of society, the established social order. Communities spawn informal and formal institutions that, in turn, spawn dissident organizations. Pinard (1968, 685) thus argues that "whenever pre-existing primary and secondary groupings possess or develop an ideology or simply subjective interests congruent with that of a new movement, they will act as mobilizing . . . agents toward that movement." Marwell and Oliver (1984, 16) concur: "Collective action, in general, is not undertaken by isolated automata: rather, it is undertaken by groups of people in social interaction with one another." In short, classes, and not masses, make protests and rebellions.

Dissident entrepreneurs therefore rarely build an organization from scratch. Dissident institutions never emerge from chaos and anarchy. The idea of the spontaneous protest or rebellion is a myth. Given that dissident groups are never created *ex nihilo*, all "immaculate conception" (Taylor 1989, 761) theories of social movements are simply wrong.[24]

Preexisting social ties have these individual and group level consequences for protests and rebellions because they reduce all three forms of transaction costs involved in a social contract. Preexisting social ties provide contacts and communication, permitting potential contractors to bargain. A dense network of social interactions provides information about everyone's actions, permitting contractors to monitor agreements. Finally, preexisting social ties provide rewards and sanctions based on social incentives (sect. 4.2.2), permitting contractors to administer agreements.

Coleman (1990) offers a compatible economic interpretation of such preexisting social relations: individuals experience externalities from one another's actions in that $a$'s actions affect $b$, $b$'s actions affect $c$, and $c$'s actions affect $a$. Any factor that increases such externalities increases what Coleman calls the "social capital" of the group. Three forms of capital are thus relevant to a dissident production function (sect. 3.4.1): "Physical capital is wholly tangible, being embodied in observable material form; human capital is less tangible, being embodied in the skills and knowledge acquired by an individual; social capital is even less tangible, for it is embodied in the *relations* among persons. Physical capital and human capital facilitate productive activity, and social capital does so as well" (Coleman 1990, 304).

In sum, preexisting social ties facilitate the social contract approach to the Rebel's Dilemma and thereby increase the chances for collective dissent.[25] Social capital also facilitates several other solutions to the Rebel's Dilemma.

- A dissident's involvement in preexisting organizations may increase his or her sense of personal efficacy. This facilitates the *Increase the Probability of Making a Difference* solution (sect. 3.7).
- Preexisting social ties provide experience in risk sharing. This facilitates the *Increase Risk-Taking* solution (sect. 3.9).
- Preexisting social ties provide traditions and experiences of people assisting one another, governing themselves, and controlling community resources. A long experience of cooperation leads people to generalize reciprocity. One gets to know "whom to trust and whom not to trust" (Calhoun 1988, 149). Moreover, members of preexisting social networks would damage their reputations by noncooperation. Trust, in turn, fosters a crucial set of beliefs: conjectural variation will be predictable, one's contribution will bear fruit, and long-term commitments and investments will pay off. Trust, as indicated in section 4.1.1, is the backbone of the *Increase Mutual Expectations* solution to the Rebel's Dilemma.[26]

- Preexisting organization facilitates a bandwagon (sect. 4.1.2). Popkin (1979, 164–65) offers an example from Vietnam: "Corporate villages, by reacting *en masse* to a new situation, can change so suddenly . . . as soon as a notable converted [to Catholicism] he had an advantage over the others in the village [i.e., an external ally was available to intercede with mandarins and provincial officials]. To nullify this advantage, the other notables were likely to follow his example quickly: thus, the chain reaction so common to corporate villages."
- Preexisting social ties create shared goals and values that reinforce group solidarity and commitment. Such values are significant to the *Overcome Pecuniary Self-Interest* solution (sect. 4.2).
- Preexisting organizations reduce the fixed costs (sect. 3.2.4) of collective dissent because many of the costs of organization have already been paid by prior contributors. As Marwell and Oliver (1984, 22) argue, "Because they have already absorbed many 'organization costs,' such organizations make resistance less costly and therefore more likely." For example, as the preexisting solidarity of dissidents increases, bloc recruitment becomes possible. Dissidents can be mobilized into collective dissent by organizations to which they already belong. This facilitates the task of entrepreneurs (sect. 6.1).

Preexisting social ties are therefore strongly associated with collective dissent: they facilitate a social contract and in addition encourage personal efficacy, risk taking, mutual expectations, bandwagons, other-regardingness, and entrepreneurship. Numerous revolutionaries[27] and academics[28] recognize such arguments.[29]

A problem, however, is the potential contradiction between the homogeneity and preexisting organization arguments. Preexisting organization implies differentiation, the antithesis of homogeneity. Calhoun (1982, 176) proposes a resolution: preexisting organizations aid the CA of a dissident group only if they do not act at cross-purposes with the group. If preexisting social ties contribute to the homogenization of a dissident community, the collectivity is reinforced, a social contract is facilitated, and collective dissent is encouraged; if preexisting social ties contribute to the social differentiation of a dissident community, the collectivity is weakened, a social contract is impeded, and collective dissent is discouraged.[30]

Keeping in mind Calhoun's understanding, we can now turn to the two types of preexisting organization that have been associated with collective dissent: formal and informal organizations. The key distinction here, as Lipset, Trow, and Coleman (1962, 176–77) point out, is between primary and secondary groups:

As an ideal type, the former is characterized by a strong sense of "we-ness"; by the personal, voluntary, and inclusive character of the relationship among its members; and by the identity of ends held by its members, among which are the primary relationships themselves. In contrast, secondary groups are characterized by more impersonal relations between members who interact fleetingly, often indirectly, and in terms of specific roles rather than as total persons. These secondary relationships are not seen by the members as ends in themselves, but as means to some defined ends which vary among the members.

The next section examines how preexisting formal organizations influence collective dissent. The following section considers the impact of preexisting informal organizations. I then consider the social and political origins of preexisting organizations.

### 5.2.3.1. Formal Organization

Formal organizations constitute one set of preexisting ties in a community. People hold multiple memberships in such voluntary organizations as labor unions, women's clubs, religious societies, churches, athletic groups, nationality groups, benevolent orders, service organizations, fraternal societies, lodges, political parties, veterans' organizations, and chambers of commerce. A formal organization corollary therefore immediately follows from the preexisting organization proposition: as the extent, intensity, and duration of preexisting formal ties among dissidents increase, collective dissent increases. Given that preexisting organizations are quite often formal associations, and that the social contract approach relies on the formation of informal community norms, an old maxim can be reversed: association facilitates community.

The formal organization corollary to the preexisting organization proposition is one of the most well-established generalizations in conflict studies. Dissidents are, indeed, likely to hold strong formal ties to their communities.[31] Members of dissident groups often turn out to be members of other community groups, as in student movements,[32] the U.S. civil rights movement,[33] farmers' movements,[34] peasants' movements,[35] working-class movements,[36] guerrilla wars,[37] and the American civil war.[38] Moreover, preexisting formal organizations are important in all revolutions, including the English,[39] American,[40] French,[41] Russian,[42] Chinese,[43] Mexican,[44] Vietnamese,[45] Iranian,[46] and Nicaraguan.[47]

The two preexisting formal organizations that have been most important to collective dissent are the church and the military. With respect to a church, it has been noted that "every great religious or spiritual movement is likely,

...er or later, to take a political direction. It will associate itself with the aspirations and the grievances of classes which are on the rise or which are oppressed" (Armstrong, cited in Hagopian 1974, 38). Indeed, nonconformist religious movements have often lead to nonconformist political movements, religious sects have repeatedly spawned political sects, and religious dissent has frequently turned into political dissent (Hobsbawm 1959, chap. 8). Several examples[48] of a church hierarchy opposing the political hierarchy may be offered.[49]

Military organization is also crucial to collective dissent. As Nordlinger (1977, 5) asserts, "A unified officer corps is virtually always capable of maintaining a civilian government in office, or taking control itself." Militaries are important in civil wars, secessionist struggles, and of course coups. A military organization has several characteristics that enable it to become politically active and help dissidents solve the CA problem: esprit de corps, solidarity, resources, hierarchy, discipline, communication networks, isolation, and self-sufficiency.[50] The military also encourages collective dissent in two other ways. First, former soldiers contribute disproportionately to dissent organizations (sect. 3.3). Second, the military is an important patron of collective dissent (sect. 6.2.3.1).

### 5.2.3.2. Informal Organization

Informal social networks are the other form of preexisting ties that often bind individuals. People form many social attachments based on primary groups, face-to-face relations, and daily routines. Subcultures of ethnicity, class, religion, kinship, workplace, and neighborhood often exist. Peer groups of age, occupation, status, race, and so on frequently determine the shared fate, parallel interests, and common activities of individuals. Such social relations typically overlap; there are relations among the relations, or what Calhoun (1982, 200) refers to as "multiplexity."

Dissidents often hold such strong informal ties to their communities via their participation in community, neighborhood, and primary groups. Hence, the more integrated an individual is into his or her community, the more likely he or she is to be a first joiner of a dissident group, participate in collective dissent, and take part in a great deal of the group's activities. An informal organization corollary therefore immediately follows: as the extent, intensity, and duration of preexisting informal ties among dissidents increase, collective dissent increases. Community, that is, facilitates contract.

Advocates of the informal organization corollary to the preexisting organization proposition are legion.[51] The informal organization-collective dissent linkage may be demonstrated by considering examples of informal social ties that often form the basis of dissident movements: friendship cliques, kinship, patron-client ties, estate, and caste.

*Friendship cliques.* Dissident groups often consist of friends. Indeed, long-standing interpersonal contact is often the richest source of recruits to a social movement (Snow, Zurcher, and Ekland-Olson 1980, 790–92). Rule (1988, 266) thus suggests that participants in protests and rebellions are likely to be well known to each other: strangers do not suddenly meet and decide to rebel. There is considerable evidence on this point.[52]

*Kinship.* Dissident groups often consist of relatives — extended families and clans are an ideal basis of protest and rebellion. Hagopian (1974, 25) describes one such a system as follows: "The clan is organized around a patriarch or matriarch and embraces cousins to the second or third degree of removal . . . In a clan-dominated society, class and sometimes status differences are considerably muted as the clan cuts across or, more precisely, cuts vertically through various social strata." Messianic movements, in Weber's view (see Bendix 1960, 146), can be rooted in "familial charisma" and hence are often organized around the extended family or clan. Hobsbawm (1959, 107) argues that such millenarian movements may become revolutionary movements, if tied to the right organization and ideology. Welch (1980, 206) considers a case from China.

*Patron-client ties.* Several types of prepolitical relations, such as client-age, serfdom, vassalage, and paternalism, are often considered the basis of personal deference and hence social stability. Such patron-client ties can also serve as the basis of collective dissent. Scott (1972) offers numerous examples from peasant movements.

*Estate.* Under feudalism, rights and duties were shared — extended to estates and corporations, rather than to individuals. Such estates often formed the basis of collective dissent against the established order. As Bendix (1969, 47) puts it, "Medieval political life consists in struggles for power among more or less autonomous jurisdictions."

*Caste.* The strongest informal ties in a community involve a caste system. Within this social framework, protest and rebellion often takes the form of demanding recognition for a new caste or renewed privileges for an old caste. Lower castes have a CA problem, however, and hence usually do not unite in opposition to the system (Kuran forthcoming).

There are well-documented examples of dissident movements that emerged from informal social ties.[53] Working-class protest is rooted in strong local communities.[54] Equally strong evidence comes from studies of peasant upheavals. Peasant villages are often characterized by a self-conscious existence and a set of self-contained organizational structures. They are therefore widely perceived as ideal vehicles for conducting a joint defense of communal autonomy against outside intervention by landlords or the state.[55] Examples are legion: there are many cases of successful peasant upheavals being rooted in strong peasant communities,[56] and also many cases of unsuccessful peasant upheavals where peasant communities were weak.[57]

In sum, strong evidence may be offered for both the formal and informal organization corollaries to the preexisting organization proposition. Moreover, the two corollaries work together and not at cross-purposes. As Lipset, Trow, and Coleman (1962, xv) put it, "Knowledge of men's informal social relations is a prerequisite to any clear or adequate understanding of their behavior in any of the formal organizations to which they belong or in which they are employed." Hence, informal ties beget formal organizations, and vice versa, and both, in turn, spawn dissident groups.

The hallmark of protest in the twentieth century, however, has been the replacement of informal social ties by formal social organizations.[58] Community has given way to association as the basis of dissident groups. The change from informal preexisting organizations to formal ones has three consequences for collective dissent. First, tactics changed. As voluntary associations replaced communal ones, the twentieth century repertoire of demonstrations and strikes replaced the eighteenth century repertoire of food riots and tax rebellions. Reactive claims and defensive mobilization, to employ Tilly's (1978, 144) terms, became proactive claims and offensive mobilization. Second, the CA problem became more severe. As Tilly (1986, 75) argues, formal organizations break with everyday routine. A formally called meeting or demonstration cannot count on people being there as a matter of course. Hence, they offer the potential rebel a sharper choice between joining or not joining CA. Finally, dissident entrepreneurs could no longer recruit people on the basis of their informal daily routines. Modern organizational techniques had to be developed.

### 5.2.3.3. Social Origins
Where do preexisting organizations come from? They are social capital (Coleman 1990, chap. 12) subject to high fixed costs, snowballing, underinvestment, depreciation, liquidity problems, and sudden destruction.

Preexisting organizations are not built up over night; the start-up, or fixed, costs (sect. 3.2.4) can be enormous. Short-lived communities (sect. 5.2.1) are therefore incapable of generating preexisting formal and informal organizations, unlikely to sustain a social contract, and hence an improbable source of collective dissent.

The creation of social capital is facilitated when preexisting organizations snowball into a bandwagon (sect. 4.1.2). By simple recursive reasoning, if a preexisting dissident organization, A, gives rise to a new dissident organization, B, then B may serve as a preexisting organization that facilitates the emergence of a new dissident organization, C. Newly created institutions, in other words, become the preexisting institutions that facilitate the growth of even newer institutions. Consider, for example, the British working class (Thompson 1966). Working conditions and social arrangements served as the basis of preexisting formal and informal organizations of workers. These helped to solidify the working class as a social formation. Workers then created nascent trade unions, which then facilitated strike activity. Protest movements followed. Finally, protest movements helped to support electorally-based political parties. Note that each working-class organization was able to draw upon *all* preexisting organizations, regardless of how far back in the chain. Hence, working conditions and social arrangements also contributed to the formation of political parties.

The construction of social capital faces a major obstacle, however: the PG–PD problem produces underinvestment (Coleman 1990, 316). Dissident entrepreneurs, in fact, continually complain about the absence of "community spirit" among their followers.

Moreover, existing social capital may depreciate. Coleman (1990, 321) points out that "social capital is one of those forms of capital which depreciate over time. Like human capital and physical capital, social capital depreciates if it is not renewed. Social relationships die out if not maintained; expectations and obligations wither over time; and norms depend on regular communication."

For social capital to be useful to dissidents, it must be liquid (Wrong 1988, 143); that is, dissidents must be able to divert collective resources from nonpolitical to political uses. Such redeployment of social capital, also referred to as fungibility, can create considerable difficulties.

Finally, social capital can be destroyed. Coleman (1990, 320) argues that a factor "which affects the creation and destruction of social capital is the stability of social structure." Anything that eliminates informal community ties reduces the possibility of collective dissent. The hallmark of the twentieth century, as indicated above, has been the eradication of such informal social ties. Taylor (1988, 93) thus suggests that "the destruction and decay of community in modern societies removes the most important social basis for collective action."

### 5.2.3.4. Political Origins

Can a movement survive without preexisting organizations and a distinctive social base or constituency? There are examples of movements that are not tied to an obvious community — the fascist movements in the interwar period and the new social movements of the 1980s, for instance. How do such groups mobilize supporters?

The traditional argument among DA theorists is that social ties beget political ties. Political sociologists are particularly likely to assume that social organization sires political organization. Zuckerman (1989, 491) reverses this argument, however, suggesting that political structures can create social structures: "Political ties and appeals may precede and help to form social affiliations. The more a political movement strives to attract the members of a particular social category, the more likely the objects of their attention are to identify with each other and to develop a shared web of understanding." Political parties, for example, helped create ethnic ties in the United States: "Ethnic loyalties have sometimes been created among immigrants where they did not previously exist by the appeals of vote-seeking politicians" (Wrong 1988, 150). Political parties have also helped create social classes. Przeworski (1985a) maintains that the strategies pursued by leaders of socialist electoral parties influence whether or not individuals come to identify themselves as workers.

This focus on dissident organization as a source of social solidarity provides a partial solution to the problem of the origin of social groups (sect. 10.2.1). Since dissident entrepreneurs recognize that preexisting social ties reduce the transaction costs of the social contract approach to the Rebel's Dilemma, they attempt to take maximum advantage of existing formal and informal organizations in the dissident community. And if such organizations are weak or nonexistent, they try to create them. I will explore both the entrepreneur's reactive and proactive strategies, and then discuss the state's response.

Dissident entrepreneurs organize their recruitment strategy so as to take maximum advantage of preexisting formal and informal organizations in the dissident community. In particular, Popkin (1979, 196) asks, "what incentives could the leaders provide to aggregate the previously existing small organizations into one large and powerful organization that could then attract hundreds of thousands of new members?" They use several strategies.

- Dissident entrepreneurs recruit heavily at regular meetings of formal and informal community organizations. Tilly (1986, 75) found that much of the pre-twentieth-century CA in Europe grew out of existing public gatherings: "People took advantage of an authorized festival, ceremony, or procession to display symbols, parade effigies, or mime solemnities" (Tilly 1986, 116).
- Dissident entrepreneurs recruit their followers based on a community's daily routines. Tilly (1986, 75) also found that a population's daily routines and patterns of internal organization led to characteristic patterns of CA and that changes in those daily routines led to changes in patterns of CA.
- Dissident entrepreneurs recognize the various subgroups and intermediate associations of their community — neighbors, ethnics, former schoolmates, and so on — and try to mobilize supporters by using, rather than overcoming, these identities. They target their

appeals to the particular subgroups. As Calhoun (1988, 163) puts it, "The task of class leaders is thus not to minimize sectional identities, but to mobilize such intermediate associations to serve the common cause."

- Dissident entrepreneurs recruit blocs of dissidents at a time, since they think of potential supporters as belonging to particular categories of contributors. Consequently, dissidents tend to join dissident organizations in groups, rather than as individuals. Recruitment thus tends to be uneven over time, with large blocs of people going over to the dissidents all at once. Moreover, dissident entrepreneurs prefer bloc to individual recruitment, because bloc recruitment reduces the probability of repression (sect. 3.2) and increases the probability of success (sect. 3.6).

- Dissident entrepreneurs try to make themselves part of the community. This is done by establishing personal contacts, relationships, and friendships with potential supporters. As Kahn (1982, 109) suggests, "Personal contacts are at the heart of any organizing drive and of any people's organization." Thus, recruitment is often done on a one-to-one basis. There is no substitute for knocking on doors.[59] Dissident entrepreneurs try to mobilize their sympathizers by establishing regularized contacts with people and building long-term relationships with the community. Kahn (1982, 123) thus suggests that "regular contacts with members is one of the secrets of building strong organizations." Hence, leaders try to involve followers in the organization's activities. Weekly meetings, for example, are used to build a sense of group solidarity, togetherness, direction, and spirit.

- Some dissident groups are exclusive. Members have no competing loyalties, having cut their ties to other organizations, renounced the outside world, and given up external relationships. Such organizations have long indoctrination periods and make heavy and very extensive demands on their followers. Other dissident groups are inclusive. Members maintain many extragroup ties and competing loyalties. Such organizations have short indoctrination periods and make minimal and very specific demands on their followers. In general, the former type of group is more capable of generating collective dissent than is the latter because its members are more dependent on the group. Dissident entrepreneurs thus try to increase the exclusivity of the dissidents' involvement in dissident-sponsored organizations and activities. Coleman (1990, 502) suggests that rebels should "cut potential recruits off from contact with nonsupporters of the revolt [and] develop a high degree of closure within groups of supporters." For their part, authorities should "reduce opportunities for closure of social structure among members of the opposition."

- One dissident group can aid recruitment into another dissident group. With new dissident groups likely to emerge out of existing dissident groups (Freeman 1979, 170-72), the newer groups tend to have a symbiotic, or parasitic, relationship with the older ones. Hence, rebels usually have a prior history of rebellion (e.g., civil rights activists become antiwar activists and then environmentalists). Rebels also typically hold simultaneous memberships in multiple rebel groups (e.g., activists on the left join women's, welfare rights, environmental, and peace groups). Examples of preexisting dissident organizations serving as "'host' institutions" (Tarrow 1989, 220) for new dissident organizations abound: the New Left emerged from the Old Left; a variety of women's, ethnic, peace, and ecology movements developed from the antiwar and civil rights movements of the 1960s; many leftist movements were built upon dissident community organizations. Dissident entrepreneurs can take advantage of a preexisting dissident group by attempting to outflank their colleagues and charging that they are insufficiently radical.[60] The idea is to use "the orderly protests of more established groups as a platform for disruption" (Tarrow 1989, 84). Dissident entrepreneurs, in other words, use a conventional form of political action organized by their less radical and older allies as an opportunity for new and more radical actions. Radical "outside" agitators may thus exploit the opportunities offered by reformist "internal" demonstrators. By trying to radicalize an existing dissident group, dissident entrepreneurs, in effect, dissent against both the government and the dissident group (sect. 6.4.2).[61]
- Finally, a dissident group must decide which preexisting social ties can be most effectively exploited. Dissident entrepreneurs gear their strategy to the particular strengths of the groups in question. They use formal community organizations where these are strong and informal community organizations where these are strong. If communal ties are strong, they try to mobilize along existing communal lines. If associational ties are strong, dissident entrepreneurs try to mobilize dissidents along existing associational lines. For example, entrepreneurs organize along ethnic lines (e.g., an ethnic group) rather than along production lines (e.g., a farmer's association of all ethnic groups) when it is easier to mobilize preexisting ethnic groups. The result is that in less developed countries dissident groups tend to be communal and in more developed countries they tend to be associational.

When dissidents lack both formal and informal community organizations, these recruitment tactics evidently cannot work. How do dissident entrepreneurs recruit in the absence of community? Zald and McCarthy

(1979c, 239) suggest that "the two primary strategies of recruitment when confronted with isolated structures seem to be direct contact with the isolates and attempts to aggregate sympathizers to make recruitment attempts more efficient." Strategies for direct contact include mass mailing, newspaper advertisements, and canvassing door-to-door and by telephone. Dissident entrepreneurs may sponsor entertaining events (sect. 4.2.1). Zald and McCarthy (1979c, 239–40) observe that "parades, entertainments, sports events, and even certain street corners may draw high proportions of sympathizers, depending upon the social change goals considered. The production of assemblies, especially when combined with side benefits such as food and entertainment, makes recruitment attempts more efficiently pursued."[62]

There is also a more aggressive approach: create a community of dissidents to make up for the lack of preexisting organizations. Taylor argues that peasant entrepreneurs often adopt this strategy:

> In some cases where the local community was less strong (because there was little cooperation amongst its members in the agricultural work which dominated their lives, for example, or relations between members were much too mediated by landlords and officials), revolutionary mobilization could not occur without entrepreneurs — who got about their work, however, by building or strengthening the local community through organizing mutual aid and undermining the dependence of the village on local landlords. (Taylor 1988, 68)

Two types of dissident organizations can be created.

One type is social. Dissident groups often create a network of voluntary social organizations (e.g., clubs) that draw people into common and cooperative activities. Such organizations hold community events, such as festivals and parties. Indeed, "Membership social activities [are] built right into Club meetings" (Messinger 1955, 9). The Nazis, for example, tried to combine existing primary groups into a larger one by employing various forms of social activities (e.g., bands, outings). The classic example of a dissident group creating a network of voluntary social organizations comes, however, from the left.[63]

The other type of organization that dissidents create is political, that is, alternative institutions for governing. Goodwin and Skocpol (1989, 493–94) argue that revolutionaries succeed where they provide "dual power," or an alternative "state within a state" that provides the PGs of security from the regime, law and order, public education, health services, and economic reforms. This is, of course, the origin of base areas (sect. 5.1.1).

In sum, dissident entrepreneurs attempt to reduce the transaction costs of social contracts. They thus employ numerous strategies to use and/or manufacture formal and informal communal organizations.

Like dissident entrepreneurs, the state is also aware of the value of having preexisting community organizations on its side. It is usually more successful coopting preexisting social networks than are the dissidents because such patron-client ties can be mutually beneficial: community leaders often lobby government officials for selective incentives (sect. 6.5.3) in exchange for delivering their followers' cooperation. Preexisting social ties are thus more often a source of political stability than of political dissent. Many scholars have noted that participation by social networks takes place *within* rather than *against* the established order. Formal and informal community ties are much more likely to lead to pragmatic bargaining with government officials than to a radical restructuring of government and society.

Sometimes states, like oppositions, attempt to create "preexisting" organizations. Levi (1988, 65) notes that "historically, rulers have promoted communal institutions as a means of administering a polity indirectly and with low cost. This in effect creates conditional cooperation among the members of the community, who then produce social order or enforce a policy among themselves." Rulers, for example, often have an interest in promoting conditional cooperation among their constituents when it comes to the collection of taxes (e.g., *ancien régime* in France) and the surveillance of dissent (e.g., Cuba). Such strategies are often successful, for example containing peasant rebellions.[64] The state's strategy sometimes backfires, however. Authorities can unintentionally create preexisting organizations that ultimately aid the dissidents,[65] in effect serving as patrons of collective dissent (sect. 6.2.3.2).

Regimes and oppositions thus compete for the loyalty of preexisting social networks; they are, in essence, struggling over control of the social infrastructure of society. Dissidents try to organize their forces, institutionalizing and structuring civil society so that it is autonomous of the regime. The state tries to atomize dissidents, deinstitutionalizing and destructuring the civil society that dissidents create. Conversely, the regime tries to organize its forces, institutionalizing and structuring civil society so that it is dependent on the state. The dissidents try to deinstitutionalize and destroy whatever civil society the regime has created.[66] If the dissidents win, preexisting organizations are destabilizing; if the regime wins, they are stabilizing. Hence, the key question: under what conditions do social networks switch from supporting to opposing the system?

Both regimes and dissidents might actually have relatively little leverage. What is most effective about the community behind a social contract is precisely that such communal organizations were *not* created by outside entrepreneurs. Coleman (1990, chap. 12) thus suggests that social capital is best achieved as a by-product of other activities rather than by direct efforts. Lipset, Trow, and Coleman (1962, 78, emphasis in original) offer an example: "What must be significant about the printers' occupational community is that *it developed without any formal connection with the union.* The various benevolent organizations, newspapers, social clubs, athletic teams, and lodges have for the most part been organized by working printers in their spare time, by men who felt the need to engage in such activities with other printers." In short, action (i.e., political origins) always operates within a set of opportunities and constraints (i.e., social origins).

### 5.2.4. Autonomy

There are rules within rules, choices within choices, games within games, and institutions within institutions. Ostrom (1990, 50) thus argues that "the constitutional-choice rules for a micro-setting are affected by collective-choice and constitutional-choice rules for larger jurisdictions." One of her design principles for self-governing arrangements, therefore, is that larger units acknowledge the rights of smaller units to organize (Ostrom 1990, 90). If the more inclusive political system does not recognize local rules, decentralized CA is difficult to sustain.

The transaction costs of arranging cooperation among dissidents through a social contract are therefore affected by the dissidents' autonomy. An autonomous dissident community is one in which dissidents enjoy de jure and de facto sovereignty from national and local authorities. It is, in short, a state within a state.

Such autonomy facilitates a social contract because autonomous dissidents form a self-contained, segregated, and independent community that can work out the long-standing relationships that aid in the development of a social contract. Autonomy, moreover, facilitates three other solutions to the Rebel's Dilemma. First, autonomous dissidents can create a base of operations to train, arm, and eventually attack the regime. This facilitates the *Increase Resources* solution to the Rebel's Dilemma (sect. 3.3). Second, as dissidents' autonomy increases, the regime's information becomes more costly, unreliable, and untimely, and locating dissidents becomes more difficult. Autonomous dissidents can therefore easily take refuge from the state's repressive apparatus. This facilitates the *Lower Costs* solution to the Rebel's Dilemma (sect. 3.2). Finally, autonomous dissidents can seek foreign support, by taking refuge in neighboring countries. This facilitates the *Locate Principals or Patrons* solution to the Rebel's Dilemma (sect. 6.2).

For all of these reasons, collective dissent becomes more likely if the dissidents are autonomous. Peasant rebellions offer an example. Moore (1966, 477–78) and Skocpol (1979, 115) argue that peasant communities that are autonomous vis-à-vis local landlords and national bureaucracies are better able to sustain peasant rebellions. New social movements offer another example; they maintain their strength in part by virtue of their autonomy, sovereignty, and independence.

Geographic isolation is an important source of dissident autonomy: it can result from great distances, inaccessible terrain, a poor transportation system, or fluid and uncertain boundaries. A corollary of the autonomy proposition thus presents itself: as the dissidents' geographic isolation from national authorities increases, collective dissent increases. The isolation corollary is well understood in conflict studies,[67] with the classic examples coming from guerrilla warfare.[68]

The nature of guerrilla wars suggests three more specific versions of the isolation corollary. First, the greater the physical distance between regimes and dissidents, the greater the levels of collective dissent. Remoteness, in other words, encourages rebellion. Chamberlin ([1935] 1987, 53) observes that "two of the most actively revolutionary of the provincial Soviets [in the Revolution of 1905] were located far away from the capital in remote parts of the country." Tong's (1988, 118) study of Ming China offers some quantitative evidence: the further away the county from Beijing, the higher the level of collective violence. Second, ecology blesses or curses dissident movements. Nations with poor transportation and communication networks have higher levels of collective dissent than nations with good ones. Gurr (1970, 263) contends that "guerrilla war is common in underdeveloped countries because of poor transportation and communication networks and the isolation of rural areas, which facilitate guerrilla incursions. Free access to rural people enables guerrillas to propagandize, control, and secure support from them." And third, political boundaries affect collective dissent. When dissidents are isolated because political control is confused, collective dissent appears. Frontiers, disputed areas, or territories at the confluence of several provincial or national boundaries are susceptible to resistance and independence movements.

Dissidents, of course, appreciate the isolation idea. They try to create sanctuaries, massing in locations remote from the regime's coercive strength. This is one factor behind base areas (sect. 5.1.1). Regimes, of course, also recognize the potential problems of isolation; counterinsurgency theorists have developed expertise in the area. Thompson (cited in Gurr 1970, 262) thus discusses the way remoteness and inaccessibility work to the guerrillas' advantage.

There is, however, a counterargument: some maintain that protective terrain is counterproductive for collective dissent. Guevara (1961) argues that if the terrain is too rugged, remote, and inaccessible, guerrillas will not be able to get supplies, find profitable targets, and locate people to mobilize. Guerrillas, in short, will be secure, but ineffective. Isolation also increases the dissidents' organizational problems. Popkin (1979, 232) observes that "the distance of Cochinchina from the Party's mountain base in northern Tonkin . . . posed severe problems of communication and coordination." Finally, isolation reduces the possibility of coalitions with actors in the cities. This makes the *Locate Principals or Patrons* solution (sect. 6.2) less feasible.

One way to resolve this controversy is to suggest that the argument and counterargument hold at different stages in the development of a dissident movement. At the beginning of a revolution, when dissidents are weak, they are best advised to locate far from the power of the regime. During the course of the revolution, as dissidents become stronger, they are best advised to locate closer to the regime's forces.

### 5.2.5. Stability

The transaction costs of arranging cooperation among dissidents through a social contract are also affected by the level of turnover, or the movement in and out of, the dissidents' community. High turnover means an unstable population. A great deal of entry and exit from the community hinders the social contract approach to the Rebel's Dilemma because dissidents cannot count on one another to be there in the future. Tit-For-Tat, for example, rests on the ability of cooperators to inflict punishment on defectors over the long-run. Such conditional cooperation can work only if dissidents can be counted on to stick around. Both students of CA and of collective dissent understand the impact of high levels of emigration and immigration on communal action.[69]

At least five factors influence stability. One source of stability is preexisting organizations (sect. 5.2.3). Conversely, one can expect high turnover where dissident groups lack linkages to preexisting organizations. Once again, the various aspects of community are interrelated.

Militancy is another source of stability. Radical groups have low turnover. Lasswell and Kaplan (1950, 37) argue that "the low accommodation (militant) groups will be most stable in membership" because they have high entry and exit requirements. More militant groups thus find it easier than less radical groups to work out a social contract approach to the Rebel's Dilemma. One therefore expects, and indeed finds, that militant groups have greater staying power and higher participation ratios that less militant groups.

A third source of stability is the work situation: as the turnover of incumbents in a particular occupation increases, the probability that the incumbents will undertake CA decreases. Hence, occupations characterized by high turnover will be less easily unionized. Migratory workers and temporary employees, who, by definition, come and go would likely be slow to unionize. Unskilled workers also turn over quickly because they can be replaced easily. Hence, there should be relatively little union organizing in relatively unskilled occupations. White collar workers also turn over quickly because they are continually moving up and down the various rungs on the promotional ladder. One expects them too to be slow to unionize. Indeed, all of these deductions seem to fit the history of union activity.

A fourth source of stability is social mobility. By definition, high levels of social mobility increase the turnover of a dissident group and therefore should decrease collective dissent. This issue was explored as part of the *Restrict Exit* solution (sect. 3.11).

A final source of stability is geographic mobility. Dissidents are likely to be the more stable and long-lived members of their communities, not recent immigrants.[70] New members of a community, in other words, are the least reliable participants in that community's social contract.

This idea of stability is applied most importantly to urban dissent (Nelson 1970). On the microlevel, one suspects that dissidents in urban areas are more likely to have been born in their city than to have migrated there from rural areas. On the macrolevel, one suspects that the growth of large cities and rapid rural-urban migration dampens, rather than intensifies, protest. This expectation holds for two reasons. First, urbanization destroys rural community. Since long-lived members of rural communities are removed, the likelihood of a social contract in rural areas is lowered. Second, rapid urbanization does not enhance protest in urban areas, because it takes a while for recent migrants to build the urban ties and create the urban associations that increase the chances for an urban social contract. In sum, urbanization destroys rural communities but does not replace them with urban communities, leading to an overall decrease in the possibilities for collective dissent. There is evidence to support the urbanization-dissent corollaries.[71]

### 5.2.6. Concentration

The ecological concentration of the dissidents' community provides the final influence on the transaction costs of arranging cooperation among dissidents through a social contract. Concentration refers to physical proximity; a densely packed set of dissidents is located in a single geographically contiguous area of a nation and a scattered set of dissidents is dispersed over several unconnected areas of a nation. As the geographic concentration of dissidents increases, a social contract, and hence collective dissent, is facilitated.

Why? As the concentration of dissidents increases, the extent and intensity of interactions among dissidents increases, which in turn increases their communications (e.g., of grievances). And this facilitates the bargaining of the terms of a contract. Moreover, as dissidents talk to one another, they increase their mutual awareness and knowledge, or what Jacob and Teune

(1964, 26) refer to as "cognitive proximity." As dissidents become more visible to one another, they are better able to monitor contributors and noncontributors (sect 6.5.2). Finally, with reduced distance between dissidents, it is easier to administer rewards for compliance and punishment for noncompliance (sect. 6.5.3).

Concentration is especially advantageous for the Tit-For-Tat form of social contract. Where Tit-For-Taters have many more interactions among themselves than with non-Tit-For-Taters, cooperation is encouraged. By contrast, cooperation becomes more difficult where they have essentially random interactions among themselves and with non-Tit-For-Taters. Axelrod (1984, 63–69) shows that even a small, but concentrated, cluster of players who use Tit-For-Tat can establish themselves in a population of non-Tit-For-Taters.

There are two other reasons, unrelated to the social contract approach, that the concentration of dissidents facilitates collective dissent. First, as dissidents become more aware of each other, they are better able to coordinate their mutual expectations (sect. 4.1.1). Thus, density facilitates both crowds and bandwagons. Second, the concentration of dissidents reduces several organizational costs of collective dissent. Concentration allows entrepreneurs to impose, monitor, and enforce agreements (sect. 6.5). Recruiting is easier, and it is easier to organize and coordinate activities. It is obviously more difficult to transport resources to a project that is remote than to one that is nearby.

The concentration proposition is indeed a powerful tool for conflict studies.[72] It allows one to predict which groups will be easy to organize for collective dissent and which ones will have difficulty forming.

Which groups, then, are concentrated? Ceteris paribus, as the size of the dissident community increases, density decreases. If potential dissidents are numerous, they are less likely to interact and, hence, to know each other very well; their trust that their fellow dissident will adhere to a social contract is low. Smaller groups permit greater interaction and communication, which decreases the noise level in the system, reduces the possibility of misinformation, and makes it easier to predict what others will do. Monitoring individual contributions and punishing noncontributors becomes easier.[73]

The largest possible dissident community is a global one. In general, CA among dissidents in several different nations is more difficult to organize than CA among dissidents in a single nation. A worldwide revolutionary movement, or one that attempts to secure the cooperation of revolutionary movements in many different countries, runs up against the concentration problem. International revolutionary efforts therefore always fail.[74]

This corollary to the concentration proposition leads to many further predictions. Consider, for instance, workers. The problem of overcoming national boundaries will seriously confound any effort on the part of "workers of the world" to unite. Contra Marxist theory, a worldwide proletarian revolution is a most unlikely event. Internationalism might be a common theme among working-class intellectuals (Thompson 1966, 828), but the working class itself will remain unmoved. Similarly doomed to failure are pan-Arab, pan-African, and pan-Latin American liberation movements, and also international student, environmentalist, and terrorist movements. The CA problems of diasporas, such as Jews and Palestinians, are particularly severe. The evidence for these predictions is overwhelming. There was little cooperation among the simultaneous revolutions in Europe in either the seventeenth (Merriman 1938) or the nineteenth centuries (Robertson 1952). Nor has there been a great deal of unity among Latin American, African, and Asian guerrilla movements. And continent-wide movements, such as pan-Africanism, have been unsuccessful.

Nationally based dissident movements, however, have a greater chance of success. But, even then, the concentration argument leads to the prediction that some of these movements are more likely to be successful than others. Thus, great geographic scope works against dissident movements. As state boundaries increase, nationally based dissident movements weaken. Madison (Madison, Hamilton, and Jay [1788] 1987) advances the argument that factions are weaker in larger social units, because they have more difficulty coordinating their activities. Olson (1982, 41) agrees. He argues that small social units encourage the cartelization of a nation, whereas large social units destroy the basis of many interest groups. This suggests two hypotheses: the disintegration or fission of an existing community leads to greater levels of CA; the integration or fusion of many existing communities leads to less CA.

In another sense, however, wide geographic scope can work to the advantage of nationwide dissident movements because it can also work against regimes that try to repress. Put otherwise: the isolation proposition (sect. 5.2.4) mitigates the concentration proposition. But the resolution is easy and insightful: expect subnational movements to predominate in nations of great geographic scope.

Separatist movements are a form of subnational movement. As they are concentrated in a single geographic area, separatists are easier to mobilize than nationalists who tend to be dispersed over the entire nation. Smith (1976, 10) thus argues that "territorially integrated and compact populations" are more likely to serve as the basis of successful nationalist movements. Hence, separatist movements will have more actual participants per potential participant than nationalist movements. Expect less free riding separatists than free riding nationalists.

Ethnic groups are another form of subnational movement. Since ethnic groups tend to be geographically concentrated and classes tend to be spread throughout the nation, the concentration proposition leads one to expect much less class solidarity than ethnic solidarity. While a class-in-itself (i.e., those in an objectively similar situation, but with no consciousness or organization) will become a class-for-itself (i.e., those who are politically self-conscious and organized) only with relative difficulty, an ethnic group-in-itself will become an ethnic group-for-itself with relative ease. Hence, more workers than ethnics will free ride.

Workers do benefit, however, from their concentration in urban areas and their concentration in factories. These residential and workplace patterns assist workers' organizations. Rural smallholders and peasants, having none of these advantages, are more difficult to organize.[75]

The concentration argument also explains why some class groupings are easier to mobilize than others. Consider the relationship between unemployment and collective dissent. As unemployment increases, collective dissent increases, because there is a greater concentration of unemployed workers. Furthermore, the more unemployment is concentrated in a particular geographic area, the more the unemployed will participate in collective dissent.

The concentration proposition also explains the variation in strike activity among workers. Kerr and Siegel (1954) find that where workers in an industry form a homogeneous group that is isolated from the larger community, the industry is strike-prone. Hence, miners around the world tend to be radical,

> in great part the result of the structure of the "occupational community" of the miners. The high degree of interaction among the miners results in a very close-knit social organization. Since they are concentrated together, and in relative physical and social isolation from the influences of the dominant social classes in the society, it is highly likely that a shared class outlook based on the recognition of their common interests will develop. (Petras and Zeitlin 1967, 580)

Further examples of geographically concentrated workers that develop high levels of CA include coal, lumber, textile, and waterfront workers.

The concentration proposition implies that the gathering of workers in large factories contributes to collective dissent. By bringing workers together in one place, capitalists create the conditions for working-class CA. Nowhere is this more true than in large factories in either densely populated urban areas or isolated rural areas: workers there are more extremist and engage in more strike activity than do workers in small factories (Kornhauser 1959, 150–58; Jenkins 1983, 531–32). A classic example is the Russian proletariat on the eve of the Russian Revolution. The proportion of the Russian workers employed in large factories was the highest in the world, and the Peterloo works in Petrograd was the largest factory complex in the world (Dunn 1989, 31).

The concentration proposition also tells us a great deal about class conflict (sect. 3.10.1.1). It is easier to concentrate capital than labor. Hence, the bourgeoisie holds a privileged position in its conflict with workers. Moreover, the concentration of capital begets the concentration of labor (i.e., factories).

The concentration argument, finally, leads one to suspect that when socioeconomic change alters the spatial-territorial distribution of workers, it affects worker CA. Tilly and Schweitzer (1982, 69) argue that changing patterns of urban residence early in the industrial revolution contributed to class solidarity: "In principle, we might reasonably expect the increasing segregation of workers from the rest of the population, and the declining division of the city into households and neighborhoods grouping together all members of a single trade from masters to servants, to have weakened trade-wide solidarities and to have strengthened solidarity on the basis of class."

The concentration argument also explains why densely packed urban areas characteristically produce much collective dissent: the cities are home to so many like-minded dissidents.[76] Suppose we apply the concentration argument, once again, to urban areas. An interesting deduction follows: concentration within urban areas increases collective dissent. Hence, Tilly's (1964, 23–24) evidence suggests that the higher the concentration of urban population in one city (the metropolis), the higher the collective dissent. Nations with a single major urban area, therefore, will have more collective dissent than nations with several important urban areas.[77]

The other side of the urbanization-dissent coin is obvious. Since peasants are typically spread out over a large geographic area, peasant revolts are harder to organize than urban rebellions.[78] Two other factors contributing to this situation are the lack of autonomy from local landlords and bureaucracies (sect. 5.2.4) and a lack of preexisting organizations (sect. 5.2.3).

But peasants do rebel. The concentration argument also holds implications for rural rebellion: it is more likely to begin in the marketplaces of towns and villages than in the isolated areas of the countryside. Indeed, this was the pattern during the early industrial revolution in France and England (Rudé 1964, chaps. 1, 2).

Social organization is another important source of concentration. One would expect more CA in institutionalized settings than in noninstitutionalized settings. It is not surprising, for example, that mutinies on ships were once common. Schools, churches, factories, and hospitals, too, should be fruitful areas for dissident groups.

Students, for example, engage in a great deal of collective dissent because they do not suffer financial hardship from the time forgone at a job. Their opportunity costs (sect. 3.2.3) are, consequently, low. And because they are young, they have a low discount rate (sect. 5.2.1). Still another reason that students engage in much collective dissent is that they are concentrated in universities and are particularly easy to mobilize. Lipset (1971b, 36) argues that "the campus is the ideal place in which to find large numbers of people in a common situation." He (1971b, xv) suggests that students are typically revolutionary because of "the relative ease with which those on campus can be reached and mobilized." Lipset (1964, 35) thereby maintains that

> like a vast factory, a large campus brings together great numbers of people in similar life situations, in close proximity to each other, who can acquire a sense of solidarity and wield real power . . . It is relatively easy to reach students; leaflets handed out at the campus gate will usually do the job. These facilitate quick communication, foster solidarity, and help arouse melodramatic action.

Moreover, students who live on campus will engage in more CA than those who live at home (Lipset 1964, 42). The political activism of students is, indeed, legend and is bolstered by argumentation,[79] examples,[80] and systematic evidence.[81]

Students constitute the classic example of how an institutionalized setting produces geographic concentration and hence can foment collective dissent. There are also some classic examples of how a geographically dispersed, noninstitutionalized setting discourages CA. For that reason, women should be hard to mobilize for collective dissent; consumers too. Both corollaries ring true for women and consumer activists.

The final set of implications of the concentration argument to be considered here relate to the idea that crowding per se should produce collective dissent. One suspects that as population density increases, collective dissent will increase. Some aggregate cross-national evidence supports this speculation (Welch and Booth 1974, 155). So does some aggregate cross-city evidence in the United States: Spilerman (1970) reports that the absolute number of blacks in a city is the best predictor of black riots in American cities in the 1960's.[82]

One also suspects that population growth leads to collective dissent. This should especially hold where there are limited resources, such as land and employment opportunities. Support for this proposition exists.[83]

One also suspects that crowds are conducive to collective dissent because crowding both increases mutual expectations (sect. 4.1.1) and reduces the probability of repression (sect. 3.2).[84] Expect crowds, in short, to precede riots.

In sum, the concentration argument offers excellent guidance as to which dissidents will organize successfully. The geographic concentration of some groups, such as miners, factory workers, subnational groups, and students, enhances their capacities for CA. The geographic dispersion of other groups, such as international movements, migrant workers, consumers' and women's groups, impedes their attempts to organize effective CA. Nonetheless, in modern societies, the concentration idea, just like the isolation idea, may be becoming less relevant. Communications networks, for one, can help overcome geographic dispersion. In principle, workers can now organize as easily as Chicagoans and doctors as easily as Coloradoans. Specialized publications (e.g., magazines, journals, newsletters), national conventions, friendship cliques, telephone contacts, and the mail are all part of the new technology (sect. 3.4.2) of organizing collective dissent.

This chapter has examined what happens to the Rebel's Dilemma when dissidents forge a social contract. Dissidents can establish three types of contracts: self-governing institutions (sect. 5.1.1), Tit-For-Tat arrangements (sect. 5.1.2), and mutual exchange agreements (sect. 5.1.3). In other words, the famous problem of social order can be overcome with the larger rationality characteristic of voluntary political associations.

This approach yields many interesting insights into protest and rebellion. The existence of a social contract as an explanation for social order, however, has been criticized. Sabine (1973, 601) write that "to ask who makes a constitution . . . is nonsense, for constitutions are not made." Thus, Hegel argues (cited in Sabine 1973, 601) that "a constitution is not just something manufactured; it is the work of centuries." The fatal flaw of the social contract approach is that social contracts must ultimately be based on community norms. Durkheim's ([1893] 1933, 211) and later Parsons's (1937, 311, 460–61) classic argument is that one cannot have voluntary, mutual arrangements between two unrelated partners *without* extracontractual understanding, such as common values about justice. Both thus argue that explicit social agreements presuppose certain norms about the agreements. What is in the contract? What can be contracted and what not? What makes a social contract valid? How are violations sanctioned? Durkheim concludes that "effective contracts depend on the existence of the *institution* of contract, which itself cannot be contractual but must be bindingly established and enforced" (Poggi 1978, 4, emphasis in original). By implication, "it is social norms rather than contracts which should be postulated as primitives in explaining how social integration comes about" (Ullmann-Margalit 1977,

75). One should, in other words, adopt a Community approach to explaining CA.[85]

This chapter has confirmed these suspicions. I have traced the social origins of social contracts directly to community. Social contracts are rooted in a community's longevity, homogeneity, preexisting organizations, autonomy, stability, and concentration. Contract alone is therefore never sufficient to solve the dissidents' CA problem; it must ultimately be backed by community. The consequence is that Contract solutions to the Rebel's Dilemma offer as incomplete an explanation of CA as Market and Community solutions did, an issue that requires elaboration (sect. 9.1).

Let us now turn to the last institution within which a dissident dwells. Perhaps a hierarchical context will provide a more complete solution to the Rebel's Dilemma.

## CHAPTER 6

# Hierarchy

Hierarchical institutions are the final context within which Market solutions to the Rebel's Dilemma operate. Such a context assumes that a dissident organization preexists collective dissent. Hierarchy solutions then seek the visible hand processes used by dissident leaders to coerce their followers into contributing to the PG. CA thus occurs, according to these explanations, because someone has the power to bring it about.

This chapter examines five sets of Hierarchy solutions to the Rebel's Dilemma. The dissident group may encourage dissident CA through the strategies pursued by certain key actors — agents or entrepreneurs (sect. 6.1) and principals or patrons (sect. 6.2). The dissident group may also encourage protest and rebellion by virtue of its structure — how the group organizes its activities (sect. 6.3) and how it competes against its allies (sect. 6.4). Finally, the dissident group may encourage collective dissent by imposing, monitoring, and enforcing agreements among its members (sect. 6.5).

## 6.1. Locate Agents or Entrepreneurs

Dissidents participate in CA when there are leaders who create organizations and pool resources. Accordingly, leaders of dissident movements, such as Mao, Lenin, or Hitler, are often considered the embodiment of their movements. I will first consider the importance of entrepreneurial activity (sect. 6.1.1), and then focus on the causes (sect. 6.1.2) and consequences (sect. 6.1.3) of such activity.

### 6.1.1. The Importance of Entrepreneurial Activity

Many have tried to identify the components of dissident organizations that are most responsible for collective dissent. Some conceive of these components in broad, functional terms. Gurr (1970, 285, emphasis in original), for example, writes that "dissident institutional support varies strongly with the cohesiveness and complexity of dissident-controlled organizations. *Cohesiveness* is the extent of goal consensus and cooperative interaction among members; *complexity* is the extent of hierarchical and functional differentiation within an organization." Huntington (1968, 12–24), too, uses functional terms: he associates "institutionalization" with "coherence," "complexity," "adaptability," and "autonomy." Others conceive of these components in specific, structural terms. Some point out that dissident groups often create a financial infrastructure. Self-financing is achieved either through robbery, hijacking, protection rackets, and drug trafficking, or legal businesses and portfolio investments. Rich patrons are solicited (sect. 6.2). There are even pension schemes for the disabled and for widows. Dissidents also occasionally create various sorts of military organizations (Gurr 1970, 268). And they may have political operatives whose purpose is to influence government policy by lobbying and negotiating with state authorities.

Most students of conflict argue, however, that it is the leadership aspect that is most crucial to the success of the dissident organization. An important solution to the Rebel's Dilemma, therefore, is to locate leaders.[1] Hence, one may suggest the following proposition: as the leadership of a dissident organization strengthens, collective dissent increases. One suspects, for example, that dissident groups with larger staffs will have more CA than those with smaller staffs and that dissident groups that can raise money centrally will have more CA than those that cannot.

The leadership proposition is true because entrepreneurs possess many skills that are necessary for the success of dissident movements. Indeed, many attribute various "roles" to revolutionary leaders. Lasswell (cited in Hagopian 1974, 329) refers to theorists, agitators, and administrators. Brinton (1965, chap. 4) refers to idealists, formulators, propagandists, agitators, and organizers. Hoffer (1951, chaps. 15–17) refers to men of words, fanatics, and practical men of action. Finally, Hopper (1950, 272, 274, 277, 278) refers to agitators, prophets, reformers, statesmen, and administrator-executives. All of the skills involved in these jobs facilitate many solutions to the Rebel's Dilemma.

- *Increase Benefits* (sect. 3.1). Charismatic leaders create zealots. Weber ([1924] 1968, 241–45) suggests that a sense of charisma may become attached to a leader with an overpowering personality. Weber holds that such a leader is by definition a revolutionary, because his or her claim to authority is always in conflict with the established bases of legitimacy. Charisma, Weber even suggests, may be the *only* source of revolution in a bureaucratic society. Such leaders stimulate their followers into action with their words (Hoffer 1951, chap. 15). Coleman (1990, 311) adds that people may vest authority in these charismatic people of words in order to create the social capital (sect. 5.2.3) needed to overcome the free-rider problem.
- *Lower Costs* (sect. 3.2). Dissident leaders deflect government repression away from the rank-and-file dissident. As Gurr (1970, 294)

argues, "The mere existence of leadership also may reduce the perceived likelihood of retaliation by a sort of lightning rod effect. The rank-and-file member of a dissident organization may believe that the brunt of negative sanctions will fall on his leaders rather than on him."

- *Increase Resources.* Entrepreneurs can provide outside resources that subsidize the costs and raise the benefits of CA.
- *Improve the Productivity of Tactics* (sect. 3.4). Leadership adapts long-range goals to immediate demands. They formulate tactics so as to achieve strategic objectives. Such planning allows dissident tactics to be productive.
- *Increase the Probability of Winning* (sect. 3.6). Entrepreneurs try to persuade their followers that victory is possible. Chong (1991, 195) offers an example from the U.S. civil rights movement: "At the turn of the twentieth century . . . [t]he forces of society — government, police, businessmen, employers, white supremacists — were so strongly united against blacks that mass protest was both futile and dangerous." Prospective participants had to be convinced that CA could achieve their goals. Civil rights leaders worked hard to assure their followers that they could indeed win.
- *Use Incomplete Information* (sect. 3.8). Concrete grievances must be interpreted. As Tarrow (1989, 114) puts it, "With varying degrees of self-consciousness, the protesters are applying general interpretative frames to concrete situations, thereby dignifying their grievances and broadening the range of their potential supporters." Such interpretive frameworks are composed of many elements. Dissident leaders attempt to interpret the discontent of followers, explaining to them "the causal context in which they are placed" (Elster 1985, 350). Leaders also try to focus that discontent on the state, by blaming the state for the evils they face. Leaders also attempt to justify their strategy and tactics, the use of political violence, for example. And they try to "synthesize a diversity of interests and discontents and put them to the service of the goals of dissident leaders" (Gurr 1970, 291). In short, as Hopper (1950, 272, 274–75) suggests, agitators "lead people to challenge and question their mode of living," prophets claim to have "a special and separate knowledge of the causes of unrest and discontent," and reformers attack "specific evils and [develop] a clearly defined program." Dissident entrepreneurs therefore take advantage of incomplete information to develop an ideology that both legitimizes and inspires the dissident group.
- *Increase Mutual Expectations* (sect. 4.1.1). Dissident leaders dispense information to their followers that cues collective dissent. In

this sense, leaders coordinate preferences. Elster (1985, 366–67) demonstrates how leadership produces significant information gains: "If one individual knows and is trusted by one hundred people, he can create the information conditions by two hundred transactions — first asking each of them about their willingness to join CA and then telling each about the willingness of everyone else. By contrast bilateral communication between the hundred will require about five thousand acts of communication."

- *Build a Bandwagon* (sect. 4.1.2). Leaders are needed to pay the start-up costs that begin a bandwagon. They may be the unconditional cooperators who are the bandwagon's initial participants.
- *Use Tit-For-Tat* (sect. 5.1.2). Entrepreneurs are not needed to mobilize small numbers of homogeneous people or groups. Entrepreneurs are needed to create the conditions of community — longevity, homogeneity, preexisting organization, autonomy, stability, concentration — that can jump-start a set of dissidents. Another important organizational task of leadership is to provide assurance to conditional cooperators that if they do their fair share, others will do likewise.
- *Impose, Monitor, and Enforce Agreements* (sect. 6.5). Dissident entrepreneurs facilitate their followers' agreements to cooperate by minimizing the organization's transaction costs, or the costs associated with capturing the gains from exchange among dissidents. Specifically, they seek to reduce the costs of devising contracts or negotiating agreements, measuring inputs or devising monitoring procedures, and enforcing contracts or providing rewards and sanctions. And they may try to overcome the problems of asymmetric information and hidden preferences with various preference-revelation techniques (sect. 9.2.2.2).

While dissident entrepreneurs *can* facilitate these many solutions to the Rebel's Dilemma, the evidence shows that leadership is neither necessary nor sufficient for collective dissent. As Gurr (1970, 291) observes, "There is no precise correspondence between the existence of leadership and the development of massive political violence. Some revolutions have failed for want of adequate leadership, others have failed in spite of it, yet some successful ones have had no effective leaders until the revolutionary process was well under way." Laqueur (1987, 402) echoes these observations: "In some guerrilla movements the personality of the leader has been of decisive importance . . . on other occasions personalities have been of little consequence."

Why does one find only a feeble relationship between dissident leadership and collective dissent? One reason is that Hierarchy is just one of four types of solutions to the Rebel's Dilemma. Another reason is that dissident

leaders choose among dissident tactics. Strong leaders might therefore negotiate an agreement with the government that accommodates the dissidents'
demands. Hence, leadership per se is not associated with collective dissent or
collective violence. Gurr (1970, 293) recognizes that tactical considerations
intervene and muddle the leadership-dissent linkage: "Competent leadership
and complex organization enhance dissident institutional support; that support may be used to minimize rather than increase political violence, depending on the commitments and tactical calculations of leaders." Strong
leadership, in short, is just as responsible for the termination as it is for the
initiation and continuation of conflict. The weakness of the dissident leader-
ship-collective dissent linkage is related to the weakness of the more general
dissident organization-collective dissident proposition (sect. 8.1).

## 6.1.2. The Origins of Entrepreneurial Activity

If organization helps to provide a PG, then organizing the dissident group is
itself the true PG. As Hechter (1988, 105) remarks, "Formal controls may be
required for the survival of large groups, but they are a second order collective good whose provision is threatened by free riders." Hence, the question:
"Why then would rational egoists agree to establish such institutions in the
first place?" (Hechter 1988, 105).

Hechter's (1988, 106) general answer is that "if the establishment of formal controls is necessary for the production of some joint good, then individuals will be led by their very interest in consuming the good to help produce
these controls." A three-stage process seems quite plausible: uncoordinated
efforts to achieve a PG begin gradually; then coordinated activities to achieve
economies of scale develop; and finally organization to reduce free riding
emerges. Such arguments are so general, however, as to mystify, rather than
clarify, the process of organizing dissidents. Three more specific processes
have been proposed to account for the emergence of dissident organization.

First, the dissident groups in a dissident movement compete (sect. 6.4)
for government's rewards (public goods) and/or to avoid government's threats
(public bads). Such competition eliminates the less-organized dissidents.
Natural selection and evolution thus solve the second-order Rebel's
Dilemma: only organized dissidents survive.[2]

Hechter offers a second evolutionary view of the development of dissident organizations. He suggests that private good (excludable) clubs (sect.
6.3.1) tend to evolve into groups producing a PG:

> Something of a two-stage theory of institutional development [occurs].
> In the first stage, individuals form groups to obtain joint *private*
> [excludable] goods, like credit and insurance, but to do so they must
> also establish formal controls, which constitute a *collective* good. Once

these controls are in place, a second stage becomes possible. The group's resources, now protected by the existence of formal controls, can be diverted (under a set of circumstances that needs to be investigated) to the production of further collective, or even *public* goods. (Hechter 1988, 123, emphasis in original)

Dissident groups have indeed followed such a path. Mutual aid societies, insurance groups, friendly societies, fraternal associations, and guilds were the bases for trade unions (Thompson 1966).

The third specific process that can account for the emergence of dissident organization is profit making by dissident entrepreneurs. If there are incentives to free ride, the collective outcome is inefficient and suboptimal: potential net gains from CA have not been captured. If there are gains to be had, there exist opportunities for someone to make a profit. These opportunities will not remain unexploited. Entrepreneurs could devise organizational strategies and institutions to eliminate the incentives to free ride. As long as total benefits exceed organizing costs and the costs of the good, a surplus exists. Hence, entrepreneurs can exploit the joint gains from CA, pass some of those gains on to the group, and retain some for themselves. The group would gain from such an arrangement and hence would be willing to subsidize the entrepreneurs (Frohlich, Oppenheimer, and Young 1971).

This last process is a particularly important explanation of the emergence of dissident organizations. Self-interested political elites undertake risk, exploit some situation, and decide to become dissident entrepreneurs. They thus create a dissident organization for one basic reason: the opportunities for profit that come from adopting leadership positions in the dissident group are greater than the opportunities for profit that come from adopting leadership positions in the regime. Both sets of benefits — to the dissident entrepreneur and to the regime entrepreneur — underlie the decision to create a dissident organization.[3]

Dissident entrepreneurship then arises, first of all, when opportunities for advancement in the regime are unavailable. As the demands of elites for power, status, wealth, and so on in a regime are blocked, the supply of dissident entrepreneurs increases. Dissident leaders therefore lack upward social mobility in the regime. As leadership positions in society become unavailable, or as the opportunities for mobility of the most talented, qualified, and ambitious individuals narrow, elites increasingly choose to lead dissident groups. Blocked and downward elite social mobility, in creating dissident entrepreneurs, thus increases collective dissent. The opposite also holds: open channels of social mobility decrease collective dissent, because in such situations fewer entrepreneurs are available to lead potential dissidents. This is a common argument in conflict studies,[4] supported by much evidence, especially from revolutions.[5]

Dissident leaders are thus often elites from the upper socioeconomic strata, among the most talented and best trained people in society. Gurr (1970, 337) thus suggests that "revolutionary leaders may be marginal, in the sense that they feel their social position and prospects for advancement precarious, but they seldom emerge from the lowest classes. A distinctive characteristic of revolutionary movements, and internal wars generally, is substantial participation by higher classes, especially at the leadership level."

Two ironies follow. First, most revolutionary leaders come from a higher socioeconomic background than their followers. As Zimmermann (1983, 312) points out, "Revolutionary leaders come by and large from middle-class origin, are better educated, have better occupations and generally more resources available than do rank-and-file revolutionaries." Greene (1990, 57) makes a similar observation: "Compared with their followers, leftist revolutionary movements are likely to be better educated, more widely travelled, and drawn from higher social classes." The second irony is that most revolutionary leaders come from the same high socioeconomic background as the leaders of the regime whom they seek to replace. Greene (1990, 41) points out that revolutionary elites are no "more representative of the social base of their society than are the political elites they seek to displace." These two ironies taken together lead to one of the great paradoxes of collective dissent: the educated lead protests against the educated in favor of the noneducated; the rich lead protests against the rich in favor of the poor. Focusing on the entrepreneurial element of collective dissent goes a long way toward helping us understand this paradox, for which there is a great deal of evidence.[6]

The second reason why self-interested political elites might assume the risk involved in becoming dissident entrepreneurs is the great opportunities for advancement and upward mobility in a dissident group. In general, as Olson (1982, 59) argues, as the opportunities and incentives for dissident entrepreneurs increase, dissident entrepreneurship increases. Thus, entrepreneurs will enter dissident movements, and new dissident groups will form, under certain circumstances: where there exists the greatest possibility of profit, lowest barriers to entry, and smallest organizational costs. Fuentes and Frank (1989, 185), for example, recognize the pecuniary motivations of dissident entrepreneurs: "Not unlike working class and peasant movements before, these popular movements often have some middle class leadership and now ironically offer opportunities for employment and job satisfaction to otherwise unemployable members of the middle class and intelligentsia — professionals, teachers, priests, etc. — who offer their services as leaders, organizers, or advisers to these community and other popular Third World social movements."

The employment opportunities in dissident groups are affected by several factors. First, as the grievances of dissidents increase, the potential profit to entrepreneurs, and, thus to entrepreneurship, increases. Entrepreneurs prefer to organize unorganized collectivities with unsatisfied demands into dissident groups. They will avoid unorganized collectivities for which they have to "manufacture" grievances (sect. 9.2.2.1). Hence, any factor that facilitates the *Increase Benefits* solution to the Rebel's Dilemma (sect. 3.1) also facilitates the *Locate Agents or Entrepreneurs* solution.

Second, in some cases, outside organizers may be required to achieve any CA at all. This makes entrepreneurs particularly valuable and potentially very well paid. Such a scenario fits two types of movements, as shown in McCarthy and Zald's (1973) entrepreneurial model of the formation of social movement organizations. First, it fits those based on a broad and diffuse, and thus disorganized, constituency characterized by dispersed benefits and concentrated costs of CA.[7] Second, the scenario fits resource-poor collectivities with lower-class participants, movements that are "centered among deprived groups with few resources, minimal political experience, and little prior organization" (Jenkins 1983, 531). Hence, entrepreneurs can help mobilize those for whom it would be almost impossible to mobilize themselves: the poor, elderly, physically or mentally handicapped, and children (Walker 1991, 13).

Also affecting the opportunities and incentives for dissident entrepreneurs is innovation in the technology of dissent (sect. 3.4.2) which can greatly improve the chances that dissident entrepreneurship will be successful. Thus, the supply of dissident entrepreneurs increases in response to technological improvements in dissident organization. Jenkins (1983, 530–42) contrasts, for example, the "classical" social movement organizations, with their indigenous leaderships, volunteer staffs, extensive memberships, resources derived from the direct beneficiaries, and mass participation, and the "new" social movement organizations, with their outside professional leaderships, full-time paid staffs, small or nonexistent memberships, resources derived from conscience constituencies, and few participants who "speak for" their larger constituencies. Indeed, with the right organization a mass base is no longer required, thus widening the scope for entrepreneurial activity.

Finally, changes in the occupational structure of society can also be responsible for an increase in the number of dissident entrepreneurs. One example comes from the United States at the turn of the twentieth century: "The growth of journalistic moral entrepreneurs . . . [meant that] muckrakers as Lincoln Steffens and Ida Tarbell become key figures in defining issues. Their position is dependent on the expansion of the mass-circulation newspapers and weeklies and the growth of a national audience" (Zald 1988, 22). Another example comes from the United States in the 1960s: many new occupations supported a commitment to social change. Lawyers could choose poverty law, consumer law, and civil rights law. Social workers could choose community organization. Priests and ministers could choose to become political activists. The supply of dissident entrepreneurs increases along with any complementary job market.

In sum, dissident entrepreneurship arises when the opportunities for profit from leadership positions in the dissident group are greater than the opportunities for profit from leadership positions in the regime. When these conditions exist, the wealthy, or those who can invest (see sect. 3.3, the *Increase Resources* solution) and the risk-acceptors, or those who want to take chances (see sect. 3.9, the *Increase Risk Taking* solution) often decide to become dissident entrepreneurs.[8]

### 6.1.3. The Consequences of Entrepreneurial Activity

Rank-and-file dissidents seeking a way out of the PG-PD game often hire a dissident entrepreneur. Agency has two important consequences for dissident groups.

First is self-perpetuation:

> From a means, organization becomes an end. To the institutions and qualities which at the outset were designed simply to ensure the good working of the party machinery (subordination, the harmonious cooperation of individual members, hierarchical relationships, discretion, propriety of conduct) a greater importance comes ultimately to be attached than to the productivity of the machine. Henceforth the sole preoccupation is to avoid anything which may clog the machinery. (Michels, cited in Lasswell and Kaplan 1950, 44)

Dissident entrepreneurs acquire an interest in maintaining their organization. Leaders who have helped overcome their group's CA problem want to continue overcoming that CA problem. For one thing, they have made specific investments in the organization and consequently are vulnerable to appropriation of quasi-rents by followers, other entrepreneurs, and regimes (Eggertsson 1990, 173). Second, entrepreneurs want to preserve the selective benefits they receive from their leadership positions. Hence, entrepreneurs eventually develop organizational goals and become preoccupied with organizational survival.

Dissident entrepreneurs pursue two strategies for preserving their organizations. First, if the group's goals are achieved or made irrelevant, whether as a result of government action or changed social conditions, its entrepreneurs can attempt to refocus the goals and keep the group active long after its initial aims are fulfilled.[9] Second, dissident entrepreneurs can emphasize solidarity incentives over purposive incentives (sect. 4.2). Zurcher and Curtis (1973, 182) point out why such a strategy works: "It can reasonably be assumed that those organizations emphasizing purposive incentives would be less prone to pressures for organizational maintenance, since the goals based on such incentives would have greater potential for tangible and terminating attainment. Those organizations emphasizing solidary incentives would be more prone to self-perpetuation since member rewards are not necessarily based upon the conclusive attainment of specific organizational goals."

Bureaucratization is the second consequence that agency holds for dissident groups. All long-lived dissident groups become bureaucratized. Hence, Weber ([1924] 1968, 246) stresses the routinization of charisma. He is especially aware of these problems in movements advocating revolutionary socialism (Giddens 1971, 135).

This second consequence of agency turns out to be historically valid. Tilly (1978, 1986; Tilly, Tilly, and Tilly 1975) observes that dissent based on community has been replaced by dissent based on association. Short-term reactive strategies undertaken by small-scale, decentralized, and informal solidarity groups have given way to long-term proactive strategies undertaken by large-scale, centralized, special purpose organizations. Billington (1980) also shows that since the nineteenth century, insurrection has become professionalized and sophisticated bureaucratic organizations have come to predominate. Revolutionaries have thus become quite self-conscious about their task. Small nineteenth century friendship cliques (e.g., Marx's League of Communists) gave way to organized revolutionary movements (e.g., Lenin's Bolsheviks). Radical organizations became better able to exploit unfavorable situations and influence the course of revolution, further increasing the opportunities for entrepreneurship.

Further institutionalization, routinization, and bureaucratization of a dissident group occurs after it seizes power. Bendix (1960, 304) indicates what this entails:

> The leader's camp followers and disciples become his privileged companions and, subsequently, fief-holders, priests, state officials, officers, secretaries, editors, publishers, and others who want to live off the charismatically-inspired institution or movement. The people, in turn, become tax- or dues-paying "subjects," whether they are members of a church or party, disciplined soldiers obligated to serve, or citizens who abide by the law. The charismatic message becomes variously dogma, theory, legal regulation, or the content of an oral or written tradition.

When the counterelite becomes the governing elite, the Thermidorean phase of the revolution is not far behind.

## 6.2. Locate Principals or Patrons

Even zealots and hegemons (sect. 3.1) are unlikely, at least in the case of large-scale protest and rebellion, to be able to assist very many other dissidents. Outsiders, however, often have the necessary resources and can make the difference between success and failure. Rebels are thus always tempted to make appeals to other political actors, such as agents/entrepreneurs or principals/patrons. As Alinsky (1971, 184) puts it, "All minority organizations . . . seek out allies." They use third parties to build a coalition against the regime (Coser 1956, 139–49). Dissidents seek to increase the breadth and depth of their linkages to such patrons. If the effort is successful, powerful allies will subsidize the dissidents' cause, allowing the Rebel's Dilemma to be overcome.

There are numerous aspects to the *Locate Principals or Patrons* solution to the Rebel's Dilemma: how patrons help dissidents (sect. 6.2.1), why they do so (sect. 6.2.2), and who does so (sect. 6.2.3). There are also implications to consider if patrons help dissidents, rather than if dissidents rely upon internal support (sect. 6.2.4). These implications raise the question of whether dissidents always seek patrons.

### 6.2.1. How Patrons Help Dissidents

Patrons can be absolutely invaluable to dissident groups by assisting dissidents (individual patronage) or the dissident organization (institutional patronage) with all of the previously discussed solutions to the Rebel's Dilemma. Patrons may, for example, increase benefits, lower costs, increase resources, improve the productivity of tactics, increase the probability of winning, increase the probability that a contribution will make a difference, and help locate entrepreneurs to organize the group.

Three of these forms of assistance bear special mention. First, patrons may help defray the costs (sect. 3.2) of collective dissent by providing potential dissidents with the resources they lack: leadership, money, arms, and so on. Moreover, as Eckstein (1989, 37) suggests, the involvement of upper-class patrons may "minimize the state's use of force against the tumultuous, because elites are much more reluctant to use repression against the middle than the 'popular' classes." When the less-privileged strata can count on the protection of the more privileged strata, the probability of repression decreases and hence their willingness to protest increases.

Second, patrons may raise the expected benefits from CA. One way to raise expected benefits, of course, is to raise the rewards from CA (sect. 3.1). Upper-class patrons, for example, "may induce lower-status people to consider as unacceptable conditions that they otherwise might tolerate" (Eckstein 1989, 37). Hence patrons, as well as entrepreneurs (sect. 6.1), may provide the ideological basis for a dissident's utility function. Patrons may also increase expected benefits by increasing the dissident's estimate of his or her probability of success (sect. 3.6). Dissidents in democratic states are acutely aware that well-off patrons may induce the government to grant them attractive concessions. Schattschneider (1960) thus argues that when a dissident group is in the minority, its activities tend to be directed toward reference publics and public opinion, as well as third parties and powerful patrons, in its attempt to expand the scope of conflict. Lipsky (1968, 1145–46, emphasis in original) picks up on this idea. He points out that dissidents seek to expand the scope of conflict in order to gain allies that will improve their chances in their struggle with the regime:

> The "problem of the powerless" in protest activities is to activate "third parties" to enter the implicit or explicit bargaining arena in ways favorable to the protestors. This is one of the few ways in which they can "create" bargaining resources. It is intuitively unconvincing to suggest that fifteen people sitting uninvited in the Mayor's office have the power to move City Hall. A better formulation would suggest that people sitting in may be able to appeal to a wide public to which the city administration is sensitive. Thus in successful protest activity the *reference publics* of protest *targets* may be conceived as explicitly or implicitly reacting to protest in such a way that target groups or individuals respond in ways favorable to the protestors.

Patrons, third, may alter the productivity of certain dissident tactics (sect. 3.4). Nonviolence is an effective strategy, for example, only when it can mobilize support among third parties to a conflict. It works, as indicated above, because it enlarges the scope of conflict. McAdam (1982, 169–79) shows how the U.S. civil rights movement adopted a strategy of nonviolence predicated upon the patronage of Northern whites and the federal government.

### 6.2.2. Why Patrons Help Dissidents

Why do some patrons help dissidents while others stand as conservative bulwarks of the regime? Churches in Germany, Russia, southern Europe, and France, for example, identified with the upper classes and the state and, hence, opposed working-class movements. By contrast, churches in England and Canada often had close ties with socialist movements (Lipset 1971a, 169).

One must presumes rationality — that patrons are principals who hire dissidents as their agents. Hence, patrons contribute to dissidents in order to maximize their own utility. Working from this premise, several propositions about the etiology of the external support of dissident groups follow.

Consider the motivations of domestic patrons. One may be the desire to gain supporters for a domestic political struggle. Splits in a ruling class (sect. 3.6.2.2) might encourage some elites to seek the support of the peasantry, for example.[10] The split might even turn into a patronage race as various segments of the elite bid for the support of certain social groups. The challenges and counterchallenges to the morality of a dissident group and the regime should be understood as part of this race. Dissidents claim that government is "self-seeking and elitist" while they themselves are "public spirited and mass based" (Wilson 1973, 293). The regime, on the other hand, claims that the dissident organization is unrepresentative of the group for which they claim to speak. The regime also often claims that while it agrees with the dissidents' ends, it disagrees with their means. The dissidents, regimes say, are wrong in their facts and inappropriate in their tactics. Such a dispute between regime and opposition is not *only* about abstract conceptions of justice. It also involves concrete appeals by potential patrons.

Now consider foreign patrons. An external actor takes account of many factors in deciding whether to give aid to dissidents in some other nation.[11] One motive for doing so might be to conduct surrogate warfare against the regime. Kaplan (1978, 241, emphasis in original) suggests that "the terrorist who actually carries out the operation is an *agent* for a *principal* who may preserve a certain disassociation from the act."

Another motive might be to counter the aid of the regime's foreign patrons. As Gurr (1970, 270) argues, "Most regimes threatened by internal war also have foreign supporters, however, who frequently respond by increasing military assistance to the regime." The result is that supporters of the regime and the dissidents are in a sort of "arms race" by proxy: as the foreign support of a regime increases, the foreign support of its dissidents increases, and vice versa. Indeed, one finds a very high cross-national correlation between external support for dissidents and for the regime (Gurr 1970, 270).

Chong (1991, 160) identifies a final motive encouraging the foreign patronage of collective dissent: "Outside assistance from sympathetic and supportive third parties tends to be conditioned upon the ability of the movement to launch and sustain itself" — that is, on the hope that the dissidents may actually succeed. Patrons, no less than dissidents, will not contribute to lost causes (sect. 3.6).

A foreign patron's estimate of the dissidents' chance for success is related to two factors. The first is the ability of the foreign patron to actually supply the dissidents. Gurr (1970, 269) argues that this is a significant constraint on external supporters of rebellion:

> Little more than refuge and training can be provided for dissidents unless they control base areas to which military supplies can be shipped; such base areas are most easily provisioned if they border a country whose regime favors the dissidents. If this condition holds, dissidents can be equipped to the extent of their capacity to make use of the equipment, subject only to limitations on the resources and international restraints on the supplying nations.

A foreign patron's expectations concerning the dissidents' chances for success are related, second, to the existing scale of dissident activities. More foreign support for dissidents will be forthcoming in campaigns that are geographically broad and temporally enduring. Hence, significantly more external support is provided for internal wars than for conspiracy or turmoil (Gurr 1970, 271). Successful dissident groups thus attract both internal supporters (sect. 3.6) and external patrons. Dissident groups that are unable to win thus face a catch-22: to be successful they need supporters and patrons, but to find supporters and patrons, they need to be successful.[12]

Patrons, of course, also recognize the downside of supporting dissident groups: they face an agency problem (sect. 6.1.3) in controlling the dissidents whom they subsidize. They know that dissidents can play off one sponsor against another and that dissidents may turn out to be more radical than suits a patron's tastes. State-sponsored collective dissent might even prove to be a Pandora's box, unleashing revolutionary forces that topple the regime.[13] It is precisely these possibilities that limit both the willingness of patrons to sponsor collective dissent and the *Locate Principals or Patrons* solution to the Rebel's Dilemma.

### 6.2.3. Which Patrons Help Dissidents

Dissident groups may find internal and external patrons. Domestic sponsors include sympathetic members of the state, such as the military, as well as nonstate actors. Foreign sponsors include governments and international actors.

#### 6.2.3.1. The Military as an Ally
One very important potential ally of a dissident group is the regime's military. As Gurr (1970, 271) observes, "At the outset of antigovernment rioting, troops and their commanders may decide that their sympathies lie with the

opposition and join them." Such a decision can turn antigovernment rioting into revolution — a military that switches sides can be decisive. Gurr thus suggests that "if only a few [join the dissidents] . . . violence can still be readily suppressed. If many but not all defect, internal war may result; if almost all defect, the regime will almost certainly collapse" (Gurr 1970, 271).[14]

A shift in military support from the regime to the dissidents alters "the balance of coercion, directly because [it] increase[s] rebel military capacity at the expense of the regime" (Gurr 1970, 271). The impacts on collective dissent are threefold. First, the shift reduces the regime's ability to repress the dissents, facilitating the *Lower Costs* solution (sect. 3.2) to the Rebel's Dilemma. As Gurr (1970, 251) puts it, "The capacity of a regime to exercise any kind of persistent coercive control over its citizens, at any level or threat or severity of sanctions, depends ultimately on the loyalty of its military and internal security forces. The greater their loyalty, the more effective the regime is likely to be, other things being equal, in exercising coercive control." Second, a military shift signals the weakness of the regime and hence increases the dissidents' estimates of the probability of winning (sect. 3.6). As Gurr (1970, 251) again puts it, "The less [the military's] loyalty . . . the more likely civilian dissidents are to think they can succeed in attacks on the regime." Third, the shift implies that the military itself may become a dissident group and try to topple the regime. To cite Gurr (1970, 253) once again: "There is also a strong inverse relationship between the loyalty of the military to civilian regimes and the likelihood of conspiracy, as distinct from other forms of political violence. The military as an institution of force can easily intervene against a civilian regime, and if its officers are both disloyal and discontented, a coup d'etat is likely to seem the most convenient means to resolve their discontents."

Consequently, one may follow Tullock (1987a, chap. II) in making a series of predictions: if the military switches sides and joins the dissidents, the dissidents will definitely win; if the military remains neutral, the dissidents will probably win; if the military remains loyal to the regime, the regime will probably win. There are many examples to support these propositions.[15]

The government is well aware of the potential threat represented by its own military establishment. To prevent coups, dictators typically try to increase the CA problem of the military by constructing a division of labor that creates competing factions and hence a balance of power. The usual technique is to develop a set of countervailing military institutions: military, paramilitary, national guard, and national police forces are formed. There may be palace military forces — an elite Praetorian Guard. Different branches of the military, such as the army, navy, and air force, might overlap.

Regimes thus use a divide-and-conquer strategy not only with their opponents, the dissident group, but also with their own supporters.

When will a military be inclined to support a dissident group and when not? The military is on the front line of the regime-opposition conflict and thus is particularly sensitive to the actual conduct and expected outcome of that conflict.

Consider the actual conduct of the regime-opposition conflict. Militaries often have a difficult time supporting dissidents because of the team competition between regime and opposition (sect. 3.10.1.2). A key factor influencing the military's support for a group of dissidents is the duration of collective dissent. In a long and drawn-out internal war between regime and opposition, dissidents are likely to inflict heavy casualties on the military. As these clashes become more widespread and deadly, the *Increase Team Competition between Regime and Opposition* solution works against the chances that dissidents will find allies in the military: "Regime forces that have suffered many casualties at the hands of dissidents are more hostile towards them, less likely to cooperate with them" (Gurr 1970, 272). If the military is to become a patron of a dissident group, it will do so at the commencement of hostilities, not at its consummation.

Now consider the expected outcome of the regime-opposition conflict. Since militaries naturally gravitate to the winning side, two factors appear critical for the military to ally itself with a dissident group. First is whether a bandwagon (sect. 4.1.2) is forming. Militaries often jump on a civilian bandwagon. The key mechanism in building this bandwagon is contacts between the military and the dissidents that are extensive and intense: "Fraternization with the population . . . can weaken army unity and lead to conversion of some of its members to revolutionary doctrines" (Gurr 1970, 254). For example, fraternization between Soviet troops and Hungarian revolutionaries in 1956 led some of the troops to shift sides (Gurr 1970, 254). A second factor influencing the military's support for a dissident group is its estimate of the dissidents' probability of success (sect. 3.6). Militaries may become patrons of collective dissent because those estimates are high. Thus, ephemeral and localized rioting is less likely to win over the military than is a large-scale guerrilla war. Another factor is the initial defection of parts of the military; when portions of the military go over to the dissidents, others may update their estimates of the dissidents' probability of success, and their conversion becomes more likely. There is, in other words, a military bandwagon (sect. 3.6.6).

### 6.2.3.2. The State as an Ally
Dissidents often appeal to one branch of government to change the actions of another (Tilly 1986, 17–18) with the result that some regime elites provide

material support for dissidents to use against other regime elites. Parts of the regime thus protect dissidents from other parts of the regime. With coalitions forming between established members of the polity and revolutionary challengers, government has, in effect, helped to organize collective dissent against itself. Examples are legion.[16]

Government patronage of collective dissent raises the question: Why would a regime subsidize antiregime behavior? Neo-Marxist theorists of the state provide one answer. Following Poulantzas (1975), classes tend to be composed of conflicting factions, who willingly sacrifice the long-term interest of their entire class for the short-term interest of their particular faction. Classes, therefore, must be organized before they can become historical forces. An "autonomous" state is often defined as one that is independent of the dominant class groups and personnel, and can implement polices that serve the fundamental interest of the entire dominant class. In short, the state often tries to solve the CA problem of the dominant class (sect. 7.2.2) by acting as its patron. More specifically, the state acts as the agent that induces coherence among class factions, since it alone has the political power to induce concessions and compromises from the constituent groupings. The state's policies may backfire, however, if the dominant class uses its new-found solidarity against the state. This happened with the aristocratic resurgence on the eve of the French Revolution. Thus, a relatively "autonomous" state may be the unwitting patron of antigovernment behavior.

Another explanation for government patronage of collective dissent is that splits in the governing elite can lead certain factions of the regime to seek allies. They may seek out dissident groups, resulting in cross-class alliances and coalitions. In the classic case of Tory radicalism, the landed elite sought to ally itself with the working class to outflank the bourgeoisie. Classic examples on the American scene were Roosevelt's New Deal and Kennedy's New Frontier. Both presidents tried to bring unrepresented social groups into the political system — Roosevelt encouraged labor unions and Kennedy stimulated civil rights organizations. Modernizing or reform leaders in less developed nations provide yet another example. The modernizers attempt to bolster their own power base by incorporating new groups into national politics. To this end, they often use the radical middle and/or working and/or peasant classes against conservative landed elites.

Governments support collective dissent for still another reason: they may support a dissident group as the lesser of two evils; the moderate wing of a movement may be preferable to the radical wing. At one point, for example, Israel supported the Muslim fundamentalist group Hamas as a "benign" alternative to the PLO.

A final explanation for government subsidy of collective dissent is that regimes often need the support and assistance of the dissident group in governing. Moe (1980a, 59) argues that whether or not government acts as a patron for a dissident group depends on what the group "can offer public officials in return (information, political support, administrative cooperation)." In this way, corporatist arrangements subsidize dissident behavior.[17]

Government can act as a patron of collective dissent by affecting the benefit and cost functions of a dissident group, thereby solving its Rebel's Dilemma.

- Government may choose to legalize a dissident group, which makes it much easier for the group to recruit followers. U.S. labor unions offer the classic example: a sequence of laws made a dissident group legal, and even privileged. The 1914 Clayton Act exempted unions from antitrust laws. The Norris-LaGuardia Act of 1932 outlawed yellow-dog contracts (e.g., ones in which workers agree to not join a union). The Wagner Act of 1935 recognized the right of unions to organize, provided electoral machinery to determine bargaining agents, required employers to bargain with duly recognized unions, and legalized closed shops. These laws were crucial to the growth of labor unions in the United States.
- Government may make membership in a dissident group compulsory. Often a scenario like the following occurs: dissidents seek access to the state; they use whatever influence they have to convince the state to coerce potential members of the dissident group into actually joining the dissidents; they succeed in making group membership compulsory; this, in turn, increases the dissidents' access to the state. The circle is thus complete. As with legalization, government's decision to make membership in a dissident group compulsory can result in a significant increase in the group's activities. This is why unions favor and businesses oppose the closed shop. Many, including Commons (cited in Wilson 1973, 120), even argue that "if they had to choose, union organizers would invariably prefer getting a union shop to getting better wages and hours."
- Government may also act as a patron by choosing to designate a dissident group as the official spokesperson for the dissidents' cause. For example, public officials in a particular unit of government (e.g., bureaucratic agency, legislative committee) may recognize a particular group as the legitimate representative of the interests in a particular policy area (e.g., economy, civil rights). Such official recognition is particularly common in corporatist systems (Schmitter 1974). Government-granted monopolies always affect markets, including the market for collective dissent. A dissident group that is designated

official spokesperson for a grievance gains a great advantage over other dissident groups in the same movement (Moe 1980a, 59–60; Wilson 1973, 82). Once the group assumes such a privileged, quasi-governmental status, self-interested dissidents join.

- Further, government may act as a patron by allowing a dissident group to exercise certain governmental powers. It may be allowed to tax its members, for example, by a dues checkoffs. Such powers can be quite important. As Rich (1980, 583) finds in his study of neighborhood groups in the United States, "Organizations enjoying greater formal powers . . . tend to be more successful . . . in attracting members."
- Government may also institutionalize the dissident group's participation in the state's decision-making process. Such institutionalization, which may occur in either the executive, legislative, or judicial branch, is often a response to pressure by the group. Dissidents often persuade the government to create bureaucracies that provide them with PGs *and* solve their Rebel's Dilemma. Freeman (1979, 176; 1973, 797) offers two examples of government serving as the preexisting organizational basis (sect. 5.2.3) of dissident movements: the welfare rights movement grew out of Community Action Programs set up under the War on Poverty; the National Organization of Women (NOW) grew out of a government commission on the status of women. Lowi (1971) reports other examples of U.S. government agencies that are the result of successful social movements.
- Government may consolidate several competing dissident groups (sect. 6.4) into one large dissident organization.[18]
- Government may assist a dissident group by allowing it to allocate government jobs. Tilly (1986, 254, emphasis in original) offers an example from the French Revolution: "With the growth of governmental administration in the Nord, the government became for some people the employer of *first* resort: revolutionary committees served, among other things, as placement offices for well-connected militants." Jobs are a significant selective incentive (sect. 6.5.3) and the ability of a dissident group to hand them out significantly increases its membership. Dissident groups thus lobby government heavily for this form of patronage. Local and regional dissident groups are particularly eager to win the right to allocate government jobs. Fights over local self-government are in fact fights over the control of local resources, money, and jobs. Bureaucracies must be staffed; grants must be made. Affirmative action schemes, development plans, public works projects, agricultural initiatives, environmental protection

programs, and tourism policies offer potentially invaluable patronage for local and regional dissident groups.[19]

- Government may provide direct monetary grants to a dissident group. There are many examples: U.S. agencies involved during the late 1960s included the Community Action Programs of the Office of Economic Opportunity, Model Cities Agencies, and Volunteers in Service to America (McCarthy and Zald 1973, 13). There are also more subtle examples: the U.S. government offers reduced postal rates for nonprofit associations, and many professional and vocational associations hold conventions that are supported by tax write-offs. McCarthy and Zald (1973, 15) add that government funding often indirectly creates employment opportunities for dissident entrepreneurs: "The major change influencing the careers of social movement leadership [is] the growing institutionalization of dissent. Briefly stated, as a result of the massive growth in funding, it has been possible for a large number of professionals to earn a respectable income committing themselves to full-time activities related to social movements." By supporting VISTA and the Peace Corps, for example, the government trained future activists who went on to community work and collective dissent. Wilson (1973, 203) cites a study that concludes that "the single most important source of organizers of the Massachusetts Welfare Rights Organization, and thus of the confrontations with government officials that it staged, were VISTA workers paid out of government funds."[20]
- Government may provide nonfinancial resources to a dissident group, for example, information, equipment, training, and organizational skills. Zald and McCarthy (1979c, 243) contend that such assistance is common:

> In the early stages, many modern movement organizations in the United States draw upon the resources of the government, both federal and local. Typically, such aid develops either through pre-existing social relations between government functionaries and movement participants or through formal programs designed to benefit or develop information concerning some segment of the population that the social movement participants claim to represent.

Nonfinancial resources can be critical to a group's success. Farm workers organized in 1965-72, whereas they had failed to organize in 1946-52, because the government (federal, state, local, police, judiciary) and various liberal organizations (labor) shifted their support to the workers and away from the growers (Jenkins and Perrow 1977).

- Government may mandate and subsidize participation in dissident-sponsored government programs. The U.S. government, for example, mandated "maximum feasible participation" of the poor in the community action programs of the War on Poverty (Nagel 1987, 145–46; Moynihan 1969). The U.S. government paid neighborhood organizers of community development programs to get people involved in such programs. The social participation grants to community groups working on housing, crime, and poverty problems include grants made by the Community Action Program of the Office of Economic Opportunity, the Model Cities Agency, Volunteers in Service to America, and the Legal Service Corporation.[21]

In sum, states can act as patrons of dissident groups in numerous ways. The government, if it is willing, can even provide resources to the relatively poor and powerless that make it possible for them to fight government itself (Levi 1988, 20; Piven and Cloward 1971, chap. 10; Levi 1974; Walker 1983, 404).

Government patronage of collective dissent is highly significant. First, it affects dissident group strategies. Dissidents attempt to get government to reduce the costs and increase the benefits of dissent; they might, for example, devote a great deal of their resources to lobbying for the repeal of repressive legislation.[22]

Second, the politics surrounding government patronage of collective dissent is intense. On the state's side, many members of government will object to such sponsorship. On the dissident's side, many dissident groups in a dissident movement will compete (sect. 6.4.2) for the patronage. As Oberschall (1979, 51) argues,

> The authorities' recognition of some, but not other, leaders and factions as legitimate spokesmen of the challenger may itself become an additional issue in the conflict, and sometimes becomes *the* principal issue. This was the case with the seating of the National Liberation Front of South Vietnam with the North Vietnamese and inclusion of the South Vietnam Government with the United States in the Paris peace negotiations.

Third, given all these possible forms of government patronage, the state turns out to have a crucial influence on the extent of protest and rebellion. The state is the organization with the greatest capacity to solve the CA problem of the dissidents. State sanctioned, subsidized, supervised, and supported CA is thus a very significant phenomenon in collective dissent. More than anyone or anything else, it is government that shapes the Rebel's Dilemma (sect. 10.2.2).[23]

The final consequence follows subtly from the others: because regimes can be so valuable to dissidents, dissidents are dependent on regimes. Regimes thus influence dissident organizations through their impact on the pathologies of collective dissent (sect. 8.2). The result is that government patronage imposes many structural uniformities on dissident groups. A version of Eckstein's (1969) congruence hypothesis is therefore almost certainly true: all dissident groups in a nation tend to look alike. Russia, China, and Vietnam, for example, had many conspiratorial organizations and secret societies before their respective revolutions.

### 6.2.3.3. Nonstate Domestic Actors as Allies

Besides the military and the state, dissidents may draw upon other possible domestic patrons. Rebels can either convert proregime forces to their side or nudge neutral actors into their corner (Gurr 1970, 278). The United Farm Workers, who organized a grape boycott in the United States, offer an example of how many different nongovernmental domestic actors can become allies of a dissident group:

> Students had to contribute time to picketing grocery stores and shipping terminals; Catholic Churches and labor unions had to donate office space for boycott houses; Railway Union members had to identify "scab" shipments for boycott pickets; Teamsters had to refuse to handle "hot cargo"; Butchers' union members had to call sympathy strikes when grocery managers continued to stock "scab" products; political candidates and elected officials had to endorse the boycott. (Jenkins and Perrow 1977, 264)

More generally, support can come from other dissident groups, labor unions, churches, the wealthy, criminal networks, and the media.

One dissident group can be an important potential domestic supporter of another dissident group. A coalition between two dissident groups in the same or a related dissident movement may enable both to overcome their Rebel's Dilemmas (sect. 6.4). Given that the level of collective dissent is a function of the possibility for the transference of resources among dissident groups, dissident groups seek cooperation with one another (Zald and McCarthy 1979a, 14-15). A Communist party, for example, can be an important ally. Cross-national evidence (Hibbs 1973, 126-27) suggests that as the size of Communist parties increase, at least one form of collective dissent (protest) increases.

A labor union can also be an important ally. One union will often subsidize the efforts of another union with money and organization. The AFL, for example, helped organize local craft unions and steelworkers supported mine workers (Wilson 1973, chap. 7). More generally, as the size of dissident labor unions increases, collective dissent also increases. Gurr (1970, 284) provides cross-national support for this proposition.

A church (sect. 5.2.3.1) is another potential domestic ally of dissident groups. The Catholic Church has sponsored urban, labor, and democratic movements in Latin America, Spain, and Poland (Levine and Mainwaring 1989). Liberal churches and/or liberal church officials (as well as liberal labor unions) in the United States have sponsored civil rights organizations (McAdam 1982; Morris 1984) and farm workers (Jenkins 1985, 127).

The wealthy are another potential domestic ally of dissident groups. Business leaders, groups, and organizations have sometimes supported rebels. Examples here are legion.[24]

The criminal class, too, is a potential domestic supporter of dissidents. Terrorist movements have been assisted by the criminal underworld. Guerrilla movements, such as the Shining Path in Peru, have linkages with drug dealers (McClintock 1984, 81).

And finally, the media are a potential domestic ally of a dissident group. Publicity is necessary for mobilizing public opinion and gaining the support of reference elites and third parties.

### 6.2.3.4. External Actors as Allies

A dissident group can ally with a foreign power. Crozier (1960, 130) argues that "at a given moment external help and advice can be of great importance to the rebels." Gurr (1970, 269) goes even further: "The greatest potential increment to dissident military capacity is external support."

Foreign assistance to dissidents takes many forms. Verbal support includes diplomatic recognition and assistance; meetings and visits; alliances, agreements, and treaties; and statements of solidarity coupled with threats to opponents. Nonmilitary support includes technical assistance and training, as well as material and financial aid (e.g., loans, bank arrangements). Military support includes arms and supplies; technical assistance, logistic planning, and advice given by military advisers and/or mercenaries in either an official or unofficial status; provision of training facilities, military bases, and areas of refuge (i.e., safe havens and sanctuary given to leadership and/or rank and file); limited combat support, in the form of blockades, patrols, and surveillance; and major combat support, in the form of military units used on a large scale.

External support in its various forms is widespread.[25] So numerous are the examples that "it is consequently difficult to see the logic behind the

argument that revolutionary movements are best described as 'internal wars'"
(Greene 1990, 129).

External support for dissidents and regimes, moreover, influences the
character and outcome of collective dissent. The United States-Soviet Union
conflict, for example, had a major impact on domestic conflicts during the
cold war era. Several more precise propositions may be offered.

Foreign involvement in domestic conflicts increases the extent of those
conflicts, as more people become involved on both sides. The key factor is
that foreign resources can reduce the costs of participation (sect. 3.2). Foreign involvement also increases the intensity of collective dissent. For one
thing, it provokes the external support of regimes, and vice versa. A revolutionary state's patronage of revolution is both a cause and a consequence of a
status quo power's patronage of counterrevolution. The result of this external
patronage race is to make a domestic conflict more deadly. Foreign involvement also increases the duration of these conflicts. As Gurr (1970, 298)
argues, "Dissidents . . . who have foreign sources of supplies are better able
to conduct protracted insurgencies than those who do not." Hence, "foreign
support is likely to be dysfunctional for terminating internal wars. It is much
more likely to increase the scale of conflict to a high level and to prolong it"
(Gurr 1970, 270). Cross-national evidence supports the idea that foreign support engenders more extensive, intensive, and prolonged civil strife (Gurr
1970, 270; Gurr and Lichbach 1979).

External patronage also affects the dissidents' tactics. With increased
resources, demands can be escalated and violence becomes feasible, so collective dissent is likely to move from protest to rebellion and then to revolution.

Finally, foreign involvement in domestic conflicts affects who wins.
Gurr (1970, 270) suggests that "if external support rapidly increases dissident coercive control well beyond that of the regime, dissidents will win
quickly and the magnitude of violence will be low." Hence, as the foreign
support of a dissident group (regime) increases, the probability that the dissidents (regime) will win increases. The impact of external support on the
outcome of domestic conflicts is best demonstrated in those cases where foreign support is terminated. If the regime can cut off the dissidents' foreign
patrons, rebellion may be fatally weakened. For example, the Yugoslavs cut
off assistance to the Greek Communists. The Communists were subsequently
defeated. Likewise, if dissidents can cut off the regime's foreign patrons,
rebellion may be dramatically encouraged. For example, the United States
cut off aid to Batista, Samoza, Marcos, and the Shah. Each dictator subsequently fell.

Both dissidents and regimes are aware of the impact that foreign support
can have on the extent, intensity, duration, form, and outcome of collective

dissent. Both are therefore concerned with the international connections among like-minded regimes and dissidents. Dissidents (the state) thus often claim that the state (dissidents) is part of an international conspiracy and therefore they too need external support.

### 6.2.4. What if Patrons Help Dissidents

First, the upside: patrons lower the costs and/or raise the benefits of CA. They therefore enable collective dissent to be more widespread, enduring, deadly, destructive — and successful. There is a good deal of scholarly support for this proposition,[26] especially with respect to peasant rebellions,[27] worker movements,[28] and interest groups.[29]

Now, the downside: outside support often means outside control — whoever pays the piper calls the tune. A sponsor, therefore, can exercise great influence over his or her benefactors, forcing a dissident group to adapt its policies to his or her demands. Dissidents who accept outside support thus risk becoming their patrons' puppets.

Examples of the cooptation of dissidents are legion. First, states coopt working classes. The political culmination of labor aristocrats (Zolberg 1986, 432) is working-class tories (Nordlinger 1967). The alternative is also possible: "German parties, having no opportunity to wield power, remained doctrinaire parties of principled world views" (Weber 1946, 46). Second, the middle class coopts peasants. Eckstein (1989, 49) cites the cases of Mexico and Bolivia and argues that "for the laboring classes, alliances with the middle classes typically are a mixed blessing. In the long run, the middle class tends to dominate multiclass movements for its own ends." Third, one-party dominant systems coopt their opponents. The MPR in Mexico has often coopted opposition groups. The PCI and DC in Italy coopted movements of landless peasants in the late 1940s (Tarrow 1989, 41). Fourth, colonial powers coopt natives. Subordinate group members become administrators, tax collectors, clerks, and police. Fifth, Communist parties coopt other Communist parties, as in the case of Stalin who controlled numerous Communist movements.

When the patron is the state, the outside control problem becomes especially acute. Edelman (1971, 180) suggests that "when discontented people organize or are helped to do so by the government, the organization is more likely to facilitate cooptation to the existing order than to foment or catalyze violent demonstrations or rebellion against it." Governments, in other words, often try to coopt dissidents into participating in legal political struggles. For example, the U. S. government institutionalized conflicts in various agencies in the hope that the locus of conflict would shift to those agencies. Part of the incorporation of the working class in the United States involved institutionalized bargaining between labor and management, supervised by executive agencies. Zald and McCarthy (1979c, 244) offer some additional examples: "An expanded Civil Rights Division in the Justice Department, the Equal Employment Opportunity Commission, the U.S. Commission on Civil Rights, and various sections and officers in other governmental agencies at the federal level certainly have the effect of shifting the ground and tactics of contention for organizations and individuals interested in pursuing civil rights change goals." Rebels entered these institutionalized struggles for power and became less doctrinaire. As they got close to power, they compromised.

Cooptation can sometimes be so complete that the upside — dissident group mobilization and success — never occurs. The more a dissident group becomes a puppet of some sponsor, the less its appeal, as its credibility weakens in the eyes of its constituents. This is the dissident's Patronage Dilemma: the weaker a dissident group, the more patronage it needs; the more patronage a dissident group receives, the weaker it becomes. Nationalistic appeals, for example, are diminished when a domestic group obtains foreign support. Dissidents can be tainted by external links because the government can accuse them of treason. Thus, South African sponsorship rendered UNITA, in Angola, and RENAMO, in Mozambique, illegitimate.

Minority groups face a particularly acute Patronage Dilemma. Coopted minority dissident groups are particularly susceptible to diminished appeal. Major group involvement in minority group movements, as allies or coalition partners, inevitably alienates some members of the minority. Minority-group dissidents come to believe, for example, that the majority group's monopoly of skills has enabled it to occupy too many powerful positions in the group. Marx and Useem (1971, 90) refer to "the privileged position of the outsiders." Some minority-group dissidents, moreover, come to see themselves as more committed to their cause than the outside majority group. Ideological disagreements between a moderate majority faction and an extreme minority faction are inevitable. To avoid splitting the group and diminishing its appeal, minority groups often advocate self-help solutions. And some dissident entrepreneurs reject the *Locate Principals or Patrons* solution to the Rebel's Dilemma altogether. The black power wing of the U.S. civil rights movement of the 1960s argued, for example, that blacks should depend more on black community organizing and less on white allies.

Minority group self-help solutions have inherent limitations, however. Minorities come up against an elementary problem of democratic politics: they cannot change government policies when they remain in the minority. Minorities must form coalitions and alliances to become majorities. Blacks in the United States, for example, have had some success at changing local policies when they have constituted a majority. When they have been a minority, they have had more difficulty changing national policies — *except* in coalition with whites (McAdam 1982, 179–80). The working class, too, has also always been a political and numerical minority in democracies and has had to form class alliances (Przeworski 1985a, 23–29).

In sum, dissidents reap decreasing marginal benefits and pay increasing marginal costs for external patronage. A little bit probably helps, a great deal probably hurts, so the tradeoffs between self-reliance and external support must be carefully weighed. A grass-roots strategy often begets a resource-poor dissident group, but one that is highly committed to the cause. A sugar-daddy strategy, by contrast, often begets a resource-rich dissident group, but the sponsors are often less committed to the dissidents' cause. The grass-roots strategy cannot work for a relatively poor and powerless constituency and the sugar-daddy strategy cannot work for a relatively militant group.

Part of this dispute over the patronage of collective dissent can be resolved if one recognizes a distinction between direct and indirect patronage. On the basis of historical studies in western Europe, Tilly (1986, 391) argues that there has probably been a decrease in the importance of *direct* patronage of dissident movements.[30] The political contests of 1650–1850 were highly patronaged. Dissidents tended to prevail upon local power-holders to convey grievances and disputes to powerful outsiders. The political struggles of 1850 and onwards were autonomous in character. Dissidents tended to challenge rivals or authorities, even national authorities and their representatives, directly rather than through local patrons. Tilly thus maintains that collective dissent from the eighteenth to the twentieth centuries is characterized by a steady decline in the use of patrons and the rise of direct challenges to rivals or authorities.

Patronage, however, has not disappeared entirely. Indeed, *indirect* patronage has grown more important. Tilly (1986) identifies a new feature in twentieth century social movements — disputes that normally involve two parties (e.g., workers and employers) are addressed to third parties (e.g., the public, the state) by means of actions that dramatize the conflict and attract the sympathetic attention of the media. One suspects that dissident entrepreneurs may find it relatively easy to reject direct patronage, but will find it relatively more difficult to reject in toto indirect external support.

### 6.3. Reorganize

The third solution to the Rebel's Dilemma based on the hierarchy approach involves reorganizing the dissident group. To this end, dissidents may form an exclusionary club (sect. 6.3.1), shape an efficacious group (sect. 6.3.2), or decentralize to a federal group structure (sect. 6.3.3).

### 6.3.1. Become Clubbish: Form an Exclusionary Club

A dissident group can in the first instance reorganize by limiting its size. It can establish clear boundaries and control its membership. A dissident group that excludes some dissidents is said to form an exclusionary club (Buchanan 1965). The free-rider problem is therefore overcome through two forms of exclusion: both club goods and selective incentives (sect. 6.5.3) motivate participation.

The success of the dissidents' efforts to form an exclusionary club depends on the costs of exclusion. These costs, in turn, are closely related to the costs of monitoring dissidents (sect. 6.5.2). As the costs of exclusion decrease, the possibility of collective dissent clubs, and hence of collective dissent itself, increases.

Assuming a dissident group can control entry and exit (sect. 3.11), what influences its calculations of its optimal size? What sorts of factors lead some dissident groups to remain small and restrictive and others to become large and catch-all (Kirchheimer 1966)? Given that dissident groups try to solve their Rebel's Dilemmas, entrepreneurs calculate how the number of dissidents in their group affects the costs and benefits of individual participation in collective dissent. These calculations, however, are not straightforward. Hence, there is much debate in the CA literature about whether large groups are less able than are small groups to provide themselves with PGs (Lichbach forthcoming, chap. 6). This debate parallels the confusion in the conflict literature over the relationship between group size and collective dissent.

On the theoretical level, some work anticipates Olson (1965) and suggests that smaller groups have greater levels of collective dissent than larger groups. Elitist theorists, such as Pareto ([1920] 1980), Mosca (1939), and Michels ([1919] 1962), tend to emphasize that minorities are more cohesive than majorities (Wrong 1988, 217). Weber ([1924] 1968, 1414) also recognizes the advantage of small numbers: "Political action is always determined by the 'principle of small numbers,' that means, the superior political maneuverability of small leading groups. In mass states, this caesarist element is ineradicable." Simmel (1955, 96) argues similarly, suggesting that the smaller a conflict group, or the more it represents a minority position in some system, the greater its internal solidarity will be. Lasswell and Kaplan (1950, 105–7) also point to the weakness of large numbers, as does Hume (cited in Olson 1965, 33–34, fn. 53).

This argument explains why political stability is more common than collective dissent. While regimes often are able to solve their CA problem due to their small numbers, oppositions often are unable to solve their CA problem due to their large numbers. Weber ([1924] 1968, 952) sets out the reasoning:

> The ruling minority can quickly reach understanding among its members; it is thus able at any time quickly to initiate that rationally organized action which is necessary to preserve its position of power. Consequently it can easily squelch any action of the masses . . . threatening its power as long as the opponents have not created the same kind of organization for the planned direction of their own struggle for domination. Another benefit of the small number is the ease of secrecy as to the intentions and resolutions of the rulers and the state of their information; the larger the circle grows, the more difficult or improbable it becomes to guard such secrets.

Group size thus determines the outcome of team competition between regime and opposition (sect. 3.10.1.2). Once again, dissidents are the losers.

Taking the opposite position are those who suggest that larger groups will have greater levels of collective dissent. Lipset (1971b, xvi), for example, argues that as the number of sympathizers increases, CA increases. For one thing, as group size increases, someone is likely to have an intense grievance and hence to be a zealot (sect. 3.1). Moreover, larger groups can better sustain a bandwagon (sect. 4.1.2). And finally, with a large group even a relatively small part of a dissident community can be enough of a critical mass to support a particular event, episode, or campaign of collective dissent (sect. 6.3.2).

Not only theoretical controversy, but also empirical disagreement characterizes discussion of the group size-collective dissent nexus. Some evidence seems to suggest that smaller groups will have greater levels of collective dissent,[31] other evidence suggests the opposite point,[32] and some evidence is mixed.[33]

No less than the academics, dissident group leaders themselves hold contradictory beliefs about the efficacy of group size. Sometimes dissident entrepreneurs believe that as group size increases, so do the chances for successfully achieving a PG — even though the free-rider ratio might increase. As groups increase in size, that is, factions coalesce, resources are pooled, and, with increasing returns to scale, a victory occurs. Moreover, large groups can better risk fights with a regime. As DeNardo (1985) argues, there is "power in numbers." Kahn (1982, 2) suggests that "the power of a lot of people working together is enough to make changes where one person can do very little." Even Olson (1990, 13) recognizes that efforts to limit the size of a dissident group will probably doom its efforts: "A group of people small enough to engage readily in collective action usually won't have enough strength to overthrow any effective government." Those dissident entrepreneurs who hold to this view seek to form as large a dissident organization as possible. They are not only after activists, so their organizations will not set strict membership requirements. Examples include many ethnic associations with nominal membership fees.

Sometimes dissident entrepreneurs believe to the contrary that as group size increases, both the free-rider ratio and the chances of success decrease — concerted action becomes difficult, while factionalism and mutinies become common. And they hold that the support of only a minority of a population is needed to sustain collective dissent. Moreover, large groups raise the costs of mutual monitoring. The need for extensive information reduces the chances that the *Use Tit-For-Tat* solution (sect. 5.1.2) will work. T. E. Lawrence thus boasted "that he could make a rebellion with 2 percent of the population active and 98 percent 'passively sympathetic'" (Desai and Eckstein 1990, 443). Luttwak (1968, 23) argues that rebel inaction is sometimes really a form of action: "As the coup will not usually represent a threat to most of the élite, the choice is between the great dangers of opposition and the safety of inaction. All that is required in order to support the coup is, simply, to do nothing — and this is what will usually be done." The power of small groups was also on the mind of a religious protest leader in Israel (quoted in Wolfsfeld 1988, 141) who said, "We start with an axiom: the smaller the group the more aggressive it is because in a large organized structure, like a party, there is a careful decision-making process. A small group can organize within a few hours with signs and shouting in (what is called) a spontaneous protest." Dissident entrepreneurs who share these views seek to form as small a dissident organization as possible. Their organizations set strict membership requirements and seek activists as members. Examples include Communist parties and terrorist groups.[34]

It is not always clear, one must conclude, when large numbers are either necessary and/or sufficient for group success. Some dissident entrepreneurs, in some times and places, are relatively unconcerned about free riding and hence adopt a *Become Small* (or *Large*) solution to the Rebel's Dilemma; other entrepreneurs, in other times and places, care a great deal about free riding and hence adopt a *Become Large* (or *Small*) solution.

Deciding on an optimal group size is therefore a difficult choice. Free riders, moreover, pose different kinds of problems, depending upon group size. Hence, dissident entrepreneurs adapt their free rider avoidance tactics to the size of the group.

First, the larger the dissident group, the more risk averse its tactics (sect. 3.9). Whereas small groups are risk prone because they are less likely to achieve the PG they seek, large groups are more reluctant to take risks. Compare terrorist groups with Communist parties.

Second, the larger the dissident group, the simpler the type of collective dissent it chooses to mobilize. A large membership imposes severe information requirements on groups that rely on individually contributed sanctions against free riding — the more one needs to know about every person in a dissident group in order to sustain CA, the harder it is to maintain CA. In large groups, dissent is thus limited to simple boycotts, strikes, and demonstrations. The importance of simplicity to collective dissent is considered in section 6.5.2.

Third, the larger the dissident group, the more likely it is to be organized. Large groups do not have the luxury that small groups often do of relying on Market solutions to the Rebel's Dilemma. They must rely instead on Hierarchy solutions.[35] Large groups that want to organize complex forms of collective dissent, and thus counter the problem noted above, are especially prone to organization.

Finally, the larger the dissident group, the more likely it is to organize mass movements rather than clandestine elite conspiracies. As Gurr (1970, 279) puts it, "If followers are few in number, conspiratorial activity is more feasible than revolutionary activity." Secret societies, revolutionary cells, and terrorist organizations tend to be clandestine and small. Protest movements, dissident trade unions, and guerrilla movements tend to be large and open. Alinsky (1971, 126) illustrates this point with a rather fatuous analogy:

> For an elementary illustration of tactics, take parts of your face as the point of reference: your eyes, your ears and your nose. First the eyes; if you have organized a vast, mass-based people's organization, you can parade it visually before your enemy and openly show your power. Second, the ears; if your organization is small in numbers, then do what Gideon did: conceal the members in the dark but raise a din and clamor that will make the listener believe that your organization numbers more than it does. Third, the nose; if your organization is too tiny even for noise, stink up the place.

Not surprisingly, large groups are based on the power of numbers (DeNardo 1985).

In sum, large and small groups face special CA problems. Dissident entrepreneurs set the size of their organization and then deal with the consequences of that decision in terms of the approaches they adopt to solving the Rebel's Dilemma.

### 6.3.2. Become Effective: Shape an Efficacious Group

Perhaps the most important issue facing a dissident entrepreneur is the nature of the dissident group itself. Section 10.2.1 explores the social origins of dissident groups. Now consider their political origins (see also sects. 5.2.3.4, and 10.1).

Recall that a dissident group was defined in section 1.3 as a group seeking a single PG. This abstract formulation masks disunity. Members of a dissident group pursue a diverse, even if interrelated set of PGs. For example, men and women, merchants and workers, young and old, and majority and minority ethnics can all be part of a nationalist coalition. Moreover, there is no such thing as a "natural" dissident group drawing upon a definite population with a fixed set of beliefs. A dissident group is an "empty slot" (Esping-Anderson 1985, 27) that *could* result from virtually any cleavage or aspect of the socioeconomic and cultural division of labor. This means that a constituency must be put together and that group goals, ideologies, and grievances require definition. In short, a group identity must be politically constructed.[36]

This is not an easy task. Dissidents do not necessarily agree on objectives and methods. Rebels debate means (i.e., solutions to the Rebel's Dilemma) because rebellions are not inevitable. Dissident groups thus may split over strategy, which often pits moderates, pragmatists, and reformists against radicals, purists, and revolutionaries. Radicals often prefer direct action to negotiation, for three reasons. They believe that difficult challenges provide the largest payoffs, if successful (sect. 3.1). They are natural risk takers (sect. 3.9). And finally because they seek challenge and inspiration, they may take costs to be benefits (sect. 4.2.1). Reformers often prefer negotiation to direct action for the opposite reasons.[37]

That there are many ways to overcome the CA problem suggests that dissident entrepreneurs have to make many choices in trying to forge a group identity.[38] CA theories and Downs's (1957, chap. 2) insights can help clarify these choices: dissident leaders formulate policies to overcome regimes, rather than overcome regimes to formulate policies. In short, dissident entrepreneurs have strong instrumental concerns about issues and ideology. Moreover, "As organizations grow, the question of choosing issues becomes more strategic" (Kahn 1982, 93).

Dissident entrepreneurs are thus not interested in group identity, per se. They seek to shape the PG sought by their group, such that the Rebel's Dilemma is minimized and an efficacious (i.e., winning) coalition results.

It follows that dissident entrepreneurs attempt to manufacture grievances to maximize their following. In fact, they can always find grievances against which people can rebel. No political, social, or economic institution is "perfect" or even "perfectible." All political, social, and economic institutions create winners and losers. Hence, a Say's Law of Collective Dissent holds:[39] the supply of dissident entrepreneurs creates its own demand for dissent. Professional revolutionaries create the demand for revolution by supplying grievances.[40] Grievances, in this sense, are not necessary for collective dissent: a creative entrepreneur can construct the grievances required to foment collective dissent. Given that preference falsification assures that grievances, identities, and common goals remain unknown, public discourse is altered. Kuran (forthcoming) draws out the many implications of this point.

We can begin to understand how entrepreneurs create, intensify, and focus grievances by borrowing Riker's (1982, chap. 9; also see Schattschneider 1960, chap. 4) basic insight: losers must somehow upset the current issue space and create a new and more favorable distribution of preferences. Dissident entrepreneurs use at least five strategies to shape the PG issue space.

First, leaders can enlarge the scope of grievances (Schattschneider 1960, chap. 4). Dissident entrepreneurs can start with a small issue and then add larger issues to the political discourse in hopes of radicalizing new members.

A second strategy is bait and switch. Leaders can mobilize the members of a dissident group on the basis of a preexisting grievance and then convince them of the importance of redressing another related grievance.[41]

A third strategy is to promise a PG that cannot be delivered. Dissident entrepreneurs try to convince their followers that anything and everything is possible. They intensify grievances by promising radical change even when they know they cannot deliver it immediately. Only through such promises are they likely to mobilize their followers. Would rank-and-file Jacobins have labored so long simply to trade Louis XVI for Napoleon? Would rank-and-file Bolsheviks have worked so hard just to exchange Nicholas II for Stalin?

Dissident entrepreneurs can, in addition, generate a new issue that divides the existing winning (i.e., dominant) coalition. They can try to "cut issues" so as to divide enemies and unify friends.[42] As Clark and Wilson (1961, 146) put it, "The continual problem of purposive organizations is to select ends that divide the association from other groups in the community without at the same time dividing the association's members from one another." Entrepreneurs thus attempt to redefine the political agenda by setting the terms of political debate. They introduce new dimensions into politics and thereby politicize social cleavages. A group identity is thus forged in opposition to the group's enemy (sect. 3.10.2). Riker (1982, chap. 9) offers an example of how this approach culminated in the U.S. Civil War.

Finally, although dissident entrepreneurs recognize that a dissident group cannot be all things to all people, it can certainly try to be. Rudé (1959, 63) reports the following of the early days of the French Revolution: "In October, *bourgeoisie* and *peuple* acted together in a common cause [capture and hold the king], the former were actuated solely by the desire to defeat the plots of the aristocracy, whereas the latter, while sharing this desire, were equally concerned with the scarcity of bread." The German Revolution of 1848–50 offers another example. For the bourgeoisie, revolution meant a parliament. For the guilds, revolution meant the return of corporations. For the peasants, revolution meant land. Alliances therefore can be formed of dissidents interested in diverse issues. Mutual exchange agreements can be forged (sect. 5.1.3). One of the tasks of entrepreneurship then is to show how that this is possible — that a single PG can actually provide different types of individual benefits.

Kahn (1982, 119, emphasis in original) puts this last strategy into particularly compelling language: "When you talk with people, one of the questions they often ask is 'what are *you* going to do for *me*?'" He maintains that

> one of the ways of approaching groups in order to get them to participate in an issue is defining the issue in such a way that it appeals to their organizational self-interests. Sometimes this is referred to in organizing talk as "cutting an issue." Take the issue of public transportation. Senior citizen groups could support it because most seniors either don't drive or don't have the income to own cars and they need access to services throughout the city. Unions might support it because it would mean additional jobs in construction and in operating an improved mass transit system. Women's organizations might support it if there were particular guarantees written into the program to assure safety at night for women using it. Minority community organizations might support a plan which assured services between their neighborhood and places where jobs were available . . . An organization of the handicapped might be interested in special provisions for access. (Kahn 1982, 279–80)

He concludes that "the process of putting allies together around an issue involves more than presenting the issue to each organization in a way that makes the members appreciate its value. It also requires dealing with each organization around what its members see as their self-interest and what they want as their price for supporting the issue" (Kahn 1982, 279).

In sum, the second basic principle of dissident reorganization is to build an efficacious group by manufacturing grievances and hence shaping the demand for collective dissent. Dissident entrepreneurs manipulate the issue space so as to find a PG that best solves the Rebel's Dilemma. Hence, at the same time the CA problem is being solved, the collectivity is being built.

### 6.3.3. Become Decentralized: Create a Federal Structure

Dissident groups may be either centralized or decentralized. Reorganizing by decentralizing and adopting a federal group structure, is another possible solution to the Rebel's Dilemma.

Decentralization affects levels of participation. A dissident group with a decentralized structure can mount greater levels of collective dissent against a regime. For example, a single hierarchically organized dissident group with fifty potential contributors will have more free riders than a dissident group composed of ten subgroups with five potential contributors apiece.[43] There is some evidence for this claim.[44]

A dissident group may decentralize in one of two ways. In fission, or decentralization from above, entrepreneurs divide their followers into subsets. Communist parties are hierarchically organized into cells, terrorist groups into squads, and guerrilla armies into platoons. The CCF, a Canadian farmers' organization, is an example of a protest organization that decentralized in this manner (Lipset 1971a, 252). A related decentralization strategy is to divide issues into subsets. Hence, entrepreneurs break abstract national questions into concrete local ones (Popkin 1988, 10).

The second approach to decentralization is fusion, or decentralization from below. Dissident organizations often begin as small-scale dissident groups that grow when local organizations form coalitions and coalesce into a national organization. Examples of mergers, trusts, and conglomerates among dissident groups are legion — American labor unions, for example (Booth 1978). Dissident groups also become large by using local organizations as building blocks. Starting with concrete local issues that offer an immediate payoff, they extract a "revolutionary" surplus from their supporters and then use the surplus to build a national organization to tackle abstract projects. Where the federal group solution is implemented by fusing locally based dissident groups, preexisting organizations obviously play an important part (sect. 5.2.3).

There is a counterargument to the federalism idea. Some maintain that centrally organized dissident groups are able to mount greater levels of collective dissent than can those that are decentrally organized. Decentralization increases bargaining costs and thus slows decision making; it also raises the possibility of unstable outcomes. Hence, the greater the decentralization within a dissident group, the greater the chance of unsuccessful CA. Autocratic dissident groups are therefore better able to sustain collective dissent than democratic ones. This controversy will be considered once again when I explore the consequences of competition among dissident organizations (sect. 6.4.4) and the intended consequences of dissident organization (sect. 8.1).

## 6.4. Increase Team Competition among Allies

Completely harmonious relations among fellow dissidents and among dissident organizations are rare. Individual rebels often compete over jobs and selective incentives (sect. 6.5.3). Among dissident organizations, splinter movements enter and exit antiregime coalitions, making for frequent defections; dissident movements form and reform, group and regroup, making policy squabbles common; and dissident factions challenge the existing hierarchy of dissident groups, making leadership changes routine.[45]

Section 6.4.1 considers the various forms that competition among dissidents take. Section 6.4.2 explores the causes, section 6.4.3 the courses, and section 6.4.4 the consequences of team competition.

## 6.4.1. The Forms of Competition

Dissidents may be organized into three subsets: an antiregime coalition consists of various dissident movements, a dissident movement consists of various dissident groups, and a dissident group consists of various factions. Competition among dissidents takes place at all three levels.[46]

At the highest level, revolutions often result from an antiregime coalition composed of diverse social and political movements. Conflict and cooperation among these movements is explored in section 7.2.1.

As for competition among dissident groups within a dissident movement, dissident ideologies compete in the "idea market" (Willer and Zollschan 1964, 140) and dissident organizations compete in the "recruitment market." Potential dissidents may thus choose from among the many moderate and radical social movement organizations within a social movement industry (Zald and McCarthy 1990). For example, various dissident groups competed in the civil rights movement in the United States during the 1960s. Blacks could choose among groups that advocated revolutionary terrorism and/or political separatism (e.g., Deacons for Defense, Black Muslims, Black Panthers), direct action and/or quasi-revolutionary change (e.g., SCLC, CORE, SNCC), and nonviolent protest and/or social integration (e.g., NAACP, Urban League).

Finally, competition occurs within a dissident group. Some dissident organizations consist of a large number of essentially separate suborganizations, or factions. Often each faction is a relatively feeble and transitory clique of dissidents based on personalistic, familial, and clientelistic ties. When such factions are linked together into an alliance, referred to here as a dissident group, the central organization can coordinate each clique's activities only very indirectly. Dissident factions, moreover, often devote more time to internal maneuvering against one another than to mobilizing people against the regime. Cliques are thus really constellations of elites. As Huntington (1968, 415) puts it, there is "interminable maneuvering in which the actors continually shift partners and antagonists without ever enlarging the number of participants." Factions therefore become "a means of linking . . . to other political activists, not a means of linking political activists to the masses" (1968, 414). There are many examples of such factionalized dissident groups.[47]

### 6.4.2. The Causes of Competition

A revolutionary's worst enemy is often another revolutionary. A revolutionary's best friend, however, is also often another revolutionary. An important question thus arises. Dissident movements within an antiregime coalition, dissident groups within a dissident movement, and dissident factions within a dissident group differ in goals and tactics and also compete for resources and leadership. Some dissident groups within a dissident movement, for example, tend to be cooperative (e.g., environmentalists), some conflictual (e.g., Marxists), and others mixed (e.g., civil rights groups in the United States during the 1960s). Under what conditions does cooperation emerge?

This is yet another instance of Olson's Problem. Cooperation among organizations is simply a different manifestation of the PG–PD game than one finds in cooperation among individuals.[48] To explain cooperation among the former, therefore, one has only to appeal to the many solutions to the Rebel's Dilemma proposed here.

*Increase Benefits.* The distribution of benefits, preferences, and goals (sect. 3.1) among dissidents explains conflict and cooperation among dissident organizations. As the dissidents' heterogeneity (sect. 5.2.2) with respect to preferences increases, organizational divisions increase. Dissidents could oppose a dissident group on a single issue and split the organization. Lipset (1971b, 94) offers the example of black students in the United States during the 1960s. He notes that while they were general!y more antiwar than white students, they participated at much lower rates in the white-dominated movement.

Realizing that splitting a dissident group will severely reduce its strength, regimes attempt to factionalize rebels. A favorite strategy is government accommodation of particular dissidents. By increasing benefits to some rebels, but not all, regimes appeal to the moderate rank and file and  coopt centrist leaders. If successful, the strategy isolates the radicals and plays off factions of the dissident group against one another.

*Reduce Costs.* Regimes also try to factionalize dissident groups and splinter dissident movements by imposing costs (sect. 3.2) on the group. One repressive-type strategy is to infiltrate the dissident group with agent provocateurs (Marx 1974, 403). This increases mutual suspicion and promotes factionalization.

*Increase Resources.* Dissident resources (sect. 3.3) also influence competition among dissident groups. A large resource base permits dissident organizations to coexist: as resources increase, the number of competing dissident associations increases (McCarthy and Zald 1977, 1225). The heterogeneity (sect. 5.2.2) of resources is also a cause of factions. Dissidents are disparate in their possession of skills. An extensive division of labor within a dissident group often creates an unwieldy and faction-prone coalition.

*Improve the Productivity of Tactics.* The distribution of preferences among dissident groups over methods (sect. 3.4) also accounts for conflict and cooperation among dissident organizations.[49] Dissidents split over both strategy and tactics.

*Increase the Probability of Winning.* Both success and failure (sect. 3.6) can generate divisions among dissident organizations. When dissidents are unsuccessful, challenges to leadership arise and these challenges increase the likelihood of internal factionalism. Hence, as a dissident group's failures mount, the number of competing dissident factions increases. As dissidents begin to succeed, however, new rival entrepreneurs enter the dissident movement (sect. 6.1.2), which increases the opportunities for new dissident groups to form. When victory appears inevitable, leaders of a dissident group become willing to damage the group by factionalizing it. Hence, as the dissident group approaches victory, the number of competing dissident factions increases. Finally, after the dissidents win, they often part company, as submerged differences reemerge with a vengeance. The CA problem may, in fact, worsen: rebels are often less united in government than in opposition.[50]

*Increase Team Competition between Regime and Opposition.* The team competition between regime and opposition (sect. 3.10.1.2) influences the factionalization of the dissidents. Consider a conflict's extent, intensity, and duration.

Extensive regime-opposition conflict draws everyone in the nation into the political struggle. All must take sides. This increase in the size of the dissident community, or increase in the demand for dissident organizations, leads to an increase in the demand for dissident entrepreneurs (sect. 6.1.2). Reciprocally, as the number of potential dissidents and dissident entrepreneurs increases, the number of dissident organizations also increase.

The intensity of conflict also affects factionalism, as in Turner's (1986, 174) rephrasing of a proposition by Coser (1956): "The more violent or intense is the conflict . . . the more conflict promotes structural and ideological solidarity among members of each conflict party." Intense conflicts therefore lead to dissident groups characterized by well-defined boundaries, internal cohesion, centralization, intolerance of deviation, and high levels of group identification and mobilized resources (sect. 3.10.3). Thus, as the conflict with the regime intensifies, the number of competing dissident factions and organizations decreases. Violent government repression therefore reduces the factionalization of the opposition.

Lastly, the duration of conflict matters. Long-lasting conflicts intensify the differences between hard-liners and soft-liners. Relatively enduring conflicts thus beget a large number of competing dissident organizations.

*Use Tit-For-Tat.* Cooperation among dissident organizations may be based on informal or formal agreements and contracts such as Tit-For-Tat (sect. 5.1.2). For example, dissident entrepreneurs can sometimes satisfy everyone by dividing up the recruitment market and differentiating their products. Instead of competing for resources and people, they can create autonomous, distinctive, and assured niches. During the 1960s, for instance, the NAACP and the Urban League served different clienteles and carried out different activities (Wilson 1973, 264).

*Locate Principals or Patrons.* Competition among patrons (sect. 6.2) for the support of a dissident group often factionalizes the group, creating a serious problem: as patronage increases, the number of competing dissident factions increases. Patrons who are members of another dissident group tend to induce particularly high levels of factionalism. Hence, a dissident organization created as an offshoot of another dissident organization tends to have more intense internal conflicts than one that arises by its own efforts. Foreign patrons also tend to induce particularly high levels of factionalism and bitter debates. The search for external support by dissidents often results in the "internalization" of "international cleavages" (Tarrow 1989, 39). The Sino-Soviet competition in Africa during the mid-1960s led to numerous divided national liberation movements, for example ZAPU against ZANU in Rhodesia, ANC against PAC in South Africa, SWAPO against SWANO in Namibia, and MPLA against FLNA/UNITA in Angola.

*Become Clubbish: Form an Exclusionary Club.* The nature of the PG sought by dissidents affects the extent of conflict among dissident organizations. If the good is nonrival in consumption, unanimous (inclusive) coalitions form and factionalism is reduced. If the good sought by dissidents is rival in consumption (i.e., it is a club good; sect. 6.3.1), minimum winning (exclusive) coalitions form and factionalism is increased.

*Administer Selective Incentives and Disincentives.* Many of a dissident group's internal squabbles concern the spoils, rather than the rationale, of victory. Disputes involve, that is, the distribution of selective incentives (sect. 6.5.3). Poorer dissidents, for example, might favor a distribution based on absolute dollars whereas wealthier dissidents might prefer a percentage-based distribution. As selective incentives increase, the number of competing dissident organizations increases.

In sum, several solutions to the Rebel's Dilemma can explain conflict and cooperation among dissident movements within an antiregime coalition, among dissident groups within a dissident movement, and among dissident factions within a dissident group. Another important issue in conflict studies may therefore be understood within the CA framework.

### 6.4.3. The Courses of Competition

The competition for followers among dissident organizations can be as intense as the competition among regimes and oppositions. Consider how dissident groups compete for followers and how followers choose among dissident groups.

Each dissident group in a dissident movement wishes to carve out its own distinctive niche by "product differentiation" of its goals and tactics. Tarrow (1989) identifies a common pattern with the example of how the New Left grew out of the Old Left in Italy.

- The Old Left, including Communist parties, labor unions, and student organizations, attempts to place an issue on the political agenda. It may, for example, organize a protest demonstration against United States involvement in Vietnam.
- The New Left seizes the opportunity of the officially organized protest demonstration to outflank its older ally. Radicals outflank moderates by outbidding them and accusing them of caving in to the establishment. They charge the moderates with being impotent, ineffective, and inept, and then put forth more extreme means and ends. This is a typical political strategy identified by Riker (1982; also see sect. 6.3.2): new dissident groups try to make inroads in an existing political market by dividing an older dissident group that currently has a monopoly over a constituency. Toward this end, new groups generate a divisive issue (e.g., lack of internal democracy within the existing party, disarming the police) to split their opponents. Dividing the existing policy "space" in new ways allows them the "space" for mobilization.
- New more radical dissident factions subsequently form within the traditional moderate dissident group. Often incited by outsiders, youth groups, for example, press their leadership to go beyond the party's traditional actions.
- Initially, the Old Left benefits from the upsurge of protest: "Unions were riding the tiger of working-class revolt" (Tarrow 1989, 241). Eventually, however, the Old Left is beset by factionalism. As Tarrow

(1989, 163) puts it, the Old Left is "torn between encouraging disorder and defending reaction," as competition with new dissident organizations increases. The Old Left thus finds itself in exactly the same political situation in which it once put the state. It must now figure out how to incorporate new political forces into an aging political organization.

Now consider this process from the dissidents' point of view. In choosing among the various groups, rank-and-file dissidents are likely to donate to two or more competing dissident groups that supply substitutable PGs rather than to only one organization. They rarely solve their optimization problem by specializing and adopting corner solutions. Dissidents contribute to multiple causes, because by splitting their contribution between several groups, they stand to gain concessions from all sides (Frohlich, Oppenheimer, and Young 1971, 94). Hence, when multiple dissident groups compete for support, dissidents donate in order to affect PG programs, not merely to attain a PG (Frohlich, Oppenheimer, and Young 1971, 95). Dissidents thus donate in order to counter fellow dissidents who seek a similar, but somewhat distinct, PG. For example, a person on the far left may donate to a group on the far left in order to counter a more moderate leftist group. Another reason for splitting one's contribution among many dissident groups is that it is often uncertain which one will win. As victory approaches, donations increase and people increasingly try to affect the PG platform of the eventual winner (Frohlich, Oppenheimer, and Young 1971, 107). A final reason for splitting contributions is that the Tit-For-Tat solution is based on mobilizing preexisting organizations (sect. 5.2.3). Such organizations tend to involve dissidents in several interrelated causes.

Two types of dissidents — those who are well-endowed and activists — are particularly amenable to such reasoning. The better endowed a dissident, the more likely he or she is to participate in many dissident groups. The more an individual participates in collective dissent, the more widely dispersed among dissident groups the participation is likely to be. Well-endowed activists thus tends to have multiple memberships in many related dissident groups rather than one membership in a single dissident group.

In deciding which groups to join, dissidents choose those that solve their Rebel's Dilemma in particularly attractive ways. The key issue is expected benefits. Hence, groups with the greatest probability of winning (sect. 3.6) will attract many supporters, as in the case offered by Popkin (1988): the Viet Minh outrecruited other organizations because it convinced potential contributors that their contributions would be most effective if channeled through the Viet Minh. In addition, groups with more and better selective incentives (sect. 6.5.3) will gain many supporters. Again Popkin (1979, 200): "Whereas both the Cao Dai and the Catholics could offer welfare and protection against the divide-and-conquer tactics of landlords and notables, only the Cao Dai could immediately offer positions of power and influence to local bonzes, administrators, and teachers; the Catholics could offer such positions only after a decade or more of special training, at best."

### 6.4.4. The Consequences of Competition

How does competition among allied dissident organizations affect the Rebel's Dilemma? Will intense competition among numerous dissident organizations who pursue essentially the same cause encourage CA and facilitate group success? Will a dissident group's monopoly status, on the other hand, stimulate collective dissent and allow victory? Unfortunately, the analytic answer provided by the PG literature is inconclusive about whether or not competition among suppliers of a PG increases the level of CA and hence the supply of the PG (Oakland 1987, 509; Lichbach forthcoming, chap. 6). This uncertainty is mirrored in the conflict literature.

Those who emphasize the malevolence of competition argue that divided dissident movements mount less collective dissent than do nondivided movements. There are several reasons for this.[51] If economies of scale exist, competition increases costs (sect. 3.2). Moreover, competition provides dissidents with better (i.e., more realistic) information about the probabilities of victory (sect. 3.6) and of making a difference (sect. 3.7). The major problem with competition, however, is that it produces ineffective dissidents; that is, their probability of victory is lower than that of nonfactionalized ones. One reason that competition lowers the chances of winning is that a single powerful dissident group is in a better position to influence the regime. Factions decrease the dissidents' abilities to bargain with the regime, which makes it more difficult to institutionalize the conflict so as to provide at least some of the PG sought by the dissidents.[52] Government, for example, tends to coopt only those dissident groups that can deliver their supporters (sect. 6.2.3.2). Another reason that a single dissident group is more likely to succeed is that a central authority settles the question of who gets the spoils of victory. By contrast, factionalized dissident groups typically fail because some of their efforts are directed toward winning the postconflict struggle rather than toward winning the conflict itself.

Those who take the opposite approach and emphasize the benevolence of competition observe that competition among dissident organizations tends towards outbidding and outflanking, which radicalizes dissident goals and means. Tarrow (1989, 19) suggests that such political maneuvering occurs when CA is expanding: "During the upward curve of the cycle, as mass participation increases, there is creative experimentation and testing of the limits of mass participation. As established groups, such as trade unions, parties and interest associations, enter the movement sector, they monopolize conventional mass forms of action, producing incentives for others to use more and disruptive forms of mass action to outflank them." Tarrow (1989, 19) also suggests that such political maneuvering occurs when CA is contracting: "As participation declines later in the cycle, the mass base for both moderate and confrontational mass actions begins to shrink. New groups who try to enter the movement sector can only gain space there by adopting more radical forms of action that do not depend on a mass base."

Supporters of competition maintain that this radicalization of collective dissent encourages protest and rebellion by competitive team mobilization (sect. 3.10.1.1): radicals stimulate moderates, and vice versa, as each seeks to become the dominant force. This has been the dynamic between the New Left (e.g., students, extraparliamentary opposition) and the Old Left (e.g., the Communist Party). Tarrow (1989, 221) suggests that "with time, and especially as mobilization ceases to expand, movement organizations increasingly compete for supporters by using new and more innovative forms of collective action. The process of competitive tactical innovation . . . is a major force in the diffusion of protest." He (1989, 184–86) also suggests that such a process increased strikes in Italy: "Though the organizational strength of the strike wave was largely due to the growing unification among the three major union confederations, its disruptiveness was in part the result of competition between them . . . the most disruptive strikes were those in which competing organizations participated" (Tarrow 1989, 92).

Supporters of competition also maintain that the radicalization of collective dissent facilitates victory and hence increases estimates of the probability of winning (sect. 3.6). Extremists present regimes with the stick, moderates offer the carrot. Dissidents need both to succeed, as Blalock (1989, 186) indicates:

> There may be certain advantages of diversity and a rather loose control system, however, especially when the more moderate members of the party of concern, here X, can make a convincing argument that they have little or no control over their extremist members. The potential actions of such extremists can, for example, be used as a bargaining weapon akin to Schelling's (1960, 36; 1966, chap. 2) notion of commitment. If X's leaders can convince Y that, if Y were to sustain its present polices or modify them in the wrong direction, then extremist elements among X's members could no longer be controlled, then X is in effect

telling Y than the onus of the risk-taking is on Y, not X. At the same time, because of their perceived or actual weakness in controlling their own extremists, moderate leaders of X are communicating to Y that they, themselves, cannot be held accountable for the action of their own deviant members.

Hence, the presence of extremists encourages patrons (sect. 6.2) to support moderates and encourages governments to recognize the moderates as the "reasonable" and "legitimate" spokespeople for a group and hence the appropriate bargaining partners (McAdam, McCarthy, and Zald 1988, 718; also see sect. 6.2.3.2). Paradoxically, therefore, the presence of radicals strengthens the hand of the moderates. Freeman (1979, 183) suggests that "the most viable movement is one with several organizations that can play different roles and pursue different strategic possibilities."

In sum, there is disagreement about the impact of the rivalry among dissidents on the levels and outcomes of protest and rebellion. Further empirical study is needed to determine how the competition of dissident movements within an antiregime coalition, dissident groups within a dissident movement, and dissident factions within a dissident group affects the level and success of collective dissent.

## 6.5. Impose, Monitor, and Enforce Agreements

Entrepreneurial agents solve the CA problem of their rank-and-file principals by coercing contributions to the PG. The last solution to the Rebel's Dilemma based on hierarchy thus entails imposing agreements on the members of a dissident group (sect. 6.5.1), monitoring defections from those agreements (sect. 6.5.2), and administering selective incentives (sect. 6.5.3) and disincentives (sect. 6.5.4) to reward compliance and sanction noncompliance with the agreements.

### 6.5.1. Impose Agreements

Dissident entrepreneurs can propose cost-sharing agreements to their followers. The rank and file, however, has a hard time agreeing on burden sharing. Everyone attempts to minimize his or her costs and all try to contribute less than their fair share. Each, that is, hides his or her wealth and pleads poverty. The result is a struggle over the costs of CA. Popkin (1979, 41) found this to be the case among Vietnamese peasants: "One would expect that peasants, instead of readily agreeing about need, ability to pay, or standards, would hide their wealth from common scrutiny and thus make it even more difficult to decide who is better off and able to pay a larger share of the load. Indeed, there is commonly a 'cult of poverty.'"

The dilemma of CA, of course, is that cost-sharing agreements are in the interests of all dissidents. Rebels therefore like the idea of having such arrangements imposed upon them. Although dissident entrepreneurs can successfully impose taxes, most such attempts fail. Zagorin (1982b, 61) reports on one of the successes: the Huguenots taxed themselves voluntarily to sustain their struggle against the French king.

What types of agreements are successful? Dissident entrepreneurs employ four types of institutions to successfully tax their rank and file. Some dissident groups create elaborate taxing bodies. Dissident neighborhood organizations, for example, use a variety of constitutional forms to apportion costs among their members. Small municipal corporations, home-owners' organizations, and condo agreements often include compulsory membership requirements (e.g, a closed shop) and membership dues. Some of these taxing bodies use less than the rule of unanimity to allocate costs (e.g., all persons living in a certain area are automatically subject to the association; see Rich 1980, 580).

A second kind of institution is the tax collector: dissidents designate one of themselves to collect contributions. Hobsbawm and Rudé (1968, 67) observe "that the one formal officer we find most frequently among the riotous mobs was such a 'treasurer.'" They report that "a 'purser' or 'treasurer' was often appointed [in protest movements of rural laborers] 'to take charge of the contributions.'"

A third alternative is the tax farmer: dissidents engage someone who specializes in collecting taxes. Sometimes these tax farmers receive a percentage of the taxes collected, for example, ten percent of all revenues. At other times, the tax collector receives a fixed fee for his or her services, for example, a commission for each member recruited. Thompson (1966, 538) cites some evidence on this point, reporting that working-class dissidents often paid those who collected subscriptions or contributions. In turning to tax farmers, the dissidents' behavior parallels that of the state. Sixteenth-century French monarchs are a case in point (Tilly 1986, 128).

The fourth institution used to impose cost-sharing arrangements is the government. Again, the state is the greatest patron of collective dissent (sect. 6.2.3.2). Lipset (1971a, 102) reports the example of dissident farmers in the Saskatchewan Wheat Pool, who asked "the provincial government to enact legislation requiring that all grain grown in Saskatchewan be marketed through one Pool, subject to the approval of two-thirds of the farmers in a special referendum."

## 6.5.2. Monitor Defections

No agreement is self-enforcing. In fact, dissidents often try to evade contract-mandated contributions to cost-sharing arrangements, forcing entrepreneurs to monitor rank-and-file compliance. Moreover, as monitoring defections from cost-sharing compacts becomes less costly and more effective, collective dissent increases. Popkin (1988, 19) thus argues that "whether an action is self-enforcing depends on how easy it is to monitor free riders and communicate their identity to others." Leaders adopt several approaches to minimizing monitoring costs.

*Simplicity.* Simple rules are easy to apply and monitor.[53] Simplicity frequently implies standardization. Dissident entrepreneurs often use simple and easy to apply formulas as seniority rules and equal contributions.[54] Simplicity also frequently implies uniform taxes. Uniform membership dues often involve a requirement to contribute, taking turns contributing, or a lottery. Simplicity also frequently implies the use of fixed, rather than variable, returns. Popkin (1979, 48) observes that "the insurance systems common in peasant society, such as labor exchanges or burial societies, have fixed returns. In these groups each peasant receives exactly what he has put into the scheme." Simplicity also frequently implies constant rules; the rules cannot be easily adjusted. Finally, simplicity frequently implies the use of exact, rather than equivalent, exchanges. Strict reciprocity, as Popkin (1979, 48) notes, is the norm in peasant societies: "Peasant exchange groups are generally for exact exchange — labor for labor, part of someone's pig this month for part of someone else's pig next month, or money for money — rather than exchanges where contributions and payouts involve agreeing on a rate of exchange on more than one item."

Simple cost sharing rules produce two results. One is unfairness. A regressive tax system, for example, does not equate the marginal costs and benefits of CA. No matter. When Pareto optimality cannot be achieved, rebels will accept a Pareto improvement. If a first-best solution is unobtainable, in other words, a second-best solution becomes attractive: "In developing decentralized collective actions the obvious approach, the approach which requires the least information, usually dominates the most fair approach because it requires less communication, less organization and less sanctioning than more complicated and more fair arrangements" (Popkin 1988, 19). Dissidents thus choose an enforceable over a fair tax code and hence taxes are regressive (Popkin 1979, 42).

Another consequence of simplicity is that a common solution to the PG problem mentioned in the theoretical literature, the use of preference revelation devices (e.g., market demand for complementary private goods; Cornes and Sandler 1986, 252–55), finds few practical applications. It is theoretically possible for an entrepreneur to use a preference revelation mechanism to discover the preferences that should be input into an agreement. Actually conducting such experiments, gathering such information, and imposing such agreements is anything but simple. Practical dissidents reject the theorists' impractical suggestions.

*Subdivision.* Monitoring costs can be minimized by a type of federal group solution (sect. 6.3.3) that might be referred to as "divide and tax." Dissident entrepreneurs subdivide their rank and file and impose a cost-sharing arrangement. When Luddites "collected money to promote their cause" (Rudé 1964, 83), they organized dues collection by dividing their sympathizers into groups and then collecting taxes from each group (Thompson 1966). Tilly (1964, 332–33) offers an example from the Vendée: "The apportionment of a quota of armed men from the top down, so that first an area was assigned its number, and then the number was subdivided among the communities of the area, mimicked the methods by which taxes had always been collected and the perennial procedures for military conscription." Thus, he (1964, 332) reports that "when the generals needed a certain number of men for an action, they apportioned the number among the communities in the areas, and each commandant filled his quota."

*Visible standards of need.* If costs are not to be apportioned and benefits are not to be provided equally, then dissidents must find some way of defining "need." Since standards based on abstract or complex conceptions of "justice" and "fairness" are hard to apply and generate a great deal of squabbling, dissident entrepreneurs avoid them. Standards based on highly visible, publicly demonstrable, and universally accepted conceptions of "justice" and "fairness" are more readily defensible and noncontroversial. They may only be proxies for what entrepreneurs would really like to measure, but they are often adopted. Popkin (1979, 47) reports as follows: "Given the problems of conflicting standards and claims of need, however, very little welfare is available for indigents or persons with bad harvests, and village welfare or subsidies are allocated mainly to the aged, widowed, or orphaned — specific categories with claims that are clear, hard to exaggerate, and clearly not due to laziness or mismanagement." Moreover, "Both rich and poor can expect to benefit from such rules of exemption during the life cycle" (Popkin 1979, 41).[55]

*Visible actions.* Ambiguity and uncertainty about their followers' contributions limits the ability of entrepreneurs to monitor rank-and-file compliance with cost-sharing arrangements. As Hechter (1988, 162) suggests, contributions must be observable if contracts are to work. Widely known and traceable dissident contributions are therefore likely to facilitate CA. For example, Popkin (1979, 256) argues that agreements among peasants to not pay high interest rates were easy to evade and, thus, hard to monitor. Detecting whether individuals secretly paid the high rate was nearly impossible.[56]

Dissident entrepreneurs use several approaches to increase the visibility of their followers' actions. One is to make contributions well defined. Contracts must make everyone's obligations absolutely clear and specific (Popkin 1979, 47–48). Another approach is to limit privacy so as to be able to measure contributions (Hechter 1988, 51). Yet another approach is to establish a division of labor so as to make contributions identifiable and traceable: "An appropriately detailed division of labour and allotment of tasks in PD-structured situations might serve as a means of social control which ensures cooperation" (Ullmann-Margalit 1977, 49). A final approach is to bring all dissidents together at the same time. Suppose draining a swamp in a peasant village requires the collective effort of thirty people. It is harder to verify contributions if each participant contributes one day a month than if all participants work on the thirtieth day, and each cleans one part. The latter strategy is thus a dissident entrepreneur's preferred option.

*Visible members.* In order to reduce monitoring costs, dissident entrepreneurs also try to increase the visibility of their followers. Such visibility is a function of the entrepreneur's ability to distinguish members from outsiders. Hechter (1988, 162) suggests that "monitoring costs are minimized by arrangements that . . . allow for minimal errors of interpretation" about who is a member and who is a nonmember of a group. Rogowski (1974, 82) suggests that groups with stigmata have a low cost of identifying members and are thus particularly easy to monitor.

One factor affecting the entrepreneur's ability to distinguish group members from outsiders is the cost of entry into the group. Lasswell and Kaplan (1950, 35) suggest that "the *permeability* of a group is the ease with which a person can become a participant." The other factor affecting the entrepreneur's ability to distinguish group members from outsiders is the cost of exit out of the group. Groups with stigmata also typically have a high cost of conversion, or of changing group affiliation. When exit (sect. 3.11) is an attractive option, CA is hard to sustain: "If everybody who disliked his social position or group affiliation could easily move to another or more preferred one, there would be no incentive for collective action . . . The more permanently one is tied to some position or social group, the stronger is the incentive to combine with those who hold similar positions to promote one's own interests" (Weede 1985, 48). Hechter (1988, 162) thus suggests that "sanctioning costs are lowered to the degree that groups . . . institute high exit costs."

Dissident groups whose members are readily identifiable because they face a high cost for conversion into and out of the dissident community are therefore highly effective at mobilizing collective dissent. Rogowski (1974, 82–86) and Rogowski and Wasserspring (1971, 21) emphasize the mobilization potential of segmented, distinct, and stigmatized social groups. For example, it is easier to mobilize ethnic than class action. Gurr (1968; Gurr and Duvall 1973; Gurr and Lichbach 1979) has indeed found that nations with distinctive minority communities are particularly prone to rebellion.

*Mutual monitoring.* Hechter (1988, 162) argues that "monitoring costs are minimized by arrangements that . . . give members an incentive to monitor each other." Mutual monitoring is, in turn, facilitated by Community:

"Exchanges and contracts are likely . . . to involve people who are in constant contact so that giving and return can be balanced at short intervals and the advantages to each partner easily assessed" (Colson 1974, 50). The factors identified in section 5.2 as facilitating community are thus relevant here. Dissident entrepreneurs, of course, do not rely solely on Community. They encourage their followers to monitor each others' actions. One approach is to reward informants. Leaders pay followers who tell of other followers' noncompliance. Another approach is to hire spies. Leaders pay outsiders to become insiders who reveal members' noncompliance. The Puritans' initiation of "holy watching" and Lenin's advocacy of informing on friends (Walzer 1979, 38–39), which survived in the Communist world after Lenin, are examples of this strategy.

*Collective punishment.* Another strategy used by dissident entrepreneurs to achieve economies in monitoring costs is the employment of collective punishment. Hechter (1988, 153) argues that this approach reduces monitoring costs for two reasons: "First the monitoring agent need not know the identity of the culprit, but merely the group to which that person belongs. Second, this kind of punishment provides all members with an incentive to monitor each other informally." Group punishment is often used by dissidents during guerrilla wars.[57]

*Clubs.* Ostrom (1990, 222, fn. 16) refers to "span-of-control problems" in which "the cost of monitoring increases with the size and diversity of a firm or a state." Given that monitoring costs are obviously lower in small groups, dissident entrepreneurs might well prefer smaller to larger organizations. A dissident entrepreneur's final strategy for lowering monitoring costs is thus to limit the number of dissidents that have to be monitored. One expects, moreover, that the more complex the agreement, the fewer the number of people able to participate. The question of optimal group size is considered in section 6.3.1.

In sum, dissident entrepreneurs adopt several strategies to minimize monitoring costs. They simplify cost-sharing rules, subdivide their rank and file, use visible standards of need, increase the visibility of actions, increase the visibility of members, encourage mutual monitoring, use collective punishment, and limit the size of the group.[58] These strategies are an important part of a rebel entrepreneur's attempt to overcome the Rebel's Dilemma as well as to control the political allegiances of his or her followers (Levi 1981, 457).[59]

## 6.5.3. Administer Selective Incentives

One of the first solutions that Olson (1965) offered to the CA problem was selective incentives. I first consider the argument (sect. 6.5.3.1) and evidence (sect. 6.5.3.2) behind the selective incentives idea. I then explore the causes (sect. 6.5.3.3) and consequences (sect. 6.5.3.4) of selective incentives.

### 6.5.3.1. The Argument: The Centrality of Selective Incentives

The CA research program teaches us that situations characterized by collectively supplied benefits and privately incurred costs will not motivate participation in collective endeavors. The CA problem thus arises whenever the goods sought by rebels are exclusively public; in such situations additional incentives are needed to move dissidents to action. The idea is simple, elegant, and yet powerful. Each dissident's self-interest prevents CA and thus works against the dissidents. Why cannot each dissident's self-interest promote CA and thus work for the dissidents?

The Rebel's Dilemma can therefore be overcome and collective dissent made likely under three conditions. First, some benefits are available to dissidents as private goods. Second, dissidents are treated differently depending on whether or not they choose to participate in CA. Third, the specific rule for differentially awarding the private goods is that a special reward is contingent upon actual participation. Participation, in short, is a necessary and sufficient condition for receiving an extra private good: extra benefits flow to rebels who join CA; a rebel who does not join receives no extra benefits. Selective incentives are consequently defined as private goods or side payments that are offered to dissidents who participate in collective dissent. Rebels thus receive multiple payoffs for their contributions: both divisible and excludable private goods as well as nondivisible and nonexcludable public goods.

Selective incentives often successfully motivate CA. Public television appeals to everyone's altruism but offers magazines and tote bags only to its contributors. Museums and zoos appeal to everyone's civic spirit but offer free admissions and newsletters and gift shop discounts only to their members. The Nature Conservancy appeals to everyone's consciousness about the environment but offers guided tours of its wilderness preserves only to its hundred-dollar sponsors. Farmers' groups appeal to the plight of all farmers but provide agricultural assistance only to their supporters. Finally, the American Political Science Association purports to represent all political scientists but offers journal subscriptions and discounted convention admission only to its members.

Students of collective dissent thus recognize several truths. Dissidents are often unconcerned with broad purposes, philosophical systems, political theories, and revolutionary organizations (Edwards 1927, 71–74). Dissident grievances are mostly specific and well defined, limited and local. Rebel actions are correspondingly designed to satisfy material self-interests. Thus, dissidents join a dissident group or participate in collective dissent because of particularistic benefits.

Perhaps the most forceful proponent of the self-interest principle in collective dissent is Saul Alinsky, the famous American community organizer.[60] Alinsky (1946, 225) argues that "in the world as it is, man moves primarily because of self-interest." He continues:

> Political realists see the world as it is: an arena of power politics moved primarily by perceived immediate self-interests, where morality is rhetorical rationale for expedient action and self-interest . . . In this world, laws are written for the lofty aim of "the common good" and then acted out in life on the basis of the common greed . . . It is a world not of angels but of angles, where men speak of moral principles but act on power principles. (Alinsky 1971, 12–13).

Alinsky draws the lesson for dissident entrepreneurs:

> *In a mass organization, you can't go outside of people's actual experience. I've been asked, for example, why I never talk to a Catholic priest or a Protestant minister or a rabbi in terms of the Judeo-Christian ethic or the Ten Commandments or the Sermon on the Mount. I never talk in those terms. Instead I approach them on the basis of their own self-interest, the welfare of their church, even its physical property.* (Alinsky 1946, xvi, emphasis in original)

*6.5.3.2. The Evidence: Rebels Seek Selective Incentives*
These claims that dissidents quite often pursue their pecuniary self-interests are supported by compelling evidence. Selective incentives appear in all forms of collective dissent. Because of the intense scholarly resistance against the idea that dissidents can be bought (Lichbach forthcoming, chap. 6), I consider this evidence in detail.

*Everyday forms of peasant resistance.* Everyday forms of peasant resistance, or "weapons of the weak" (Scott 1985), are subtle Brechtian or Schweweikan forms of resistance. Peasants often resort to these strategies when they are involved in a conflict with either landlords (for example, over wages, equipment, labor, rents, irrigation systems) or the state (for example, over taxes, the forced contribution of property, the forced requisition of labor). The strategies thus originate in perceived exploitation and injustice.

In using everyday forms of peasant resistance, a peasant seeks to manipulate the system so as to maximize his or her material benefits. Colburn (1989b, 194) refers to "the rational but self-interested maximization of welfare by the rural poor" and suggests (1989a, x) that peasants "work the system to their maximum advantage (or minimum disadvantage, per Hobsbawm), ever testing the limits of the possible." He (1989, 177) thus maintains that "the weapons of the weak are employed whenever and to the extent conditions permit the augmentation of meager earnings, the seizure of any possible windfall, and — most importantly — for deflating exactions." Esman (1989, 222) agrees: "These weapons [of everyday forms of peasant resistance] can be material or ideological. If material, they attempt to reduce the labor required or increase the share of the produce available to workers, their families, and kinfolk." Many everyday forms of peasant resistance involve the receipt of material selective incentives by peasants.

One type of resistance that offers selective incentives is called "opportunism" or "moral hazard" in the economics literature (Eggertsson 1990, 44–45). These techniques involve such activities as shirking, foot dragging, slacking off, working slowly, showing up late, and taking long lunch breaks. The techniques also include false compliance, dissimulation, and feigned ignorance or stupidity. A final set of techniques entails the careless performance of one's obligations. Examples here are eating grain instead of feeding it to livestock and using the worst tools or animals for manor work.

Robbery, another everyday form of peasant resistance, offers obvious selective incentives. Examples of pilfering landlord's property include the theft of wood in forests and poaching (for example, fish from ponds, game birds, and fruit from trees; Kochanowicz 1989, 44–51). Economic crimes against government are smuggling, selling animals that are soon to be requisitioned, illegal land clearing, underreporting of land, misreporting of crop patterns and yields, making exaggerated claims about the theft and spoilage of grain, and hoarding grain for personal consumption (e.g., Brown 1989, 106). The more dramatic examples here involve squatting and land invasions.

Exit (sect. 3.11) is a final everyday form of peasant resistance that holds out the promise of selective incentives. Via desertion, defection, flight, and escape the peasant hopes to trade a situation that offers few material rewards for a situation that offers greater material advantage.

*Unorganized rural protest.* Some peasant protests and rebellions occur without the assistance of preexisting dissident organizations.[61] Many of these forms, including peasant jacqueries, food riots, social banditry, charivari, and preindustrial crowds, involve selective incentives.

Peasant jacqueries often involve three types of activities. Peasants invade, seize, and occupy commons (for example, forests). They also seize private property. And they renounce manorial dues and burn manor houses, with the goal of destroying deeds and archives that show who owes payments to whom.[62] For example, Landsberger and Landsberger (1974, 120) report that peasants tried to tear up and burn manor rolls, court records, and tax lists during the English Rising of 1381: "It seems correct to say that there was not a county where any action occurred — and this included a majority of counties of England — where manor rolls and court records were not destroyed. Almost everywhere sheriffs, escheators, justices and tax collectors were

sought out for threats and actual punishment." Even though all peasant jacqueries involve some type of plunder, what peasants want most is land; once
they think they have obtained title to their land, their jacqueries grind to a
halt. Pettee ([1938] 1971, 62) thus reports that "after the burning of the cha-
teaux in France by the peasants, for instance, destroying the documents on
which many of the privileges and abuses rested, the peasants never again had
as much interest in the revolution, and never really supported the Jacobins."

Food riots are another type of unorganized rural protest in which private
motives lie behind dissident actions. During food riots peasants would often
assemble, seize grain, and sell it at a "fair" price. Rudé (1959, 23) thus refers
to food riots as "*taxation populaire*" or "unofficial price control by collective
action." Sometimes peasants did not compensate owners. Mousnier (1970,
43) reports, for example, that food riots among peasants in seventeenth century France sometimes involved "taking bread without paying for it." The
key point is that regardless of the particular type of food riot, food is available *only* to the riot's participants.

Social banditry is a third form of unorganized rural protest in which
peasants seek both public goods and private profit (Hobsbawm 1959, chap.
2). In cases in which social bandits lack political ambition and emphasize
private goods at the expense of public goods, social banditry shades into robbery. The roving bandit is one example. Mousnier (1970, 283) provides an
instance from seventeenth century Ming China: "It seems that we see here
men in arms to assuage their hunger by way of plunder. They appear all to
have become professional bandits." The fixed bandit is another example.
Mafia-type organized robbery is the classic instance here. Sometimes, however, social bandits become more than mere plunderers and assume the role
of Robin Hoods, agents of social protest who right social wrongs. Such
social banditry succeeds, as Mousnier (1970, 179) reports of seventeenth
century Russia, because of implicit and explicit support by peasants:

> The people saw these bandits as their avengers. The peasants refused to
> cooperate with the authorities against them. On the contrary, they acted
> as guides and scouts for the bandits, gave them shelter, and harbored
> their stolen goods for them. Sometimes an *ataman* would become a
> popular hero, and his legendary feats would be celebrated in songs.

Charivari, or "rough music," was an eighteenth century form of unorganized rural protest. Peasants typically directed it against public officials who
engaged in familial, sexual, or marital immorality. It, too, had a selective
incentive component. Tilly (1986, 30) reports that people "assemble in the
street outside a house; make a racket with songs, shouts, and improvised
instruments such as saucepans and washtubs; require a payoff from the people inside the house; then leave if and when the people pay."

Preindustrial crowds are a final form of unorganized rural protest in which peasants are often motivated by selective incentives. Rudé (1964, 253) notes "the remarkable single-mindedness and discriminating purposefulness of [preindustrial] crowds, even those whose actions appear to be most spontaneous." Preindustrial rioters thus chose their targets and means carefully, for example, breaking into prisons to find and release supporters, leaders, and friends.

Even more interestingly, pre-industrial crowds often rioted because someone, often dissident entrepreneurs, paid them to riot. They were hired, in effect, as mercenary revolutionaries (Ireland 1967, 52). While such compensation might horrify contemporary academics, Rudé (1964, 227) argues that preindustrial crowds fully expected to be rewarded for their efforts: "The people might also expect to be paid for carrying out such duties" even if they "were morally justified and performed as a kind of solemn public duty." Rudé (1964, 217) points out that "this was the well known device of 'raising a Mob.'" Several instances of preindustrial rioters who were directly compensated for their activities come to mind. Hilton (1973, 217) offers an example from the English Rising of 1381: "James of Bedingfield, a leading rebel, put pressure on the chief constable of Hoxne Hundred in Suffolk to muster ten archers from the hundred to join the rebels, at the usual rate of pay, sixpence a day." Many late eighteenth-century British mobs were "hired bands operating on behalf of external interests" (Thompson 1966, 75). One example is the antirevolutionary "Church and King" mobs, employed from 1792 onward, to terrorize wealthy and prominent English Jacobins and reformers. These mobs were operated legally, financed by local authorities and conservative gentry. They were provided, in effect, with "bribery and license" (Thompson 1966, 113). Rudé (1964, 162, 227) offers three additional examples from England: "Swing" rioters charged a fee for smashing threshing machines; Gordon rioters collected money "for the poor mob," and the Rebecca riots eventually "tended to fall into the hands of professionals who charged a price for their services." Thompson (1966, 574) offers a final English example: "According to other accounts, this final phase of Luddism was the work of one or two almost 'professional' gangs, who were called in and paid by lodges of the now-underground union." Examples also come from eighteenth century France. The September "massacrers" in Paris, for example, "exacted their reward in terms of food and drink" (Rudé 1964, 227). Brown (1989, 101) reports a modern version of this very direct use of selective incentives: Egyptian villagers hired professional criminals to do the dirty work of rebelling for them.

*Organized rural rebellion.* Some peasant struggles involve fairly high levels of organization. One form of organized rural rebellion involves guerrilla armies. It is well known that guerrillas are often brigands and pirates.

Thus, peasants involved in guerrilla armies often seek booty, captives, and the other spoils of victory. Peasant armies are often built around raiding, marauding, looting, pillaging, and sacking. The more organized the peasants, it often seems, the more organized the plunder and the rape, as in the following examples.

One example of demobilization comes from the Philippines. Walton (1984, 48) reports the following of a peasant rebellion in the Philippines: "In December 1897 Aguinaldo [the rebel] agreed to peace terms that included vague words about reform and the very concrete sum of 800,000 pesos, which Aguinaldo and nineteen associates took with them in exile to Hong Kong."

China provides a set of examples of mobilization. In Ming China, pecuniary motives and demands were behind provincial revolts against imperial clansmen, bondservant revolts against masters, and tenant revolts against lords (Tong 1991, chap. 7). In twentieth century China, warlords established patron-client ties, or a patronage system, to distribute plunder. A warlord thus "had to reward his officer-followers with money, weapons, and control over military units and territorial subbases" (Skocpol 1979, 237).

Russia provides a final set of examples. Mousnier (1970, 189) offers the following description of the "second Dmitri," part of the Russian peasant revolts during the "Time of Troubles" in the seventeenth century: "A small army gathered round the 'Brigand' — Cossacks, vagrants, and Polish adventurers, including several generals. These men had no illusion about their figurehead, any more then he had himself: the Brigand was an impostor whom his soldiers treated as a joke. The name of Dmitri provided cover for the operations of a band of plunderers." The importance of plunder to Russian peasant upheavals is also well documented by Avrich (1972, 156) who writes that "Bulavin appealed to all who wanted to 'roam the open fields with him, to go in style, to drink sweetly, eat well, and ride fine horses.'" He (1972, 232) reports of one peasant upheaval that "the overriding objective was plunder . . . In every Volga district granaries were pillaged, livestock confiscated, timber felled, and manor houses burned. In the towns treasuries were emptied and the houses of the wealthy sacked and burned." Of another occasion, Avrich (1972, 89) recounts that "officials were executed, property confiscated, prisons thrown open, taxes abolished, records [title deeds] destroyed." Avrich (1972, 87) indicates further that "once in [their] hands the towns were given over to plunder. The rebels confiscated the government treasury and pillaged the cathedral, the bazaars, and the houses of the wealthy. Then, in accordance with Cossack tradition, they divided up the loot in equal shares."

Rural guerrilla warfare thus mixes politics and crime, the pursuit of public goods and the pursuit of private goods, the search for social justice and the search for selective incentives. Avrich concludes that in less developed states the line between robbery and rebellion, the brigand and the dissident, is a fine one. He (1972, 70) points to "that peculiar mixture of brigandage and revolt which characterized all the mass uprisings of the period. At first, to be sure, piracy was the dominant element; but the latent forces of insurrection were not slow to emerge, so that what began chiefly as an expedition of plunder was soon to be transformed into a full-scale social rebellion."

The modern form of organized rural rebellion involves revolutionary organizations. Selective incentives may be found here too.[63] Goodwin and Skocpol (1989, 494) maintain that

> in addition to collective goods, revolutionary organizations may also offer selective incentives to encourage participation in various sorts of activities, particularly dangerous ones like actual guerrilla warfare. Such incentives for actual or potential cadres and fighters, and their families, may include extra tax or rent reductions or an additional increment of land beyond that allocated to supporters in general. In any event, it is the ongoing provision of such collective and selective goods, not ideological conversion in the abstract, that has played the principal role in solidifying social support for guerrilla armies.

Migdal (1974, 233) maintains that "like the other types of political organizations that peasants join, revolutionary movements must trade off inducements to individual peasants in return for their participation and support." Thus he (1974, chap. 9) reports that peasants joined organizations in exchange for cigarettes, bath towels, soap, lines of credit, party or government jobs, and agricultural assistance. Peasants also joined to gain assistance in pleading their case for special government favors, such as subsidies and tax exemptions, before officials of the state. Popkin (1979, 255) argues that peasant organizations with excludable benefits, or benefits restricted only to contributors, are self-enforcing; that is, "when a member fails to pay or do his share, he loses his benefits." Hence, such organizations are more likely to succeed. Popkin (1979, 240) thus offers the following account of a Vietnamese communist peasant:

> [Before joining] I thought about my grandmother. I worried that she would live in misery if I went off and joined the army because no one would be left to look after her. I brought these apprehensions up with the cadres and they said that they were certain that the village authorities would take care of my grandmother. After I left my grandmother was given 0.6 hectar of ricefield.

*Early worker movements.* Thompson (1966) reports several fascinating examples of selective incentives in the British working class movement of the late eighteenth and early nineteenth centuries. Delegates to conventions were compensated for their time and travel expenses (p. 125). Committee meetings of early British trade unions "were well lubricated with ale paid for out of union funds" (p. 514). Some "small Luddite bands were actually subsidised out of union funds" (pp. 540–41). At a working class insurrection, "some reluctant recruits [were there because of] promised 'roast beef and ale', rum, and even a pleasure trip on the Trent" (p. 660).

There were good reasons for the provision of such selective incentives. Rank-and-file workers often lived a marginal existence. They simply could not afford to give up a day's pay in order to join a protest. Leaders were hard to find. They had to be compensated to keep them from falling in with the opposition. Thompson (1966, 154) thus observes that a local British working-class organization insisted that its representative to the larger national organization be paid for his time and effort because the "principle of payment for services [was designed] to prevent the taking over of its affairs by men of means or leisure."

While selective incentives became an accepted part of collective dissent among the emerging British working class, such rent seeking was often carried to an extreme. The result was public scandals. Thompson (1966, 626) reports that the early Radical leadership in Britain drew no clear line "between their private business concerns and the finances of the movement. Questions as to the use and trusteeship of Radical Funds, or the confusion of public and private interests became . . . subjects of humiliating public recrimination." He (1966, 626) offers a fascinating example: one leader sold "radical breakfast powder," a "concoction based on roasted corn, which was sold as a substitute for tea or coffee, and which was recommended to Radicals as a means of boycotting taxed articles."

*Modern strikes.* Contemporary workers follow the precedents established by the early working class. For example, "when strike pay is tied to picketing, attendance on picket lines will increase" (Hechter 1988, 19).

*Modern riots.* Contemporary urban riots are neither entirely acts of "irrational" and "mindless" destruction, nor entirely symbolic efforts at protest, nor entirely efforts at achieving a concrete PG for an aggrieved community. Contemporary rioters often loot, or seize valuable property. They tend not to destroy it. Consider, for example, black rioting in the United States during the 1960s. The most important factor affecting the choice of targets was the "attractiveness of merchandise" (Berk and Aldrich 1972, 534). Hence, "patterns of attack during civil disorders strongly imply choice by some rioters . . . We are not arguing that the overall events were planned, but rather that individual participants appear to have been selecting many of their targets" (Berk and Aldrich 1972, 545). During black riots, for example, property and retail establishments were attacked; schools and banks were not

(Tom Hayden, cited in Bienen 1968, 30). Such riots were evidently fed, at least in part, by concrete pecuniary motives.

*Revolutions.* Revolutionaries are quite willing to divide the spoils of victory among themselves. The Great Revolutions thus offer many examples of revolutionaries confiscating the property of "counter-revolutionaries" and redistributing it to themselves (Edwards 1927, 187; Brinton 1965, 241–43). Brinton (1965, 184) writes that "the property of many, if not most, of those openly and stubbornly identified with the beaten parties is confiscated for the benefit of the successful parties, usually identified as 'the people.' Furthermore, as the different moderate groups are defeated their property, too, is commonly confiscated in the same way." During the American Revolution, for example, Loyalist lands were confiscated.

*Coups.* A military leader who expects to be deposed as chief of staff will often stage a coup to preserve his position. Indeed, many have argued that pecuniary self-interest often lies behind military coups. Nordlinger (1977, 66) maintains that "the personal interests of officers — their desire for promotions, political ambitions, and fear of dismissal — are important motivating factors in a significant number of coups." He (1977, 127) suggests that "military governments are on the whole no less corrupt and self-serving than civilian ones." Finer (1976, 50) argues that "a powerful motive in military intervention may be the material interests of the individual officers," which include better pay and easier promotion. Thompson (1973, 26) also argues that coup participants have individual or personal grievances, interests, and ambitions: "Military coup-makers apparently perceive a threat to their personal position(s) and resource base(s) within the military organization, the political system, or both." Tullock (1979, 58) argues that the greater the expectation of a high position in a postcoup regime, the more likely a dissident is to participate in the coup. There is considerable empirical evidence of personal ambitions lying behind coups (Thompson 1973, 26–28; Greene 1990, 121, fn. 29; Finer 1976, 50–52).

*Terrorism.* Laqueur (1987, 96–101) reports that terrorism is a profitable business for terrorists and that they live quite well off of it. As a result, there are many who believe that if ransom (or protection money) is regularly paid to terrorists, terrorism will increase. In fact, the U.S. government does not *officially* pay ransom whereas U.S. businesses usually do — and indeed businessmen are the most common targets in South America (Amos and Stolfi 1982, 78).

*Antisemitism.* Rebels and revolutionaries often expropriate the resources of established classes and organizations. The Nazis, for example, were particularly vigorous in confiscating the wealth of Jews (Jones 1974, 120–21).

*Welfare rights campaigns.* The National Welfare Rights Organization (NWRO) used pecuniary incentives to mobilize supporters. As Jenkins

(1983, 537) suggests, "The NWRO was initiated by professional organizers who used the selective incentives of assistance in securing special cash benefits to mobilize welfare recipients." Wilson (1973, 65, emphasis in original) reports the typical recruitment strategy of the NWRO: "To persuade a potential member in a face-to-face conversation at her doorstep that she would receive a direct material benefit within a very short time after coming to the first meeting, but *only* if she came to the meeting." Jenkins (1983, 537) reports how the loss of selective incentives affected the organization:

> When organizers shifted to nonmaterial incentives, few prospective members were receptive. In line with Olson's theory, as soon as members learned how to secure the welfare benefits for themselves, contributions to the NWRO trailed off, leaving behind a core of activists motivated largely by the selective benefits of social recognition. When welfare administrators abolished the cash benefit program, the NWRO virtually collapsed.

*Neighborhood groups.* Wilson (1973, 68) cites evidence of the selective incentives available to those who join community organizations: "Other studies have shown that many low-income participants in neighborhood [Community Action Programs] have been paid for their involvement (a fee for attending meetings, plus carfare) and that when this payment stops their participation declines sharply."

*Biblical protests and rebellions.* The Lord tells Moses that selective incentives will help to mobilize Hebrews wary about the value and prospects of their slave revolt: "And I will give this people favor in the sight of the Egyptians. And it shall come to pass, that, when ye go, ye shall not go empty; but every woman shall ask of her neighbor, and of her that sojourneth in her house, jewels of silver, and jewels of gold, and raiment; and ye shall put them upon your sons, and upon your daughters; and ye shall spoil the Egyptians" (*Exodus* 3, 21–22). Mordecai uses a mixture of selective incentives and disincentives to convince an uncertain Queen Esther to risk to her position and rebel in order to help save her people: "Think not with thyself that thou shalt escape in the King's house, more than all the Jews. For if thou altogether holdest thy peace at this time, then will relief and deliverance arise to the Jews from another place, but thou and thy father's house will perish; and who knoweth whether thou art not come to royal estate for such a time as this?" (*Esther* 4, 13–15).

In sum, selective incentives can be found in everyday forms of peasant resistance, unorganized rural protests, organized rural rebellions, early worker movements, modern strikes, modern riots, revolutions, coups, terrorism, antisemitism, welfare rights campaigns, neighborhood groups, and biblical protests and rebellions. Olson (1965) was obviously right. The *Use Selective Incentives* solution to the Rebel's Dilemma should be one of the first, if not *the* first, CA approaches that students of conflict investigate.

### 6.5.3.3. The Causes: Politics

The level of selective incentives in any dissident struggle is a function of demand and supply. Rebels demand selective incentives. Potential suppliers include one or more dissident rebel organizations and the authorities (e.g., the state and its allies). The selective incentives market[64] faces cutthroat competition, as each supplier bids for rebel support with selective incentives and tries to become a monopoly. This fight over alternative sources of supply helps to define the politics of collective dissent.

I will first consider how each of the relevant actors — rebels, rebel organizations, and the authorities — influence the selective incentives market. I will then consider the political implications of this market.

*Rebels.* A dissident's interest in material selective incentives is a function of his or her income. Wealthier dissidents can better afford to be ideologues who are motivated by nonmaterialistic considerations. They have the luxury of responding to appeals that solely emphasize political rights, social justice, public morality, and economic fairness. Poorer dissidents are forced by their economic position to demand material selective incentives in return for their support of dissident movements.[65]

Since many dissidents are poor, the search for private benefits in exchange for participation influences many dissident activities. Their particular demands are affected, as are the quality, quantity, timing, and direction of contributions.

First, dissidents demand compensation for any personal costs they incur while participating in collective dissent. Few rebels make sacrifices willingly. Few accept short-run private costs without short-run private benefits. Most such potential dissidents are just like the peasant who exclaimed to Colburn (1989b, 192), "I don't get involved in politics unless I get something out of it." The same idea holds for elites. Luttwak (1968, 73–74) suggests that appeals to a potential coup participant emphasize the private rewards rather than the public virtues of the coup. Coup leaders thus attempt to recruit officers disgruntled over pay and promotions rather than those disgruntled over policies and ideologies.

Second, the availability of selective incentives determines whether or not potential dissidents decide to join protests or rebellions. Rebels are more likely to protest when public benefits are accompanied by private rewards. The many examples of selective incentives cited earlier are evidence on this point.

Third, rebels time their participation in dissident movements to the availability of selective incentives. That is, they will join a dissident group only after the group can offer selective incentives. Given that groups that succeed and become the government have more resources available than movements that have not yet succeeded, one expects dissident movements to experience their greatest growth *after* the revolution. This proposition holds for the Mexican Revolution after the 1910s and the Bolsheviks after 1917 (Hagopian 1974, 306); it is also true of the successful peasant revolutions in China and Vietnam.

Finally, rebels choose to participate in certain types of actions and not in others because of the relative selective incentives available. For example, some everyday forms of peasant resistance (Scott 1985) do not offer material selective incentives. Symbolic or ideological resistance occurs when peasants reject demeaning labels and withdraw deference. Verbal attacks on village elites involve gossip, slander, the use of nicknames, and character assassination. The use of force includes attacks on village elites (for example, beatings and murder), as well as attacks on their property (for example, arson and sabotage against crops, livestock, and equipment). One expects peasants to participate more frequently in those everyday forms of peasant resistance that yield selective benefits than in those forms that yield none. Thus, peasants employ symbolic resistance, a war of words, and the use of force less frequently than shirking, false compliance, and poaching. In short, peasants would rather steal than destroy property: everyday forms of peasant resistance involve more theft than arson, more extortion than murder, more foot-dragging than slander. Brown (1989, 115) indeed reports that "resistance to the state through attacks on officials involved a small number of individuals."

This line of reasoning leads to two other conclusions. During everyday forms of peasant resistance the destruction of property will be a pretext or cover for the theft of property.[66] I do not know of any examples, however. One also expects peasants not to destroy property they need. Guha (1989, 82) reports that peasants burn forests that are worked commercially but not forests that they use:

> There is no evidence that the vast extent of broad-leaved forests, also under the control of the state, were at all affected. As in other societies in different historical epochs, this destruction by arson was not simply a nihilistic release but carefully selective in the targets attacked. As Eric Hobsbawm has argued, such destruction is never indiscriminate, for "what is useful for poor men" — in this instance broad-leaved species far more than chir — is spared.

*Rebel Organizations.* I now turn to supply considerations. Two types of dissident organizations must be considered: those that are self-organized and those that are organized by outsiders. Both organizations aim to provide selective incentives efficiently.[67]

Self-governing institutions (sect. 5.1.1) are prominent, for example, during everyday forms of peasant resistance. Such institutions are created in order to minimize the costs of obtaining selective incentives. Five cost-minimization techniques are employed. First, peasants adopt a tacit "conspiracy of silence." Scott (1989, 7) suggests that everyday forms of peasant resistance "cannot be sustained without a fairly high level of tacit cooperation among the class of resisters." Brown (1989, 109) suggests that "the peasantry's conspiracy of silence consisted of three elements: the refusal to report crime, the refusal to identify criminals, and the refusal to tell the truth about crime." He (1989, 117) concludes that "the conspiracy of silence brought the costs to atomistic action far lower than they would have been without community support." Second, peasants do not employ formal organizations. Most everyday forms of peasant resistance are, in fact, unplanned and unsystematic. Third, peasants do not make their everyday forms of resistance part of an openly declared struggle; rather, they keep things quiet. They do not seek a direct confrontation with authorities; nor do they offer a symbolic public challenge to the existing power structure. Fourth, peasants keep everyday forms of peasant resistance on a small scale, which avoids the organizational costs of simultaneously mobilizing all potential sympathizers. Finally, peasants disguise their everyday forms of resistance by keeping their activities clandestine, concealed, and surreptitious. Scott (1989, 24) points out several "nocturnal threats by masked men." Such instances occurred during Captain Swing, the Rebecca Riots, and Les Memoiselle. In addition, peasants often try to avoid notice and detection by making anonymous threats.

In sum, everyday forms of peasant resistance are rooted in institutions that are cooperative, informal, undeclared, small-scale, and secretive. These arrangements serve the needs of the peasantry because they keep down the costs of selective incentives, costs that are paid in terms of economic oppression and political repression.

Selective incentives also explain another self-organized institution underlying collective dissent: bandwagons of protest and rebellion (sect. 4.1.2). Mousnier (1970, 45) offers the following account of the peasants of the French countryside during the seventeenth century: "Having, during one of the riots, managed to plunder some houses in the town, [they] withdrew with the loot to their villages, and their neighbours were soon stirred up by their bad example to engage in plundering . . . In a moment, all the villagers dropped their ploughs and took up arms instead." Bandwagons of peasant protest, the spatial contagion and temporal diffusion of peasant upheavals, may therefore well be traceable to the perceived availability of selective incentives.

There are other examples of dissidents organizing and governing themselves during protests and rebellions so as to provide selective incentives: the structure of mafias, peasant armies, social bandits, and base areas have been discussed in the literature. Worthy of further investigation are the study of the self-organizing and self-governing institutions (sect. 5.1.1) created by dissidents to carry out their campaigns of collective dissent, how dissidents organize themselves to obtain selective incentives, and how they govern themselves to distribute those selective incentives.

Now consider externally organized rebels. Entrepreneurs recognize a simple truth: successful organizations require rule-enforcing mechanisms that induce followers to act in certain ways. Organizations therefore achieve "mobilization by manipulation" (Hannigan 1985, 441). That is, their success is contingent upon their ability to offer private rewards. To assure that they can control the flow of selective incentives to a wary clientele, entrepreneurs design dissident organizations that are able to perform at least three tasks: obtain resources, recruit new members, and retain existing members.

How do dissident entrepreneurs find the resources needed to offer their followers selective incentives? According to Fireman and Gamson (1979, 18), "Organizers may offer selective incentives even though they lack the resources to provide them right away. Like entrepreneurs, organizers try to create or pool resources by using their skills and connections to convince constituents that they will be able to deliver selective incentives in the future." Dissident entrepreneurs use six techniques to obtain and manage resources that are convertible into selective incentives.

First, they urge their followers to plunder. For example, supporters will be urged to rebel against their masters and to take their possessions. Entrepreneurs encouraged Russian serfs, for instance, to murder their masters, burn title deeds, and then take food, money, and wives (Avrich 1972, 30).

Second, dissident entrepreneurs redistribute resources, a strategy that may be seen as "from each according to his or her politics, to each according to his or her politics." The idea, in other words, is to take from those outside the movement and give to those inside the movement. Popkin (1979, 225) provides evidence on how the forced redistribution of resources creates selective incentives: "The Viet Minh collected large 'donations' from the well-to-do (protection money, in the eyes of the rich) and used some of this money to support the teachers." As one of their followers (Popkin 1979, 240) reported, "The Viet Minh came through on their promises. They actually took the land from the landlords and distributed it among their followers." Another example of this strategy (McClintock 1984, 81) comes from a Peruvian guerrilla organization:

Sendero has provided significant benefits to its supporters. Of course, it promised a better life. But the movement has also taken action — violent action — to benefit the peasants materially. After blacklisting relatively well-to-do landowners, shopkeepers, and intermediaries, and either killing them or causing them to flee, Sendero distributed their property among villagers, and canceled debts to them.

Third, dissident leaders attempt to privatize a good, issue, or grievance in which the group is interested. This solves the rebel's CA problem by making benefits excludable and rival. Entrepreneurs can control such benefits. For example, a dissident group can sell services on a fee-for-service basis and develop into a business enterprise. McClintock (1984, 81) reports that Sendero, the Peruvian guerrilla organization, "offered recruits basic subsistence (probably possible as a result of Sendero's economic levies on the drug trade)."

Fourth, dissident leaders can break the elites' monopoly on political institutions. Entrepreneurs may intervene for their supporters in local government (Popkin 1979, 240); they may also create new village organizations (Popkin 1979, 238). Local courts established by the Viet Minh to arbitrate local disputes, for instance, often provided selective incentives.

Fifth, dissident entrepreneurs seek patrons who can provide selective incentives. The regime, of course, is a potentially wealthy benefactor (sect. 6.2.3.2), since governments often reward rebels. Dissident entrepreneurs attempt to turn these rewards into selective incentives that they can control. Bates (1990, 43) observes, for example, that entrepreneurs often "demand divisible benefits [from government] such as schools, roads, and clinics) rather than collective benefits such as higher prices." This is because entrepreneurs can parcel out divisible benefits to their peasant supporters. Entrepreneurs also prefer the government to distribute private rather than communal land because they can then parcel out the private land to their peasant supporters. Government thus turns out to be a particularly important patron of rural peasant organizations.

Finally, recall that selective incentives are always in short supply and are always demanded by the poorer rebels. Dissident entrepreneurs must therefore ration selective incentives: they reserve the expensive material incentives for mobilizing a few important elite participants and use the relatively costless selective incentives to mobilize the many nonelite participants. Wilson (1973, 37) suggests that "exclusive material benefits are useful for attracting and holding members, but not for motivating present members to take on additional burdens or to perform particular tasks; individual material incentives, on the other hand, are designed precisely to secure, not new members, but specific contributions of time and effort." Marwell and Oliver (1984, 15) conclude similarly, that "money can buy time, but it is mostly used to buy large amounts of time from full-time activists, and is almost never used to buy small amounts of time from a large number of people." Osanka (1971, 411) reports of the guerrilla wars he studied that expensive selective incentives were offered only to elites:

> The *paid* procedure of guerrilla recruitment is the least practiced procedure of the three [e.g., paid, forced, persuaded]. Guerrilla leadership will usually resort to this method only in cases where a unique technical skill is needed and the individual possessing the unique skill cannot be persuaded to perform the needed task by ideological or moral argument. Professional people such as chemists, pharmacists or doctors of medicine are the most common types that might be induced to serve the guerrillas by these means.

In short, while dissident entrepreneurs might offer expensive private benefits to activists, they rarely offer costly rewards for simply joining the group.

Recruitment strategies are a second aspect of dissident organization affected by selective incentives. Entrepreneurs do not try to overcome the Rebel's Dilemma solely by ideology and appeal to a dissident's sense of duty and obligation. All dissident groups appeal to material self-interest. Since dissident entrepreneurs prefer to use each follower's self-interest rather than to overcome that self-interest with appeals to the collective interest, the typical dissident organization devotes more resources to materialistic than to ideological appeals (Tullock 1979, 53).

The consequences for recruitment strategies are clear. First, entrepreneurs emphasize PGs that are specific and concrete, rather than general and abstract. For example, dissident peasant organizations will emphasize their fight for a road and a bridge and not their struggle for "socialism" and "justice." In short, entrepreneurs seek benefits that are tangible, visible, and unambiguous (for example, food, jobs, and houses) rather than intangible, invisible, and ambiguous (for example, socialism, justice, and world revolution). Second, entrepreneurs appeal to a dissident's immediate concerns rather than to their long-run interests. Third, entrepreneurs forge narrow, short-term, single-issue coalitions, finding them to be more successful than long-term multiple-issue coalitions. Finally, dissident organizations capitalize on community and local experience (Alinsky 1946, chap. 5). Consider former Speaker of the House Tip O'Neil's maxim of American politics: all politics are local. The CA approach implies two related maxims: all grievances are local; all collective dissent is local.[68] Dissident struggles are thus rooted in local quarrels or grievances rather than national struggles or issues. Several expectations follow. Dissident organizations that attach local issues to national ones will be more successful than organizations that rely solely on national issues. Local revolts are more likely to succeed than national revolutions. Indigenous and native leaders who can tap into local issues are more likely to succeed in organizing peasants than are outside leaders.

These recruitment strategies are indeed found in organized rebellions. Skocpol (1979, 114) comments accordingly on the limited appeal of ideology in the Great Revolutions: "Peasants participated in these Revolutions without being converted to radical visions of a desired new national society, and without becoming a nationally organized class-for-themselves. Instead they struggled for concrete goals — typically involving access to more land, or freedom from claims on their surpluses." Wesson (1967, 202) observes that "Chinese rebel movements usually begin in opposition to local officials, remaining nominally loyal to the emperor until forced into total opposition." Popkin (1979, 262) reports that in Vietnam successful peasant entrepreneurs organized individual villages around important local problems. They first won support for less risky, small-scale projects that provided immediate and concrete benefits. They then tried to organize peasants for more uncertain, large-scale projects that could provide abstract benefits in the long-run:

> The initial organization of peasant focused on local goals and goods with immediate payoffs. This suggests that an important way to increase peasants' estimate of success, and therefore, the probability of contribution is to decrease the scope of the project for which he is being recruited — and thus shorten the interval before benefits are received. The profits derived from local organizing can then be directed by the leadership to larger, more national goals and projects, which take longer to pay off.

Thompson (1966) and Rudé (1959, 1964) offer many examples of peasants' concrete grievances and specific rent-seeking activities. Such examples, as Scott (1985, 317–18) suggests, may be multiplied manyfold: "A historical examination of the rank and file of nearly any manifestly revolutionary movement will show that the objectives sought are usually limited and even reformist in tone, although the means adopted to achieve them may be revolutionary. Thus 'trade-union consciousness' is not, as Lenin claimed, the major obstacle to revolution, but rather the only plausible basis for it."

Many recruitment strategies employed by dissident entrepreneurs therefore find their origin in the search for selective incentives. Recruitment cannot sustain an organization indefinitely, however. To retain recruits, dissident entrepreneurs must provide selective incentives over the long haul. This means, quite simply, that entrepreneurs offer activists the opportunity to turn their activism into a career.

A study of career patterns in collective dissent offers some final implications of the idea that dissidents seek material selective incentives. Kahn (1982) observes that "the best organizers in the world tend to become unhappy when they miss their paychecks for three weeks in a row." In short, whereas activists initially volunteer their time, they quickly attempt to become paid staff and thereby make a career out of membership in a dissident group. Such efforts snowball, as each participant argues, "Look, if *they* are going to get paid for doing this, why should *I* do it for free?" (Kahn 1982, 70, emphasis in original). Dissident entrepreneurs can appreciate and exploit careerism by providing patronage in exchange for support. In the short run, entrepreneurs offer activists positions in the dissident organization. Tarrow (1989, 230) reports, for example, that "the movement press . . . provided jobs for people in the movement sector who needed to support themselves 'outside the system.'" In the long run, entrepreneurs promise activists positions in the postrevolutionary regime. Hagopian (1974, 230) reports, for instance, that "in the French Revolution, many *sans culotte* militants, 'even if they were not moved by ambition alone, considered the procurement of a position as the legitimate payment for militant activity.'" Academics have observed this iron law of professionalism and careerism in collective dissent.[69] The professionalization of protest is considered in section 6.2.3.2.

Dissident entrepreneurs are, moreover, farsighted in their careerism. They will be concerned with their future careers once they leave the dissident group. Many dissident leaders use the skills, training, and contacts gained from their affiliation with a dissident group to obtain a "better" job. A dissident may even join a dissident group specifically to advance his or her career. Hence, as careers related to a dissident group's activities become available before and after membership in the dissident group, the supply of dissident entrepreneurs increases (sect. 6.1.2).

Further evidence of careerism is therefore the subsequent career choices of political activists who market their acquired skills in areas "that would tolerate or reward unconventional attitudes and behavior" (Fendrich 1974, 98). Such careers include public, social, and human services. Teaching is one example. Erlanger (1977, 243) offers a second example, the Legal Services lawyer:

A second component of socialization experience by the Legal Services Lawyer is training in skills relevant to the legal problems of poor people, with the relative absence of training in legal skills relevant to corporations and wealthy individuals. The Legal Services lawyer, in much the same way as other lawyers who have worked in a particular area, becomes a specialist of sorts and, thus, has limited attractiveness to some potential clients, employers or colleagues and enhanced attractiveness to others.

A third example of a career that might be aided by experience in a dissident group is conventional politics. Professional dissidents often become professional politicians. Leaders of dissident groups therefore tend to be those who can get selective political incentives — politicians: "Rural politicians in search of office have a strong incentive to contribute to the formation of political movements in support of peasant demands" (Bates 1978, 356). Leaders of dissident groups, just like leaders of political parties (Weber [1924] 1968, 1398) have career-oriented, as well as substantive, goals.[70]

*The authorities.* The state and its allies also influence the supply of selective incentives. In fact, it is much easier to find examples of selective incentives offered by elites and authorities than by nonelites and dissidents. Governments respond to protests and rebellions by offering private rewards to two sets of actors.

Regimes offer selective incentives to the forces of "order": armies, police, and militia. Two examples illustrate the significance of mercenaries and soldiers of fortune to collective dissent. Mousnier (1970, 43) reports that a seventeenth century French king offered selective incentives to those of his troops who put down peasant disturbances: "The soldiers broke into larders and wardrobes; stole money, clothes, jewels, food, and wine; slaughtered the poultry, carried off the cattle, threw furniture and doors into the fire; raped women and girls; and manhandled or murdered their husbands and fathers." Second, local governments, business leaders, and large landowners financed the fascist thugs who intimidated peasants in pre-Mussolini Italy.

Regimes also offer private rewards to the forces of "disorder," hoping to coopt potential dissidents into becoming "paid riders" (Lee and Sandler 1989) and hence to turn rebellions into dissident-dissident struggles (sect. 6.4). Three examples illustrate the point. Mousnier (1970, 66) reports that a French king often put down peasant revolts by recruiting soldiers among the rebelling regions, "reducing thereby the number of rebels." Scott (1985, 11-12) reports that Razak, one of his peasant villagers,

paid the M$1 subscription to join the village branch of the ruling party, which dominates politics and the division of whatever loaves and fishes filter down to the village level . . . Razak's logic, shared by some but by no means all of the village poor, has paid the expected dividends. When a drought, a year earlier, forced the cancellation of the irrigated paddy season, the government created a work-relief program. Politics weighted heavily in the selection of workers and Razak was a winner. The local Farmers' Association office hired him to take care of their poultry for forty days at M$4.50 a day, and he was paid M$50 to help clear weeds from a section of the irrigation canal. None of the poor villagers who were on the wrong side of the political fence did nearly as well.

The Mexican Partido Revolucionario Institucional is a final example of how government provides selective incentives in order to contain popular participation. This governing party controls worker and peasant unions through an elaborate system of payoffs and patron-client ties.

In addition to offering their own selective incentives, regimes try to limit the opposition's supply of selective incentives. For example, the PLO smuggled funds into the Territories to keep the Intifada going:

> According to Muhammad Milhim, head of the Occupied Territories Section of the PLO's Executive Committee, in 1988 the damage sustained in the Territories by inhabitants and institutions totaled $571 million. This represented the salaries of activists, PLO compensation to families of martyrs (an initial payment of about 2,000 Jordanian dinars and then 100 dinars a month) and to the owners of houses demolished by the IDF (their equivalent value, for purchasing or building a new house), and payments to the families of detainees (about 50 dinars a month if the detainee is unmarried, and 60 dinars to the family of a married detainee). (Shalev 1991, 95)

The Israelis were keenly aware of this and took a variety of measures to limit this flow of funds into the rebellion.

Local elites also react to the success of material selective incentives at mobilizing rebels. For example, how might landlords respond to Brechtian or Schweikan forms of resistance? The problem of and solution to everyday forms of peasant resistance that involve opportunism are well identified in the new institutional economics literature (Eggertsson 1990, 44–45). Landlords face a moral hazard problem: they have a difficult time discovering whether meager returns from their land are caused by bad luck or the poor performance of their peasant laborers. Landlords confronted by opportunism will thus try to impose on their tenants a form of contract, such as fixed rent, share, wage, that is designed to minimize such tactics. If landlords dominate village legal institutions, one expects that contract law will take account of landlord interests in this matter. The problem and solution to everyday forms of peasant resistance that involve theft are well identified in the economics of crime literature (Becker 1968). Landlords confronted by theft will employ various monitoring and policing behaviors. They will attempt, for example, to increase the severity and certainty of punishment. Furthermore, if land-lords dominate village police institutions, one expects policing policies to take landlord interests into account.

The state influences the level of selective incentives in collective dissent in yet another way. In states where political corruption is widespread, the translation of political into economic power is both crude and direct. For example, where the typical sources of economic power, such as landowner-ship and control of mineral resources, are inaccessible and static, govern-ment is often the sole means of achieving wealth and power. Post-World War II examples of parasitic and predatory states include Cuba under Batista, Nicaragua under Samosa, Haiti under Papa Doc, Iran under the Shah, and the Philippines under Marcos. Kling (1956, 33) suggests that under such regimes, "government does not merely constitute the stakes of a struggle among rival economic interests . . . government itself is a unique base of eco-nomic power." Nkrumah's dictum (cited in McKown 1975, 193), "seek ye first the political kingdom," is therefore particularly relevant.

Predatory states thus encourage rent seeking among dissidents. For example, coups become a way of political life. As Kling (1956, 33) suggests, "As political office provides a uniquely dynamic opportunity to acquire an economic base of power, however, sufficiently large segments of the popula-tion are prepared to take the ultimate risk, the risk of life, in a revolt, in a *coup d'etat*." Contemporary "rentier states," such as rich oil-producing ones like Iran, provide a particularly rich payoff for a coup and hence offer fertile ground for coups (Skocpol 1982). Historical examples of corruption and rent seeking by government officials, and the associated coups and countercoups, occurred in many aristocratic empires (Wesson 1967, 293–308).

*The Politics of Selective Incentives.* In sum, government, the private sec-tor and a variety of dissident groups can provide selective incentives. Given that dissidents have more than one potential supplier, they can comparison shop for their best deal[71] and opt to join certain rural movements rather than others based on the relative selective incentives available. Popkin (1988) shows how various dissident groups in Vietnam competed for supporters by offering selective incentives. He also shows why the Communist Party was successful: it organized itself to provide selective incentives far more effec-tively than any other group.

In the competition among dissident organizations (sect. 6.4), the opti-mal way to offer selective incentives is to be the only supplier. Entrepreneurs realize that selective incentives are less effective at overcoming their group's CA problem under two conditions: someone (government, the private sector, or another dissident group) can provide the same selective incentives that they can; someone can provide selective incentives more cheaply. The consequences are clear. Dissident organizations will find that more dissidents join their group if they ensure that the only way to obtain selective incentives is to join the group (Rogowski 1985, 89). Dissident organizations that have exclusive access to selective incentives will be better able to mobilize supporters than groups that do not monopolize access. The lesson for potential dissident leaders is clear: entrepreneurs who control excludable selective incentives will be more successful than those who cannot. Competing dissident organizations therefore seek to end the competition, as each attempts to become the monopoly supplier of selective incentives.

One might assume (based on elementary microeconomic theory) that efforts to monopolize the supply of selective incentives would reduce the supply of selective incentives. It might appear further that competition among the suppliers of selective incentives favors appeals based on selective incentives rather than appeals based on collective benefits. The reality is otherwise, however; competition among dissident organizations, and competition between the regime and dissident organizations, actually decreases the supply of selective incentives; and it is monopoly that offers dissident organizations the better opportunities to win support by materialistic appeals.

The reason is that competition makes ideological appeals relevant — dissidents must pay attention to the different programs. The success of one side rather than the other will help to define the national agenda and hence affect the rebel's personal situation and his or her local community. When multiple dissident groups compete for support, dissidents therefore donate to affect PG programs and not merely to obtain the good (sect. 6.4.3). If, however, either a dissident organization or the authorities exercise a monopoly in some local community, there is no incentive to pay attention to the various stands on great national issues. Rebels will instead most likely strike their best deal with the existing powers.[72]

Competition between the state and a dissident organization damages the use of selective incentives for an additional reason: regimes can usually easily outbid dissidents. Hence, dissident organizations, unable to enter a bidding war, are likely to emphasize collective benefits over selective incentives.[73] In order to mobilize support with selective incentives, dissident organizations thus need to be geographically remote from the regime. When they are far removed from the regime they can use selective incentives to convert the apathetic to the involved, the nonactivist to the activist.

In sum, the struggle over the *Administer Selective Incentives* solution to the rebel's CA problem is a crucial aspect of the political struggle between rebels and their opponents. It helps determine whether material selective incentives or nonmaterial collective benefits will be emphasized in mobilizing dissidents. Materialistic appeals will be made to poorer rebels, especially when one supplier of selective incentives gains a monopoly. Such appeals are particularly attractive in states with widespread political corruption. Ideological appeals will be made to wealthier rebels. They will be especially prominent when the competition among suppliers is fierce. They are particularly attractive in states without a strong tradition of political corruption.

### 6.5.3.4. The Consequences: A Non-Solution?

The centrality of selective incentives to dissident groups has so far been demonstrated here in two ways: by providing evidence of the widespread existence of selective incentives in collective dissent and by tracing the origins of selective incentives to the political struggles of the dissidents. A nagging problem remains. Colburn (1989, 195) puts his finger on it: "It is an embarrassment that the supposed benefactors of the revolution prove to be as selfish as the economic elite of the old order."[74] Two questions thus arise. First, does not the pursuit of material self-interest automatically disqualify dissident behavior from being considered "political," let alone truly "revolutionary"? And second, does not the pursuit of material self-interest hurt rather than help the dissidents' collective cause?

The first question can be divided into the issues of whether the goals and/or the means of materially self-interested rebels are political. In addressing these two issues, one confronts the limitations of CA theories: they do not allow for an a priori determination of whether the dissidents' aims are political. This issue can only be decided a posteriori by empirical work. CA theories assume that some group exists in the sense that common goals exist. Hence, if rebels do not share common goals that extend beyond the pursuit of material self-interest; if rebels do not pursue a PG in addition to selective incentives; if rebels are not interested in social justice as a complement to personal aggrandizement; or if rebels have no political ambitions but only criminal ones, then the theory developed here *does not apply.*[75] For example, where peasants do not use a conception of right and wrong (e.g., "the norm of reciprocity," "the right to subsistence"; Scott 1976), and where they do not see their actions as directed toward righting those wrongs, CA theories are not relevant. No PG, after all, is being sought. The search for selective incentives can supplement but not replace the search for collective gains.

Whether the dissidents' means are political is also an empirical question, not an analytical one. CA theories assume that a series of individual actions helps to achieve some PG. If such a dissident production function (sect. 3.4.1) does not exist; if dissidents have no sense that they are working collectively toward some common end; or if dissidents are oblivious to their interactions, then the theory developed here also *does not apply.* For instance, if peasants who loot manors during a jacquerie do not believe that their activities further their collective cause *as well as* offer personal enrichment, then they are indeed thieves and not rebels. No collective dissent, after all, is being undertaken.

One example of the controversy over whether materially self-interested peasants pursue common or political goals and use common or political means is the debate over whether everyday forms of peasant resistance are political. In those situations, self-help schemes do result in self-aggrandizement, but common/political goals and common/political actions definitely exist as well. Brown (1989, 108) maintains that peasants who use everyday forms of peasant resistance pursue political goals. As he puts it, "Almost all political acts were self-interested in the sense that they were designed to redress individual grievances." Brown (1989, 108) also maintains that peasants who use everyday forms of peasant resistance pursue political means, which he sees in the implicit cooperation among peasants:

> Atomistic acts should be considered political because they were made thinkable by the consensus and support of the community . . . A shoplifter helps himself in a way that is not political. A group of shoppers who, in an atmosphere of distress over high prices, simultaneously refuse to pay for their groceries or stand back while a few attack the grocer are helping themselves in a communitarian — and political — fashion.

In other words, the conclusion that "PGs or political goals are not sought; collective action or political means are not employed" does not necessarily follow from the premise "peasants are pursuing their self-interest." Self-interested behavior does not automatically imply apolitical behavior. The pursuit of selective incentives does not diminish the politics of the rebels' goals or means. This issue, as indicated earlier, must be settled outside of the CA framework.

The pursuit of self-interest and the pursuit of class interest are thus not contradictory. As Scott (1989, 22) argues, "If class domination is a process of systematic appropriation, then the measures devised to thwart that appropriation constitute a form of resistance. All class struggle must necessarily join self-interested material needs with conflict." The generalization of Scott's argument was offered by Hillel: "If I am not for myself, who will be for me? And if I am for myself only, what am I? And if not now, when?"[76]

Now consider the second question: does the pursuit of material self-interest actually further collective political goals? Critics charge that the selective incentives idea implies that PGs are unnecessary for protests and rebellions. Some[77] rebels who are unconcerned with political goals could be led to CA by the lure of selective incentives. Such people contribute toward the PG, but can they serve as the foundation of a political movement?

If disinterest in the PG characterizes many dissidents, any achievement of the PG by the dissidents occurs despite the fact that many dissidents are pursuing a private agenda. Here we note a great irony: self-interest and not collective interest can lead to collective success. That CA can be the unintentional by-product of the pursuit of private interests was one of Olson's (1965) most original and most important insights. We can now understand an often observed syndrome in dissident struggles: dissidents do not formally, explicitly, or consciously pursue a common goal; collective goals, ideologies, and policies are only remotely connected to CA; dissidents take individual actions for personal aggrandizement; the dissidents are somehow able to overcome these difficulties and alleviate their burdens. The unintended consequences of individual actions are again at work. For example, peasants in the tsar's army deserted en masse during World War I. Three collective goals, one might speculate, were sought: bring down the tsar, conclude the war, and end conscription. No soldier had to think to himself, If I desert, the war will end. Each soldier wanted only to end his own involvement with the tsar's army. Deserting was thus the selective incentive available to each of the peasant soldiers. This selective incentive ultimately allowed all of them to achieve the three PGs they all sought.

Successful CA thus appears fragile, an unintended consequence of self-interest. However, might the glass be half full rather than half empty? The other side of the coin is that self-interest can indeed further the collective interest. Even if a PG is obtained as a by-product of the pursuit of private goods, a PG *is* obtained. In this sense, the selective incentives argument combines Smith and Marx. Class struggle, the organizing principle of Marxian analysis, is pursued through maximizing one's utility subject to constraints, the organizing principle of neoclassical economics. There is no contradiction between the pursuit of material self-interest and the pursuit of class struggle (compare Scott and Hillel). The pursuit of material self-interest need not hurt CA—indeed, it may even be the *sine qua non* of successful CA.

Two conclusions follow. First, a PG alone is never enough to start a dissident group. The prospect of material selective incentives must somehow enter the picture. Second, selective incentives alone are never enough to sustain a dissident group. To be effective, selective incentives must be tied to ideological appeals. Selective incentives without political ideology are counterproductive. Like everything else, they have a diminishing marginal utility. And like almost everything else, they have complements and substitutes.

Hence, dissident entrepreneurs who provide material selective incentives must also emphasize goals. This principle explains why unorganized peasant upheavals and rural banditry almost always degenerate: participants are too easily attracted to selective incentives. Organization is thus the *sine qua non* of successful peasant upheavals because it rations selective incentives. Peasant organizations would limit selective incentives even if they did not have limited resources.

In sum, the *Administer Selective Incentives* solution to Olson's Problem no doubt expresses part of the truth. There are numerous examples of selective incentives proving to be absolutely essential to collective dissent. The intended consequences of selective incentives include successful mobilization and the successful achievement of a PG. However, counterexamples can just as easily be found where selective incentives were much less relevant to protests and rebellions. The unintended consequences of selective incentives include cooptation, reformism, and the diversion from revolutionary goals. The key then is to discover where and when the solution works. Under what conditions do selective incentives actually mobilize rebels? Where and when do they achieve the PG sought? My argument is that successful dissident organizations are able to balance appeals to material selective incentives with appeals to the PG.[78] Neither exclusively romantic nor exclusively rationalist views of dissidents are justified. Rebels, no less than anyone else, need a head and a heart. CA theories reveal the flaws of a disembodied focus on one to the exclusion of the other.

Dissident CA is thus a dilemma wrapped inside a paradox wrapped inside an irony. The dilemma is that rebels would be better off cooperating, yet they do not. The paradox is that rational rebels should not cooperate, but they do. The irony is that selfishness both explains the paradox and solves the dilemma. Selfishness, that is, often permits cooperation that facilitates the emergence of purportedly selfless goals.

Our appreciation of rebel CA is enriched by our understanding of these truths. Rebels, just like the rest of us, like to be paid for what they do. And rebels, just like the rest of us, attempt to balance the public and the private spheres of their lives.

## 6.5.4. Administer Selective Disincentives

As the expected value of a dissident's punishment for noncontribution to a dissident group increases, his or her contribution, and hence collective dissent, increases. This idea that successful dissident entrepreneurs employ coercion to punish defectors and exact contributions has a long history in social thought[79] and conflict studies.[80]

Where does the expected value of punishment come from?[81] Dissident entrepreneurs influence their followers' expected value calculations in the following ways: they establish rules to punish defectors; they attempt to monitor dissidents' participation in collective dissent; if they detect defectors, they attempt to catch them and then penalize them; they attempt to impose a punishment that is severe enough (e.g, long sentences, heavy fines) to deter future defectors; and finally, they attempt to implement those penalties. A dissident's estimate of the expected value of punishment is based on this rule making-detection-capturing-sentencing-penalizing-implementation scenario. For example, as the dissident group's probability of capturing defectors increases, participation in collective dissent increases.

What strategies towards selective disincentives are employed by dissident entrepreneurs? First, entrepreneurs often publicize the names of noncontributors, a form of extortion that can be very effective. For example, picketing at strikes makes scabs highly visible and thereby discourages strikebreakers. Such an approach carries the *Social Incentives* solution to the Rebel's Dilemma (sect. 4.2.2) to its limit.

A second technique is to ostracize noncontributors. There is considerable empirical support for the proposition that the forced exit (sect. 3.11) or exile of disobedient dissidents can be effective.[82] Scott (1985, 262) recounts the impact of the selective disincentives that the poor are able to impose on one another:

> The most level of restraint that has been achieved makes ample use of social sanctions such as gossip, character assassination, and public shunning. There is no surer way for poor men or women to call scorn upon themselves than to work at a lower wage than the prevailing rate or to take a job that "belongs" by custom to others. Nor is it merely a question of reputation, for the offender will find that he or she is shunned in labor exchange (*derau*), not included in share groups, not told about possibilities of finding work, denied the petty jobs that the poor can occasionally offer, and not invited to join "rotating credit associations" (*kut*) in the neighborhood. Each of these material sanctions, taken separately, is fairly trivial, but collectively they represent a potential loss of some magnitude. Nor is the threat of violence entirely absent from these sanctions, as we shall see. Thus, the poor man who is tempted to break ranks must measure very carefully his short-term gain against the losses his angry neighbors may be able to impose. By their opinion and by their sanctions, the poor have erected a set of customary prohibitions that symbolize the acceptable limits of self-seeking.

Thus, excommunication limits the Hobbesian struggle among the poor during their larger struggle with the rich.

While shame and ostracism are powerful selective disincentives, dissident entrepreneurs have one ultimate weapon in their recruitment arsenal: force. In general, as Buchanan (1979, 69) argues, force might be applied either during the revolutionary struggle or after it. In the former case, some group would threaten the imminent use of violence against those proletarians who refrain from revolutionary activity. In the latter, some group would threaten to use violence against non-contributors once the proletariat achieves power.

Whether the dissidents win or lose, in other words, dissident entrepreneurs make it clear that those who support the regime will be punished. Dissident entrepreneurs thus often enlist the support of contributors to force noncontributors into participating in collective dissent. Examples of the use of violence against dissident noncontributors, informants, collaborators, and traitors abound.[83]

Dissidents' opponents indeed often charge that dissident entrepreneurs coerce people into rebellion by threats of physical violence. Rebels are said to be motivated by only two things: fear (i.e., selective disincentives) and greed (i.e., selective incentives). Some counterinsurgency theorists speak of "the use of coercion by rebels to obtain popular support" (Gurr 1970, 261) during guerrilla wars. One important goal of government, they suggest, should be to protect villagers from the dissidents' reprisals. More resources should be devoted to protecting neutrals than to killing and capturing dissidents (Coyle 1985, 75).

While many examples of selective disincentives may be offered, the many solutions to the Rebel's Dilemma discussed in this book discredit such a one-motivation theory of collective dissent. Others, however, have gone to the opposite extreme. Critics contend that selective disincentives are *never* a way to solve the Rebel's Dilemma. Selective disincentives are thought to be irrelevant, for example, to guerrilla movements,[84] peasant upheavals,[85] and movements of the left.[86]

In addition to finding selective disincentives ineffective, critics find them counterproductive. They worry about two important negative consequences of dissident coercion. First, they are concerned that dissidents' liberty, in the sense of purely negative freedom from force and control, will be restricted. Second, they are concerned that a dissident group that coerces its followers will become, if successful, a dissident regime that coerces its people. Dissident leaders who forcibly capture state authority will come to recognize that their continuance in office depends upon their ability to establish a state strong enough to suppress the former elite. Hence, dissidents who take power violently retain power violently.[87]

This chapter has examined what happens to the Rebel's Dilemma when rebels are organized. Agents or entrepreneurs (sect. 6.1) and principals or patrons (sect. 6.2) can provide leadership. These leaders can reorganize the dissidents (sect. 6.3), compete more effectively with their allies (sect. 6.4), and impose, monitor, and enforce agreements on their followers (sect. 6.5). The famous problem of social order, in other words, can be overcome by a hierarchical organizational structure.

This approach has yielded many interesting insights into protest and rebellion. The reference to hierarchy as an explanation for social order has been extensively criticized, however. Hierarchy solutions are thought to be an insufficient basis for social order, because the use of force to maintain social order presumes that one can, in fact, use force. But the use of social control mechanisms, as indicated in section 6.1.2, itself requires that the problem of social order be solved. As Arrow (1974, 72) puts it,

> The control mechanisms are themselves organizations, composed of people. Their use to enforce authority is itself an exercise of authority. Even the most absolute dictator requires that the secret police follow orders in purging opponents. He cannot do the job himself.

The consequence is that Hierarchy solutions to the Rebel's Dilemma offer as incomplete an explanation of CA as Market, Community, and Contract solutions did, an issue I explore in section 9.1.

We have finally run out of contexts within which to place Market solutions to the Rebel's Dilemma. The time for elaborating the CA approach to collective dissent, the time for establishing the microfoundations of the rational actor or resource mobilization approach to conflict studies, is over. It is now time to assess my theoretical project. The next section draws out my themes of CA solutions as politics and pathologies. The concluding section employs several analytical and empirical criteria to evaluate CA theories of collective dissent.

# Part 3
# Themes

CHAPTER 7

# Solutions as Politics:
# The Origins of Collective Action

Part 2 demonstrated that there are many solutions to the Rebel's Dilemma. Part 3 elaborates my two principal theses about these solutions. Chapter 7 explores the origins of various solutions to Olson's Problem and the theme that solutions involve politics. Chapter 8 explores the outcomes of various solutions to the CA Problem and the theme that solutions involve pathologies.

Politics *is* the struggle over solutions to CA problems. Someone will always be interested in solving a group's CA problem, just as someone else will invariably be interested in exacerbating that group's problem.[1] *Regimes and oppositions thus struggle over every CA solution introduced here* (see the summary in sect. 2.3). More generally, they struggle over two basic political processes by which dissidents obtain their PG. First, dissidents may try to induce an existing regime to supply the PG through reform. As Wilson (1973, 289) argues, "Protest succeeds because the target concedes." Alternatively, dissidents may become the regime and supply the PG themselves through revolution. Neither reform nor revolution is a straightforward process. The theoretical and empirical analysis of policy change is still in its infancy, as is the "science" of overthrowing and replacing regimes. This chapter offers a preliminary exploration of both processes. Section 7.1 explores reformist cooperation between state and opposition, or the nexus of institutionalized and noninstitutionalized politics. Section 7.2 explores revolutionary conflict between revolutionary and antirevolutionary coalitions, or the struggle between the Rebel's Dilemma and the State's Dilemma.

## 7.1. The Reformist Cooperation between States and Dissidents

Political competition between states and oppositions often turns into reformist cooperation; it has even been suggested that collective dissent is a necessary condition for reformist political change.[2] I argue (sect. 7.1.1) that CA models lack a theory of reformist politics and propose (sect. 7.1.2) ways to develop such a theory.

### 7.1.1. Apolitical Production Functions

The question of a "theory of the state" arises quite naturally in all research programs in political science (sect 10.2.1). In rational actor theories one asks, How do political institutions, mechanisms, and processes aggregate demands? In public policy theories one asks, How can we account for the supply of government policies? In systems theories one asks, How are the demands of the socioeconomic subsystem mapped into the outputs of the political subsystem? In theories of authority patterns one asks, What is the relationship between participation by subordinates and responsiveness by superordinates? In neo-Marxist theories of the state one asks, What determines the relative autonomy of the state vis-à-vis society?

The PG–PD models employed here to study collective dissent assume a particularly primitive theory of the state (Lichbach forthcoming, chap. 2). Their idea is that a simple production function links a dissident's resource input to a state's PG output: a unit of input valued at cost $c$ by a rebel induces a regime to produce a unit of output valued by the rebel at benefit $b$. This highly simplified production function is woefully inadequate, because it leaves almost all of the important political questions unanswered. Politics is also missing in the more complicated production functions introduced earlier as part of the *Shape an Efficacious Group* solution (sect. 6.3.2). No one has yet been able to demonstrate how lumpy PGs, Minimum Winning Coalitions, step functions, and so on, translate into *actual* political processes. Both simple and complex CA models thus tend to produce an "alchemy" (Marx, cited in Avineri 1968, 201; Rubenstein 1987, 59) of the production process surrounding collective dissent rather than a true chemistry.

Many scholars therefore criticize CA models for failing to explain how dissidents get (or do not get) the PG they want from a regime. Tarrow (1988, 429) argues that existing theories "black box" the politics of dissent by adopt an "anti-institutional persuasion" that assumes "a basic opposition between movements and institutions" and produces "an underspecification of the institutional structures within which movements emerged" (Tarrow 1991, 13). The CA research program therefore does not explore the mechanisms by which political demands are revealed to those who supply political outputs and the mechanisms by which the suppliers respond to the demands. In Lowi's (1971, 54, emphasis in original) words, CA theories do not ask how protests "*activate the mechanisms of formal decision-making.*" They neglect the "'terms of exchange' between political and economic command" (Arrighi, Hopkins, and Wallerstein 1989, 63).[3] In CA jargon, the multiperson social composition function must be elaborated. In social choice nomenclature, the aggregation of individual action by dissidents into a collective outcome provided by government must be studied.

The production function of the group, or the group's power equation, includes many actors outside of the group: the general public, specific allies, key opponents, the government, outside powers, and so on. The operational question thus is the following: exactly who in the state, for what reasons, and located in which institutions determines where, when, and how much of the dissidents' demands (i.e., the PG) are met? This is a political, and not merely a technical, question. As Marwell and Oliver (1984, 18) put it, "Movement technologies are more complex than industrial technologies in that they generally act on other people who can and do change their responses over time."

Adding reformist politics to CA models is thus no simple task for the theorist. At least six specific problems arise. First, the most comprehensible public choice processes occur within a given institutional setting. Although there are many rational actor theories of legislatures, elections, and voting, collective dissent by definition (sect. 1.1) takes place outside of traditional institutional settings and yet activates processes in those settings. This structure complicates the formal modeling of collective dissent.

Second, a dissident production function may involve multiple tactics. It makes a great deal of difference, for example, whether terrorism is the sole strategy used by dissidents (e.g., the Baider-Meinhoff gang in West Germany) or whether it is part of a broader overall strategy in a guerrilla war (e.g., the FLN in Algeria).

Third, a dissident production function often involves multiple groups. In general, failed revolutions involve a single dissident group, whereas successful revolutions unite many such groups (sect. 7.2.1). Coalitions and alliances among dissidents can be crucial to the dissidents' cause.

Fourth, dissidents debate the production function and the future of the "movement" or of the "revolution." Examples include the debate between Lenin, the Economists, and the Social Revolutionaries (DeNardo 1985, 179–81) and the debate among the Left in postwar Italy (Tarrow 1989, 233). A model that assumes a simple production function, as in Lichbach (forthcoming, chap. 2), ignores these tactical and strategical disputes among dissidents and hence offers no insights into how a set of dissidents actually selects strategies and tactics. Tilly (1985, 747) thus criticizes CA theories for failing to specify the linkages between individual and collective actions and decisions. The social choice process by which a production function is actually chosen must eventually be modeled.

Fifth, some dissidents lack a predetermined strategy for seizing power and producing a PG. Terrorist doctrine, for example, is unclear as to how bombings and assassinations will bring about the desired revolutionary change. Will the active participation of the masses, or the army, be needed eventually? If so, then how will terrorist actions facilitate conversion? Jenkins (1982, 16) argues that "terrorists have failed to articulate a comprehensive strategy for taking power. They are bombers and shooters, tacticians at best, not strategists." Hobsbawm (1959, 101) offers another example: "The precise way in which the new world would come about was uncertain" in millenarian movements. Participants just knew that the revolution would succeed and the millennium would come. For this reason, terrorists and millenarians constantly change their production function in their search for successful tactics.

Finally, some dissidents misunderstand strategy. It is rare for collective dissent to result directly in political change. Political processes and debates, coalition formation and realignment, intervene. However, rebels sometimes act as if they believe that collective dissent produces political change in a mechanical and predictable dialectic of action and reaction. Many eighteenth- and nineteenth-century European dissidents believed that if they merely made their grievances known to the benevolent despot, he or she would acknowledge the problem and promptly solve it. As Hobsbawm (1959, 119) puts it,

> Though it is patent that local lords, officials, clergymen and other exploiters suck the blood of the poor, this is probably because the monarch does not know what is done in his name. If the Tsar or the King of France only knew he would doubtless sweep through the country to shrivel up the unjust officials with his eagle eye, and to dispense justice to his loyal commons. A score of folk-myths express this attitude.

The dissidents' PG is therefore sought by multiple groups that pursue multiple tactics outside of conventional channels of government. Many of these groups lack or misunderstand strategy and tactics and yet debate them incessantly. Is it surprising that students of conflict have not yet developed a theory of conflict outcomes? Thus, we know much more about group mobilization (why people rebel) than about group success (how groups triumph).

More specifically, the field is beset by three controversies.[4] The first concerns the efficacy of various tactics — whether scope, duration, or intensity of collective dissent is the most effective in achieving the desired PG, for example. Are six villages who revolt at time $t$ more likely to achieve their demands than if one village revolted at time $t$, a second at time $t+1$, a third at time $t+3$, and so on? A related debate over tactics was sparked by Piven and Cloward's (1979, chap. 1) case for disruption — that group disturbances can lead to political success, and hence that the poor should interfere with normal political processes. Second, there is a dispute over Gamson's (1990, appendix A) explanation of group success. Our major systematic and quantitative examination of group success raises more questions than it answers. Third, there is a dispute over the significance of free riding. How serious a problem is it (Gamson 1990, 152), and when does it actually damage a group's chances for achieving a PG? After all, a large absolute and/or relative number of free riders can hurt some causes and not others (sect. 6.3.1).[5]

This lack of knowledge leads to many surprising and paradoxical outcomes (Lichbach forthcoming, chap. 8). Regimes are obstinate and do not accommodate dissidents when it appears that they will concede (e.g., China in 1989), but regimes accommodate dissidents when it appears that they will be obstinate (e.g., Eastern Europe in 1989).[6] Regimes that appear shaky persist (e.g., the Austro-Hungarian empire in the middle of the nineteenth century), whereas regimes that appear strong topple (e.g., Samoza in 1978, the Shah in 1979). And regimes that are powerful defeat determined but weak opponents (e.g., the Weathermen in the United States), yet seemingly weak dissidents defeat powerful regimes (e.g., Castro in Cuba in 1958, the IRA in Ireland in 1921, and the Jews in Palestine in 1948).

## 7.1.2. Political Games

For all of these reasons, it is difficult to model a production function for collective dissent with greater specificity than is used in Lichbach (forthcoming, chap. 2). Nevertheless, some preliminary ideas about the linkage of collective dissent to reformist political change can be suggested. A dissident production function must be based on both a theory of dissident beliefs and a theory of the institutional structures within which dissidents operate.

Dissidents who engage in collective dissent aimed at obtaining reformist political change must hold four beliefs about their production function. First, they must believe that the state *should* provide the PG and that therefore it is responsible in some causal, legal, or moral sense for their grievances. The issue is whether or not "government is held responsible by acts of commission or omission for discontent" (Gurr 1970, 159). Attributing some blame to government for, say, poor economic conditions, seems essential to collective dissent.

Second, rebels must believe that the state *can* provide the PG and remedy the grievance. Must things remain as they always have been, or are alternatives possible? Pre-Enlightenment thought tends to see the social world as immutable and God-given. Post-Enlightenment thought tends to see the social world as a human construct and hence alterable. Hirschman (1982b, 1463, emphasis in original) thus points out that the idea of a perfectible social order, one in which "happiness could be *engineered* by changing the social order," is new; in the past, "most tended to attribute their unhappiness to concrete and fortuitous happenings — ill luck, ill health, the machinations of enemies, an unjust master, lord or ruler — or to remote general and unchangeable causes, such as human nature or the will of God." Some Post-Enlightenment thinking seems essential to collective dissent.

Third, rebels must believe that the state *has not* yet provided the PG. As Welch (1980, 27) puts it, "The more the negative consequences of natural events are ascribed to government than to God, the greater their potential political effects." Theories of subjective attribution processes, or how a dissident comes to hold the state responsible for not remedying grievances, are needed.

Fourth, rebels must believe that the existing state or some new state can be made responsive to collective dissent and thus that under pressure government *will* provide the PG. Pettee ([1938] 1971, 66) suggests that "the individual may adjust himself to the system, or he may seek to adjust the system to himself. It is this latter alternative which produces all revolutionary ideas." CA, therefore, must be perceived as a feasible solution to a dissident's problems, the issue being the dissidents' beliefs about how his or her inputs produce outputs (i.e., how the production function actually operates).

In sum, dissidents must believe that the state should and can provide reformist political change. They must also believe that protest can turn an unresponsive government into a responsive one. Understanding such beliefs is necessary, but not sufficient, for understanding the political game between regime and opposition. One must also investigate the institutional context within which such beliefs occur.

One context is democratic elections. Dissident groups that can influence electoral outcomes attract the attention of political parties. Tilly (1985, 735) notes that "the proper analogy to a social movement is neither a party nor a union but a political campaign." Piven (1976, 322; see Piven and Cloward 1979, 15–18) also recognizes the importance of electoral processes in democratic states: "The political impact of institutional disruptions depends upon electoral conditions. Even serious disruptions such as industrial strikes will force concessions only when the calculus of electoral instability favors the protesters."

Social movements in democracies have thus often succeeded by aligning with established political parties. The Kerner Commission (1968, 230–31) concludes that the civil rights protests of the early 1960s were successful mainly where blacks could decide elections by voting with the Democrats. The activities of dissident groups, moreover, often merge into the activities of political parties. At the local level in the United States, for example, various social movements have captured local party organizations. Dissident movements, finally, can generate third parties.[7] Protest, guerrilla, and terrorist movements have, on occasion, become political parties and competed in elections. Examples include the Tupamaros in Uruguay and the Irgun in Israel.

Almost no systematic work has been done on the question of how collective dissent and the electoral process affect one another. Students of conflict should investigate any electoral processes, such as direct referendums and general elections, involving traditional political parties that have been influenced by dissident movements. A particularly relevant question is how protest groups form coalitions and enter politics as political parties and/or interest groups (Lipset and Rokkan 1967).

Formal negotiations are the second institutional area in need of study. Direct strategic interaction between representatives of the state and the opposition can sometimes bypass conventional political processes and produce public policies. As Sandler and Scott (1987, 35–36) point out, "Terrorists attempt to circumvent legislative and election processes, and make their demands directly to government officials. These demands are made credible when terrorists are successful in taking hostages, bombing, assassinating, and so forth." Any bargaining processes, such as lobbying between leaders of a state and a dissident group, that determine the PG supplied by the regime to the dissidents should be considered. An examination of formal negotiations to end internal wars seem a particularly fruitful way to begin this inquiry (Moore 1991).

These ideas are but preliminary thoughts about how to add reformist politics to CA models.[8] To be convincing, CA theories of collective dissent must show how the institutional processes of democratic politics interact with the noninstitutional processes of collective dissent to produce a PG sought by dissidents. The influence of collective dissent on public policy will always be somewhat unclear: the unintended effects of group action often overwhelm the intended ones; the long-range consequences of group action often outweigh the short-term ones.[9] However, CA theories must try to account for reformist political change. Apolitical production functions must be replaced by political games.

### 7.2. The Revolutionary Conflict between States and Dissidents

Part 2 has demonstrated, I trust, that the CA research program can explain a relatively short-lived and geographically isolated incident of collective dissent. Such incidents typically involve one dissident group employing one form of collective dissent to achieve one goal — a meeting, rally, demonstration, riot, or coup. What I have not yet shown is that the CA research program can explain a complex constellation of temporally and spatially linked incidents of collective dissent. Such incidents — a protest campaign, social movement, civil war, or social revolution — typically involve several dissident groups employing several different forms of collective dissent in order to achieve several different goals. The larger and more significant the conflict, the more interesting it is to students of conflict. Thus, the Great Revolutions have always been central to conflict studies (Edwards 1927; Brinton 1965; Pettee [1938] 1971; Moore 1966; Skocpol 1979; Dunn 1989; Goldstone 1991).[10] To be credible, the CA research program must address the more major incidents of conflict.

This difference between the minor and major explananda in conflict studies raises the aggregation, micro-to-macro, or level of analysis problem. In Zald and McCarthy's (1990) terms, the challenge is to explain the progression from an incident of collective dissent to a social movement organization to a social movement industry to a social movement sector. How, for example, do separate guerrilla attacks turn into a struggle for national liberation? Understanding large-scale social movements and social revolutions thus poses special challenges, a problem understood by conflict theorists.[11]

Scholars generally agree, however, on how revolution must be understood. Eckstein (1965, 145–48) advises that we scrutinize both insurgents and incumbents; Huntington (1968), that we analyze the relationship between social mobilization and political institutionalization; and Skocpol (1979), that we study the dialectic of popular mobilization and state breakdown.[12] The CA version of these arguments is that revolution involves conflict between revolutionary and antirevolutionary coalitions, or a struggle between the Rebel's Dilemma and the State's Dilemma.

### 7.2.1. The Revolutionary Coalition: The Rebel's Dilemma

The revolutionary movement, of course, faces a particularly acute Rebel's Dilemma, because a revolution involves so many people paying such high costs. How is the Revolutionary's Dilemma solved?

Several CA solutions appear to be particularly well suited to explaining how individual incidents of collective dissent coalesce into episodes, campaigns, and movements of greater extent, intensity, duration, and scope, eventually culminating in revolution.

- *Improve the Productivity of Tactics* (sect. 3.4). Larger and more successful dissident movements resort to multiple tactics and assume multiple forms. Revolutionary movements are thus strengthened as the number of different tactics used by a dissident group increases.
- *Increase the Probability of Winning* (sect. 3.6). Signs of government weakness encourage and embolden dissidents to redouble their efforts. Thus, as a regime weakens, revolutionary movements strengthen.
- *Increase Team Competition between Regimes and Oppositions* (sect. 3.10.1.2). Enduring team competition between regimes and opposi-

tions politicizes all social forces, isolates government from those social forces, generates new divisive issues, and reduces the willingness and ability of leaders to compromise. If the team competition between a regime and an opposition persists, revolution becomes more likely.

- *Build a Bandwagon* (sect. 4.1.2). Small localized conflicts sometimes diffuse over time and space to become large nationalized conflicts. An urban riot, for example, can become a regional rebellion. The reverse can also happen, as big conflicts engulf little ones and further enlarge the conflict. An internal war, for example, may come to subsume coups and protests. Either process facilitates revolution.
- *Use Mutual Exchange* (sect. 5.1.3). Different types of dissidents and their entrepreneurs have multiple, mixed, and changing goals, targets, and tactics. Cooperation among these various groups may be fruitful. As dissidents exchange participation in collective dissent on one issue for participation on another, revolution becomes more likely.
- *Use Tit-For-Tat* (sect. 5.2). The basis of Tit-For-Tat is a strong community and a long-run commitment to collective dissent. As dissidents adopt Tit-For-Tat norms, revolutionary movements strengthen.
- *Locate Agents or Entrepreneurs* (sect. 6.1). Complex events spread over space and time may be the result of leadership. Alternatively, such events may eventually acquire leadership. Strong revolutionary movements are associated with strong leadership.
- *Locate Principals or Patrons* (sect. 6.2). External support can provide the resources that allow dissidents to broaden a conflict. As external support for dissent increases, revolutionary movements strengthen.

Revolution may thus arise as principals or patrons provide outside resources that allow agents or entrepreneurs to improve the productivity of their tactics. It is equally possible that revolution may begin after the regime has alienated so many segments of society that team competition intensifies, mutual exchange and Tit-For-Tat among dissidents increase, and a bandwagon of collective dissent emerges as dissidents come to believe that they have a good chance of winning. All such solutions should be pursued.

There is one other important political process behind revolution: coalition formation. Dissident groups can cooperate and form alliances. Revolutions often result from such antiregime coalitions that pool diverse social forces.

Revolution is therefore a two-step process. The first step involves CA: dissidents achieve cooperation within each dissident group (i.e., the formation of a dissident organization). The second step involves coalition formation: dissidents achieve cooperation among dissident groups (i.e., the formation of an antiregime coalition). According to Elster (1985, 15–16), dissidents thus may be thought of as playing two games: the first is a CA game aimed at forming collective actors; the second is a coalition game among those collective actors. Hence, "once collective actors have been formed and have achieved some stability, we may look at the way in which they confront one another in the social and political arena" (Elster 1985, 16).

Coalitions of dissidents are probably behind revolution, because coalitions can combine the aforementioned solutions to the Rebel's Dilemma. Dissident coalitions are often led by entrepreneurs, who locate wealthy patrons and find followers who can make a unique contribution to the movement. Moreover, coalitions of dissidents facilitate mutual exchange and Tit-For-Tat, creating a bandwagon and increasing the dissidents' estimates of their probability of winning. As a consequence, the dissident's coalition comes into intense competition with the regime's coalition. This combination of solutions (Lichbach forthcoming, chap. 7) to the Rebel's Dilemma might well hold the key to explaining revolution.

In sum, revolution involves more than a disgruntled collective actor engaging in group CA. Revolution results from an antiregime coalition that consists of multiple disgruntled collective actors overcoming multiple CA problems with multiple solutions. Revolution can occur only in the presence of such a diverse and heterogeneous coalition of social forces.

All major students of revolution, including Barrington Moore (1966), Samuel Huntington (1968), and Theda Skocpol (1979), concur.[13] Indeed, much evidence underlies the coalition-revolution proposition: no *central* organization solved one *single* CA problem in any Great Revolution; rather, many separate revolutionary movements solved many separate CA problems. A revolution, such as the French,[14] Russian,[15] and several Latin American revolutions,[16] as well as counterrevolutions,[17] is best described as an interrelated series of localized revolts from below. Failed revolutions, moreover, often result from aborted inter-class coalitions.[18] The coalition-revolution proposition is thus supported by a wealth of argumentation and evidence. Somewhere in the combination of CA and coalition processes lies the key to understanding the complexity of a revolution. Coalition formation is a critical link between collective dissent and revolution and hence theories of CA need to be supplemented by theories of coalition formation.

### 7.2.2. The Antirevolutionary Coalition: The State's Dilemma

The other part of the formula for revolution involves incumbents (Eckstein 1965, 145–48), political institutionalization (Huntington 1968), and state breakdown (Skocpol 1979). Consider, in short, the antirevolutionary coalition.

Counterrevolutionaries are often called lackeys, hirelings, puppets, mercenaries, agents provocateurs, infiltrators, spies, and informants. They work for the conservatives. It is difficult to account for their behavior; we have, after all, many more theories of revolution than of counterrevolution.[19]

CA theories fill this important gap in the literature, by recognizing that the regime faces a CA problem with respect to its supporters. This CA problem will be referred to here as the State's Dilemma.[20] Again, Olson (1965, 105–6) understood the key issue early on: "If a person is in the bourgeois class, he may well want a government that represents his class. But it does not follow that it will be in his interest to work to see that such a government comes to power." Olson later (1990, 15, emphasis in original) isolates the regime's CA problem very neatly:

> Just as it does not normally pay a typical individual to rebel, so it also does not pay for the typical policeman or soldier or bureaucrat who happens to believe in the regime to go out of his way to help the regime survive simply because he favors the regime. It does not pay the typical official of a regime to carry out the orders of the leadership unless there is some incentive for him to do that *separate from* his belief in the established system. Think of a society where there are huge numbers of people who want a revolution, but also huge numbers who want to preserve the status quo. The logic of collective action applies to one side as much as to the other.

Recall one of the principal themes of this book: all CA problems are political. Someone will be interested in solving a group's CA problem; someone else will be interested in exacerbating the problem. Politics is in part the struggle over solutions to CA problems. This theme is particularly evident in the case of the State's Dilemma. While regimes work hard to implement solutions to the State's Dilemma and hence prevent revolution, dissidents work just as hard to impede those solutions and hence foment revolution.

Revolutionaries try to intensify the State's Dilemma by appealing to the government as a patron (sect. 6.2.3.2). This strategy works when elite divisions (sect. 3.6.2.2) lead some members of the polity to seek advantage by bringing revolutionaries into the governing elite. Such elites may even be willing to sponsor rebellion to encourage the incorporation of new social forces (Tilly 1978, 213–14; Piven and Cloward 1979, chap. 1; Skocpol 1979; Jenkins and Schock 1992). One finds examples in all types of regimes. In liberal democratic regimes closely fought electoral competition encouraged a center-left government to support the labor movement in the 1930s (Jenkins and Brents 1989), the civil rights movement in 1960s (McAdam 1982, 77–82), and farmworkers in the 1960s (Jenkins 1985, 217–22). In absolutist states fiscal crises produced elite divisions that facilitated revolutionary coalitions between landowning nobility and political outsiders (Kimmel 1988, 15–16). In bureaucratic-authoritarian states divisions within the military and between the military and upper classes led to revolutionary coalitions between polity members and outsiders (Stepan 1985).

Regimes, for their part, try to mitigate the State's Dilemma and forestall revolution. Any of the general solutions to the CA problem are potentially applicable to the State's Dilemma. Quite naturally, self-government (sect. 5.1.1) appears to be a particularly important approach. The CA problem of the dominant class is often solved by creating a representative assembly, a forum that the governing class then uses to forge an agreement about how to coerce (i.e., tax) themselves. Brewer (1988, 347) argues that after 1688 British landlords recognized the foreign policy dangers to their state and responded in Parliament with a new tax policy. Such forums, however, can also work against the regime. In France, regional parliaments facilitated cooperation by the nobles against the state (Brustein and Levi 1987, 478–9).

### 7.2.3. The Rebel's Dilemma and the State's Dilemma

In sum, the key to understanding the revolutionary struggle between regimes and oppositions is to understand their struggle over solutions to the Rebel's Dilemma and the State's Dilemma. The real competition is over their respective CA problems. As one side tries to implement solutions to its dilemma, the other side tries to impede those solutions, and vice versa. The relative capacity for solving and creating, diminishing and magnifying, CA problems decides the outcome of the game — as evolution and revolution, persistence and change, hang in the balance.

The state holds the privileged position in this competition. "One's intuition tells one," Olson (1990, 15) observes, "that the situation is different when we are looking at the existing government, and so it is." A hierarchy or state is in fact one category of solution to the CA problem. The state can draw upon selective incentives and disincentives to mobilize its supporters:

> The existing government, after all, pays salaries to its policemen and its soldiers, pays higher salaries to its higher officials, and gives promotions to those who serve it especially well. If the functionaries do not do what the leadership wants, they will lose those salaries. On top of that, the policemen are, of course, paid to arrest and punish people who act in ways that are offensive to the people in charge. Thus the pay of the sol-

diers, policemen, and officials — and the punishment the regime can impose — are the positive and negative selective incentives that make the regime work. Regimes can often survive when they are unpopular because they have the selective incentives arising from their guns, their tax receipts, their monopoly of the printing press, and so on. These selective incentives make the bureaucrats, soldiers, and policemen carry out the orders of the leadership, whether they like the existing regime or not. (Olson 1990, 15)

Thus, states have the advantage over dissidents, because they can more easily implement solutions to their own CA problem and impede solutions to their opponents' CA problem. This reality can explain both the existence of the state and the infrequency of revolution. The regime does not have the necessary force to invoke against all dissidents at once. Force is never enough to ensure that regimes stay in power (Lichbach forthcoming, chap. 7). Legitimacy is also insufficient because the regime's supporters face Olson's Problem and need not come to the regime's defense.

Revolutions are therefore infrequent only because of the dissidents' CA problem. Rebels, that is, cannot all mobilize at once because of many little and one big Rebel's Dilemma. The state survives because it can more easily solve its CA problem with respect to its supporters than can dissident groups.

This line of thought is important for the study of revolution, in particular, and important for conflict studies, more generally. The focus on *both* the Rebel's Dilemma *and* the State's Dilemma allows one to move from a theory of collective dissent to a theory of domestic political conflict — from a focus on what dissidents do to a focus on the ongoing process of challenge and response by dissidents and regimes (Gurr and Lichbach 1979; Lichbach and Gurr 1981). Future applications of CA theories to collective dissent therefore should focus on the strategies and tactics that regimes and oppositions take toward the CA problems of regimes and oppositions.

This chapter has examined the two basic political processes in which regimes and dissidents are involved: reform and revolution. I have explored the political competition, cooperation, and conflict between regimes and oppositions over the many solutions to PG–PD problems. Before evaluating what the "solutions as politics" theme has accomplished, I turn to my second perspective on the many ways to solve the Rebel's Dilemma.

## CHAPTER 8

# Solutions as Pathologies: The Outcomes of Collective Action

This chapter asks the *what if* question about solutions to the Rebel's Dilemma. Section 8.1 addresses the "solutions as intended consequences" subtheme. Intended consequences include group mobilization and group success. Section 8.2 addresses the "solutions as unintended consequences" subtheme. Unintended consequences involve the pathologies of group organization.

## 8.1. The Intended Consequences of Dissident Organization

Hierarchy solutions to the Rebel's Dilemma are used to win followers and redress grievances. Under what conditions are the intended consequences of dissident organization achieved?[1]

Some would argue that dissident organization is needed to solve the Rebel's Dilemma by removing obstacles to CA. Large groups that wish to sustain geographically dispersed and temporally persistent collective dissent require organization. Any collective dissent that manages to mobilize large numbers of people over a wide territory without dissident organization will be short-lived (O'Brien 1974, 237–38). A movement might be able to arouse participation in response to a crisis (sect. 3.1) with appeals to ideology (sect. 3.8.2.3) or to the dramaturgy and fun of conflict (sect. 4.2.1). Inevitably, however, the initial excitement passes, obstacles arise, and frustration sets in. As McAdam, McCarthy, and Zald (1988, 722) put it, "The creation of a revolutionary consciousness hardly ensures the survival of this consciousness over time." To sustain participation, the movement needs organization to supply leadership, financing, ideology, communication, strategies, and tactics. In short, enduring dissident action requires dissident organization.

The literature offers two specific propositions. First, the better the organization of the dissidents, the more collective dissent becomes nonrandom and disciplined. Demonstrations, marches, and strikes, for example, replace riots and brawls (Frank and Kelly 1979, 601). Second, the better the organization of the dissidents, the greater the collective dissent. Deadly and long-lived guerrilla wars, for example, replace terrorism.

There is an enormous body of argumentation and evidence behind these ideas. Many dissidents[2] and academics[3] accept both propositions. Case studies,[4] historical analyses,[5] and cross-national studies[6] provide support.

There is nevertheless a counterargument that downplays the importance of organizing. Many revolutionaries, including Blanqui, Bakunin, Sorel, Luxemburg, and Cohn-Bendit, argue that spontaneity fosters creativity and thus success. Many academics, including Piven and Cloward (1979, 36–37) and Touraine (1985), also argue that organization ultimately limits spontaneity and actually contributes to a decline of collective dissent.

The problem, they believe, is that dissident organization forecloses other solutions to the Rebel's Dilemma. First, it reduces a dissident's estimate of the probability of making a difference (sect. 3.7): "The existence of formal organizations often contributes to a sense that someone else is carrying the burden of protest, and one need not sacrifice one's own resources" (Calhoun 1988, 170). Second, the selective incentives (sect. 6.5.3) and disincentives (sect. 6.5.4) made available by organizations induce dissidents to make a tradeoff. As private benefits (i.e., the dissident entrepreneur's implicit or explicit purchase of a dissident's services) and private costs (i.e., the dissident entrepreneur's coerced and extorted taxes) increase, voluntary contributions decrease. In effect, dissidents are encouraged to participate opportunistically rather than ideologically. As any one form of contribution increases, the other two decrease. The effect on the total resources available to the dissident group is difficult to predict (Frohlich, Oppenheimer, and Young 1971, 7). Finally, dissidents' formal organization hurts the dissidents' naturally occurring pluralism, mutual conciliation, communication, and cooperation. Given that these factors are all necessary to sustain social contracts (chap. 5), the thinking is that Hierarchy eventually destroys Community.

Hence, the paradox of organization: the bureaucratic dissident organization smothers and suffocates the spontaneity and excitement of the dissident movement.[7] There is indeed evidence (sect. 5.1) that indicates large-scale and long-lived CA can occur without elite entrepreneurs,[8] that organized dissident groups can be propelled to action by unorganized dissidents,[9] and that organization is the dependent variable, not the independent variable, because dissident CA reinforces community and hence builds the dissident organization.[10]

The question of the necessity of dissident organization has thus been debated among practitioners of conflict. Which is more important to revolution, dissidents wonder, individual acts of heroism or long-term planning and mobilization? The nineteenth century saw many competing proposals for dissident organization: utopian communities practicing withdrawal, cadre parties practicing conspiratorial and rapid insurrection, and secret societies practicing terrorism (Billington 1980; Wallerstein 1984, 112–13). The first great debate in Marxist circles concerned the question of whether communism could be achieved only by an organized party. The Marxists ultimately defeated the Anarchists and created the Second International. Once it was decided to create an organization, the second great debate in Marxist circles focused on the issue of whether communism could be achieved only by an elitist party. The Bolsheviks defeated the Mensheviks and created a centralized and disciplined organization. Contemporary debates among the New Left and the new social movements revisit these earlier debates.

Students of conflict, too, have debated the question.[11] The debate has been particularly intense with respect to revolution[12] and peasant upheavals.[13]

Given all of the conflicting arguments and evidence, Gurr (1970, 275) simply maintains that "neither the extent nor the kinds of organization in a society have an invariant relationship with the extent or forms of political violence." The analysis here supports Gurr's judgment: there are *many* solutions to the Rebel's Dilemma — some involve organization and some do not. Hierarchy solutions (chap. 6) imply that formal dissident organization precedes dissident action. Community solutions (chap. 4) imply that informal dissident organization precedes dissident action. Contract solutions (chap. 5) imply that dissident action precedes dissident organization. Market solutions (chap. 3) imply that dissident action can occur without organizational antecedents or precedents. No one category of solution to the Rebel's Dilemma exercises a monopoly. All are viable approaches.

## 8.2. The Unintended Consequences of Dissident Organization

As indicated above, critics of dissident organizations stress their unwanted negative impacts on dissident movements. But each type of solution to the Rebel's Dilemma can backfire. I will now consider the problem of the unintended consequences of CA solutions more closely.

### 8.2.1. The Iron Laws

I refer to the self-defeating nature of solutions to the Rebel's Dilemma as the "pathologies" or "iron laws" of dissident groups. These pathologies are deep and wide-ranging and affect dissident leaders, followers, organization, policies, and leader-follower linkages.

I identify five iron laws about dissident leaders. These concern rent seeking, the professionalization of protest, coerciveness, manipulativeness, and hypocrisy.

*Rent seeking.* Given that dissident entrepreneurs seek selective incentives, one expects that greedy leaders will manipulate their followers for their own personal aggrandizement. Dissident leaders, one suspects, sacrifice the interests of their followers for their own personal gain. An inevitable and unavoidable concomitant of dissident entrepreneurship, therefore, is the agency problem of corruption and rent-seeking behavior (sect. 6.1.3; Lichbach forthcoming, chap. 6).

*The professionalization of protest.* Dissident entrepreneurs are ambitious and attempt to make a career out of their participation in a dissident group. Furthermore, dissident leaders often use their experience with dissident groups to prepare for their subsequent careers (sect. 6.5.3.3). Dissident followers are also careerist: many attempt to become paid staff. Thus, as dissident groups age, there often emerges a professional cadre of dissident entrepreneurs — full-time salaried fund-raisers, for example.

*Coerciveness.* The selective disincentives solution to the Rebel's Dilemma implies that dissident leaders coerce their followers into contributing to the dissident group (sect. 6.5.4). Coerciveness may also result from the application of the *Increase Team Competition between Enemies* solution to the Rebel's Dilemma (sect. 3.10). Coercive dissident groups that achieve power, moreover, are likely to become regimes that coerce their peoples.

*Manipulativeness.* Dissident entrepreneurs often manipulate their followers. For example, they use insincere demands and policy statements to mobilize their rank and file (sect. 6.3.2).

*Hypocrisy.* Wildavsky (1984, 220) tells us that "hierarchies must be hypocritical; there is no other way." So it is. Dissident leaders interested in shaping an efficacious group often hypocritically hide tactical policy shifts behind high-sounding principles (sect. 6.3.2). Furthermore, they are more concerned with convincing potential supporters that their cause will succeed than that their cause is just, and more interested in asserting that the group is strong than that the group is right. All dissident entrepreneurs thus claim widespread, enduring, and intense support. They predict eventual victory, just as they struggle to make true their inflated claims (sect. 3.6.5). Dissident entrepreneurs are hypocrites in yet another sense: they hide their own selective incentives (sect. 6.5.3). They may enjoy them in locations not frequented by their followers; or they may create complex rules, full of details and loopholes, to distribute the benefits of CA. Yet another way is to claim that their private interests are equivalent to the public interest. Finally, dissident entrepreneurs may mask selective incentives by eschewing a few private rewards in a very public display of self-sacrifice. This tactic is especially useful when private rewards are very conspicuous and controversial, and hence difficult to hide.

Dissidents' attempts to overcome their Rebel's Dilemma also have unintended negative consequences for dissident followers. They, too, are subject to five iron laws: mendacity and the decline of revolutionary zeal, altruism, reciprocity, and voluntarism.

*Mendacity.* Rank-and-file dissidents are also often liars and hypocrites. Dissident followers do not reveal their true demand for PGs (sect. 9.2.2.2). Moreover, their publicly stated (i.e., collective) purposes are often not the same as their privately held (i.e., individual) motives. Kuran's (1989, 1991a) important work demonstrates that preference falsification is basic to collective dissent. Rioters typically deny the profit motive behind collective dissent in order to establish the legitimacy of their grievances, attract third-party support, and have their actions defined as social protest and not economic crime (sect. 6.5.3). A final element of hypocrisy comes in ritualistic demands for participation. Dissidents often claim to hold postmaterialist values of participatory democracy, according a high priority to "seeing that the people have more say in how things get decided at work and in their communities" and "giving the people more say in important government decisions." The rhetoric, however, outweighs the action: only infrequently do dissidents seek to participate in a dissident group's decision-making processes (sect. 2.1).

*The decline of revolutionary zeal.* Dissidents try to profit from their participation in collective dissent. Before the revolution, they create organizations that encourage the "growth of careerism, corruption, and self-serving at the expense of revolutionary idealism" (Hagopian 1974, 228). Hierarchy solutions (e.g., *Administer Selective Incentives*, sect. 6.5.3) to the Rebel's Dilemma thus foreclose Market solutions (e.g., *Locate Zealots*, sect. 3.1). One thus expects that as selective incentives and disincentives increase, the intensity of support for collective dissent will decrease. Revolutionary organizations, in short, are responsible for the decline of revolutionary zeal.[14] Profit-making, and hence the decline of revolutionary zeal, accelerates in the postrevolutionary society. Political apathy and passivity reemerged in the Thermidorean phase of all the Great Revolutions. As a consequence, revolutionary leaders typically did not have to exclude the mass of dissidents from postrevolutionary politics — most withdrew voluntarily. As some (e.g., DA theorists) would put it, the basis of legitimacy in postrevolutionary societies shifts from charisma (i.e., emotion) to legality (i.e., rationality).

*The decline of altruism.* Taylor (1982) argues that Hierarchy destroys Community by undermining the personal, direct, and unmediated relations typical of a close-knit group of potential cooperators. Hierarchy solutions (e.g., *Administer Selective Incentives*, sect. 6.5.3) to the Rebel's Dilemma thus foreclose Community solutions (e.g., *Overcome Pecuniary Self-Interest*, sect. 4.2). Hence, one expects that as selective incentives or disincentives increase, altruism will decrease. Hierarchy solutions shift the CA problem, they do not solve it.

*The decline of reciprocity.* By destroying Community, Hierarchy solutions to the Rebel's Dilemma also damage reciprocity and hence such Contract solutions as Tit-For-Tat (sect. 5.1.2). One therefore expects that as selective incentives or disincentives increase, the effectiveness of Tit-For-Tat will decrease. Once again, Hierarchy solutions have shifted but not solved the CA problem.

*The decline of voluntarism.* Given that Hierarchy solutions to the Rebel's Dilemma destroy Market (e.g., zeal), Community (e.g., altruism), and Contract (e.g., reciprocity) solutions, one must conclude that dissident organizations reduce voluntarism and hence impede rather than promote participation in collective dissent. For this reason, many argue that dissident organizations intensify rather than solve the CA problem (sect. 8.1).

The dissidents' attempts to overcome the Rebel's Dilemma also have unintended negative consequences for dissident organizations. There are four iron laws about dissident organization: disunity, secretiveness, bureaucratization, and self-perpetuation.

*Disunity.* Factionalism marks dissident groups, dissident movements, and antiregime coalitions (sect. 6.4) because attempts to solve the CA problem often generate a new divisive issue. For example, debates over tactics to improve the dissident's production function (sect. 3.4) often make the group less effective, not more so. Such differences are often papered over and the coalition fragments once it takes power.

*Secretiveness.* In order to improve the productivity of their tactics (sect. 3.4), dissident entrepreneurs often keep their strategy a secret from the regime. Crozier (1960, 157) maintains that "absolute secrecy in the phase of preparation is an essential condition of success." One consequence is that dissident leaders are also secretive with their followers. Failure to obey this iron law of secrecy may lead to failure, as the anti-Sukarno and anti-Batista rebels discovered (Crozier 1960, 157).

*Bureaucratization.* Enduring cults are called churches. So it is with dissident groups. Spontaneous dissident organizations (e.g., revolutionary communes, soviets, cooperatives, assemblies, conventions, committees; sect. 5.1) become institutions (e.g., interest groups, neighborhood organizations, community councils, labor unions, political parties, terrorist groups, guerrilla organizations; sect. 6.1). Agitators become administrators; charismatics, organizers.

*Self-perpetuation.* Some dissident groups are latecomers. Those who find the field occupied tend to have difficulty mobilizing internal sympathizers and locating external patrons. The initial failure rate of new dissident groups is therefore high. For example, UNITA in Angola formed after the FNLA and the MPLA and faced numerous obstacles. Once a dissident group forms, however, dissident entrepreneurs acquire a vested interest in the group's rewards (sect. 6.5.3). For this reason, dissident organizations tend to persist even when they become anachronistic, and the failure rate of dissident groups diminishes with age.

Dissidents' attempts to solve their CA problem lead to another set of unanticipated and unwanted consequences: policy change. Dissident groups tend to become opportunistic, coopted, depoliticized, deradicalized, particularistic, and expediency-oriented.

*Opportunism.* Dissident entrepreneurs alter their policy positions in order to mobilize supporters, often to the point of becoming a catch-all party (sect. 6.3.1). Dissident entrepreneurs also shift policy positions, in order to participate in legal political struggles (sect. 6.1). Dissident followers are equally opportunistic. They move from left to right and back again, support both sides of a conflict, flock to the side that looks like the winner, and then finally join the side that actually does win (sect. 9.2.2.2).

*Cooptation.* Dissident groups that rely on domestic and foreign patrons are likely be coopted (sect. 6.2.4). Regimes can also be coopted. This leads to an external patronage race, as the external support of dissidents provokes the external support of regimes, and vice versa. A peaceful resolution of the conflict becomes that much more difficult to achieve.

*Depoliticization.* Dissidents who seek only selective incentives (sect. 6.5.3) are nothing more than nonpolitical robbers — social bandits and not revolutionaries (sect. 6.5.3.4). An acquired taste for plunder, moreover, accelerates a transformation of political protest and rebellion into social banditry.

*Deradicalization.* Both success and failure have deradicalized dissident organizations. Lack of success often breeds deradicalization because of generational change: first-generation leaders mellow as they age; second-generation leaders are less likely to be radical. They tend to focus less on societal issues and more on the organization and its constituency (Tucker 1969, chap. 6). Furthermore, lack of success weakens the group's support (sect. 3.6.2.1), which leads group entrepreneurs to try to maintain the group (and the prerogatives they receive from it) by widening the group's base of support. Often this means adopting less radical goals and means. Finally, as unsuccessful dissident groups redouble their efforts to find selective incentives (sect. 6.5.3) that can mobilize followers, and as they renew their efforts to locate patrons (sect. 6.2) who can turn things around, the groups' commitment to radical goals and means can be diminished

Success, too, may breed deradicalization. Hirschman (1982a, 94) poses the question, "What is there left to do for a republican after the fall of the monarchy, or for the separatist after successful secession?" Those who seize state power often turn out to be satisfied with the benefits to be derived from reforming the system, even at the cost of strengthening it. Successful dissident movements thus try to consolidate their gains, rather than pursuing an even greater break with the past. Every successful revolution becomes a conservative, even counterrevolutionary, force that endeavors to preserve the status quo it has created — the new social order (i.e., the rents finally achieved). Tocqueville ([1856] 1955, vii) suggests that revolutions typically destroy their predecessors and then wind up rebuilding the Old Regime: "Though nothing was further from their intentions, they used the debris of the old order for building up the new." A Thermidorean slowdown and an eventual rollback of social change has, indeed, occurred in all of the Great Revolutions.

In sum, both successful and unsuccessful dissident groups deradicalize. Success breeds embourgeoisement. Lack of success breeds changes that entrepreneurs hope will bring success. Both successful and unsuccessful dissidents eventually tend to become less radical and hence "channeled" (Jenkins and Eckert 1986, 828). Religious movements,[15] leftist movements,[16] and the Townsend movement in the United States[17] are classic examples.

*Particularism.* One solution to the Rebel's Dilemma is to become small (sect. 6.3.1). Small dissident groups are likely to be homogeneous groups that narrowly pursue a local community's parochial interest. They are unlikely to be heterogeneous groups that fight for the interests of the entire national community. Such dissident groups view themselves as players in a zero-sum game who are fighting over the distribution of a pie. By the same token, they are unlikely to see themselves as players in a nonzero-sum game who are out to increase the size of the pie (Olson 1982, 42).

*Expediency oriented.* To ensure the survival of their group, and, consequently, of the prerogatives that they receive, dissident entrepreneurs often sacrifice principle for expediency, trading ends for means.[18] For a large and heterogeneous dissident group, which has a hard time holding its coalition together, expediency often becomes the most important principle (Friedrich 1950, 416). One finds classic illustration of this phenomenon in pre-WWI Europe: once hostilities began, Socialist parties reversed their position on war. And in interwar Germany and Italy many Social Democrats eventually came to terms with the Nazis and Fascists.

Dissidents' attempts to overcome their Rebel's Dilemma lead to one final set of unintended negative consequences: the estrangement of leaders and followers. There are several iron laws concerning the leader-follower linkage. Dissident groups are likely to be characterized by nonparticipation, which in turn is partially responsible for nonrepresentativeness, nonresponsiveness, inequality, oligarchy, and authoritarianism.

*Nonparticipation.* The CA problem also holds *within* a dissident group. Dissidents have an interest in shaping the group's goals. But since those goals are for a PG, dissidents will not voluntarily participate in the group's decision-making processes. Coleman (1990, 362) points out that "an organized opposition party which presents the membership with an alternative that can overcome the oligarchic monopoly of agents of the corporate body is a public good, which no member or set of members will have the incentive to bring into existence." Moreover, as Lipset, Trow, and Coleman (1962, 86, emphasis in original) point out, leaders construct their organizations so as to make mass participation costly: "It is perhaps paradoxical that the very organizations which allow workers to act collectively in their relations with employers are ordinarily so constructed that *within* them the members are usually unable to act collectively in dealing with their leaders." The result is that dissident followers typically do not try to influence dissident leaders. Hence, the next iron law: most dissidents do not participate in the affairs of the dissident group; those who do participate will participate little; any participation will be short-term; low-cost activities will be preferred (sect. 3.2.2). Membership in a dissident group is thus "inclusive" rather than "exclusive."

What about the revolutionary rhetoric that advocates richer and less perfunctory participation in the affairs of dissident organizations? This rhetoric comes from leaders who claim to have offered their followers the opportunity to participate in the dissident group's business. The rhetoric also comes from followers who claim the right to influence their leaders. In fact, both leaders and followers almost always employ the rhetoric but also almost always have no interest in the reality. Appeals to participatory democracy within dissident groups typically fail. Olson's (1965) logic of collective inaction is thus as inexorable within dissident groups as within societies more generally. It can explain the absence of internal dissent against dissident groups as easily as it can explain the absence of collective dissent against regimes.

But one group of dissidents does participate in a dissident group: leaders. This process is "the main dynamic behind the 'Iron Law of Oligarchy'" (McMahon and Camilleri 1975, 617), a point recognized by Michels ([1919] 1962). Differential rates of participation result from differences in rewards, preference intensity, and resource endowment. First, whereas dissident leaders often receive selective rewards (sect. 6.5.3) in return for their participation, followers commonly receive nothing more than the PG of a better dissident organization. The differential reward system leads to differential rates of activism. Second, leaders are more likely than followers to have intense preferences. As a dissident's intensity of demand for a PG increases, the extensiveness of his or her participation increases (sect. 3.1). Those with less intense preferences will exploit those with more intense preferences because of the latter's willingness to contribute toward the PG. Finally, leaders are more likely than followers to control resources. Those who provide more resources will be able to exploit those who provide less resources, because they will be better able to rent seek from the dissident group (sect. 3.3). In sum, well-rewarded, well-motivated, and well-endowed dissidents make comparatively greater efforts at participation than do those who are less so. They will thus be more successful at influencing group policy. The small will exploit the great (Olson 1965, 29, 35). One must conclude that dissident groups are always captured by *someone*: either those who are well rewarded and endowed (and thus are better able to bear the costs) or those who are zealots and ideologues (and thus have special interests) gain control.

*Nonrepresentativeness*. One consequence of differential rates of participation is that a dissident group's policies do not necessarily reflect the underlying common interests of the dissident group's community. Another reason that dissidents are unrepresentative of their community is that dissident entrepreneurs are often elites (sect. 6.1.2). Sampling also creates nonrepresentativeness. The selection of dissidents is, of course, the result of a nonrandom sampling procedure in which participants self-select. One reason for a biased sample is that participants in collective dissent are particularly risk-prone individuals (sect. 3.9) and are thus atypical members of the dissidents' community. But let us lay aside this sampling problem and assume that the process of selecting dissidents from their community is essentially random. Sampling theory tells us that if random sampling is used, the larger the sample, the more representative it is likely to be. This rule holds, at least until sample size reaches approximately one thousand cases. After this point, the marginal benefits of adding another member to the sampling frame diminish dramatically. Since small dissident groups are therefore less representative of the larger dissident population than are large dissident groups, the *Become Clubbish* solution to the Rebel's Dilemma (sect. 6.3.1) produces less representative dissident groups. As Olson (1982, 47-50) suggests, as the dissident group decreases in size, its demands become more extreme and more concerned with the specific, rather than the general, interest. Another consequence is often referred to as the tyranny of small communities: informal social pressures lead to enforced uniformity. In short, a dissident group is a biased sample of its constituency; a dissident group's leadership is a biased sample of the dissident group.

*Nonresponsiveness*. Dissident leaders are often unresponsive to their followers. Leaders often constrain followers, but followers are often unable to constrain leaders, due to differential rates of participation. Once again we have an agency problem (Lichbach forthcoming, chap. 6). The goals of the leadership are therefore not necessarily the goals of the group. On the contrary, "The behavior of persons who lead or speak for an organization can best be understood in terms of their efforts to maintain and enhance the organization and their position in it" (Wilson 1973, 9), not as a conduit for their followers' desires. A dissident group's policies do not necessarily respond to the underlying common interests of rank-and-file dissidents. A dissident group's demands do not necessarily reflect its membership's demands.

*Inequality.* Another result of an active leadership and a passive followership is inequality. In fact, the CA problem, however it is solved, generates inequality. Hierarchy and stratification are the inevitable concomitants of solutions to the Rebel's Dilemma.

Consider Market and Hierarchy solutions to the CA problem. Both solutions generate inequality. When Market solutions are applied, contributions are not forced. Costs are instead shifted from the tempted to the suckered, the result of an anarchic environment of free riding and unequal burden sharing. As Olson (1965, 29, 35) puts it in his classic formulation, the great will be exploited by the small, the few will be exploited by the many. Hierarchy solutions also generate inequality. Since a controlled environment often leads to fixed and uniform fees for a PG, unequal burden sharing results as costs are shifted from the zealots to the uncaring. In sum, whether none are forced to pay or all are forced to pay, resources are always shifted unfairly.

Now consider two levels of popular involvement in the affairs of the dissident organization. A low level of participation generates inequality because it allows the few who do participate to rent seek and accrue more gains from collective dissent. Therefore, under low levels of participation, redistribution favors those who have an incentive to become politically involved. Inequality also arises when there is a high level of participation, as each person or group seeks to privatize its benefits and socialize its costs. The result, as O'Donnell and Schmitter (1986, 12) note, is that "higher levels of participation in some institutions, through such devices as workers' councils and corporatist forums, can result in an increase rather than a decrease in the overall inequality of benefits."

One must conclude that the very act of overcoming the CA problem generates privilege and causes inequality. The particular solution to the Rebel's Dilemma is irrelevant, as is the level of participation. Dissident entrepreneurs are always better paid than followers; they always find ways to rent-seek, or to exploit their position to extract extra benefits. Any gains from CA are always distributed unequally.[19] The Russian and Chinese Revolutions, for example, produced a redistribution of resources to a postrevolutionary new class — the Leninist elite. Revolutions, that is, simply transfer power and control from one small minority to another. Inequality is thus more often the consequence than the cause of revolution (Lichbach 1989).

*Oligarchy.* The result of an active leadership and a passive followership is also that leaders are independent of followers. The dissident group may thus be said to be oligarchical.

*Authoritarianism.* Dissident organizations, finally, tend toward authoritarianism. Permanent organizations (i.e., Hierarchy solutions) become despotic. Lenin's vanguard party was an authoritarian means to a radical end, for example. Armed dissident organizations are especially likely to become authoritarian (Fuentes and Frank 1989, 181). Impermanent organizations also tend toward despotism. For example, large and undifferentiated crowds (i.e., Market solutions) are vulnerable to demagogues. Cleon, Marius, and Alcibiades are the classic examples from antiquity of demagogues leading followers astray (Dobel 1978, 968). The attempt to increase team competition between regime and opposition (sect. 3.10.1.2) only intensifies the authoritarian tendency of dissident groups and leads to restricted liberty for dissidents. Coser's (1956) proposition, as summarized by Turner (1986, 174) rings true: "The more violent or intense is the conflict, the more conflict leads to the suppression of dissent and deviance within each conflict party as well as forced conformity to norms and values."

Accordingly, dissident groups are almost always opposed to internal dissent. Thus, revolutionaries attack moderation, reformism, pragmatism, and compromise; and they will also attack radicalism, putschism, left-deviationism, and ultrarevolutionism. This search by leadership for ideological purity and revolutionary truth is really an effort to prevent opposition to its policies. As Brinton (1965, 194) observes of all the Great Revolutions, opposition entrepreneurs are intolerant of any internal opposition.

Postrevolutionary societies also tend toward authoritarianism.[20] The Left's rhetoric of revolution is negative — abolish private property, create a classless society, and let the state wither away. The reality of revolution is positive — the dictatorship of the proletariat, the new class, and the strengthening of the state (Skocpol 1979, 161–62). The irony of revolution is thus that those who support dissent against others eventually oppose dissent against themselves.[21] Dissident victory finishes off collective dissent and one tyranny replaces another.

In sum, CA theories imply that collective dissent will probably not occur. If protest and rebellion were to occur, however, the avowedly lofty aims of the participants would probably not succeed. Strategies to overcome the Rebel's Dilemma generate as many problems as they solve. Dissidents who adopt solutions to the Rebel's Dilemma are thus like the sorcerer's apprentice: they set in motion mechanisms that they do not understand and cannot stop. Solving the Rebel's Dilemma produces a stream of unintended and unwanted pathologies that eventually engulf dissident groups — a Pandora's box of iron laws results. Elster (1989, 18) notes the irony: "Sometimes it might have been better for all if the original [CA] problems had been left unsolved." Dissidents who solve their Rebel's Dilemma always get less than they hoped for and more than they bargained for.

## 8.2.2. The Universality of the Iron Laws

The structure and development of dissident groups, CA theories would lead us to believe, are subject to two general laws. Law Number One: only evil dissidents can win.[22] Law Number Two: you cannot change Law Number One.

But do such iron laws really exist? Are all revolutions betrayed, all dissident groups evil, and all dissidents corrupt? Surely, honest, self-effacing, and self-sacrificing dissidents may be found. Alexander Solzhenitsyn and Anatoly Sharansky come to mind. Dedicated and committed dissident organizations may be located: the Paris Commune, the Petrograd Soviet, the "Yenan Way" in base areas under Chinese Communist control, and the agrarian collectives of the Spanish Revolution, for example. Small and unsuccessful movements do remain ideologically pure and committed. Trotskyists and certain ecological movements might be cases. Protest movements do manifest all that is good in humanity. The foresight, courage, and altruism of some in the U.S. civil rights movement and others in the Jewish resistance to the Holocaust are indisputable. Moreover, processes of rebellion leads to social revolution: youth and women, for example, might find greater equality and liberation. Processes of rebellion also lead to political revolution: in the United States, for example, "social movements have contributed to the freeing of the slaves, the end of child labor, the suffrage of blacks, women, and 18–20 year olds, the eight-hour work day and the forty-hour week, direct election of U.S.senators, the graduated income tax, social security, collective bargaining, prohibition, the end of prohibition, and the desegregation of public facilities and schools" (Stewart, Smith, and Denton 1984, ix). Are not CA theories blind to these positive outcomes because they deny the possibility of mass mobilization? Is not the picture produced by the CA research program, therefore, overdrawn and one-sided?

Each of the iron laws may indeed be called into question.[23] The iron laws are not universal, as has been recognized in two branches of conflict studies. First, the new "history from below" emphasizes the distinctive perspectives of rank-and-file revolutionaries. Rudé (1959, 5), for example, observes "social groups with their own distinctive identity, interests, and aspirations, whose actions and attitudes can no longer be treated as mere echoes or reflections of the ideas, speeches, and decrees" of leaders. Second, the Resource Mobilization perspective provides an important corrective to an earlier literature, influenced by the Weber-Michels theory of the routinization and oligarchization of social movements, that stressed the inevitable institutionalization of dissident groups.[24] In short, the iron laws are not an iron cage that imprisons all dissidents. Yes, CA solutions impose constraints on dissidents, but they do not dictate outcomes. The future, as always, is open to human intervention.

### 8.2.3. Overcoming the Iron Laws

"True" or "ultra" revolutionaries know that the iron laws are not inevitable, that they can be overcome (Hagopian 1974, 236–43). They claim to know how context influences the operation of such laws and, hence, the laws' boundaries. Marx's means (Avineri 1968, 142) for breaking the iron laws was a "workers' association. It does not have a narrowly political, nor a trade unionist significance: it is the real constructive effort to create the social texture of future human relations." Lenin looked to a vanguard party to overcoming the laws (especially that of reformism). Luxemburg relied on the spontaneity of the masses. And Mao adhered to a "mass line" philosophy.[25]

The search for ways to repeal the iron laws has thus influenced a great deal of revolutionary thought and practice. Examples may be found in the Great Revolutions,[26] the New Left,[27] and Israeli kibbutzim.[28]

The CA research program offers a deeper understanding of how the iron laws may be overcome than do either the theorists or practitioners of revolution. It helps explain what makes dissident leaders responsive to their followers, and offers insights into how followers may constrain leaders (i.e., the idea of reducing agency costs as considered in Lichbach forthcoming, chap. 6).

### 8.2.4. The Lessons

More generally, the CA research program teaches us to investigate the applicability of the iron laws. We must ask several questions. Are evil dissidents the core or the rump of dissident groups? How do dissident groups actually work? What does their internal organization actually look like?

We should treat the authority structure of a dissident group as a dependent variable. We need to know, in other words, about the origins of dissident organization, about the structures and processes that are created, and about the consequences of its authority patterns. Which solutions to the Rebel's Dilemma tend not to be subject to the iron laws and which tend to reinforce them? Are Community solutions any better than Hierarchy solutions, for example? More generally, we would like to know how a specific CA solution operating under specific conditions generates a specific pathology.[29]

A dissident group's authority structure should also be treated as an independent variable. We need to know, following the intended consequences argument of section 8.1, about the impacts of various organizational patterns on the extent and type of collective dissent. What sort of authority structures in dissident groups best promote CA? Which are more effective and which are less effective at mobilizing supporters or achieving goals? Do the purported negative consequences of solving the Rebel's Dilemma — the iron laws — ultimately help or hurt CA?

It would be valuable to investigate the causes and consequences of dissident organization in utopian dissident organizations. We should study soviets, communes, base areas, revolutionary committees, and new social movements to test the claims of their proponents (e.g., Kitschelt 1989). Some suggest that "the iron law of oligarchy is very gradually being repealed" (Inglehart 1990, 340). Given that the iron laws teach us to look for hypocrisy in all revolutionary organizations, those who claim to have overcome the iron laws cannot be taken at their word.

The CA research program has thus led us to a theory of authority for systems in revolution (Zald and Ash 1966; Stinchcombe 1978, chap. 2). The External Rebel's Dilemma begets the Internal Rebel's Dilemma, an area of inquiry sorely neglected by students of collective dissent.

In sum, solutions to the Rebel's Dilemma produce both intended and unintended consequences. Dissident organizations do not always generate their intended purpose of mobilizing supporters and achieving success. Yet, dissident organizations do not always produce unintended iron laws. A pressing question for CA theorists of domestic political conflict is thus to investigate the conditions under which various solutions to the Rebel's Dilemma produce one or the other consequence.

# Part 4
# Appraisal

## CHAPTER 9

# Evaluating Collective Action Theories of Collective Dissent

Parts 2 and 3 used solutions to the CA problem to understand collective dissent. How valuable has been this juxtaposition of two fields of inquiry? CA theories do not fare well on two standards for evaluation. Section 9.1 offers an analytical criterion, intersolution comparison, with the result that each type of CA solution offers a logically incomplete explanation of collective dissent. Section 9.2 offers an empirical standard, the predictability of particular outbreaks and aggregate levels of collective dissent, with the result that CA theories do not produce a general theoretical statement of the etiology of protest and rebellion. Section 9.3 proposes two empirical criteria, based on Lakatos and Popper, on which CA theories of collective dissent fare better. The theories account for several *additional* and *true* observations about protest beyond merely asserting that rational people, at least under the right circumstances, do (not) rebel. The theories also explain these observations *differently* and *better* than competing DA theories. Section 9.4 offers a summary evaluation of the accomplishments and limitations of CA theories of protest and rebellion.

## 9.1. An Analytical Criterion: Intersolution Comparison

Each of the four categories of solutions to the Rebel's Dilemma has its classic proponents. Market was championed by Adam Smith, Community by Emile Durkheim, Contract by John Locke, and Hierarchy by Thomas Hobbes. The result was great debates in social thought. It is now generally recognized (Cohen 1968) that each category has critical shortcomings. CA theorists must surely agree with this assessment, since the existence of so many different solutions to the Rebel's Dilemma implies that *any one category of solution must be an incomplete explanation of CA.*

The major difficulty is that each type of solution presupposes the existence of at least one of the other types. Consider this syllogism: Contract requires Market, because beneficial mutual exchange permits parties to arrive at the terms of a contract; Market requires Community, because common values create the trust needed to conduct market transactions; Community requires Hierarchy, because common values must be authoritatively enforced and passed on to future generations; and Hierarchy requires Contract, because in the very long run only mutually agreed upon coercion will be accepted. Or consider this syllogism: Community requires Market, because beneficial mutual exchange is one important basis of common values; Market requires Hierarchy, because the terms of exchange must be enforced; Hierarchy (again) requires Contract, because in the very long run only mutually agreed upon coercion will be accepted; and Contract requires Community, because common values permit parties to arrive at the terms of a contract. Other syllogisms are possible as well, so the point is clear: trying to solve the problems of social order and CA leads one in a vicious circle.

Hence, the problem with *all* categories of solutions to the Rebel's Dilemma is that *all* types of solutions simply push the explanation of CA one step further back. One cannot escape the fundamental question, How were the institutions required for the particular type of solution themselves created, maintained, and transformed? As Elster (1985, 367, emphasis in original) puts it, "To answer the fundamental question about collective action — *how is it all possible?* — we cannot begin by assuming a situation in which it has already taken place." All categories of solutions to the Rebel's Dilemma are therefore fundamentally incomplete, in that they presume the existence of at least one other category of solution to the problem of CA. While each type of solution might be necessary to either create, maintain, or transform CA, taken independently none is sufficient.

If no category of solution to the Rebel's Dilemma can guarantee rebellion, then how *is* the rebel's CA problem solved? Given that each approach is insufficient to bring about social order, and "all social order rests on a combination of coercion, interest and values" (Cohen 1968, 32), a new approach immediately suggests itself: investigate *combinations* of solutions to the Rebel's Dilemma. Such combinations explain an individual dissident's participation in CA. Elster (1989, 49) thus suggests that "for any given situation, [we cannot] expect to find one type of motivation to provide the major explanation of successful collective action . . . mixed motivations are essential for cooperation. Certain motivations act as catalysts for others, while the latter act as multiplicators for the former." Such combinations also explain CA by a dissident group. Successful CA results from the interactions of people who participate for many different reasons. Hence, Elster (1989, 202) believes that "in any given case we will observe that the individuals who make a voluntary contribution have different motives. A successful campaign, strike, lobbying effort or election cannot be traced to a single, homogenous motivation that animates all the contributors."

Thus, many ways of overcoming pecuniary self-interest (sect. 4.2) are often adopted simultaneously. Participation in collective dissent may result from high levels of group consciousness that are reinforced by the belief that protest is a self-actualizing political experience. Elster (1989, 202–14, emphasis in original) suggests several other CA bandwagons based on different motives. He points out that "*everyday Kantianism and the norm of fairness interact to produce much more cooperation than either could do by itself,*" (Elster 1989, 205) and that "*the strength of utilitarianism and that of fairness vary inversely with each other*" (1989, 206)

I have argued elsewhere (Lichbach forthcoming, chap. 7) that starting from the premise that solutions to the Rebel's Dilemma are as often complements as substitutes, one discovers many possible combinations and permutations of solutions. Whereas the categories of solutions to the CA problem may be collectively exhaustive, they are definitely not mutually exclusive. Each solution to the Rebel's Dilemma is therefore a Weberian ideal type, a tool for understanding reality. CA problems, in practice, are solved by mixtures and modifications of the two dozen sets of pure or ideal solutions.

## 9.2. One Empirical Criterion: Predictability

Let us now turn from an analytical criterion for evaluating CA theories of collective dissent — logical completeness — to an empirical criterion — predictability. The classic example of a predictive theory of collective dissent, consisting of a set of direct and indirect causes, is of course Gurr (1970), who argues that grievances, justifications, and mobilized resources produce protest and rebellion. Numerous other general theories of conflict have been proposed. Dahl (1966, 370) suggests that objective, subjective, and attitudinal variables produce behaviors such as collective dissent. Tilly (1978) argues that collective dissent is produced by interests, beliefs, organization, mobilization, opportunity, facilitation, power, and solidarity. There are also inductive statistical models (e.g., Hibbs 1973).

Since the CA research program does tell us a great deal about how states and oppositions interact, one might be tempted, as Gurr, Dahl, Tilly, and Hibbs, to use the approach to offer a general statement about the etiology of conflict. One could, for example, suggest how interests become politicized, how politicization leads to mobilization, how mobilization is met by government assistance and resistance, and how conflict between state and opposition takes shape as other actors enter into the fray.

The results of this book belie such a simple story. A general theory of why people rebel will fail for one simple reason: *aggregate levels and particular outbreaks of collective dissent are largely unpredictable.* The complexity of the Rebel's Dilemma (sect. 9.2.1) and the weakness of grievances (sect. 9.2.2) render forecasting problematic, which has major consequences for evaluating CA theories of protest and rebellion (sect. 9.2.3).[1]

### 9.2.1. The Complexity of the Rebel's Dilemma

This book has demonstrated that rebels find themselves in a very complicated situation. They confront many potential solutions to the Rebel's Dilemma and many contexts in which the solutions operate.

Consider the many forecasting difficulties created by the fact that the Rebel's Dilemma may be solved in so many ways. First, there are many sufficient conditions for rational rebellion, but no necessary ones. Second, "in different cases different models could be appropriate. There is no reason why the same set of assumptions should explain cartel formation and union formation, peasant revolts and urban strikes" (Elster 1985, 16). Finally, because dissidents often adopt a combination of solutions, the same solution may lead to one result in one case and the opposite result in another case.

Now consider the forecasting difficulties created by the fact that the Rebel's Dilemma operates in so many different contexts. The classic thought experiments by Hobbes ([1651] 1988), employing the "state of nature," and by Rawls (1971), employing the "original position," lacked institutions. Perhaps in some original state of nature, there existed neither economic power (property rights), nor political power (police and armies), nor cultural power (hegemony), but it is inconceivable that these institutions would never develop. They always emerge and come to affect protest and rebellion.

The truth about collective dissent is thus highly contingent upon solution and environment. Happenstance determines context; politics decides solutions (chap. 7). Ergo, aggregate levels and particular outbreaks of collective dissent are unpredictable.

### 9.2.2. The Weakness of Grievances

CA theories offer a second reason for the unpredictability of aggregate levels and particular outbreaks of collective dissent. Given that grievances are neither necessary nor sufficient for collective dissent (sect. 9.2.2.1) and that dissidents falsify their preferences (sect. 9.2.2.2), grievances are only weakly correlated with collective dissent (sect. 9.2.2.3).

#### 9.2.2.1. Neither Necessary nor Sufficient for Collective Dissent
Several scholars argue that grievances are crucial for collective dissent. Hobbes's ([1640] 1969, 168) first condition of revolution is "discontent; for as

long as a man thinketh himself well, and that the present government stan-
deth not in his way to hinder his proceeding from well to better; it is impossible for him to desire the change thereof." Gottschalk (1944, 5) identifies the
"demand" for change as a principal "cause" of revolution. Edwards (1927,
30) suggests that rebellion occurs when "people gradually realize that 'there
is something rotten in the state of Denmark.'" Such arguments about public
bads (sect. 3.12.1) are central to the DA tradition (sect. 1.2).

CA reasoning implies that these expectations are misleading, that grievances are neither necessary nor sufficient for the occurrence of active opposition to a regime. I have already shown how dissident entrepreneurs can
manufacture grievances (sect. 6.3.2) and provide selective incentives (sect.
6.5.3) or disincentives (sect. 6.5.4) for participation. Hence, grievances are
not necessary for collective dissent. Now consider that grievances are also
not sufficient.

Suppose that a dissident cares a great deal about the issue at hand. His
or her passion for righting wrongs is boundless, and his or her concern for
the downtrodden legendary. Jane Smith, our dissident from chapter 1, makes
Mother Teresa look like a disciple of Adam Smith. The Rebel's Dilemma,
nevertheless, still holds. If the benefits, however massive, accrue to a dissident regardless of his or her actions, why pay *any* costs? The real issue, in
short, is costs and not benefits.[2] Where personal cost is involved, dissidents
are reluctant to support the concerns, causes, and principles of a dissident
group. They are often unwilling to make *any* sacrifices for the collectivity.

Attitudes, therefore, do not automatically lead to behaviors. Shared
grievances may be strong but need not result in protest or rebellion. Popular
dissatisfaction does not always translate into collective dissent, because preference for a dissident group is not the same as willingness to work for it. CA
theories thus suggest that "we may stand Gramsci on his head; subordinate
classes — especially the peasantry — are likely to be more radical at the
level of ideology than at the level of behavior, where they are more effectively constrained by the daily exercise of power" (Scott 1985, 331).

In sum, while DA theories tend toward the view that gripes, criticisms,
and ideologies are much more important than plans, resources, and organizations for rebellion, CA theories take the opposite position.[3] Political grievances, then, are only a minor political force; they are not the mother of revolt
(Elster 1985, 352–53).

One thus expects that dissident leaders will constantly complain about
the absence of "collective spirit" among their followers. One also expects a
rhetoric that promises increased benefits to all if participation by many can
be obtained. However, the implications of Olson's ideas are harsh: mere
exhortation of followers to participate will not bring participation. Dissident

groups whose only recruitment device is to emphasize shared grievances cannot succeed, because grievances are neither necessary nor sufficient for protest and rebellion.

### 9.2.2.2. Preference Falsification

CA models assume that dissidents always act strategically. This implies that rebels do not reveal their preferences sincerely. A dissident's expressed demands and preferences are not the same as his or her privately held goals and feelings. Dissidents do not signal their true preferences for CA, because demands are made efficaciously, with an eye to their consequences. Preference falsification by dissidents is manifested in many ways. Dissidents will support a side in which they do not believe, remain neutral, support both sides, switch sides, switch among opposition groups, and take sides only after the conflict is over.

- Dissidents support a side in which they do not believe. A dissident may sympathize with a dissident group (the regime) but provide support to the regime (a dissident group), because his or her abstract and long-term ideologies conflict with concrete and short-run benefits. Hence, dissident loyalties cannot be surmised from their participation on one side of a conflict.
- Dissidents remain neutral. Most dissidents will not have strong loyalties. Coleman (1990, 481–82) cites evidence that in Vietnam

   there was little support for the Viet Cong and somewhat more for the government; there was an absence of intense support for either side, an absence of patriotic fervor for defense against the North Vietnamese and of revolutionary fervor for overthrow of the regime. In both of these cases the absence of strong support for either the revolutionaries or the regime is consistent with the general thesis of the [CA] theorists. The hearts and minds of the general populace seem not to have been fought over by the revolutionaries and the regime, nor did the people strongly support one side or the other.

- Dissidents support both sides. Stone (1972, 144) offers an example from the English Revolution: "Some contemporary cynics argued that these family divisions [one side Parliamentarian, the other Royalist] were part of a carefully arranged insurance policy, so that whichever side won there would always be someone with influence among the victors to protect the family property from confiscation and dismemberment."

- Dissidents switch between regime and opposition. Dissidents' loyalties are unstable for still another reason: the regime bids for the dissidents' supporters and the dissidents bid for the regime's supporters. People thus move from one side to the other and then back again — for many reasons. They switch sides as they update their estimates of the probability of victory: they bet on the winner (sect. 3.6.1). Dissidents also switch sides as they recalculate the relative benefits: they defect to the group offering the better selective incentives (sect. 6.5.3.2). Conflicts between regimes and dissident groups are thus marked by intrigue, betrayal, defection, deceit, bickering, spying, and informing. As Machiavelli ([1514] 1961, 52) writes, "The populace is by nature fickle; it is easy to persuade them of something, but difficult to confirm them in that persuasion." Examples are legion.[4]
- Dissidents switch among opposition groups. Their loyalties are unstable and cannot be surmised from their participation in one dissident group, rather than another. A dissident may well sympathize with one dissident group but provide support or defect to another.[5] A dissident may move from Left to Right and from Right to Left with little or no ideological discomfort (Laqueur 1976, 302). Mussolini, for example, was one of many prewar Socialists who became interwar Fascists.
- Dissidents take sides only after a conflict is over. Movements that succeed and become the government have access to more resources than do movements that have not yet succeeded. One thus expects dissident groups to experience their greatest growth after they win (sect. 3.6.1). Many rebels become rebellious and revolutionaries revolutionary only after the rebellion or revolution. People will go along with the crowd in the Old Regime and say that the Old Regime was good, then go along with the crowd in the New Regime and say that the Old Regime was bad (Kuran forthcoming, chap. 15).[6] Moreover, revolutionaries often become revolutionary only after joining the revolutionary party. DeNardo (1985, 26, emphasis in original) thus reports that "most of Mao's followers only became revolutionary *after* they joined the movement."

In sum, dissidents are notoriously insincere in expressing their preferences.[7] They are also insincere in their choice of tactics (sect. 3.4) and group policies (sect. 6.3.2). Hence, they will say almost anything if there is political gain to be had. Of course, rebels deny that their statements cannot be taken at face value. They often hide tactical shifts behind high-sounding principles. Marxism is the classic example: fidelity to Marxism in theory is accompanied by its abandonment in practice. Marxist parties talk a good game of revolution.[8]

### 9.2.2.3. The Grievance-Collective Dissent Linkage

These last two problems — that grievances are neither necessary nor sufficient for collective dissent and that preferences are revealed strategically —
have three major implications for collective dissent. First, ideological commitment is not needed to sustain a dissident movement (Scott 1985, 348). As
Oberschall (1973, 195) argues, "Revolutionary ideas and radical ideologies
are not required to create revolts and rebellion." When the right selective
costs (sect. 6.5.4) are imposed, people will rebel even without intense grievances. Hence, in conflict situations "many are bullied and coerced into
choices that are contrary to their predispositions" (Oberschall 1973, 29). CA
thus occurs because of force and exchange processes; values (i.e., grievances) are not irrelevant but can be overcome. Second, eliminating grievances does not eliminate collective dissent; nor is it so that collective dissent
persists unless structural conditions change. Rebels, after all, can be bought
or forced to join dissident movements.[9] Third, one must not confuse "the
demands of the rebels for the cause of rebellion" (Brustein and Levi 1987,
471). An inventory of motives behind protest and rebellion is not the same as
an etiology of protest and rebellion. Terrorism, for example, must be
explained by reference to more than simply the terrorists' reasons (e.g.,
Leites 1979).

In sum, a dissident's grievances neither completely direct nor totally
constrain his or her behavior. Rebels may feel one thing and say and do
another. Political dissatisfaction is somewhat independent of collective dissent.

A dissident's loyalties, therefore, cannot be inferred from his or her nonparticipation in collective dissent. Given that grievances are not sufficient for
dissent, a dissident might not join a dissident group, even if he or she agrees
with its goals. Even antiregime zealots (sect. 3.1) may refrain from joining.
The absence of dissident behavior thus does not prove that the government is
popular and/or that a dissident group lacks support. As Crozier (1960, 158)
argues, "The apparent absence of agitation after a long period of warning
signs may be the deceptive calm before a storm. Calm may conceal conspiracy, and secrecy is often the prelude to violence." Or, as Brinton (1965, 252,
emphasis in original) maintains, "It may be that the majority of people are
discontented, loathe the existing government, wish its overthrow. Nobody
knows. They don't commonly take plebiscites just *before* revolutions." The
implications for regimes are profound: authorities may well interpret the lack
of collective dissent as "social peace" or "value consensus," when in reality
there is an "imposed armistice" due to oppression and repression (O'Donnell
and Schmitter 1986, 48–49). There are several lessons here: do not mistake
the passive behavior of potential dissidents for implicit support of a regime; a
silent majority may be a silent opposition; nonparticipation often represents
self-interested acquiescence, a Rebel's Dilemma — not legitimacy.[10]

A dissident's loyalties, moreover, cannot be surmised from his or her participation in collective dissent. The presence of dissident behavior does not prove that the government is unpopular and/or that a dissident group has strong support. Given that grievances are not necessary for rebellion, one expects that a dissident might join a dissident group even if he or she disagrees with its goals. Apathetics may thus join dissident groups, and it is theoretically possible that even proregime zealots will participate in collective dissent.

Hence, both the presence and the absence of collective dissent are poor mechanisms of preference revelation. Dissidents engage in too much strategizing for their (non)actions to be taken as definitive indicators of their sentiments. One may never infer a dissident's feelings of legitimacy and support for the regime from his or her (non)action. While collective violence may imply that something politically important is happening, preference falsification (Kuran 1987, 1989, 1991a, 1991b, 1993, forthcoming) is so widespread that it will never be clear exactly what *is* happening. Collective dissent, on this account, is not a valid poll of popular opinion about a regime.

One concludes that the political grievance-collective dissent linkage is quite weak. This makes it difficult for regimes and oppositions to judge their popular support and for DA theorists and forecasters to predict collective dissent.

But this does not stop both sets of people from trying. Consider the practitioners. In their effort to gauge their "true" popular support,[11] regimes use various monitoring and preference revelation methods. One example from the Vietnam War is the survey: "President Lyndon Johnson commissioned a survey of the population of South Vietnam, to discover the extent of support for the Viet Cong, for the South Vietnamese government, and for American intervention" (Coleman 1990, 481). Another example from Vietnam is control of villages: "The progress of revolutionary war in South Vietnam is assessed by both participants and observers in terms of the proportion of population or number of villages under Saigon and National Liberation Front control" (Gurr 1970, 284). States concerned about the possibility of revolution are particularly likely to develop elaborate monitoring systems. The British monitor Northern Ireland, the South Africans monitor black townships, and the Israelis monitor the West Bank and Gaza. Since all three regimes are on constant alert, they are difficult to topple. Nevertheless, there is still the possibility of the unexpected flare-up, such as the Intifada, which defies prediction. Dissident groups also employ preference revelation methods. Not surprisingly, regimes and dissidents almost invariably offer competing assessments of their struggle (sect. 3.6.5).

Now consider the academics. The weakness of the political grievance-collective dissent nexus helps to discredit DA theories. Knowing that a dissident does or does not participate in protest or rebellion tells us very little about the dissident's underlying values, demands, or goals. Given that grievances are largely irrelevant to collective dissent, that grievances are neither necessary nor sufficient for rebellion, and that both leaders and followers make insincere demands, one should not mistake nonaction for nongrievances, nor participation for dissatisfaction. Of what value, then, is a focus on deprivations?

The weakness of the political grievance-collective dissent linkage thereby creates forecasting problems. Consider that grievances are neither necessary nor sufficient for rebellion. Given that revolutionary intentions are not "good predictors of revolutionary activity" (Calhoun 1988, 155), there will be little observed correlation between aggrieved attitudes and dissident behavior (Oberschall 1970, 79). As the extent and intensity of grievances in a collectivity increase, collective dissent may or may not increase. Moreover, as the extent and intensity of grievances remain constant, collective dissent may either increase, decrease, or stay the same. Tilly (1974, 302) is right: "Grievances are fundamental to rebellion as oxygen is fundamental to combustion. But just as fluctuations in the oxygen content of the air are not of major account in the overall distribution of fire in the world, fluctuations in grievances are not a major cause of the presence or absence of rebellion." Chamberlin ([1935] 1987, 420) is also right: human misery is not "an infallible barometer of revolutionary action." The inability of grievances to predict collective dissent severely damages our ability to forecast collective dissent.

Now consider strategic preference revelation. A dissident who dislikes the regime will hide his or her feelings as long as the dissident group appears weak and the regime strong. If many have falsified their preferences, regime support can crumble rapidly in the face of some external event or shock, especially one that reveals dissidents to be strong and the regime to be weak (sect. 3.6). On the other hand, the sudden power deflation of the Old Regime is matched by the hastily achieved legitimacy of the New Regime as people flock to the powers-that-be. In short, small events can trigger large outcomes. Strategic preference revelation hence damages our ability to anticipate collective dissent.

Most collective dissent is therefore unanticipated.[12] Hindsight and foresight on the probability of revolution diverge considerably. As Kuran (forthcoming, chap. 15) asks, "Plausible as at least some of the explanations [of the Iranian Revolution] seem, none makes clear why hindsight and foresight should diverge. Why, in particular, did a revolution that now appears as the inevitable outcome of an array of powerful social forces surprise so many of its leaders, participants, victims and observers?" Revolution thus always surprises everyone and no one. Collective dissent comes as a collective surprise.

It comes as a surprise even to the dissidents themselves. Their estimates of the probability of victory (sect. 3.6) and the probability of making a difference (sect. 3.7) are uncertain. Calculations of self-interest, including safety (e.g., repression, sect. 3.2) and monetary returns (e.g., opportunity costs, sect. 3.2.3), can change rapidly. This explains public/private preference cycles (sect. 9.3.2.1). Finally, perceptions of the cues for collective dissent (sect. 4.1.1) are also highly variable. In sum, dissidents themselves face formidable difficulties in forecasting their own conflict behavior, let alone that of their colleagues.

Much evidence supports the conclusion that collective dissent is unpredictable.[13] One of the few things predictable about revolution is that it is unpredictable.

## 9.2.3. The Consequences for Evaluating CA Theories

The parallel to Riker (1982) is now complete. His focus on the politics of collective choice leads to the conclusion that collective choice is inherently unstable and unpredictable. My focus on CA solutions as politics and pathologies, as well as the preference falsification problem, leads to the conclusion that CA is equally unstable and unpredictable.

While the inability to predict aggregate levels and particular outbreaks of collective dissent might appear to dampen enthusiasm for the CA approach, there are three important points in defense of CA theories. First, as indicated with respect to Riker (1982), these conclusions parallel the conclusions reached in the rational actor research program more generally;[14] the paradox of similar causes producing dissimilar effects, due to contexts or institutions, is well known.

Second, these conclusions parallel those reached in structural theories of revolution. Consider, for example, Trimberger's (1978, 1) caveats:

> This emphasis on both structural and historical determinants of revolution from above indicates that there can be no general theory of revolution (or of social change) applicable to all societies at all times. Any general theorizing about the causes and consequences of different types of revolution is invalidated by the distinct historical and international contexts in which particular revolutions occur. Every revolution is unique in some respects, and each revolution changes the parameters facilitating and hindering the next one.

Skocpol (1979, 288) makes a similar point.[15]

Third, the inability to predict either aggregate levels or particular outbreaks of collective dissent does not imply that CA ideas about collective dissent are immune to empirical scrutiny. Although one might not know it from the quantitative work, there is a lot more to collective dissent than aggregate levels and particular outbreaks. The common CA processes behind the unpredictable outcomes are equally important and can be studied. As indicated in chapters 7 and 8, the problematique of the CA research program is to determine the conditions under which a particular CA solution is adopted and those under which a particular CA solution is effective or pathological. We thereby bypass the initial problem of why rational people rebel and never reach the ultimate problem of a *complete* explanation of aggregate levels and particular outbreaks of rebellion. A midrange approach best elaborates CA ideas. It is possible, for example, to study the conditions under which foreign patronage of rural rebellion occurs and the conditions under which it succeeds at mobilizing peasants and achieving the PG sought by the peasantry. It is also possible to investigate the conditions under which repression occurs and the factors that allow repression to depress the protest and rebellion of particular groups in a society. One can also determine which types of participants join which types of dissident movements, under which conditions (sect. 8.1). One can, finally, determine how dissidents, dissident movements, and postdissident societies eventually become corrupt.[16]

Hence, a variety of general propositions about collective dissent, as part 2 has shown, may be derived from CA theories. What is not fruitful, however, is integrating these propositions, summarized in a complex arrow diagram of "why *all* people rebel" or "why *all* dissident groups mobilize," into a general predictive theory of aggregate levels or particular outbreaks of collective dissent. How solutions and environments interact in overcoming *all* possible manifestations of the Rebel's Dilemma cannot be neatly summarized in a single model. The propositions developed here cannot be grouped together, used to construct a general model of collective dissent, and then used to explain and predict *all* of the collective dissent that occurs days, weeks, months, years, or decades from now. Such an exercise would leave much of the variance unexplained (Gurr and Lichbach 1979, 1986) and much of the truth misunderstood.

Even attempting such an exercise would be counterproductive, because it would not assist in deriving further falsifiable propositions. These come from the assumptions behind the CA research program, rather than from a collation of propositions derived from the assumptions and labeled a general "theory." Nor would such an exercise aid in interpreting particular cases. Manufacturing such a middle-range theory of conflict based on the CA research program produces a whole series of constructs that get in the way of linking CA theories with the empirical world. Such constructs, moreover, would become a point of dispute, pushing both CA arguments and the empirical world into the background. In short, *The Rebel's Dilemma* focuses on the CA research program for collective dissent, rather than on a CA theory of collective dissent. The Big Questions concern an explanation sketch, rather than a general explanation (Eckstein 1980).

Given the limitations of predicting aggregate levels and particular outbreaks of collective dissent, a question arises: how should the hypotheses derived from the CA approach be investigated? The propositions developed in this book should guide quantitative, many-case studies. Statistical tests of the propositions, both at the individual level, using survey data, and the collective level, using aggregate data, will usefully elaborate the CA research program. Survey, cross-national, and time series techniques have an important place in conflict studies.

I have argued, however, that CA theories imply that collective dissent is highly unpredictable, contingent, and relative. Hence, we should explore the specific institutional details relevant to individual cases of collective dissent. Context must provide the concrete actors who have specific goals, means, constraints, and decision-rules, and who interact in some well-defined game. Qualitative single-case and comparative-case studies thus also have an important place in conflict studies (King, Keohane, and Verba 1994).

CA theorists would therefore do well to adopt some of Weber's methodological precepts. Theory, for Weber, is not a goal of inquiry but rather a means for the analysis of concrete historical cases. One uses theories to explain the unique outcome of each case, to compare for the purpose of establishing both differences as well as similarities. Weber ([1896] 1988, 385–86) offers an example of this approach:

A genuinely analytic study comparing the stages of development of the ancient *polis* with those of the mediaeval city would be welcome and productive . . . Of course I say this on the assumption that such a comparative study would not aim at finding "analogies" and "parallels," as is done by those engrossed in the currently fashionable enterprise of constructing general schemes of development. The aim should, rather, be precisely the opposite: to identify and define the individuality of each development, the characteristics which made the one conclude in a manner so different from that of the other. This done, one can then determine the causes which led to these differences. It is also my assumption that an indispensable preliminary to such a comparative study would be the isolation and abstraction of the individual elements in each development, the study of these elements in the light of general rules drawn from experience, and finally, the formation of clear concepts . . . Without these preliminary steps no causal relationship whatever can be established.

Weber also argues that "one can only define the specific characteristics of, for example, the mediaeval city . . . after one has established which of these characteristics were lacking in other cities (classical Chinese, Islamic). That is a general rule. The next task of historians is to give a causal explanation of those specific characteristics" (cited in Weber [1896] 1988, 21).

The CA research program thus teaches us, as does Weber, to explain particular and unique outcomes of collective dissent — concrete and histori- cally grounded dissident individuals, groups, and events — using the general understanding that can be gained through a study of CA processes. Since each CA solution is an "ideal type," to understand an actual historical situa- tion one must bring various types to bear on the specific case, or approximate the historical case by showing how each type works in practice.

Moreover, we should address questions and puzzles that are historically situated in time and place. For example, what accounts for the victory of socialism in Russia but not in Germany in 1917? Why did certain segments of the Chinese Communist Party resist bureaucratization, while almost no such resistance appeared in the Soviet Communist Party? Why did revolution come to France in 1789 but not to England? Why did so many more revolu- tions follow the revolution in France in 1848 than in 1830? We could com- pare the adoption of CA strategies by similarly situated groups: the CCP versus KMT, Vietminh versus Cao Dai, and Kadets versus Bolsheviks. Given the wealth of data and contradictory perspectives available, studies of the Great Revolutions — Dutch, English, American, French, Mexican, Russian, and Chinese — seem particularly feasible. Finally, we can model particular CA problems as particular games. One can develop models, for example, of the drive for civil rights in the U.S. South during the 1950s (Chong 1991) or of eastern Europe during the late 1980s (Kuran 1991a).

In sum, any case or comparative case study of collective dissent should follow the historical waning and waxing of CA by continually repeating a four-step process:

1. We begin with the five percent rule (sect. 1.5): CA is the exception and not the norm. Hence, we try to observe collective action *and* inaction, what did *and* did not happen, or the dog that barked *and* the one that remained silent, in some particular context. Following Walker (1991, 1–3), we consider the whole range of dissident groups that are and are not active, and then ask how so many groups came into being and why so many others did not. In short, we must com- pare the preference distribution of the population to the constellation of dissident groups. CA theories thus focus on the meso level of groups rather than on the micro level of individuals or the macro level of societies.

2. The question then becomes: which of the many plausible rival solu- tions to the CA problem actually did the work of mobilizing or demo-

bilizing a *particular* set of dissidents? In other words, which CA solutions, under which conditions, mobilized or demobilized which CA?

3. We then inquire into politics: how did competing interests try to shape their contexts, structures, and institutions so as to initiate, sustain, and terminate CA processes?

4. We finally inquire into pathologies: what are the unintended consequences of group mobilization and group success?

Hence, solutions to the CA problem are the basic building blocks in a certain type of theory of collective dissent. What is really useful about CA theories is that they lead to comparative and historical analyses of the causes and consequences of the CA processes that drive *particular* groups.[17]

In conclusion, *The Rebel's Dilemma*, does not propose a general predictive theory of collective dissent. Protest and rebellion are best understood as outcomes of abstract processes general to all CA, not as outcomes of middle-level processes unique to collective dissent. There is thus no need to subsume many general propositions about protest and rebellion under one theoretical umbrella, develop a general predictive theory of a type of CA (e.g., political violence), and then apply the general theory to a large number of randomly chosen cases. Given that we already have a set of general CA processes, the research task is to apply specific theories to specific cases by considering initial conditions, structures, institutions, and groups.[18]

Moreover, just because we cannot develop general theories that predict *all* collective dissent does not mean that the science of rebellion is no better than the pseudosciences of physiognomy and astrology, nor no different than religion. General propositions valid across many different forms of collective dissent, as proposed in part 2, can be developed. Moreover, qualitative or quantitative case and comparative studies of these propositions can be done. The CA research program does lead to a science of collective dissent. However, it is not a science that exclusively seeks to explain the variance in aggregate levels of protest and rebellion across a random sample of cases. The science will consist of applying general CA processes to specific initial conditions, both contextual and institutional, in order to explain the causes and consequences of particular solutions to particular Rebel's Dilemmas.

### 9.3. Two More Empirical Criteria: Lakatos and Popper

This chapter has demonstrated that CA theories of collective dissent do not fare well on the analytical criterion of logical completeness or on the empirical criterion of predictability. There are, however, other important empirical standards by which CA theories of protest and rebellion can be judged. To have value for conflict studies, the CA research program must accomplish two tasks. First, it must account for some *additional* and *true* observations about protest beyond merely asserting that rational people, at least under the right circumstances, do rebel. Second, it must explain these observations *differently* and *better* than competing DA theories. I will consider (sect. 9.3.1) and then apply (sect. 9.3.2) both criteria.

### 9.3.1. The Criteria

The *additional* and *true* criteria asks the following: *What, besides that protest groups do form and that their participants are rational, does the CA research program tell us about collective dissent?* Each solution to the free-rider problem must tell us something *additional* and *true* about protest. CA solutions are potentially rich in their implications, focusing as they do on the group's actions (e.g., rhetoric, deeds), internal organization (e.g., membership characteristics, entrepreneurs), and external relations (e.g., competition with enemies such as the regime, cooperation with allies such as patrons). Showing that the CA research program can tell us more about conflict than simply that rational people rebel demonstrates the heuristic value of the approach. It reveals the range of observations, or the multiple outcroppings (Webb et al. 1981, 66–68), about conflict that the approach can explain. And it enables us to take a fresh look at theoretical arguments and empirical evidence.

The agenda of the CA research program is thus to seek the many causes and consequences of CA solutions. In short, the challenge is to ask "Why?" and "What if?" a solution is adopted. *Why* questions, as noted chapter 7, involve us in the politics of collective dissent. They lead us to the struggle over the Rebel's Dilemma. *What if* questions, as noted in chapter 8, involve us in the intended and the unintended consequences of solving the Rebel's Dilemma in particular ways. They lead us to the struggle over the Organizational Dilemma.

Consider, for example, an evaluation of the selective incentives idea (sect. 6.5.3). This solution to the Rebel's Dilemma anticipates many stylized facts about protest and rebellion. (1) Rioters typically loot stores. (2) Voluntary members of a dissident group often attempt to become paid staff and make a career out of their participation (i.e., over time there is a professionalization of protest). (3) Long-lived dissident organizations usually become oligarchical, with leaders receiving the majority of the benefits. (4) Government commonly coopts leaders and "buys off" followers, and thus long-lived dissident organizations regularly become deradicalized. (5) Organizing manuals written by protest leaders frequently suggest that appeals emphasize self-interest, and hence immediate, specific, and concrete issues, rather than altruism, and hence ideology, programs, and self-sacrifice. (6) Organizational meetings and protest demonstrations routinely include food, drink, and entertainment.

These ideas tell us more than that participation in collective dissent is rational. The existence of selective incentives determines what the various actors (e.g., participants, opposition leaders, government, patrons) do and how opposition groups become corrupt and change over time. While the *Administer Selective Incentives* solution to the free-rider problem was initially designed to explain why rational people participate in rebellion, it explains much more — why protest and rebellion take particular courses and have particular consequences. The focus upon *additional* and *true* statements about conflict is thus a particularly useful perspective for evaluating the CA research program's approach to collective dissent.

This first standard for evaluating the CA research program comes close to the criteria proposed by the philosopher of science, Imre Lakatos (1970). He suggests that we characterize each modification of a research program (e.g., a solution of the free-rider problem). A modification of a research program is "progressive" (1) if it can account for previous findings in the field; (2) if it can predict "novel content," or some hitherto unexpected or counterintuitive observations in the field; and (3) if some of these excess predictions resist falsification.[19] A modification of a research program is "degenerative" if it is merely patchwork to explain an internally generated anomaly of the program and offers no new substantive insights. Degenerative programs are, accordingly, autonomous and self-perpetuating, farther and farther removed from reality.[20]

The Lakatosian approach is not without its critics, however. Many would argue that the deductive fertility of the CA research program — the large number and fascinating variety of propositions that it can yield — is a necessary but not sufficient condition for its value to conflict studies.[21] While valuable and important, there are several reasons why one should not overestimate the significance of the CA research program's ability to produce *additional* and *true* observations about collective dissent.

First, the CA research program is only one of many research programs in the social sciences. Each program has a more or less fertile agenda of topics for study. Some parts of the agendas of different research programs do not coincide. "Breakdown theories," for example, tell us that protest will occur during periods of personal pathology and anti-social behavior; *ergo*, the concomitants of protest will be suicide, divorce, alcoholism, drug abuse, and vagrancy. Nothing in the CA research program leads one to study these phenomena as covariates of protest. Other parts of the agendas of different research programs do coincide. Both CA and DA theories, for example, have been used to explain the same observations about the impact of economic inequality on collective dissent (Lichbach 1989, 1990)

Second, almost all the proponents of research programs claim that they can explain much of the empirical world by subsuming the important parts of other competing research programs. Consider, once again, the case of collective dissent. Gurr (1970, 321) is obviously correct, from a philosophy of science perspective, when he argues that "one determinant of the adequacy of theoretical generalization is the degree to which it integrates more specific explanations and observed regularities." But claims about the deductive fertility and integrative capacity of the core ideas of research programs in conflict studies have been heard too many times. Gurr (1970), for example, too easily integrates status discrepancy, cognitive dissonance, value disequilibrium, and relative deprivation ideas under the frustration-aggression rubric. Tilly (1971, 416) thus likens *Why Men Rebel* to a "sponge" and maintains that "the spongelike character of the work comes out in Gurr's enormous effort to subsume — to make every other argument, hypothesis, and finding support his scheme, and to contradict none of them." Students of conflict are thus justifiably suspicious about claims by supporters of the latest research program that the program is the key that "unlocks all conceivable doors" (Hirschman 1970b, 330). Exaggerated claims succeed "only in provoking the readers' resistance and incredulity" (Hirschman 1970b, 331). The derivation of innumerable "true" propositions from a research program is thus seen as a breathless search, with elements of gimmickry and gadgetry. Hirschman (1970b) understandably councils modesty when engaged in the difficult search for truth and understanding. Only a simple minded positivism would lead one to try to subsume all theories under a single favorite theory (Lloyd 1986, 216).

Third, it is always easy to make deductions that support theories. If, for example, collective dissent occurs, DA theories conduct an ex post facto search for grievances while CA theories undertake an ex post facto search for CA solutions. If, on the other hand, collective dissent does not occur, DA theories conduct an ex post facto search for the weakness of grievances while CA theories look for the Rebel's Dilemma. Hence, accounts of the beginning of CA always seem to confirm DA theories; accounts of the end of CA always seem to confirm CA theories. An example from Thompson (1966, 572) illustrates the point: "Yorkshire Luddism petered out amidst arrests, betrayals, threats, and disillusionment." CA theorists are all too easily trained to read "selective disincentives" and the "improbability of making a difference" into Thompson's diagnosis of why Yorkshire Luddism failed. Runciman's (1989, 367) warnings against "self-confirming illustrations preemptively immunized against awkward evidence" is quite relevant here.

Fourth, it is easy to produce numerous deductions by adding numerous assumptions. Assumptions that mechanically entail deductions deserve no honors, much "like a conjurer putting a rabbit in a hat, taking it out again and expecting a round of applause" (Brian Barry, cited in Hechter 1990, 243). Such underachievement is a real possibility because scholars often seek cognitive consistency. They try to interpret new information from their old perspective. The result is that research programs in the social sciences appear deductively fertile only because their assumptions are hedged so as to be able to account for much of the empirical world. They are deductively fertile only at the cost of an inelegant eclecticism. The problem is that theories with assumptions that are imprecise and eclectic yield deductions which are informal and synthetic. Unless the assumptions behind a research program are parsimonious, nothing of value has been accomplished, for Anything can be derived from Everything.

The consequence of eclectic theories is therefore that testing becomes impossible. Eckstein (1980) discovered this truth in conflict studies when he tried but failed (not *his* fault) to separate two important research programs, Gurr's (1970) version of DA theories and Tilly's (1978) version of rationalist theories, by determining which theory better explains the known facts about how social cleavages, the economy, repression, urbanization, and so on influence collective dissent. Eckstein points out that both Gurr and Tilly built a "protective belt" around their core assumptions by arguing that both grievances and mobilizable resources are required for collective dissent. Both theories thus turned out to be eclectic. Gurr's theory was consciously so, mixing rational and nonrational assumptions about individual motivation. The attempt by Tilly to produce a countertheory suffered a similar eclecticism.

Given these difficulties with the *additional* and *true* criterion, students of conflict must answer a second question about CA theories: *compared to other approaches, does the CA approach tell us things about collective dissent that are unique and more valid?* One must show, in other words, that its implications are (1) original and pioneering and hence unexpected and counterintuitive, given the traditional wisdom in the field; and (2) more valid than that traditional wisdom. The *additional* and *true* propositions about conflict, that is, must also be *different* and *better* than those offered by alternative theories.

Truth, Popper (1968) tells us, comes out of the confrontation of ideas. CA models must therefore be tested against the competition. Consequently, I am less interested in finding the best solution to the free-rider problem than in comparing the competing theories of collective dissent. This point is well recognized by philosophers of science[22] and practicing social scientists.[23]

The *different* and *better* criterion is particularly relevant here, for two important reasons. First, many recent solutions to the PG–PD problem have tried to push back the limits of rational choice explanations. Bates and Bianco (1990, 351) observe the recent trend toward "the synthesis and reinterpretation of noneconomic variables that have traditionally been studied by the behavioral sciences." CA arguments, for example, have been extended to explain norms, trust, ideology, reputation, institutions, and leadership. These recent extensions of the rational actor paradigm to new frontiers, collated above as Community solutions (chap. 4), lead one to question whether such extensions truly represent "progress." Miller (1990, 343) argues that, given the way many have tried to solve repeated PD games, "the choices of 'homo economicus' in repeated, personal, norm-constrained, social interaction becomes virtually indistinguishable from the behavior attributed to 'homo sociologicus.' This leads us to ask if there is anything left in the classic distinction between economics and sociology."

Second, the principal competitor to rational actor theories in conflict studies is Gurr's (1970) DA theory, *Why Men Rebel*. The controversy over whether rebels are frustrated or rational has motivated much of resource mobilization theory (Snyder 1978). Eckstein (1980) produces a classic test of rational actor versus DA theories of protest and rebellion — a competition that seems essential to a full appraisal of the CA approach to conflict studies.[24]

In sum, Lakatosians advocate a full elaboration of a single research program to determine its progress over time (i.e., the *additional* and *true* criterion); Popperians advocate an examination of stylized versions of competing research programs to determine their relative worth (i.e., the *different* and *better* criterion). Given the problems with both types of evaluations, and given the current state of conflict studies, the only safe course is to do both. One must elaborate one research program to discover its utility and at the same time, one must compare predictions to a stylized version of an alternative research program. Hence, one should seek from the CA research program deductions that help us to address the major problems and puzzles concerning the causes, courses, and consequences of collective dissent. One should determine for each modification of the CA research program (i.e., each proposed solution to the free-rider problem) what the proposed solution has to say about collective dissent beyond simply that rational people rebel. One should also investigate whether these *additional* and *true* propositions about collective dissent are *different* and *better* than those offered by alternative, especially DA, theories.

## 9.3.2. The Criteria Applied

The last section offered two criteria by which to evaluate the various solutions to the Rebel's Dilemma. I will now examine each of the solutions introduced here with Lakatos's and Popper's criteria in mind. The principal foil, as indicated above, will be Gurr's *Why Men Rebel.*

### 9.3.2.1. Market

The following Market solutions to the CA problem were examined in chapter 3: increase benefits, lower costs, increase resources, improve the productivity of tactics, reduce the supply of the PG, increase the probability of winning, increase the probability of making a difference, use incomplete information, increase risk taking, increase team competition among enemies, restrict exit, and change the type of PG.

*Increase Benefits.* There are three important problems with accepting the idea that a dissident's personal benefits from a PG explain his or her contribution to that PG.

First, as Hirschman (1974, 9) observes, "The preference for participation in public affairs over the 'idiocy' of private life is much more unstable, and subject to much wider fluctuations, than the preference for, say, apples over pears or for present over future consumption." For the *Increase Benefits* solution to be useful, we must explain the timing of private interest-public interest cycles: why do people become frustrated and unhappy with private pursuits at one time, and then become disappointed and disillusioned with public pursuits at another time (Hirschman 1982a, 15)? Moreover, preferences for public participation vary greatly among individuals. For this solution to be useful, we must also explain why some people have more publicly-oriented preferences than others. Unless we can explain individual and aggregate preferences for PGs, the problems with the *Increase Benefit* solution becomes similar to the problems Weber ([1904–5] 1985, 88) finds with national character arguments, "The appeal to national character is generally a mere confession of ignorance," or to the problems some find with culturalist explanations, that they tend to become "a catch-all to end all catch-alls."

Another problem with this solution is that many of its propositions are heartily endorsed by DA theorists. Consider Gurr's arguments. He (1970, 279) writes that "if followers are intensely hostile to the regime and prepared to make great sacrifices to the dissident cause, leaders can organize conspiratorial or revolutionary movements . . . But if followers are not so intensely committed, whatever their numbers, overt action probably will be limited to turmoil, for example antigovernment riots and general strikes." He (1970, 335) also writes that "if there is intense mass discontent in a society, revolutionary leaders are more likely than not to be able to wage internal wars; if discontent is limited largely to the revolutionary elite, conspiratorial activity is their most feasible recourse." These arguments are hard to distinguish from CA arguments about increasing benefits. Since both DA and CA theories agree that as the intensity of grievances increases, collective dissent increases, the proposition and its corollaries may well be true. But this situation of mutually compatible predictions from ostensibly incompatible research programs does not lend credibility to CA theories of collective dissent. Such propositions might be *additional* and *true* modifications of the CA research program but are clearly not *different* and *better* than what appears in DA theories.

A final problem with the *Increase Benefits* solution to the Rebel's Dilemma is that one would expect it to inform us how government accommodation of dissidents influences collective dissent, since government is the biggest potential supplier of benefits. Unfortunately, it does not.

That the *Increase Benefits* solution to the Rebel's Dilemma is not a particularly fruitful avenue of research for CA theorists is not unexpected. Most of the interesting propositions in economics come from the comparative statics of costs, rather than from the comparative statics of benefits. Moreover, this solution contradicts a basic CA problem, that grievances are supposed to be irrelevant to collective dissent (sect. 9.2.2.1). CA theorists thus might have more luck focusing on the costs, rather than on the benefits, of collective dissent — on what dissidents will pay for a PG instead of on what benefits dissidents derive from that good.

*Lower Costs.* The *Lower Costs* solution to the Rebel's Dilemma proves to be particularly insightful. One can find many subtle examples of how costs affect collective dissent, leading to propositions that constitute numerous nonobvious extensions of the Rebel's Dilemma. It seems then that Tilly (1978, 6) is wrong in arguing that "it is also hard to build purposive models which specify the constraints limiting the pursuit of interests, grievances, and aspirations." The CA research program can easily suggest fruitful micromodels of rational action in which costs constrain preferences.

A glance at sections 3.1 and 3.2 (and the index) thus confirms that rational actor approaches are more fruitful when used to dissect the costs rather than the benefits of rational choice. This is not surprising. Costs, after all, often occur immediately and without equivocation while benefits often come later and are uncertain. There are nevertheless three important limitations of the *Lower Costs* solution to the Rebel's Dilemma.

First, arguments about costs (e.g., repression) have been made by theorists — Gurr (1970), for example — working primarily in the DA research program. But such arguments tend to be ad hoc; the propositions offered here cannot easily be derived from the DA research program. In contrast, the *Lower Costs* solution is a direct extension of CA assumptions.

Second, assessments of the costs of collective dissent are not always clear-cut. The costs produced by government repression, for example, are rather complex and can have ambiguous effects upon collective dissent

(Lichbach 1987). Unfortunately, the CA research program does not appear to resolve many of the theoretical and empirical ambiguities surrounding the repression-dissent nexus.

Attributing opportunity costs to certain demographic categories is also tricky. Consider gender. Many terrorists are female (Jenkins 1982, 15). The predominance of women has been noted in the crowds of the French Revolution (Rudé 1964, 220) and the disorders of the Russian Revolution (Chamberlin [1935] 1987, 28). Women have also played a more prominent part in insurgencies in the developing world than in the developed world. In general, however, males engage in more collective dissent than females.

CA theories do not provide an adequate explanation for this. One speculation is that males are more likely to see their career choices as being involved in collective dissent, thus facilitating the *Administer Selective Incentives* solution (sect. 6.5.3). Reif (1986, 148) offers another explanation, based on the opportunity costs of family responsibilities:

> In the occupational sphere, as well as in all areas of social organization, the energy, time, and freedom of movement available to most women is greatly limited: men generally do not face the double burden of participating in nondomestic areas and primary responsibility for the domestic area. Women's role in reproductive activities thus constitutes a major barrier to their involvement in nondomestic political action such as guerrilla struggle.

Others make the opposite point, that the absence of employment responsibilities outside the home has allowed women to mobilize. Thus, Navarro (1989, 257) reports that Latin American women were able to protest about the "disappeared" because

> they also had more time than men to search for their missing children, or at least they could find time more easily. Men could not spend endless hours making the rounds of ministries and precincts, waiting for an audience with yet another official who might provide information. They had to earn a living, and although they could take some time off, they could not risk losing their jobs, so they eventually had to return to work. On the other hand, after taking care of their housework, women could find the time to go once more to the Interior Ministry, follow a lead that might prove useful, get another writ of habeas corpus, collect money or signatures for an advertisement, contact women in the places whose children had also disappeared, help those who had been left destitute, and so forth.

In sum, one does not know whether the increasing rates of women's participation in the labor force will reduce the male-female participation gap in collective dissent. Family responsibilities and the costs of forgone wages work themselves out in complex ways.

Thus, CA theories can only partially account for the observation that young, single males participate in collective dissent disproportionately.[25] CA theories can account for the disproportionate activity of the young (sect. 5.2.1) and singles (sect. 3.2.3) but not the males. Hence, focusing on the opportunity costs of participating in collective dissent yields only a limited series of speculations about the "biographical availability" (McAdam, McCarthy, and Zald 1988, 709) of certain demographic groups.

Finally, a certain fundamental puzzle about costs and collective dissent remains unsolved. Why do potential dissidents choose to participate in collective dissent, even when it is a high-cost alternative to less costly private activities? Also puzzling is the fact that dissidents often choose high-cost forms of collective dissent rather than strategies that impose fewer costs on their members. What explains radical groups who pursue unattainable goals and demand great sacrifices from their members? Why do such dissident groups not pursue a reformist strategy that imposes fewer costs on their members? For answers to this riddle, we evidently must turn to other solutions to the Rebel's Dilemma.

*Increase Resources.* A microeconomic perspective leads one to believe that the income effect will greatly influence collective dissent. We learn from the *Increase Resources* solution to the Rebel's Dilemma, for example, that the high levels of participation of former soldiers could be explained in this manner. Unfortunately, this solution, too, has its shortcomings.

For one, both the individual-level and aggregate-level evidence about the impact of income and wealth on collective dissent is decidedly mixed (Zimmermann 1983). Moreover, the CA research program does not appear to contribute to the resolution of the empirical and theoretical ambiguities surrounding this income-dissent nexus.

A further limitation of this solution is that DA theorists have also employed such arguments. Gurr (1970, 28) recognizes that money, cadres, and the communications media are the resources by which dissident leaders broaden their support. He argues, for example, that "there are only two inherent limitations on the escalating spiral of force and counterforce: the depletion of either group's resources for coercion, or the attainment by one of the capacity for genocidal victory over its opponents" (Gurr 1970, 232). In fact, Gurr (1970) treats the resource issue in depth. His discussions of "the coercive balance" (1970, chap. 8) and "the balance of institutional support" (1970, chap. 9) are almost always neglected by his critics. The basic reason is that Gurr's arguments about dissident resources did not follow from his core assumptions about individual dissidents. He introduces resources in a somewhat ad hoc manner, as contextual factors that do not affect individual-level motivations. The resource argument and its implications are, on the other hand, quite consistent with the CA approach.

In spite of its weak empirical support and overlap with some DA ideas, the *Increase Resources* solution to the Rebel's Dilemma has already shown its value. It deserves further exploration.

*Improve the Productivity of Tactics.* This solution turns out to be a particularly fertile approach to Olson's Problem. It explains a great deal about the dissidents' choice of targets and tactics, especially with regard to the tactical choice between collective dissent and collective violence.

However, the CA research program has no monopoly on such arguments. Gurr (1970, 156–57) also argues that collective violence is used efficaciously: "The potential for political violence varies strongly with the intensity and scope of utilitarian justifications for political violence among members of a collectivity . . . *Utilitarian justifications* for political violence are the beliefs men hold about the extent to which the threat or use of violence in politics will enhance their overall value position . . . and that of the community with which they identify." He is thus concerned about the relative utility of collective violence versus other tactics. In another statement that resembles the CA approach, Gurr (1970, 211) writes that

> the utilities of political violence are not likely to be perceived in all-or-nothing terms, neither by individuals nor by all members of a collectivity. Men make more or less explicit calculations about prospective benefits vis-à-vis the prospective costs of violence as a tactic. Such calculations are likely to be more explicit among leaders, more implicit among potential followers. The greater they believe the potential gains to be, the more justifiable violence is likely to appear to them.

DA theorists also argue that tactics can often substitute for one another. Thus, "milder forms of protest may function as an alternative to more violent conflicts" (Zimmermann 1983, 49). One tactic, in other words, is either a safety valve or a functional alternative for another (Zimmermann 1983, 429–30). Turmoil, for example, often prevents internal war: "A plausible explanation for the apparent substitutability but infrequent simultaneity of [turmoil and internal war] is that if revolutionary organizations are active in a society, they serve as means for the expression of popular discontent that otherwise lead to turmoil" (Gurr 1970, 335). Coups also prevent internal war: "A coup d'état in a prerevolutionary situation can forestall massive violence, for example, by removing hated symbols and political repression and offering hopes for the alleviation of deprivation" (Gurr 1970, 293).

Finally, DA theorists argue that tactics complement one another. There are "stages" and "sequences" in dissident movements, so that one form of dissent might precede another form, or even become another form. Gurr (1970, 341–47) holds that turmoil, conspiracy, and internal war really reflect differences of degree in scale and organization. One form thus often turns into another.

Such arguments, however, are not well integrated into Gurr's micro-model of relative deprivation and the politicization of dissent. By contrast, they flow directly from the CA research program.

There is one other limitation of the *Improve the Productivity of Tactics* solution to the Rebel's Dilemma. Although regimes should be able to reduce collective dissent by improving the productivity of alternative means of collective participation (for example, by elections), the democracy-collective dissent nexus is bogged down in a theoretical and empirical muddle (Zimmermann 1983, 102–5). The CA research program, moreover, does not appear to offer any simple resolution to these ambiguities.

*Reduce the Supply of the Public Good.* Since dissidents and regimes are fighting over the supply of the PG, one hopes that this solution can explain a great deal about protest and rebellion. It should help piece together a picture of government response strategies toward collective dissent: the *Lower Costs* solution should tell us about repression; the *Increase Benefits* solution and the *Reduce the Supply of the Public Good* solution, about accommodation. These hopes, unfortunately, have not been realized. The accommodation-dissent and repression-dissent puzzles remain puzzles.

*Increase the Probability of Winning.* The *Increase the Probability of Winning* solution offers several keys to understanding the Rebel's Dilemma. Both regimes and dissidents try to convince potential dissidents that they will be the eventual victors — a competition that reveals much about collective dissent. Moreover, the dissident group's actual victories and defeats, as well as the regime's actual strengths and weaknesses, contribute to dissidents' estimates of the probability of winning.

The probability of winning is also important in DA reasoning. According to Gurr (1970, 216), "One of the most potent and enduring effects of 'revolutionary appeals' is to persuade men that political violence can provide value gains commensurate to or greater than its costs in risk and guilt." Hence, "utilitarian justifications" for collective dissent figure prominently in his (1970) magnum opus. Moreover, many of the factors behind estimates of the probability of winning are associated with DA thinking. For example, DA theorists such as Eckstein and Gurr (1975) would probably argue that leadership crises often precede collective dissent, because widely accepted patterns of executive recruitment serve as an important basis for the legitimacy of a regime.

More specifically, a focus on an the probability of winning raises three issues that fall squarely within the purview of DA theories. First is socialization — how people are socialized into beliefs about the probability of winning. Second is cognitive failures — wishful thinking and unrealistic expectations about success.[26] And the third is symbols — signals that reinforce beliefs.

Calculations about the probability of winning also explain two phenomena that have been central to the DA research program. Such estimates explain the basic observation undergirding Gurr's relative deprivation theory: rebels are frustrated. Coleman (1990, 484) points out that high estimates of the probability of winning lead to both frustration and collective dissent. A spurious correlation between frustration and collective dissent is thus a by-product of the rebels' sense of imminent victory: "If opponents of an authority system come to have a strong belief in their own power to overthrow the regime, one consequence will be a sense of frustration that the regime remains in power. But this frustration will be only an epiphenomenon, an incidental consequence of the opponents' increased belief in their own capabilities." Estimates of the probability of winning also explain the J-curve phenomenon. As Coleman (1990, 480–81) argues, improved conditions might increase or decrease frustration, but definitely increase estimates of the probability of winning, because they add resources (sect. 3.3) to the dissidents.

The paths of CA and DA theories evidently cross in many strange ways. While *Increase the Probability of Winning* arguments are consistent with some DA positions, such "utilitarian justifications" for collective dissent do not really accord well with the nonrational thrust of Gurr's relative deprivation arguments. The many interesting and important propositions derived from probability of winning arguments do, however, grow quite neatly out of the CA approach.

*Increase the Probability of Making a Difference.* This solution has generated far fewer insights into collective dissent than the previous one. This is because the rank and file do *not* personally make much of a difference in a large group of dissidents. The task of convincing individual dissidents otherwise is an arduous one. Quite simply, there are few ways to increase the probability of making a difference, a point noted by early proponents of this idea (Tullock 1971a, 51–52). Hence, the truth, that the success of rebellion depends much more on the efforts of all of the others than on one's own efforts, cannot be hidden from all of the dissidents all of the time.

Moreover, rebels with inflated "probability of making a difference" calculations are harder to explain within the CA program than within the DA research program. DA theorists can study expectations, especially unrealistic ones, by exploring socialization, cognitive failures, and symbols. CA theorists lack the tools to do this. Hence, CA attempts to understand such calculations do not lead, as the brevity of section 3.7 attests, to many insights into collective dissent. The DA approach, consequently, can resolve an internally generated CA problem. Score one for DA theories.

*Use Incomplete Information.* The assumption of the *Use Incomplete Information* solution — that dissidents act under incomplete, uncertain, and asymmetric information — yields several interesting ideas about collective dissent. Many interesting observations about dissidents, dissident groups, regimes, and the competition between regime and opposition were derived from this solution to the Rebel's Dilemma. Nevertheless, the approach has some difficulties.

First, DA theorists also heartily embrace this solution. Gurr (1970, 214–15), for example, argues that many "utilitarian justifications [rest] on untested beliefs about the efficacy of action," that dissidents are likely to hold diverse and questionable assumptions about the consequences of collective dissent, and that "actors' calculations about the effects of their actions are widely disparate" for different actors in the *same* situation. His (1970, 210) explanation for such "miscalculations" is drawn from social psychology: "Evidence examined here suggest that many participants in strife perceive violence in a utilitarian way, but that their perceptions of utility are not often 'rational' in the sense of being based on accurate calculations about the effects of alternative courses of action. Instead they tend to be derived from ideological assumptions or perceptions that violence has been successful in other situations." Gurr (1970, 193) concludes that "the more immediate psychological determinants of how we respond to specific deprivations are our cognitive maps of social causality and responsibility, by which we attribute blame, and our beliefs about the justifiability and consequences of specific kinds of actions in response to those situations . . . We also are likely to make calculations, whether shrewd or self-deceiving, about the gains we can achieve through violence." Thus, both CA and DA approaches can explain why revolutionary movements contain nonlogical and romantic elements (e.g., rituals, flags, slogans), making the *Use Incomplete Information* solution to the Rebel's Dilemma easily reconciled with DA theories.

The second problem with the *Use Incomplete Information* solution is one of consistency of assumptions. That dissidents hold erroneous views does not enhance the credibility of the CA research program. Rebels may be fooled in the short run but it is more difficult to make the case that they can be fooled in the long run. Why would they keep committing the same error, never revising their beliefs? While such a model might explain why dissidents choose to participate in CA in the first place, it cannot explain why they continue to participate every day in ongoing CA. Moreover, some dissidents perhaps can be fooled, but can most? Such a model might explain why some hold incorrect information, but it cannot explain why correct information does not eventually diffuse to everyone.

A final problem with this solution is the evidence that highly educated people join dissident groups more frequently than those who are less educated (e.g., Verba, Nie, and Kim's 1978, 64, evidence on "socioeconomic resource level"). The joiners, then, are the ones least likely to be fooled by dissident leaders.

How do proponents of the *Use Incomplete Information* solution to the Rebel's Dilemma respond to these critiques? In general, whenever individual decisions are interdependent, errors and efficiencies can coexist. One rebel's error is not independent of another rebel's error. Collectively, they can keep each other in error. Moreover, both dissident entrepreneurs (e.g., those with mechanisms for producing fiscal illusion) and regime elites (e.g., those with techniques for inducing underestimations of dissident strength) maximize errors. Dissidents, however, minimize such errors (e.g., with specific approaches to the optimal gathering of information). In short, the CA research program can surpass the DA program by explaining how expectations of the parameters in the rebel's decision calculus are formed.

Consider, for example, calculations of the probability of winning. DA theorists would have us believe that such calculations often lead to highly "irrational expectations": self-fulfilling prophecies of imminent victory (perhaps leading all to participate), self-denying prophecies of imminent victory (perhaps leading no one to participate), and self-deluding prophecies of imminent victory (perhaps leading some to participate). Some CA theorists would have us believe, to the contrary, that dissidents gather information optimally and that probability of winning calculations are made "rationally," so that rational expectations emerge. Other CA theorists approach the DA point of view. Kuran's (1989, 1991a) work on expectations prior to revolution shows that underestimation of the probability of winning is the norm. More empirical work is needed in this area.

*Increase Risk Taking.* Some DA theorists believe that dissidents seek danger, prefer stress, and are recklessness and impulsive. Hence, Jenkins (1982, 15) suggests that terrorists are risk takers, and Crenshaw (1986, 388) that "terrorists may be 'stress seekers'" who relish intensely emotional activities. This psychological profile is offered by CA theorists, as well. The CA research program goes further, however, and grounds these ideas in the theory of rational decision making under risk. The resulting propositions offer interesting and testable insights into the behavior of dissidents. Even so, additional modeling of the implications of risk taking is needed if one is to judge whether this approach to the Rebel's Dilemma is superior to existing DA theories.

*Increase Team Competition between Enemies.* Consider four DA versions of the *Increase Team Competition between Enemies* solution to the Rebel's Dilemma. One emphasizes ethnocentrism as a nonrational motivation behind conflict. Blalock (1989, 168) writes that

> nearly all groups are ethnocentric, in the sense of believing that their own group's ways are superior to those of others. Ethnocentrism obviously varies by degree, however, and we are certainly aware of many groups, as well as entire nations, that consider themselves inferior to others in selected ways. Extremely high levels of ethnocentrism, as for example a "chosen people" orientation, are likely to produce a reciprocated reaction on the part of nearly all actors with whom the party in question has contact, thereby increasing the probability of conflicts with them but also feeding back to reinforce any paranoid interpretations placed on their reactions.

A second type of DA argument holds that team competition leads to identity formation which is then responsible for CA. Theorists of the new social movements stress that self-identity is created through the process of challenging and engaging in conflict with the establishment. Participants in the new social movements form goals, interests, and life-styles as a by-product of their conflict with the regime.[27] A third type of DA argument about team competition is more structural; it contends that domination, exploitation, inequality, and, of course, relative deprivation are the basis of unequal "team competition." These forms of social conflict are thought to beget political conflict. A final type of DA argument is more psychological, stressing that people need to personalize their problems. Since problems cannot be the result of inexorable trends, abstract social forces, and unintended consequences, a specific target must be located.[28]

Although these DA arguments are interesting, the *Increase Team Competition between Enemies* solution to the Rebel's Dilemma provides numerous additional ideas. For example, the CA research program points to a neglected subfield of conflict studies: counterrevolution (sect. 7.2.2). Further modeling of the team competition between regimes and oppositions is required.

*Restrict Exit.* This solution generates many insights into protest and rebellion. Withdrawal, secession, and migration appear to be common substitutes for collective dissent that bear further investigation.

Gurr (1970, 75–76) discusses this tradeoff between emigration and dissent. But, once again, the discussion is not well integrated into his DA research program. By contrast, such arguments fit squarely within the CA approach to conflict studies.

*Change the Type of Public Good.* What have the *Seek Public Bads* and *Seek Nonrival Public Goods* solutions to the Rebel's Dilemma contributed to our understanding of protest and rebellion?

Dissidents have different types of grievances and hence seek different types of goods: private, public, mixed, ambiguous, quasi-public, nonrival but excludable, rival but nonexcludable, and so on (Mason 1984). This approach to the Rebel's Dilemma makes three suppositions: the type of PG sought affects the type of CA problems that result; these problems, in turn, lead to different ways of overcoming the Rebel's Dilemma; the solutions, finally, lead to differential group mobilization and success. These suppositions yield highly interesting conjectures. Section 3.11 thus examined nonrival but excludable PGs, while section 3.12 examined nonexcludable but rival PGs. The application of the *Restrict Exit, Seek Public Bads*, and the *Seek Nonrival Public Goods* solutions to the Rebel's Dilemma leads to the speculation that both excludability and nonrivalness increase collective dissent. It also suggests that seeking to avoid public bads, rather than seeking to obtain public goods, generates more collective dissent. These intriguing ideas have had little impact on conflict studies, but bear further serious consideration. They are, after all, at the heart of the CA research program.

### 9.3.2.2. Community
Two sets of Community solutions to the Rebel's Dilemma were examined in chapter 4: common knowledge, or overcoming mutual ignorance, and common values, or overcoming pecuniary self-interest.

*Common Knowledge.* Dissidents must overcome mutual ignorance in situations that involve simultaneous choice. Eckstein (1965, 140–143) offers a classic perspective on such cases, maintaining that conflict theorists can never develop a theory of the "precipitants" of outbreaks of collective dissent. In comparison with "preconditions," they are supposedly too numerous and too varied. Who, after all, can predict the timing of protest or rebellion (sect. 9.3)? The *Increase Mutual Expectations* solution to the Rebel's Dilemma offers an interesting and insightful perspective on these precipitants as "calls to action." Przeworski (1986, 55) even goes so far as "to suggest that several factors that are often viewed as 'causes' should be regarded precisely as such signals." These might include secession crises, economic downturns, foreign pressures, and so on. Given that the precipitants of collective dissent can be understood within the CA research program, the perspective has accomplished something Eckstein thought impossible.

Another situation where dissidents must overcome mutual ignorance is one involving sequential choice — the *Build a Bandwagon* solution to the Rebel's Dilemma. DA theorists maintain that the spatial and temporal contagion of collective dissent occurs through the diffusion of norms and values. For instance, collective behavior theorists suggest that heightened personal interactions — mingling, mixing, fraternizing, gossiping, socializing — can produce bandwagons of collective dissent. One finds examples in Le Bon's "suggestions and hypnotic effects," McDougall's "exciting of an instinct in one individual by another's expression of the same emotion," Allport's "social facilitation," Miller, Dollard, and Blumer's "circular reactions," and Park and Burgess's "rapport" (Coleman 1990, 201).

Interestingly, Gurr emphasizes the utilitarian basis for the temporal diffusion of protest and rebellion: "The intensity and scope of utilitarian justifications for political violence vary strongly with the extent to which a collectivity has increased its average value position in the past through violence" (Gurr 1970, 221). A variable that has consistently appeared in Gurr's empirical work is the historical success of dissidents in internal wars, conspiracies, and group protest (Gurr 1968; Gurr and Duvall 1973; Gurr and Lichbach 1979).

Gurr (1970, 222) also emphasizes the utilitarian basis for the spatial diffusion of protest: "A related source of utilitarian perspectives on violence is provided by the demonstration effect of other groups' successful use or threat of violence . . . If the residents of one black ghetto see members of another looting successfully, or protesting successfully to local officials about their grievances, they will readily see the advantages of doing so themselves." Gurr also generalizes: "The intensity and scope of utilitarian justifications for political violence in a collectivity vary moderately with the extent to which similar collectivities elsewhere are thought to have increased their average value positions through political violence" (Gurr 1970, 223).

However, Gurr again does not integrate his "utilitarian" arguments about diffusion with his nonutilitarian arguments about relative deprivation. He has simply suggested two quite reasonable dissident motivations and never questions whether the assumptions behind the arguments are consistent with one another. By contrast, propositions about the spatial and temporal diffusion and contagion of collective dissent flow directly from CA ideas.

Moreover, DA and CA theories of bandwagons can be distinguished. The CA research program suggests three propositions about the temporal diffusion of protest and rebellion. First, there will be a very strong correlation between a dissident group's past successful collective dissent and its future collective dissent. Second, there will be a weak correlation between a dissident group's past successful and unsuccessful collective dissent and its future collective dissent. Third, there will be no (or even a negative) correlation between a dissident group's past unsuccessful collective dissent and its future collective dissent. DA theories lead to the first proposition, perhaps to the second. They do not lead to the third.

Similarly, the CA research program suggests three propositions about the spatial diffusion of protest and rebellion. First, there will be a very strong correlation between past successful collective dissent by one dissident group and future collective dissent by other dissident groups. Second, there will be a weak correlation between a dissident group's past successful and unsuccessful collective dissent and future collective dissent by other dissident groups. Third, there will be no (or even a negative) correlation between past unsuccessful collective dissent by one dissident group and future collective dissent by other dissident groups. Again, DA theories might yield the first two propositions, but not the third.

Thus, there can be a clear test of the competing approaches to the temporal and spatial diffusion of protest using the *different* and *better* criterion.

*Common Values.* There is much evidence that dissidents are concerned with more than their pecuniary self-interest. Jailed dissidents do not always inform on their fellow supporters, even to save their own lives (Thompson 1966, 584). Looting is discriminate: targets are selected and pinpointed, adjoining targets are avoided. Property is broken and not stolen. Finally, confiscated property is often sold and the proceeds given to the owners. During bread riots and taxation populaire, for example, bread was not stolen; it was sold at a "just" price and the money given to the bakers.

Many in conflict studies point to such observations and conclude that dissidents are not motivated exclusively by pecuniary self-interest. As Thompson (1973, 27) puts it: "Nor is politics, even in the coup zone, quite the Hobbesian jungle of constant competition for spoils and prizes one might expect if events were understood primarily in terms of avarice, lust for power, and survival of the fittest."

DA theorists generalize such observations and suggest that a crucial solution to the CA problem is the legitimacy of the dissident group. If dissidents' orientations toward the dissident group include an obligation to obey its authority, which may result from the specific processes discussed here — altruism, communal consciousness, Kantian ethics, or fairness — they are likely to participate in the group's activities. Elsewhere (Lichbach forthcoming, chap. 7) I have cautioned against such arguments, suggesting that we should be quite selective about expanding rationality to take into account such motivations as a process orientation and other-regardingness.

### 9.3.2.3. Contract

The following Contract solutions to the Rebel's Dilemma were examined in chapter 5: *Self-Government*, *Tit-For-Tat*, and *Mutual Exchange*. Do they contribute much to conflict studies?

The examples of more or less elaborate dissident self-government are legion, yet little systematic work has been done on the problem of dissident organization. The only quantitative attempts to assess dissident authority relations are Gamson (1990) and Gurr (1968; Gurr and Duvall 1973; Gurr and Lichbach 1979). Hence, we know little about how the revolutionary group and the revolution are governed. Not much is known, for instance, about monitoring and enforcing arrangements (sect. 6.5), or for that matter about the conditions that permit dissident self-government and organization without external leaders and patrons (i.e., hierarchical dissident organizations are unnecessary; see sect. 8.1). In short, CA theories once again suggest a new avenue of research: the institutions that govern collective dissent.

Tit-For-Tat agreements, or the idea of contingent cooperation, and mutual exchange agreements, or the idea of trade, are also two important ideas in the CA research program. They lead directly to a focus on the social origins of social contracts. Hence, the three contract solutions to the Rebel's Dilemma are of the most deductively fertile of all of the solutions examined in this book. The transaction costs of arranging cooperation through a social contract lead to the study of the dissidents' community: its longevity, homogeneity, preexisting organizations, isolation, stability, and concentration. A community of dissidents which is long-lived, distinct, interconnected, separate, self-contained, and dense will be able to mobilize more collective dissent than one that is short-lived, heterogeneous, unintegrated, proximate, mobile, and diffused. Dozens of corollaries follow from this basic argument.

While a good deal of collective dissent may be understood by reference to the social contract idea, this approach manifests two weaknesses that have occurred time and time again in this chapter: DA theorists, especially Gurr, have interpreted the same evidence as supporting *their* theory.

Consider the homogeneity argument. Gurr (1970, 287) observes that "much of the literature on crowd behavior and mob violence can be interpreted in terms of the effects of crowds in enhancing group cohesiveness." He (1970, 288) thus argues that homogeneity increases collective dissent, because it facilitates highly interactive crowd-type behavior in which dissidents lose their own individual identity, come to identify with the group, and are susceptible to the behavioral contagion of actions. Note how close this sort of thinking is to CA propositions about homogeneity — that similarity produces solidarity, solidarity produces CA, and hence similarity produces CA. Has not the message behind CA theories always been, however, that solidarity is not enough for CA? By advocating the homogeneity argument CA theorists thus appear to adopt the very same position as their opponents.

Now consider the preexisting organization argument. Stinchcombe (1990, 302) points out that "a basic generalization from political sociology is . . . that the more one associates with workers, the more left one's opinions and voting will be and the more likely one is to be drawn into those activities that are connected to working-class milieux." In other words, preexisting organizations may affect patterns of socialization, rather than processes of CA. Where Gurr sees only community, CA theorists see contract rooted in community —"shared Reason" (Seligman 1992, 60) or a "community of Reason" (Seligman 1992, 196). Hence, Moore (1978) and Scott (1976) attribute revolution to the violation of a social contract among dominated and subordinate groups and CA theorists attribute revolution to the implementation of a social contract among members of the subordinate group.

Consider the argument about discount rates. DA theories contend that young people participate disproportionately in protest and rebellions because it is in the nature of youth to combine a restless and searching soul with high energy. From the CA point of view, the basic reason is that young people have more to gain and less to lose than their older counterparts.

Finally, consider the remoteness and concentration arguments. Gurr (1970, 267) suggests that "the likelihood of internal war varies with the geographical concentration of dissidents in areas to which regime forces have limited access." One reason is that if supporters are concentrated, dissident groups can "obtain supplies and move with relative freedom and anonymity" (Gurr 1970, 264). Gurr (1970, 264) also maintains that "some kind of protective terrain is almost essential if dissidents, even if concentrated, are to maintain persistent opposition to a strong regime." While Gurr's proposition might well summarize sections 5.2.4 and 5.2.6, DA reasoning does not bridge the gap between the macro-observation (i.e., remoteness and concentration) and the microprocesses (i.e., dissident motivations). CA reasoning offers a tighter linkage.

DA and CA theories again cross in many ways. There is, however, a major disagreement with respect to the implications of a high discount rate. Recall that Deprived Actors are frustrated by grievances. Rebels, therefore, should strike out immediately against the source of their grievances, rather than rationally plan a long-term response. Impatience and a sense of urgency, in other words, are more likely to produce collective dissent than are patience and the ability to delay gratifications. Hence, DA theorists would expect most dissidents to seek short-run rather than long-run benefits, and to rebel if they do not get them.[29]

A dissident's discount rate, in sum, unleashes contradictory forces. A short-term horizon may lead not only to frustration with a regime but also to the inability to adopt Tit-For-Tat strategies with other dissidents. Concomitantly, a long-term horizon may lead not only to "giving the regime a chance," but also to the willingness to adopt Tit-For-Tat strategies. Both sets of theorists may, of course, be right. Perhaps those with high discount rates and those with low discount rates seek different PGs and engage in different forms of collective dissent. Those who heavily discount the future might seek PGs that can be produced and consumed quickly, such as the end to a particular government program, while those with low discount rates might seek PGs that take a long time to produce and consume, such as revolution. Those who heavily discount the future might engage in such spontaneous collective dissent as riots, while those with low discount rates might engage in such planned collective dissent as protest campaigns. Such speculation, aimed at reconciling DA and CA theories, could serve as the foundation of survey-based tests of the competing approaches.

Beyond these comparisons with DA theories, contract arguments have a further difficulty. If one explains collective dissent with reference to preexisting social organizations, for example, one is still left with explaining the preexisting social organizations. Cohen (1985, 676–77) argues that assuming that organizations already exist begs the key question in Olson's analysis:

> The standard response by resource-mobilization theorists is that Olson errs in assuming that those who are mobilized into CA are unorganized individuals (the market model) whereas, in fact, they are already organized into solidarity groups. But this reply simply finesses the problem by displacing it to a different level: what remains unclear is why individuals acting rationally in pursuit of interests get involved in groups and what makes them solidarity in the first place . . . Indeed, as Parsons pointed out long ago in his critique of utilitarianism, an analytic perspective that focuses on strategic-instrumental action cannot provide an answer to the question of the origin and logic of group solidarity.

It is therefore one thing to argue that community solves the CA problem; it is another, and more difficult, task to suggest the conditions under which community emerges. This chicken-and-egg question — Which comes first, preexisting organization or CA? — is considered in section 9.1.

The more fundamental perspective of the contract approach may equally be questioned. I have argued that the transaction costs of arranging cooperation among dissidents through a social contract is affected by several structural aspects of the dissidents' community (i.e., longevity, homogeneity, preexisting organization, isolation, stability, concentration). Community, in sum, facilitates mutual monitoring which in turn facilitates contract. Therefore, community facilitates contract. What this means is that the "alternative" approaches to social order rely upon one another, an issue I discuss in Lichbach (forthcoming, chap. 7).

One must conclude that the social contract argument is no Philosopher's Stone for students of conflict. Repeated games do not explain all collective dissent. Nonetheless, the three contract approaches to the Rebel's Dilemma do yield numerous insights into collective dissent. Students of conflict might well begin to unravel the puzzle they face by looking at self-governing arrangements, norms of conditional cooperation, and trade.

## 9.3.2.4. Hierarchy

The following Hierarchy solutions to the Rebel's Dilemma were considered in chapter 6: locate entrepreneurs, locate patrons, reorganize, increase team competition among allies, and impose, monitor, and enforce agreements.

*Locate Agents or Entrepreneurs.* One might think that the *Locate Agents or Entrepreneurs* solution to the Rebel's Dilemma could differentiate between the DA and the CA research programs, since bureaucracy is intimately connected with rationality (Weber 1946, chap. 8). However, Gurr (1970, 356) stresses the importance of organizational structures for collective dissent: "Whereas the first task of revolutionaries is to intensify discontent and focus it on the political system, the most essential task of pragmatic dissidents thus is to organize: to expand the scope of their organizations, elaborate their internal structure, develop the sense and fact of common purpose, and maximize the use of their collective resources, not for violent action but for value-enhancing action." Unfortunately, he never integrates his arguments about dissident leadership and organization into his basic assumptions about relative deprivation. By contrast, arguments about dissident entrepreneurship fit squarely into the CA perspective.

Nevertheless, CA arguments about entrepreneurs are themselves incomplete and suffer from two logical problems. First, since the organization of collective dissent is itself a PG, the *Locate Agents or Entrepreneurs* solution simply pushes explanation one step further back: CA theorists now have to account for the PG of institutions instead of the PG itself. Instead of asking how the CA problem is overcome, the question is how dissident organization is built. As with the Great Man theory of the origins of the state,[30] not much appears to have been accomplished. Second, entrepreneurship may not yield a Pareto-optimal supply of the PG. As Bates (1988, 397) argues, "If the fates of third parties are not linked to the outcome, they may choose to impose systems of plunder. If they do possess a stake in the outcome, then the institution will not yield individually rational outcomes — ones supporting Nash equilibria — that are socially efficient."

The *Locate Agents or Entrepreneurs* solution to the Rebel's Dilemma must therefore be coupled with theories of the origin of entrepreneurial activity (sect. 6.1.2) and the implementation of leadership plans (sect. 6.5). Only then will this solution become a powerful tool for understanding collective dissent.

*Locate Principals or Patrons.* Patrons can be a decisive factor in the development of collective dissent and hence this solution holds numerous implications for conflict studies. This solution has its limitations, however.

First, DA theorists, such as Gurr (Gurr and Lichbach 1979, 1986), have also stressed the importance of patrons for collective dissent. Gurr never really integrates, rather than simply adds on, the argument into his theory. By contrast, the ideas flow very easily out of CA assumptions.

Second, the *Locate Principals or Patrons* solution to the Rebel's Dilemma appears to be a *deus ex machina*. Why does a PG–PD–CA problem not exist between the dissident organization and its patron? Before one can make a convincing case that patronage solves the Rebel's Dilemma, once must show how the relationship between principal (patron) and agent (dissidents) arises.

Third is the idea that patrons of social revolution, peasant rebellion, class conflict, and political terrorism are sugar daddies and external supporters. Regimes think of them as outside agitators and political incendiaries, and conservatives often charge that revolutionaries are motivated by money and/or bribed by (foreign) agents. The "devil" or "hidden hand" theory of revolution (Rudé 1964, 215) thereby suggests that "the twin agents of riot and rebellion were bribery and 'conspiracy.'" Rubenstein (1987, xv) refers to this view of terrorism as the "'Manchurian Candidate' theory of terrorism," or that terrorists are "suicidal robots programmed by foreign manipulators." In short, external intervention arguments can lead to conspiracy theories of collective dissent. They link domestic dissent to foreign machinations, international conspiracies of the left and right, and global networks of revolutionaries or counterrevolutionaries. But one of the central messages of *The Rebel's Dilemma* is that there are *many* solutions to the Rebel's Dilemma. A monocausal theory of collective dissent focused on *only* the patronage argument simply takes the *Locate Principals or Patrons* solution too far. Eckstein (1989, 37) points out that "'well-situated' individuals rarely succeed in inciting rebellion when subordinate groups do not already feel aggrieved. Instead, their importance rests with the direction and coordination they give to rebellious sentiments." Hence, external patronage of revolution and counterrevolution often fails. Walt (1992, 356) thus remarks: "Revolutions are a relatively poor export commodity . . . efforts to reverse a revolution from outside are [also] usually more difficult that their advocates anticipate. Ironically, then, both sides' perceptions of threat are usually mistaken." An exclusive focus on principals or patrons emphasizes the supply side of collective dissent to the neglect of the demand side.

One must conclude that if the *Locate Principals or Patrons* solution to the Rebel's Dilemma degenerates into conspiracy theories, the approach will not help conflict studies. The patronage solution should be used, but judiciously. The concrete contributions that patrons make to collective dissent must be verified empirically, so that the counterfactual question — what would have happened in the absence of patronage — can be given serious consideration.

*Reorganize.* There are three forms of reorganization. Dissident organizations can become clubbish, effective, or decentralized.

Participants in the theoretical, empirical, and policy debates around the importance of group size assume that one can develop unconditional propositions of the form, "as group size increases (decreases), collective dissent increases (decreases)." The *Become Clubbish* solution to the Rebel's Dilemma challenges this assumption. CA theorists can produce no universal prediction about how group size affects CA; conflict theorists can produce no universal prediction about how the size of a dissident group affects collective dissent. The reason is that the group size-collective dissent nexus depends upon the assumptions one makes about how group size affects individual costs and benefits. The key relationships are therefore the rivalness of consumption, economies of scale, and club and exclusion propositions.[31]

By clarifying what one can and what one cannot explain, the *Become Clubbish* solution contributes to conflict studies. It also raises two important questions: Will the dissident group try to recruit anyone, or exclude someone? How large a dissident group will dissident entrepreneurs seek?

The second basic approach to dissident reorganization is to build an efficacious group. Dissident entrepreneurs do this by manufacturing grievances and shaping the demand for collective dissent by finding a PG that best solves the Rebel's Dilemma.

This is, of course, a strategic perspective on group identity. While many interesting observations about the behavior of dissident entrepreneurs were derived from this approach, it has its limits. DA theorists prefer to focus on the social, rather than political, origins of dissident groups. CA theories are notably silent about the social origins of dissent. Given that entrepreneurs must start someplace, the lack of a theory of preferences implies that CA theories can only offer partial insights into questions of group identity and coalition formation (sect. 10.2.1).

Finally, a federal group structure is a potentially important organizational characteristic of dissident groups. Further empirical work is required, however, to determine how many dissident groups actually adopt this approach to the Rebel's Dilemma. Once again, the CA research program points to a new set of empirical questions that students of conflict should address.

It is also important to note, once again, that a solution to the Rebel's Dilemma is woefully incomplete. To create a federal group structure by fusion is, of course, to assume that dissident groups ready to fuse already exist — precisely what the CA problem takes as problematic. This difficulty is, more generally, a flaw in all three of the solutions offered in section 6.3. To reorganize is to be organized already. A dissident group that becomes clubbish and forms an exclusionary club, or becomes effective and shapes an efficacious group, or becomes decentralized and creates a federal group must have already solved its Rebel's Dilemma. The incompleteness of so many solutions to Olson's Problem is a topic that is considered more fully in Lichbach (forthcoming, chap. 7).

*Increase Team Competition among Allies.* Competition within antiregime coalitions, dissident movements, and dissident groups is ubiquitous. Given that collective dissent against organizations dedicated to collective dissent is widespread, one would expect that examining conflict and cooperation within and among dissident groups would be a topic of high priority for conflict theorists. DeNardo (1985) analyzes this issue using spatial theory. Empirical studies of the division of a dissident movement into various dissident organizations, however, are rare (McAdam, McCarthy, and Zald 1988, 718).

CA theories provide numerous insights into the causes of competition (sect. 6.4.2), the ways in which dissident entrepreneurs compete, and the principles by which dissidents choose among dissident groups (sect. 6.4.3). They unfortunately do not yield firm conclusions about the effects of competition among suppliers of a PG on either the level of CA or the supply of the PG, on either group mobilization or group success. Students of conflict need to resolve these theoretical issues in order to advance the study of how the market structure of dissent affects protest and rebellion.

*Impose, Monitor, and Enforce Agreements.* The first part of this solution to the Rebel's Dilemma implies that one should examine the structure of dissident groups from the point of view of cost-sharing arrangements. One should try to determine how agreements are selected, which agreements tend to be chosen, and why they are effective.

Not much work in conflict studies has been aimed at addressing these issues, although some suggestive studies have been done: Zagorin (1982b) on the Huguenots, Lipset (1971a) on Canadian farmers, Rudé (1964) on the Luddites, Tilly (1964) on the Vendée, Rich (1980) on neighborhood organizations, and Thompson (1966) on the working class. Clearly, the *Impose Agreements* solution shows promise.

The second part of this approach involves monitoring defections from agreements. This solution, too, leads analysts to consider the organization of the dissident group; but to date the work along these lines has been woefully meager.

The final part of this approach involves rewarding compliance with agreements and punishing deviance. That dissidents seek selective incentives explains a great deal about protests and rebellions. First, it can explain much about the dissidents' strategy and tactics. Rioters typically loot stores in towns; rebels typically burn manorial records. This "petty" looting and arson often becomes associated with the "lofty" aims of protest and rebellion. The demands of rebels are often local and concrete. Selective incentives can also account for the level of participation in political disturbances, the activities in which dissidents participate, the dissident groups that they join, and the timing of their membership decisions. Second, selective incentives can explain how socioeconomic and political institutions come to influence protest and rebellion. Land and resource inequality may become associated with dissent when peasants see an opportunity to redistribute resources themselves. Government uses selective incentives to demobilize its opponents and mobilize its own supporters. For example, regimes often try to coopt dissident leaders and "buy off" their followers. Long-lived dissident organizations are thus prone to deradicalization.

Finally, selective incentives can also explain the operation of institutions created to conduct collective dissent. The self-organization of peasant rebels is affected. Everyday forms of peasant resistance (Scott 1985), for example, often involve a "conspiracy of silence" to cover dissident activities. Bandwagons — the spatial contagion and temporal diffusion of protest — may emerge when word leaks out of the rebels' success at obtaining pecuniary rewards. Selective incentives also affect externally organized dissident organizations. Dissident entrepreneurs often seek outside patrons to offer selective incentives. If they find themselves in competition for the same base of support, each will try to monopolize the supply of selective incentives. Organizing manuals written by rebel leaders advise appealing to the peasant's material self-interest and focusing on immediate, specific, and concrete issues, rather than on altruism, ideology, and self-sacrifice. Organizational meetings and protest demonstrations often include food, drink, and entertainment. Voluntary members of revolutionary peasant organizations attempt to become paid staff and make a career out of their participation. Long-lived dissident organizations are thus prone to a professionalization of protest. They tend to become oligarchical, with rent-seeking leaders receiving the majority of the benefits.

The selective incentives solution to the Rebel's Dilemma is indeed rich in its implications for studies of collective dissent. It tells us much more than simply that participation in collective dissent is rational, and it accounts for much more than the motivations of rebels. Selective incentives determine the strategies and tactics of various actors (e.g., rank-and-file dissidents, dissident leaders, government, the dissidents' opponents such as their landlords, and the dissidents' supporters such as their patrons). They also determine the institutions rebels use to conduct rebellion — addressing the question of how revolutionary organizations become professionalized and corrupt over time. Protests and rebellions have particular causes, take particular courses and have particular consequences *because* selective incentives are employed. The study of selective incentives thus leads us to many *additional* and *true* statements about political conflicts, statements that are also *different* and *better* than alternative theories. The selective incentives idea, in short, is a particularly useful tool for explaining peasant CA.

The selective disincentives solution to the Rebel's Dilemma once again raises the question of whether revolutionaries seek social justice or self-interest. DA theories tend toward the former view, CA theories toward the latter (with the caveat of sect. 4.2). Is it possible to resolve this controversy?

As section 6.5.4 indicates, the views of Marx, Gurr, and Esping-Anderson on the general irrelevance of selective disincentives to collective dissent run directly counter to the perspective of the CA research program. An investigation of the efficacy of selective disincentives therefore holds more promise for resolving the controversy than does an investigation of the efficacy of selective incentives, because the issue of costs separates DA and CA perspectives more neatly than does the issue of benefits.

Students of conflict can gain much from this solution, but should realize that it is not the *only* solution to the Rebel's Dilemma. To say that selective disincentives *never* solves the Rebel's Dilemma is as misleading as to claim that they *always* solve the Rebel's Dilemma. The real issue is the context within which the approach succeeds. In short, analysts must establish the approach's boundaries (Lichbach forthcoming, chap. 9).

### 9.3.3. The Criteria's Results

How well do CA theories perform by the criteria of Lakatos and Popper? One never knows how far a good idea will take you. Part 2 has shown that there are untold riches in the CA approach, that it illuminates more about collective dissent than anyone has hitherto imagined. Numerous problems and puzzles concerning the causes, courses, and consequences of collective dissent were addressed.

The *additional* and *true* as well as the *different* and *better* statements found in part 2 address many of the Big Questions in conflict studies. Four of these questions relate to solutions as politics (chap. 7).

- *What sorts of individuals participate in what sorts of dissident groups under what conditions?* The CA research program offers many interesting suggestions about the conditions under which specific people, such as government officials, former soldiers, youths, singles, nationalists, separatists, communal group members, workers, the unemployed, professionals, and students join specific dissident groups.
- *What actions do dissident leaders take to promote collective dissent, and what actions does government take to prevent it?* Oppositions are kept from power because of their CA problem; regimes stay in power because of their opponents' CA problem. Both sides recognize solu-

tions to the Rebel's Dilemma and act accordingly. The dissident group works hard to implement solutions, and the regime works just as hard to impede those solutions. CA theories thus focus on how the state shapes conflict.

- *What actions do dissidents' allies take to promote collective dissent, and what actions do dissidents' enemies take to prevent it?* The CA research program focuses on how intervention by foreign and domestic powers — on the side of both dissidents and the regime — shapes conflict.
- *How does collective dissent become revolution?* The CA research program can explain a relatively short-lived, geographically isolated incident of collective dissent — a well-defined meeting, rally, demonstration, riot, or coup, for instance. The program can also explain a constellation of temporally and spatially linked incidents of collective dissent, for instance, a protest campaign, political movement, civil war, or social revolution.

Two of the Big Questions addressed by CA theories relate to solutions as intended and unintended consequences (chap. 8).

- *Are dissident organizations really necessary?* There are many categories of viable solutions to the Rebel's Dilemma. Some involve organization and some do not.
- *Do dissidents become corrupted once they rebel, dissident groups oligarchical once they form, and postdissident societies evil once they are achieved?* Michels' (1962) "iron laws of oligarchy" and Weber's ([1924] 1968, 246) "routinization of charisma" were early recognitions of the problems inherent in the transformations from dissident individuals to dissident movement and finally to postdissident society. The CA research program delves more deeply into the flaws of revolutionary leaders, revolutionary groups, and post-revolutionary societies. Solutions to the Rebel's Dilemma are in many ways self-defeating in that they lead to numerous pathologies of collective dissent. In probing the unintended and unwanted consequences of dissidents' attempts to overcome their CA problem, CA theories explain why revolutions are so often betrayed, why dissident groups are so often the lesser of two evils, and why dissidents are so often rent seekers.

In sum, the CA research program tells us that certain types of dissidents will participate in certain types of dissident groups under certain types of conditions. It explores the actions of dissident entrepreneurs and the responses of government. It explains how isolated incidents of collective dissent become revolution and addresses the issue of when dissident organizations are really necessary. It forecasts what happens to dissident groups once they form and to postdissident societies once they are achieved. The CA research program, in short, provides numerous *additional* and *true* statements about protest and rebellion, statements which are also *different* and *better* than those offered by the DA research program. It thus meets Lakatos's and Popper's tests for productive research programs.

CA theories do not, however, explain everything that we would like to know. Some major puzzles about the causes, courses, and consequences of collective dissent remain. For example, government accommodation, government repression, good economic times, and political democracy sometimes increase collective dissent but sometimes they decrease it. Unfortunately, the CA research program has yet to clarify the accommodation-, repression-,[32] income-, and democracy-dissent connections, that is, the conditions under which these structures encourage or discourage protest and rebellion.

The major reason that CA theories have not solved some of the important puzzles in conflict studies is the micro-macro problem, or the fit between structures and processes. Structural arguments are incomplete unless supplemented by CA processes that show how they operate. However, since there are so many solutions and combinations of solutions to the Rebel's Dilemma, explaining empirical contradictions is easy. There is no trick in demonstrating that given some structure, one CA process yields a positive effect on collective dissent while another CA process yields a negative effect. Making predictions, or showing the conditions under which we should expect the positive or negative effect, is a much more difficult task. There are so many CA processes that collective dissent is unpredictable, simple structural determinism often fails, and conflict puzzles remain puzzles — even after applying CA reasoning.

Two important points may be made in defense of CA theories. First, accommodation, repression, economics, and democracy are broad variables and must be operationalized as more precisely defined institutions, if one wants to determine their effects on a particular group's protest and rebellion. Second, many of these puzzles and questions were generated by DA theories. Why should CA theories be expected to solve internally generated DA problems? The CA research program cannot answer all of the questions raised by all of the other perspectives in the field. Furthermore, from the point of view of CA theories, some of these puzzles are neither important nor interesting. Olson's approach has its own fertile research agenda: CA theories point in new directions, away from many of the old puzzles. Such a redirection of research brings new insights into a field. In short, evaluating a research program by explaining existing puzzles is too limited an approach.

It must be admitted, however, that the CA research program's inability to solve more of the traditional puzzles in conflict studies is quite unfortunate. Given that each of these relationships *is* probably fundamental to understanding conflict, one would have hoped that the CA research program could resolve the empirical and theoretical confusion that surrounds the relationships. It may yet do so. The current inability of the CA research program to resolve the ambiguities in the etiology of collective dissent has cost it credibility among conflict theorists. The research agenda of CA theorists should thus include efforts to resolve these puzzles.

## 9.4. Summary Evaluation

What, then, is the bottom line — the accomplishments and limitations of CA theories of protest and rebellion?

First the good news: CA theories of protest and rebellion are powerful. They offer many *additional* and *true* as well as *different* and *better* observations about collective dissent. They address Big Questions.

Now the bad news: CA theories of protest and rebellion are incomplete. First, each solution category is a logically incomplete explanation of protest and rebellion (sect. 9.1). Complex combinations of the pure solutions are required to explain a concrete case. Second, the theories leave aggregate levels and particular outbreaks of collective dissent unpredictable (sect. 9.2). They offer no general theoretical statement of the etiology of protest and rebellion. Third, the theories leave important substantive questions unaddressed (sect. 9.3.3). Key puzzles are unresolved.

The theories, in short, have boundaries (Lichbach forthcoming, chap. 9). Both a little pride and a little modesty on the part of CA theorists of collective dissent are in order.

CHAPTER 10

# Improving Collective Action Theories of Collective Dissent

The last chapter argued that the PG–PD approach to the Rebel's Dilemma yields many important insights into collective dissent. I maintained that the many hypotheses advanced in *The Rebel's Dilemma*, hypotheses that are *additional* and *true* as well as *different* and *better* than those developed by DA theorists, and hypotheses that are at the root of the rational actor or resource mobilization approach, establish the value of the CA research program in conflict studies.

I do not expect these insights and hypotheses to win over critics. Some of the critics are avowed opponents of the CA approach to conflict studies. Skocpol (1979, 14–18), for one, explicitly denies any useful place for "voluntarist" or "purposive" theories of revolution. The critics also include the key developers of the rational actor approach to conflict studies (sect. 1.4). Both groups emphasize the weaknesses — especially the incompleteness — of CA theories of collective dissent. The two strategies for making the theories more complete are deepening their microfoundations (sect. 10.1) and exploring their macrocontext (sect. 10.2).

## 10.1. Deepen the Micro

The psychologists are right: CA theorists should deepen the microfoundations of PG–PD models and explore the idea of rationality. Many conflict theorists have taken this approach. Debates in conflict studies focus on whether certain types of dissidents — revolutionaries, rioters, coup makers, secessionists, peasants, and so on — are *really* rational. Unfortunately, the debaters talk past one another.

Consider terrorism. Many argue that terrorists are rational. Crenshaw (1986, 385) maintains that "the most important terrorist events are part of campaigns led by organizations." Stohl (1988a, 8–11) argues that many terrorist groups have particular goals that are part of an ongoing political struggle, offering examples of negotiations leading to the peaceful settlement of hostage incidents. Hutchinson (1972, 394) suggests that "paradoxically terrorism, which must appear irrational and unpredictable in order to be effective, is an eminently rational strategy, calculated in terms of predictable costs and benefits." Many formal models of terrorism, supported by considerable evidence, are based on the assumption of rationality (Atkinson, Sandler, and Tschirhart 1987, 3).[1] The counterargument is that terrorists are not rational. Both Lenin and Trotsky (Rubenstein 1987, 174–75), in discounting the utility of terrorism, reject its rationality. Laqueur (1987, 153) rejects rational choice models of terrorism on other grounds: they do not make sense, because "few people would go into a business in which the chances of success are as dim as they are in terrorism."

Some students of conflict have tried to resolve such disagreements by synthesizing the two assumptions and arguing that dissidents can act both rationally and nonrationally. Several examples of this perspective on building theories of protest and rebellion are illustrative.

- Extending rationality. Blalock (1989, 61) advocates a broader notion of rationality: "Merely characterizing a riot participant as 'irrational' because he or she wishes to destroy property or gain vicarious excitement may simply indicate that the analyst has a very inadequate understanding of that actor's goal hierarchy."
- The strategic use of irrationality. Some note that irrationality can be used strategically. Coleman (1990, 510, footnote 5) observes that displays of emotions can be purposive: "That this is true in some circumstances is indicated by terms such as 'crocodile tears' which implicitly recognize the existence of a strategy." Unpredictability, too, can be used strategically. If dissidents are believed to be irrational and unpredictable, if they have a reputation for being risk prone, or if they are believed to use trip-wire mechanisms to precommit themselves to action, then the regime must act carefully.
- Typologies of actors. Others try to synthesize the two perspectives by suggesting that dissident leaders can act rationally, but that their followers cannot (Gurr 1970, 211). Coleman (1990, 483), for example, points out that "it is possible, of course, to overlay purposive action on expressive action, by imputing strategic behavior to leaders and expressive behavior to the followers."
- Typologies of conflict. Still others develop typologies of conflict. Coser (1956, 48–55) argues that there are two types of conflict, "realistic" and "nonrealistic." Tarrow (1989, 14) suggests that Coser's two types are often combined in practice: "Though they use unconventional actions in expressive ways, protesters are *strategic* in their choice of issues, targets, and goals." He also maintains that cycles of rational protest followed by expressive protest often occur.

- Levels of rationality. Other scholars contend that the level of rationality employed in a conflict situation is an important determinant of the outcome of the conflict. Two of Simmel's (1955) propositions (as summarized by Turner 1986, 141) are that "the more that conflict is a means to a clearly specified end, the less likely is the conflict to be violent" and that "the greater is the degree of emotional involvement of parties to a conflict, the more likely is the conflict to be violent."[2]
- Dual political attitudes. Several scholars (Barnes and Kaase 1979; Gamson 1990) argue that a combination of trust and efficacy influences collective dissent. Lipset (1959, 86) maintains that democratic stability is a function of legitimacy and effectiveness: effectiveness is primarily instrumental and assessed in terms of self-interest; legitimacy is more affective and evaluative. Wrong (1988, chap. 5) argues that coercion and legitimation interact in determining political stability.
- Dual motivations. One may argue, finally, that both Gurr's (1970) and Tilly's (1978) classics are vague about motivations and thus combine rationality with nonrationality (Eckstein 1980; Lichbach 1989). Gurr (1970, 156), for example, argues that rebels are guided by both normative and utilitarian calculations. He develops each theme separately and at length.[3]

These syntheses are often advocated but have never been widely accepted. This is because turning to such combinations of assumptions *at the start of inquiry* is premature. I have advocated elsewhere (Lichbach, forthcoming) a different approach to theory building: taking pecuniary self-interest as a baseline model and selectively expanding the conception of rationality as that baseline model fails to illuminate reality. In this way the weakness of CA theories, the admittedly narrow approach to rationality, turns out to be its strength: the theories can offer a systematic and comprehensive approach to explanation.

However one deepens the microfoundations of CA theories, the exercise has implications for the macrostructures within which the theories operate. If motivation is based solely on pecuniary self-interest, the issue of social order need arise only indirectly, as unintended (market) and intended (contract) consequences. If motivation is based on nonpecuniary and other-regarding values, however, the question of social order must be confronted quite directly. Values, by definition, must be held in common. As Alexander (1990, 1) puts it, "There is subjective order rather than merely subjective action because subjectivity is here conceived as a framework rather than intention, an idea held in common rather than an individual wish, a frame-

work that can be seen as both the cause and the result of a plurality of interpretive interactions rather than a single interpretive act per se." Deepening
the micro therefore leads to the question of the interrelationship of culture
and protest.[4]

This analysis has provided numerous examples of how cultural values
and orientations drive CA processes.

- A general ethos, vision of the future, or moral code can create zealots
  and hence influence the *Increase Benefits* solution (sect. 3.1).
- Adaptability and openness to innovation affects both dissidents and
  regimes. The dissidents' ability to adopt innovations in the technology
  of dissent affects the *Improve the Productivity of Tactics* solution
  (sect. 3.4.2). The government's inefficiency and ineffectiveness
  affects the state's weakness and hence drives the *Increase the Probability of Winning* solution (sect. 3.6.2.2).
- Orientations to political efficacy influence a dissident's calculus of
  the probability of success and hence drive the *Increase the Probability of Winning* solution (sect. 3.6.1).
- A group ethos of risk-proneness can affect dissidents' willingness to
  take risks and hence the *Increase Risk Taking* solution (sect. 3.9).
- Incommensurate value systems drive communal competition and
  hence affect the *Increase Team Competition between Enemies* solution (sect. 3.10.1.1).
- Nationalism can unite dissidents against an external enemy and hence
  affect the *Increase Team Competition between Enemies* solution
  (sect. 3.10.1.3).
- Dissidents are more sensitive to losses than to gains, a factor that
  drives the *Seek Public Bads* solution (sect. 3.12.1).
- A tradition and culture of violence influences the temporal diffusion
  of collective dissent and hence affects the *Common Knowledge* solution (sect. 4.1.2.1).
- A variety of common values, such as Kantian ethics, fairness, and a
  group consciousness, offer very direct solutions to the Rebel's
  Dilemma (sect. 4.2).
- Trust allows predictability and hence facilitates the generation of both
  the *Increase Mutual Expectations* solution (sect. 4.1.1) and the social
  contact approach (sect. 5.1).
- Norms of reciprocity, developed for example by peasants (Scott
  1976), aid cooperation and hence facilitate the *Tit-For-Tat* approach
  (Section 5.1.2).
- Eras with future-oriented ideologies encourage low discount rates
  and hence facilitate the social contract approach (sect. 5.2.1).

- Community norms help reduce the bargaining, monitoring, and enforcement costs of dissident agreements and hence drive the social contract approach (sect. 5.2).
- Orientations toward political morality and political corruption influence the demand for rent-seeking and hence affect the *Administer Selective Incentives* solution (sect. 6.5.3.3). Such values can also influence government inefficiency and ineffectiveness and hence affect state weakness, which in turn drives the *Increase the Probability of Winning* solution (sect. 3.6.2.2).

CA theories thus recognize that culture matters. The theories, however, can offer more than this obvious depiction of culture as a *deus ex machina* that hovers over regimes and dissidents. They offer a uniquely political perspective on the question of culture and dissent. What dissidents think and believe are affected by strategic factors. Various political actors try to persuade dissidents about their interests and convince them about various aspects of their struggle. Preferences and cognitions are politics. Moreover, the themes and orientations of protest, or the articulation of dissidents' values, are driven by strategic considerations. Rhetoric is also politics. More specifically, this analysis has demonstrated that dissident preferences and cognitions, and the articulation of the themes of protest, are affected by three political struggles: regime vs. opposition, leaders vs. followers, and opposition vs. opposition.

The strategic struggle between regime and opposition shapes dissident preferences and cognitions. Regimes and opposition struggle over information (sect. 3.8). Both try to foster illusions, ideologies, and symbols. The root of this struggle is a battle over community. Common values are at issue. Hence, regimes and oppositions try to manipulate a process orientation and other-regardingness (sect. 4.2). Structures are also at issue, as both regimes and oppositions try to define and redefine the dissidents' community. Formal and informal dissident organizations have their origins in politics (sect. 5.2.3.4). The strategic struggle between regime and opposition also affects the articulation of the themes of protest. Political violence is a form of political communication (sect. 3.4.5.1). Dissidents try to express their demands, publicize their group's existence, and pierce the government's veil of legitimacy. Dissidents also try to generate new issues to divide a regime's coalition (sect. 3.4.5.1). Radical and reformist political demands are therefore advanced strategically (sect. 3.4.5.2).

The strategic struggle between the principals (followers) and agents (leaders) of dissent also influences dissident preferences and cognitions. Dissident entrepreneurs try to create an efficacious dissident group (sect. 6.3.2), which involves putting together a coalition of like-minded dissidents. Hence, dissident entrepreneurs try to shape their followers' grievances, goals, and identities. The strategic struggle between the principals and agents of dissent also influences the articulation of the themes of protest. Dissident leaders and followers express their values, regarding both goals and means, strategically. Preference falsification is therefore a major part of collective dissent (sect. 9.2.2.2).

Finally, the strategic struggle among dissident groups within a dissident movement also influences how the themes of the protest are articulated. Dissident groups in a dissident movement try to "product differentiate" their goals and tactics, attempting to create their own niche (sect. 6.4.3). It is particularly important for a new and smaller dissident group to do this. Often the new group tries to outflank and outbid its older and larger "ally" by charging that it is insufficiently radical (sect. 5.2.3.4).

In sum, the CA approach, with its uniquely political perspective on culture and dissent, can contribute to the interpretive turn in conflict studies, specifically, and in the social sciences, more generally. CA theorists can remind the culturalists that the origins of dissident preferences and cognitions, as well as the articulation of the values of protest and rebellion, involve strategic considerations.[5]

## 10.2. Explore the Macro

The sociologists are right: CA theorists should explore the macrostructures within which PG–PD models operate. Individual choice presupposes the existence of a structure of constraints within which individual choices are made.[6] Hence, deductions from the CA approach, as discussed in section 2.2, are obtained by comparative statics. One takes a CA model, places it in a specific communal, contractual, or hierarchical context, and obtains predictions. One then goes on to a second context, and then a third, and so on. Finally, one takes a second CA model and repeats the procedure. Predictions from the models are obtained, in other words, by varying highly specific solutions to *and* highly specific environments for the Rebel's Dilemma. Solution + context = predictions. Moreover, institutional arrangements for CA are not immutable. Communal, contractual, and hierarchical institutions change. Hence, any student of collective dissent interested in CA theories must also be interested in the comparative and historical analysis of institutions.

This analysis has indeed pointed out numerous examples of how the macrostructures of state and society drive CA processes.

- The economic dependency of rebels on authorities affects dissident opportunity costs and hence influences the *Lower Costs* solution (sect. 3.2.3).

- The coercive capacity of the state determines the level of repression that can be brought to bear on dissidents and hence influences the *Lower Costs* solution (sect. 3.2.5).
- The state's weakness affects dissidents' estimates of their chances of success and hence drives the *Increase the Probability of Winning* solution (sect. 3.6.2.2).
- Weakly institutionalized procedures for leadership succession can influence regime weakness. This, in turn, influences dissidents' estimates of their chances of success and hence drives the *Increase the Probability of Winning* solution (sect. 3.6.2.2).
- Fixed resources and limited growth generate zero-sum competition and hence influence the *Increase Team Competition between Enemies* solution (sect. 3.10.1.1).
- Modernization, industrialization, migration, urbanization, demographic change, and state penetration can increase ecological competition and hence affect the *Increase Team Competition between Enemies* solution (sect. 3.10.1.1).
- Urbanization affects the homogeneity (sect. 5.2.2) and the stability of a dissident community (sect. 5.2.5) and hence the social contract approach.
- Overlapping social cleavages enforce dissident homogeneity and hence assist the social contract approach (sect. 5.2.2).
- A nation's geographic endowment — if it includes great distances, inaccessible terrain, a poor transportation system, or fluid and uncertain boundaries — increases dissident autonomy and hence facilitates the social contact approach (sect. 5.2.4).
- Industrialization concentrates workers and hence facilitates social contracts (sect. 5.2.6).
- Population growth and population density affect concentration and hence facilitate social contracts (sect. 5.2.6).
- Socioeconomic change and population growth affect the spatial distribution of workers (i.e., their concentration, sect. 5.2.6) and hence the social contract approach.
- The occupational structure of society affects the supply of dissident entrepreneurs and hence influences the *Locate Agents or Entrepreneurs* solution (sect. 6.1.2).
- Blocked channels of upward elite social mobility, or even the existence of downward mobility, encourage dissident entrepreneurship and hence activate the *Locate Agents or Entrepreneurs* solution (sect. 6.1.2).
- Changes in the occupational structure of society, such as a movement toward jobs that reward the skills that entrepreneurs acquire in dissi-

dent groups, encourage dissident entrepreneurship and hence activate the *Locate Agents or Entrepreneurs* solution (sect. 6.1.2).
- The global structure of interstate competition influences the external patrons of regimes and oppositions and hence affects the *Locate Principals or Patrons* solution (sect. 6.2.3.4).
- States with widespread political corruption increase the demand for rent seeking and hence affect the *Administer Selective Incentives* solution (sect. 6.5.3.3).

Given that CA theories are inherently political (chap. 7), these macrostructures set the context for the power struggle between regime and opposition. Three contexts deserve close scrutiny. First, CA models must be imbedded in a theory of civil society (sect. 10.2.1), since those who are struggling for power need to be identified. Second, CA models must be imbedded in a theory of the state (sect. 10.2.2), since dissidents operate within the framework established by the state, even as they try to change the incumbents, policies, and/or structures of that state. Finally, CA models must be imbedded in a theory of state-society linkages (sect. 10.2.3), since collective dissent pits parts of civil society that are aligned with parts of the state against other parts of civil society that are also aligned with the state.

## 10.2.1. A Theory of Civil Society: Groups

To apply CA theories of collective dissent to a given situation, one must identify the key actors who are competing for power and what it is that they want. As Zald (1988, 24–25) argues, "To predict the orientation of the social-movement sector, the major goals of social movements, requires a juxtaposition of emerging social cleavage lines of class, race, religion, age, sex, and culture as they relate to the definition of actionable issues in the political system." In short, one must link the structural aspects of the domestic and international society in which dissidents find themselves to the common goals sought by the dissidents.

This issue is central to all research programs in political science (sect. 7.1.1). Pluralists ask what explains the emergence of one group rather than another. Political sociologists ask which social cleavages become politicized. Culturalists ask into which collective goals dissidents are socialized. Systems theorists ask how interests are mapped from the economic, social, or cultural system into the political system. Finally, CA theorists ask which of many possible PGs are sought.

Students of CA have provided three types of answers to such questions. One group of CA theorists, as indicated in section 10.1, offers a distinctly political perspective: regime and dissident entrepreneurs try to persuade dissidents about their interests and convince them about their values. Preferences are therefore politically constructed.

A second group of CA theorists treats preferences as a *deus ex machina*: preferences provide an explanation while themselves remaining unexplained. Tastes, goals, appetites, and desires, that is, are taken as given.[7] Such theorists presume that groups already exist and try to explain how they are set in motion. Olson (1990, 24) summarizes the approach: "The logic of collective action focuses on what does or does not take place after people have defined their interests in a particular way."

The idea that one can explain the relationship between individual and collective action without understanding the relationship between individual and collective goals is far fetched. Consequently, this group of CA theorists has ignored important questions about the origins of dissident grievances, revolutionary ideologies, collective identities, and social cleavages. Because of these gaps, this particular CA approach cannot address many important puzzles in conflict studies.

- Which groups become dissident. Take, for example, certain key problems in the etiology of revolution. The most influential social force behind revolution has been variously identified as the working class (Marx and Engels [1848] 1968), the peasantry (Huntington 1968), and the landed upper classes (Moore 1966). These CA theories have nothing to suggest about which group, under which circumstances, will prove decisive. Moreover, Moore (1966) outlines various possible social alignments among government bureaucrats, landed elites, urban bourgeoisie, industrial workers, and rural peasants, that might lead the revolution. These CA theories also cannot explain which of the several possible revolutionary class coalitions will form. Finally, while Moore (1966) argues that the commercialization of agriculture sets revolution in motion, Skocpol (1979) stresses international political competition and state building. These CA theories cannot explain how various groups react to either state building or the commercialization of agriculture (or even why any of these groups should be the focus of analysis).
- The alignment of social forces behind dissident groups. Why do some people become Communists and others Fascists? How can the typical patterns be explained: that support for leftist revolutionary parties come from peasants and workers, that support for bourgeois revolutionary parties comes from the middle class, and that support for rightist revolutionary parties comes from the lower middle classes. These CA theories are silent on the alignment in interwar Europe — that Fascist parties were supported by the lower middle classes, small

peasants, former officers and soldiers, and not the working class and the upper middle classes. They therefore cannot shed any light on one of the great historical puzzles in conflict studies: who voted, who marched, who worked, and who killed for Hitler? Or, consider collective dissent in interwar China. Over time the Kuomintang and Communist party elites became socially polarized (Hagopian 1974, 299). Both started out with a healthy proportion of intellectuals of middle- and upper-class backgrounds. Eventually the sons and daughters of peasants flocked to the Communists, while the sons and daughters of business and commercial elites joined the Kuomintang. These CA theories are silent on the question of why this realignment occurred.

- The relationship between the social backgrounds of dissident leaders and followers. Leaders and followers of bourgeois movements are often very close in social background (Greene 1990, 43–45). On the other hand, leaders and followers of leftist movements are often very far apart in social background (Greene 1990, 42–43). To complete the puzzle, leaders and followers of rightist movements often fall in the middle, and are only somewhat close in social background. They tend to be drawn primarily from the middle and lower middle classes and hence approximate their social base (Greene 1990, 45–47). Here, too, these CA theories do not account for important patterns.

- The relationship between the social backgrounds of revolutionary leaders and regime leaders. The evidence shows that bourgeois revolutionary leaders are closest in social background to the regime elites, rightist revolutionary leaders the furthest, and leftist revolutionary leaders somewhere in the middle (Greene 1990, chap. 4). These CA theories offer no hypothesis as to why this is so.

- Who will be the radicals and who the moderates in a dissident group. Consider, for example, revolutionary movements (Hagopian 1974, 210–13). In some movements it is hard to distinguish radicals from moderates on the basis of social background. In France it was hard to distinguish Girondists from Montagnards; in England, separating the Presbyterians from the Independents was no easy task. In other revolutions, it was much easier. In Russia it was easy to distinguish Kadets from Bolsheviks; in Spain, separating the Radicals from the Socialists was easy. Given a group of dissidents, why are some moderate and some radical? Again, these CA theories are silent, even where social background would seem to provide an important clue.

- Why peasants are sometimes revolutionary and sometimes conservative. In general, as Huntington (1968, 435) argues, "The support for the governing party, if there is a governing party, comes form the countryside; the support for the opposition from the cities." The city, therefore, is usually the center of instability and opposition. But this implies that "the peasantry may thus play either a highly conservative role or a highly revolutionary one" (Huntington 1968, 293). When, then, will peasants be revolutionary and when will they be counter-revolutionary? These CA theories offer no suggestions.

- Which peasants are revolutionary. Some maintain that those peasants with landed property are likely to be the most revolutionary (Wolf 1969; Scott 1976). Others follow Lenin and Mao and maintain that the landowning peasantry is inherently conservative and those peasants who are propertyless laborers or sharecroppers are likely to be the most revolutionary (Paige 1975, 11). Why? Do not look to these CA theories for an answer.
- Which urbanites are revolutionary. Huntington (1968, 301) suggests that after one generation the urban lumpenproletariat will become revolutionary because it will not be able to find jobs in the modern industrial sector. He also suggests that the urban middle class will become conservative because it will have acquired new professions that are more technical and business-oriented. These CA theories do not help us to understand this pattern.
- The many relationships between socioeconomic status and conflict. Income, education, and occupation are linked to collective dissent through the calculation of costs and benefits. However, socioeconomic status has many direct and indirect effects and thus produces many different costs and benefits. These CA theories therefore cannot offer any definite conclusions about the income-, education-, and occupation-dissent linkages.
- The rise and fall of interest in particular issues and grievances. These CA theories cannot explain what accounts for Downs's (1972) "issue attention cycle": the cycle characterized by the development of public concern around an issue, followed by group formation, and then the growth of public boredom, followed by group stagnation.

In sum, this particular CA approach offers no theory of the origins of preferences and hence no answers to some very important puzzles in conflict studies. This gives CA theories a static quality: there is a fixed set of actors, with fixed goals, means, constraints, costs and benefits, courses of action, and so on. The unanswered questions also give the analysis an expost flavor: all of the really crucial things have been decided and the results merely set in motion.

Stronger assumptions produce stronger deductions. In order to endogenize a dissident's decisions and yield more precise deductions about his or her participation in collective dissent, CA theories require more specific assumptions about dissident goals. These goals must be rooted in a conception of the civil society that gives rise to the groups that are struggling for power. Restricting a dissident's utility function in this manner will yield more exact and far-ranging empirical propositions about collective dissent. Making general assumptions about CA and adding to these auxiliary assumptions about preferences may thus allow the development of even more useful applications of CA theories to conflict studies.

A third group of CA theorists is moving in this direction. Materialist theories of preferences are important in the analyses of Bates (1989) and Rogowski (1989). Kuran's (1987, 1989, 1991a) work on preference falsification treats both public and private preferences as endogenous within a CA framework. Such work may open up entirely new avenues for the study of protest and rebellion.

### 10.2.2. A Theory of the State: Politics

In order to apply CA theories of collective dissent to a given situation, one must understand the framework established by the state within which dissidents struggle. State institutions matter. Federalism, local governments, legislative structures, government bureaucracies (especially the military and police), legislative-executive relations, and constitutional courts all affect dissident groups.

States thus structure conflicts. Class formation, ethnic relations, women's rights, and countless other types of social protest are a function of the state institutions within which conflict occurs. Three examples illustrate the point. The American state, which is weak, fragmented, and decentralized, is partially responsible for the low level of class consciousness among American workers (Lipset 1977a, 1977b). The state in prerevolutionary France, which was monarchical, bureaucratic, centralized, and sharply differentiated from society, influenced the political capacities of the landed upper classes and peasantry (Skocpol 1979). The state in postrevolutionary France, which is even more bureaucratic, centralized, and sharply differentiated from society than its predecessor, "fostered anarchist or Marxist orientations and political militancy among French workers, whereas the centralized but less differentiated British 'establishment' encouraged British workers and their leaders to favor parliamentary gradualism and private contractual wage bargaining" (Skocpol 1985, 26).

The most important general argument along these lines derives from Schattschneider (1960) and can be traced to the social choice literature (Riker 1982). Schattschneider argues that political institutions are not neutral but rather have an independent influence on the transmission of preferences into outcomes. Institutions channel participation into particular directions and affect the relative distribution of power among groups. In short, institutions mobilize bias. For example, consider the CA problems of large and diffuse interests and of special interests under two forms of democracy: federal systems and unitary polities. Under federalism, large and diffuse interests are disadvantaged and highly organized special interest groups favored. Under unitary polities, the situation is reversed: power tends to fall into the hands of large national constituencies and it is local special interest groups that have difficulty mobilizing.

CA theories of collective dissent must therefore include a more institutionally rich theory of politics. Suggestions along these lines appear in section 7.1.2.

## 10.2.3. A Theory of State-Society Linkages: Domination and Legitimacy

Finally, in order to apply CA theories of collective dissent to a given situation, one must also understand the connections between civil society and the state. After all, collective dissent implies a challenge to the state's domination of civil society: parts of civil society consider the state's authority illegitimate in that the state does not represent some of the interests of civil society. In short, the influence of civil society is not matched by the responsiveness of the state.

The representation of social forces within the state, and hence the legitimation of state domination, is affected by electoral laws, party systems, systems of interest intermediation, channels of political recruitment, and mechanisms of political participation. More generally, the state and civil society are linked by a dense network of interacting, interlocking, and interdependent structures and organizations. State-society relationships involve networks of networks, connections of connections, organizations of organizations, and linkages of linkages.

Such relationships have a direct bearing on collective dissent. In the case of the working class, for example, federalism influences workers' CA. The business community, the working-class community, and capital-labor connections also influence workers' CA. Finally, capital-government and labor-government relationships, too, influence workers' CA.

Moreover, states are not simply passive observers of state-society relations. Governments engage in policies of social control to maintain their dominance and the dominance of their allies in civil society. These policies (Lichbach 1984, 1987) include accommodation (sect. 3.5) and repression (sect. 3.2). Thus, state actions create more or less favorable "political opportunities" for dissident groups (McAdam 1982, 51).

In sum, collective dissent pits parts of civil society that may be aligned with parts of the state against other parts of civil society that also may be aligned with parts of the state. CA processes are therefore imbedded in state, societal, and state-societal structures. These structures, and the historical forces that produce them, are the macrocontexts that drive CA. Microfoundations (i.e., CA processes) need macrostructures (e.g., state-society linkages), and vice versa.

CA theories must therefore contribute toward the resolution of the structure-agent problem in collective dissent. Theories of collective dissent have been, at root, either theories of action or theories of structure. In Gurr (1970), the prime cause of collective dissent is the mental state and the mediating factors are institutions. In Skocpol (1979), the prime cause of collective dissent is the institution and the mediating factors are (implicitly) mental states. Given that a satisfying explanation of collective dissent must eventually explain both dissident preferences and actions, CA theorists need theories of structure that supplement Olson's theories of action. Both types of theories contribute to the explanation of collective dissent: structure without action has no mechanism; action without structure has no cause.

Such a synthesis will help to solve the incompleteness problem (sect. 9.1). Deepening the microfoundations of rationality and exploring the macrostructures within which rationality operates will produce more logically complete explanations of dissident CA. Case and comparative studies (sect. 9.2.3) must consider the historically specific situation and context within which CA processes operate. Such efforts, quite naturally, deepen the micro and explore the macro.

# CHAPTER 11

# A Final Perspective

This book has elaborated the CA approach to collective dissent and has therefore provided the microfoundations of the rational actor or resource mobilization approach to conflict studies. I hope that students of social order, CA, and collective dissent are convinced that examining the interrelationships among Hobbes's Dilemma, the Prisoner's Dilemma, and the Rebel's Dilemma has definite, albeit circumscribed, value. More specifically, the CA approach to collective dissent has two virtues.

*Conflict studies enrich CA studies.* The preface suggests that it is probably more appropriate to use the CA research program to explain collective dissent, or seek the origin of social order, than to explain most other social phenomena. Thus, my focus on protest and rebellion has clarified many outstanding issues in the CA research program. I have pointed out, for example, that the issue of the relative importance of solutions based on planned order and solutions based on unplanned order is of great concern to students and practitioners of collective dissent (sect. 8.1). I have also shown how the question of the origin of preferences is a central problem in conflict studies (sect. 10.2.1). In short, the application helps us to understand the theory.

*CA studies enrich conflict studies.* This book has also demonstrated that the CA research program illuminates many paths in conflict studies. These wide-ranging theories explain many puzzles about dissidents and dissident groups, as well as about their allies and enemies. More specfically, the theories demonstrate that CA problems are a ubiquitous feature of collective dissent, that particular groups have particular CA problems, and that CA processes are the microfoundations of many behavioral relationships.

First, everywhere that we looked we found CA problems. Consider the many instances of Olson's Problem that this analysis has uncovered.

- Dissidents face Olson's Problem when participating in collective dissent against a regime. Contributing to the dissidents' cause, in other words, is a PG (sect. 1.3). Economic competition and the competition for selective incentives (sect. 6.5.3) intensify this CA problem.
- Exit may occur as individual exit (a private refuge) and as collective exit (a "Mayflower Compact," sect. 3.11).

- Dissident movements, groups, and factions face a CA problem (sect. 6.4). The factors that account for cooperation among factions of a dissident group and among dissident groups themselves also account for cooperation among individual dissidents. Cooperation among individual dissidents, dissident factions, and dissident groups are thus three manifestations of the same underlying PG–PD problem — the Rebel's Dilemma. Competition among dissident entrepreneurs, both within and among dissident groups, intensifies this CA problem.
- Different dissident movements face a CA problem in forming an anti-regime coalition. The revolutionary coalition also faces a PG–PD situation (sect. 7.2.1).
- Now consider the counterrevolutionary coalition. Supporters of the regime face Olson's Problem in assisting the regime: contributions to the regime are a PG. Supporters also face Olson's Problem in participating in regime organizations: becoming informed about regime affairs and trying to influence and control regime leaders is yet another PG (sect. 3.10.2). There is competition among regime entrepreneurs (sect. 6.1). A dictator organizes his or her military apparatus such that potential coup makers face a considerable CA problem (sect. 6.2.3.1). All of these phenomena are manifestations of the regime's CA problem — the State's Dilemma (sect. 7.2.2).
- International revolutionary (and counterrevolutionary) coalitions confront CA problems (sect. 6.2.3.4).
- The agency problem (Lichbach forthcoming, chap. 6) in collective dissent is that dissidents as principals face a CA problem in controlling their agent, the dissident entrepreneur. This problem arises because rank-and-file dissidents are numerous, dispersed, and self-interested. Followers thus face a PG problem of not acquiring information about their leaders (i.e., rational ignorance, sect. 3.8.1). Dissidents also face a PG problem of not trying to influence leaders (i.e., rational nonparticipation). The dissidents' agency costs are thus the result of an Internal Rebel's Dilemma: while it is in the interest of all principals (i.e., rank-and-file dissidents) to control their agent (i.e., the dissident entrepreneur), each principal wishes to free ride on the contributions of others to the collective cause. The dissidents' agency problem is responsible for many of the unintended consequences of collective dissent (sect. 8.2).
- A dissident group's patrons face Olson's Problem in aiding the dissidents. A regime's patrons face Olson's Problem in aiding the regime. Patronage, in short, is a PG (sect. 6.2).

CA problems in collective dissent are thus widespread. Indeed, Olson's Problem affects all aspects of protests and rebellions. No facet is immune.

Moreover, we have found competition — the reverse of CA problems — everywhere. There is economic competition among dissident followers (sect. 5.1.3). There is competition among regime followers for rewards or selective incentives (sect. 6.5.3). There is competition among regime entrepreneurs (sect. 6.1). There is competition among dissident entrepreneurs, both within and among dissident groups (sect. 6.4). There is competition between dissident entrepreneurs and regime entrepreneurs (sect. 3.10.1.2). Finally, there is competition between patrons of the regime and patrons of the dissidents (sect. 6.2.4).

Second, we have come to understand the CA problems of various sorts of groups and have been able to make predictions about the sorts of people who, given certain conditions, will join particular dissident groups.

- Government officials will participate in more collective dissent than will nongovernmental officials. This is because government officials receive extensive benefits from government (sect. 3.1), have a higher probability of making a difference (sect. 3.7), and are more likely to receive selective incentives for their participation (sect. 6.5.3).
- Former soldiers will participate in more collective dissent than will those who are not former soldiers, because demobilized soldiers have more skills that increase the productivity of their tactics (sect. 3.4).
- The young will participate in more collective dissent than will the old, because the young have a lower discount rate (sect. 5.2.1).
- Single people will participate in more collective dissent than will married people, because singles face no opportunity costs arising from family responsibilities (sect. 3.2.3).
- Nationalist movements will have more participants than will cross-national movements, because movements that cross national boundaries do not concentrate dissidents (sect. 5.2.6).
- Separatist movements will have more participants than will nationalist movements, because separatist movements concentrate dissidents (sect. 5.2.6).
- Members of distinct, segmented, and stigmatized social groups will participate in more collective dissent than will those who are not members of such groups, because members of distinct social groups are better able to monitor each other's participation (sect. 6.5.2). Mobilization is also facilitated because such groups tend to have a concentrated population (sect. 5.2.6). One thus expects there to be more ethnic-based collective dissent than class-based collective dissent. One also expects that nations with distinctive minority communities to be particularly prone to protest and rebellion.
- Workers' movements in the mining, coal, lumber, textile, and waterfront industries will have more participants than will workers' move-

ments in other industries, because such workers are more concentrated (sect. 5.2.6).

- Workers' movements in large factories will have more participants than will workers' movements in small factories, because large factories concentrate workers (sect. 5.2.6).
- The unemployed will participate in more collective dissent than will the employed, because the unemployed face no opportunity costs from losing time at an income-producing job (sect. 3.2.3). If the unemployed are concentrated in a particular geographic area (sect. 5.2.6), expect them to engage in particularly high levels of protest.
- People with independent incomes will participate in more collective dissent than will people without independent incomes. Hence, free professionals (e.g., lawyers, journalists, artists, writers, professors, physicians, intellectuals) will have high participation rates in collective dissent. Those in more exposed occupations (e.g., lower civil servants, white-collar employees, the peasantry, agricultural workers, tenants) will have low participation rates. This is because people with independent incomes have lower opportunity costs (sect. 3.2.3) and can take more risks (sect. 3.9).
- Students will participate in more collective dissent than will nonstudents, because students, for the most part, are not yet employed and hence have a lower opportunity cost of collective dissent (sect. 3.2.3). They are also concentrated in schools (sect. 5.2.6). Another factor is their relative youth and hence low discount rate (sect. 5.2.1).

The CA problems of different groups of people are thus different. Different people are mobilized into collective dissent by different CA processes.

Third, we have seen how CA processes lurk behind the association of various factors with collective dissent. CA theories provide the microfoundations for the linkage of adaptable dissident groups (sect. 3.4.4), unsuccessful dissident groups (sect. 3.6), elite disunity (sect. 3.6.2.2), wars (3.6.2.2), symbols (sect. 3.8.2.4), preplay communication (sect. 4.1.1), temporal diffusion of dissent within dissident groups (sect. 4.1.2.1), spatial diffusion of dissent among dissident groups (sect. 4.1.2.2), base areas (sect. 5.1.1), mutual exchange agreements (sect. 5.1.3), age structures of a population (sect. 5.2.1), homogeneous dissident communities (sect. 5.2.2), preexisting dissident organizations (sect. 5.2.3), autonomous dissident communities (sect. 5.2.4), concentrated dissident communities (sect. 5.2.6), dissident leadership (sect. 6.1.1), patronage of dissident groups (sect. 6.2.1), shifts in the military (sect. 6.2.3.1), and competition among dissidents (6.4.4) with protest and rebellion.

In sum, the most noticeable feature of the CA research program is that it keeps expanding. The insights abound. Starting from a few simple principles about CA, a great deal, but certainly not all, of the shady areas of collective dissent are illuminated. The Rebel's Dilemma is consequently a rich perspective to bring to the problem of collective dissent. CA theories do indeed offer many *additional* and *true* statements about collective dissent.

Many of these propositions are *different* and *better* than those offered in DA studies. The CA solution to Hobbes's Dilemma, moreover, does not impoverish important questions by foreclosing alternative approaches. It enriches the study of social order by allowing us to see the possible significance of rival answers. The rational actor model, after all, is the great baseline model in the social sciences (Lichbach forthcoming, chap. 7). CA and DA approaches thus cross in many strange ways (sect. 9.3.3).

Hence, the CA research program meets both Lakatos's (1970) and Popper's (1968) criteria for a progressive and important research program in conflict studies. Paraphrasing Churchill, the CA approach offers the worst explanation of collective dissent, except for all the other explanations that have been tried from time to time. CA theories, accordingly, should be a principal guide for students of protest and rebellion.

At least for the moment. It is important to put such a conclusion into perspective. Hegel's famous dictum is that "the owl of Minerva spreads its wings only with the falling of the dusk" (cited in Avineri 1972, 128). One of Parkinson's Laws (1957, 60) is that "a perfection of planned layout is achieved only by institutions on the point of collapse." The implication is that one can achieve a clear understanding of a social system only when the system is well on the road to extinction. Just as understanding is achieved, that understanding is no longer needed and must be transcended.

There is a poignant message here. The history of social science indicates that all of our research programs run their course and contribute to their own demise. Academic theories change just as the political winds blow in a new reality that the theories must confront. Academic formulations also change as the theories try to overcome internal roadblocks.

This may be happening with the CA research program. I have argued that CA theories should be supplemented by two sets of auxiliary theories: microtheories of motivation that extend thin rationality and macrotheories of structure that extend a sparse conception of state, society, and state-society relations (chap. 10). But if these suggestions are adopted, have we not gone well beyond the CA research program? Might they not distort the approach? Perhaps the addition of these supplementary theories to the CA framework will no longer reveal much about protest and rebellion that is *additional* and *true*, and certainly not anything that is *different* and *better,* than can be found in the alternative approaches from which the auxiliary theories are borrowed.

But this takes us far into the future. Much progress has been made, and there is still much progress that can be made, by accepting a relatively thin version of rationality and a relatively sparse conception of state and society.

We need to push back the boundaries of the approach, but there is no need as yet to knock down the walls.

Some will dissent from this judgment. The empirical implications of the CA approach will always disturb some people, who will continue to argue that dissidents are simply not rational. I believe, however, that Machiavelli (cited in Lasswell and Kaplan 1950, 24) was closer to the truth: "Where men's lives and fortunes are at stake they are not all insane." If my advocacy of CA theories makes me appear to be a cynic, or someone who believes that dissidents are often motivated by pecuniary self-interest, so be it.

The normative implications of the CA approach will always disturb some people as well, who will continue to argue that dissidents should not be concerned only with their own pecuniary self-interest. I believe, however, that Hillel[1] was closer to the truth: "If I am not for myself, who will be? If I am for myself only, what am I? If not now, when?" Nevertheless, I am not an advocate of pecuniary self-interest and an opponent of altruism. As Aumann (1989, 45) puts it, "Blaming game theory — or, for that matter economic theory — for selfishness is like blaming bacteriology for disease. Game theory studies selfishness. It does not recommend it."

I therefore find assumptions about rational dissidents to be neither always true nor always good, merely almost always useful. Hardin (1982, xv) captures the equivocation very well: "I am generally concerned with pushing cynical explanations to their limit, to see what they cannot explain as well as what they can; I am not sure what to feel about the fact that they can explain as much as they can." A famous detective was once asked, "You always assume the worst about people. Do you really think that *everyone* is evil?" "No," the detective replied, "but it sure helps me solve crimes." I do not think that *all* dissidents are pecuniary seekers of self-interest. Nor do I think that Olson's Problem lurks behind *every* domain of social life. Yet, entertaining such beliefs certainly helps me to understand collective dissent.

# Notes

## PREFACE

1. *Exodus* 1: 42; *Numbers* 83: 88; *Numbers* 98: 99. For a more complete list of opposition to authority in the Bible, see Lehman-Wilzig 1990, 137–39.

2. All citizens may not agree that social order is a PG (Taylor 1982, 47). The current social order might perpetuate existing property rights, whereas a free-for-all might redistribute property rights. Thus, the poor might see social order as a public bad in which those who dominate and exploit are able to coerce those who are dominated and exploited. Hence, Moore (1966, 353–54) argues that "a policy of law and order favors those who already have privileges, including some whose privileges are not very large." Rothman (1970, 81) replies that "a policy of violence and disorder favors those who are both aggressive and strong, including those who are just a little more aggressive than the vast majority of the people." A synthesis of the "social order is a public good" and the "social order is a public bad" viewpoints is, at least in principle, straightforward: rational people are motivated by distributive and redistributive considerations and hence social order should be evaluated according to the considerations of efficiency and equity.

## CHAPTER 1

1. Some further terminological clarifications are needed. The term *dissidents* or *rebels* is defined herein as a collectivity whose members wish to prevent some public bad or gain some public good. Their objectives may be either reformist (e.g., a new road supplied by the existing government) or revolutionary (e.g., taking over the government and supplying their road). In short, dissidents share goals. They need not share every goal. All dissidents might pursue a single PG while subsets of the dissidents might pursue different PGs that bring them into competition with one another. For example, a nationalist movement might pool the young and the old, workers and bourgeoisie, and majority and minority ethnics. Moreover, dissidents do not necessarily share means. The actual level of participation by dissidents may range from none (e.g., staying home), to relatively passive (e.g., a green con-

sumer who recycles), to moderately aggressive (e.g., everyday forms of peasant resistance, as in Scott 1985), to downright belligerent (e.g., terrorism). Hence, the term *dissidents* should be read *aggrieved population of potentially active dissidents*. They are those who *sympathize* (sect. 2.1) with some dissident group. The CA problem relates to turning an *aggrieved population of potentially active dissidents* from mere *sympathizers* into actual *contributors*.

The use of Dahl's (1966, 370) terminology can help clarify this perspective. Dissidents must share more than an objectively similar position and a subjective identification with one another; they must also share attitudes in the sense of a common demand on government. The question is then whether they act together. Hence, the Rebel's Dilemma refers to the turning of attitudinal groups into action groups.

A *dissident group* or an *opposition group* is defined herein as the organizational manifestation of a set of *dissidents*, or the more or less formal association purporting to represent some aggrieved population. I distinguish between various sets of dissidents (i.e., antiregime coalitions, dissident movements, dissident groups, and dissident factions) in section 6.4.

Three last points need to be made. For clarity, I sometimes distinguish between *potential dissidents* and *active dissidents*. For variety, I sometimes refer to collective dissent as a *revolt, protest, rebellion,* or *conflict*. Where relevant, my footnotes contain references to participation in conventional interest groups and political parties.

2. The flip side is that dissidents are trying to prevent a public bad. The essence of a public bad is captured by the proverb from the American Revolution, "We will all hang together or surely we will hang separately," and the Jewish proverb, "What will befall all Jews, will befall each Jew" (Dawidowicz 1986, 221).

3. As Tocqueville (quoted in Elster 1993, 15) argues, "I have always thought that in revolutions, especially democratic revolutions, madmen (not those metaphorically called such, but real madmen) have played a very considerable political part. At least it is certain that at such times a state of semi-madness is not out of place and often leads to success."

4. Some scholars argue that the CA problem has been central to rational actor or resource mobilization approaches to protest and rebellion. Zald (1992, 334) writes that "we also have a literature that takes the Olson problematic seriously, detailing free-rider effects and arguing about the role of solidarity and selective incentives offered by entrepreneurs in overcoming any free-rider problems." Mueller (1992, 5) maintains that "the key social psychological issue for the resource mobilization [approach] has centered on the problem of the free rider of rational choice theory." I believe that Marwell and Oliver (1984) are closer to the truth. Resource mobilization theorists might have started with Olson, but they ignored much of the work that

Olson spawned. The flaw in this literature, as I see it, is not an overpreoccupation with Olson's Problem but an underappreciation of CA solutions. As a consequence the microfoundations of resource mobilization theory are exceedingly weak. This book, in any event, is based on two assumptions: first, that the microfoundations of resource mobilization theory consist of a set of CA processes; second, that exploring how CA processes operate tells us a great deal about collective dissent.

5. Such scholars are well aware of each others' efforts. The consequence is that the use of variants of Tullock's (1971a) model is one of the two truly cumulative modeling approaches in studies of domestic political conflict (Lichbach 1992, 348).

6. In a personal communication (April 7, 1992) Mancur Olson has responded as follows:

> At the time *The Logic of Collective Action* was circulating in draft, the reactions to it were often those of startled people. Thus many objected that the argument was only true by tautology [and thus my great care to distinguish the non-refutable logical form of the argument (which clearly covered *every* type of collective action) from narrower and easily refutable formulations]. Others thought the argument reached too far and claimed too much, even in its obviously non-tautological form, and urged me to claim less. I am actually most gratified that our sort of argument is more widely acceptable now.

7. For DA theorists, the CA question is usually posed as follows: How are deprivations and exploitations activated and politicized? Gurr thus recognizes that grievances are insufficient for rebellion. He writes about the "politicization of dissent" (1970, 177) and even suggests that "most discontents in the modern world are not political but politicized" (1970, 179). Welch (1980, 131) follows Gurr and maintains that "few discontents are narrowly political — but most are politicizable."

8. Marx raises a similar question. His concern is how to move from class condition to class consciousness to class action. He argues that internal contradictions within the working class reduce CA. To overcome internal contradictions is to solve the Rebel's Dilemma. Rule (1988, 69) thus states the key CA question in Marxist terms:

> Class interest, for most people most of the time, manifests itself in pursuit of private ends, as people act out their often antagonistic roles in various social hierarchies. When do these antagonisms become bases for collective action, rather than simply for private tensions?

Katznelson (1986, 14–19) makes distinctions among Class 1, or structure;

Class 2, or way of life; Class 3, or dispositions; and Class 4, or organization. Jasay (1989, 132) points out that the CA problem is inherent in the Marxist dictum of communism: in order to achieve the benefit of "to each according to his or her needs," the costs of "from each according to his or her abilities" must be imposed.

9. Weber ([1924] 1968, 929) suggests that "the emergence of an association or even of mere social action from a common class situation is by no means a universal phenomenon." Hence, classes "are not communities; they merely represent possible, and frequent, bases for social action" (Weber [1924] 1968, 927). The issue for Weber is thus how class and status become party. Dahrendorf (1959, 173–79) ponders the means by which groups move from latent to manifest interests, from a quasigroup to a full-fledged conflict group. Political sociologists (e.g., Lipset and Rokkan 1967; Zuckerman 1975) raise the basic CA question of the linkage between social cohesion and political cohesion: how are social ties and ideological position within a group translated into political action and organization?

10. Strickland and Johnston (1970, 1069) want to know what accounts for "issue elasticity" in political systems. Zald and McCarthy (1979b, 4) ask "What activates reference publics and elites. Why does an atrocity in one decade receive bland acceptance and in another crystalize movement activity? What are the mechanisms of selection amongst issues, and why do some issues remain prominent longer than others?" Downs (1972, 39–40) thus focuses on the issue-attention cycle: an "alarming" problem is discovered; audience attention is attracted and "euphoric enthusiasm" to do "something" is expressed; once some change is attempted, there is a "gradually spreading realization that the cost of 'solving' the problem is very high indeed"; the consequence is a "gradual decline of intense public interest," as the problem moves once again to the background.

## CHAPTER 2

1. CA theories are thus theories of "political 'apostasy'" (Thompson 1966, 176). As Calhoun (1988, 129) puts it,

> That revolutions are risky undertakings poses a problem for theorists of popular insurrections. Why, it has often been asked, would reasonable people place their lives and even their loved ones in jeopardy in pursuit of a highly uncertain goal? Neither the success of uprisings nor the desirability of post-revolutionary regimes has appeared likely enough to outweigh the probability of privation and the physical harm.

Maranto (1987, 16) thus suggests that "in radical perspectives, free-riders are moderates who choose less risky (and less violent) means of carrying out the struggle against the regime."

2.  Thomas Jefferson recognizes that mass apathy hurts the prospects for revolution. He writes in the Declaration of Independence that "all experience hath shewn, that mankind are more disposed to suffer, while evils are sufferable, than to right themselves by abolishing the forms to which they are accustomed."

3.  Saul Alinsky, a famous community organizer in the United States, recognizes that self-interest often impedes protest. He (1946, 95) bitterly condemns dissidents who think only of their own self-interest: "Such self-interest is based a good deal on the law of the jungle, and certainly the survival of the fittest does not lend itself to thinking and acting according to co-operative and self-sacrificing for-the-other-guy philosophy." He (1946, 94) thus sympathizes with the frustrations of those who try to organize mass movements: "Many exponents and supporters of People's Organizations bitterly denounce self-interest as one of the main obstacles that must be crushed if people are to be organized into a co-operative fellowship. Both liberals and organizers have attributed the failure of their attempts to the rampant spirit of individualism and selfishness."

4.  Karl Marx also recognizes that self-interest poses a major problem for mass movements. He understands the free-rider issue and believes that both the capitalist and laboring classes face distinctive PG–PD problems (Elster 1985, 409). Some scholars (Przeworski 1985; Sabia 1988) are trying to provide a rational actor microfoundation for Marxism. Elster (1985, 347, emphasis in original) thus believes that he is following Marx in defining positive class consciousness as "*the ability to overcome the free-rider problem in realizing class interests.*" Marx, and more so Lenin, understands that most people will be passive supporters of the regime, few will be reformers, still fewer will ever become revolutionaries. Left to their own devices, the vast majority of workers will never fulfill their "revolutionary destiny." Worker consciousness and organizing might emerge but at best it will result in a "trade union mentality." Moreover, Marx argues that the CA problem is not a historical constant but rather a peculiar product of capitalism which imbues workers with an individualistic "rationality" that impedes group efforts. The false consciousness of self-interest creates the CA problem. Were it to be replaced by the revolutionary consciousness of collective interest, CA would be forthcoming (Arrighi, Hopkins, and Wallerstein 1989, 20–21). Transcending self-interest therefore allows the working class to move from a class *an sich* (in itself) to a class *für sich* (for itself). The debate among Marxist revolutionaries about how to solve the Worker's Dilemma has produced many of the solutions that are investigated here (e.g., spontaneous dissident self-government, sect. 5.1.1; a vanguard party, sect. 6.1).

5. It is theoretically possible for dissident groups to create more members than sympathizers by using the selective disincentives of terrorism and intimidation (sect. 6.5.4).

6. One can falsify the five percent rule by adopting a relatively passive definition of participation. For example, "participants" in the environmental movement may be defined by states of mind (e.g., identification with environmental causes) or symbolic acts (e.g., the display of bumper stickers). As indicated in section 3.2.2, as the costs of participation increase, levels of participation decrease and hence dissident groups must locate themselves on an intensity/extensiveness curve.

7. Scholars overwhelmingly accept the five percent rule. Greene (1990, 74) argues that "a revolution involves minorities fighting minorities." Coleman (1990, 489) maintains that "revolts and revolutions are not ordinarily mass uprisings. Typically a revolution involves only a very small part of the population as activists, either on the side of the revolutionaries or on the side of the authorities." Hagopian (1974, 219) observes that "in many places, in many revolutions, most of the people would prefer neutrality and noninvolvement to exertions and sacrifices in favor of any of the forces in contention. Cavaliers and Roundheads, Jacobins and Royalists, Reds and Whites, Loyalists and Nationalists, Communists and KMT — all have found local populations who have wished a plague on the two houses." Brinton (1965, 252) maintains that "in the actual clash — even Bastille Day, Concord, or the February Days in Petrograd — only a minority of the people is actively engaged." Finally, Moore (1978, 156–57) observes that

> the overwhelming majority of those whose "objective" situation would qualify them as being somehow the victims of injustice took no active part in the events of the period. As far as it is possible to tell now, they just sat tight, tried to make do in their daily lives, and waited for the outcome. Although in the twentieth century, the degree of popular participation has undoubtedly increased, I strongly suspect that doing nothing remains the real form of mass action in the main historical crises since the sixteenth century.

8. While the number of active dissidents is usually quite small, the number who die as a consequence of collective dissent is frequently quite large (Gurr 1970, 3; Goldstone 1991, 477).

9. The only exceptions to the five percent rule that I have come across are very short-lived episodes in the political life of highly mobilized states. One out of every seven Israeli Jews protested in Tel Aviv's Municipality Square against the war in Lebanon (Sachar 1990, 811). The Eastern Euro-

pean Revolutions of 1989 included several events that mobilized over ten percent of the population. An analysis of these deviant cases should be high on the research agenda of CA theorists.

10. Olsen, Perlstadt, Fonseca, and Hogan (1989, 1) report that "a critical problem faced by most neighborhood associations is that only a small proportion of the residents within the geographic area typically belong to or participate in them. Surveys in Detroit and Chicago found that only 8 to 12 percent of the residents belonged to neighborhood improvement associations, and even fewer were active participants."

11. Coleman (1990, 490) reports that "in community conflicts which constitute revolts against local government or school authorities, the fraction of the population that is actively involved is small — despite the fact that such conflicts are ordinarily resolved by a vote by the citizens, creating strong incentives for the authorities and their opponents to mobilize the population."

12. Brooks (1974, 268) reports the following about black protest in the United States: "There were, between June 1967 and May 1968, 236 riots and disturbances resulting in 8,133 casualties and 49,607 arrests, but involving less than one percent of the total black population, approximately 200,000, according to the National Commission on Causes and Prevention of Violence."

13. The proportion of students who actually became involved in the student revolts of the 1960s was small. Coleman reports the following about a prominent student revolt in the United States:

> In the Columbia University crisis of 1968, which was one of the largest campus revolts, less than 10% of the student body was involved as active participants in the conflict; the SDS, which constituted the principal activist body, was composed of only about 50–100 students, out of a total student body numbering 13,000. Within the SDS was "a tiny group of students" (Cox Commission, 1968, p. 58) whose aim was wholly revolutionary: to destroy the university as part of the authority structure of society. The Cox Commission report estimated (p. 165) that at the height of the conflict, on April 29, there were 700–1000 students inside the buildings and 2000 outside. Most of those outside were not active participants. (Coleman 1990, 490)

The French student movement in 1968 was also relatively small. Greene (1990, 75) reports that "of the 160,000 students in Paris during the events of May–June 1968, no more than 40,000 participated in the demonstrations. Of the 600,000 students in all of France, only about 10 percent played an active role in a movement (initiated by the students) that seriously threatened the Gaullist state."

14. Lipset, Trow, and Coleman note the following about trade union activity:

> Ordinarily, however, few members show much interest in the day-to-day political process within the union; apathy of the members is the normal state of affairs. There are good reasons for this. Most union members, like other people, must spend most of their time at work or with their families. Their remaining free time is generally taken up by their friends, commercial entertainment, and other personally rewarding recreational activities. (Lipset, Trow, and Coleman 1962, 10)

15. Laqueur (1976, 317) suggests that "this has been one of the traditional weaknesses of rural guerrilla warfare; peasants cannot easily be turned into professional revolutionaries willing to give up their ties and roots." Greene (1990, 75) thus reports that "a study of the percentage of participants in seven insurgencies between 1940 and 1962 again shows the very small number of the total population involved in revolution. Including both insurgents and government forces, the average is 7 percent, with a range of 0.7 percent in the Philippines to 11.2 percent in Greece."

16. Lipset (1971a, 244) describes a rural populist movement as follows: "The Saskatchewan CCF has succeeded in involving more people in direct political activity than any other party in American or Canadian history, with the possible exception of certain similar farmers' parties. In 1945 the party had a dues-paying membership of 31,858, or approximately 4 per cent of the total population and 8 per cent of the 1944 electorate . . . One can hardly speak here of mass passivity." Note how scholars have come to expect that few will participate in collective dissent. Lipset's low expectations evidently led him to consider four percent participation as a glass half full rather than one half empty.

17. Greene reports the following:

> It has been estimated that throughout most of the American Revolution one-third of the 2.5 million population was neutral, another third was pro-British, and only the remaining third supported the Patriot cause. Of the approximately 700,000 men of fighting age (18 to 60) the maximum strength of the Continental Army was around 90,000. But for the greater part of the military conflict that extended over seven years, the Continental Army managed to enlist only about one man for every sixteen of fighting age. (Greene 1990, 74)

18. Greene reports the following:

> Only about 12,000 persons were active in the Russian Social Demo-
> cratic party between 1898 and 1905. On the eve of the February Revolu-
> tion in 1917, the Bolsheviks numbered no more that 30,000 members in
> all of Russia. The population of Petrograd was 2 million, with 600,00
> employed as workers. Events in the February Revolution began with
> strikes and demonstrations by 90,000 workers, most of whom did not
> intend a revolution. On the third day of strike activity, government fig-
> ures estimated the total number of demonstrators at 240,000 or 12 per-
> cent of the total population of Petrograd . . . The October Revolution in
> Petrograd was carried out by no more than 25,000 to 30,000 armed
> insurrectionists. (Greene 1990, 75)

19. Greene (1990, 74) notes that "the Algerian rebellion was initiated in
1954 by no more than 500 men, 300 of them in the Aurés Mountains with
fewer than fifty shotguns."

20. Greene (1990, 74) reports that "some authorities put the maximum
size of Castro's army at even less than the 2,000 cited above. And while his
urban supporters also could be numbered in the thousands, they were never
organized and there was nothing approximating mass participation in the revolution until its successful end was a foregone conclusion."

21. Greene (1990, 74–75) reports that "with 100,000 members in 1920,
the Italian fascists had only 2.5 members per 1,000 population . . . Compara-
ble ratios for the German Nazis was 1.6 in 1928, 5.8 in 1930, 12.2 in 1931,
and, prior to the capture of power in 1933, 1.4 million party members or 21.4
per 1,000 population."

22. I point out in section 6.2.3.2 that government, or at least parts of government, can also aid collective dissent.

23. Practitioners of collective dissent know that dissidents compete to
evolve successful solutions to the Rebel's Dilemma. This is why debates in
dissident circles are so vicious.

24. Michels's ([1919] 1962) "iron law of oligarchy" and Weber's ([1924]
1968, 246) "routinization of charisma" were early recognitions of the problems inherent in the transformations from dissident movement to dissident
institution to postdissident society. Weber ([1922] 1991, 226) remarks on
"the altogether universal experience that . . . the employment of violence
against some particular injustice produces as its ultimate result the victory,
not of the greater justice, but of the greater power or cleverness." He (cited in
Alexander 1987, 237) thus issued a famous warning: revolutions are not
"trolley cars you can get on and off at will." Once you choose revolution, you

will have to live forever with both its good and bad consequences. Marable (1991, 85) notes that "in the process of social transformation, there are always bitter seeds of defeat hidden within the fruit of victory." Lowi (1971) writes of an "iron law of decadence": all established groups lose their militancy, become conservative, and are absorbed into the political system. Touraine (1985, 762) sums up the phenomenon rather well: "Every revolutionary creation of a new order is led to destroy the social movement it is based on. Saturn ate his children, revolutions eat their fathers." A considerable literature in political sociology and organizational theory is devoted to such questions of the polarity of movement and institution (Olofsson 1988, 22–23).

25. Engels (in a letter of 1885 reprinted in Laqueur 1978, 208) suggests that "people boasting that they have made a revolution are always convinced next day that they did not know what they were doing and that the revolution they have made is not at all the one they wanted to make." Luxemburg, Trotsky, and Gramsci articulate fears about the bureaucratization of the revolutionary party. For example, Trotsky's famous warning is that "the organization of the Party takes the place of the Party itself; the Central Committee takes the place of the organization; and finally the dictator takes the place of the Central Committee" (cited in Sabine 1973, 735).

26. One last preliminary issue related to the appraisal of CA theories of collective dissent must be mentioned. My use of examples from a variety of different historical and comparative contexts will invite the (good-natured?) gibe, "history without the dates and anthropology without the details" (Runciman 1989, 60). The criticism of "exampling" (Glaser and Strauss 1967, 5) goes back to complaints against Machiavelli, who "used history exactly as he used his own observation to illustrate or support a conclusion that he had reached quite without reference to history" (Sabine 1973, 320). My long response to this charge is this book. My short response is that I use examples from a variety of comparative and historical contexts in order to propose, develop, and elaborate CA theories, not to evaluate, appraise, or test them. I sometimes mention exceptions and negative instances, but never analyze them in depth because I am interested in the step-by-step development of the internal logic of CA ideas. As indicated above, I suggest criteria by which to appraise CA theories in chapter 9. I argue, in particular, that the hypotheses developed here should be tested in comparative historical studies of collective dissent (sect. 9.2.3).

## CHAPTER 3

1. The term originates in a dissident struggle. Zealots were Jewish dissidents who considered their subjection to Rome intolerable. They rebelled in 66–73 c.e., until their fortress at Masada was captured.

2. Students of conflict who adopt a resource mobilization perspective accept the *Increase Benefits* solution to the Rebel's Dilemma. Freeman (1979, 173) suggests that "whenever a deprived group triumphs over a more privileged one without major outside interference, it is because the deprived group's constituencies have compensated with a great deal of time and commitment." Conflict practitioners also often accept the *Increase Benefits* idea. Kahn (1982, 259) observes that

> it's almost always easier to raise money in the early days of an organizing campaign than farther down the road. When feelings are running high, people are willing to dig into their own pockets. Two years later, when things have slowed down, it becomes harder and harder to come up with the same amount that is needed to get by.

3. There is some evidence to support this proposition (Mason 1984; Muller and Opp 1986).

4. Too much zealotry, however, produces burnout. Hence, entrepreneurs also seek to limit zealotry. Dissident leaders recognize the difficulties of waging an all-out-war against the regime and thus carefully pace their activities. For example, Palestinian leaders during the Intifada avoided exaggerated demands and unachievable goals. They took a long-term view and only asked for sacrifices that their followers could reasonably make. Setting the pace of the insurgency had an additional benefit: it demonstrated to the Israelis that it was the Palestinians who controlled the conflict.

5. I owe this last point to Peter Sederberg.

6. Evidence from the U.S. civil rights movement supports these contentions. More blacks were involved in civil rights demonstrations than in riots, and more were involved in riots than in armed resistance and revolution (Gurr 1989, 16). Wilson (1973, 181) attributes the greater relative success of the NAACP as compared with that of CORE and SNCC to the fact that the former required less intense participation. The latter picked harder targets, had less moderate goals, and could not win enough victories to sustain the intense commitment required of their members.

7. As Walker (1991, 19) writes, "Most people, most of the time, are able to find better things to do than participate in politics. Even if some method could be devised to allow all citizens to be consulted on every governmental decision, few people would have the time or inclination to participate." Roller-derby will thus always be more popular than C-span.

8. One must also consider the opportunity costs of passivity. Five examples illustrate this mode of reasoning. Potential dissidents threatened with economic hardship and subsistence crises have little to lose (Tong 1988, 115). The impact of individual efforts to improve wages in a segregated soci-

ety may be nil. Those who face injury and death as a normal part of their working conditions (e.g., American railroad workers in the nineteenth century) have less to fear from the injuries and deaths that result from regime repression. Actual dissidents hounded by the regime and threatened with death will fight to the death. Finally, regicides have sealed their fate and thus will fight to the bitter end.

9. For example, by 1990 Palestinians had become integrated into the Israeli economy (Shalev 1991, 84–88). Approximately one-half of the Palestinian workforce in Gaza and the West Bank were employed in Israel. The Palestinians have been unwilling to return to the pre-1967 period in which there was 30 percent male unemployment in the West Bank and 36 percent in Gaza. Hence, the PLO has targeted collaborators: informers, those who sell land to the Israelis, people with close social relations with Israelis, and those who advocate policies that "conflict" with Palestinian national interests. However, it has not attacked those who are either employed by Israelis or engaged in commerce with them. In addition, the PLO has asked for resignations only in those jobs that do not affect the local economy and day-to-day life. Policemen employed by the Israelis have resigned, but teachers and medical personnel have not. More generally, the PLO has not called for an extended general strike, a total boycott of Israeli goods, or mass resignations from jobs with Israeli employers. It realizes that the Palestinians are not self-sufficient and therefore that it cannot destroy and replace the entire Israeli administration at once. Palestinian dependence on the Israeli economy has thus closed off many avenues of dissent. Whereas individual Palestinians are willing to risk personal injury, and even death, to end Israeli control, most Palestinian organizations are unwilling to risk mass unemployment. If civil disobedience were all-embracing, it would pauperize the population, produce mass starvation, and enfeeble the rebels, thus weakening the revolt. In short, the financial opportunity costs would be too high.

10. A similar constraint holds for academics. They too must locate themselves somewhere on the praxis (theory/action) curve.

11. There is another way of looking at a dissident's opportunity costs that is revealing. In a PG–PD game, if all others cooperate, the opportunity costs of defection is the difference between the payoff for defection (called "Temptation") and the payoff for cooperation (called "Reward"). Hence, as the benefits of mutual cooperation increase relative to the benefits of unilateral defection, CA increases. In short, raise the payment to unilateral inaction (i.e., make protest less of a self-actualizing political experience, sect. 4.2.1) and lower the payment for mutual action (i.e., make government accommodation less valuable), and fewer dissidents will protest. Alternatively, in a PG–PD game, if all others defect, the opportunity costs of defection is the

difference between the payoff for defection (now called "Punishment") and the payoff for cooperation (now called "Sucker"). Hence, as the benefits of unilateral cooperation increase relative to the benefits of mutual defection, CA increases. In short, raise the payment to mutual inaction (i.e., make government repression more deadly) and lower the payment for unilateral action (i.e., make protest less of a fairness issue, sect. 4.2.2), and fewer dissidents will protest.

12. The military is not the only training ground that allows people to acquire valuable experience that assists collective dissent. Other "specialists in violence" acquire a great deal of just the right human capital that make them attractive to dissident entrepreneurs. Those who fought in guerila wars tend to be recruited for subsequent guerila wars. For example, some members of the Zapatist National Liberation Army in Mexico during 1994 were said to be recruited from the leftist guerila wars of the 1980s in Nicaragua and El Salvador. Former convicts are often as well trained as former soldiers. Participants in the Intifada thus disproportionately tend to come from released security and administrative prisoners.

13. Lawyers offer an interesting parallel. Political parties, interest groups, and government bureaucracies provide a market for legal skills. Lawyers thus gravitate to these job markets, just as demobilized soldiers gravitate to the collective dissent job market.

14. Former Roman soldiers helped bring down the Republic (Runciman 1989, 292). Demobilized soldiers made an important contribution to the fascist movements of the interwar period (Carsten 1967, 232). Soldiers turned bandits turned rebels were critical in numerous preindustrial peasant upheavals (Mousnier 1970, 80, 327). Three cases may be cited. The rebels who opposed the King's new taxes in seventeenth century France were former soldiers in the King's armies (Mousnier 1970, 58). The Chinese peasant revolts of the 1630s and 1640s that preceded the fall of the Ming Dynasty were launched by army deserters (Mousnier 1970, 282). Finally, peasant disruptions in Turkey and China in the seventeenth century are also traceable to former soldiers (Goldstone 1988, 126–27).

15. Heterogeneous dissident groups are likely to have more resources than homogeneous groups. To understand why, recall that in discussing the *Increase Benefits* solution (sect. 3.1), I suggested that heterogeneous groups are more likely to have someone who derives great benefits from the PG. Such heterogeneous groups are also likely to have someone with great resources to provide the PG. Hence, as the heterogeneity of a group of dissidents increases, and consequently the likelihood of an individual with great resources increases, collective dissent increases. Unequal resources among dissidents thereby lead to CA by dissidents. A balance of power among dissi-

dents is thus not necessary for cooperation. The literature on political integration offers an interesting parallel. Deutsch et al. (1957, 38–39) report that nation-states formed from both equal units that lacked a core area (e.g., United States, Swiss Confederacy) and highly unequal units with a single strong core area (e.g., Germany, Italy, and the United Kingdom).

16. Note the similarity of this argument to the one about the relationship between gun control and crime.

17. Zald (1988, 34, emphasis in the original) writes that "there is a *production function* for tactics." Marwell and Oliver (1984, 17–18, emphasis in the original) suggest that "we may think of a movement *technology* as a set of information about cause-effect relations, i.e., as knowledge about the probabilities of success of various courses of action." Hirshleifer (1983, 1987) argues that there is a technology of conflict — a relation between a set of inputs (e.g., armies, guns, lawyers) and a set of outputs (e.g., income, resources).

18. The forms of patronage also changed (sect. 6.2.4).

19. There is evidence to support this proposition. McAdam (1982, 164–66) and Chong (1991, 178) attribute the success of the U.S. civil rights movement to its many tactical innovations: the bus-boycott, freedom ride, sit-in, community-wide protest organization, and so on. These innovations kept the opponents off balance and hence enhanced the prospects for success.

20. General strikes organized around economic issues occurred in Belgium (1902), Sweden (1909), France (1920), Norway (1921), and England (1926). After these strikes were defeated, union membership declined and repressive legislation was passed. Socialist parties then focused almost exclusively on electoral tactics.

21. Ninety-five percent of terrorism consists of "bombings, assassinations, armed assaults, kidnappings, barricade and hostage situations, and hijackings" (Jenkins 1982, 14). Terrorists choose among the tactics in this repertoire based on cost-benefit considerations. Risk, time, and the likelihood of capture influence their choices (Mickolus 1980, xix–xxviii). Government response strategies are the chief factors in these cost-benefit considerations: "Governments under pressure, resulting from public reaction to a particularly effective terrorist mode of operation, often focus their countermeasures on the troublesome event, thus creating the alteration in relative costs which should encourage terrorists to replace one mode with another" (Im, Cauley, and Sandler 1987, 243).

Thus, measures designed to curb one type of terrorism induce terrorists to switch to another type of terrorism. In general, if government represses terrorist mode of operation $i$, terrorist mode of operation $j$ becomes popular (Sandler and Scott 1987, 38). Three examples may be cited. As airport screening devices increased, skyjacking decreased but hostage taking increased. After metal detectors were installed in airports, attempted sky-jacking in the United States dropped from 27 in 1972 to 1 in 1973 (Landes 1978, 3). Similarly, as embassy security measures increased, embassy take-overs decreased, but diplomatic assassinations and kidnappings increased. Finally, there was a change in the targets of terrorism from the nineteenth to twentieth century. Because of increased security, targeting kings, tsars, and presidents gave way to targeting lesser public officials.

22. Defeat has often led to the rejection of old ideas about how to start a revolution and the adoption of new approaches. For example, should the revolutionaries target the city or the countryside? In Huntington's (1968, 266) "Western" revolutions (e.g., French Revolution), the central cities are captured first, the countryside second. In his "Eastern" revolutions (e.g., the second phase of the Chinese Revolution), the countryside is captured first, the cities second. One expects dissident groups to shift between the one and the other, trying to discover where their tactics are most productive (i.e., where the free-rider problem is easiest to overcome). Mao and the Chinese Communist Party thus experimented with the city before turning to the countryside. As rural counterinsurgency became more effective in Latin America during the 1960s, for another example, rural guerrilla warfare declined and urban terrorism increased (Laqueur 1987, 22–23).

23. There are limits, however, to the adaptability of dissident groups. One important qualification relates to the time frame involved. In the short run, no inputs into the dissidents' production function are variable; in the long run, all inputs are variable. Hence, dissident tactics are more likely to change in the long run than in the short run.

24. The theory of one-person games applied to dissidents as consumers assumes that dissidents maximize their utility function, subject to a budget constraint. The result is a system of demand equations in which collective dissent of types $i$ and $j$ are both functions of a set of exogenous price and income variables. As the resources (e.g., arms, equipment, training, coercive potential) of a dissident (or dissident group) increase, the use of the repertoire by all members increases. Hence, given increasing resources, the extent of several collective dissent tactics may increase simultaneously. The theory of one-person games applied to dissidents as producers assumes that dissidents maximize profit. The result is that certain forms of collective dissent are complements or substitutes in the dissidents' production process. The theory of n-person noncooperative games assumes that dissidents make best replies to the strategies of other dissidents. The result is a set of reaction functions in which collective dissent of type $i$ is a function of collective dissent of type $j$. Finally, the theory of n-person cooperative games assumes that dissidents form coalitions. The result is that coalitions combine different types of dissidents who engage in different types of dissident activities. The

deductions from all of these models are generally ambiguous. They do not yield consistent predictions about the signs of the correlations among tactics.

25. Some studies have found only weak relationships among conflict variables whereas others have discovered fairly strong positive relationships (Zimmermann 1983, 42–47). For example, hijacking and kidnapping in terrorist groups may be positively correlated with one another. There is also a positive correlation between democratic participation (e.g., voting, campaign activities) and aggressive participation (e.g., violent protesting); see Muller 1977, 459; Barnes and Kasse 1979.

26. This point is widely recognized. Wilson (1961, 292) maintains that "the problem of many excluded groups is to create or assemble the resources for bargaining. Many often select a strategy of protest." Lipsky (1968) suggests that protest is a "political resource." Zimmermann (1983, 47–48) observes that "by using violent protest, dissidents may want to improve their bargaining position (and not just react to adverse social conditions)." Wilson (1973, 282) defines protest as "a process whereby one party seeks by public display or disruptive acts to raise the cost to another party of continuing a given course of action." Gurr (1970, 211–12) observes "less direct uses of violence are protests, like anti-government riots and strikes, designed to induce rulers to change undesirable policies."

27. Hagopian (1974, 20) argues that a riot "serves as a barometer of the feelings of a strategically located segment of the population." Huntington (1968, 357) writes that "relatively decentralized and spontaneous violence is a common means through which disadvantaged groups call attention to their grievances and their demands for reform." Gurr (1970, 212) suggests that "the occurrence of violence within the state, even if it is sporadic and unplanned, and even if it has nonpolitical targets, can be used by leaders and regarded by rulers as evidence of the intensity of the discontenteds' demands for change." Section 9.2.2.2, however, points out the limitations of collective dissent as a preference revelation technique. Governments recognize that collective violence is used strategically and therefore discount some proportion of it.

28. Hagopian (1974, 20) maintains that "before the days of popular representation the mob employed violence to communicate its demands to the political authorities . . . Should conditions deteriorate, riot was the way the mob recalled its rulers to their 'duty' . . . In short, recourse to violence was the normal method of articulating demands, and both sides knew and accepted this fact." Gurr (1970, 212) writes that "a common indirect use of violence is to demonstrate symbolically the demands of those who use it." Zimmermann (1983, 47) suggests that "turmoil may often be used as a means of introducing certain demands into the political process and thus be understood not only as a dependent variable but also as an independent variable."

29. An implication of the shock value argument for collective violence is that "repeated use of the same tactics reduces their impact" (Huntington 1968, 361). Hence, as collective violence is used more frequently, it becomes less effective. Tilly (1986, 349–50) thus argues that "on the general principle that powerholders learn at least as fast as their challengers, and have much greater means to put their learning into practice, the probable result is this: the collective-action repertoire inherited from the nineteenth century has become less and less effective as a way of changing the structure of power, more and more effective as a signal of preferences within that structure of power." Huntington (1968, 359) illustrates this point with two interesting examples:

> In 1963 racial riots in the United States and monkish self-immolations in Vietnam helped to produce significant changes in governmental policy and political leadership. Three years later similar events failed to produce similar consequences. What had once seemed a shocking departure from the political norm now seemed a relatively conventional political tactic. In many praetorian political systems, of course, violence becomes an endemic form of political action and consequently completely loses its capacity to generate significant change.

30. The civil rights movement in the United States is a case of collective violence that was productive only in conjunction with nonviolence:

> The early riots occurred almost simultaneously with the peaceful protests of the civil rights movement, intensive lobbying, campaigns on behalf of major civil rights legislation, increased black electoral participation, and other conventional political activities. By late in the decade, however, the riots appeared to have pre-empted other strategies. Urban violence assumed the position of primary tactic of urban blacks, and it proved to be noticeably less successful. (Button 1978, 176)

31. Several have adopted this view. Crozier (1960, 159) argues that "terrorism is a weapon of the weak." Wilkinson (1986, xiii) cites the argument that "terrorism is a weapon of the weak pretending to be strong." Edelman (1971, 137) argues that the "resort to violence as a form of militant protest is apparently stimulated by the absence of formal organization among the disaffected." Devine and Rafalko (1982, 39) offer an "Economy of Scale argument," suggesting that resource constraints lead to terrorism, a cheap form of warfare.

32. Hobbes's ([1640] 1969, 168) third condition of revolution is the "hope of success; for if it were madness to attempt without hope, when to

fail is to die the death of a traitor." Gottschalk (1944, 5) identifies "hopeful-ness of success" as a cause of revolution. Lasswell and Kaplan (1950, 46–47) argue that "in the face of the necessity of continued sacrifice without expec-tations of ultimate success, solidarity may progressively weaken and ulti-mately break down completely as conflict continues. A differentiation between 'we' and 'they' emerges *within* the group . . . 'their' interests do not coincide with ours, 'they' are responsible for the conflict or at any rate for the defeat, and so on." Hoffer (1951, 18) argues that dissidents must maintain an "extravagant hope" that victory is not far away. Johnson (1966, 99) recog-nizes that one accelerator of revolution is "an ideological belief held by a protesting group that it can . . . succeed in overcoming the elite's armed might." Wesson (1967, 339–40) argues that "with apathy comes fatalism, a belief that life is a lottery, or a destiny over which it is not worth exerting oneself very much and which may be influenced more by mysterious influ-ences than by one's own efforts." Edelman (1971, 122) points out that "defeatism about the prospects of success from militant political action inhibits mass resort to militancy, while optimism about the prospects of suc-cess encourage it." Additional examples from the rational choice school include Finkel, Muller, and Opp (1989), Fireman and Gamson (1979), Muller and Opp (1986, 1987), Oberschall (1980), and Brustein and Levi (1987).

33. It is also possible that some dissidents commit the fallacy of sunk costs (sect. 3.2.4), refusing to give up on a lost cause for which they have made great sacrifices.

34. Some dissidents will gravitate toward the winning side, because win-ners can eventually offer more benefits and impose greater costs. As a citi-zen's expected returns from the dissidents (relative, of course, to his or her expected returns from government) increase, more support goes to the dissi-dents. Part of expected returns is the probability of winning. Hence, there is one further counterargument: expectations of the probability of winning only influence the participation of those who expect to receive selective incentives (Lichbach forthcoming, chap. 3). The propositions I subsequently put for-ward thus apply especially to those who get most of the spoils from the dissi-dents' victory: leaders and entrepreneurs (sect. 6.1), elites and patrons (sect. 6.2).

35. Each of the solutions proposed here is, after all, a sufficient but not necessary condition for collective dissent (sect. 9.1).

36. Muller (1972, 947) reports a correlation of .46. Klandermans (1984, 592) finds that potential participants in workers' strikes in the Netherlands were more likely to participate if they thought the strike would succeed.

37. Gurr's (1970, 210–23) work on utilitarian justifications for violence is relevant here.

38. Cues and thus precipitants are important in affecting perceptions of the probability of winning. See the *Increase Mutual Expectations* solution (sect. 4.1.1).

39. The argument that dissidents gravitate toward the winning side has a long pedigree. Rule (1988, 87–88) points to Hobbes's classic argument that individuals seek the winner, to be on the safe side in contests between dissidents and regimes: "People are calculating which of two systems of sovereignty - one struggling to stay alive, the other struggling to be born - is more likely to provide the safety they ultimately desire for their own private pursuits of self-interest. Once a clear winner emerges out of the flux of events, a Hobbesian might argue, most people will accept the winner as sovereign and return to the private pursuits of self-interest that sovereignty affords." Pettee ([1938] 1971, 133) refers to "the great mass [during a revolution] whose consent will go unquestioningly to the victor."

40. One can, of course, trace dissident victories back to their resources; hence, resources are an important factor influencing a dissident's estimate of the probability of victory (sect. 3.3). As a dissident group's resources/cost ratio increases, its ability to achieve a PG will increase. Given "rational" expectations, dissidents' subjective estimates of the possibility of achieving the PG will increase when they see this ratio increase.

41. The state strength-collective dissent proposition is very common in conflict studies (Gurr 1970, 285–86). Gottschalk (1944, 8) asserts that state weakness "demonstrates clearly that conservative forces are no longer able to resist the revolutionary tide." Baechler (1975, xii) suggests that "the decisive factor in the theory of revolution, therefore, seems to me to be the analysis of the fragility of political systems." Huntington (1968) argues that a well-organized and institutionalized regime allows citizens to be mobilized peacefully into politics. A more general version of the idea is the loads/capabilities metaphor (Deutsch et al. 1957, 41–42): revolution occurs when the loads on a government exceed the government's capabilities.

42. Hagopian (1974, 165–66) observes that revolutions often occurred after state centralizers attempted financial reforms aimed at overcoming a weak tax base. Merriman (1938, 89) confirms this point: all of the revolutions of the sixteenth century — in England, France, the Netherlands, Spain, Portugal, and Naples — began as protests against taxation. Brinton (1965, 30) also supports this idea. He argues that the revolutions in England, the United States, France, and Russia occurred in "a rich society with an impoverished government." More systematic evidence for this proposition is found in Gurr (1970, 298) and Goldstone (1991).

43. Anderson (1977, 77) argues that "an insurrection will only succeed if the repressive apparatus of the State itself divides or disintegrates — as it did in Russia, China or Cuba. The consensual 'convention' that holds the forces

of coercion together must, in other words, be breached."

44. Hagopian (1974, 160) observes that in England, France, and Russia "the government political class or the Court was on the whole less competent than the men who" made revolutions against them. Edwards (1927, 51) suggests that immorality, moral decay, licentiousness, and extravagance preceded all the modern revolutions. He thus observes (1927, 29) that scandals and rumors about the dominant class increased before the American, French, and Russian revolutions. Brinton (1965, 51–53) argues that inefficiency, not despotism, produces revolution. Hence, Charles I, George III, Louis XVI, and Nicholas II were more incompetent than tyrannical.

45. Tong (1991, chap. 5) summarizes the argument. New dynasties were characterized by competent, rigorous, energetic, and vigilant administration. This produced a golden age of economic, cultural, social, and political accomplishments. Military capability was strengthened. Tax and welfare policies were paternalistic and benevolent. There was, in short, state building. As time went on, however, decadent and slovenly management appeared. Absentee and neglectful leaders, capricious and frivolous sovereigns, sly and devious rulers, as well as nepotistic and corrupt elites eventually produced dynastic breakdown. Consequently, those Ming Dynasty emperors most subject to rebellion were juvenile, senile, or imbeciles. The result was that more and more peasants were squeezed by increasing taxes and diminishing welfare relief. Encouraged by government weakness, the rebellious peasants contributed to the overthrow of the dynasty.

46. Wesson (1967, 286) points out the flaws of the administrative apparatus of the bureaucratic empires of antiquity: "Lack of initiative and avoidance of responsibility, slowness, excessive attention to precedent, a formalistic approach to problems, the stupidity of routine, remoteness from and indifference to people, waste of manpower, and corruption." Complementing this bureaucracy were leaders best characterized as "evil, deranged, stupid, or lazy" (Wesson 1967, 277).

47. Many have argued that revolution is produced by the division of the ruling class, elite fragmentation, and the appearance of numerous leaders who are "traitors to their class." Elite coordination, consensus, and compromise, it is also maintained, prevent revolution. Huntington (1965, 403) suggests that "unity, esprit, morale, and discipline" lend coherence and stability to government. Ake (1967, 492) points out that consensus among the ruling class helps to minimize the potentially disintegrative effects of popular mobilization. Lijphart (1969, 1975, 1977), in his work on consociational democracy, argues that elite disunity leads to revolution whereas elite integration limits collective dissent. Tilly (1986, 140) maintains that "one requisite for large-scale popular rebellion was division among established authorities." Brinton (1965, 39) refers to the "transfer of allegiance of the intellectuals."

Deutsch et al. (1957, 90) argue that integration is a result of elites skilled in compromise. Wesson (1967, 200) argues that "against the great machine and the custom of law and obedience, dissension can succeed only if the ruling apparatus is ready to fall apart." Fireman and Gamson (1979, 30) maintain that "disarray in the target of collective action can dramatically increase chances for successful collective action," by showing that the target is incapable and incompetent. Higley and Burton (1989) argue that elite unity leads to democratic stability. Eckstein and Gurr (1975, 132–47) stress the importance of the "decision behavior" of the ruling classes, including their consensus, unity, and willingness to compromise, to a state's ability to manage conflict. Tarrow (1991, 15) suggests that the "political opportunity structure" for collective dissent can expand or contract "when political alignments are in disarray and new re-alignments have not yet been formed" and "when there are major conflicts within the political elite that challengers can take advantage of." Eckstein (1989, 40) suggests that "elites competing for dominance may seek the support of the lower classes, and in so doing both raise poor people's hopes that change is possible and weaken the legitimacy of the institutions that oppress them. Competing political elites may even unwittingly stir up tumult when candidates and parties that command political loyalty raise rank-and-file hopes and aspirations." McAdam, McCarthy, and Zald (1988, 721) suggest that it is important to examine "the interplay of different branches and geographical units of government in accounting for the success or failure of [campaigns of the civil rights movement]. Southern sheriffs and voter registrars were restrained by federal laws and Justice Department suits. Governor Orville Faubus of Arkansas was constrained by President Eisenhower's calling out of the National Guard in the Little Rock school desegregation crisis." In addition to these authors, see Hagopian (1974, 156–58), Burton (1977, 1984), Johnson (1966, 103), Pettee ([1938] 1971, 51–59), Edwards (1927, 80), Brinton (1965, 51), Gottschalk (1944, 7–8), Waterman (1981, 577–78), Eisenstadt (1978), Trimberger (1978), and Jenkins and Perrow (1977).

48. Sparta and the Venetian Republic had ruling elites with the collective determination and power to preserve themselves for long periods of time (Runciman 1989, 136). Political quiescence in Britain "is conventionally credited to the evolution of complex and responsive political institutions, supported by widespread, fundamental agreement on the procedures if not necessarily the purposes of political activity" (Gurr 1970, 286). Stability in Norway is attributed by Eckstein (1966) to consensual and cooperative patterns in all sectors of Norwegian society.

49. The quarrel within the French ruling classes over representation in the Estates General provoked the revolution. As Skocpol (1979, 124) contends,

> Another major condition facilitating the spread of [peasant] revolts from 1789 was the disorganization and division of the upper strata, including those in charge of police and army. Especially after the Municipal Revolution in July, the propertied classes were in a poor position to repress the rural disturbances. Many *intendants* had been chased from their posts. Urban militias had seized arms and ammunition. Desertions from the army were increasing.

The weakness of the Provisional Government in Russia radicalized the revolution and thus led to a "deepening of the revolution" (Chamberlin [1935] 1987, 142). Seventy years later divisions within the Communist party produced a coup that proved fatal to the Soviet Communist regime. Government crises of authority precipitated the German peasant war and Kett's rebellion (Zagorin 1982a, chap. 7). The incoherence of U.S. policy making during the war in Vietnam has been blamed for both its policy failure and the antiwar movement (Burton 1977). Tilly (Shorter and Tilly 1974; Tilly, Tilly, and Tilly 1975; Tilly 1978; Snyder and Tilly 1972) shows that spikes of strike activity and peaks of protest action typically occur during periods of political disorder. Tarrow (1991, 14) argues that collective dissent in postwar Italy occurred during a period of elite disunity and political crisis: "My work on Italy in the late 1960s and early 1970s showed that its major cycle of postwar protest differed from others in the West both by its length and its expansion of social actors other than students and workers . . . The reason can be found in the partial de-alignment of the Italian party system in the 1960s and its incomplete re-alignment around a modern left-right axis in the 1970s." Goldstone (1980) reanalyzes Gamson's (1990) data and shows that the majority of successful conflict groups arise in a few crisis periods, characterized by critical elections and elite conflict.

50. Gurr's (Eckstein and Gurr 1975; Gurr and McClelland 1971) term for leadership or succession crises is "stability of procedures for authority maintenance."

51. Wesson (1967, 277–85) offers examples of succession crises in historical autocratic empires. Goldfrank (1975, 430) points to Mexico on the eve of the revolution. Even the turnover of prison administration has been cited as a frequent cause of prison riots (Colvin 1982, 452, 457).

52. A temporal bandwagon is also a factor here; see section 4.1.2.1.

53. Tilly (Rule and Tilly 1975, 69; Tilly and Lees 1974, 1064) offers interesting quantitative evidence on this point. He demonstrates that particularly high levels of violence occurred in France after 1830 and 1848.

54. For a review and evaluation of this literature, see Starr (1994).

55. Laqueur (1987, 405) observes that "guerrilla war against domestic rulers has succeeded in the past — with one exception (Cuba) only during a general war or immediately following it, with the collapse of central state

power." Hunter (1940, 33–43) locates many revolutions and revolutionary situations between 1204 and 1926 that occurred immediately after a military defeat. For instance, Hagopian (1974, 163–65) points out that World War I was "the midwife of revolution." All the defeated nations, Russia, Austria, Hungary, Germany, and Turkey, underwent revolutions that ended long-standing autocratic empires. The effects of the war, moreover, were long run. The Nazi takeover in Germany in 1933 has been attributed to Germany's defeat in World War I. World War II also produced numerous revolutions. The wartime resistance movements in China, Yugoslavia, Albania, Vietnam, Malaya, the Philippines, and Burma evolved into postwar insurrections. As Laqueur (1987, 405) suggests, "During the Second World War guerrilla movements had limited success against overextended enemy units; but they used the war to consolidate their power and in the political vacuum after the war they emerged as the chief contender for power."

56. Sorokin ([1925] 1967, 376), for example, reports a positive relationship between international conflict and domestic conflict in Europe, from the Hellenic Age to 1933.

57. Alinsky (1946, 209, emphasis in original) suggests that "*this has always been the prime task of the organizer - the transformation of the plight into the problem*. The organizer must be able to communicate and convince people that, if they find a way to join together, they need not fatally accept their plights but will have the power to affect the shape of their world." Alinsky (1971, 120) thus suggests that "organizations are built on issues that are . . . realizable." Kahn also emphasizes this theme. He (emphasis in original) writes that "*a good issue is winnable*" (1982, 95), that "*a good tactic is winnable*" (1982, 195), and that "people are also easier to organize when they see a chance of winning" (1982, 16). Fanon (1967) suggests that belief in the omnipotence of Europeans was the principal barrier to colonial uprisings. Collective violence against European colonialists challenged this myth and convinced colonials that they could win.

58. Walt (1992, 338–39) offers several examples of this strategy:

Khomeni argued that "it is only through the active, intentional pursuit of martyrdom that unjust rulers can be toppled," and Lin Biao reminded his readers that although U.S. imperialism was vulnerable, "the task of the national-democratic revolution can be fulfilled only through long and torturous struggles." Similarly, Mao Zedong warned his followers to "despise the enemy strategically while taking full account of him tactically," meaning that overcoming the enemy would require careful preparation and repeated sacrifice but that victory was assured because the enemy was vulnerable. Lenin similarly warned his followers against overconfidence; victory, though assured, could not be won without setbacks and tactical retreats along the way.

Another example (Walt 1992, 350) comes from Mao, who "warned his followers to avoid both 'right deviations' (passivity and fear of struggle) and 'left deviations' (overconfident recklessness)." Stewart, Smith, and Denton (1984, emphasis in original) report some more systematic evidence on this point: 24 percent of protest songs *"assured movement supporters that victory would come ultimately for their efforts,"* (1984, 155) but only 11 percent *"predicted that victory was at hand"* (1984, 153).

59. He writes that "given the existence of politicized discontent, magnitudes and forms of political violence vary with the balance of institutional support between regimes and dissident organizations" (Gurr 1970, 274). Hence, "the magnitude of political violence varies strongly and directly with the ratio of dissident institutional support to regime institutional support to the point of equality, and inversely beyond it" (Gurr 1970, 277). The consequences of this relationship, according to Gurr (1970, 277), are as follows:

> If regime institutional support is high vis-à-vis dissident institutional support, political violence is likely to be limited in scope, duration, and intensity. If dissident institutional support approaches that of the regime, both are likely to have the capacity to maintain prolonged conflict. If dissidents have markedly greater institutional support than does the regime, they are likely to win, or secure desired concessions, with relative ease.

60. He argues that "the magnitude of political violence varies strongly and directly with the ratio of dissident coercive control to regime coercive control to the point of equality, and inversely beyond it" (Gurr 1970, 234). Gurr also argues that the balance of coercive control influences the type of collective dissent. If both sides have roughly equal forces, internal war (e.g., civil war) results; if the balance of forces favors the dissidents, conspiracy (e.g., a coup) results; if the balance of forces favors the regime, turmoil (e.g., a riot) results.

61. This is a widely recognized point. O'Kane (1981, 294) suggests that "the decision of a group of conspirators to intervene, however, is based upon calculation of the chances of success." Nordlinger (1977, 105) maintains that "the decision of the uncommitted officers — whether to resist the praetorians, to join them, or to remain neutral — is almost always based upon a single consideration: Will the coup succeed or fail?" Finer (1976, 54) argues that a cause of military coups is "a sense of overwhelming power, the knowledge that, in the peculiar circumstances of that moment or that particular country, there is nothing that can prevent them having their own way." Finally, Luttwak (1968, 22) argues that "the course of action followed by [senior bureaucrats, army, and police officers in a coup] will depend on their individual assessments of the balance of forces on the two sides."

62. Gurr (1970, 271–72) writes that "the delicate negotiations that precede coup attempts, especially in Latin America, in fact resemble bargaining sessions; the purpose of the participants is to ascertain and if possible to alter the balance of coercive control."

63. Needler (1966, 620) suggests that "given the range of political orientations within the military services, then, the task of the organizer of a successful coup d'état is thus to build a coalition of officers of a size and character adequate to execute the successful coup. The prime mover or movers in organizing the coup must therefore be engaged over a period of time in the process of building a coalition which will eventually exceed, in size and 'weight', the minimum necessary to insure success."

64. Huntington (1968, 219) writes that "the seizure of power, in this sense, represents the end of a political struggle and the recording of its results, just as takes place on election day in a democratic country." He (1968, 218–19) continues: "The colonel who plans a coup, if he is wise, prepares the way in much the same manner that the majority leader of the U.S. Senate prepares for a roll-call vote on a crucial bill: he trades on past favors, promises future benefits, appeals to patriotism and loyalty, attempts to distract and to divide the opposition, and when the chips are down, makes doubly sure that all his supporters are mobilized and ready to act."

65. Gurr (1970, 272) observes that "if the dissidents gain the ascendancy, incumbents are so informed and, if gentlemen, are usually willing to be displaced with a minimum of open conflict. If dissidents fail to gain a sufficient advantage, by their estimation, they are likely to refrain from action until they can do so." Huntington (1968, 219) makes a similar observation:

> It is precisely this careful preparation — this painstaking construction of a political majority — which makes the coup painless and bloodless. The actual seizure of power itself may be the action of only a small group of men, but normally the support of a fairly large proportion of the total number of political actors in the society is achieved before the coup is launched. In the most successful coup, indeed, the targets offer no resistance whatsoever: they know they are beaten when the coup is announced; quietly and quickly they head for the airport.

For the usual sequence of events, see Finer (1976, 142).

66. This holds for other forms of collective dissent as well. One reason that the Eastern European revolutions of 1989 were successful is that they happened so fast that the regimes had little time to choose an appropriate response strategy.

67. Note that this proposition refers to personal efficacy, whereas a similar proposition in section 3.6.1 refers to group efficacy (i.e., the efficacy of protest, in general).

68. Survey work on personal efficacy and participation in protest (Muller 1972, 463–64; 1979, 74–75; Barnes and Kasse 1979) provides some support for these ideas.

69. While solid evidence on the closeness-dissent proposition is hard to come by, some indirect evidence from electoral competition does exist. Survey results show that turnout increases as elections look close (Riker and Ordeshook 1968, 38). There is also evidence of a rational choice calculus of voting, involving closeness of elections and the calculation of party positions, for radical and ethnoregional political parties (Levi and Hechter 1985, 138–43).

70. An example provided by Alinsky (1946, 167–69) is the Back of the Yards Neighborhood Council in Chicago, which sought information on school lunch subsidies offered by federal and state authorities.

71. All of the Great Revolutions were unanticipated: "Revolutionaries are often surprised when they gain power, which suggests that they were not motivated by expectations of personal future gain" (Walt 1992, 335, fn. 43). The French Revolution was thus "so inevitable yet so completely unforeseen" (Tocqueville [1856] 1955, 1). That the Russian Revolution took everyone by surprise (Chamberlin [1935] 1987, 73) is evidenced by Lenin himself: "Lenin told a socialist youth group in January 1917 that 'we of the older generation may not live to see the decisive battles of this coming revolution'" (Walt 1992, 335, fn. 43). And Sandinista leader Daniel Ortega admitted that "as late as July 1979 he did not expect to see the revolution succeed in Nicaragua" (Walt 1992, 335, fn. 43). Kuran (1989, 43–45; 1991a, 7–13) provides further evidence that the French, Russian, Iranian, and Eastern European revolutions were unanticipated.

72. Coser's (1956) proposition, as rephrased by Turner (1986, 172), is that "the more clear-cut are the indexes of defeat or victory in a conflict, the more likely are leaders to perceive the high costs of complete attainment of goals," and hence the shorter the conflict. Conversely, "The less the parties in a conflict can interpret their adversary's symbolic points of victory and defeat, the more prolonged is the conflict." Welch (1980, 224) thus observes that "negotiation often came only after both parties had paraded their strengths."

73. Laqueur (1987, 328) offers two examples: "First, from the ideological pronouncements of the IRA one would not learn that sectarian elements were prominently involved in their strife; secondly, the one major tactical innovation of the Palestinian guerrillas was their operations were mainly conducted outside Israel. But official pronouncements almost invariably proclaim the opposite. The IRA and the Palestinian Arab spokesmen no doubt have sound political reasons for preferring fiction to fact."

74. Margolis (1982, 13) argues that "even if I am narrowly self-interested, it is often not easy to judge how various policies affect my interests...

Hence it is not surprising to note that politically active people devote a large portion of their time and political resources to efforts which may generally be termed *persuasion*: efforts to influence others' patterns of preferences by means of arguments, manipulation of symbols, dissemination of information, and so on." Taylor (1990, 226) indicates that such persuasion involves "providing information and arguments about the alternatives, about the consequences of adopting the various courses of action, about others' attitudes and beliefs, and so on."

75. As Huntington (1968, 345) points out, "The aim of the revolutionary is to polarize politics, and hence he attempts to simplify, to dramatize, and to amalgamate political issues into a single clear-cut dichotomy between the forces of 'progress' and those of 'reaction'. He tries to cumulate cleavages . . . the revolutionary produces rigidity in politics." Blalock (1989, 137) agrees that the simplicity of belief systems, a "good versus bad" or "we versus them" orientation, is what dissident leaders wish to instill in their followers: "Many kinds of ideological devices are well-known. The opposing party or enemy is likely to be blamed for a large number of offenses, past and present, and to be depicted in an extremely unfavorable light: as immoral, dangerous, treacherous, inhumane, and generally deserving of even more punishment than is currently being meted out . . . Motives of those on both sides are oversimplified by seeing the opposing party as [the exact opposite of the party]."

76. Many have recognized the frequent juxtaposition of ideology and collective dissident. Sassoon (1984, 871) sees dissident groups as "media for different, alternative ways of perceiving, codifying, constructing the social world." Dunn (1989, 245) recognizes that elite ideologies must be marketed to the masses. Goldfrank (1979, 138) refers to the "opportunistic sophistry" attached to ideology. Kuran (1989, 65) argues that a leader tries "to mold people's private preferences. To this end, he finds wrongs in the existing order, brings them to the non-activists' attention, and drums into their consciousness that the order advocated by the opposition would serve them better." Stewart, Smith, and Denton (1984, chap. 5) show how dissidents use rhetoric to overcome the CA problem.

77. As Jefferson (quoted in Alinsky 1946, 155) suggests, "Enlighten the people generally, and tyranny and oppression of body and mind will vanish like spirits at the dawn of day." Coleman (1990, 502), for another example, suggests that rebels should "find and promulgate a utopian ideology that challenges the values expressed by the current authority structure, and provide an alternative vision for the future." Further examples of the value of ideology to the free rider problem may be found in Siegenthaler (1989).

78. These include social banditry in Europe (Hobsbawm 1981), the French Jacquerie in 1358, and Mexican revolutionaries under Zapata. A particularly powerful example comes from Russia. Peasant rebellion characterized Russian dissent in the sixteenth, seventeenth, and eighteenth centuries.

Intellectual revolution characterized Russian dissent in the nineteenth century. In the early twentieth century, the two strands fused. Thus, the earlier efforts at a mass movement without ideas and vice versa failed; only the later effort, which fused ideas and a mass movement, succeeded.

79. Hobsbawm (1959, 152) asserts that "meetings, processions, joint acts of worship or the like" serve to "reaffirm the unity of the members." Rudé (1964, 245) argues that "slogans served to unify the crowd itself and to direct its energies toward precise targets and objectives," and "by such means groups and individuals with widely varying motives and beliefs may be rallied in support of a common cause and to focus their protests on a common target" (Rudé 1964, 245–46). Stewart, Smith, and Denton (1984, 98) argue that "leaders and superiors must create and use symbols that unite and transcend individual and collective differences." Finally, Gurr (1970, 294) argues that "a major function of the doctrines articulated by leaders is to provide their followers with normative justifications for opposition. Followers' awareness that they are members of an organized group of like-minded individuals reinforces group cohesion and provides a sense of security in the face of external pressure."

80. In his 1938 edition, Brinton adds that they are "always trying for a home run. No good revolutionary leader would ever bunt."

81. Several scholars suggest that people living a marginal existence are too worried about seeking food to risk participating in collective dissent (Migdal 1974, chap. 10; Scott 1976; Mason and Krane 1989). Welch (1980, 54) maintains that "peasants lived close to the margins of existence. Tawney's famous remark about cultivators in China applied equally well to those in Telengana: 'There are districts in which the position of the rural population is that of a man standing permanently up to the neck in water, so that even a ripple is sufficient to drown him.'" Feeny (1983, 782) argues that "peasant revolt is another form of investment in seeking security. A revolt can be viewed as a lottery, with large gains if it is successful. Thus, peasants with small surpluses or those who are better organized are more willing and able to gamble on success." Scott (1975, 512) maintains that a situation of insecure poverty, where people cannot always provide for their own sustenance, leaves little time for CA. Huntington (1968, 53) writes that "those who are concerned about the immediate goal of the next meal are not apt to worry about the grand transformation of society. They become marginalists and incrementalists concerned simply with making minor but absolutely essential improvements in the existing situation." Gurr (1970, 131) suggests that "there is nonetheless a natural threshold below which economic impoverishment will not lead to revolt, whatever men's expectations, namely the 'starvation threshold.' If economic deprivation is so great that men are reduced to or

below the level of physical subsistence, they are literally incapable of rebellion."

82. Zald (1979, 6) argues that "the mobilization of one side in a conflict issue creates the conditions for the mobilization of the other side." Tilly (1964, 61) maintains that "two groups which never meet cannot fight" and hence (1975a, 495) that "an important portion of collective violence pits contenders for power against one another, rather than rebels against regimes."

83. Simmel's (1955) work implies that as the extent (number of participants), intensity (level of violence), and duration (longevity) of conflict between groups increase, the requirement for self-defense, and, consequently, the internal solidarity of the conflict groups, increases. Coser (1956, 33–48) agrees, arguing that a positive function of conflict to society is to set moral boundaries and strengthen in-group solidarity. Several other students of conflict have taken up this theme. Pruitt and Rubin (1986, 105–8) hypothesize that conflict leads to in-group unity, solidarity, effectiveness, and cohesiveness. Masters (1983, 187) maintains that "intergroup competition places a premium on within-group cooperation." Wesson (1967, 337) suggests that "group solidarity is directly proportional to feelings of hostility to or difference from outsiders." Thompson (1966) points out the relationship between "solidarity *with*" and "solidarity *against*."

84. An outside enemy leads dissidents to stress the importance of mutual aid, mutual reinforcement, and competitive mobilization. Collective defense thus promotes collective offense. This idea may be found in Deutsch (1973, 75–77), who reviews the argument that external threats lead to ingroup solidarity. It is also found in Lasswell and Kaplan (1950, 46), who argue that intergroup conflict creates a common enemy who, in turn, produces ingroup consciousness: "Group consciousness initially increases with conflict with other groups with equal or higher degrees of consciousness." They (1950, 46) argue, further, that "defense against the common enemy is an interest in common, facilitating the recognition of other shared interests." For a further review of the idea that external conflict increases internal cohesion, the ingroup/out-group hypothesis, see Stein (1976).

85. Groups do not always return violence for violence. Other response strategies, such as exit (sect. 3.11), are possible. For example, during the later part of the nineteenth century several European governments provided symbolic and material support to anti-Jewish pogroms. The result was the Zionist movement.

86. The Catholic League's countermobilization against the Huguenots is an interesting example (Zagorin 1982b, 75). Counterrevolutionaries appeared during the Great Revolutions (e.g., royalists in England, loyalists in the American Revolution, Whites in Russia, the KMT in China). Interwar

Europe saw the growth of communist and fascist movements, most explosively in the case of the Spanish Civil War. Countermobilization also occurs in labor-management conflicts (Wilson 1973, 150–51): trade unions (labor) beget trade organizations (business). Coleman (1990, 491) offers an example from student revolts: "In the student revolts of the late 1960s, there was ordinarily a group of students who actively supported the university authorities. At Columbia University these were known as 'the jocks'; in the 1968 revolt of French university students at Nanterre, they were known as 'Occident.'" Tilly (1986, 348) offers this particularly vivid example of opposition and counteropposition in Paris on May Day, 1983: "After the left marched on the Right Bank, the right marched on the Left Bank." Subsequently, the *Internationale* provoked the *Marseillaise* and the *Marseillaise* provoked the *Internationale* (Tilly 1986, 370). A final series of examples come from the recurring pattern of protest and counterprotest in American history. Protests about abortion, abolition, nuclear power, civil rights, gun control, and war have usually brought counterprotests. And the majority of American race riots follow an actual or a reported interracial assault (Lieberson and Silverman 1965, 889).

87. Marx's views on this issue of team competition and collective dissent have been widely adopted by his numerous followers. Przeworski (1985b, 390) argues that "the problem of organizing each class (and other collectivities) cannot be considered in isolation from the relation of the individual members of one class to the other class." Hilton (1973, 11) writes that "a necessary condition for the existence of the peasantry as a class of small-scale agricultural producers has always been the existence of other classes who, to put it crudely, live off the surplus product of peasant labour. This involves the peasantry in a wide network of relationships with these other social groups, relationships which inevitably generate antagonism." Even Weber ([1924] 1968, 930), Marx's sometime intellectual nemesis on questions of class, agrees with Marx on this point: "Class situations emerge only on the basis of social action. However, social action than brings forth class situation is not basically action among members of the identical class; it is an action among members of different classes."

88. Lipset, Trow, and Coleman (1962, 172) thus indicate that "over a hundred years ago Marx noted that workers in small craft shops, who work side by side with their employers, associate with them informally and develop personal ties with them, are markedly less class-conscious and less involved in workers' organizations than are workers in large industry. The personal ties of small-shop men with their employers tend to weaken their identification with organizations predicated on a conflict of interests between workers and employers."

89. Hagopian (1974, 147, emphasis in original) asserts that "*nationalism in some manifestation is always involved in modern revolutions.*" Laqueur (1987, 396) comments on the appeal of nationalism: "Guerrillas succeed with much greater ease against foreign domination than against national incumbents." Huntington (1968), too, stresses that nationalist movements solve the Rebel's Dilemma: "The common cause which produces the revolutionary alliance or revolutionary parallelism [of city and countryside] is usually nationalism and the catalyst is usually a foreign enemy" (1968, 304); "nationalism is the cement of the revolutionary alliance and the engine of the revolutionary movement" (1968, 308); and, "no society can carry out a revolution in isolation. Every revolution is, in some measure, against not only the dominant class at home but also against the dominant system abroad" (1968, 306).

90. Foreign intervention galvanized the revolution and kept it going in France, Russia, Mexico, China, Yugoslavia, Vietnam, and Cuba. Examples of alien rule generating collective dissent also abound. The statist nobilities of a number of Eastern European countries in the nineteenth century are interesting cases in this regard.

91. The *invent an enemy* solution to the Rebel's Dilemma is related to a popular strategy used by regimes to stay in power: conduct foreign wars to divert attention from domestic problems.

92. Mansbridge (1986, 2) holds that both proponents and opponents of the Equal Rights Amendment mobilized activists by exaggerating the amendment's importance. Walt (1992, 337) offers three additional examples of this approach:

> Lenin broke with the "Economists" in Russia and with Social Democrats like Karl Kautsky over the possibility of reforming tsarism and capitalism, and Mao Zedong told his followers that "'imperialism is ferocious' . . . [I]ts nature will never change, the imperialists will never lay down their butcher knives . . . they will never become Buddhas." Similarly, the Ayatolloh Khomeini opposed compromise with the Shah by warning Iranians that "if you give this fellow a breathing spell, neither Islam nor your country nor your family will be left for you. Do not give him the chance; squeeze his neck until he is strangled."

93. This is not unlike what happens when police protection is inadequate and citizens respond by purchasing security devices and hiring private security agencies.

94. Secessionism by some can ignite collective dissent by others. For example, political separatism and secessionism often provokes civil war.

95. Exit and voice can increase together. Hirschman (1993) observes that this was the case in the East German Revolution.

96. Revolution by some can ignite emigration by others. An example is the emigration of French nobles during the French Revolution (Tilly 1964, 192).

97. Europe is rich with examples. Hilton (1973, 74) submits a case from the European Middle Ages: "Seigneurially directed colonization of new land during a period of population growth" was followed by reduced levels of collective dissent, a linkage readily explained by the increased availability of the exit option. Hobsbawm (1975, chap. 11) advances a case from the second half of the nineteenth century: the decline of working-class and nationalist movements in Europe is related to rising emigration. The United States offers a final set of examples. The frontier and the availability of free land reduced the possibility of violence and revolution in the United States. This is, in part, the Turner thesis on the importance of the American frontier to American democracy (Moore 1966, 130–31). Exit dampened collective dissent during the Vietnam era: draft resisters moved to Canada. Voice or exit bears, in fact, a remarkable similarity to the old taunt of the Right, "America: love it or leave it." For other examples of the exit/voice choice, see Barry (1974, 83-85), Gurr (1970, 75–76), and Hirschman (1974; 1978, 102–3).

98. The emigration literature offers a variety of explanations that due to space constraints cannot be developed here.

99. Yet the evidence on this point so far is negative. Tilly (1978, chap. 5) reports that the trend of violence from the nineteenth to twentieth centuries has run in the opposite direction: proactive violence has replaced reactive violence. This evidence, however, should not be interpreted solely in terms of the *Seek Public Bads* solution.

100. PGs are both nonrival and nonexcludable. Rivalness always hurts collective dissent. Hence, the rivalness issue yields one solution to the Rebel's Dilemma: *Seek Nonrival Public Goods*. The impact of excludability on dissident CA, however, is more complex. The repercussions depend upon who is controlling the exclusion. If dissident entrepreneurs can control exclusion, they can use this power to promote participation in collective dissent. If others control exclusion, dissident groups are in worse shape than if the good were completely nonexcludable. Thus, three solutions to the Rebel's Dilemma relate to excludability. The first is to control excludable goods. Dissident entrepreneurs who offer selective incentives (sect. 6.5.3) and form clubs (sect. 6.3.1) are carving out excludable goods, and thereby enhancing the prospects for collective dissent. A second solution is to turn nonexcludable goods into excludable goods that the dissidents can control. If dissidents seek a nonexcludable good, the prospects for collective dissent are weakened, because benefits are not contingent upon contributions. Hence, dissi-

dent entrepreneurs always try to turn nonexcludable goods into excludable goods that they can control. For example, dissident entrepreneurs who cut off the exit (sect. 3.11) option enhance the prospects for collective dissent. A third solution is to eliminate excludable goods controlled by others. Dissident entrepreneurs thus attempt to prevent other dissident entrepreneurs or the regime from offering selective incentives to their potential clientele. Dissident leaders who can do so enhance their group's prospects for success.

## CHAPTER 4

1. Gottschalk (1944, 5) suggests that "the fact that I am discontented will not lead me to revolution unless I am aware that quite a number of other people are equally discontented and are likely to unite with me in the expression of my discontent." Edelman (1971, 130) asserts that

> there must be a perception that if some defy the laws, the authorities, or conventional behavior, others will join in the action and the still larger public will be supportive. Aggressive impulses stemming from frustrations occur frequently in everyone. Rarely do they eventuate in collective physical aggression. They do so when there is reason for people to believe that physical aggression is a norm, to be regarded by a larger public — some present and some a reference public — as proper, laudable or conventional behavior in the specific situation.

Deutsch et al. (1957, 46, 56) suggest that an "essential requirement for the establishment of an amalgamated security community" is "mutual predictability of behavior." Milgram's (1974) experiments demonstrate that resistance to domination increases markedly when there is even the slightest possibility that peers will support it.

2. Brown (1965, 753–56) analyzes a lynch mob as an assurance game. To assure coordination, the participants go though a "milling" phase during which they try to convey their preferences to others and to ascertain the preferences of others. They are looking for cues signaling that there are the numbers to guarantee success. He (1965, 758–59) offers supportive examples. Edelman (1971, 124) also reports that "case studies of riots consistently note an increase in the frequency and intensity of the rumors before the outbreak of disturbances." The nature and content of such rumors are thus important to CA theorists of collective dissent.

3. How regimes react to this proposition bears further investigation. One suspects that regimes will ban gatherings at focal points in order to upset dissident coordination.

4. Preference falsification (sect. 9.2.2.2), however, mitigates the value

of preplay communication. If people are falsifying their preferences, they do not realize how easily they can topple a regime.

5. Tilly (1978, 157) suggests that a contender's own experience with collective dissent counts in his or her future use of collective dissent. In describing incidences of student and worker militancy, Mann (1973, 45–55) remarks upon the phenomenon of "explosions of consciousness" in which each new CA forms the basis for the next, more militant, CA. Blalock (1989, 48), in this spirit, offers a domino theory, or a theory of the snowballing of disaffected units of a nation into a movement of national integration:

> Imagine, for example, a situation involving a large number of small political units, each of which is weakened because of continual conflicts with its immediate neighbors. Should any one of these small units be able to dominate its closest rivals and pull them into an effective coalition, however, a snowball effect may be set in motion. Gaining in resources, it will be able to incorporate more and more territory.

Others (Parsons 1963, 1964; Johnson 1966; see the discussion in Rule 1988, 154–60) think of bandwagons of collective dissent in terms of the gradual breakdown of government authority. A "power deflation" is seen as the political equivalent to a "run" on a bank. The more power deflates, the more it continues to deflate. Eventually the challenge to the state is so great that all governmental authority is lost.

6. Knighton's (cited in Hilton 1973, 216) description of the English Rising of 1381 is a clear example of a chain reaction among successful dissidents:

> Thomas Baker of Fobbing (so called because of his trade) took courage and began to make speeches and to find supporters among some of the men of the village. Then others joined them, and then each of them sent messages to their friends and relatives, and so further, from village to village, district to district, seeking advice and asking them to bring prompt help with respect to those needs which they had in common and which bore so heavily on them. And so they began to gather together in companies with a great show of jubilation, as was their wont.

Tong (1991) shows how early success led dissidents in Ming China to broaden their movement: successful local bandits evolved to become full-fledged rebellious movements, which, if they remained successful, became dynastic contenders.

7. Many postwar insurrections grew out of successful wartime resistance movements. In Yugoslavia, China, Malaysia, the Philippines, and Vietnam, the wartime "resistance movements provided a model for methods of

guerrilla warfare and terrorism; that they provided some of our rebels with experience of guerrilla conditions and with arms for future use; and that, even when they did not have direct experience of the resistance, it helped to condition their conduct of operations" (Crozier 1960, 107). Temporal diffusion was, moreover, taken one step further: where independence was achieved violently, the nation tended to have subsequent violent collective dissent (e.g., coups and secessionism). One can therefore locate linkages between prewar social movements, wartime resistance movements, postwar struggles for power, and postregime coups and secessionism. The state's weakness is also a factor here (sect. 3.6.2.2).

8. It is widely recognized that successful coups tend to breed more coups: "The recurrence of coups d'etat in many Latin American countries may be largely attributable to the success of previous plotters in seizing power and, through it, status and wealth" (Gurr 1970, 219). Witness Argentina, where "the military which originally intervened out of reluctant necessity, found coups an increasingly satisfactory means of resolving their own discontents and those of segments of the upper and middle classes that supported them. More and more Argentineans became resigned to the occurrence of coups, especially after 1955, and growing numbers of officers became convinced by their relative success in national management that intervention was justifiable in utilitarian terms" (Gurr 1970, 220).

9. Wrong (1988) offers an interesting discussion of cycles in democratic (p. 204) and autocratic (p. 207) polities.

10. As Im, Cauley, and Sandler (1987, 241-42) argue, "Not only do terrorists imitate one another's proven strategies, but governments also learn from one another, thus diffusing effective countermeasures. This diffusion will, in time, reinforce the downturn in terrorist activities. As with terrorist groups, a government's development of an effective countermeasure confers external benefits to other governments."

11. As Zimmermann (1983, 429) asks,

> Do weaker forms of violent protest, such as strikes, sit-ins, and demonstrations, because they frequently occur in democratic societies, serve as a safety valve, thus preventing the build-up of protest potentials of a much larger size? . . . The French fruit-grower who dumps his surplus products, with a certain regularity, on the *routes nationales* might express his discontent in what he considers to be the appropriate form of protest . . . As Stanley Hoffmann argues, "the protest movement is both the safety valve of a society divided by deep conflicts and the traditional French form of democracy."

12. See Gurr (1970, 168–77), Lichbach and Gurr (1981), and Lichbach (1985a, 1985b).

13. Nations tend to have traditions of certain forms, properties, and targets of collective dissent. Coups and countercoups in Thailand, factional violence in Venezuela and Colombia, and racial violence in the United States are examples.

14. Dissident groups also tend to have traditions of certain forms, properties, and targets of collective dissent. Revolutionary movements thus have persisted over long periods of time. The predecessor and successor organizations of the Viet-Minh, the Irish Republican Army, Basques separatists, Parisian workers and shopkeepers, and food rioters and machine breakers in eighteenth and nineteenth century England and France are examples. Gurr (1970, 315–16) reports that "rebel bands in the Burma hills, in central Luzon, in India's Naga Hills, and in the Colombian state of Tolima have maintained insurgencies for twenty years or more." The Mann-Giddens thesis attributes the radicalism of the French labour movement to its past: "Their central thesis is that the major historical source of the radicalism of the French labour movement lay in the existence of profound social conflicts in the countryside that generated bitter and enduring traditions of agrarian radicalism. French workers, it is held, were distinctive in that they entered the industrial workplace *already* radicalized by their experiences in the rural sector" (Gallie 1982, 150, emphasis in original).

15. Dissidents often have a history of prior dissident activities (McAdam, McCarthy, and Zald 1988, 708). Members of the new labor movement in Canada, for example, tended to be immigrants who had been active in the labor movement in the United Kingdom (Lipset 1971a, 110). McAdam's (1986, 81–82) follow-up study of the Freedom Summer applicants, for another example, found that a person's level of activism between 1964 and 1970 was among the best predictors of his or her current activism. Moreover, previous levels of civil rights activism were powerful predictors of whether people withdrew from the project.

16. Im, Cauley, and Sandler (1987, 241) thus note that "one group's development of an effective operating procedure confers an external benefit on the other groups. Learning by doing also assists successful groups to perfect their operating procedures, and this perfection also helps increase the number of incidents." Tilly also recognizes diffusion among groups. He (1978, 155) argues that other contenders' experience counts, and hence the repertoire of collective action spreads from one group to another. Wallerstein (1983, 70), too, sees the spatial diffusion of protest as an important cause of the growth of revolutionary movements: "A key factor in the strength of any given movement has always been the existence of other movements."

17. This is Wallerstein's (1983, 70) argument: "The ability of a given strong state to intervene against an anti-systemic movement located in a weaker state, for example, was always a function of how many other things were on its immediate political agenda. The more a given state was preoccu-

pied with a local antisystemic movement, the less ability it had to be occupied with a faraway antisystemic movement." Wallerstein (1984, 108) thereby maintains that "the success of one has created more political space for the other. Each time an antisystemic movement has come to partial or total power, it has altered the balance of power of the interstate system such that there has been more space for other antisystemic movements."

18. As Tilly (1978, 155) writes, "That is no doubt one of the main reasons 'waves' of strikes or demonstrations occur: the fact that a given sort of group gets somewhere with the tactic spreads the expectation that employers or governments will be vulnerable to the same tactic in the hands of other similar groups." Wallerstein (1983, 70) agrees: "Movements learned from each other's errors and were encouraged by each other's tactical successes. And the efforts of the movements worldwide affected the basic worldwide political ambiance — the expectations, the analysis of possibilities." Wallerstein (1984, 108) thus maintains that

> these movements have, first of all, quite clearly served as inspiration and reinforcement for analogous neighboring movements, particularly at the very beginning of their phase of achieved power. One cannot imagine the political history of the twentieth century without taking into account this spread effect. Mobilization has bred mobilization, and the success of one has been the source of hope of the other.

19. All the Great Revolutions consequently produced civil and foreign wars.

20. Bendix (1984, 115) notes that "once the English king had been overthrown and Parliament declared supreme, other monarchies became insecure and the idea of parliamentary government was launched." Zagorin (1982b, 38) attributes the Scottish and Irish revolutions to the English Revolution.

21. The French Revolution was an inspiration to many subsequent revolutionary efforts. Pettee ([1938] 1971, 96) remarks that

> the French Revolution was the revolution which cracked the modern consciousness and made men realize that revolution is a fact, that a great revolution may occur in a modern progressive society. After the French Revolution no other revolution could ever be carried out by men so innocently naive about the significance of their own acts. It is after the French Revolution that we find professed revolutionaries working for revolution in the future and studying those in the past.

22. Wickham-Crowley (1989, 139) notes "the symbolic impact of the Cuban revolution, then, exemplified Max Weber's portrait of ideas acting as historical 'switchmen,' which redirect the paths down which (class) interests

express themselves. All Latin American revolutions since 1959 must be understood historically as post-Cuban (and now post-Nicaraguan) in nature."

23. Chong (1991, 96) points to the bandwagon in the collapse of Communist regimes in Eastern Europe in 1989–1990:

> By the time the wave of popular protest swept Czechoslovakia, events there were almost a replay of earlier protests in Poland, Hungary, and East Germany, 'only a month later and a bit faster' . . . Czechoslovakia may have benefited most from these precedents. Not only did it take Czech citizens only a week of demonstrations to remove the Communist Party leader, but it seemed as though the entire population became convinced all at once of the need for major reforms.

24. Demonstration effects, facilitated by exiles, were responsible for the spread of the Reformation (Zagorin 1982b, 72, 99). Demonstration effects also helped spread dissent during the Swing movement in England (Hobsbawm and Rudé 1968, chap. 9). The 1848 revolutions were the product of diffused demonstration effects. As Gurr (1970, 97) notes, "The February 1848 revolution of Parisian workers and liberal bourgeoisie that overthrew Louis Philippe clearly was the inspiration for subsequent rising by Germans, Italians, Czechs, and Magyars later in the year." Demonstration effects also influenced African national liberation struggles: "Ghana's attainment of independence in 1957 intensified expectations of political independence among African leaders throughout the continent and thus indirectly contributed to political violence in regions like the Belgian Congo and Angola where progress toward effective African political participation was dilatory or nonexistent" (Gurr 1970, 97). Tarrow (1989, 90) observes that "the Italian student movement refused to stay in school." He (1989, 20–21) also points out a correlation between nonreligious and religious protest in Italy from 1966 to 1973. Petras and Zeitlin (1967, 578) demonstrate "the impact of organized workers in Chile on the development of political consciousness in the peasantry." The traditionally radical miners and trade union organizations radicalized the traditionally conservative peasants. People active in the U.S. civil rights struggles contributed to the student revolts in Berkeley and the opposition to the war in Vietnam. More generally, U.S. blacks were the early arrivers during the 1950s and 1960s; religious fundamentalists, women, students, animal rights activists, gays, and so on, were the latecomers during the 1960s and 1970s. Additional examples of demonstration effects can be found in Greene (1990, 147–49).

25. One example comes from Western Europe:

> A turning point came when unions in West Germany lost a six-week strike for a shorter work week. After that Dutch unions no longer

believed they would succeed in attaining a shorter work week in the Netherlands. First they moderated their demands (thirty-nine hours instead of thirty-five) and then dropped the shorter-work-week demand altogether. (Klandermans 1988, 81)

26. Spatial contagion of protest raises Galton's problem: the nonindependence of cases due to emulation, contagion, spillover, and diffusion. See Ross and Homer (1976).

27. These include the women's, youth, gay and lesbian, ecological, antinuclear, environmental, peace, religious fundamentalist, and citizen-action movements. They seek direct participation or "politics of the first person" for communal members. All forms of representation of interests are spurned: "Since what is at stake is the appropriation of identity all mediation is rejected as likely to produce the mechanism of control and manipulation against which the struggle is directed in the first place. Hence the importance of direct action and of direct participation, in other words, of the spontaneous anti-authoritarian anti-hierarchical nature of the protests originating in the movement" (Meluci 1980, 220).

28. Political violence facilitates psychological liberation by allowing the individual to break out of the identity created by one's oppressors and adopt the identity of some reference community. Hence, Blalock (1989, 52) refers to "the utility attached to aggression or to injuring the other party," Sorel (1950) stresses the personal experience of engaging in collective violence, and Fanon (1967) argues that violence builds one's identity.

29. I am indebted to Timur Kuran for this observation.

30. Tullock (1971a; 1979, 51) points to this aspect of protest and even argues that where there is little probability of success and nontrivial costs, the entertainment value of participation in collective dissent must be high before people join protests and rebellions. Banfield (1974, chap. 9) discusses "rioting mainly for fun and profit" and participation in CA for "sport." Leites (1979, 37), too, argues that CA is "fun." De la Hodde (cited in Laqueur 1987, 185) argues that dissidents are fond of "noise, fracas and sudden events." Zolberg (1972, 202–3) argues that some individuals yearn "for a more dramatic political process in which fulfillment could be achieved through the act of participation itself." H. L. Menken (cited in Brown 1965, 709) argues that lynchings in the old rural South "often take the place of the merry-go-round, the theater, the symphony, and other diversions common to larger communities." As the chorus in the play *Marat/Sade* sings, "And what's the point of a revolution without general copulation copulation copulation" (Weiss 1965, 92).

31. Marwell and Oliver (1984, 20–21) observe that "persons whose daily lives are boring and unsatisfying often derive great intrinsic pleasure from their participation in collective action." Zolberg (1972, 200) refers to "a rev-

olution against boredom." Anderson, von der Mehden, and Young (1967, 93, emphasis in original) stress the importance of "*boredom - restlessness - the romanticism of guerrilla life*. We have a number of instances, particularly in Southeast Asia, where young men have admitted joining a revolutionary organization because of the boredom of their peasant, urban, or school existence." Tarrow (1989, 35) describes Italian student demonstrators as follows: "Out of school and out of spirits in the December gloom [they] wander aimlessly around the old city." Revolution overcomes boredom asserts Abbie Hoffman (1968) in *Revolution for the Hell of It*. Also see De la Hodde (cited in Laqueur 1987, 185).

32. They can be found in terrorism. Rapoport (1984, 675) argues that "the people attracted to [terrorism] may be so intrigued by the experience of perpetrating terror that everything else is incidental." Fascism is another case in which the entertainment value of collective dissent can be seen. Linz (1976, 34) refers to the attempt to overcome boredom and the search for fun, adventure, and activism that enabled fascism to attract recently demobilized veterans and university students: "Fascism had a strong romantic component — an appeal to emotion and sentiment, to the love of adventure and heroism, the belief in action rather than words, the exultation of violence and even death." Guerrilla warfare is yet another form of collective dissent in which there is an element of entertainment value. Popkin (1979, 239) writes the following of the Viet Minh: "A people's culture and art movement was founded. It recruited heavily from among the wandering troupes that performed traditional Sino-Vietnamese shows at village festivals, from vagabond musicians, and from village guitar teachers. Much like the bands at Tammany Hall election rallies, these groups helped attract large crowds for Viet Minh village rallies." The civil rights movement in the United States used entertainment— scripture reading, prayer, Old Negro Spirituals, hand clapping, shouting, and hymns — to attract participants. As one leader, E. D. Nixon (cited in Morris 1984, 47), says: "If you are going to continue to lead a group of people you are going to have to put something into the program that those people like. A whole lot of people came to the . . . meetings for no other reason than just to hear the music, some came to hear the folks who spoke." A final form of collective dissent whose entertainment value attracts people is a protest demonstration. Tilly (1978, 144–45) reports that many nineteenth-century demonstrations were quite entertaining. People enjoyed the experience of "rough music," parades, spectacles, and brawls. Many contemporary demonstrations also have spectator appeal. Dissidents often stage parades and sporting matches that provide food and entertainment. Music and song, as well as art and literature, are essential. Dissidents, for example, often organize street theater. They put on mock political trials. People, quite literally, come to watch the show.

33. Weber ([1924] 1968, 24–25) defines "value-rational" motivations as a conscious belief in an absolute value purely for its own sake, independent of its consequences.

34. Turner's (1986, 141) restatement of one of Simmel's (1955) propositions is that "the more that conflict is perceived by members of conflict groups to transcend individual aims and interests, the more likely is the conflict to be violent." Coser (1956, 33–38) argues that individuals obtain a sense of belonging to a group from engaging in conflict as members of the group, and that such belonging reinforces their behavior. Chong (1991, 74) suggests that dissidents seek to "share in the excitement of a group effort." Zald and McCarthy (1979c, 239) suggest that "the more closely sympathizers in any social change goal approximate a solidary group, the more easily mobilizable they are." Fireman and Gamson (1979, 31) argue that people are more likely to contribute their fair share "when group interest, solidarity, and urgency combine." Wilson (1973, 63) argues that "membership in voluntary organizations can most economically be explained by the principle that 'likes attract likes.'" Coleman (1990, 158) refers to "the organization of action through identification, which I call affine agency" and argues that "unity of purpose and unity of action among those in association, with no dissension about overall aims, can provide mutual rewards. Records of this are found in accounts of revolutionary and rebellious activity" (1990, 494). Cohen (1985, 693) suggests that social movements create new social meanings and solidarities: "Religious communities, secular communes, political sects, and the like stage expressive and ritualistic actions to secure their identities." Finally, Gurr (1970, 208) also suggests that group consciousness may be a solution to the Rebel's Dilemma:

> The effectiveness of new justificatory beliefs about political violence also varies with the extent to which they provide the discontented with a sense of community. That sense can be created or reinforced by use of symbols that make men aware of their common discontents, of the worthiness of their group or organization, and of their potential for cooperative actions against their oppressors.

35. Several commentators suggest that fascists sought a new purpose, identity, and community. Barbu (cited in Woolf 1968, 111–12) claims that "one of the most fruitful approaches was to conceive of the [fascist] party as a type of primary community, a corporate morality, which tries to reinforce the feeling of belonging to something, the primary emotional involvement of the individual . . . the fascist movement appealed to people who needed strong bonds . . . The fascist party offered a type of solidarity; it appealed to people who suffered from the disintegration of traditional or any kind of

social solidarity." Carsten (1976, 423) reports along similar lines that fascist paramilitary organizations operated as youth gangs, with primary ties of kinship and friendship. Communal consciousness, for example, was very important in the Nazi movement: "A persistent theme of Nazi ideology, ritually emphasized in innumerable Nazi ceremonies, was the historical community and accomplishments of the Germanic people. Traditions symbolizing German unity were revived or created out of whole cloth, Germanic culture was glorified, and the evils in German society projected onto non-Germanic groups - the Jews, the international bankers, the communists, hostile international forces" (Gurr 1970, 208).

36. Laqueur (1987, 89) argues that the terrorist group "provided love, friendship and protection while it replaced the family, culture and politics. It had its own language, symbols and value system." It is thus easy to understand why, as the Task Force on Disorders and Terrorism (1976, 15) argues, "for some, terrorism has become a way of life."

37. One of the principal problems with organizing peasant movements is thought to be a lack of a communal identity. Giap and Truong Chinh (cited in Popkin 1979, 252), for example, suggest that

> peasants also have the mentality of private ownership . . . They are suspicious of talk of collective work. Most of them do not like the idea of contributing money for common goals. Traditional peasant organizations . . . are all characterized by individual profit for each member of the group. None have a society nature, *i.e.*, a common advantage for the entire group or for society . . . We have yet to see peasants spontaneously organize societies which have common usefulness.

38. Many suggest that a shared and distinctive youth subculture contributes to CA by young people. The student revolt of the 1960s is thus thought to be an expression of youth's need for separateness, to reject the adult world, and to create its own modes of communication and lifestyles. Coleman (1990, 494) observes that "students who engaged in the occupation of university buildings or other prolonged collective actions during the protests of the 1960s have reported afterward that the spirit and the collective euphoria they experienced made the period a high point in their lives." Hobsbawm (1981, 159) offers the example of the Symbionese Liberation Army in the United States: "The members were personally 'reborn' in the group, chose new names, and evolved a private symbolism."

39. Millenarian movements are another classic example of how communal consciousness overcomes the dissident's CA problem. Smelser (1962, 313) suggests that such movements try to "restore, modify or create values in

the name of generalized belief. Such a belief necessarily involves all components of action, that is, it envisions a reconstruction of values, a redefinition of norms, a reorganization of the motivation of individuals and a redefinition of situational facilities." These movements tend to be cultural, romantic, utopian, antirational, and religious. Lewy (1974, 3) sums up the importance of religion to solving the Rebel's Dilemma: "Religion has also been an important force facilitating radical political and social change, providing the motivation, ideological justification, and social cohesion for rebellions and revolutions. Religiously inspired revolutionary movements have occurred throughout history; the search for the Millennium, often led by a messianic figure, has sparked numerous revolutionary movements many of which have produced significant political and social innovation."

40. Communal consciousness has played a prominent part in the new social movements, which are essentially moral crusades engaged in a quest for community (Eder 1982). It has been widely argued that followers of the new social movements positively value communal consciousness and social solidarity over formal organization and hierarchical structures. Melucci (1984, 822–23) observes that "participants in collective action are not only motivated by what I would call an 'economic' orientation, calculating costs and benefits of action. They are also looking for solidarity and identity." Melucci (1980, 220) argues that for these individuals "the struggle centers around the issue of group identity; there is a return to the criterion of ascriptive membership (sex, race, age, locality) which is the form taken by revolt against change directed from above." Eder (1982, 9) suggests that new social movements seek "particularistic collective identity" and Habermas (1981, 36) maintains that the key issue behind the movements is the "establishment and delimitation of communities."

41. See Klandermans (1984, 596), Knoke (1988), Opp (1986; 1989, 65, 68), Mitchell (1979, 110), Muller and Opp (1986), and Tillock and Morrison (1979).

42. The success of the Grange and the failure of most other nineteenth century farmers' movements in the United States are partially due to the fact that the Grange, in particular, was able to provide solidary incentives to its members (Salisbury 1969, 18). Social bandits are motivated by considerations of social respect (Hobsbawm 1981, 35–36). Labor unions capitalize on social incentives: "Given their strong pride of craft and sense of craft solidarity, the printers were able at an early date to discipline by ostracism those of their workmates who violated the norms of the group" (Lipset, Trow, and Coleman 1962, 30). A final example of the impact of social incentives on collective dissent is offered by Scott (1985, 262). He points out that Malaysian peasants who did not join CA were "shunned in labor exchange (*derau*),

not included in share groups, not told about the possibilities of finding work, denied the petty jobs that the poor can occasionally offer, and not invited to join 'rotating credit associations'.

## CHAPTER 5

1. For example, the Huguenots constructed a counterstate with many of the characteristics of later dissident organizations (Zagorin 1982b, 64). Soldiers' councils formed in the New Model Army in England in the 1640s, in France in 1789, and in the Russian, German, and Austrian armies during the First World War. Spontaneous revolutionary organizations took control in several European cities in 1848 and in Paris in 1871, during the Commune. Chamberlin ([1935] 1987, 246–47) points out that spontaneous organizations formed during the Russian Revolution:

> The city workers had the Soviets and the factory committees. The army was covered with a network of organizations, representing units of varying size from a company to several armies on one of the fronts. And the peasants, despite their political ignorance and their high percentage of illiteracy, also found their representative organizations in the shape of *volost*, or township, committees, which often assumed the functions of local government; peasant Soviets, which supplemented the township committees, and land committees.

French students, in their revolt of 1968, formed *comités d'action lycéen*. South Korean students formed clandestine study groups to oppose their government. Fuentes and Frank (1989, 184) point out the spontaneous organizations behind urban social movements in Third World nations:

> Among the most numerous, active, and popular of these social movements are a myriad of apparently spontaneous, local rural and urban organizations/movements, which seek to defend their members' survival through cooperative consumption, distribution, and production. Examples are soup kitchens; distributors and producers of basic necessities like bread; organizers, petitioners, or negotiators, and sometimes fighters for community infrastructure, like agricultural and urban land, water, electricity, transport, etc. There are over 1,500 such local community movements in Rio de Janeiro alone, and they are increasingly wide-spread and active in India's 600,000 villages.

2. Not all spontaneous peasant uprisings achieve such a high level of organization. Mousnier (1970, 340–41) reports that spontaneous peasant

uprisings in fourteenth and fifteenth century Russia and China never realized the same level of organization as their French counterparts: "In China there do not appear to have been any peasant organizations in the strict sense. The only organs of revolt seem to have been bands with a military-type structure," as was the case with the roving bandits in China in the 1640s who "imposed a strict discipline on themselves" (Mousnier 1970, 282). As to Russia during the Time of Troubles,

> it is hard to perceive any distinct peasant organization . . . Grouped around their emblem, the supernatural hero Stenka Razin, they adopted the democratic and egalitarian institutions of the Cossacks: the general assembly of all the people, which elects its own leaders; the division of the people into thousands, hundreds, and tens, with leaders chosen by the general assembly. But this organization remained strictly local. Peasants and Cossacks did not try to set up a hierarchy of provincial assemblies crowned by a national assembly, with a system of representation. When the hero had been beaten and was in flight, the insurrection broke up into an infinite number of disconnected local revolts. (Mousnier 1970, 340)

3. Skocpol (1979, 254–55) provides a diagnosis of the Chinese Communists' basic problem:

> The central dilemma in the Chinese Communists' quest for victory through rural guerrilla warfare [was] how to achieve direct and stable contact with the settled and productive peasants . . . In principle, the Communists could offer a variety of policies — such as tax or rent reduction, seizure and redistribution of gentry property, provision of local social services, and protection against marauding armies — that might appeal to the felt needs of the settled peasantry. But the actual implementation of such policies depended upon gaining direct access to the peasants in their communities, which meant working around and under — and ultimately displacing — the local gentry and rich peasants and their supporters. That, in turn, was an intricate political process that could only be successfully carried through by Communist cadres working right in the village under the security of at least a minimal military-administrative shield.

The solution was the "Yenan Way" (Selden 1971). The Chinese Communists penetrated local villages in North China and established a direct link to the peasantry. With a program of administrative and agrarian reform, they set out to rebuild the political, social, and economic institutions of the village

(Hagopian 1974, 288–89). Mao describes the various institutions created by the Communists:

> [Each area] must be subdivided and individual companies or battalions formed to accord with the subdivisions. To this "military area," a military commander and political commissioners are appointed. Under these, the necessary officers, both military and political, are appointed. In the military headquarters, there will be the staff, the aides, the supply officers, and the medical personnel. These are controlled by the chief of staff . . . In the political headquarters, there are bureaus of propaganda organization, people's mass movements, and miscellaneous affairs. Control of these is vested in the political chairmen. (Mao 1961, 77)

4. They, too, reorganized the daily life of the village, altering such institutions as property rights, contractual relations, insurance schemes, tax collection, social welfare, and communal land (Popkin 1988). They also organized "literacy and self-help programs [that] became an important recruiting ground for lower level officials and Party members" (Popkin 1979, 239). They even organized self-help organizations, built around friendship cliques, to build straw huts and celebrate local holidays. The Vietnamese Communists also reorganized village politics by developing a parallel government:

> Not one but two systems of organization linked sympathizers to followers and leaders: a territorial system of personnel drawn from villages grouped into districts, with each district subordinated to a provincial committee, the provincial committees organized into zones, and each zone reporting to the Central Committee of the Communist Party; and a cross-cutting system of special-interest organizations focused on peasants, workers, women, youth, and urban cultural associations directed especially at students and intellectuals. Each member of a clientele organization was responsible for maintaining a loose relationship with three nonmembers, thereby extending further the movement's reach into the grass roots of Vietnamese society. (Greene 1990, 95)

This political apparatus included an adjudication process to resolve conflicts over contributions to their cause. The Vietnamese Communists also reorganized military life in the village by creating self-defense units and security teams. And finally, they reorganized the village economy by creating collective enterprises. A by-product was an expanded tax base, the profits of which were used to fund their organization. In sum, the Vietnamese Communists were social, political, military, and economic entrepreneurs who tried to realize the full potential of village-level cooperation for promoting collective dissent.

5. Two other aspects of community facilitate social contracts: size (sect. 6.3.1) and internal competition (sect. 6.4).

6. But no one can wait forever. After a while, people begin to think that the group is a loser (sect. 3.6) and participation falls (e.g., Trotskyites in the United States).

7. While protest decreases with age, voting turnout increases.

8. One might also expect those who have children to care more about future generations than those who do not, and hence to be amenable to contractarian solutions. Consanguinity implies, in a certain sense, that the game is endless. One of Ostrom's (1990, 88) design principles for enduring, self-governing Common Property Resource institutions holds that such institutions work best where people expect their children to inherit the land. But collective dissent can be quite dangerous and time consuming. For people with children, cost considerations overwhelm discount rate considerations; those with family responsibilities therefore participate in little collective dissent (sect. 3.2.3).

9. An additional factor is a low probability of repression. Students "enjoy a special immunity because they are students and for that reason are expected, in the normal course of their college career, to indulge in a certain amount of rabble-rousing activity" (Chong 1991, 75).

10. Laqueur (1987, 77–78) reports that terrorists are mostly young people. Youth are also heavily involved in nationalist movements — Young Italy, Young Egypt, Young Turkey, and so on. Goldstone (1991, 136) cites some relevant literature.

11. Support for the homogeneity proposition among students of conflict is widespread. Zald and Berger (1978, 843–44) argue that mutually reinforcing cleavages, cohesiveness, symmetries, and equalities among subordinates lead them to challenge superordinates. Gurr (1970, 289) argues that "interaction is facilitated to the extent that the discontented are or see themselves as being alike." Turner (1986, 172) rephrases one of Coser's (1956) propositions as follows: "The fewer are the internal cleavages within conflict parties, the greater is a leader's capacity to persuade followers." Looking at the situation from the organizer's point of view, Kahn (1982, 81) raises the question, "How do you build a majority movement out of a group of minorities, many of whom conflict with, don't get along with, or don't share interests with each other?"

12. According to Dahrendorf (1959, 239, propositions 4.1.1.2–4.1.1.4) reinforcing cleavages superimpose one conflict on another and hence lead to violence. Turner (1986, 148) rephrases a proposition in Weber ([1924] 1968) as "the greater is the correlation of membership in class, status group, and

party (or alternatively, access to power, wealth, and prestige), the more intense is the level of resentment among those denied membership (or access), and hence, the more likely are they to withdraw legitimacy." Deutsch (1973, 82–84) argues that cross-cutting cleavages reduce CA and overlapping cleavages increase CA. Dahl (1966, 357–59) discusses how subcultural pluralism influences dissent. Gluckman (1960) argues that heterogeneity in dissident groups reduced conflict in Africa, a point modeled by Bates (1983, chap. 1). Eckstein (1989, 33) puts the argument as follows:

> The more local social and cultural ties are mutually reinforcing . . . the more likely villagers are to engage in collective defiance . . . When . . . communities are differentiated socially and economically into two distinct camps, commonly shared injustices are likely to be collectively resisted. By contrast, the more complex the local class structure, the less likely it is that grievances will be perceived to be collectively shared and collectively correctable. When kinship, patronage, and ritual ties crosscut class lines, collective solidarity is rare.

For more on the crosscutting cleavage argument, see Pruitt and Rubin (1986, 77). The parallel argument in voting studies is that people subject to crosspressure are less likely to vote (Berelson, Lazarsfeld, and McPhee 1954).

13. The success of student demonstrations is often associated with the homogeneity of students: "The frequency of student demonstrations and insurrections is partly attributable to the relative homogeneity and high degree of interaction characteristic of student culture" (Gurr 1970, 290).

14. On the success of ghetto riots in the United States, Gurr (1970, 290) observes that "the enforced homogeneity of the ghetto poor similarly has facilitated riots by black Americans."

15. Homogeneity is a characteristic that binds revolutionaries together. For example, "The American Revolution could scarcely have succeeded had it not been for the consensus on goals among young men of the colonial upper-middle classes, based on their common schooling and similar socioeconomic backgrounds, and their interaction in colonial politics and later in the Committees of Correspondence" (Gurr 1970, 290).

16. The success of worker movements is often attributed to homogeneity. Marx, for instance, argues that the homogenization of workers facilitates CA by workers (Sabia 1988, 53). Historians of the labor movement concur:

> The spectacle of uniform poverty suffered under identical conditions promoted the mutual awareness of the dispossessed. The working mass, meeting at the factory, met again in the sordid shacks and unhealthy sidestreets of the great industrial cities . . . That feeling of belonging to the same category of rejects, separated from the rest of the nation, was

to help give all the sense of belonging to a single class of pariahs, living outside the collectivity. (Gerard Dehove and Edward Dolleans, cited in Gurr 1970, 289)

17. Heterogeneity among peasants works against peasant CA. Scott (1985, 244) makes the following point with respect to a village in Malaysia: "The very complexity of the class structure of Sedaka mitigates against collective opinion and, hence, collective action on most issues."

18. Society-wide movements in caste-based societies are notoriously difficult to organize, as Welch (1980, 55) suggests: "The social divisions inherent in caste provided social strain and complicated collective action; although individual castes (*jati*) might be mobilized in favor of joint objectives, cooperation across *jati* lines was often difficult."

19. The failure of worker movements is often attributed to the development of a "labor aristocracy," or a privileged stratum within the working class (Katznelson 1986, 11). As Marshall (1983, 264) puts it, "Since labor is divided into segments with different market and work situations, and hence with different life-experiences, the absence of a unified class consciousness can readily be explained by the rise of labor aristocracies, by the division between new and traditional working classes, by the cleavages created by discrimination against minority groups, by the operation of dual or segmented labor markets, and so on." In the United States, for example, social diversity led to a fragmented labor movement and competition among workers, which left union organizers facing an uphill struggle (Hall and Ikenberry 1989, 45–46).

20. There is some evidence to support the differentiation-integration-action linkages. Slater (1967, 176) argues that studies of group psychology show that "a group . . . cannot effectively revolt so long as it perceives itself as a mob or mass, but only when it can differentiate clearly among its members." Michels's ([1919] 1962) classic study demonstrates that the success of dissident political parties depends upon the differentiation of their memberships (Nielsen 1985, 145).

21. Marwell, Oliver, and Prahl (1988, 508) suggest a resolution of the competing expectations: given a high level of mean interest in a PG, as heterogeneity increases, CA decreases; but given a low level of mean interest in the PG, as heterogeneity increases, CA increases (with a caveat for a skewed distribution).

22. Dissident entrepreneurs, in this respect, face the same tradeoff as leaders of democratic political parties. As Rose and Urwin (1969, 23) put it,

Within a somewhat protected market, leaders of political parties face a continuing dilemma. As the size of a party's vote increases, supporters tend to become increasingly heterogeneous in their characteristics and form increasingly difficult coalitions to manage . . . The more socially homogeneous the supporters become, the more limited is the party's potential and actual support within a society. This makes the task of internal party management easier, but reduces electoral success.

23. Such a test appears in the voting literature. Powell's (1982, 115–20) study of democracies found that nations that had a stronger social cleavages-voter turnout relationship also had higher levels of voter turnout.

24. So are corresponding theories of the origins of states. Levi (1988, 41) writes that "rarely, if ever, in history has a state emerged full blown from society. In general, the term *state formation* refers to the consolidation or takeover of an organization that already performs at least some of the functions of a state."

25. The key problem in using Tit-For-Tat is that the collective sanctions required to sustain conditional cooperation create a second-order free-rider problem: locating and punishing defectors may be prohibitively costly for the group (Coleman 1990, 270–73). These transaction costs are minimized by strong social ties.

26. Mutual expectations, moreover, help solve the multiple equilibria problem of Tit-For-Tat. Mutual expectations of conditional cooperation exist when conditional cooperation is familiar to dissidents, as when some preexisting organization provides experience in reciprocity. Such experience implies that people have reliable information about the preferences of others (and hence about their probability of cooperating).

27. Marx's followers realize that

> stratification cannot lead to collective action unless it also promotes informal organization among the stratified population. Peasants who live on their separate plots of land and only come together to exchange in a distant market place are unlikely to develop collective solidarity. On the other hand, workers who interact with each other regularly in the factory or Jews who are forced to live together in a ghetto possess communication networks and bases of trust that are essential for the development of a political organization. (Levi and Hechter 1985, 131–32)

As Alinsky (1946, 86) puts it, the protest group must be an "organization of organizations."

28. There are numerous supporters of the preexisting organization proposition. An early proponent was Chorley ([1943] 1973, 85):

> History shows that successful revolutions have invariably taken off from a springboard of properly organized community life. Whether the community life is organized in the interests of this or that class is of no

moment. The point is that it is organized. It is a fallacy to suppose that revolutions are ever the offspring of chaos and foul night.

Tilly has been a particularly forceful advocate of the preexisting organization proposition. He (1986, 4) argues that conflict is not disorder, and the closer we look at conflict "the more we discover order." Tilly (1978, 62–63) thus suggests that dissident groups utilize existing organizations and interpersonal networks. He refers to the combination of both factors as a community's "cat-net," or category plus network. (Related typological efforts include Tönnies's [1963] *gemeinschaft* or Oberschall's [1973, 120] horizontal dimension of community and Tönnies' [1963] *gesellschaft* or Oberschall's [1973, 120] vertical dimension of association). Tilly (1985, 730) therefore stresses the importance of "the prior existence of a social structure that already connects most individuals, and that changes and becomes more elaborate as a result of repeated communication among individuals . . . ties may well multiply and reinforce each other in the course of collective action, but previously existing ties form the mass base for mobilization and collective action." Many other supporters exist. Compared to the resource mobilization model of Zald and McCarthy (1990; also see McCarthy and Zald 1973, 1977) and Obserschall (1973), the political process model of McAdam (1982) emphasizes the importance of indigenous organization. McAdam (1982, 51) thus refers to the "indigenous organizational strength" that resides in the institutions and networks of cooperation among individuals. Curtis and Zurcher (1973) argue that protest organizations can be structurally integrated with informal and formal community organizations, creating a multiorganizational field. Zald and Berger (1978, 829, 845) suggest that "the preexisting networks, associations, and organizations of involved groups may facilitate or hinder collective action. The greater the associational density and the higher the proportion of organizational participants who are members of associations, the easier it is to mobilize." Fireman and Gamson (1979, 18) stress the importance of "long-standing organizations with a surplus of resources that they are ready and willing to contribute for the provision of a collective good. The surplus is a 'byproduct' of past mobilization maintained by the ongoing provision of selective incentives." Calhoun (1982, 176) maintains that "the larger a population aggregate, the more likely it is to depend on intermediate levels of association in order to act collectively; if it lacks such intermediate levels, or if they seek purposes conflicting with those desirable for the largest aggregate, the largest aggregate loses its capacity to act." Jackson, Peterson, Bull, Monsen, and Richmond (1960, 37) argue that "if a movement is to grow rapidly it cannot rely upon its own network of communication, but must capitalize on networks already in existence." Eschen, Kirk, and Pinard (1971, 530) maintain that "disorderly politics has an organizational substructure dragging people into activity just as does routine politics." Donati (1984, 843) argues that "the decision to join always involves a pre-existing relationship (friendship, kinship, association ties, etc.) with another individual already participating in the collective action." Hobsbawm and Rudé (1968, 58) suggest that "the stimulus for action was more likely to work where men habitually and daily met in large numbers." Others (also see Pollock 1982, 485) who point out that preexisting organizations are agents of mobilization include Lipset, Trow, and Coleman (1962), Taylor (1988, 68), Verba and Nie (1972, chap. 11), and Verba, Nie, and Kim (1978, chaps. 6, 7).

29. The preexisting organization proposition runs counter, however, to Kornhauser's (1959) classic argument. He maintains that high rates of oppositional mass mobilization are most likely where nonelites are available for direct mobilization by elites. Such a condition occurs where associational groups that mediate between elites and nonelites are lacking. Kornhauser, in effect, argues that as the preexisting organization of a community increases, collective dissent decreases.

30. Calhoun (1982, 176–77) thus writes that

> if the intermediate associations collectively act toward other goals than those of the class, these goals, whether or not they actually conflict, will divert attention and resources from the class as a whole, and its capacity for collective action is correspondingly reduced. A large potential collective actor, therefore, such as a class, may be internally differentiated into groups of such a size that their members may be fairly closely knit with each other; for the class rather than the groups to be the relevant locus of collective action, the different subgroups must be linked together in such a way that they are cohesive at the highest level. For class action to take place, the component units of the class, such as communities and crafts, must be strong, but their in-group association must not so completely predominate over their affiliation with other groups that they are not densely knit into a web of class relations.

31. See McAdam, McCarthy, and Zald (1988, 708), Barnes and Kasse (1979), Eschen, Kirk, and Pinard (1971), and Walsh and Warland (1983, 774–75). Systematic evidence for these claims appears in Gurr's cross-national studies of collective dissent. He (1970, 275) reports that dissidents usually come from groups with a preexisting formal organization, usually a political party. Participation in nonpolitical formal organizations is also strongly associated with participation in legal political organizations such as political parties and interest groups (Lipset, Trow, and Coleman 1962; Nie, Powell, and Prewitt 1969a, 1969b; Verba, Nie, and Kim 1978, 100–6).

32. Student movements emerge from student organizations. Orum (1972, 50) reports a positive relationship between the number of campus organiza-

tions to which a student belongs and participation in the student sit-in movement.

33. This movement's success has often been attributed to the prior growth of black colleges and black churches (Jenkins 1983, 532; McAdam 1982, 98–106, 125–28). McAdam (1986, 86) reports some more precise evidence: participants in the Freedom Summer project belonged to more organizations than nonparticipants. The formal organization corollary to the preexisting organization proposition was intuited by black power advocates of the late 1960s who argued that blacks must control their own community institutions before they could use those institutions as bases for protest.

34. The mode of production in the Canadian wheat belt led to many challenges and crises of production. Grain growers have tried to resist the fluctuations of the market economy by forming production and marketing cooperatives. These include "local, county, and state agencies for the purchase of implements and supplies and the sale of farm products, local grain elevators, and cooperative stores, the manufacture of farm machinery, banking, insurance, and even organizations for bringing direct trade between the American producer and the European consumer" (Buck, cited in Lipset 1971a, 19). The remote and isolated nature of production also forced grain growers to build their own community institutions. Lipset (1971a, 54) observes that "farmers have been forced to unite cooperatively to obtain telephone service, local roads, medical and hospital facilities, and other social services. Today 125,000 farmers hold almost 500,000 cooperative memberships; that is, on the average a farmer belongs to four or five cooperatives." Both economic and community organizations provided the basis for movements of agrarian social protest.

35. Hilton (1973, 217–18) demonstrates that prior organizational experience, gained from collecting taxes, running the manor court, and enforcing the bylaws of guild organizations, aided villagers in the English Rising of 1381.

36. Calhoun (1982, 176) argues that "for workers to be organized for class action requires a hierarchy of intermediate foci of association, each incorporating those below it. Without such intermediate associations, the possibility of class action is replaced by, at most, the simultaneous action of a number of mobs sharing common external characteristics." More specifically, almost all types of CA by workers have been attributed to preexisting formal organizations among workers.

- Working-class solidarity. Where social conditions included preexisting formal organizations, the "emergence" of the working class was facilitated. For example, preexisting formal organizations of journeymen, masters, and artisans were the backbone of the British working class. Community-based craft guilds, for instance, proved amenable to political mobilization. More generally, several preexisting social, religious, and economic organizations, such as Friendly Societies of workers that covered sickness, unemployment, and funeral expenses, combined with Methodists and Guilds to create the British working class (Thompson 1966).

- Trade unions. Labor organizations have often drawn upon the many social institutions created by the working class. A solidified working class helped create, for example, the British trade unions.
- Political parties. Electoral organizations, in turn, often draw upon economic organizations. Thus, British trade unions helped to create the British Labour party.
- Protest organizations. Trade unions also facilitate dissident protest organizations. Many other preexisting formal organizations also inspired working class protest organizations. As Thompson (1984) reports, preexisting Working Men's Associations, Radical Associations, branches of the Great Northern Union, Democratic Associations, and Political Unions underlay the Chartist movement.
- Strike activity. Not only trade unions, but also other preexisting formal organizations facilitate strike activity by workers. One of Shorter and Tilly's (1974) principal themes is that the extent and intensity of strike activity in a locale is a function of the prior organization of workers in that locale, and the existence of a context or structure which identifies and accumulates grievances as well as facilitates CA.

37. Fuentes and Frank (1989, 184) argue that many communities in the developing world organize to provide themselves with basic services (e.g., health, hygiene, child care, illiteracy programs, food distribution) and that these organizations form the basis for social movements and guerrilla organizations. Walton (1984, 144) points out that the precursors to the Mau Mau in Kenya were certain national associations (the EAA and KA), the forerunners of La Violence in Colombia were political parties (UNIR), and the progenitors to the Huks in the Philippines were political groupings (Sakdal). Labor organizations are often predecessors of guerrilla organizations. Walton (1984, 58) writes, for example, that "the Hukbalahap resistance movement was formed in March 1942, drawing its cadre and organizational base directly from preexisting confederations of peasants and labor such as the KPMP, PKM, AMT, and CLM, as well as the Socialist and Communist parties." Martic (1975, 132) offers another example from guerrilla warfare in Africa: "Cabral looked to the longshoreman of Guinea and Cape Verde for the nucleus of his guerrilla forces. These workers had already acquired significant experience in the strikes and protest against the police."

38. The American Civil War mobilized preexisting formal organizations. Olson (1990, 25) observes that the southern states were organized. Each "had a governor, a legislature, and bit of a bureaucracy. In other words, there were already selective incentives — people on the payroll. There were state taxes already being collected, and this meant that the southern states could overcome the problem of collective action and put on a real fight."

39. The preexisting organization of the independent churches, the New Model Army, and county militias were important to the English Revolution. The Country "party" in England, moreover, was particularly crucial to the revolution (Hagopian 1974, 182).

40. Merchants' committees, committees of correspondence, colonial legislatures, New England town meetings, sons of liberty, committees of safety, the first Continental Congress, and local militias were important to the American Revolution. Freemasonry, quasi-masonic fraternities, masonic lodges, and secret revolutionary brotherhoods may also have played an important part.

41. Numerous preexisting formal organizations helped start the French Revolution. Skocpol (1979, 123) observes that the following was part of the calling of the Estates-General in France just before the Revolution: "In each rural community every man twenty-five or older who paid any amount of taxes was eligible to participate in a meeting of the elected representatives to the *bailliage* assembly and drew up a *cahier de doléances* expressing local grievances." Preexisting organizations that assisted bourgeoisie activism included societies de pensée, free masons, Jacobin clubs, revolutionary clubs, citizen guards, agricultural societies, philanthropic academies, teaching institutions, reading rooms, mesmerist societies, political clubs, "national" or "patriot" clubs, and the committee of thirty. For the nobles, preexisting organizations included *parlements*, provincial estates, and seigneurial courts. Preexisting formal organizations also helped to sustain the Revolution once it began. Organizations active during the Revolution that supported the municipal rioters included journeymen's unions, craft guilds, local committees, militias, district assemblies, the commune of Paris, and city-wide councils. Those supporting the bourgeoisie included unofficial municipal governments, both in small towns and in Paris, and reorganized local civic guards (Lefebvre 1947; Rudé 1959).

42. Preexisting organizations important to the February Revolution included local and provincial dumas, zemstvos, and landed estates (elected popular representative organs). Several preexisting organizations were specifically important to the outbreak of the Revolution on February 23: food queues, off-duty soldiers, workers locked out of a large factory complex, and women workers leaving factories to celebrate Women's Day (Kuran 1989,

63). The preexisting organizations most important to the October Revolution were the soviets. As Trotsky (cited in Greene 1990, 101) writes, "Attempts to lead the insurrection directly through the party nowhere produced results." Hence, "Power was not won by the Bolshevik party, but by the Bolshevik party working through the dual power structure represented by the soviets" (Greene 1990, 101).

43. The key preexisting organizations for the Revolution of 1911 included gentry-led self-defense associations and study groups, as well as newly elected local, provincial, and national representative assemblies.

44. Goldfrank (1979, 153–56) indicates the important of village organizations to this revolution.

45. Popkin (1979, 215) reports that "returning to Asia, [Ho Chi Minh] formed a Revolutionary Youth League (1925–1929) from several hundred young Vietnamese, most of who were either members of preexisting, anticolonial organizations like the Tam Tam Xa (Heart to Heart Association) and the Tan Viet (Revolutionary Party) or lycée students expelled for anti-French activities." Popkin (1979, 262) also indicates that several religiously-oriented movements that competed with the Communists drew upon preexisting organizations: "All three religions utilized preexisting religious organizers to make contact with persons able to relate their message and vouch for them with other villagers." For example, "a major source of the Cao Dai base were the small-scale sects and secret societies already in existence" (Popkin 1979, 196). Cao Dai was thus able to consolidate many local sects into a nation-wide movement (Popkin 1979, 247).

46. Preexisting formal organizations were equally important to the Iranian Revolution. Formal religious organizations mattered (Snow and Marshall 1984, 138–42). Farhi (1990, 94–95) writes that

> the Iranian religious community has always had certain economic and political resources that have given the ulama the organizational independence to react again state encroachments. Economic resources have included control over charitable/religious endowments (*awgaf*) given to institutions like schools, mosques, shrines, and hospitals. The ulama have also kept direct control over certain religious taxes, the so-called *khums* (one-fifth of agricultural and commercial profits) and *zakat* (levied on various categories of wealth and spent on purposes specified in the Quran), and the voluntary payments, *sadaga* (spent for purposes of charity) and *nuzur* (made for vows).

Formal economic organizations also mattered. Farhi (1990, 17) argues that "opposition to the shah was made possible by the existence of autonomous, urban communal enclaves connected to the traditional centers of petty-commodity production." Preexisting religious and economic institutions combined into a network of relationships. This provided the Revolution's urban infrastructure. Farhi (1990, 70) thus maintains that religious "bonds were constantly reinforced, since many of the regularly employed members of these communities were employed in the bazaars . . . The religious establishment, which continued to adjudicate commercial disputes and provide religious education for the bazaars, in turn, used the religious taxes received from well-to-do bazaaris to provide personalized welfare services for the devout urban poor."

47. The FSLN developed strategic alliances with Christian-based communities. The church was thus at the center of a network of underground urban institutions that supported the guerrillas: "Clerics working in poor barrios, in the countryside, or with university and high school student protesters became contact points between the FSLN and the Christian neighborhood organizations throughout Nicaragua" (Booth 1985, 136). The FSLN operated in the following way: it "did not enter urban communities as a political party and attract support on that basis. Instead, it operated through local or intermediate organizations embedded in, and respectful of, everyday practices and beliefs of the people" (Farhi 1990, 78). These local power structures assisted the guerrillas in raising fighters, stockpiling food, and locating medical supplies.

48. Methodism assisted Chartism and Radicalism in Britain (Hobsbawm 1959, 130). Methodism aided the organization of the working class in England by increasing its familiarity with organizational techniques: raising money; making rules, policies, and platforms; communicating with fellow workers, allies, and other organizations; and holding caucuses and meetings (Thompson 1966, 42). Religious leaders soon became political leaders: "The early leaders of British trade unions and labor political groups were men who had first served as officers or Sunday-school teachers in the Methodist or other nonconformist churches" (Lipset, Trow, and Coleman 1962, 262). Hobsbawm (1959, 140) calls Methodism "a school of cadres." Zagorin (1982a, 159) observes that "the structure of the Calvinist communities facilitated their adaptation to political activism" in the rebellions of sixteenth and seventeenth century Europe. The Catholic Church in Poland assisted Solidarity. Gurr (1970, 313) recounts the importance of the church to Argentinean collective dissent:

Even so well-institutionalized an organization as the Catholic Church of Argentina supported and provided one of two organizational foci — the other being the Army — for the anti-Perón movement in 1954 and 1955.

The Church shifted from its neutrality toward the regime to active opposition, by the rank-and-file and activists if not the hierarchy, after the suppression of religious schools, the burning of several churches, and verbal attacks on the Church by Perón. In June 1955, 250,000 members of Catholic Action demonstrated against the regime in Buenos Aires, and Church members were widely active in the conspiratorial activity that laid the groundwork for the coup d'etat in September.

There are many other examples of church-led protest in Latin America (Levine and Mainwaring 1989).

49. Religiously inspired protest has often taken the form of various other-worldly social movements that are only weakly rooted in formal organizations. One may distinguish three types of other-worldly social movements. The first is millenarianism, or "the general category of movements which claims to replace the sinful, corrupt, and soon to be destroyed community with one that is directly inspired and informed by a religious rebirth" (Hagopian 1974, 24). The second is messianism, which is "characterized by the exalted position of a charismatic leader or messiah over the community of adepts" (Hagopian 1974, 24). The third is nativism, which is "any conscious, organized attempt on the part of a society's members to revive or perpetuate selected aspects of its culture" (Ralph Linton, cited in Hagopian 1974, 21). All three types of other-worldly social movements have spawned this-worldly political movements. Examples include the Taiping rebellion in China and the Cao Dao Sect in Vietnam. Welch (1980, 65) argues that this pattern was common in Africa:

> Religious movements provided many African societies means of coping with the strains imposed by colonial rule, as a surrogate for political protests banned by the administration. Adaptation of Christian messages — especially those dealing with equality of believers — cloaked criticism of British rule. Religious protest was a step toward political action. Several Mau Mau participants have suggested in their memoirs that indigenous sects derived from Christian teachings . . . marked a stage of their pilgrimage toward rebellion.

50. Finer (1976, 5) writes that "the armed forces have three massive political advantages over civilian organizations: a marked superiority of organization, a highly emotionalized symbolic status, and a monopoly of arms." Gurr (1970, 268) argues that the most important contribution that preexisting military organization makes to collective dissent is equipment and training. This argument was put forth earlier by Mosca (1939, 212), who asserts that "a serious insurrection by peasants is possible only in places where they have a

certain habit of handling arms, or at least where hunting or brigandage, or family and neighborhood feuds, have kept people familiar with the sound of gunfire." Prior military experience and organization was important in both the English and American revolutions. The military experience and organization acquired fighting the Japanese was particularly important to the subsequent rebellions in Indonesia, Vietnam, Malaya, China, and the Philippines. Chorley ([1943] 1973, 181) argues a different point: "It is segregation from civilian life which emasculates the soldier as a citizen. The more he is segregated and subjected to the military machine the more he is likely to forget his citizenship."

51. Taylor (1982, 67) implies that where collective dissent is based on kinship, lineage, or clan it has a good chance of being successful. Wilson (1973, 204) suggests that "neighborhood organizations are easier when they can grow upon preexisting informal social networks — friendship, cliques, ethnic ties, political affiliations, or church membership." Waterman (1981, 563) observes "the omnipresence of primary, usually communal, ties at the core of" collective dissent, maintaining that "failed rebellions, social movements, and interest groups [are] replete with examples of the absence of such durable primary groups." Finally, Calhoun (1988, 135–36) holds that "the informal bonds of community relationships may provide powerful selective incentives, and a form of pre-existing organization ready to mobilize in a variety of actions." Calhoun (1988, 131) thus refers to the "radicalism of tradition" and suggests that "traditional communities provide the social foundations for widespread popular mobilizations."

52. McAdam (1986, 79–81) found that participants in the 1964 Freedom Summer project had "stronger ties" to other participants than to those who ultimately decided not to participate. Bolton (1972, 558) found that members of two peace groups "were already associated with persons who belonged to or were organizing the peace group, and were recruited through these interpersonal channels." Lipset, Trow, and Coleman (1962, 77) argue that the printers had a variety of formal and informal friendship cliques — sporting clubs, teams, lodges, and veteran's organizations — which brought printers together in their leisure time. Such informal associations assisted the printers' union, strikes, and political activities. McAdam, McCarthy, and Zald (1988, 707–9) review some further evidence on this point.

53. The importance of informal social networks (McAdam, McCarthy, and Zald 1988, 707–9) has been examined for the case of the women's movement (Evans 1979) and the U.S. civil rights movement (Wilson and Orum 1976). Preexisting informal networks, according to Pinard (1971, chap. 11), were significant to the Social Credit party in Quebec. In their study of two antipornography organizations, Curtis and Zurcher (1973) likewise were struck by the prominence of preexisting informal networks. Waterman

(1981, 563) reports that "the religious community of the Sokagakkai is the basis for a movement-party." Nagel (1982, 38) claims that American Indians mobilize, at least partially, along tribal lines. Finally, informal social cliques are often behind military coups. As Finer (1976, 30) indicates,

> The armed forces has always been — by the closed and intimate nature of the personal relations they foster — peculiarly susceptible to infiltration and the establishment of networks of conspiracy. Often there we have, every so often, fascinating glimpses which attest to their existence but do little more: the Freemason network in the Spanish army of 1820; the secret patriot societies that began to honeycomb the Japanese army after 1930; the Grupo de Officiales Unidos in Argentina in 1943, likewise the military leagues in the pre-1939 Balkans, such as the "Black Hand" and the "White Hand" in Serbia, the officers league in Bulgaria (1922), and in Greece (1909 and later).

54. Thompson (1984, 118–19) emphasizes that traditional values and informal community ties aided working class protest at the beginning of the industrial revolution in Britain:

> In the towns and villages of Britain thousands of anonymous men and women organised the Chartist movement, using traditional forms of processions, carnivals, theatrical performances, camp meetings, sermons and services to put across the message of the six points. Flags, banners, caps of liberty, scarves, sashes and rosettes appeared on public occasions. Slogans from the Bible, from literature and from earlier radical movements decorated the banners and placards they carried. Hymns and songs were written and sung, poems were declaimed. Every aspect of the religious and cultural life of the communities was brought into service to press home the Chartist message.

Calhoun (1982) is particularly concerned with how tradition and community served as "the social foundations of popular radicalism during the industrial revolution." He (1982, 8) maintains that "reactionary radicals were able to base a good deal of collective action on the sound foundations which their local and craft communities gave them. From the beginning of the nineteenth century through Luddism and the parliamentary reform agitation of the 1810s these personal bonds among kin, neighbors, friends and co-workers provided the primary basis for mobilization." Calhoun (1982, 7) therefore stresses tradition and community over ideology and class: "In the early part of the industrial revolution, community was the crucial social bond unifying workers for collective action. Only gradually were either formal or informal patterns of organization extended to unify the class subjected to capitalist exploitation."

55. Taylor (1988, 81) refers to the "wide agreement amongst historians that the local communities provided the social basis and organizational framework of peasant rebellion." Moore (1966, 475–76) observes that there are two types of peasant solidarity: conservative solidarity results from peasant/landlord ties that facilitate social control; revolutionary solidarity results from ties that facilitate collective dissent. Moore also suggests that patterns of peasant interaction determine patterns of peasant solidarity that, in turn, influence peasant struggles. Landsberger (1974, 46) reports that strong communities with previous experience in cooperation were essential for peasant rebellions. Zagorin (1982a, 86) suggests that "agrarian rebellion almost invariably began in the mobilization of village communities, their members summoned to rise by the violent ringing of church bells in the parishes and then flowing together in growing crowds fed from all parts of the countryside."

56. The best documented examples may come from historical studies in Europe. Zagorin (1982a, 194) reports that in the German peasant war, "mobilization followed communal lines as crowds of peasants belonging to a particular lordship, district, or jurisdiction streamed together carrying arms. Communities seem sometimes to have decided as a body to rebel. They then formed bands, or *Haufen*, which were organized and chose leaders paralleling the familiar *Dorf*, or village organization." Thus, according to Zagorin (1982a, 261), "the German peasant war . . . was fundamentally a *Gemeinde* movement, or revolution of communities, dedicated to the formation of *new* communities reflecting the common good." Brenner (1976, 49) also argues that the sixteenth century German peasant rebellion was decisively influenced by the strength of communal institutions. Hobsbawm and Rudé (1968, 67) report that Friendly Societies (benefit clubs providing mutual exchange and aid) proved important to many local rural movements in medieval Europe. Rudé (1964, chaps. 1, 2) shows that eighteenth century grain riots followed the principal communal lines of communication and transportation. Zagorin (1982a, 86) suggests that seventeenth-century agrarian rebellions in France were rooted in the union of peasant communities. Hilton (1973, 212) reports that in the English Rising of 1381 rebels seized "on those elements in the literary and homiletic tradition which would legitimize their actions." Skocpol (1979, 120) suggests that French peasants enjoyed communal lands and self-governing political organizations. The cooperative economic and political relations that they learned assisted their rebellion during the French Revolution. Skocpol (1979, 129, 132) also suggests that Russian peasants

enjoyed the collective ownership of land through *obshchina* and the rights of self-government through *mir.* These relations facilitated their rebellion during the Russian Revolution. There are also examples from contemporary less developed countries. Wolf (1969, 28) points out that socially cohesive villages were the basis of Zapata's support during the Mexican Revolution. Eckstein (1989, 33) uses studies of peasant upheavals in Latin America to make a similar point: "Agriculturals who maintain ties through community-based cultural and social institutions, and not merely or even necessarily through production, tend to perceive grievances as commonly shared." Finally, Bates (1983) demonstrates that preexisting communal organization influenced collective dissent and rural politics in Africa.

57. Moore (1966, 330–41) suggests that the lack of relatively strong and cohesive village-level institutions in India was a key factor in the absence of a peasant revolution in India. Hechter and Brustein (1980, 1080) cite evidence from fourteenth and fifteenth century Europe that a feudal mode of interaction imbued a petty commodity mode of solidarity which, in turn, induced sedentary peasant politics.

58. Tilly (1986) describes this process in great detail. He reports that the recruitment of dissidents from informal social gatherings — markets, fairs, processions, festivals, hangings, and local electoral assemblies — has declined, to be replaced by deliberately organized meetings, strikes, rallies, and demonstrations.

59. Note that a similar lesson has been learned in voting studies: door-to-door canvassing by local precinct workers has a demonstrable impact on aggregate voter turnout and hence the margin of victory (Price and Lupter 1973, 433).

60. DeNardo (1985) shows how the spatial distribution of dissident preferences affects the political opportunities inherent in this strategy.

61. Italy was witness to two examples of the radical left joining the moderate left's demonstrations to exploit the opportunity to radicalize a large dissident group. Tarrow (1989, 246) reports that "industrial disputes, which were led by the unions, were used as occasions for the New Left groups to expose their 'betrayal' of the workers." Similarly, the Italian Communist party's relatively passive demonstrations against U. S. involvement in Vietnam were radicalized by leftist groups (Tarrow 1989, 249).

62. A frequent aggregation strategy used by interest groups is that of holding dinners honoring prominent supporters.

63. Esping-Anderson (1985, 5) points out that many leftist movements created social organizations as separate institutions, in opposition to the state: "Many social democratic parties were originally 'ghetto' parties. Until World War I, all three Scandinavian social democratic parties followed the

model of the later communist parties, building a separate socialist world by means of athletic associations, boy scout movements, educational institutions, organized leisure activities and so forth." Waterman (1981, 563) recounts another example: "The efforts to create local entertainments, clubs, concerts, fêtes, community singing, parades, auxiliary services, meeting rooms, welfare provisions, etc . . . tied the workers in the textile industry of the Nord to the Socialist party while at the same time tying them to each other." Communist-controlled "front" organizations have typically included groups for youths, students, women, trade unionists, and professionals. The Mensheviks founded trade unions and workers' clubs. More recently, the new social movements have created communal institutions, self-help projects, shops, and so on, to permit their isolation and autonomy from the state. Melucci (1984, 830) suggests that in new social movements "people are offered the possibility of another experience of time, space, interpersonal relations." He maintains that

> the normal situation of today's "movement" is to be a network of small groups submerged in everyday life which requires a personal involvement in experiencing and practising cultural innovation. They emerge only on specific issues as for instance the big mobilizations for peace, abortion, against nuclear policy etc. The submerged network, although composed of separate small groups, is a system of exchange (persons and information circulating along the network, some agencies such as local free radios, bookshops, magazines providing a certain unity). (Melucci 1984, 829)

64. Perry (1984, 447) asserts that the reason there are no peasant rebellions under communism is that "the very policies of socialist agriculture thus worked to encourage Wolf's closed corporate community, Scott's Moral economy and Migdal's inward-oriented village in the Chinese countryside. Rather than set peasants adrift from the familiar bonds of local society, state building under socialism meant a reinforcement of traditional kinship and community ties." Eckstein makes a similar point with regard to Mexico:

> In post-revolutionary Mexico, village structures have to date not sparked much collective defiance among economically hard-pressed peasants. There, local groups have lost much of their autonomy through incorporation into national government and party institutions, and local leadership has been coopted through patronage into national institutional structures . . . Thus, the experience of Mexico and Bolivia suggests that agrarian revolutions that both strengthen village ties and

preserve local institutional autonomy are more likely than those that do not to spark subsequent village-based mobilizations. (Eckstein 1989, 34–35)

65. As Farhi (1990, 18) notes,

During ordinary periods in peripheral cities, popular organizations aimed at improved social relations for subordinate classes are generally closely allied with, if not controlled by, state bureaucracies. In revolutionary situations, however, the state loses its ability to continue its clientelist relationship with these organizations, and important bonds are forged between subordinate classes and organizations linked to other social groupings. It is within this context the preexisting social bonds and the organizational potential existing in the poor urban communities (long established or more recent) become important and decisive. The weakening of the state allows for the loosening of methods developed to control potentially volatile poor sectors. This, in turn, eases the transformation of friendship and kinship networks, as well as neighborhood and religious organizations, into political organizations or opens the way for strategic alliances among external organizations operating within the poor urban settlements.

66. Moore (1966, 217), for example, argues that in the conflict between Chinese bandits and Imperial authorities during the peasant rebellion of 1852–68, "both rebels and Imperial authorities could manipulate the local social structure with about the same degree of ease or difficulty."

67. Machiavelli ([1514] 1961, 42, 47) argues that the Prince's absenteeism from the far-flung parts of his realm leads people to believe that their interests are being disregarded or neglected and hence encourages collective dissent. Weber ([1924] 1968, 1051) recognizes that geographically dispersed states are harder to administer and hence encourage collective dissent: "Even under purely bureaucratic patrimonialism no administrative technique could prevent that, as a rule, the individual parts of the realm evaded the ruler's influence the more, the farther away they were from his residence." More modern versions of the argument exist. Goodwin and Skocpol (1989, 497) maintain that

the growth of revolutionary movements is made even easier when rebels can operate in peripheral areas that the authoritarian regimes they oppose are unable to control. This happens when authoritarian regimes have never fully penetrated certain areas (as in Central American and

Lusophone Africa), when they lose control of areas due to war or invasion (as in Southeast Asia), or when they are unable to prevent neighboring countries from harboring revolutionaries . . . If a kind of administrative vacuum already exists on the exclusionary regime's territory, or it suddenly emerges, then the task of the armed revolutionaries will be easier.

Welch (1980, 24) suggests that

> in such marginal areas, the writ of government receives little attention. Inhabitants prize their distinctive way of life, and resent infringements of it. Able to take refuge in readily-defended redoubts, they resist the intrusion of "outside" ways — including, naturally enough, the taxes, conscription, and legal codes of the central government. In short, these settings encourage a sense of psychological separation from the national political system that parallels, and to a large extent is reinforced by, the physical separateness of the regions themselves. They become reservoirs for potential rebellion.

Laqueur (1987, 393) also recognizes the advantages that an inaccessible terrain holds for dissidents, arguing that "guerrilla movements have usually preferred regions that are not easily accessible such as mountain ranges, forests, jungles, and swamps, in which they are difficult to locate and in which the enemy cannot deploy his full strength."

68. Goldfrank (1979, 156) stresses rebels' geographical advantages during the Mexican Revolution. Wolf (1969, 291) suggests that peasants living "in a peripheral area outside the domains of landlord control [and hence] whose settlements are only under marginal control from the outside" are potential rebels. He (1969, 293) also maintains that "frontier areas quite often show a tendency to rebel against the central authorities, regardless of whether they are inhabited by peasants or not." He offers the examples of China, Mexico, Vietnam, and Cuba. Migdal (1974, 236) reports that border areas and rear areas in China scored the majority of Communist successes. Distance from the capital and the corresponding difficulties in communications were important factors in the French, Russian, and Chinese peasant revolts of the seventeenth century (Mousnier 1970, 337). For additional examples, see Gurr (1970, 263).

69. In the CA literature, Taylor (1982, 32) argues that Tit-For-Tat requires a stable community (e.g., one in which dissidents are likely to meet each other again in the future); Olson (1982, 41) suggests that stable boundaries contribute to the cartelization of a nation; and one of Ostrom's (1990,

88) design principles for enduring, self-governing Common Property Resource institutions is a stable population. In the conflict literature, Lasswell and Kaplan (1950, 35) suggest that "the morale of a group varies inversely with its circulation." For an alternative model that suggests that exit does not damage the Tit-For-Tat solution, see Schuessler (1989).

70. An exception is where immigrants carry traditions of dissent with them (e.g., the U.S. Communist movement in the 1920s and 1930s drew much support from recent immigrants).

71. Some comes from less developed nations. Huntington (1968, 278–81) reports that new urban migrants — the lumpenproletariat of urban shanty towns, *fauelas, ranchos, barriadas* — are conservative and not revolutionary. For the unskilled, political radicalism increases as the length of residence increases (Huntington 1968, 281–83). Hence, second-generation urban dwellers are more revolutionary than those of the first generation. Additional evidence on the urbanization-dissent corollaries comes from studies of the U.S. civil rights movement. Coleman (1957, 21–22) maintains that more integrated groups tend to be the first to join community conflicts. There is also evidence that participants in black riots were more likely to have been raised in the ghetto than to have been recent migrants from the rural South (Gurr 1970, 99). Hence, as length of residence in the ghetto increased, participation in riots in the United States increased. Finally, there is evidence on the urbanization-dissent corollaries from eighteenth-and nineteenth-century France. Tilly (1969, 26–29) argues that there is no direct correlation between the rate of urbanization and political violence. Moreover, the participants in urban upheavals were not new migrants acting outside of established communal institutions, but rather were established urban workers, acting within the context of organized political movements. Hence, rapid urbanization dampened, rather than spurred, violent protest.

72. Tilly (1964, 86) points out that several students of conflict in the nineteenth century accepted the concentration argument (e.g., Vidal de la Blache and Siegfried). The contemporary supporters of this proposition are also numerous. Freeman (1979, 176) maintains that "a major factor affecting the costs of mobilizing resources is their density . . . Enormous resources are required to reach, let alone mobilize, aggrieved groups that are atomized and scattered throughout the population. Those that are concentrated can be mobilized fairly easily." Taylor (1982, 27) argues that "the total amount of communication, or the relative density of communication channels, or the members' capacity for communication with each other" facilitates Tit-For-Tat among dissidents. One of Ostrom's (1990, 88) design principles for enduring, self-governing Common Property Resource institutions is that individuals live side by side. The concentration proposition is also consistent

with Deutsch et al.'s (1957, 51) view of the importance of "unbroken links of social communication" for the origins of national integration. For a more intensive review of this literature, see McAdam, McCarthy, and Zald (1988, 703).

73. The size issue is considered in section 6.3.1.

74. International counterrevolutionary efforts will also mostly fail. Hegemons or zealots (sect. 3.1) are probably crucial for overcoming the counterrevolutionaries' CA problem.

75. Marx held these views. See Elster (1985, 354–55), Sabia (1988, 53), Calhoun (1988, 132–37), and Weede (1985, 48).

76. As Gurr (1970, 265) puts it, "Crowds of dissidents are most likely to form in cities, not in rural areas." This corollary to the concentration proposition finds support in the urban studies literature. Park and his followers emphasize the importance of the physical layout of a community for CA. Tilly (1964, 86) points out that "recent analyses of French political geography . . . have uniformly shown the tendency for 'agglomerated' communities to have higher proportions voting in national elections than 'dispersed' communities do."

77. There are, however, two qualifications to the urbanization-dissent linkage. Recall that the preexisting organization proposition (sect. 5.2.3) implies that new migrants to cities will not engage in much collective dissent. The implication is that urbanization initially dampens, but eventually accelerates, collective dissent. A second qualification is that police and militaries are also concentrated in urban areas. Hence, Gurr (1970, 266) argues that "the urban environment facilitates turmoil, but not internal war."

78. "As I read the evidence," Moore (1966, 475, emphasis in original) writes, "the absence of solidarity (or more precisely a state of weak solidarity, since some cooperation always exists) puts severe difficulties in the way of *any* political action." Moore (1966, 477) thus suggests that "Marx caught the essence of the situation when he compared French villages made up of small peasant holdings to sacks of potatoes." And many others arrive at the same conclusion. Banfield (1958), for example, argues that the lack of peasant solidarity in Italy, or what he calls the presence of "amoral familism" (competition among village families), inhibited cooperative village action.

79. Huntington (1968, 290), in particular, stresses the point: "The city is the center of opposition within the country; the middle class is the focus of opposition within the city; the intelligentsia is the most active opposition group within the middle class; and the students are the most coherent and effective revolutionaries within the intelligentsia." He (1968, 371) maintains that "if there is any cleavage which is virtually universal in modernizing countries, it is the cleavage between government and university. If the presi-

dential palace is the symbol of authority, the student union building is the symbol of revolt."

80. A classic example of student involvement in revolution occurred in Russia: "Russian students were in the vanguard of the revolutionary movement in the last decades of the nineteenth century and were quite active in the abortive revolution of 1905. Afterwards, however, changes in educational policy and in the social background of students so altered their political inclinations that they ended up as a 'relative bastion of patriotism and order against the Bolshevik trend'" (Hagopian 1974, 301). Another classic example of student involvement in revolution occurred in China. The May 4th Movement in China in 1919 was launched by students and educators. Barnett (1968, 47) reports that in 1948 students were the most active and vocal opposition group. He notes "an increasing alienation of students from the Central Government and a definite shift to the Left, in the sense that more and more students are showing sympathy toward the Chinese Communist Party, and now regard Communist takeover as the only alternative to what they consider an intolerable situation."

81. Wickham-Crowley (1989, 141–42) reports a positive relationship between the expansion of university enrollments in Latin America and leftist guerrilla movements. Goldstone (1986b, 302–3) observes a positive relationship between the expansion of university enrollments and the Puritan Revolution in seventeenth century England.

82. For further arguments and evidence on the urban population density-collective dissent relationship, see Galler, Gove, and McPherson (1972).

83. For the English and French revolutions, see Goldstone (1991). Greene (1990, 155) offers two additional examples: "The population of Paris grew rapidly between 1800 and 1850 and thereby laid the basis for the mass participation that marked the revolutions of 1830 and 1848. Between 1800 and 1900 the population of Moscow increased by 400 percent and the population of St. Petersburg increased by 500 percent."

84. As Gurr (1970, 265) argues, "If the dissident group is also compact, the crowd setting provides its members with a shield of anonymity that temporarily can be" effective for dissent. A principal reason is that in crowds, people "are likely to think that they can get away with [expressing dissent] because they cannot readily be identified by security personnel" (Gurr 1970, 265).

85. The incompleteness of social contract theories of social order have made them a subject of some clever derision. Pufendorf (cited in Sabine 1973, 491) observes that "the fiction of a social contract must be helped out with the further fiction of unanimous consent." Okun (cited in Rosen 1985, 1149) suggests that there is an "invisible handshake" that parallels the invisi-

ble hand. And Steiner (1978, 295) asks, "Can a social contract be signed by an invisible hand?"

## CHAPTER 6

1. Weber ([1924] 1968, 241–45) maintains that in times of crisis and stress, charismatic leaders appear who express, explain, and solve discontent in a revolutionary way. Dahrendorf (1959, 179) suggests that leadership is important to "quasi-groups." Wesson (1967, 78) insists that "political parties, movements or rebellions usually look to a strong individual for positive action and clear policy." Gamson (1990, 311, col. 39) tries to assess how important a dominant leader is to a challenging group's success.

2. A similar argument has been used to explain the emergence of nation-states (Taylor 1982, 129–39).

3. Note that the question, When will entrepreneurs arise?, is similar to the question, Which solution to the Rebel's Dilemma will be used, Planned or Unplanned Order, Association or Community? And it is similar to the question, Is spontaneous collective dissent possible? The former issue is discussed in section 9.1, the latter one in section 8.1.

4. Many argue that "the desertion of the intellectuals" is a precursor of dissent and revolution. An early proponent was Pareto ([1920] 1980, 272–79). He argues that collective dissent is due to an established, but declining elite that faces an aggressive insurgent elite who could not achieve ruling positions in the old regime. More recently, Gurr (1970, 336) writes of "elite relative deprivation," which "is perhaps most common among men who have elite characteristics but not high value positions — the intrinsic elite, in Pareto's term — for example, the unemployed intelligentsia in less-developed countries, and competent men and women barred from advancement by discriminatory barriers in Western societies. Elite [relative deprivation] is also common among members of extrinsic elites: political leaders barred from electoral activity, entrepreneurs subject to restrictive legislation, military officers given what they regard as inadequate resources." Kling (1956) argues that Latin American elites lack adequate opportunities for upward economic mobility and hence turn to political office in order to satisfy their ambitions. A syndrome of coups and countercoups results.

5. Brinton (1965, 60) observes that large parts of the middle and upper classes faced limited mobility opportunities in all of the classical European revolutions. North with Pool (1965, 320) reports that "to a notable extent, [Kuomintang and Communist] leadership elites were composed of culturally alienated intellectuals - men and women of well-to-do families who had removed themselves from the orthodox stream of their society's traditional culture." Both elite groups, moreover, derived largely from families descend-

ing, rather than ascending, on the social hierarchy. Skocpol (1979, 164–68) attributes revolutionary outcomes to the actions of "marginal social elites." Further evidence that revolutionary leaders were upwardly immobile comes from the predominance of Jews in European movements of the Left. Jews are a classic example of an excluded minority. Given tsarist antisemitism, for example, one should not be surprised to find Jews overrepresented among Russian revolutionaries (Chamberlin [1935] 1987, 35; Zimmermann 1983, 308).

6. AlRoy (1966, 16–21) observes that very few peasant struggles are led by peasants and that peasant leaders who have rural origins acquire military and organizational experience outside of the peasant village. Laqueur (1987, 329) reports that most Latin American guerrilla leaders come from a middle- or upper-class background. More generally, studies of revolutionary leaders demonstrate that most leaders come from the higher classes, the middle and upper socioeconomic strata, and especially from the intelligentsia (Hagopian 1974, 298; Greene 1990, 42–43). Seton-Watson (1951, 263), for example, finds that the intelligentsia has dominated most twentieth-century revolutionary and conspiratorial movements.

7. Hence, neither the general public nor middle class consumers are likely to organize without the help of entrepreneurs (Jenkins 1983, 531). The experience of Common Cause and other public interest lobbies are examples.

8. Knight (1921) and Barzel (1987) identify wealth and risk-taking as preconditions for entrepreneurship.

9. An example of a group adapting its goals (and hence surviving) is the American Red Cross. A recent American example is H. Ross Perot's "volunteers." Examples of nonadaptation (and hence demise) are the Women's Christian Temperance Union and the Townsend Organization (Wilson 1973, 206).

10. Lord (cited in Migdal 1974, 209) argues that "in all three countries under study [Bolivia, Venezuela and Mexico] a political role for the peasantry has developed because political leaders needed its vote, its militia, or its general support in order to promote political stability and to keep political control away from potential opposition groups. Thus, political leaders have organized the peasantry and brought it into the political system to serve their own purposes." Migdal (1974, 210) also suggests that "government can organize the peasantry to serve its purposes, whether to keep the status quo or to institute reforms."

11. Idiosyncratic factors may play an important part. For example, states support terrorists for economic reasons, such as to encourage trade with Arab states, or for political reasons, such as to avoid terrorism on their own soil.

12. The CA perspective leads to many more propositions about foreign sponsorship of collective dissent. An external patrons' calculus of interven-

tion, moreover, may be similar to the regime's calculus of accommodation and repression (Lichbach 1984). One place to begin developing these propositions is the literature on external intervention in domestic conflict (Goldstone 1986a).

13. Regimes also unintentionally create preexisting organizations that aid dissidents (sect. 5.2.3).

14. Many others recognize the importance of the military as a potential ally of a dissident group. Johnson (1964, 14) stresses "the central position of armed forces in revolutions." Lasswell and Kaplan (1950, 265) argue that the regime's control over the coercive apparatus of society is a fundamental determinant of collective dissent. Russell (1974, 80) suggests that "successful rebellions require some defections on the part of the armed forces" and that "armed-force disloyalty is necessary for a successful outcome of [mass] rebellion, but it is not a sufficient condition" (1974, 79). Zimmermann (1983, 315–16) also stresses the importance of the military to revolution.

15. Skocpol (1979, 136), for instance, argues that the Russian Revolution of February 1917 succeeded because the military turned on the tsar, whereas the Russian Revolution of 1905 failed because the military remained loyal. More systematic, quantitative evidence is provided by Gurr (1970, 253):

> If dissidents think that factions of the military are not completely loyal, they may enlist their support for conspiratorial activity rather than resorting to turmoil or internal war. In the 1961-65 cross-national study of civil strife cited previously, for example, military or police personnel were reported to have participated in 48 percent of those conspiracies in which participants were identified, 30 percent of internal wars, but in only one percent of turmoil events. Moreover they participated in 53 of 58 coups and coup attempts identified in the 114 countries studied.

The Iranian Revolution may be an exception.

16. In seventeenth-century France, according to Tilly (1986, 17–18), "every popular movement provided an opportunity for some fragment of the ruling classes to press its advantage against the crown. The clientele of one great noble or another often formed the basic units among warriors or rebels. Crowds that moved against royal exactions . . . found sympathy or even support among local authorities." Lipset (1971a, 169) reports that many former ministers were part of a Canadian agrarian populist party (CCF). Gamson (1990) provides evidence in the United States. He found that collective dissent tended to be more successful when dissidents' demands were modest; when they coincided with powerful members of the polity; when those polity members split from other polity members; and when dissident polity members and outside dissidents formed alliances.

17. Wilson (1973, 81) offers two interest-group examples:

> Before the British government decided it was necessary to regulate and increase food production, the National Farmers' Union (NFU) was a small group trying, not very successfully, to lobby Parliament on behalf of farmers. Wartime necessities led to a vast increase in the scope of activity of the Ministry of Agriculture, and this in turn led to a rapid growth in the size and influence of the NFU. The British Medical Association, though publicly often quarreling with the Ministry of Health, privately and routinely has an informal partnership with the Ministry for the purpose of interpreting and carrying out the policies of the agency that oversees the complex, state-supported and state-controlled health services.

18. Wilson (1973, 81) offers an example from the field of interest groups:

> After World War I, there were a variety of veterans' organizations in Britain, distinguished one from the other by their members' rank, service, extent of war injuries . . . But the government ministry charged with administering the Pension Act, desirous of dealing with one organization rather than many, was able to stimulate the merger of the competing groups into the British Legion.

19. Levi and Hechter (1985, 137) suggest that "the size of ethnoregional party membership will increase when the party is able to provide more patronage to its members . . . The possibility of patronage is largely determined by the region's institutional autonomy." Hence, "Federal systems and the devolution of administration to the local or regional level means that jobs in the administrative, educational, and legal systems are capable of coming under the control of an ethnoregional party" (1985, 136). Examples include the Parti Quebecois in France and several Spanish political parties.

20. Moynihan's (1969) argument was a precursor to Wilson's (1973) and McCarthy and Zald's (1973) emphasis on government funding of dissident entrepreneurs and the consequent professionalization of protest. As Perrow (1979, 200) puts it,

> The white middle class, quite unbidden, took up the cause of the poor. In particular, professional reformers with social science backgrounds created new careers out of a mixture of the surplus funds in the federal budget and a conviction that they could solve intractable social problems. Promise much and deliver little was the recipe for the disorder that followed.

21. Government-sponsored political participation, referred to as "mobilization from above," is also quite common in authoritarian Third World states. Participation was also often government-sponsored in former Communist states, where ceremonial and support activities were manipulated. People marched in parades, worked hard on development projects, participated in government-organized youth groups, and voted in elections. Such participation was of course designed to prevent protest and rebellion.

22. Fireman and Gamson (1979, 34) offer a parallel example from the field of labor relations: "When unions succeeded in reducing the work week, they increased the discretionary time of their constituents; when unions succeeded in raising wages, they increased the discretionary income of their constituents. These struggles reduced the subsequent costs of contributing time and money to the union."

23. Government might be the primary solution to most types of CA problems, not only those dealing with collective dissent. Voluntary price-fixing arrangements, for example, most often fail; government mandated price-fixing often works (for a while, at any rate). Wilson (1973, 151–52) thus argues that "business associations have on the whole been most successful when they have been able to reach their objectives through obtaining favorable legislation and least successful when they have had to rely on voluntary agreements."

24. Fascist movements in Germany and Italy received money from the bourgeoisie. Rebels during the French Revolution were supported by wealthy patrons: "We may be sure that at least part of the upper bourgeoisie helped organize resistance. Bankers like Laborde and wealthy merchants like Boscary, who boasted of it later, advanced funds to pay insurrectionists for their lost days' wages and to equip them with arms and ammunitions" (Lefebvre 1947, 98). Zapata's wealthy patrons included "disaffected intellectuals with urban ties" (Wolf 1969, 31). Finally, the upper class in towns were opportunistic allies of the peasants in the English Rising of 1381; they used peasant disturbances to settle their own ancient grievances, achieve a redistribution of power, and play partisan politics (Hilton 1973, 203).

25. Gurr (1970, 271) reports that, from 1961 to 1965, 30 out of 54 "internal wars" experienced external interventions. Numerous examples of foreign patrons of dissident groups may thus be offered. Patronage of terrorism, for instance, includes hiring terrorists to work abroad (e.g., Libya), offering humanitarian aid (e.g., Sweden), serving as a host government (e.g., France and Switzerland), and opting not to prosecute offenders (e.g., Greece). Bianco (1971, 13) points out that Japanese patrons of Sun Yat-Sen provided "money, arms and advice." Gurr (1970, 269–70) observes that Guatemala, Nicaragua, Honduras, Ghana, Algeria, Cuba, China, France, Britain, and the United States have supported protests and rebellions outside of their own

borders. For additional instances, see Greene (1990, chap. 9).

26. Tarrow (1991, 15) suggests that political opportunity structures can expand or contract "when challengers are offered the help of influential allies from within, or outside the system." Opp and Gern (1992, 1) maintain that the "collective action of aggrieved groups can be accounted for by 'external resources' (Jenkins and Perrow 1977, 255), i.e., by support from other organized groups." Eckstein (1989, 37) argues that

> in both the city and the countryside, economically subordinate groups are more likely to defy conditions that they dislike collectively if they have the support of more advantaged individuals or groups. This strategy of support may come from the more economically well-to-do, political parties of considerable standing, or religious leaders. Protest movements do not necessarily and inevitably emerge out of the contradiction in economic or other structural arrangements, even when subordinate groups perceive their situation to be unsatisfactory and unjust. Better-situated individuals help arouse the masses and shape the demands of the aroused in such a way that individual discontent is collectively channeled.

27. Migdal (1974, 209) argues that peasants are capable of organizing but almost always need outside leadership and direction: "In practically all cases of effective organization of peasants, the initiative is from above, from those outside the peasant class." Eckstein (1989, 38, emphasis in original) agrees: "Outside leadership is of particular consequence in turning localized rural rebellions into nationally coordinated revolutionary movements . . . In all Latin American revolutions, cultivators rebelled against intolerable *local* conditions; their support for *national* movements hinged on alliances with the urban intelligentsia."

28. Elster (1984, 101, emphasis in original) points out that one class may act as a principal or patron for another class: "We are so accustomed to the Hegelian-Marxist dichotomy between classes existing *in themselves* and classes existing *for themselves* that we forget the importance of the intermediate stage where classes exercise their influence through their existence *for others*." At certain points in English history, for instance, the landed elite assisted the workers.

29. Walker (1983) argues that such outside patrons as wealthy individuals, private foundations, associations, and government account for a great deal of the origin and maintenance of interest groups in America.

30. Other ways in which protest modernized are discussed in section 3.4.2.

31. Popkin (1979, 48–49) reports that "peasant schemes generally tend to involve small groups in which only self-management with little leadership (or actuarial skills) is required." He (1979, 25) concludes that "there are times when many collective goods (including insurance or welfare schemes) will be provided by small groups, although large groups could do better — because neither the necessary skills nor incentives systems exist to maintain larger groups."

32. There were relatively more civil rights demonstrations in large than small cities (Spilerman 1970). The same holds for student protests: "In dealing with protests which occurred during 1968–1969, Astin and Bayer reported that given the same type of student body, large universities are more likely to have demonstrations than small ones" (Lipset 1971b, 95). Furthermore, "on the whole, the large village was more likely to riot than the smaller" during Captain Swing in nineteenth Century Britain (Hobsbawm and Rudé 1968, 180).

33. The evidence about the impact of prison overcrowding on prison riots is mixed (Garson 1972, 550–51; Colvin 1982, 452, 457). The evidence about the relationship between military coups and group size is also mixed. Thompson (1978, 93) questions the findings of Sigelman (1975) and Feit (1975) and asks, "Are small armies more likely to intervene in politics than large armies?" Size appears irrelevant to the success of military coups for three reasons. One reason is that a whole region or regime can be overcome by a handful of troops (Finer 1976, 145). Another reason is secrecy. Finer (1976, 225) also suggests that "the conspirators do not dare seek the complicity of the entire forces, since this would breach security. For this same reason the strike-force must be as small as appears consistent with success." A third reason is that the dissidents' estimate of the coup's probability of success (sect. 3.6.6) leads many military leaders to stand on the sidelines. The consequence is that most coups turn out to be short (often one day), bloodless (often no casualties), and small in size (often a handful of men). Luttwak (1968, xii) and Finer (1976, 220) offer several examples: 150 infantrymen in Gaban and Togo in 1963, 500 troops out of 10,000 in Ghana, 500 men and 30 officers in the Northern region of Nigeria in 1966, and 3500 troops out of 600,000 in Korea, overthrew regimes.

34. Examples of social groups that have sought to control entry into their ranks are legion. Many ruling classes have practiced endogamy to prevent outsiders from entering the elite via intermarriage and thereby diluting group privileges. The English nobility used primogeniture, disinheriting a large proportion of their own children, and Indian castes restricted marriages to insiders. Other examples of exclusive coalitions that seek to restrict their membership so as not to dilute their benefits include doctors, lawyers, and

Ph.D's in political science.

35. Hence, the expansion of suffrage in western democracies led to an increase in party organization (Duverger 1959; Cox 1987, 126).

36. An ancient set of rebels, Israeli slaves in Egypt, faced this problem acutely: "The first dilemma is that the identity the Israelites hope to achieve by liberation also is its precondition. Without identity, there can be no action. They must be able to say something about who they are before there is a 'they' to make a revolution" (Wildavsky 1984, 29–30).

37. Terrorist groups provide an example of this divisive potential of differing preferences with regard to strategies. There are often tensions between the political and terrorist wings of the Palestine Liberation Organization (PLO) and the Irish Republic Army (IRA). Laqueur (1987, 76) thus suggests that "the (terrorist) tail was eventually wagging the (political) dog."

38. There is another way of looking at this phenomenon: rebels face a collective choice problem in solving their collective action problem. How do radicals and reformers come to an agreement? How do dissident groups choose strategies? How are rank-and-file preferences reflected in dissident policies? There have been few studies of decision making within dissident groups. The nature of the Rebel's Collective Choice problem remains a mystery. However, the Rebel's Collective Action problem and the Rebel's Collective Choice problem are interrelated. The latter issue thus merits some discussion here.

Any explanation of dissident group policies must begin with rank-and-file preferences. Two hypotheses about the influence of rank-and-file demands come to mind. A dissident group's demands may reflect, on the one hand, the lowest common denominator of the group. As DeNardo (1985) suggests, dissident groups may appeal to the median dissident. Hence, as the demands of the median dissident becomes more radical, the demands of the dissident group also become more radical. The rank and file thereby pushes the dissident entrepreneur to the center; when that center changes so does the position of the dissident group. On the other hand, the center of rebel politics often does hold, and a dissident group's demands may reflect the most intense preferences in the group. Special interests may push the dissident group to extreme positions. Lipset (1971b, 78) suggests that "a kind of Gresham's Law of extreme politics operates in which the more aggressive constantly drive out the more moderate, which means that they also press the sympathetic periphery to withdraw from politics." Gurr (1970, 293–94) explains why:

> The needs of intensely discontented followers for expressive hostility will force leaders into more violent action than they consider desirable on tactical grounds, on pain of losing control. They may then develop

more routinized, less violent means of symbolic protest of the kinds used by regimes to minimize the destructive consequences of protest... The ritual use of antigovernment demonstration and strike, accompanied by high levels of verbal hostility, is one possible outcome of this process.

We do not know the conditions under which the DeNardo median dissident hypothesis or the Lipset-Gurr extremist dissident hypothesis hold. Two sets of factors, however, seem relevant. First, actors besides rank-and-file dissidents are important. Entrepreneurs (sect. 6.1), patrons (sect. 6.2), allies (sect. 6.4), and the regime (sect. 3.10.1.2) may influence whether the center or the extremes win. Second, the context of the conflict in which dissidents find themselves may also be decisive. Two factors seem most relevant.

The first is the duration of the conflict, since demands change over time. One pattern is that of escalating demands at the outset as leaders use a vision of future benefits to mobilize dissidents; then as a conflict ends, demands deescalate and leaders may negotiate a compromise with the regime. An alternative pattern is that initial demands are moderate and only become more radical if they are not fulfilled. Demands also escalate in long-lived conflicts, because long-lasting conflicts bring both regime and dissident hard-liners to power.

The second contextual factor is the degree of the dissident group's success (sect. 3.6). With increasing success, the dissident group's demands may escalate and expand; when students won during the 1960s on the issue of "free speech," for example, they moved on to the issues of military recruiting and the role of the ROTC on campus (Martic 1975, 222). The demands of the dissident group may become more extremist, as well, as the probability of victory decreases. This is because the group must appeal on the basis of the PG to be supplied, and not on the basis of the probability of the good actually being supplied. Dissident leaders who are losing may therefore try to appeal to a homogeneous group of activists who are differentiated from all others (Frohlich, Oppenheimer, and Young 1971, 107). Huntington (1968, 368), following Lasswell and Kaplan (1950, 267), offers a resolution of these alternative views. He suggests that dissident groups

> are more likely to make revolutionary demands in their phases of minimal power and of maximal power. In the former phase, they have little incentive to accept reforms and concessions because the latter are so small in comparison to their aspirations for the total reconstruction of society. In the latter phase, on the other hand, their willingness to accept reforms or concessions is small because of their closeness to the acquisition of total power: they are in a position to demand unconditional

surrender. With intermediate power, however, the counter elite may be interested in acceptance into the existing power structure. Its members may well want to share in the rule — to achieve some gain immediately — rather than to hold to the hope of overthrowing the entire system.

39. There is also a Say's Law of interest groups (Hansen 1985, 94).

40. The idea that grievances expand to meet the resources of dissident entrepreneurs is common in conflict studies. McCarthy and Zald's (1977, 1215) entrepreneurial model of the formation of social movement organizations implies that "grievances and discontent may be defined, created, and manipulated by issue entrepreneurs and organizations." Tilly (1964, ix) also recognizes the possibility that "manipulative leaders direct the diffuse anger of their countrymen to their own ends." He (1985, 728) thus asks, "Can we, for example, take the demands made in the group's name as evidence of the motives for individual involvement? Does the process of mobilization itself predictably transform individual motives?" Gurr also suggests that dissident leaders can create a demand for collective dissent by focusing and channeling their followers' grievances. He (1970, 278) offers the examples of the Dravidian separatist movement in southern India and the 1960 Japanese opposition to the security treaty with the U. S.

41. Coleman (1990, 390) recounts an interesting example of this approach:

> Around 1950 a small group of citizens in Pasadena, California, was opposed to the superintendent of schools and wanted either to remove him from office or to change the "progressive" educational practices he had instituted in the system . . . One of their actions was to call a meeting of "concerned parents" (they were not themselves parents of children in school) to discuss the problems that children were having with learning to read. In that meeting, to which a number of parents came, the members of the instigating group did not attempt to find others who shared their interest in opposing the superintendent and his progressive practices; instead they focused attention on another event with which the parents were interested: their children's failure to learn to read.

42. There might, of course, be a tradeoff: an issue might split one's supporters and one's opponents.

43. Note that decentralization does not mean no organization at all. Decentralized organizations can be quite organized. Section 8.1 considers the general dissident organization-collective dissent nexus.

44. Migdal (1974, 262) reports that "successful revolutionaries have decentralized administration by placing its cadres within villages and dis-

tricts." During the Intifada the Israelis successfully repressed all central Palestinian organizations located in the Occupied Territories. Palestinians thereby created a series of local and popular committees to carry on their struggle. Moreover, there is evidence that hierarchical leadership is often brittle and lacking in resilience. When the leadership is beheaded, the organization is rendered powerless. For example, the activities of the Muslim Brotherhood in Egypt declined after the death of its founder, Shaykh Hasan al-Banna, in 1948 (Luttwak 1968, 142).

45. A number of scholars have commented upon these problems. Pettee ([1938] 1971, 64) suggests that "classes having everything to gain by common action may be torn by indecision and internal faction." Gamson (1990, 316, col. 65) assesses competition among dissident groups. McCaughrin (1983, 406) refers to "dissent within dissent — deviance from dissents' own norms by splinter groups." Huntington (1968, 414) observes that the factions of a dissident organization often "form and re-form in a confusing series of permutations and combinations which are no less factions for being equipped with ponderous names and lengthy manifestos."

46. Zald and McCarthy (1990) offer a roughly parallel terminology. They refer to an antiregime coalition as a social movement sector, a particular dissident movement as a social movement industry, and a particular dissident group as a social movement organization.

47. Revolutionary armies are notoriously hard to coordinate. For example, the Vendée was composed of autonomous and locally based dissident movements. Region-wide coordination was resisted (Tilly 1964, 331). Guerrilla movements are plagued by internal competition. Laqueur (1976, 404) points out that "guerrilla movements have frequently been beset by internal strife, within their own ranks or between rival groups." The Afghan resistance movement, for example, was a loose confederation of resistance groups. Communist parties are often factionalized. Before the seizure of power, Communists in Russia were beset by factional strife. Ulam's (1965, 197) wry comment on Lenin's innumerable and interminable propaganda battles is that "in the fantastic garden of Marxist heresies a new evil weed appeared." Working-class movements are almost always divided. Economic and political unions of workers in western Europe during the nineteenth century were also beset by ideological and organizational battles. Thompson (1966, 626) reports, for example, that in England "nearly all the reform leaders were quick to impugn the motives of their fellows at the first sign of disagreement." Finally, terrorist movements are beset by factionalization. All major terrorist movements, such as the PLO and the IRA, are splintered alliances of narrow factions. Laqueur (1987) observes, moreover, that most terrorist groups originate in a split between moderate and extremist wings of an already-existing dissident organization. The notorious difficulty of arranging

coalitions among the many black or among the many Jewish organizations in the United States is a further example.

48. Hence, Walker (1991, 49) reminds us that members of dissident groups can be autonomous individuals representing themselves or organizational delegates representing some group. The later arrangement can generate a more severe CA problem. Recall from section 2.1 that Wilson (1973) argues that the PG problem is more severe among organizations than among individuals.

49. A formal model of the relationship between dissident preferences and the mobilization of collective dissent is offered by DeNardo (1985). He models the tradeoff between the extent of violence and the number of supporters.

50. Examples come from the Great Revolutions. Brinton (1965, 122) observes that "the honeymoon was in these revolutions short; very soon after the old regime had fallen there began to be evident signs that the victors were not so unanimous about what was to be done to remake the country as had appeared in the first triumphant speeches and ceremonies." War intensified this factionalization. The revolutionaries who seized power were often confronted by hostile foreign powers. War radicalized the revolution and split the victors. It thus partially accounts for the fall of the moderates in the revolutions in England (1642), France (1792), and Russia (1917).

51. This is simple PG reasoning: cooperation increases industry profits, while conflict reduces those profits.

52. As Dahrendorf (1959, 226) suggests, "So long as conflicting forces are diffuse, incoherent aggregates, regulation [of conflict] is virtually impossible." Deutsch (1973, 377–78, emphasis in original) thus claims that "*unless each party is sufficiently internally coherent and stable to act as an organized unit so that the actions of its components are controlled and unified in relation to the conflict, it is evident that regulation cannot be effectively developed or maintained.*"

53. Ostrom (1992, 305) points out the value of "a small set of simple rules." Olson (1982, 56) argues that entrepreneurs tend to adopt simple cost-sharing rules. Popkin (1979, 42) observes that "it is extremely difficult for villagers with even the best intentions to agree on ability to pay — they therefore tend to rely on easily coordinated strategies to avoid interminable conflict."

54. This is the reason why cartels fix prices or wages and leave quantities to market determination.

55. Another example of measurement by proxy is the use of price in oligopoly. Measurement by proxy generates the indicator problem in command economies (Eggertsson 1990, 43).

56. Support for the visibility idea also comes from experimental work. Fox and Guyer (1978, 474) and Jorgenson and Papciak (1981, 378) show that publicly visible contributions lead to more CA than anonymous contribu-

tions. Actions that were anonymous (i.e., it was not known who inflicted damages and who provided benefits) promoted less CA.

57. Collective punishment is, of course, the antithesis of selective disincentives. It might therefore be a flawed strategy for assuring compliance because it creates a collective interest among those punished to avoid the public bad, rather than an individual incentive to avoid personal punishment.

58. Ostrom (1992) points out several other factors that contribute to the ease of monitoring contracts: commonly understood and precisely defined goals, a well defined stream of benefits, a clear production technology, mutual trust and reciprocity, low transaction (e.g., decision-making, bargaining) costs, specific rights and duties, and clear decision-making arrangements.

59. Traditional political parties also monitor political allegiances. The introduction of the secret ballot, for example, ruined the monitoring capabilities of political machines in urban America and thus seriously weakened them. Roll-call voting allows monitoring of back benchers by parties in Britain and thus encourages a responsible party system.

60. There are many others. Gamson (1990, 317, col. 70) is concerned with selective incentives in challenging groups. Blalock (1989, 143) suggests that in conflict situations "selective incentives or some ideological substitute are likely to be required to reduce free riding and to motivate reluctant members to make substantial personal sacrifices. To some extent this may be accomplished through tangible rewards such as increased salaries, promotions, medals of honor, or notoriety." Greene (1990, 149) maintains that "the majority of those who support or participate in a revolutionary movement are mobilized initially by their self-interest and by their immediate concerns for personal well-being." Coleman (1990, 493–94) states that benefits from participation in protest and rebellion come from a successful revolt (i.e., the PG), and from one's participation (i.e., citizen duty), as well as from a successful revolt *and* one's participation in it (i.e., selective incentives).

61. Tilly (1964, vii–viii) characterizes the findings on these types of peasant struggles as follows: "In contrast with an older picture of rural rebellions as unfocused reactions to hardship or to rapid social change, the last two decades' work on the subject has revealed a general pattern of response to specific violations of well-established rights." Scott (1985, 342–45) thus proposes that the aims of the peasantry are typically limited and concrete, suggesting (1985, 295) that "to ignore the self-interested element in peasant resistance is to ignore the determinate context not only of peasant politics, but of most lower-class politics." Colburn (1989b, 192) agrees: "The political apathy in rural Nicaragua seems largely a matter of selfish calculations about benefits and costs: the benefits are reckoned to be for 'government' and the costs are personal."

62. Destruction of documents, of course, has a PG component to it: it is

not possible to exclude a taxpayer from the benefits of a fire. Selective incentives thinking would thus have us expect more looting and fewer fires, and fires that are preceded by looting.

63. In addition to the examples cited below, additional examples may be found in Roeder (1982, 6).

64. A market may exist in a more or less formal sense. The existence of a "selective incentives market" thus does not necessarily imply a formal market with distinct producers (such as rebel entrepreneurs or the state) who "offer" selective incentives to distinct consumers (that is, peasant followers). Moreover, market strategies always operate within the context of a set of structural factors that determine the underlying functions of supply and demand. As in any social-choice problem, opportunities/constraints plus strategies produce outcomes. These two clarifications can best be understood in the context of two forms of peasant struggles. In spontaneous peasant struggles, a formal market will hardly exist. Under such circumstances, selective incentives are self-offered in that peasants take advantage of some situation, such as a peasant jacquerie, to rent seek. Structural factors, such as the nature of the state and the form of property and wealth, affect the demand and supply of selective incentives and hence drive peasant behavior. In organized peasant struggles, a more formal market can be located. Under such circumstances, selective incentives *are* actually offered by rebel entrepreneurs to their peasant followers. Structural factors, however, still affect demand and supply considerations and hence drive market strategies and ultimately peasant behavior.

65. Two related observations follow. First, poorer dissidents are also likely to demand material selective incentives in exchange for their support of conventional political parties. Hence, there is a parallel here to the "neoclassical theory of patronage" that appears in the political parties literature. Shefter (1977, 405–7) summarizes the argument that immigrants, the poor, and displaced peasants are especially likely to demand patronage in exchange for their votes. Second, material selective incentives are likely to be more prominent in poor people's movements than in rich people's movements. This is one reason why discussions of material selective incentives appear more often in accounts of peasant movements than, for example, in accounts of the new social movements.

66. The L.A. riots may be an exception. People burned the only stores in their neighborhoods.

67. They are limited by resource constraints. In particular, as the size of a dissident group increases, entrepreneurs find it more difficult to provide selective incentives to all of their followers.

68. This idea is, of course, consistent with Olson's federal group solution (sect. 6.3.3).

69. Hagopian (1974, 230), for example, writes that "it is not only the topmost rungs of the revolutionary elite who feel tempted to use office for personal and mundane purposes. The transformation of the ordinary militant into the functionary is a good part of the later history of most revolutions." McCarthy and Zald (1973) note that over time more and more activists are paid for their activities. A leadership cadre of paid professionals typically emerges. Indeed, dissidents themselves have noticed this iron law. Thus, Kahn (1982, 8–9) observes that "there are professional organizers, such as the author of this book, who earn a living helping people organize themselves." Laqueur (1976, 396–97) argues that "the leadership of nineteenth- and early twentieth-century guerrilla movements was usually in the hands of men of the people . . . In backward countries they were traditionally led by rival chief or religious dignitaries. More recently they have become, by and large, the preserve of young intellectuals or semi-intellectuals."

70. Careerism offers some of the classic examples of selective incentives in interest groups. Professional associations, for example, provide selective incentives by facilitating contracts for professional advancement.

71. Rebels who are bullied and brutalized into joining dissident movements have, of course, relatively little "choice." The market metaphor is not meant to demean the experiences of the millions who have been maimed and murdered in the name of revolution.

72. For a parallel argument about political parties in the American South, see Key (1950); for one about Kenyan political parties, see Bates (1989, 91–92).

73. There is again a parallel in the political parties literature. Shefter (1977, 417) argues that internally organized parties (e.g., those that are formed by dissident government elites) are more likely than are externally organized parties (e.g., those that are formed by counterelites) to use patronage. The great ideologies that often emerge in externally organized parties are thus a substitute for government-provided patronage. Stinchcombe (1975, 569) offers a similar argument:

> Parties largely created and run by office holders and candidates . . . tend to be opportunistic . . . Contrariwise those parties in which elected officials are subordinated to militants, such as the Communist parties of France and Italy, tend to exhaust their natural constituency and then rely on "education" rather than compromise to bring them to power. Parties created as offshoots of other movements with active, aware, and powerful leaders, such as the socialist parties (offshoots of a much wider labor movement) and religious parties (offshoots of church organizations) of western Europe, tend to have severe recurrent internal conflicts about how much opportunism they ought to show.

74. Or, to quote a line from a Woodie Guthrie song, "Some rob you with a six-gun, some with a fountain pen."

75. In short, no collective goal, no collectivity. The CA action model thus fits Thompson's (1966) notion of class = class consciousness. Other theorists of class argue differently. Marx's notion was that class = means of production. Anderson (1980, 43) defends this later position: "Social classes may not become conscious of themselves, may fail to act or behave in common, but they still remain — materially, historically — classes." CA theories therefore take a particular point of view on the issue of group formation. However, a collectivity in which virtually none of the members realize that there is a collectivity might, quite literally, have the biggest CA problem of all. The question of group identity is considered in sections 6.3.2 and 10.2.1.

76. *Ethics of the Fathers* 1: 14.

77. But not all, for then there would be no CA problem.

78. Desai and Eckstein (1990) reach a similar conclusion via a different route. They argue that peasant insurgency combines the millenarian "spirit" of traditional peasant rebellion with the "rational" ideologies, organizations, and tactics of the modern era. More generally, we must explore how ideas shape interests and how interests shape ideas (Weber 1946, 61–65).

79. Hobbes ([1651] 1988, 196) assumes that "the bonds of words are too weak to bridle mens ambition, avarice, anger, and other Passions." People, therefore, do not voluntarily comply with cost-sharing arrangements: "Covenants, without the sword, are but words, and of no strength to secure a man at all." Hobbes ([1651] 1988, 202) thus argues that contracts must be enforced by the coercive power of some authority: "Therefore before the names of Just and Unjust can have place, there must be some coercive Power, to compell men equally to the performance of their Covenants, by the terrour of some punishment, greater than the benefit they expect . . . by the breach of their Covenant."

80. Walzer (1979, 43, emphasis in original) refers to the "revolutionary law" that "*no vanguard victory is possible without radical coercion.*" Buchanan (1979, 70) refers to the "revolutionary police whose function is to bully the proletariat into action." Moore (1978, 321) also observes that "there is liable to be a good deal of bullying by militants to force laggards into line and sustain the appearance of solidarity."

81. Given that dissident entrepreneurs seek to increase the expected value of punishment, they substitute between the probability and magnitude of punishment.

82. There is also analytic support for this approach to the Rebel's Dilemma. Hirshleifer and Rasmusen (1989) demonstrate that the expulsion of defectors from a group is a credible threat that can produce cooperation in finite or infinite games.

83. Olson (1965, 66-76) discusses violence and coercion in American

labor history. Repression by dissidents occurred during the reign of terror and virtue in the Great Revolutions. Brinton (1965, 177) remarks that "political indifference, that mainstay of the modern state, becomes impossible for even the most selfish, the most unworldly." Rudé (1964, 159) claims that during the Rebecca riots "farmers were summoned to make contributions and to attend nocturnal meetings; and failing compliance were threatened with reprisals." Landsberger and Landsberger (1974, 120) report that "in many instances — especially was this frequent in East Anglia — they forced people to join their bands by threat of death or destruction of property, sometimes other peasants, sometimes large property owners." Mousnier (1970, 133) reports of fourteenth- and fifteenth-century peasant disturbances in France that "the rebel peasants forced, by means of threats, other peasants to go along with them, parish priests to march at their head . . . and gentlemen to put on peasant dress and take command of armed bands." Mousnier (1970, 106) concludes that "it seems that many of the peasants jointed the rebels only under coercion, forced by threats against their cattle, their money, and their houses" and that "it seems that the number of peasants who took part in the revolt reluctantly was substantial" (1970, 138). During the English and American civil wars recruitment was facilitated by the use of conscription (i.e., selective disincentives) and mercenaries (i.e., selective incentives). Hobsbawm and Rudé (1968, 209) offer another example. "Press gangs" were roving mobs that forced people to join dissident movements. They were a particularly effective solution to the Rebel's Dilemma: "The typical agent of propagation [of Swing] was the itinerant band, which marched from farm to farm, swelling its numbers by 'pressing' the labourers working in the fields or in their cottages at night." Hobsbawm and Rudé (1968, 212) conclude that "'pressing' was, in fact, an essential measure both to bring about a general stoppage of work and to muster a sufficiently imposing force." Thompson (1966, 515) offers several examples of coercion by dissident leaders against followers. Osanka (1971, 412) argues that "professional people are often the individuals forced to serve the guerrillas" because their services are so valued. Finally, Papagos (1962, 231) offers an example from the Greek civil war:

> Force was used both directly, by the compulsory enlistment of the population, and also indirectly. Using the latter method, individuals refusing to join the Communist ranks were dubbed collaborators of the enemy, a charge which involved the death penalty or at least the burning down of the delinquent's home. Peasants who saw this happen and feared similar treatment joined the Communist ranks.

84. Gurr (1970, 355) suggests that "even if their coercive capacities are low relative to the regime, selective terrorism can be used to demonstrate the

incapacity of the regime to defend its citizens. Such terrorism is dysfunctional to the revolutionary cause if it affects neutral or innocent people; it is more effective if directed against those who are widely disliked." Gurr (1970, 260–61) thus maintains that "like dissident troops, most rank-and-file followers of dissident leaders are followers by choice, against whom few negative sanctions need to be employed." Most theorists of counterinsurgency accept Gurr's arguments and often include an examination of the limits of selective disincentives.

85. White (1988, 51) reports that in nineteenth century Japan, peasant protest seldom involved selective disincentives "(1) within villages (neighboring villages that did not join were threatened with destruction); (2) against average, or potential 'follower,' villagers (although village headmen who prevented their villagers from joining were frequently attacked); or (3) at the outset of protest — coercion became more frequent after the bandwagon began to roll." White (1988, 51) does qualify his view of the limits of selective disincentives: "Of course, it may be that the mere call to gather carried a latent threat regarding noncompliance, but this is difficult to ascertain. I have seen no evidence of sanctions other than those mentioned above, and on at least some occasions allegations of coercion formed the basis for subsequent assertions of innocence. How much coercion was real and how much constituted a license to riot is thus impossible to tell." White (1988, 57) also notes that "in contrast to the case of the average villager, coercion was a major factor in the calculations of village leaders. Examples abound of village officials' homes put to the torch and their belongings destroyed because they did not throw their lot in with neighboring villages."

86. Marx argues that revolutionary terror and violence is a sign of frustration and failure, and not confidence and success. Avineri (1968, 193) sums up Marx's view: "If a revolution can be carried out, it can be carried out without terror. What one wishes to accomplish through terror cannot ultimately be accomplished under the given circumstances." Esping-Anderson (1985, 32) accepts Marx's views: "Ostracism, ridicule, peer group pressure, even violence against 'deviants' are powerful ways of closing the ranks. But in the long run such methods prove costly, and the carrot is more efficient."

87. Femia (1987, 239) suggests that rebels are usually unable to free themselves from their violent birthmarks:

> In the revolutionary process, it is fatuous to posit a radical disjunction between ends and means; i.e. there is no escaping the intimate connection between the method used to make the revolution and the character of the subsequent society. No doubt, violence does generate its own momentum, and history teaches us that violent revolutions tend to lapse into paranoia and barbarism. The weapons used on the old oppressors often become the weapons of a new form of oppression.

Both Marx and Weber also accept this argument. Avineri (1968, 238) sums up Marx's view: "Political power retained through terror would be unable to emancipate itself from its terroristic birth marks, and would certainly cease to implement those ends for which it had been instituted." On Weber, see Giddens (1971, 135).

## CHAPTER 7

1. Conflict theorists (Rex 1961; Coser 1956; Dahrendorf 1959; Korpi 1974; Blalock 1989) and students of resource mobilization (Gamson 1990; Oberschall 1973; Zald and McCarthy 1990; Tilly 1978; McAdam 1982) also see conflict as universal, the inevitable outgrowth of state and society.

2. Huntington (1968, 357) argues that "in no society do significant social, economic, or political reforms take place without violence or the imminent likelihood of violence." He also maintains that "in most societies, civic peace is impossible without some reform, and reform is impossible without some violence" (Huntington 1968, 358–59). Moore (1966, 3–4) offers England as the somewhat unconventional example of the use of violence to rid a nation of its old institutions, and thus permit reform.

3. CA theories are thus no better than the pluralist theories they sought to replace. Both assume that government policies are a function of the parallelogram of group interests and forces (Truman 1951). This insight, however, is never developed into an institutionally rich theory of politics.

4. It is not surprising that students of conflict have not discovered the conditions under which various dissident tactics bring about political change. Political scientists, after all, have not yet agreed upon a theory of the state or an etiology of public policy. Recall, for example, the debate over "power" in New Haven (Dahl 1961).

5. One might offer the following speculations. Antiwar protestors during the 1960s in the United States could tolerate ninety-five percent free riders because of the large number of constituents. Strikers can tolerate ten to twenty percent free riders because a company will not try to hire new workers unless a large number of scabs are available. A coalition of civil rights groups may not be able to tolerate *any* free riders because if one group is coopted, others will follow, because of the fear of being cut out of government-supplied selective incentives. In the absence of an empirically sustained theory of reformist political dissent, these remain speculations.

6. For a theory of regime accommodation and repression, see Lichbach (1984).

7. Why this transformation occurs is clear (Eckert and Willems 1986, 148). Major parties are often involved in an oligopolistic competition for votes. Social movements are often relatively small actors with no hope of winning elections. They can therefore specialize in one particular issue and

fill a niche left by the major, catch-all parties. This strategy allows them to attract "discretionary resources" and become the vehicles for "voicing objection" (Hirschman 1970a).

8. Other ideas exist. DeNardo (1985) demonstrates that there is power in numbers. Rabushka and Shepsle (1971, 1972) show that the political salience of social cleavages is a function of political entrepreneurs. Blalock (1989, 27) suggests that a group's production function consists of the amount of group resources, the degree to which these resources are mobilized, and the efficiency of the mobilization effort. Spatial theorists of elections (Riker 1982) demonstrate that institutions affect the conversion between group actions and social outcomes, or between the number of people and public policies.

9. Similar difficulties arise when studying the consequences of political participation (Salisbury 1975, 325).

10. H. L. Mencken (cited in Kimmel 1990, 1) explains why: "Revolution is the sex of politics."

11. As Marwell and Oliver (1984, 6) put it:

> In our view, the key immediate problem for social movement research is to link a theory about single actions with a phenomenon that entails many actions. Social movements are made of collective events, but the distance between these two phenomena is immense. Any particular collective event is an isolated snowflake, an insignificant ripple on the ocean of history. A social movement is more like the whole winter, or the whole ocean. Even if we can say quite a bit (and we believe we can) about why and how people engage in some single collective event, this will not necessarily tell us why a social movement came about.

The aggregation problem has also been raised with respect to the aggregate data approach in conflict studies (e.g., Gurr 1968; Hibbs 1973): How does one sum conflict events that differ by actors, goals, means, and so on, into a meaningful score for, say, Bolivia in 1978? Hence, "The links between these violent events and the larger movements for social change are not clear" (Marwell and Oliver 1984, 9). A revolutionary movement, it is said, is much more than the arithmetic sum of the number of actions undertaken by its supporters.

12. Dissident entrepreneurs express similar views. Tucker (1969, 150, emphasis in original) reports that Lenin in *Leftwing Communism* states a

> "fundamental law of revolution," which had been confirmed by all revolutions, including three Russian revolutions of the twentieth century, that "only when the *'lower classes' do not want* the old way, and when

the 'upper classes' *cannot carry on in the old way* — only then can revolution triumph. This truth may be expressed in other words: revolution is impossible without a nationwide crisis (affecting both the exploited and the exploiters)." Such a crisis, he went on, is characterized by the fact that at least a majority of the class-conscious, politically active workers fully understand that revolution is necessary and that the ruling classes are going through a government crisis which draws even the most backward masses into politics, weakens the government, and makes it possible for the revolutionaries to overthrow it rapidly.

13. For Moore (1966), developmental coalitions among the nobility, peasants, bourgeois, workers, and state hold the key to revolution. In Huntington's (1968, 277) assessment,

It takes more than a revolutionary group to make a revolution. A revolution necessarily involves the alienation of many groups from the existing order. It is the product of "multiple dysfunction" in society. One social group can be responsible for a coup, a riot, or a revolt, but only a combination of groups can produce a revolution.

Goodwin and Skocpol (1989, 492) hold that revolutions are the product of "conjunctures of struggles." Dix (1984, 432) argues that what distinguishes successful from unsuccessful revolutions is the ability to put together a coalition that overcomes the regime. Deutsch et al. (1957, 88, 112) suggest that all successful integration movements are cross-class movements. Greene (1990, 66) maintains that diverse coalitions are always behind successful revolutionary movements: "Revolutionary movements do not succeed where only the workers are mobilized, or only the peasants, or only the middle classes. They succeed only where a critical mass of most or all of the major classes in the society is mobilized in the revolutionary process. The dustbin of history is filled with revolutionary leaders and followers who thought only in terms of the parochial interests of their special clienteles." Hirschman (1982a, 76) suggests that "perhaps one can define a revolutionary situation precisely as one in which the dissatisfaction of the have-nots converges with the disappointment of the haves." Tilly (1982, 18) maintains that "the main differences between everyday struggles and great revolts do not lie in the form or content of the individual actions which make them up, but in the connections and coalitions among local groups." Eisenstadt (1978) questions how different and isolated protest movements coalesce into a revolution. Finally, Goldstone (1986b, 311) suggests that a revolution is really a conjuncture of many separate revolutionary struggles: "The convergence of these events has always posed a difficult question for the theory of revolutions: Is such convergence of different conflicts a chance phenomenon, a fatal confluence of separate causal streams, or has it an underlying rationale?"

14. The fall of the French monarchy stimulated the growth of many local and regional bodies. The French Revolution thus consisted of actions taken by nobles, the "enlightened" parts of the haute bourgeoisie, the Parisian proletariat, petite bourgeoisie, and peasants. Different actors with different goals using different tactics coalesced at one time: nobles in parliaments, bourgeoisie in representative institutions, *sans-culottes* in the streets of Paris, and peasants in rural uprisings. The urban and peasant revolts, moreover, probably saved the bourgeoisie from an alliance of the monarchy and aristocrats aimed at stopping the Revolution. The French Revolution, in short, was the sum of many separate revolutions. The Rebel's Dilemma in the French Revolution, therefore, was the sum of many separate Rebel Dilemmas.

15. The fall of the Russian monarchy led to grass-roots collectivities of peasants, workers, and soldiers who tried to confiscate land, increase wages, run factories, and obtain soldiers' rights. Workers, peasants, and soldiers thus attempted to seize local control and provide specific local PGs. Pettee ([1938] 1971, 85) reports that "the Russian Revolution was no mere proletarian rising, but the simultaneous revolt of the proletariat, the peasantry, the army, and the bourgeoisie." The coalition that made the Russian Revolution consisted of "the mutinous armed forces [who wanted peace], the turbulent workers [who wanted higher wages, shorter hours and control of industry], the land hungry peasants, the dissatisfied minor nationalities [who wanted autonomy]" (Chamberlin [1935] 1987, 63). Hence, spontaneous peasant *and* urban revolts were both necessary. Neither alone would have been sufficient because the regime could have contained either a peasant jacquerie or an urban insurrection (Huntington 1968, 293–95).

16. Eckstein (1989, 49) summarizes the experiences of the four major Latin American revolutions as follows:

> Revolutionary movements succeeded in Mexico, Bolivia, Cuba, and Nicaragua when not only "popular" groups but also sectors of the middle class — including professionals, educators, and certain businessmen — defied the old regime. By contrast, when the urban middle classes have not joined in, agrarian movements have never ushered in regime transformation . . . The diverse socioeconomic groups that rebelled in Mexico, Bolivia, Cuba, and Nicaragua had different reasons for defying the government in power, but the net effect of their combined defection was the breakdown of the existing political and economic order.

17. The Vendée, for example, consisted of "a coalition of peasants, rural artisans, priests, and nobles lining up in different ways, at different times, for

different reasons, against a bourgeoisie" (Tilly 1964, ix).

18. Three examples may be offered. Autonomous peasant rebellions, as in the Russian case (Avrich 1972), almost always fail; successful peasant revolutions are virtually never just peasant revolutions (Zimmermann 1983, 341). Revolution failed in late eighteenth century Britain; the alliance that brought about the French Revolution (i.e., a radical industrial bourgeoisie and a nascent proletariat) did not form. Finally, coalitions of regional power-holders (i.e., local lords) plus a peasantry opposed to taxes initiated the rebellions of sixteenth century France; as the lords dropped out of the coalition, the rebellions petered out (Tilly 1986).

19. Tilly (1963, 30) suggests that this imbalance is unfortunate and should be redressed:

> Just as a theory of heredity which could not account for the occasional appearance of dramatically new genetic traits would be considered incomplete, a theory of revolution, or an analysis of a specific revolution, which provides no understanding of the presence of counter-revolutionary forces in the midst of a society in revolt must leave us unsatisfied. If a theory purports to tell us when and why a society is ready for rebellion, it also ought to tell us which sectors of the society will resist the rebellion, and why. Exceptions prove the rule. Counter-revolutions test our explanations of revolution.

20. CA problems of dominant classes and ruling coalitions, especially the bourgeoisie, are discussed by Levi (1981, 445–46), Przeworski (1985b, 390), and Bowman (1982, 1985).

## CHAPTER 8

1. It is interesting to note how this question about organization and action appears in three parallel literatures. Sociology debates statist approaches to the problem of social order. Social choice debates Hierarchy solutions to the problem of CA. Conflict studies debates the value of dissident organization. I discuss the first and second debates in Lichbach (forthcoming).

2. Marx recognizes the importance of organization. He is skeptical about the ability of the working class to formulate and realize its own goals without outside intellectual leadership. He accepts the idea that revolutions do not originate with the "masses" but with "elite groups" in society (Avineri 1968, 63). Turner (1986, 136) thus cites one of Marx's propositions: "The greater the ability of subordinate groups to develop a political leadership structure, the more likely they are to join in conflict." Lenin went even further than Marx in accepting both propositions. If Marx stresses the primacy

of economics over politics, Lenin stresses the primacy of politics over economics. Lenin argues that a closely knit, strictly organized, vanguard party of professional revolutionaries is required to produce a revolution. Lenin thus agrees with Olson's (1965, 102–10) criticism of Marx: a large and latent group, such as the working class, cannot organize itself; it must be activated by a revolutionary elite (Birnbaum 1988, 25). Kahn (1982, 8) accepts the arguments of both Marx and Lenin. He maintains that organization "*is* good as a tool, a weapon, a means. But it is also an end in itself." Bendix (1978, 576) summarizes the argument as follows: "The upgrading of what the professional revolutionary can do goes hand in hand with the downgrading of working-class spontaneity."

3. Academics also argue that the spontaneous tendencies of rank-and-file dissidents are most often insufficient and self-defeating. They too stress the importance of dissident organization. Crozier (1960, 8) maintains that "rebellions are made by rebels." Organization is crucial in McCarthy and Zald's (1973) "professional organizer" model of protest. Eschen, Kirk, and Pinard (1971, 531, 538) suggest that "organizations drag people into routine politics" and that "organizations, not massification, are responsible for the size of direct action movements." Freeman (1973, 794) maintains that "masses alone don't form movements, however discontented they may be." Pichardo (1988, 99) stresses the importance of elites to McCarthy and Zald's (1973) "professional organizer" model of the formation and maintenance of social movements. Lasswell and Kaplan (1950, 267) argue that "the stability of a rule varies inversely with the degree of organization of a counterelite." Huntington (1968, 461) concludes his classic book with the following classic aphorism: "Organization is the road to political power . . . Either the established elites compete among themselves to organize the masses through the existing political system, or dissident elites organize them to overthrow that system. In the modernizing world he controls the future who organizes its politics."

4. Wallerstein (1984, 116) suggests that "the October Revolution [in Russia] could be said to be the only serious example of the successful application of Blanquist ideas." Gurr (1970, 293) points out that "a comparative study of rural banditry in Colombia and urban terrorism in Venezuela concludes that effective organizational unity is a prerequisite for the pursuit of goal-oriented revolutionary policy and that highly politicized leadership is necessary if dissidents are to sustain a campaign opposed by both government and the majority of citizens." Zagorin (1982a, 269) reports that "with all too few exceptions, like the German peasant war, early modern revolutions did not get very far without strong elite support. The leadership and participation of the nobilities and aristocracies of the kingdom were crucial in the origin and development of nearly all bigger revolutionary conflicts."

5. Dissident organization has gradually developed over time. The first example of a revolutionary organization was the one that overthrew patrician rule in Italian cities during the middle ages: "The Italian *popolo* was not only an economic category, but also a political one. It was a separate political community within the urban commune with its own officials, its own finances, and its own military organization. In the truest sense of the word it was a 'state within the state' — the first *deliberately nonlegitimate and revolutionary* political association" (Weber [1924] 1968, 1302, emphasis in original). Further examples were slow to develop. Tilly (1986) reports that a key change from eighteenth to twentieth century forms of CA was that dissidents acted in the name of special interest groups and named associations or pseudoassociations (e.g., Coalition for Action, Londoners United Against) rather than in the name of corporate groups and communities. As we pass from the English to the French to the Russian Revolution, we find that revolutions are better organized, and hence more short-lived, violent, and consequential. A final example of the development of dissident organization over time is found in the working-class movement. The thought driving workers' movements has evolved from traditional to ideological, the foundation from Community to Hierarchy.

6. Hibbs (1973, 130-31) finds that "sizable Communist parties in non-Communist nations serve to promote mass protest but have no systematic impact on the incidence of Internal War." Gurr and Lichbach (1979) find that the strength of dissident organizations is related to the level of collective dissent. As the size, cohesiveness, and coercive capacity of Communist parties, labor unions, and dissident socio-economic groups increase, collective dissent increases.

7. Piven and Cloward (1979, 36–37) suggest that centralized dissident organizations reduce the possibility of direct action tactics. Parsons (1951, 529) suggests that "a revolutionary movement must pay the price of success. It cannot both have the cake of the motivational advantages of revolt, and eat it by being the focus of institutionalization of an orthodoxy too." Hannigan (1985, 446) argues that this tradeoff "can sometimes act as an albatross around the movement."

8. Communal disturbances between religious, ethnic, and subnational groups are often unplanned and uncoordinated. Hobsbawm (1959) and Rudé (1959, 1964) report numerous instances of authentic grass-roots activism: the perpetrators are the same as the dissident organizers and the dissident constituency; each episode has a different group of perpetrators.

9. Thompson (1984, 73) suggests that "popular revolutions do not as a rule begin by disciplined armed attacks on the centres of authority. The mass movement of poorly armed crowds has been the precipitant of nearly every popular uprising." For example, spontaneous revolts, not a planned upheaval,

sparked the Russian Revolution in February 1917.

10. Marx holds that "the economic struggles, i.e., trade union activities, strikes, etc., create out of their own dialectics the political emergence of the proletariat" (Avineri 1968, 146). Hilton (1973: 146) argues that "in conflicts with the local lord over local customs, village communities gained experience of common action."

11. On the advantages and disadvantages of organized and disorganized dissidents, see Chorley ([1943] 1973, 40–41).

12. Conspiracy and voluntarist theories of revolution coexist (Hagopian 1974, 177–84). To what extent are revolutionaries' actions spontaneous and natural, or organized and incited? Does leadership represent the heavy hand of dictatorship or the helping hand of guidance? Voluntarist theories of revolution maintain that "revolutions are not *made*, they *happen*" (Hagopian 1974, 178, emphasis in original). In this view, revolution requires no prior organization and only minimal current leadership. Individuals with many diverse objectives who lack a formalized, enduring organization can coordinate collective dissent on their own, without outside assistance. This view is Blanquist in its inspiration, deterministic in its etiology, and fatalistic in its implications. Conspiracy theories of revolution maintain that revolutions are made. This view emphasizes the importance of organization, planning, leadership, plotting, propaganda, and agitation to collective dissent. Proponents point to the importance of a small vanguard party of cohesive professionals providing guidance to revolution. Conspiracy theorists are suspicious of the masses and stress the importance of outsiders. This view is elitist in its inspiration, opportunistic in its etiology, and manipulative in its implications.

13. The issue of the importance of outsiders to peasant revolution is a particular instance of the voluntarist-conspiracy controversy. Wolf (1969), Scott (1976), and Paige (1975, 11) suggest that spontaneous revolution by peasants is possible. However, all maintain that outside leadership has been helpful. Migdal (1974, 209) and Popkin (1979) thus stress the importance of outside parties providing leadership, or "the classic Marxist postulate that peasants cannot launch a real revolution under their own initiative" (Hagopian 1974, 18). Landsberger (1974, 47) agrees: "The more extensive and national, and the more permanent the movement becomes, the less likely is it to be, or at least to remain, in the hands of peasants." Peasants have indeed obtained patrons (sect. 6.2) from urban areas in all major revolutions. Peasant disturbances thus followed, rather than led, collective dissent by the working, urban, bourgeoisie, and noble classes in the French, Russian, Bolivian, and Mexican revolutions (Landsberger 1974, 60).

14. This is a widespread observation. Piven and Cloward (1979, 36–37) argue that formalized poor-people's organizations merely divert energies from mass defiance, mainly because they provide political elites with a platform for offering symbolic reassurances that demobilize masses. Barnes

(1968, 114) suggests that "although ideology undoubtedly motivates many individuals, organizational considerations generally predominate: the history of mass movements is full of examples of the triumph of organizational technicians over ideologues." Walzer (1979, 41) suggests that "the routinization of vanguard consciousness" occurs as dissidents become disillusioned with the pragmatism and compromises of their leaders.

15. Spontaneous religious fervor slowly becomes bureaucratic denominationalism (Weber [1922] 1991).

16. Wallerstein (1983) points out that if such parties make the seizure of state power the central goal of the movement, two consequences follow. First, to achieve power they must find less radical domestic allies. According to Wallerstein (1983, 69), this need "pushed each movement towards entering into tactical alliances with groups that were in no way 'anti-systemic' in order to reach its strategic objective. These alliances modified the structure of the anti-systemic movements themselves." Second, once in power, as Wallerstein (1983, 69) continues, "these successful movements were then confronted with the realities of the limitations of state power within the capitalist world-economy. They found that they were constrained by the functioning of the interstate system to exercise their power in ways that muted the 'antisystemic' objectives that were their raison d'être." Antisystemic movements thus made compromises once in power because of their wish to compete in the world economic system. They found it virtually impossible to govern and remain antisystemic at the same time. Hence, the following contradiction confronted antisystemic movements: to succeed domestically, such movements must strengthen their state; but strengthening one's state reinforces one's ties to the world system; the antisystemic character of the movement is consequently undermined. Esping-Anderson (1985) makes a related argument about the reformist parties of the Left. He notes that when working-class parties won elections, they typically destroyed their own base of support. Social democratic parties became governing parties and adopted reformist policies that eventually deradicalized the working class. The electoral success of left-wing parties thus moderated the party's demands and eventually undermined its success. Leaders of left-wing movements, unions, and parties are thus often called "class betrayers," "mis-leaders of labour," and "sell-outs" by their more radical colleagues.

17. Messinger (1955) indicates that this movement's traditional manner of fund-raising changed: instead of distributing materials that presented the group's program (e.g., bumper stickers, buttons, newspapers, books), the group sold consumable items bearing its name (e.g., coffee, soap, candy, foods, vitamins). Issues changed: new programs were adopted to replace the movement's original concerns. Leadership changed: committed leaders were replaced by opportunistic ones. Recruitment changed: instead of seeking active members or converts, the group sought any supporters or customers.

Finally, membership activities changed: instead of an activist commitment to the movement, members held a recreational involvement with a club. As Messinger (1955, 10) puts it, "What were once the incidental rewards of participation [were turned] into its only meaning."

18.  Lasswell and Kaplan (1950, 43–44) make three observations: "Principled interests are modified as they come into conflict with expediency interests"; "groups are more accommodating with regard to principled than expediency interests"; and "expediency interests are relatively more constant than principled interests."

19.  This iron law is widely recognized. Elitist theorists, such as Mosca (1939), Michels ([1919] 1962), and Pareto ([1920] 1980), argue that old elites are always ousted by new elites. Writing on the Russian Revolution, Trotsky (1937, 89) notes that "the ebb of 'plebeian pride' made room for a flood of pusillanimity and careerism. The new commanding caste rose to its place upon this wave." Welch (1980, 233) observes that "independence won, the division of the spoils started to differentiate those who profited from those who paid." Runciman (1989, 145, emphasis in original), referring to the "paradox of 'permanent revolution'," or the extension of inequality over generations, suggests the problem faced by the new revolutionary elite: "Once previously subordinate [groups] have been raised as high as they can and as many of those born into them promoted individually into higher ranked [groups] as there is room for, what is to be done about *their* children?"

20.  The American Revolution is a counterexample. The Eastern European revolutions of 1989, at the time of this writing, also offer partial counterexamples.

21.  Zagorin (1982a, 145–46) offers an example from a religious rebellion:

> Protestant authorities themselves were no less hostile to dissent, which they too endeavored to repress. The chief denominations to emerge in the Reformation — the Lutheran or Evangelical, the Calvinist or Reformed, and the Anglican churches — alike claimed an exclusive religious dominion where they held say. Despite the differences in the way they conceived the church and its relation to secular authority, each rejected toleration and pluralism.

22.  While evil *might* be necessary for success, the world is spared it being sufficient. There is no iron law that says the bad guys (gals) always win.

23.  For instance, the demands of some dissident organizations have been influenced by the group's rank and file. Two examples may be cited. Many

black civil rights organizations were initially composed of middle-class blacks whose "efforts were mainly directed toward public accommodations. In the North this meant integration of facilities that required the expenditure of money: clubs, swimming pools and above all suburban middle-income and upper-income housing" (Oppenheimer and Lakey 1964, 13). These goals eventually changed:

> In the effort to integrate basically middle-class facilities, it became necessary to recruit larger numbers of people, especially Negroes, to gain more power. And as large numbers of Negroes were recruited into the active movement, organizations such as CORE became more working class in composition. The new composition was quickly reflected in new demands: better slum housing, better schools in Negro neighborhoods, more jobs."

Another example of the responsiveness of dissident entrepreneurs to their rank and file comes from the French Revolution. According to Rudé (1964, 248–49), "Leaders . . . were at times compelled, in order to maintain their authority, to trim or adapt their policies to meet the wishes of the crowd."

24. McAdam, McCarthy, and Zald (1988, 718) summarize this view:

> Zald and Ash argued that the model was limited and that a more inclusive and dynamic model of organization-environment relations allowed one to expect a variety of other [social movement organization] trajectories, including demise, radicalization, schism, and movement organization becalmed . . . As one adopts an organization-environment model for the study of ongoing movement development, it becomes apparent that [social movement organizations] exist in a larger macroenvironment that greatly constrains their actions. The net impact of these constraints is never so simple as to yield a single outcome — such as institutionalism — in the case of all [social movement organizations]. Rather, at the macrolevel, we are encouraged to analyze the process of movement development as turning on a complex process of interaction between [social movement organizations] and a variety of other organizational actors. The structural impact of this interaction process is expected to vary from [social movement organization] to [social movement organization].

25. Not all of these revolutionaries, however, fully understood the iron laws. Miliband (1981, 120) writes that "although Marx did not reject all forms of organization, he nevertheless greatly underestimated how much organization a socialist movement — let alone a socialist revolution —

required; and that Lenin, for his part, altogether underestimated the problems that the organization which he wanted and brought into being must in all circumstances produce."

26. All of the Great Revolutions had their Left oppositions: the English Revolution had its Diggers and Fifth Monarchy Men, the French Revolution its conspiracy of equals under Babeuf, and the Russian Revolution its anarchists. All of the Great Revolutions also had their "lord protectors," who used coercion to secure what they saw as the "gains" of the revolution: the rule of the major generals occurred in England under Cromwell, the second directory occurred in France under Robespierre, state-led industrialization and the collectivization of agriculture occurred in Russia under Stalin, and the Great Leap Forward of 1958–59 and the Great Proletarian Cultural Revolution of 1966–69 occurred in China under Mao.

27. The New Left of the 1960s tried to free itself from what it saw as the dehumanizing consequences of large organizations. The Port Huron statement, the Manifesto of the Students for a Democratic Society (SDS), and the efforts of the Student Nonviolent Coordinating Committee (SNCC) were self-consciously populist and egalitarian. The new social movements of the 1980s were trying, similarly, to alter organizational forms. Sassoon (1984, 871–72) notes that these groups stressed antibureaucratic, antihierarchical, and anti-institutional themes that challenged

> the organizational forms inherited from a not too distant past when social movements aimed at a coherent action in the political system. As long as they pursued the idea of organizing – during the season of the revolutionary dream — in order to better resist in the class struggle against capitalism and its repressive forces, social movements groups stiffened in constrained formulas, that were clearly inspired by the industrial production model: hierarchial structures, the subdivision of offices and responsibilities, committees, boards, and the subordinate role of the mass (the mass as raw material). It was really a mechanical articulation of revolutionary energy, that reflected the structural forms of industrial machinery and its political organization . . . Today, the organization forms of social movement groups take for granted the fact that power cannot any longer be "dialectically" contrasted, but it must rather be symbolically, paradoxically, spectacularly defied.

New social movements thus make a conscious effort to overcome the old iron laws of dissent.

28. As Avineri (1968, 142) notes, the Israeli *kibbutzim* "have perceived that the modes and forms of present social organization will determine the structure of future society."

29. One approach to addressing these questions is to explain the dissident group in a manner similar to the way that one describes a firm in the market (Eggertsson 1990, 138, 163, 178–88). A typology of the common forms of dissident organizations could be created, and one could then explain the major forms of contracts among dissidents with a transaction costs argument.

## CHAPTER 9

1. There is an important second-order unintended consequence of the unpredictability of collective dissent: given that the downfall of regimes is one possible outcome of collective dissent, regime change is equally hard to predict. Thus, the fragility of regimes results, for example, from quickly changing estimates of the probability of victory (Sect. 3.6.1). As Arrow (1974, 73) writes, "The emphasis on convergent expectations as the source of authority implies its fragility. Indeed, one can point to startling changes where the collapse of long-established authority swiftly followed recognition that it was no longer authoritative." In particular, the "fragility of autocracies" results from changing perceptions of the omnipotence of despotic rule (Olson 1990, 16).

2. Technically, the level of aggregate benefits does not affect a dissident's decision to participate. He or she may value the outcome of collective dissent more than he or she regrets the expense of his or her individual contribution, but still not participate. As Tullock (1979, 51) argues, dissidents ignore the PG in deciding whether or not to participate in collective dissent.

3. Many rational choice approaches to collective dissent are also challenged. For example, Dahl (1956) and DeNardo (1985) are misleading: preferences are not sufficient for mobilization and rebellion.

4. Hobsbawm (1959, 121) writes that "a good deal of the mob's reputation for fickleness is due to this empiricism. It wants a king who does his duty, as it wants a saint who does his duty: anyone will do." Migdal (1974, 212) observes that "the same Mexican peasants have supported one of the major progressive revolutions in history under the leadership of Zapata and later Cardenas, and they have also supported the highly repressive regime of the last twenty years." Avrich (1972, 31) notes that Liapunov, a peasant rebel in one of Russia's many peasant rebellions, switched sides. Similarly, Luttwak (1968, 21) observes that people often applaud the regime and then applaud the dissidents who overthrow it. The popular support for fallen idols, such as Nkrumah, is underwhelming, indeed.

5. One explanation for this infidelity is that when dissident groups compete, individuals donate in order to gain concessions and selective incentives (Frolich, Oppenheimer, and Young 1971).

6. This proposition holds for the Bolsheviks after 1917 (the November Revolutionaries; Hagopian 1974, 306). The proposition is also true of the successful peasant revolutions in China and Vietnam. Mousnier (1970, 84–85) offers yet another example: "This was practically the end of the great revolt. Up to this time, the duc de La Vallette had been helped only by a few gentlemen . . . After his victory, however, La Vallette found more than three hundred of them coming to join him."

7. Given that preference falsification assures that grievances, identities, and common goals remain unknown, public discourse is altered. Kuran (forthcoming) draws out the many implications of this point.

8. Tucker (1969, 192–93) sums up the Marxists' deception:

> But for subjective reasons as well as vulnerability to accusations of hypocrisy from within the movement, the leadership is uncomfortable in the presence of this discrepancy and does what it can to lessen or blur it. While rejecting the formal revisionism that would disavow the radical principles or eschatological elements of the movement's ideology, the orthodox leaders modify the *tactical* part of the ideology by stressing immediate short-term objectives and nonradical means of attaining them. And in their exegeses of the authoritative writings and pronouncements of the founders, they highlight those statements that give (or seem to give) sanction to such a development of the tactical doctrine.

9. Laqueur (1987, 6) makes these points with respect to terrorism.

10. Coser (1956, 39–48) argues, from another point of view, that the absence of conflict is an indication of the weakness, not the strength, of regimes. Minor conflict can encourage reform and hence prevent revolution. Such "rituals of rebellion" act as a "safety valve" that allows "people to release their tension in ways that do not directly challenge the basic structure of power and authority" (Sederberg 1994, 29) .

11. Regimes, however, often unintentionally encourage preference distortion. Given that you can gain by convincing your rulers that your preferences are their preferences, people do not reveal their true preferences. While the regime might appear to have considerable popular support, an exogenous shock or signal can lead people to reveal their true preferences and begin a bandwagon (sect. 4.1.2) of revolt. Authoritarian systems offer particularly strong incentives to those who feign support. Conformity under authoritarianism is thus often a facade. People will say they are for an authoritarian regime when it is in power and that they were really against the regime when it falls. Kuran (1991a) argues that this scenario accounts for the rapid collapse of the Communist states in Eastern Europe.

12. CA theories come to this conclusion, even though they offer insight into the precipitants of outbreaks of collective dissent (sect. 4.1).

13. Farhi (1990, 67) writes of the Nicaraguan Revolution that "the intensity and timing of insurrection in the barrio of Monimbo even took the revolutionary leadership by surprise." Both the Western student movement of the 1960s and the Czech movement in November 1989 surprised everyone (Tarrow 1991, 15). Coleman (1990, 481) indicates that "for the election in El Salvador in the spring of 1982, foreign journalists were unable to predict even the general direction of the outcome (which supported the rightist parties more than had been anticipated by the journalists)." Many other surprises in conflict exist (Kuran 1989, 1991a; Goldstone 1991, 35). The problem is especially severe under authoritarian regimes that suppress information (Kuran forthcoming, chap. 19). These findings validate the results of the many stochastic models of collective dissent: outbreaks of protest and rebellion are largely random events (Midlarsky, Crenshaw, Yoshida 1980; Lichbach, 1985a, 1985b, 1992).

14. Another example may be found in theories of rational expectations (Williams 1990). These theories imply "that the theory itself, a result of purposive action, can have no effect on future action. Any attempt to use the theory purposefully will consequently be, according to the theory, destined to fail" (Coleman 1990, 17).

15. It is interesting to reflect on why students of rational choice and of structural analysis downplay the possibility of predicting collective dissent, while DA theorists engage wholeheartedly in such exercises (Gurr and Lichbach 1979, 1986; Goldstone 1991; on the other hand, see Bueno de Mesquita 1984). The DA research program combines theories of structure and action. Proponents of the DA research program thus tend to claim that they can both understand and predict collective dissent. As indicated above, the CA research program generates theories of action that must use auxiliary assumptions about structure and the structuralist research program generates theories of structure that must use auxiliary assumptions about action. The CA and structuralist research programs are thus more rigorously delimited than the DA program. Proponents of the CA and structuralist research programs therefore recognize that they may possibly explain certain aspects of collective dissent but could never successfully predict aggregate levels and particular outbreaks of protests and rebellions. DA theorists combine structure and action so nimbly that they think they hold the key to the future.

16. My position, therefore, is that Elster (1993) is not theoretically ambitious enough. Elster (1993) argues that we should study "nuts and bolts" or "mechanisms," or what I call "CA processes," that reappear across various CA situations. Elster (1993, 5) also argues that we cannot offer any general

explanations of how these mechanisms are triggered: "In the real world, however, the number of possible permutations of conditions is too great for us to be able to establish the characteristic mechanism operating in each of them." Hence, "In any given historical case, the most one can do is to provide a post factum identification of individual motivations and the ways in which they interact to produce the final outcome. The very idea of creating a general theory of revolutions that would enable us to predict or, for that matter, manipulate the behavior of the masses is absurd" (Elster 1993, 23). Elster is arguing, in effect, that we cannot link up structure and action. I believe, however, that we can study how the comparative statics of context affects particular CA processes. Hence, this book tries to establish the conditions under which one CA process rather than another (e.g., selective incentives rather than altruism) operates in protests and rebellions. If Elster was right, there would be very little in the CA approach that would interest theoretically inclined comparative historians. What, after all, would be the value added to the study of CA by comparative and historical work? Tilly's (1993, 17) "social mechanisms" and Goldstone's (1991, 53) "robust processes in history" are, therefore, also more theoretically ambitious than Elster's "nuts and bolts." Comparative historians, however, would agree with Elster, the always-insightful philosopher, that an understanding of how the interaction of various CA processes produce macroevents like protests, rebellions, and revolutions may be beyond us. We would disagree on the possibility of developing a comparative and historical explanation of some relevant parts of those macro events (e.g., Tit-For-Tat, the rise of dissident entrepreneurship).

17. This approach of starting with CA processes and locating their causes and consequences is a useful alternative to Coleman's (1987) and Boudon's (1987) approach of starting with structural propositions and locating their microfoundations. Either approach has the virtue, to paraphrase Socrates, of emphasizing that an unexamined hypothesis is not worth testing.

18. These problems with constructing a single highly general and abstract predictive theory of either CA or conflict have been understood by others. CA theorists have recognized the difficulty of developing a general theory of CA. Elster (1989, 205) points out that "we will never have a general theory of collective action. The variety of interacting motivations is simply too large for any equilibrium theorems to be provable." Conflict theorists have recognized the difficulty of developing a general theory of conflict. Tilly (1985, 718) refers to all efforts, including his own, to create comprehensive accounts of CA as "miscellaneous flabbiness."

19. A Nobel prize winning physicist, Feynman (1965, 171), expresses a similar idea: "If you can find any other view of the world which agrees over

the entire range where things have already been observed, but disagrees somewhere else, you have made a great discovery." Feynman (1965, 39, emphasis in original) thus suggests that "every theory that you make up has to be analyzed against *all* possible consequences, to see if it predicts anything else." Feynman (1965, 158) also suggests that to find a new law, discover trouble with an old one. And to discover trouble with an old one, extend the law beyond previous tests:

> One of the ways of stopping science would be only to do experiments in the region where you know the law. But experimenters search most diligently, and with the greatest effort, in exactly those places where it seems most likely that we can prove our theories wrong. In other words we are trying to prove ourselves wrong as quickly as possible, because only in that way can we find progress.

Feynman's ideas are consistent with those of Eckstein's (1975) regarding case studies. Eckstein urges that we should look most diligently for tests that either are *most* likely to prove our ideas wrong (i.e., lead to confirmation of theories) or *least* likely to do so (i.e., lead to rejection of theories).

20. The CA research program is a perfect candidate for such a Lakatosian evaluation. The "solutions" to the free rider problem are really "modifications" of the program in that all have the same identifiable core assumptions but a different protective belt of auxiliary assumptions. It appears likely, moreover, that the internally generated anomaly of the program (i.e., only irrational people will join groups) will be fixed by a mere patchwork of rationalizations of individual participation.

21. A sufficient condition for the CA research program to be progressive in Lakatos's sense is if it meets the above tests for, say, collective dissent. Such tests, however, are not necessary. There are many substantive areas, such as interest group activity and voting behavior, where the CA research program may yield insights. Whether the program is valuable for protest and rebellion says nothing about whether or not it is valuable for these other fields. A Lakatosian analysis of the CA research program therefore cannot be limited to a single domain of study because limiting the empirical focus deprives the analyst of the most novel implications of the program. Focusing on a single field does not yield the full picture of the progressivity of a research program. A Lakatosian evaluation would, on the contrary, determine the impact of the program on a number of different fields: CA theories are thus progressive if they yield many diverse implications in many different substantive domains. As a consequence, my goal here is not a "rational reconstruction" of the CA research program. I do not attempt to answer the

question, "Is the CA research program progressive or degenerative?," because this question cannot be addressed with respect to a single substantive domain like collective dissent.

22. Given that theories are underdetermined by the facts, no amount of accumulated facts can lead to acceptance or rejection of a theory (Giddens 1979, 243). Only a better theory beats a theory. Feyerabend (1988, 24) thus suggests that scientists "proliferate" inconsistent theories rather than eliminate rivals. He counsels pluralism and competition rather than authoritarianism and monopoly.

23. Rule (1988, 43) argues that "rational choice models only move from the provocative and intriguing to the convincing by identifying sets of data for which the models provide better accounts that do alternative possibilities. We need more serious efforts to confront the models with such pertinent evidence." Mueller (1989, 193) maintains that "unless public choice-derived models can outperform the 'traditional, ad hoc' models against which they compete, the practical relevance of public choice theories must remain somewhat in doubt." Eckstein (1980) offers a classic test of rational actor vs. deprived actor theories of protest and rebellion. Arrow's (1974, 65) comments about competition and authority systems also apply to competition and research programs: "The owl of Minerva flies not in the dusk but in the storm."

24. The Popperian approach is also not without its critics, as many students of conflict are suspicious of efforts to evaluate competing theories. Merkl (1986a, 2) argues, for example, that "social scientists, however, must be . . . quite aware that the choice of method may determine the character of what they find. If we look for high ideals and high-minded idealists in a revolution, we shall find some, and if we look for brutal coercion and cold executioners, they will be found as well." Moreover, many students of rational choice are suspicious of efforts to compare cultural and rational choice explanations. It is often argued that economic theory contains hypotheses of the following form: under conditions $C$, individuals with preferences $P$ choose alternative $A$. For example, under any situation less than totalitarian repression, zealots will choose to rebel (sect. 3.1). But individuals have an incentive to misrepresent their preferences (sect. 9.2.2.2). Hence, we must assume that preferences are invariant across conditions and test hypotheses of the following form: given $P$, $C$ implies $A$. For example, given a group of zealots, any situation less than totalitarian repression will produce rebellion. The problem is that if this hypothesis turns out to be false, we do not know whether the maintained hypothesis "$P$" or the research hypothesis "$C$ implies $A$" is false. Multiple tests is a solution to the second challenge; survey research a solution to the first.

25. Evidence shows that the probability of protest and rebellion in a locality is positively related to the number of single young males in that

locality (Mason and Krane 1989, 184). Hobsbawm (1981, 31–33) reports that social bandits are by and large single young males. Hobsbawm and Rudé (1968, 62) also report that most of the people involved in Captain Swing were young unmarried males. Tilly (1964, 316) observes that "young unattached men predominated in the earliest outbreaks" of the Vendée.

26. CA theorists focus on rational expectations about success (sect. 3.8).

27. Three examples of this argument may be cited. Donati (1984, 838) suggests that conflict leads to identity: "Without being structured, collective action would not be possible; it would have neither unity nor continuity. But on the other hand, the very fact of defining a structure requires shaping and redefining the action itself." Touraine (1985) emphasizes that participants in new social movements find their identities in the course of an ongoing fight with the regime over the social control of the main cultural patterns of a society. It is only through such conflict that dominated collective actors are able to understand their situation, define their prospects, and organize themselves for action. Lastly, Cohen (1985, 689) argues that new social movements "defend spaces [versus government and market] for the creation of new identities and solidarities" and thus (1985, 690) "contemporary collective actors consciously struggle over the power to socially construct new identities, to create democratic spaces for autonomous social action, and to reinterpret norms and reshape institutions."

28. Hence, dissident entrepreneurs should not attack institutional racism, but rather a racist.

29. Support for such a counterargument to CA thinking is quite common among students of conflict. Gunning (1972, 41) argues that, as time preferences change from the long to the short term, the chances for collective dissent increase, because people expect immediate satisfaction of their wants. Alinsky (1971, 120) argues that "organizations are built on issues that are... immediate."

30. This was Hegel's view (Avineri 1972, 110).

31. The inherent theoretical ambiguity surrounding the issues of group size, exclusivity, collective action, and collective effectiveness was captured by Marx (this time Groucho, not Karl), who quipped, "I don't care to belong to any club that would have me as a member" (Marx 1967, 8).

32. The issue of government repression is partially addressed in Lichbach (1987).

## CHAPTER 10

1. Also see Fitzgerald (1978), Leites (1979), Osayimwese (1983), Kirk (1983), and Sandler, Tschirhart, and Cauley (1983).

2. Coser (1956, as summarized by Turner 1986, 160) proposes two similar propositions. First, "the more groups engage in conflict over realistic

issues (obtainable goals), the more likely are they to seek compromises over the means to realize their interest, and hence, the less violent is the conflict." Second, "the more groups engage in conflict over nonrealistic issues, the greater is the level of emotional arousal and involvement in the conflict, and hence, the more violent is the conflict."

3. Gurr (1970, 210, fn. 54) apparently attributes this approach to Olson: "I am indebted to Mancur Olson, Jr., for his persistent and ultimately persuasive arguments that utilitarian justifications for political violence are highly consequential and can be integrated into a theoretical model that emphasizes nonrational motivations for strife."

4. Scott (1976) offers a classic statement of how at the structural level material conditions drive culture and hence at the individual level motivations drive protest behavior. He argues that peasants are not profit maximizers because their condition (living close to the margins of subsistence) forces them to be concerned with survival and not profits. Hence, peasant decision rules are risk averse. The behavioral consequence is that peasants are reticent to adopt new technologies that could increase crop yields but could also fail to produce any crops at all. Peasant conditions also work against pure individualism. Help from neighbors is likely to be needed at any time. Hence, peasant decision rules also include reciprocity. The behavioral consequence is that peasants share resources and always come to their neighbor's assistance. Finally, peasant conditions are such that they are concerned with not falling below minimum living standards. Hence, peasant decision rules include the right to subsistence. The behavioral consequence is that peasants accept high taxes as long as the taxes are structured such that peasants are allowed to survive in lean years.

5. Cultural or interpretive theories are split between efficiency (culture is a PG that provides a framework of meaning for human interaction) and equity (culture is contested by dominant and subordinate groups) perspectives. Edgerton (1985, 7–16) explores whether "rules are sovereign" or whether there is "strategic manipulation of rules"; Scott (1985, 38–39) is concerned with "a debate that centers on the extent to which elites are able to impose their own image of a just social order"; and Laitin (1986, 11–16) is concerned with "culture's two faces." Equity or strategic perspectives on norms are consistent with my approach to the Rebel's Dilemma.

6. This is a general situation with game theory: one must place a game within a well defined context. Wildavsky (1992, 10) argues that "the rationality of the prisoners, like rationality in general, is context dependent." Hechter (1992, 33) points out "the insufficiency of game theory for the resolution of real-world collective action problems" because one must figure out how to link the model with reality, the abstract categories with actual social structures. Friedman (1992, 48, emphasis in the original) suggests that

no one game is *the correct game* independent of context. As social scientists we must tailor the games we use so that they are descriptive of the situations we wish to analyze. My own experience has been that "off the shelf" game-theoretic models have not been useful for my work in oligopoly. There is an approach which has been useful that a person trained in game theory brings to a situation. There are also basic concepts such as move, *strategy, game,* and *noncooperative equilibrium* that have also been useful. But new models have had to be forged to suit the economic circumstances that were under analysis.

7. The justification for this assumption is *de gustibus non est disputandum* (Stigler and Becker 1977). As Hobbes ([1651] 1988, 120) puts it, there is no "common Rule of Good and Evill, to be taken from the nature of the objects themselves." Utilitarian thought thus implies that "desires are random" (Parsons 1937, 89).

## CHAPTER 11

1. *Ethics of the Fathers* 1: 14.

# References

Adams, Tom. 1991. *Grass Roots: How Ordinary People are Changing America*. New York: Citadel.

Ake, Claude. 1967. "Political Integration and Political Stability: A Hypothesis." *World Politics* 19 (April): 486–99.

Alexander, Jeffrey C. 1987. *Twenty Lectures: Sociological Theory Since World War II*. New York: Columbia University Press.

———. 1990. "Analytic Debates: Understanding the Relative Autonomy of Culture." In *Culture and Society: Contemporary Debates*, ed. Jeffrey C. Alexander and Steven Seidman, pp. 1–27. Cambridge: Cambridge University Press.

Alinsky, Saul D. 1946. *Reveille For Radicals*. New York: Vintage Books.

———. 1971. *Rules For Radicals: A Pragmatic Primer for Realistic Radicals*. New York: Vintage Books.

AlRoy, Gil Carl. 1966. "The Involvement of Peasants in Internal Wars." Princeton, N.J.: Center of International Studies, Woodrow Wilson School of Public and International Affairs, Princeton University.

Amos, John W. II, and Russel H. S. Stolfi. 1982. "Controlling International Terrorism: Alternatives Palatable and Unpalatable." *Annals* 463 (September): 69–83.

Anderson, Charles W., Fred R. von der Mehden, and Crawford Young. 1967. *Issues of Political Development*. Englewood Cliffs, N.J.: Prentice-Hall.

Anderson, Perry. 1977. "The Antinomies of Antonio Gramsci." *New Left Review* 100 (Nov.–Jan.): 5–78.

———. 1980. *Arguments Within English Marxism*. London: New Left Books.

Armstrong, John A. 1976. "Mobilized and Proletarian Diasporas." *American Political Science Review* 70 (June): 393–408.

Arrighi, Giovanni, Terence K. Hopkins, and Immanuel Wallerstein. 1989. *Antisystemic Movements*. London: Verso.

Arrow, Kenneth J. 1974. *The Limits of Organization*. New York: W. W. Norton.

Atkinson, Anthony B, and Joseph E. Stiglitz. 1980. *Lectures on Public Economics*. New York: McGraw-Hill.

Atkinson, Scott E., Todd Sandler, and John Tschirhart. 1987. "Terrorism in a Bargaining Framework." *Journal of Law and Economics* 30 (April): 1–21.

Aumann, Robert J. 1974. "Subjectivity and Correlation in Randomized Strategies." *Mathematical Economics* 1 (March): 67–96.

———. 1989. "Game Theory." In *The New Palgrave: Game Theory*, ed. John Eatwell, Murray Milgate, and Peter Newman, pp. 1–53. New York: W. W. Norton.

Austen-Smith, David. 1980. "Individual Contributions to Public Goods." *Economic Letters* 5 (No. 4): 359–61.

Avineri, Shlomo. 1968. *The Social and Political Thought of Karl Marx*. Cambridge: Cambridge University Press.

———. 1972. *Hegel's Theory of the Modern State*. Cambridge: Cambridge University Press.

Avrich, Paul. 1972. *Russian Rebels: 1600–1800*. New York: W. W. Norton.

Axelrod, Robert. 1984. *The Evolution of Cooperation*. New York: Basic Books.

Baechler, Jean. 1975. *Revolution*. New York: Harper Torchbooks.

Banfield, Edward C. 1958. *The Moral Basis of a Backward Society*. Glencoe, Ill.: Free Press.

———. 1974. *The Unheavenly City Revisited*. Boston: Little, Brown & Co.

Barnes, Samuel H. 1968. "Party Democracy and the Logic of Collective Action." In *Approaches to the Study of Party Organization*, ed. William J. Crotty, pp. 105–38. Boston: Allyn and Bacon.

Barnes, Samuel H., and Max Kaase. 1979. *Political Action: Mass Participation in Five Western Democracies*. Beverly Hills: Sage.

Barnett, A. Doak. 1968. *China on the Eve of Communist Takeover*. New York: Praeger.

Barry, Brian. 1965. *Political Argument*. London: Routledge & Kegan Paul.

———. 1974. "Review Article: 'Exit, Voice, and Loyalty'." *British Journal of Political Science* 4 (January): 79–107.

Barzel, Yoram. 1987. "Knight's Moral Hazard Theory of Organization." *Economic Inquiry* 25 (No. 1): 117–20.

Bates, Robert H. 1978. "The Issue Basis of Rural Politics in Africa." *Comparative Politics* 10 (April): 345–60.

———. 1983. *Essays on the Political Economy of Rural Africa*. Berkeley: University of California Press.

———. 1988. "Contra Contractarianism: Some Reflections on the New Institutionalism." *Politics and Society* 16 (June–September): 387–401.

———. 1989. *Beyond the Miracle of the Market: The Political Economy of Agrarian Development in Kenya*. Cambridge: Cambridge University Press.

———. 1990. "Macropolitical Economy in the field of Development." In

*Perspectives on Positive Political Economy*, ed. James E. Alt and Kenneth A. Shepsle, pp. 31–54. Cambridge: Cambridge University Press.

Bates, Robert H., and William T. Bianco. 1990. "Applying Rational Choice Theory: The Role of Leadership in Team Production." In *The Limits of Rationality*, ed. Karen Schweers Cook and Margaret Levi, pp. 349–57. Chicago: University of Chicago Press.

Becker, Gary S. 1968. "Crime and Punishment: An Economic Approach." *Journal of Political Economy* 76 (March/April): 169–217.

Bell, David V. J. 1973. *Resistance and Revolution*. Boston: Houghton Mifflin Company.

Bendix, Reinhard. 1960. *Max Weber: An Intellectual Portrait*. Garden City, N.Y.: Doubleday.

———. 1969. *Nation-Building and Citizenship: Studies of Our Changing Social Order*. Garden City, N.Y.: Anchor.

———. 1978. *Kings or People: Power and the Mandate to Rule*. Berkeley: University of California Press.

———. 1984. *Force, Fate, and Freedom: On Historical Sociology*. Berkeley: University of California Press.

Bercé, Yves-Marie. 1987. *Revolt and Revolution in Early Modern Europe: An Essay on the History of Political Violence*. Trans. Joseph Bergin. New York: St. Martin's Press.

Berelson, Bernard R., Paul F. Lazarsfeld, and William N. McPhee. 1954. *Voting: A Study of Opinion Formation in a Presidential Election*. Chicago: University of Chicago Press.

Berk, Richard A., and Howard E. Aldrich. 1972. "Patterns of Vandalism During Civil Disorders as an Indicator of Selection of Targets." *American Sociological Review* 37 (October): 533–47.

Bianco, Lucien. 1971. *Origins of the Chinese Revolution, 1915–1949*. Stanford, Calif.: Stanford University Press.

Bienen, Henry. 1968. *Violence and Social Change: A Review of Current Literature*. Chicago: University of Chicago Press.

Billington, James H. 1980. *Fire in the Minds of Men*. New York: Basic Books.

Birnbaum, Pierre. 1988. *States and Collective Action: The European Experience*. Cambridge: Cambridge University Press.

Bittner, Egon. 1963. "Radicalism and the Organization of Radical Movements." *American Sociological Review* 28 (December): 928–40.

Blalock, Hubert M., Jr. 1989. *Power and Conflict: Toward a General Theory*. Beverly Hills: Sage.

Blau, Peter. 1964. *Exchange and Power in Social Life*. New York: Wiley.

Bobo, Kim, Jackie Kendall, and Steve Max. 1991. *Organizing for Social Change: A Manual for Activists in the 1990s*. Washington, D.C.: Seven Locks Press.

Bolton, Charles D. 1972. "Alienation and Action: A Study of Peace Group Members." *American Journal of Sociology* 78 (November): 537–61.

Bonanate, Luigi. 1979. "Some Unanticipated Consequences of Terrorism." *Journal of Peace Research* 16 (No. 3): 197–211.

———. 1979. "Terrorism and International Political Analysis." *Terrorism* 3 (Nos. 1–2): 47–67.

Booth, Douglas E. 1978. "Collective Action, Marx's Class Theory, and the Union Movement." *Journal of Economic Issues* 12 (March): 163–85.

Booth, John A. 1985. *The End and the Beginning: The Nicaraguan Revolution*. 2nd Ed. Boulder, Colo.: Westview.

Borge, Tomás, Carlos Fonseca, Daniel Ortega, Humberto Ortega, and Jaime Wheelock. 1982. *Sandinistas Speak*. New York: Pathfinder Press.

Bornstein, Gary, and Amnon Rapoport. 1988. "Intergroup Competition for the Provision of Step-Level Public Goods: Effects of Preplay Communication." *European Journal of Social Psychology* 18 (April–June): 125–42.

Boudon, Raymond. 1987. "The Individualistic Tradition in Sociology." In *The Micro-Macro Link*, ed. Jeffrey C. Alexander, Berhard Giesen, Richard Münch, and Neil J. Smelser, pp. 153–73. Berkeley: University of California Press.

Bowman, John. 1982. "The Logic of Capitalist Collective Action." *Social Science Information* 21 (No. 4/5): 571–604.

———. 1985. "The Politics of the Market: Economic Competition and the Organization of Capitalists." *Political Power and Social Theory* 5: 35–88.

Brenner, Robert. 1976. "Agrarian Class Structure and Economic Development in Pre-Industrial Europe." *Past and Present* 70 (February): 30–75.

Breton, Albert, and Raymond Breton. 1969. "An Economic Theory of Social Movements." *American Economic Review* 59 (May): 198–205.

Brewer, John. 1988. "The English State and Fiscal Appropriation, 1688–1789." *Politics and Society* 16 (June–September): 335–85.

Brinton, Crane. 1965. *The Anatomy of Revolution*. Rev. and Exp. Ed. New York: Vintage Books.

Brooks, Thomas R. 1974. *Walls Come Tumbling Down: A History of the Civil Rights Movement, 1940–1970*. Englewood Cliffs, N.J.: Prentice-Hall.

Brown, Nathan. 1989. "The Conspiracy of Silence and the Atomistic Political Activity of the Egyptian Peasantry, 1882–1952." In *Everyday Forms of Peasant Resistance*, ed. Forrest D. Colburn, pp. 93–121. Armonk, N.Y.: M. E. Sharpe.

Brown, Roger. 1965. *Social Psychology*. New York: Free Press.

Brustein, William, and Margaret Levi. 1987. "The Geography of Rebellion:

Rulers, Rebels, and Regions, 1500–1700." *Theory and Society* 16 (July): 467–95.

Buchanan, Allen. 1979. "Revolutionary Motivation and Rationality." *Philosophy and Public Affairs* 9 (Fall): 59–82.

Buchanan, James M. 1965. "An Economic Theory of Clubs." *Economica* 32 (February): 1–14.

———. 1987. *Public Finance in Democratic Process: Fiscal Institutions and Individual Choice*. Chapel Hill, N.C.: University of North Carolina Press.

Bueno de Mesquita, Bruce. 1984. "Forecasting Policy Decisions: An Expected Utility Approach to Post-Khomeini Iran." *PS: Political Science and Politics* 17 (Spring): 226–36.

Burton, Michael G. 1977. "Elite Disunity and Collective Protest: The Vietnam Case." *Journal of Political and Military Sociology* 5 (Fall): 169–83.

———. 1984. "Elites and Collective Protest." *The Sociological Quarterly* 25 (Winter): 45–66.

Button, James W. 1978. *Black Violence: Political Impact of the 1960s Riots*. Princeton, N.J.: Princeton University Press.

Calhoun, Craig Jackson. 1982. *The Question of Class Struggle: Social Foundations of Popular Radicalism During the Industrial Revolution*. Chicago: University of Chicago Press.

———. 1988. "The Radicalism of Tradition and the Question of Class Struggle." In *Rationality and Revolution*, ed. Michael Taylor, pp. 129–75. Cambridge: Cambridge University Press.

Carsten, Francis L. 1967. *The Rise of Fascism*. Berkeley: University of California Press.

———. 1976. "Interpretations of Fascism." In *Fascism: A Reader's Guide; Analyses, Interpretations, Bibliography*, ed. Walter Laqueur, pp. 415–34. Berkeley: University of California Press.

Chalmers, James A., and Robert B. Shelton. 1975. "An Economic Analysis of Riot Participation." *Economic Inquiry* 13 (September): 322–36.

Chamberlin, William Henry. [1935] 1987. *The Russian Revolution, 1917–1918*. Volume 1. Princeton, N.J.: Princeton University Press.

Chong, Dennis. 1991. *Collective Action and the Civil Rights Movement*. Chicago: University of Chicago Press.

Chorley, Katharine. [1943] 1973. *Armies and the Art of Revolution*. Boston: Beacon Press.

Cicchetti, Charles J., A. Myrick Freeman III, Robert H. Haveman, and Jack L. Knetsch. 1971. "On the Economics of Mass Demonstrations: A Case Study of the November 1969 March on Washington." *American Economic Review* 61 (September): 719–24.

Clark, Peter B., and James Q. Wilson. 1961. "Incentive Systems: A Theory of Organizations." *Administrative Science Quarterly* 6 (June): 129–66.

Coase, R. H. 1960. "The Problem of Social Cost." *Journal of Law and Economics* 3 (October): 1–44.

Cohen, Jean L. 1985. "Strategy or Identity: New Theoretical Paradigms and Contemporary Social Movements." *Social Research* 52 (Winter): 663–716.

Cohen, Percy S. 1968. *Modern Social Theory.* New York: Basic Books.

Colburn, Forrest D. 1989a. "Introduction." In *Everyday Forms of Peasant Resistance*, ed. Forrest D. Colburn, pp. ix–xv. Armonk, N.Y.: M. E. Sharpe.

———. 1989b. "Foot Dragging and Other Peasant Responses to the Nicaraguan Revolution." In *Everyday Forms of Peasant Resistance*, ed. Forrest D. Colburn, pp. 175–97. Armonk, N.Y.: M. E. Sharpe.

Coleman, James S. 1957. *Community Conflict.* New York: Free Press.

———. 1978. "A Theory of Revolt Within an Authority Structure." *Papers of the Peace Science Society (International)* 28: 15–25.

———. 1987. "Microfoundations and Macrosocial Behavior." In *The Micro-Macro Link*, ed. Jeffrey C. Alexander, Berhard Giesen, Richard Münch, and Neil J. Smelser, pp. 153–73. Berkeley: University of California Press.

———. 1990. *Foundations of Social Theory.* Cambridge, Mass.: Belknap.

Colson, Elizabeth. 1974. *Tradition and Contract: The Problem of Order.* Chicago: Aldine.

Colvin, Mark. 1982. "The 1980 New Mexico Prison Riot." *Social Problems* 29 (June): 449–63.

Cornes, Richard, and Todd Sandler. 1986. *The Theory of Externalities, Public Goods and Club Goods.* Cambridge: Cambridge University Press.

Coser, Lewis A. 1956. *The Functions of Social Conflict.* New York: Free Press.

Costain, Anne N. 1992. *Inviting Women's Rebellion: A Political Process Interpretation of the Women's Movement.* Baltimore, Md.: Johns Hopkins University Press.

Cox, Gary W. 1987. *The Efficient Secret: The Cabinet and the Development of Political Parties in Victorian England.* Cambridge: Cambridge University Press.

Coyle, R. G. 1985. "A System Description of Counter Insurgency Warfare." *Policy Sciences* 18 (March): 55–78.

Crenshaw, Martha. 1986. "The Psychology of Political Terrorism." In *Political Psychology*, ed. Margaret G. Hermann, pp. 379–413. San Francisco: Jossey-Bass.

Crozier, Brian. 1960. *The Rebels: A Study of Post-War Insurrections.* Boston: Beacon Press.

Crozier, Michel. 1973. *The Stalled Society.* New York: Viking Press.

Curtis, Russell L., Jr., and Louis A. Zurcher, Jr. 1973. "Stable Resources of Protest Movements: The Multi-Organizational Field." *Social Forces* 52 (September): 53–61.

Dahl, Robert A. 1956. *A Preface to Democratic Theory.* Chicago: University of Chicago Press.

———. 1961. *Who Governs? Democracy and Power in an American City.* New Haven, Conn.: Yale University Press.

———. 1966. "Some Explanations." In *Political Oppositions in Western Democracies,* ed. Robert A. Dahl, pp. 348–86. New Haven, Conn.: Yale University Press.

———. 1970. *After the Revolution? Authority in the Good Society.* New Haven, Conn.: Yale University Press.

Dahrendorf, Ralf. 1959. *Class and Class Conflict in Industrial Society.* Stanford, Calif.: Stanford University Press.

———. 1968. *Essays in the Theory of Society.* Stanford, Calif.: Stanford University Press.

Davis, Otto, and Andrew B. Whinston. 1967. "On the Distinction Between Public and Private Goods." *American Economic Review* 57 (May): 360–73.

Dawidowicz, Lucy S. 1986. *The War Against the Jews: 1933–1945.* New York: Bantam Books.

Debray, Régis. 1967. *Revolution in the Revolution? Armed Struggle and Political Struggle in Latin America.* New York: Grove Press.

DeNardo, James. 1985. *Power in Numbers: The Political Strategy of Protest and Rebellion.* Princeton, N.J.: Princeton University Press.

Desai, Raj, and Harry Eckstein. 1990. "Insurgency: The Transformation of Peasant Rebellion." *World Politics* 42 (July): 441–65.

Deutsch, Karl W., et al. 1957. *Political Community and the North Atlantic Area: International Organization in the Light of Historical Experience.* Princeton, N.J.: Princeton University Press.

Deutsch, Morton. 1973. *The Resolution of Conflict: Constructive and Destructive Processes.* New Haven, Conn.: Yale University Press.

Devine, Philip E., and Robert J. Rafalko. 1982. "On Terror." *Annals* 463 (September): 39–53.

Dix, Robert H. 1984. "Why Revolutions Succeed & Fail." *Polity* 16 (Spring): 423–46.

Dobel, J. Patrick. 1978. "The Corruption of a State." *American Political Science Review* 72 (September): 958–73.

Donati, Paolo R. 1984. "Organization Between Movement and Institution." *Social Science Information* 23 (No. 4/5): 837–59.

Downs, Anthony. 1957. *An Economic Theory of Democracy.* New York: Harper & Row.

———. 1972. "Up and Down with Ecology—The 'Issue Attention Cycle.'"

*Public Interest* 28 (Summer): 38–50.

Dunn, John. 1989. *Modern Revolutions: An Introduction to the Analysis of a Political Phenomenon.* Cambridge: Cambridge University Press.

Durkheim, Emile. [1893] 1933. *The Division of Labor in Society.* New York: Free Press.

Duverger, Maurice. 1959. *Political Parties: Their Organization and Activity in the Modern State.* Trans. Barbara and Robert North. 2nd English Ed. Great Britain: McMuen & Co.

Eckert, Roland, and Helmut Willems. 1986. "Youth Protest in Western Europe: Four Case Studies." *Research in Social Movements, Conflicts and Change* 9: 127–53.

Eckstein, Harry. 1965. "On the Etiology of Internal Wars." *History and Theory* 4 (No. 2): 133–65.

———. 1966. *Division and Cohesion in Democracy: A Study of Norway.* Princeton, N.J.: Princeton University Press.

———. 1969. "Authority Relations and Governmental Performance: A Theoretical Framework." *Comparative Political Studies* 2 (October): 269–325.

———. 1975. "Case Study and Theory in Political Science." In *Handbook of Political Science: Volume 7—Strategies of Inquiry,* ed. Fred I. Greenstein and Nelson W. Polsby, pp. 79–137. Reading, Mass.: Addison–Wesley.

———. 1980. "Theoretical Approaches to Explaining Collective Political Violence." In *Handbook of Political Conflict: Theory and Research,* ed. Ted Robert Gurr, pp. 135–66. New York: Free Press.

Eckstein, Harry, and Ted Robert Gurr. 1975. *Patterns of Authority: A Structural Basis for Political Inquiry.* New York: Wiley.

Eckstein, Susan. 1989. "Power and Popular Protest in Latin America." In *Power and Popular Protest: Latin American Social Movements,* ed. Susan Eckstein, pp. 1–60. Berkeley: University of California Press.

Edelman, Murray. 1971. *Politics as Symbolic Action: Mass Arousal and Quiescence.* Chicago: Markham Publishing.

Eder, Klaus. 1982. "A New Social Movement?" *Telos* 52 (Summer): 5–20.

Edgerton, Robert B. 1985. *Rules, Exceptions, and Social Order.* Berkeley: University of California Press.

Edwards, Lyford P. 1927. *The Natural History of Revolution.* Chicago: University of Chicago Press.

Eggertsson, Thrainn. 1990. *Economic Behavior and Institutions.* Cambridge: Cambridge University Press.

Eisenstadt, S. N. 1978. *Revolution and the Transformation of Societies: A Comparative Study of Civilizations.* New York: Free Press.

Ellis, Desmond P. 1971. "The Hobbesian Problem of Order: A Critical Appraisal of the Normative Solution." *American Sociological Review* 36 (August): 692–703.

Elster, Jon. 1984. *Ulysses and the Sirens: Studies in Rationality and Irrationality.* Cambridge: Cambridge University Press.

———. 1985. *Making Sense of Marx.* Cambridge: Cambridge University Press.

———. 1989. *The Cement of Society: A Study of Social Order.* Cambridge: Cambridge University Press.

———. 1993. *Political Psychology.* Cambridge: Cambridge University Press

Emerson, Richard M. 1983. "Charismatic Kingship: A Study of State-Formation and Authority in Baltistan." *Politics and Society* 12 (No. 4): 413–44.

Erlanger, Howard S. 1977. "Social Reform Organizations and Subsequent Careers of Participants: A Follow-up Study of Early Participants in the OEO Legal Services Program." *American Sociological Review* 42 (April): 233–48.

Eschen, Donald Von, Jerome Kirk, and Maurice Pinard. 1971. "The Organizational Structure of Disorderly Politics." *Social Forces* 49 (June): 529–44.

Esman, Milton J. 1989. "Commentary." In *Everyday Forms of Peasant Resistance,* ed. Forrest D. Colburn, pp. 221–28. Armonk, N.Y.: M. E. Sharpe.

Esping-Andersen, Gosta. 1985. *The Social Democratic Road to Power.* Princeton, N.J.: Princeton University Press.

Etzioni, Amitai. 1970. *Demonstration Democracy.* New York: Gordon & Breach.

Evans, Sarah. 1979. *Personal Politics: The Roots of Women's Liberation in the Civil Rights Movement and the New Left.* New York: Alfred A. Knopf.

Falcoff, Mark. 1976. "Why Allende Fell." *Commentary* 62 (July): 38–45.

Fanon, Frantz. 1967. *The Wretched of the Earth.* Harmondsworth, England: Penguin Books.

Farhi, Farideh. 1990. *States and Urban-Based Revolutions: Iran and Nicaragua.* Urbana, Ill.: University of Illinois Press.

Feeny, David. 1983. "The Moral or the Rational Peasant? Competing Hypotheses of Collective Action." *Journal of Asian Studies* 42 (August): 769–89.

Feigenbaum, Susan, Susan Lynn Karoly, and David Levy. 1988. "When Votes are Words Not Deeds: Some Evidence from the Nuclear Freeze Referendum." *Public Choice* 58 (No. 3): 201–16.

Feit, Edward. 1975. "A Comment on Sigelman's 'Military Size and Political Intervention.'" *Journal of Political and Military Sociology* 3 (Spring): 101–2.

Femia, Joseph V. 1987. *Gramsci's Political Thought: Hegemony, Consciousness, and the Revolutionary Process.* Oxford: Clarendon Press.

Fendrich, James M. 1974. "Activists Ten Years Later: A Test of Generational Unit Continuity." *Journal of Social Issues* 30 (3): 95–118.

Feyerabend, Paul. 1988. *Against Method*. Rev. Ed. London: Verso.

Feynman, Richard. 1965. *The Character of Physical Law*. Cambridge, Mass.: M.I.T. Press.

Finer, Samuel E. 1976. *The Man On Horseback: The Role of the Military in Politics*. 2nd Ed. Harmondsworth, England: Penguin Books.

Finkel, Steven E., Edward N. Muller, and Karl-Dieter Opp. 1989. "Personal Influence, Collective Rationality, and Mass Political Action." *American Political Science Review* 83 (September): 885–903.

Fireman, Bruce, and William A. Gamson. 1979. "Utilitarian Logic in the Resource Mobilization Perspective." In *The Dynamics of Social Movements: Resource Mobilization, Social Control and Tactics*, ed. Mayer N. Zald and John D. McCarthy, pp. 8–44. Cambridge, Mass.: Winthrop.

Fitzgerald, Bruce D. 1978. "The Analytical Foundations of Extortionate Terrorism." *Terrorism* 1 (Nos. 3–4): 347–62.

Forst, Brian, and Judith Lucianovic. 1977. "The Prisoner's Dilemma: Theory and Reality." *Journal of Criminal Justice* 5 (Spring): 55–64.

Fossum, Egil. 1967. "Factors Influencing the Occurrence of Military Coups D'etat in Latin America." *Journal of Peace Research* 4 (No. 3): 228–51.

Fox, John, and Melvin Guyer. 1978. "Public Choice and Cooperation in n-Person Prisoner's Dilemma." *Journal of Conflict Resolution* 22 (September): 469–81.

Frank, J. A., and Michael Kelly. 1979. "'Street Politics' in Canada: An Examination of Mediating Factors." *American Journal of Political Science* 23 (August): 593–614.

Freeman, Jo. 1973. "The Origins of the Women's Liberation Movement." *American Journal of Sociology* 78 (January): 792–811.

———. 1979. "Resource Mobilization and Strategy: A Model for Analyzing Social Movement Organization Actions." In *The Dynamics of Social Movements: Resource Mobilization, Social Control, and Tactics*, ed. Mayer N Zald and John D. McCarthy, pp. 167–89. Cambridge, Mass.: Winthrop.

Friedman, James W. 1992. "Views on the Relevance of Game Theory." *Rationality and Society* 4 (Janury): 41–50.

Friedrich, Carl J. 1950. *Constitutional Government and Democracy: Theory and Practice in Europe and America*. Rev. Ed. New York: Blaisdell.

Frohlich, Norman, and Joe A. Oppenheimer. 1970. "I Get By With a Little Help from My Friends." *World Politics* 23 (October): 104–20.

———. 1973. "Government Violence and Tax Revenue." In *Violence as Politics: A Series of Original Essays*, ed. Herbert Hirsch and David C. Perry, pp. 72–88. New York: Harper & Row.

————. 1978. *Modern Political Economy.* Englewood Cliffs, N.J.: Prentice-Hall.

Frohlich, Norman, Joe A. Oppenheimer, and Oran R. Young. 1971. *Political Leadership and Collective Goods.* Princeton, N.J.: Princeton University Press.

Fuentes, Marta, and Andre Gunder Frank. 1989. "Ten Theses on Social Movements." *World Development* 17 (February): 179–91.

Galler, Omer R., Walter R. Gove, and J. Miller McPherson. 1972. "Population Density and Pathology: What Are the Relations for Man?" *Science* 176 (4030): 23-30.

Gallie, Duncan. 1982. "The Agrarian Roots of Working-Class Radicalism: An Assessment of the Mann-Giddens Thesis." *British Journal of Political Science* 12 (April): 149–72.

Gamson, William A. 1974. "Violence and Political Power: The Meek Don't Make It." *Psychology Today* 7 (July): 35–41.

————. 1990. *The Strategy of Social Protest.* 2nd Ed. Belmont, Calif.: Wadsworth.

Garson, G. David. 1972. "The Disruption of Prison Administration: An Investigation of Alternative Theories of the Relationship Among Administrators, Reformers, and Involuntary Social Service Clients." *Law and Society Review* 6 (May): 531–61.

Gauthier, David P. 1986. *Morals By Agreement.* Oxford: Clarendon Press.

Geertz, Clifford. 1973. "Thick Description: Toward an Interpretive Theory of Culture." In *The Interpretation of Cultures*, ed. Clifford Geertz, pp. 3–30. New York: Basic Books.

Gerlach, Luther P. 1971. "Movements of Revolutionary Change." *American Behavioral Scientist* 14 (July/August): 812–36.

Giddens, Anthony. 1971. *Capitalism and Modern Social Theory: An Analysis of the Writings of Marx, Durkheim and Max Weber.* Cambridge: Cambridge University Press.

————. 1979. *Central Problems in Social Theory: Action, Structure and Contradiction in Social Analysis.* Berkeley: University of California Press.

Glaser, Barney G. and Anselm L. Strauss. 1967. *The Discovery of Grounded Theory: Strategies for Qualitative Research.* New York: Aldine De Gruyter.

Gluckman, Max. 1960. *Custom and Conflict in Africa.* Oxford: Basil Blackwell.

Goldfrank, Walter L. 1975. "World System, State Structure, and the Onset of the Mexican Revolution." *Politics and Society* 5 (No. 4): 417–39.

————. 1979. "Theories of Revolution and Revolution Without Theory: The Case of Mexico." *Theory and Society* 7 (January–March): 135–65.

Goldscheider, Calvin and Alan S. Zuckerman. 1984. *The Transformation of the Jews*. Chicago: University of Chicago Press.

Goldstone, Jack A. 1980. "The Weakness of Organization: A New Look at Gamson's *The Strategy of Social Protest*." *American Journal of Sociology* 85 (March): 1017–42.

———. 1986a. "Revolution and Superpowers." In *Superpowers and Revolution*, ed. Jonathan R. Adelman, pp. 38–48. New York: Praeger.

———. 1986b. "State Breakdown in the English Revolution: A New Synthesis." *American Journal of Sociology* 92 (September): 257–322.

———. 1988. "East and West in the Seventeenth Century: Political Crises in Stuart England, Ottoman Turkey, and Ming China." *Comparative Studies in Society and History* 30 (January): 103–42.

———. 1991. *Revolution and Rebellion in the Early Modern World*. Berkeley: University of California Press.

Goodwin, Jeff, and Theda Skocpol. 1989. "Explaining Revolutions in the Contemporary Third World." *Politics and Society* 17 (December): 489–509.

Gottschalk, Louis. 1944. "Causes of Revolution." *American Journal of Sociology* 50 (July): 1–8.

Granovetter, Mark. 1978. "Threshold Models of Collective Behavior." *American Journal of Sociology* 83 (May): 1420–43.

Green, Leslie. 1982. "Rational Nationalists." *Political Studies* 30 (June): 236–46.

Greene, Thomas H. 1990. *Comparative Revolutionary Movements: Search for Theory and Justice*. Third Ed. Englewood Cliffs, N.J.: Prentice-Hall.

Guevara, Ernesto. 1961. *Che Guevara on Guerrilla Warfare*. New York: Praeger.

Guha, Ramachandra. 1989. "Saboteurs in the Forest: Colonialism and the Peasant Resistance in the Indian Himalaya." In *Everyday Forms of Peasant Resistance*, ed. Forrest D. Colburn, pp. 64–92. Armonk, N.Y.: M. E. Sharpe.

Gunning J. Patrick. 1972. "An Economic Approach to Riot Analysis." *Public Choice* 13 (Fall): 31–46.

Gurr, Ted Robert. 1968. "A Causal Model of Civil Strife: A Comparative Analysis Using New Indices." *American Political Science Review* 62 (December): 1104–24.

———. 1970. *Why Men Rebel*. Princeton, N.J.: Princeton University Press.

———. 1979. "Some Characteristics of Political Terrorism in the 1960s." In *The Politics of Terrorism*, ed. Michael Stohl, pp. 23–49. New York: Marcel Dekker.

———. 1985. "On the Political Consequences of Scarcity and Economic Decline." *International Studies Quarterly* 29 (March): 51–75.

————. 1989. "The History of Protest, Rebellion, and Reform in America: An Overview." In *Violence in America. Volume 2: Protest, Rebellion, Reform*, ed. Ted Robert Gurr, pp. 11–22. Newbury Park, Calif.: Sage.

Gurr, Ted Robert, and Raymond Duvall. 1973. "Civil Conflict in the 1960s: A Reciprocal Theoretical System With Parameter Estimates." *Comparative Political Studies* 6 (July): 135–69.

Gurr, Ted Robert, and Mark Irving Lichbach. 1979. "Forecasting Domestic Political Conflict." In *To Augur Well: Forecasting in the Social Sciences*, ed. J. David Singer and Michael D. Wallace, pp. 153–93. Beverly Hills: Sage.

————. 1986. "Forecasting Internal Conflict: A Competitive Evaluation of Empirical Theories." *Comparative Political Studies* 19 (April): 3–38.

Gurr, Ted Robert, and Muriel McClelland. 1971. *Political Performance: A Twelve Nation Study*. Beverly Hills: Sage Professional Papers in Comparative Politics, 01–018.

Guttman, Joel M. 1978. "Understanding Collective Action: Matching Behavior." *American Economic Review* 68 (May): 251–55.

Habermas, Jürgen. 1981. "New Social Movements." *Telos* 49 (Fall): 33–37.

Hagopian, Mark N. 1974. *The Phenomenon of Revolution*. New York: Dodd, Mead and Co.

Hall, John A., and G. John Ikenberry. 1989. *The State*. Minneapolis, Minn.: University of Minnesota Press.

Hannigan, John A. 1985. "Alaine Touraine, Manuel Castells and Social Movement Theory: A Critical Appraisal." *The Sociological Quarterly* 26 (No. 4): 435–54.

Hansen, John Mark. 1985. "The Political Economy of Group Membership." *American Political Science Review* 79 (March): 79–96.

Hardin, Russell. 1982. *Collective Action*. Baltimore, Md.: Johns Hopkins University Press.

————. 1990. "The Social Evolution of Cooperation." In *The Limits of Rationality*, ed. Karen Schweers Cook and Margaret Levi, pp. 358–78. Chicago: University of Chicago Press.

Hechter, Michael. 1988. *Principles of Group Solidarity*. Berkeley: University of California Press.

————. 1990. "On the Inadequacy of Game Theory for the Solution of Real-World Collective Action Problems." In *The Limits of Rationality*, ed. Karen Schweers Cook and Margaret Levi, pp. 240–49. Chicago: University of Chicago Press.

————. 1992. "The Insufficiency of Game Theory for the Resolution of Real-World Collective Action Problems." *Rationality and Society* 4 (Janury): 33–40.

Hechter, Michael, and William Brustein. 1980. "Regional Modes of Production and Patterns of State Formation in Western Europe." *American Journal of Sociology* 85 (March): 1061–94.

Hibbs, Douglas A., Jr. 1973. *Mass Political Violence: A Cross-National Causal Analysis.* New York: Wiley.

Higley, John, and Michael G. Burton. 1989. "The Elite Variable in Democratic Transitions and Breakdowns." *American Sociological Review* 54 (February): 17–32.

Hilton, Rodney. 1973. *Bond Men Made Free: Medieval Peasant Movements and the English Rising of 1381.* London: Methuen.

Himes, Joseph S. 1980. *Conflict and Conflict Management.* Athens, Ga.: University of Georgia Press.

Hirschman, Albert O. 1970a. *Exit, Voice, and Loyalty: Responses to Decline in Firms, Organizations, and States.* Cambridge, Mass.: Harvard University Press.

———. 1970b. "The Search for Paradigms as a Hindrance to Understanding." *World Politics* 22 (April): 329–43.

———. 1974. "'Exit, Voice, and Loyalty': Further Reflections and a Survey of Recent Contributions." *Social Science Information* 13 (February): 7–26.

———. 1978. "Exit, Voice, and the State." *World Politics* 31 (October): 90–107.

———. 1982a. *Shifting Involvements: Private Interest and Public Action.* Princeton, N.J.: Princeton University Press.

———. 1982b. "Rival Interpretations of Market Society: Civilizing, Destructive, or Feeble?" *Journal of Economic Literature* 20 (December): 1463–84.

———. 1993. "Exit, Voice, and the Fate of the German Democratic Republic: An Essay in Conceptual History." *World Politics* 45 (January): 173–202.

Hirshleifer, David, and Eric Rasmusen. 1989. "Cooperation in a Repeated Prisoners' Dilemma with Ostracism." *Journal of Economic Behavior and Organization* 12 (August): 87–106.

Hirshleifer, Jack. 1983. "From Weakest-Link to Best-Shot: The Voluntary Provision of Public Goods." *Public Choice* 41 (No. 3): 371–86.

———. 1987. "The Economic Approach to Conflict." In *Economic Imperialism: The Economic Approach Applied Outside of the Field of Economics,* ed. Gerald Radnitzky and Peter Bernholz, pp. 355–64. New York: Paragon House.

Hobbes, Thomas. [1640] 1969. *Elements of Law, Natural and Politic.* 2nd Ed. Ferdinand Tönnies, ed.. Cambridge: Cambridge University Press.

———. [1651] 1988. *Leviathan.* London: Penguin.

Hobsbawm, Eric J. 1952. "The Machine Breakers." *Past and Present* 1 (February): 57–70.

———. 1959. *Primitive Rebels: Studies in Archaic Forms of Social Movement in the 19th and 20th Centuries.* New York: W. W. Norton.

———. 1975. *The Age of Capital: 1848–1875.* New York: Charles Scribner's Sons.

———. 1981. *Bandits.* Rev. Ed. New York: Pantheon Books.

Hobsbawm, Eric J., and George Rudé. 1968. *Captain Swing: A Social History of the Great English Agricultural Uprising of 1830.* New York: W. W. Norton.

Hoffer, Eric. 1951. *The True Believer: Thoughts on the Nature of Mass Movements.* New York: Harper & Row.

Hoffman, Abbie. 1968. *Revolution for the Hell of It.* New York: Dial Press.

Hoffmann, Stanley. 1979. "Fragments Floating in the Here and Now." *Daedalus* 108 (Winter): 1–27.

Hopper, Rex. 1950. "The Revolutionary Process: A Frame of Reference for the Study of Revolutionary Movements." *Social Forces* 28 (March): 270–79.

Hunter, Robert. 1940. *Revolution: Why, How, When?* New York: Harper & Brothers.

Huntington, Samuel P. 1965. "Political Development and Political Decay." *World Politics* 17 (April): 386–430.

———. 1968. *Political Order in Changing Societies.* New Haven, Conn.: Yale University Press.

———. 1974. "Postindustrial Politics: How Benign Will It Be?" *Comparative Politics* 6 (January): 163–91.

Hutchinson, Margaret Crenshaw. 1972. "The Concept of Revolutionary Terrorism." *Journal of Conflict Resolution* 16 (September): 383–96.

Im, Eric Iksoon, Jon Cauley, and Todd Sandler. 1987. "Cycles and Substitutions in Terrorist Activities: A Spectral Approach." *Kyklos* 40 (Fasc. 2): 238–55.

Inglehart, Ronald. 1990. *Culture Shift in Advanced Industrial Society.* Princeton, N.J.: Princeton University Press.

Ireland, Thomas. 1967. "The Rationale of Revolt." *Papers on Nonmarket Decision Making* 3: 49–66.

Jäckel, Eberhard 1982. *Hitler's World View: A Blueprint for Power.* Trans. Herbert Arnold. Cambridge, Mass: Harvard University Press.

Jackson, Maurice, Eleanora Peterson, James Bull, Sverre Monsen, and Patricia Richmond. 1960. "The Failure of an Incipient Social Movement." *Pacific Sociological Review* 3 (Spring): 35–40.

Jacob, Philip E., and Henry Teune. 1964. "The Integrative Process: Guidelines for Analysis of the Bases of Political Community." In *The Integration of Political Communities*, ed. Philip E. Jacob and James V. Toscano, pp. 1–45. Philadelphia, Pa.: J. B. Lippincott Company.

Jasay, Anthony de. 1989. *Social Contract, Free Ride: A Study of the Public Goods Problem*. Oxford: Clarendon Press.

Jeffrey, Richard C. 1983. *The Logic Of Decision*. 2nd Ed. Chicago: University of Chicago Press.

Jenkins, Brian Michael. 1982. "Statements About Terrorism." *Annals* 463 (September): 11–23.

Jenkins, Brian, Janera Johnson, and David Ronfeldt. 1978. "Numbered Lives: Some Statistical Observations from 77 International Hostage Episodes." *Conflict* 1 (Nos. 1 and 2): 71–111.

Jenkins, J. Craig. 1983. "Resource Mobilization Theory and the Study of Social Movements." *Annual Review of Sociology* 9: 527–53.

———. 1985. *The Politics of Insurgency: The Farm Worker Movement in the 1960s*. New York: Columbia University Press.

Jenkins, J. Craig, and Barbara G. Brents. 1989. "Social Protest, Hegemonic Competition, and Social Reform: A Political Struggle Interpretation of the Origins of the American Welfare State." *American Sociological Review* 54 (December): 891–909.

Jenkins, J. Craig, and Craig M. Eckert. 1986. "Channeling Black Insurgency: Elite Patronage and Professional Social Movement Organizations in the Development of the Black Movement." *American Sociological Review* 51 (December): 812–29.

Jenkins, J. Craig, and Charles Perrow. 1977. "Insurgency of the Powerless: Farm Worker Movements (1946–1972)." *American Sociological Review* 42 (April): 249–68.

Jenkins, J. Craig, and Kurt Schock. 1992. "Global Structures and Political Processes in the Study of Domestic Political Conflict." *Annual Review of Sociology* 18: 161–85.

Johnson, Chalmers. 1964. *Revolution and the Social System*. Stanford, Calif.: The Hoover Institution on War, Revolution, and Peace, Stanford University.

———. 1966. *Revolutionary Change*. Boston: Little, Brown and Company.

Jones, Anthony James. 1974. "Fascism: The Past and the Future." *Comparative Political Studies* 7 (April): 107–33.

Jorgenson, Dale O., and Anthony S. Papciak. 1981. "The Effects of Communication, Resource Feedback, and Identifiability on Behavior in a Simulated Commons." *Journal of Experimental Social Psychology* 17(July): 373–85.

Kahn, Si. 1982. *Organizing: A Guide for Grassroots Leaders*. New York: McGraw-Hill.

Kanter, Rosabeth Moss. 1972. "Commitment and the Internal Organization of Millennial Movements." *American Behavioral Scientist* 16 (November/December): 219–43.

Kaplan, Abraham. 1978. "The Psychodynamics of Terrorism." *Terrorism* 1 (Nos. 3–4): 237–54.

Kaplowitz, Stan A., and Bradley J. Fisher. 1985. "Revealing the Logic of Free-Riding and the Contributions to the Nuclear Freeze Movement." *Research in Social Movements, Conflicts and Change* 8: 47–64.

Katznelson, Ira. 1986. "Working-Class Formation: Constructing Cases and Comparisons." In *Working Class Formation: Nineteenth-Century Patterns in Western Europe and the United States*, ed. Ira Katznelson and Aristide R. Zolberg, pp. 3–41. Princeton, N.J.: Princeton University Press.

Keniston, Kenneth. 1968. *Young Radicals: Notes on Committed Youth*. New York: Harcourt, Brace & World.

Kennedy, Gavin. 1974. *The Military in the Third World*. London: Duckworth.

Keohane, Robert O. 1984. *After Hegemony: Cooperation and Discord in the World Political Economy*. Princeton, N.J.: Princeton University Press.

Kerner Commission. 1968. *Report of the National Advisory Commission on Civil Disorders*. New York: Bantam Books.

Kerr, Clark, and Abraham Siegel. 1954. "The Interindustry Propensity to Strike." In *Industrial conflict*, ed. Arthur Kornhauser et al., pp. 189–212. New York: McGraw-Hill.

Key, V. O. 1950. *Southern Politics*. New York: Knopf.

Kimmel, Michael S. 1988. *Absolutism and its Discontents*. New Brunswick, N.J.: Transaction.

———. 1990. *Revolution: A Sociological Interpretation*. Philadelphia, Pa.: Temple University Press.

King, Gary, Robert O. Keohane, and Sidney Verba. 1994. *Designing Social Inquiry: Scientific Inference in Qualitative Research*. Princeton, N.J.: Princeton University Press.

Kirchheimer, Otto. 1966. "The Transformation of the Western European Party Systems." In *Political Parties and Political Development*, ed. Joseph LaPalombara and Myron Weiner, pp. 177–200. Princeton, N.J.: Princeton University Press.

Kirk, Richard M. 1983. "Political Terrorism and the Size of Government: A Positive Institutional Analysis of Violent Political Activity." *Public Choice* 40 (No. 1): 41–52.

Kitschelt, Herbert. 1989. *The Logics of Party Formation: Ecological Politics in Belgium and West Germany*. Ithaca, N.Y.: Cornell University Press.

Klandermans, Bert. 1984. "Mobilization and Participation: Social-Psychological Expansions of Resource Mobilization Theory." *American Socio-*

*logical Review* 49 (October): 583–600.

————. 1988. "Union Action and the Free-Rider Dilemma." *Research in Social Movements, Conflicts and Change* 10: 77-91.

Kling, Merle. 1956. "Towards a Theory of Power and Political Instability in Latin America." *Western Political Quarterly* 9 (March): 21–35.

Knight, Frank H. 1921. *Risk, Uncertainty and Profit.* Boston: Houghton Mifflin.

Knoke, David. 1988. "Incentives in Collective Action Organizations." *American Sociological Review* 53 (June): 311–29.

Kochanowicz, Jacek. 1989. "Between Submission and Violence: Peasant Resistance in the Polish Manorial Economy of the Eighteenth Century." In *Everyday Forms of Peasant Resistance,* ed. Forrest D. Colburn, pp. 34–63. Armonk, N.Y.: M. E. Sharpe.

Kornhauser, William. 1959. *The Politics of Mass Society.* New York: Free Press.

Korpi, Walter. 1974. "Conflict, Power and Relative Deprivation." *American Political Science Review* 67 (December): 1569–78.

Kreps, David M., Paul Milgrom, John Roberts, and Robert Wilson. 1982. "Rational Cooperation in Finitely-Repeated Prisoners' Dilemma." *Journal of Economic Theory* 27 (August): 245–52.

Kuran, Timur. 1987. "Preference Falsification, Policy Continuity and Collective Conservatism." *The Economic Journal* 97 (September): 642–65.

————. 1989. "Sparks and Prairie Fires: A Theory of Unanticipated Political Revolution." *Public Choice* 61 (April): 41–74.

————. 1991a. "Now Out of Never: The Element of Surprise in the Eastern European Revolution of 1989." *World Politics* 44 (October): 7–48.

————. 1991b. "Cognitive Limitations and Preference Evolution." *Journal of Institutional and Theoretical Economics* 147 (June): 241–73.

————. 1993. "The Unthinkable and the Unthought." *Rationality and Society* 5 (October): 473–505.

————. Forthcoming. *Private Truths, Public Lies: The Social Consequences of Preference Falsification.* Cambridge, Mass.: Harvard University Press.

Laitin, David D. 1986. *Hegemony and Culture: Politics and Religious Change Among the Yoruba.* Chicago: University of Chicago Press.

Lakatos, Imre. 1970. "Falsification and the Methodology of Scientific Research Programs." In *Criticism and the Growth of Knowledge,* ed. Imre Lakatos and Alan Musgrave, pp. 91–196. Cambridge: Cambridge University Press.

Landes, William M. 1978. "An Economic Study of U.S. Aircraft Hijacking, 1961–1976." *Journal of Law and Economics* 21 (April): 1–31.

Landsberger, Betty H., and Henry A. Landsberger. 1974. "The English Peasant Revolt of 1381." In *Rural Protest: Peasant Movements and Social Change*, ed. Henry A. Landsberger, pp. 95–141. London: Macmillan.

Landsberger, Henry A. 1974. "Peasant Unrest: Themes and Variations." In *Rural Protest: Peasant Movements and Social Change*, ed. Henry A. Landsberger, pp. 1–64. London: Macmillan.

Laqueur, Walter. 1968. "Revolution." In *International Encyclopedia of the Social Sciences*, vol. 13, ed. David L. Sills, pp. 501–7. New York: Macmillan.

———. 1976. *Guerrilla: A Historical and Critical Study*. Boston: Little, Brown and Co.

———. 1978. *The Terrorism Reader: An Historical Anthology*. New York: Meridian.

———. 1987. *The Age of Terrorism*. Boston: Little, Brown and Co.

Lasswell, Harold D., and Abraham Kaplan. 1950. *Power and Society: A Framework for Political Inquiry*. New Haven, Conn.: Yale University Press.

Lee, Dwight R., and Todd Sandler. 1989. "On the Optimal Retaliation Against Terrorists: The Paid-Rider Option." *Public Choice* 61 (May): 141–52.

Lefebvre, Georges. 1947. *The Coming of the French Revolution*. Princeton, N.J.: Princeton University Press.

Lehman-Wilzig, Sam N. 1990. *Stiff-Necked People, Bottle-Necked System: The Evolution and Roots of Israeli Public Protest, 1949–1986*. Bloomington, In.: Indiana University Press.

Leites, Nathan. 1979. "Understanding the Next Act." *Terrorism* 3 (Nos. 1–2): 1–46.

Leites, Nathan, and Charles Wolf, Jr. 1970. *Rebellion and Authority: An Analytic Essay on Insurgent Conflicts*. Chicago: Markham Publishing Co.

Levi, Margaret. 1974. "Poor People Against the State." *Review of Radical Political Economics* 6 (Spring): 76–98.

———. 1981. "The Predatory Theory of Rule." *Politics and Society* 10 (No. 4): 431–65.

———. 1988. *Of Rule and Revenue*. Berkeley: University of California Press.

Levi, Margaret, Karen S. Cook, Jodi A. O'Brien, and Howard Faye. 1990. "Introduction: The Limits of Rationality." In *The Limits of Rationality*, ed. Karen Schweers Cook and Margaret Levi, pp. 1–16. Chicago: University of Chicago Press.

Levi, Margaret, and Michael Hechter. 1985. "A Rational Choice Approach to the Rise and Decline of Ethnoregional Political Parties." In *New Nation-*

*alisms of the Developed West: Toward Explanation*, ed. Edward Tiryakian and Ronald Rogowski, pp. 128–46. Boston: Allen and Unwin.

Levine, David H., and Scott Mainwaring. 1989. "Religion and Popular Protest in Latin America: Contrasting Experiences." In *Power and Popular Protest: Latin American Social Movements*, ed. Susan Eckstein, pp. 203–40. Berkeley: University of California Press.

Lewis, David. 1969. *Convention: A Philosophical Study.* Cambridge, Mass.: Harvard University Press.

Lewy, Guenter. 1974. *Religion and Revolution.* New York: Oxford University Press.

Lichbach, Mark Irving. 1984. "An Economic Theory of Governability: Choosing Policy and Optimizing Performance." *Public Choice* 44 (No. 2): 307–37.

———. 1985a. "Protest in America: Univariate ARIMA Models of the Postwar Era." *Western Political Quarterly* 38 (September): 388–412.

———. 1985b. "Protest: Random or Contagious? The Postwar United Kingdom." *Armed Forces and Society* 11 (Summer): 581–608.

———. 1987. "Deterrence or Escalation? The Puzzle of Aggregate Studies of Repression and Dissent." *Journal of Conflict Resolution* 31 (June): 266–97.

———. 1989. "An Evaluation of 'Does Economic Inequality Breed Political Conflict' Studies." *World Politics* 41 (July): 431–70.

———. 1990. "Will Rational People Rebel Against Inequality? Samson's Choice." *American Journal of Political Science* 34 (November): 1049–76.

———. 1992. "Nobody Cites Nobody Else: Mathematical Models of Domestic Political Conflict." *Defence Economics* 3 (No. 4): 341–57.

———. 1994a. "Rethinking Rationality and Rebellion: Theories of Collective Action and Problems of Collective Dissent." *Rationality and Society* 6 (January): 8–39.

———. 1994b. "What Makes Rational Peasants Revolutionary? Dilemma, Paradox and Irony in Peasant Collective Action." *World Politics* 46 (April): 382–417.

———. forthcoming. *The Cooperator's Dilemma.* Ann Arbor, Mich.: University of Michigan Press.

Lichbach, Mark Irving, and Ted Robert Gurr. 1981. "The Conflict Process: A Formal Model." *Journal of Conflict Resolution* 25 (March): 3–29.

Lieberson, Stanley, and Arnold R. Silverman. 1965. "The Precipitants and Underlying Conditions of Race Riots." *American Sociological Review* 30 (December): 887–98.

Lijphart, Arend. 1969. "Consociational Democracy." *World Politics* 21 (January): 207–25.

———. 1975. *The Politics of Accommodation: Pluralism and Democracy in the Netherlands.* 2nd Ed. Berkeley: University of California Press.

———. 1977. *Democracy in Plural Societies: A Comparative Exploration.* New Haven, Conn.: Yale University Press.

Linz, Juan J. 1976. "Some Notes Toward a Comparative Study of Fascism in Sociological Historical Perspective." In *Fascism: A Reader's Guide; Analyses, Interpretation, Bibliography,* ed. Walter Laqueur, pp. 3–121. Berkeley: University of California Press.

Lipset, Seymour Martin. 1959. "Some Social Requisites of Democracy: Economic Development and Political Legitimacy." *American Political Science Review* 53 (March): 69–105.

———. 1963. *Political Man: The Social Bases of Politics.* New York: Anchor Books

———. 1964. "University Students and Politics in Underdeveloped Countries." *Minerva* 3 (Autumn): 15–56.

———. 1967. "Introduction: Students and Politics in Comparative Perspective." In *Students in Revolt,* ed. Seymour Martin Lipset and Philip G. Altbach, pp. xv–xxxiv. Boston: Beacon Press.

———. 1971a. *Agrarian Socialism: The Cooperative Commonwealth Federation in Saskatchewan, A Study in Political Sociology.* Berkeley: University of California Press.

———. 1971b. *Rebellion in the University.* Boston: Little, Brown and Company.

———. 1977a. "Why No Socialism in the United States?" In *Radicalism in the Contemporary Age. Volume 1: Sources of Contemporary Radicalism,* ed. Seweryn Bialer and Sophia Sluzar, pp. 31–149. Boulder, Colo.: Westview.

———. 1977b. "American 'Exceptionalism' in North American Perspective: Why the United States Has Withstood the Worldwide Socialist Movement." In *The Idea of America: A Reassessment of the American Experiment,* ed. E.M. Adams, pp. 107–61. Cambridge, Mass.: Ballinger.

Lipset, Seymour Martin, and Stein Rokkan. 1967. "Cleavage Structures, Party Systems, and Voter Alignments: An Introduction." In *Party Systems and Voter Alignments,* ed. Seymour Martin Lipset and Stein Rokkan, pp. 1–64. New York: Free Press.

Lipset, Seymour, Martin Trow, and James Coleman. 1962. *Union Democracy: The Internal Politics of the International Typographical Union.* Garden City, N.Y.: Anchor Books.

Lipsky, Michael. 1968. "Protest as a Political Resource." *American Political Science Review* 62 (December): 1144–58.

Lloyd, Christopher. 1986. *Explanation in Social History.* New York: Basil Blackwell.

Lowi, Theodore J. 1971. *The Politics of Disorder*. New York: Basic Books.

Luttwak, Edward. 1968. *Coup D'Etat: A Practical Handbook*. Greenwood, Conn.: Fawcett Premier Book.

McAdam, Doug. 1982. *Political Process and the Development of Black Insurgency 1930–1970*. Chicago: University of Chicago Press.

———. 1986. "Recruitment to High-Risk Activism: The Case of Freedom Summer." *American Journal of Sociology* 92 (July): 64–90.

McAdam, Doug, John D. McCarthy, and Mayer N. Zald. 1988. "Social Movements." In *Handbook of Sociology*, ed. Neil J. Smelser, pp. 695–737. Beverly Hills: Sage.

McCarthy, John D., and Mayer N. Zald. 1973. *The Trend of Social Movements in America: Professionalization and Resource Mobilization*. Morristown, N.J.: General Learning Press.

———. 1977. "Resource Mobilization and Social Movements: A Partial Theory." *American Journal of Sociology* 82 (May): 1212–41.

McCaughrin, Craig. 1983. "Statics and Dynamics of Dissent." *Comparative Political Studies* 15 (January): 405–23.

McClintock, Cynthia. 1984. "Why Peasants Rebel: The Case of Peru's Sendero Luminoso." *World Politics* 37 (October): 48–84.

McFarland, Andrew. 1991. "Why Interest Groups Organize: A Pluralist Response to Olson." Paper Presented at the Annual Meeting of the Western Political Science Association. Seattle, Washington, March 21–23.

McGinnis, Michael D. 1986. "Issue Linkage and the Evolution of International Cooperation." *Journal of Conflict Resolution* 30 (March): 14–70.

Machiavelli, Niccolo. [1514] 1961. *The Prince*. London: Penguin.

Mack, Raymond W., and Richard C. Snyder. 1957. "The Analysis of Social Conflict: Toward an Overview and Synthesis." *Journal of Conflict Resolution* 1 (June): 212–48.

McKown, Roberta E. 1975. "Domestic Correlates of Military Intervention in African Politics." *Journal of Political and Military Sociology* 3 (Fall): 191–206.

McMahon, Anne M., and Santo F. Camilleri. 1975. "Organizational Structure and Voluntary Participation in Collective-Good Decisions." *American Sociological Review* 40 (October): 616–44.

McNall, Scott G.. 1988. *Road to Rebellion: Class Formation and Kansas Populism 1860-1900*. Chicago: University of Chicago Press.

Madison, James, Alexander Hamilton, and John Jay. [1788] 1987. *The Federalist Papers*. Issac Kramnick, Ed. New York: Penguin.

Mann, Michael. 1973. *Consciousness and Action Among the Western Working Class*. London: Macmillan.

———. 1987. "Ruling Class Strategies and Citizenship." *Sociology* 21 (August): 339–54.

Mansbridge, Jane J. 1986. *Why We Lost the ERA*. Chicago: University of Chicago Press.

———. Ed. 1990. *Beyond Self-Interest*. Chicago: University of Chicago Press.

Mao Tse-tung. 1961. *Mao Tse-tung On Guerrilla Warfare*. Trans. Samuel B. Griffith. New York: Praeger.

Marable, Manning. 1991. *Race, Reform, and Rebellion: The Second Reconstruction in Black America, 1945–1990*. 2nd Ed. Jackson, Miss.: University Press of Mississippi.

Maranto, Robert. 1987. "The Rationality of Terrorism." In *Multidimensional Terrorism*, ed. Martin Slann and Bernard Schechterman, pp. 11–18. Boulder, Colo.: Lynne Rienner.

Margolis, Howard. 1982. *Selfishness, Altruism and Rationality: A Theory of Social Choice*. Chicago: University of Chicago Press.

Marsh, David. 1976. "On Joining Interest Groups: An Empirical Consideration of the Work of Mancur Olson, Jr." *British Journal of Political Science* 6 (July): 257–71.

———. 1978. "More on Joining Interest Groups." *British Journal of Political Science* 8 (July): 380–84.

Marsh, Robert M. 1967. *Comparative Sociology: A Codification of Cross-Societal Analysis*. New York: Harcourt, Brace and World.

Marshall, Gordon. 1983. "Some Remarks on the Study of Working-Class Consciousness." *Politics and Society* 12 (No. 3): 263–301.

Martic, Milos. 1975. *Insurrection: Five Schools of Revolutionary Thought*. New York: Dunellen.

Marwell, Gerald, and Pamela Oliver. 1984. "Collective Action Theory and Social Movements Research." In *Social Movements, Conflicts and Change*, vol. 7, ed. Louis Kriesberg, pp. 1–27. Greenwich, Conn.: JAI Press.

Marwell, Gerald, Pamela E. Oliver, and Ralph Prahl. 1988. "Social Networks and Collective Action: A Theory of Critical Mass. III." *American Journal of Sociology* 94 (November): 502–34.

Marx, Gary T. 1974. "Thoughts on a Neglected Category of Social Movement Participant: The Agent Provocateur and the Informant." *American Journal of Sociology* 80 (September): 402–42.

Marx, Gary T., and Michael Useem. 1971. "Majority Involvement in Minority Movements: Civil Rights, Abolition, Untouchability." *Journal of Social Issues* 27 (No. 1): 81–104.

Marx, Groucho. 1967. *The Groucho Letters: Letters From and To Groucho Marx*. New York: Simon and Schuster.

Marx, Karl. [1895] 1964. *Class Struggles in France, 1848–1850*. New York: International Publishers.

Marx, Karl, and Friedrich Engels. [1848] 1968. *The Communist Manifesto.* Middlesex, England: Penguin.

———. [1846] 1970. *The German Ideology.* New York: International Publishers.

Mason, T. David. 1984. "Individual Participation in Collective Racial Violence: A Rational Choice Synthesis." *American Political Science Review* 78 (December): 1040–56.

Mason, T. David, and Dale A. Krane. 1989. "The Political Economy of Death Squads: Toward a Theory of the Impact of State–Sanctioned Terror." *International Studies Quarterly* 33 (June): 175–98.

Masters, Roger D. 1983. "The Biological Nature of the State." *World Politics* 35 (January): 161–93.

Melucci, Alberto. 1980. "The New Social Movements: A Theoretical Approach." *Social Science Information* 19 (No. 2): 199–226.

———. 1984. "An End to Social Movements?" *Social Science Information* 23 (No. 4/5): 819–35.

Merkl, Peter H. 1986a. "Prologue." In *Political Violence and Terror: Motifs and Motivations*, ed. Peter H. Merkl, pp. 1–15. Berkeley: University of California Press.

———. 1986b. "Approaches to the Study of Political Violence." In *Political Violence and Terror: Motifs and Motivations*, ed. Peter H. Merkl, pp. 19–59. Berkeley: University of California Press.

Merriman, Robert B. 1938. *Six Contemporaneous Revolutions.* Oxford: Clarendon Press.

Messinger, Sheldon L. 1955. "Organizational Transformation: A Case Study of a Declining Social Movement." *American Sociological Review* 20 (February): 3–10.

Michels, Robert. [1919] 1962. *Political Parties: A Sociological Study of the Oligarchical Tendencies of Modern Democracy.* New York: Free Press.

Mickolus, Edward F. 1980. *Transnational Terrorism: A Chronology of Events, 1968–1979.* Westport, Conn.: Greenwood Press.

Midlarsky, Manus I., Martha Crenshaw, and Fumihiko Yoshida. 1980. "Why Violence Spreads: The Contagion of International Terrorism." *International Studies Quarterly* 24 (June): 262–98.

Migdal, Joel S. 1974. *Peasants, Politics, and Revolution: Pressures Toward Political and Social Change in the Third World.* Princeton, N.J.: Princeton University Press.

Milgram, Stanley. 1974. *Obedience to Authority.* New York: Harper Torchbooks.

Miliband, Ralph. 1981. "Kolakowski's Anti-Marx." *Political Studies* 29 (March): 115–22.

Miller, Gary J. 1990. "Managerial Dilemmas: Political Leadership in Hierarchies." In *The Limits of Rationality*, ed. Karen Schweers Cook and Margaret Levi, pp. 324–48. Chicago: University of Chicago Press.

Mitchell, Robert Cameron. 1979. "National Environmental Lobbies and the Apparent Illogic of Collective Action." In *Collective Decision-Making: Applications from Public Choice Theory*, ed. Clifford S. Russell, pp. 87–121. Baltimore, Md.: Johns Hopkins University Press.

Moe, Terry M. 1980a. *The Organization of Interests: Incentives and the Internal Dynamics of Political Interest Groups*. Chicago: University of Chicago Press.

———. 1980b. "A Calculus of Group Membership." *American Journal of Political Science* 24 (November): 593–632.

Moore, Barrington, Jr. 1966. *The Social Origins of Dictatorship and Democracy: Lord and Peasant in the Making of the Modern World*. Boston: Beacon Press.

———. 1978. *Injustice: The Social Bases of Obedience and Revolt*. White Plains, N.Y.: M. E. Sharpe.

Moore, Will. 1991. *Why Internal Wars End: The Decision to Fight, Negotiate or Surrender*. Ph. D. Dissertation. University of Colorado, Boulder.

Morris, Aldon. 1984. *The Origins of the Civil Rights Movement: Black Communities Organizing for Change*. New York: Free Press.

Mosca, Gaetano. 1939. *The Ruling Class*. Trans. Arthur Livingston. New York: McGraw-Hill.

Mousnier, Roland E. 1970. *Peasant Uprisings in Seventeenth Century France, Russia, and China*. Trans. Brian Pearce. New York: Harper & Row.

Moynihan, Daniel P. 1969. *Maximum Feasible Misunderstanding: Community Action in the War on Poverty*. New York: Free Press.

Mueller, Carol McClurg. 1992. "Building Social Movement Theory." In *Frontiers in Social Movement Theory*, ed. Aldon D. Morris and Carol McClurg Mueller, pp. 3–25. New Haven, Conn.: Yale University Press.

Mueller, Dennis C. 1989. *Public Choice II*. Cambridge: Cambridge University Press.

Muller, Edward N. 1972. "A Test of a Partial Theory of Potential for Political Violence." *American Political Science Review* 66 (No. 3): 928–59.

———. 1977. "Behavioral Correlates of Political Support." *American Political Science Review* 71 (July): 454–67.

———. 1979. *Aggressive Political Participation*. Princeton, N.J.: Princeton University Press.

Muller, Edward N., Henry A. Dietz, and Steven E. Finkel. 1991. "Discontent and the Expected Utility of Rebellion: The Case of Peru." *American Political Science Review* 85 (December): 1261–82.

Muller, Edward N., and Karl-Dieter Opp. 1986. "Rational Choice and Rebellious Collective Action." *American Political Science Review* 80 (June): 471–87.

————. 1987. "Rebellious Collective Action Revisited." *American Political Science Review* 81 (June): 557–64.

Nagel, Jack H. 1987. *Participation*. Englewood Cliffs, N.J.: Prentice-Hall.

Nagel, Joane. 1982. "The Political Mobilization of Native Americans." *The Social Science Journal* 19 (July): 37–45.

Navarro, Marysa. 1989. "The Personal is Political: Las Madres de Plaza de Mayo." In *Power and Popular Protest: Latin American Social Movements*, ed. Susan Eckstein, pp. 241–58. Berkeley: University of California Press.

Needler, Martin C. 1966. "Political Development and Military Intervention in Latin America." *American Political Science Review* 60 (September): 616–26.

Nelson, Joan. 1970. "The Urban Poor: Disruption or Political Integration in Third World Cities?" *World Politics* 22 (April): 393–414.

Nie, Norman, G. Bingham Powell, Jr., and Kenneth Prewitt. 1969a. "Social Structure and Political Participation: Developmental Relationships, Part I." *American Political Science Review* 63 (September): 361–78.

————. 1969b. "Social Structure and Political Participation: Developmental Relationships, Part II." *American Political Science Review* 63 (September): 808–32.

Nieburg, H. L. 1962. "The Threat of Violence and Social Change." *American Political Science Review* 56 (December): 865–73.

————. 1969. *Political Violence: The Behavioral Process*. New York: St. Martin's.

Nielsen, Francois. 1985. "Toward a Theory of Ethnic Solidarity in Modern Societies." *American Sociological Review* 50 (April): 133–49.

Niskanen, William A., Jr. 1971. *Bureaucracy and Representative Government*. Chicago: Aldine Atherton.

Nordlinger, Eric A. 1967. *The Working-Class Tories: Authority, Deference and Stable Democracy*. Berkeley: University of California Press.

————. 1977. *Soldiers in Politics: Military Coups and Governments*. Englewood Cliffs, N.J.: Prentice-Hall.

North, Douglass C. 1981. *Structure and Change in Economic History*. New York: W. W. Norton.

North, Robert C., with Ithiel de Sola Pool. 1965. "Kuomintang and Chinese Communist Elites." In *World Revolutionary Elites: Studies in Coercive Ideological Movements*, ed. Harold D. Lasswell and Daniel Lerner, pp. 319–455. Cambridge, Mass.: M.I.T. Press.

Oakland, William H. 1987. "Theory of Public Goods." In *Handbook of Public Economics. Volume II*, ed. Alan J. Auerbach and Martin Feldstein, pp. 485–535. Amsterdam, Netherlands: Elsevier Science.

Oberschall, Anthony. 1970. "Group Violence: Some Hypotheses and Empirical Uniformities." *Law and Society Review* 5 (August): 61–92.

―――. 1973. *Social Conflict and Social Movements*. Englewood Cliffs, N.J.: Prentice-Hall.

―――. 1979. "Protracted Conflict." In *The Dynamics of Social Movements: Resource Mobilization, Social Control and Tactics*, ed. Mayer N. Zald and John D. McCarthy, pp. 45–70. Cambridge, Mass.: Winthrop.

―――. 1980. "Loosely Structured Collective Conflict: A Theory and An Application." *Research in Social Movements, Conflicts and Change* 3: 45–68.

O'Brien, David J. 1974. "The Public Goods Dilemma and the 'Apathy' of the Poor toward Neighborhood Organization." *Social Service Review* 48 (June): 229–44.

O'Donnell, Guillermo, and Philippe C. Schmitter. 1986. *Transitions from Authoritarian Rule: Tentative Conclusions About Uncertain Democracies*. Baltimore, Md.: Johns Hopkins University Press.

O'Kane, Rosemary H. T. 1981. "A Probabalistic Approach to the Causes of Coups d'Etat." *British Journal of Political Science* 11 (July): 287–308.

Olofsson, Gunnar. 1988. "After the Working-class Movement? An Essay on What's 'New' and What's 'Social' in the New Social Movements." *Acta Sociologica* 31 (No. 1): 15–34.

Olsen, Marvin, Harry Perlstadt, Valencia Fonseca, and Joanne Hogan. 1989. "Participation in Neighborhood Associations." *Sociological Focus* 22 (February): 1–17.

Olson, Mancur, Jr. 1965. *The Logic of Collective Action: Public Goods and the Theory of Groups*. Cambridge, Mass.: Harvard University Press.

―――. 1969. "The Relationship Between Economics and the Other Social Sciences: The Province of a 'Social Report'." In *Politics and the Social Sciences*, ed. Seymour Martin Lipset, pp. 137–62. New York: Oxford University Press.

―――. 1982. *The Rise and Decline of Nations: Economic Growth, Stagflation, and Social Rigidities*. New Haven, Conn.: Yale University Press.

―――. 1990. "The Logic of Collective Action in Soviet-Type Societies." *Journal of Soviet Nationalities* 1 (Summer): 8–27.

―――. 1991a. "Can Saddam Win By Losing." Unpublished manuscript. University of Maryland.

―――. 1991b. "The Strategic Plan." *Wall Street Journal*, Monday, February 25.

―――. 1991c. "Why Saddam Hasn't Been Assassinated." *Wall Street Journal*, Friday, February 22.

―――. 1991d. "Strong Ground Assault Must Break Hussein's Grip." *New York Newsday*, Monday, February 4.

Olzak, Susan. 1985. "Ethnicity and Theories of Ethnic Collective Action." *Research in Social Movements, Conflicts and Change* 8: 65–85.

Ophuls, W. 1977. *Ecology and the Politics of Scarcity: Prologue to a Politi-*

*cal Theory of the Steady State*. San Francisco: W. H. Freeman.

Opp, Karl-Dieter. 1986. "Soft Incentives and Collective Action: Participation in the Anti-Nuclear Movement." *British Journal of Political Science* 16 (January): 87–112.

———. 1989. *The Rationality of Political Protest: A Comparative Analysis of Rational Choice Theory*. Boulder, Colo.: Westview.

Opp, Karl-Dieter, and Christiane Gern. 1993. "Dissident Groups, Personal Networks, and Spontaneous Cooperation: The East German Revolution of 1989." *American Sociological Review* 58 (October): 659–80.

Oppenheimer, Martin, and George Lakey. 1964. *A Manual For Direct Action: Strategies and Tactics for Civil Rights and Other Nonviolent Protest Movements*. Chicago: Quadrangle Books.

Orum, Anthony M. 1972. *Black Students in Protest*. Washington, D. C.: American Sociological Association.

Osanka, Franklin Mark. 1971. "Social Dynamics of Revolutionary Guerrilla Warfare." In *Handbook of Military Institutions*, ed. Roger Little, pp. 399–416. Beverly Hills: Sage.

Osayimwese, Iz. 1983. "An Economic Analysis of International Violence." In *International Violence*, ed. Tunde Adeniran and Yonah Alexander, pp. 182–97. New York: Praeger.

Ostrom, Elinor. 1990. *Governing the Commons: The Evolution of Institutions for Collective Action*. Cambridge: Cambridge University Press.

———. 1992. "The Rudiments of a Theory of the Origins, Survival, and Performance of Common-Property Institutions." In *Making the Commons Work: Theory, Practice, and Policy*, ed. Daniel W. Bromley, pp. 293–318. San Francisco: Institute for Contemporary Studies Press.

Paige, Jeffery M. 1975. *Agrarian Revolution: Social Movements and Export Agriculture in the Underdeveloped World*. New York: Free Press.

Papagos, Alexander 1962. "Guerrilla Warfare." In *Modern Guerrilla Warfare*, ed. Franklin Mark Osanka, pp. 228–42. New York: Free Press.

Pareto, Vilfredo. [1920] 1980. *Compendium of General Sociology*. Abridged by Giulio Farina, Edited by Elisabeth Abbott. Minneapolis, Minn.: University of Minnesota Press.

Parkinson, C. Northcote. 1957. *Parkinson's Law and Other Studies in Administration*. Boston: Houghton Mifflin.

Parsons, Talcott. 1937. *The Structure of Social Action*. New York: Free Press.

———. 1951. *The Social System*. New York: Free Press.

———. 1963. "On the Concept of Political Power." *Proceedings of the American Philosophical Society* 107 (No. 3): 232–62.

———. 1964. "Some Reflections on the Place of Force in Social Process." In *Internal War*, ed. Harry Eckstein, pp. 33–70. Glencoe, Ill.: Free Press.

Perrow, Charles. 1979. "The Sixties Observed." In *The Dynamics of Social Movements, Resource Mobilization, Social Control, and Tactics*, ed.

Mayer N. Zald and John D. McCarthy, pp. 192–211. Cambridge, Mass.: Winthrop.

Perry, Elizabeth J. 1984. "Collective Violence in China, 1880–1980." *Theory and Society* 13 (May): 427–54.

Petras, James, and Maurice Zeitlin. 1967. "Miners and Agrarian Radicalism." *American Sociological Review* 32 (August): 578-86.

Pettee, George Sawyer. [1938] 1971. *The Process of Revolution*. New York: Howard Fertig.

Pichardo, Nelson A. 1988. "Resource Mobilization: An Analysis of Conflicting Theoretical Variations." *Sociological Quarterly* 29 (No. 1): 97–110.

Pinard, Maurice. 1968. "Mass Society and Political Movements: A New Formulation." *American Journal of Sociology* 73 (May): 682–90.

————. 1971. *The Rise of a Third Party: A Study in Crisis Politics*. Englewood Cliffs, N.J.: Prentice-Hall.

Piven, Frances Fox. 1976. "The Social Structuring of Political Protest." *Politics and Society* 6 (No. 3): 297–326.

Piven, Frances Fox, and Richard A. Cloward. 1971. *Regulating the Poor*. New York: Vintage Books.

————. 1979. *Poor People's Movements: Why They Succeed, How They Fail*. New York: Pantheon.

Poggi, Gianfranco. 1978. *The Development of the Modern State: A Sociological Introduction*. Stanford, Calif.: Stanford University Press.

Pollock, Philip H. III. 1982. "Organizations as Agents of Mobilization: How Does Group Activity Affect Political Participation?" *American Journal of Political Science* 26 (August): 485–503.

Popkin, Samuel L. 1979. *The Rational Peasant: The Political Economy of Rural Society in Vietnam*. Berkeley: University of California Press.

————. 1988. "Political Entrepreneurs and Peasant Movements in Vietnam." In *Rationality and Revolution*, ed. Michael Taylor, pp. 9–62. Cambridge: Cambridge University Press.

Popper, Karl R. 1968. *The Logic of Scientific Discovery*. New York: Harper & Row.

Poulantzas, Nicos. 1975. *Political Power and Social Classes*. Atlantic Highlands: Humanities.

Powell, G. Bingham, Jr. 1982. *Contemporary Democracies: Participation, Stability, and Violence*. Cambridge, Mass.: Harvard University Press.

Price, David E., and Michael Lupfer. 1973. "Volunteers for Gore: The Impact of a Precinct-Level Canvass in Three Tennessee Cities." *Journal of Politics* 35 (May): 410–38.

Pruitt, Dean G., and Jeffrey Z. Rubin. 1986. *Social Conflict: Escalation, Stalemate, and Settlement*. New York: Random House.

Przeworski, Adam. 1985a. *Capitalism and Social Democracy*. Cambridge: Cambridge University Press.

————. 1985b. "Marxism and Rational Choice." *Politics and Society* 14 (4): 379–409.

————. 1986. "Some Problems in the Study of the Transition to Democracy." In *Transitions from Authoritarian Rule: Comparative Perpsectives*, ed. Guillermo O'Donnell, Philippe C. Schmitter, and Laurence Whitehead, pp. 47-63. Cambridge: Cambridge University Press.

Pye, Lucien W. 1956. *Guerrilla Communism in Malaya: Its Social and Political Meaning*. Princeton, N.J.: Princeton University Press.

Quattrone, George A., and Amos Tversky. 1988. "Contrasting Rational and Psychological Analyses of Political Choice." *American Political Science Review* 82 (September): 719–36.

Rabushka, Alvin, and Kenneth A. Shepsle. 1971. "Political Entrepreneurship and Patterns of Democratic Instability in Plural Societies." *Race* 12 (April): 461–76.

————. 1972. *Politics in Plural Societies: A Theory of Democratic Instability*. Columbus, Ohio: Charles E. Merrill Publishing Co.

Rapoport, Amnon. 1985. "Provision of Public Goods and the MCS Experimental Paradigm." *American Political Science Review* 79 (March): 148–55.

Rapoport, Amnon, and Gary Bornstein. 1989. "Solving Public Goods Problems in Competition between Equal and Unequal Size Groups." *Journal of Conflict Resolution* 33 (September): 460–79.

Rapoport, David C. 1984. "Fear and Trembling: Terrorism in Three Religious Traditions." *American Political Science Review* 78 (September): 658–77.

Rawls, John. 1971. *A Theory of Justice*. Cambridge, Mass.: Belknap.

Reif, Linda L. 1986. "Women in Latin American Guerrilla Movements." *Comparative Politics* 18 (January): 147–69.

Rex, John. 1961. *Key Problems in Sociological Theory*. London: Routledge & Kegan Paul.

Rich, Richard C. 1980. "The Dynamics of Leadership in Neighborhood Organizations." *Social Science Quarterly* 60 (March): 570–87.

Riker, William H. 1982. *Liberalism Against Populism: A Confrontation Between the Theory of Democracy and the Theory of Social Choice*. San Francisco: W. H. Freeman.

Riker, William H., and Steven J. Brams. 1973. "The Paradox of Vote Trading." *American Political Science Review* 67 (December): 1235–47.

Riker, William H., and Peter C. Ordeshook. 1968. "A Theory of the Calculus of Voting." *American Political Science Review* 72 (March): 25–42.

Robertson, Priscilla. 1952. *Revolutions of 1848: A Social History*. Princeton, N.J.: Princeton University Press.

Rochon, Thomas R. 1972. "Direct Democracy or Organized Futility? Action Groups in the Netherlands." *Comparative Political Studies* 15 (April): 3–28.

Roeder, Philip G. 1982. "Rational Revolution: Extension of the 'By Product' Model of Revolutionary Involvement." *Western Political Quarterly* 35(March): 5–23.

Rogowski, Ronald. 1974. *Rational Legitimacy: A Theory of Political Support*. Princeton, N.J.: Princeton University Press.

———. 1985. "Causes and Varieties of Nationalism: A Rationalist Account." In *New Nationalisms of the Developed West: Toward Explanation*, ed. Edward Tiryakian and Ronald Rogowski, pp. 87–108. Boston: Allen and Unwin.

———. 1989. *Commerce and Coalitions: How Trade Affects Domestic Political Alignments*. Princeton, N.J.: Princeton University Press.

Rogowski, Ronald, and Lois Wasserspring. 1971. *Does Political Development Exist? Corporatism in Old and New Societies*. Beverly Hills: Sage Professional Papers in Comparative Politics, 01–024.

Rose, Richard, and Derek Urwin. 1969. "Social Cohesion, Political Parties and Strains in Regimes." *Comparative Political Studies* 2 (April): 7–67.

Rosen, Sherwin. 1985. "Implicit Contracts: A Survey." *Journal of Economic Literature* 23 (September): 1144–75.

Ross, Jeffrey Ian and Ted Robert Gurr. 1989. "Why Terrorism Subsides: A Comparative Study of Canada and the United States." *Comparative Politics* 21 (July): 405–26.

Ross, Marc Howard, and Elizabeth Homer. 1976. "Galton's Problem in Cross-National Research." *World Politics* 29 (October): 1–28.

Rothenberg, Lawrence S. 1988. "Organizational Maintenance and the Retention Decision in Groups." *American Political Science Review* 82 (December): 1129–52.

Rothman, Stanley. 1970. "Barrington Moore and the Dialectics of Revolution: An Essay Review." *American Political Science Review* 64 (March): 61–85.

Rubenstein, Richard E. 1987. *Alchemists of Revolution: Terrorism in the Modern World*. New York: Basic Books.

Rudé, George. 1959. *The Crowd in the French Revolution*. London: Oxford University Press.

———. 1964. *The Crowd in History, 1730–1848*. New York: John Wiley & Sons.

Rule, James B. 1988. *Theories of Civil Violence*. Berkeley: University of California Press.

Rule, James B., and Charles Tilly. 1975. "Political Process in Revolutionary

France, 1830–1832." In *1830 in France*, ed. John M. Merriman, pp. 41–85. New York: New Viewpoints.

Runciman, W. G. 1989. *A Treatise on Social Theory. Volume II: Substantive Social Theory*. Cambridge: Cambridge University Press.

Russell, Charles A., Leon J. Banker, Jr., and Bowman H. Miller. 1979. "Out-Inventing the Terrorist." In *Terrorism: Theory and Practice*, ed. Yonah Alexander, David Carlton, and Paul Wilkinson, pp. 3–42. Boulder, Colo.: Westview.

Russell, D. E. H. 1974. *Rebellion, Revolution, and Armed Force: A Comparative Study of Fifteen Countries With Special Emphasis on Cuba and South Africa*. New York: Academic Press.

Sabia, Daniel R., Jr. 1988. "Rationality, Collective Action, and Karl Marx." *American Journal of Political Science* 32 (February): 50–71.

Sabine, George H. 1973. *A History of Political Theory*. Revised by Thomas L. Thorson. 4th Ed. Fort Worth: Holt, Rinehart and Winston.

Sachar, Howard M. [1958] 1990. *The Course of Modern Jewish History*. New Rev. Ed. New York: Vintage Books.

Salert, Barbara. 1982. "On the Concept of Threshold." In *Missing Elements in Political Inquiry: Logic and Levels of Analysis*, ed. Judith A. Gillespie and Dina A. Zinnes, pp. 61–80. Beverly Hills: Sage.

Salisbury, Robert H. 1969. "An Exchange Theory of Interest Groups." *Midwest Journal of Political Science* 13 (February): 1–32.

———. 1975. "Research on Political Participation." *American Journal of Political Science* 19 (May): 323–41.

Sandler, Todd, and John L. Scott. 1987. "Terrorist Success in Hostage-Taking Incidents: An Empirical Study." *Journal of Conflict Resolution* 31 (March): 35–53.

Sandler, Todd, John T. Tschirhart, and Jon Cauley. 1983. "A Theoretical Analysis of Transnational Terrorism." *American Political Science Review* 77 (March): 36–54.

Sassoon, Joseph. 1984. "Ideology, Symbolic Action and Rituality in Social Movements: The Effects on Organizational Forms." *Social Science Information* 23 (No. 4/5): 861–73.

Schattschneider, E. E. 1960. *The Semi-Sovereign People*. New York: Holt, Rinehart and Winston.

Schelling, Thomas C. 1960. *The Strategy of Conflict*. London: Oxford University Press.

———. 1966. *Arms and Influence*. New Haven, Conn.: Yale University Press.

Schmitter, Philippe C. 1974. "Still The Century of Corporatism?" *Review of Politics* 36 (January): 85–131.

Schuessler, Rudolf. 1989. "Exit Threats and Cooperation Under Anonymity." *Journal of Conflict Resolution* 33 (December): 728–49.

Schwartz, Michael. 1976. *Radical Protest and Social Structure: The Southern Farmers' Alliance and Cotton Tenancy, 1880–1890*. New York: Academic Press.

Schwartz, Thomas. 1987. "Your Vote Counts on Account of the Way It is Counted: An Institutional Solution to the Paradox of Not Voting." *Public Choice* 54 (No. 2): 101–21.

Scott, Andrew, et al. 1970. *Insurgency*. Chapel Hill, N.C.: University of North Carolina Press.

Scott, James C. 1972. "Patron-Client Politics and Political Change in Southeast Asia." *American Political Science Review* 66 (March): 91–113.

———. 1975. "Exploitation in Rural Class Relations." *Comparative Politics* 7 (July): 489–532.

———. 1976. *The Moral Economy of the Peasant: Rebellion and Subsistence in Southeast Asia*. New Haven, Conn.: Yale University Press.

———. 1985. *Weapons of the Weak: Everyday Forms of Peasant Resistance*. New Haven, Conn.: Yale University Press.

———. 1989. "Everyday Forms of Resistance." In *Everyday Forms of Peasant Resistance*, ed. Forrest D. Colburn, pp. 3–33. Armonk, N.Y.: M. E. Sharpe.

Sederberg, Peter C. 1994. *Fires Within: Political Violence and Revolutionary Change*. New York: HarperCollins.

Selden, Mark. 1971. *The Yenan Way in Revolutionary China*. Cambridge, Mass.: Harvard University Press.

Seligman, Adam B. 1992. *The Idea of Civil Society*. New York: Free Press.

Seton-Watson, Hugh. 1951. "Twentieth Century Revolutions." *Political Quarterly* 22 (July): 251–65.

Shalev, Aryeh. 1991. *The Intifada: Causes and Effects*. Boulder, Colo.: Westview.

Shefter, Martin. 1977. "Party and Patronage: Germany, England, and Italy." *Politics and Society* 7 (No. 4): 403–51.

Shin, Eui Hang, and Ik Ki Kim. 1985. "Variations in the Duration of Reign of Monarchs." *Comparative Political Studies* 18 (April): 104–22.

Shorter, Edward, and Charles Tilly. 1974. *Strikes in France, 1830–1968*. New York: Cambridge University Press.

Shubik, Martin. 1971. "Games of Status." *Behavioral Science* 16 (March): 117–29.

———. 1982. *Game Theory in the Social Sciences: Concepts and Solutions*. Cambridge, Mass.: M.I.T Press.

Siegenthaler, Hansjörg. 1989. "Organization, Ideology and the Free Rider

Problem." *Journal of Institutional and Theoretical Economics* 145 (March): 215–31.

Sigelman, Lee. 1975. "Military Size and Political Intervention." *Journal of Political and Military Sociology* 3 (Spring): 95–100.

Simmel, Georg. 1955. *Conflict and the Web of Group Affiliation*. Trans. K. H. Wolff. Glencoe, Ill.: Free Press.

Skocpol, Theda. 1979. *States and Social Revolutions: A Comparative Analysis of France, Russia and China*. Cambridge: Cambridge University Press.

———. 1982. "Rentier State and Shi'a Islam in the Iranian Revolution." *Theory and Society* 11 (May): 265–83.

———. 1985. "Bringing the State Back In: Strategies of Analysis in Current Research." In *Bringing the State Back In*, ed. Peter B. Evans, Dietrich Rueschemeyer, and Theda Skocpol, pp. 3–37. Cambridge: Cambridge University Press.

Slater, P. 1967. *Microcosm*. New York: Wiley.

Smelser, Neil J. 1962. *Theory of Collective Behavior*. New York: Free Press.

Smith, Adam. [1759] 1976a. *The Theory of Moral Sentiments*. Oxford: Clarendon Press.

———. [1776] 1976b. *An Inquiry into the Nature and Causes of the Wealth of Nations*. Chicago: University of Chicago Press.

Smith, Anthony D. 1976. "Introduction: The Formation of Nationalist Movements." In *Nationalist Movements*, ed. Anthony D. Smith, pp. 1–30. New York: St. Martin's.

Snitch, Thomas H. 1982. "Terrorism and Political Assassinations: A Transnational Assessment, 1968–80." *Annals* 463 (September): 54–68.

Snow, David A., and Susan E. Marshall. 1984. "Cultural Imperialism, Social Movements, and the Islamic Revival." In *Social Movements, Conflicts and Change*, vol. 7, ed. Louis Kriesberg, pp. 131–52. Greenwich, Conn.: JAI Press.

Snow, David A., Louis A. Zurcher, Jr., and Sheldon Ekland-Olson. 1980. "Social Networks and Social Movements: A Microstructural Approach to Differential Recruitment." *American Sociological Review* 45 (October): 787–801.

Snyder, David. 1978. "Collective Violence: A Research Agenda and Some Strategic Considerations." *Journal of Conflict Resolution* 22 (September): 499–534.

Snyder, David, and Charles Tilly. 1972. "Hardship and Collective Violence in France, 1830 to 1960." *American Sociological Review* 37 (October): 520–32.

Sorel, Georges. 1950. *Reflections on Violence*. London: Collier Books.

Sorokin, Pitrim. [1925] 1967. *Sociology of Revolution*. New York: Howard Fertig.

Spilerman, Seymour. 1970. "The Causes of Racial Disturbances: A Comparison of Alternative Explanations." *American Sociological Review* 35 (August): 627–49.

Staples, Lee. 1984. *Roots to Power: A Manual for Grassroots Organizing.* New York: Praeger.

Starr, Harvey. 1994. "Revolution and War: Rethinking the Linkage Between Internal and External Conflict." *Political Research Quarterly* 47 (June): 481–507.

Stein, Arthur A. 1976. "Conflict and Cohesion: A Review of the Literature." *Journal of Conflict Resolution* 20 (March): 143–72.

Steiner, Hillel. 1978. "Can a Social Contract be Signed by an Invisible Hand?" In *Democracy, Consensus and Social Contract*, ed. Pierre Birnbaum, Jack Lively and Geraint Perry, pp. 295–316. London: Sage.

Stepan, Alfred. 1985. "State Power and the Strength of Civil Society in the Southern Cone of Latin America." In *Bringing the State Back In*, ed. Peter B. Evans, Dietrich Rueschemeyer, and Theda Skocpol, pp. 317–43. Cambridge: Cambridge University Press.

Stevens, Evelyn P. 1975. "Protest Movement in an Authoritarian Regime: The Mexican Case." *Comparative Politics* 7 (April): 361–82.

Stewart, Charles, Craig Smith, and Robert E. Denton, Jr. 1984. *Persuasion and Social Movements*. Prospect Heights, Ill.: Waveland Press.

Stigler, George J., and Gary S. Becker. 1977. "De Gustibus Non Est Disputandum." *American Economic Review* 67 (March): 76–90.

Stinchcombe, Arthur L. 1975. "Social Structure and Politics." In *Handbook of Political Science: Volume 3—Macropolitical Theory*, ed. Fred I. Greenstein and Nelson W. Polsby, pp. 557–622. Reading, Mass.: Addison-Wesley.

———. 1978. *Theoretical Methods in Social History.* New York: Academic Press.

———. 1990. *Information and Organizations*. Berkeley: University of California Press.

Stohl, Michael, 1988a. "Introduction: Demystifying Terrorism: The Myths and Realities of Contemporary Political Terrorism." In *The Politics of Terrorism*, ed. Michael Stohl, pp. 1–28. 3rd Ed. New York: Marcel Dekker.

———. 1988b. "Conclusion: Responding to the Terrorist Threat: Fashions and Fundamentals." In *The Politics of Terrorism*, ed. Michael Stohl, pp. 579–99. 3rd Ed. New York: Marcel Dekker.

Stone, Lawrence. 1972. *The Causes of the English Revolution: 1529–1642.* New York: Harper Torchbooks.

Strickland, D. A., and R. E. Johnston. 1970. "Issue Elasticity in Political Systems." *Journal of Political Economy* 78 (September/October): 1069–92.

Tarrow, Sidney. 1988. "National Politics and Collective Action: Recent Theory and Research in Western Europe and the United States." *Annual Review of Sociology* 14: 421–40.

———. 1989. *Democracy and Disorder: Protest and Politics in Italy 1965–1975*. Oxford: Clarendon Press.

———. 1991. "'Aiming at a Moving Target': Social Science and the Recent Rebellions in Eastern Europe." *PS: Political Science and Politics* 24 (March): 12–20.

Task Force on Disorders and Terrorism. 1976. *Disorders and Terrorism*. Washington, D.C.: U.S. Department of Justice.

Taylor, Charles Lewis, and David A. Jodice. 1983. *World Handbook of Political and Social Indicators. Volume 2: Political Protest and Government Change*. New Haven, Conn.: Yale University Press.

Taylor, D. Garth. 1986. *Public Opinion and Collective Action: The Boston School Desegregation Conflict*. Chicago: University of Chicago Press.

Taylor, Michael. 1976. *Anarchy and Cooperation*. New York: Wiley.

———. 1982. *Community, Anarchy and Liberty*. Cambridge: Cambridge University Press.

———. 1988. "Rationality and Revolutionary Collective Action." In *Rationality and Revolution*, ed. Michael Taylor, pp. 63–97. Cambridge: Cambridge University Press.

———. 1990. "Cooperation and Rationality: Notes on the Collective Action Problem and Its Solutions." In *The Limits of Rationality*, ed. Karen Schweers Cook and Margaret Levi, pp. 222–40. Chicago: University of Chicago Press.

Taylor, Verta. 1989. "Social Movement Continuity: The Women's Movement in Abeyance." *American Sociological Review* 54 (October): 761–75.

Thompson, Dorothy. 1984. *The Chartists: Popular Politics in the Industrial Revolution*. New York: Pantheon Books.

Thompson, E. P. 1966. *The Making of the English Working Class*. New York: Vintage Books.

Thompson, William R. 1973. "The Grievances of Military Coup-Makers." Beverly Hills, Ca.: *Sage Professional Papers in Comparative Politics*, 01–047.

———. 1978. "Another Look at the Feit-Sigelman Dispute over the Relative Military Size-Coup Propensity Hypothesis." *Journal of Political and Military Sociology* 6 (Spring): 93–99.

Tiebout, Charles M. 1956. "A Pure Theory of Local Expenditures." *Journal of Political Economy* 64 (October): 416–24.

Tillock, Harriet, and Denton E. Morrison. 1979. "Group Size and Contributions to Collective Action: An Examination of Olson's Theory Using Data From Zero Population Growth Inc." *Research in Social Movements, Conflicts, and Change* 2: 131–58.

Tilly, Charles. 1963. "The Analysis of a Counter-Revolution." *History and Theory* 3 (No. 1): 30–58.

————. 1964. *The Vendée*. Cambridge, Mass.: Harvard University Press.

————. 1969. "Collective Violence in European Perspective." In *Violence in America: Historical and Comparative Perspectives*, ed. Hugh Davis Graham and Ted Robert Gurr, pp. 5–34. Washington, D.C.: National Commission on the Causes and Prevention of Violence.

————. 1971. "Review of *Why Men Rebel*." *Journal of Social History* 4 (Summer): 416–20.

————. 1974. "Town and Country in Revolution." In *Peasant Rebellion and Communist Revolution in Asia*, ed. John Wilson Lewis, pp. 271–302. Stanford, Calif.: Stanford University Press.

————. 1975a. "Revolutions and Collective Violence." In *Handbook of Political Science. Volume 3—Macropolitical Theory*, ed. Fred I. Greenstein and Nelson W. Polsby, pp. 483–555. Reading, Mass.: Addison-Wesley.

————. 1975b. "Reflections on the History of European State-Making." In *The Formation of National States in Western Europe*, ed. Charles Tilly, pp. 3–83. Princeton, N.J.: Princeton University Press.

————. 1978. *From Mobilization to Revolution*. Reading, Mass.: Addison-Wesley.

————. 1982. "Routine Conflicts and Peasant Rebellions in Seventeenth-Century France." In *Power and Protest in the Countryside: Studies of Political Unrest in Asia, Europe and Latin America*, ed. Robert Weller and Scott E. Guggenheim, pp. 13–41. Durham, N.C.: Duke University Press.

————. 1984. *Big Structures, Large Processes, Huge Comparisons*. New York: Russell Sage.

————. 1985. "Models and Realities of Popular Collective Action." *Social Research* 52 (Winter): 717–47.

————. 1986. *The Contentious French*. Cambridge, Mass.: Belknap Press.

————. 1993. *European Revolutions, 1492–1992*. Oxford: Blackwell.

Tilly, Charles and Lynn Lees. 1974. "Le peuple de Juin 1848." *Annales: Économies, Sociétés, Civilisations* 29 (Septembre–Octobre): 1061–91.

Tilly, Charles, and R. A. Schweitzer. 1982. "How London and Its Conflicts Changed Shape: 1758–1834." *Historical Methods* 15 (Spring): 67–77.

Tilly, Charles, Louise Tilly, and Richard Tilly. 1975. *The Rebellious Century: 1830–1930*. Cambridge, Mass.: Harvard University Press.

Tocqueville, Alexis de. [1856] 1955. *The Old Régime and The French Revolution*. Garden City, N.Y.: Doubleday.

Tong, James W.. 1988. "Rational Outlaws: Rebels and Bandits in the Ming Dynasty, 1368–1644." In *Rationality and Revolution*, ed. Michael Taylor, pp. 98–128. Cambridge: Cambridge University Press.

————. 1991. *Disorder Under Heaven: Collective Violence in the Ming Dynasty*. Stanford, Calif.: Stanford University Press.

Tönnies, Ferdinand. 1963. *Community and Association*. London: Routledge & Kegan Paul.

Touraine, Alain. 1985. "An Introduction to the Study of Social Movements." *Social Research* 52 (Winter): 749–87.

Trimberger, Ellen Kay. 1978. *Revolution From Above: Military Bureaucrats and Development in Japan, Turkey, Egypt, and Peru*. New Brunswick, N.J.: Transaction Books.

Trotsky, Leon. 1937. *The Revolution Betrayed: What is the Soviet Union and Where is it Going?* Trans. Max Eastman. Garden City, New York: Doubleday, Doran & Co.

————. [1932] 1974. *The History of the Russian Revolution*. Ann Arbor, Mich.: University of Michigan Press.

Truman, David B. 1951. *The Governmental Process: Political Interests and Public Opinion*. 2nd Ed. New York: Alfred A. Knopf.

Tsebelis, George. 1990. *Nested Games: Rational Choice in Comparative Politics*. Berkeley: University of California Press.

Tucker, Robert C. 1969. *The Marxian Revolutionary Idea*. New York: W. W. Norton.

Tullock, Gordon. 1971a. "The Paradox of Revolution." *Public Choice* 11 (Fall): 89–99.

————. 1971b. "A Model of Social Interaction." In *Mathematical Applications in Political Science, V*, ed. James F. Herndon and Joseph L. Berd, pp. 4–28. Charlottesville, Va.: University Press of Virginia.

————. 1979. "The Economics of Revolution." In *Revolutions, Systems, and Theories*, ed. H. J. Johnson, J. J. Leach, and R. G. Muehlmann, pp. 47–60. Dordrecht, Holland: D. Reidel.

————. 1987a. *Autocracy*. Dordrecht, Holland: Kluwer Academic Publishers.

————. 1987b. "Autocracy." In *Economic Imperialism: The Economic Approach Applied Outside of the Field of Economics*, ed. Gerard Radnitzky and Peter Bernholz, pp. 365–81. New York: Paragon House.

Turner, Jonathan H. 1986. *The Structure of Sociological Theory*. 4th Ed. Belmont, Calif.: Wadsworth.

Ulam, Adam B. 1965. *The Bolsheviks: The Intellectual and Political History of the Triumph of Communism in Russia*. New York: Macmillan.

Ullmann-Margalit, Edna. 1977. *The Emergence of Norms*. Oxford: Clarendon Press.

Verba, Sidney, and Norman H. Nie. 1972. *Participation in America: Political Democracy and Social Equality*. New York: Harper & Row.

Verba, Sidney, Norman H. Nie, and Jae-On Kim. 1978. *Participation and Political Equality: A Seven Nation Comparison.* Cambridge: Cambridge University Press.

Walker, Jack L., Jr. 1983. "The Origins of Interest Groups in America." *American Political Science Review* 77 (June): 390–406.

———. 1991. *Mobilizing Interest Groups in America: Patrons, Professions, and Social Movements.* Ann Arbor, Mich.: University of Michigan Press.

Wallerstein, Immanuel. 1974. *The Modern World-System: Capitalist Agriculture and the Origins of the European World-Economy in the Sixteenth Century.* New York: Academic Press.

———. 1983. *Historical Capitalism.* New York: Verso.

———. 1984. *The Politics of the World-Economy: The States, the Movements and the Civilizations.* Cambridge: Cambridge University Press.

Walsh, Edward J., and Rex H. Warland. 1983. "Social Movement Involvement in the Wake of a Nuclear Accident: Activists and Free Riders in the TMI Area." *American Sociological Review* 48 (December): 764–80.

Walt, Stephen M. 1992. "Revolution and War." *World Politics* 44 (April): 321–68.

Walton, John. 1984. *Reluctant Rebels: Comparative Studies of Revolution and Underdevelopment.* New York: Columbia University Press.

Walzer, Michael. 1979. "A Theory of Revolution." *Marxist Perspectives* 2 (Spring): 30–44.

Waterman, Harvey. 1981. "Reasons and Reason: Collective Political Activity in Comparative and Historical Perspective." *World Politics* 33 (July): 554–89.

Webb, Eugen J., et. al. 1981. *Nonreactive Measures in the Social Sciences.* 2nd Ed. Boston: Houghton Mifflin.

Weber, Max. 1946. *From Max Weber: Essays in Sociology.* Trans. and Ed. H. H. Gerth and C. Wright Mills. New York: Oxford University Press.

———. [1924] 1968. *Economy and Society.* Two Volumes. Berkeley: University of California Press.

———. [1904–5] 1985. *The Protestant Ethic and the Spirit of Capitalism.* Trans. Talcott Parsons. London: Unwin Paperbacks.

———. [1896] 1988. *The Agrarian Sociology of Ancient Civilizations.* Trans. R. I. Frank. London: Verso.

———. [1922] 1991. *The Sociology of Religion.* Trans. Ephraim Fischoff. Boston: Beacon Press.

Weede, Erich. 1985. "Dilemmas of Social Order: Collective and Positional Goods, Leadership and Political Conflicts." *Sociological Theory* 3 (Fall): 46–57.

Weiss, Peter. 1965. *The Persecution and Assassination of Jean-Paul Marat as Performed by the Inmates of the Asylum of Charenton under the Direction of the Marquis de Sade*. Trans. Geoffrey Skelton. New York: Atheneum.

Welch, Claude E., Jr. 1980. *The Anatomy of Rebellion*. Albany, N.Y.: State University Press of New York.

Welch, Susan, and Alan Booth. 1974. "Crowding As A Factor in Political Aggression: Theoretical Aspects and An Analysis of Some Cross-national Data." *Social Science Information* 13 (August–October): 151–62.

Wesson, Robert G. 1967. *The Imperial Order*. Berkeley: University of California Press.

White, James W. 1988. "Rational Rioters: Leaders, Followers, and Popular Protest in Early Modern Japan." *Politics and Society* 16 (March): 35–69.

Wickham-Crowley, Timothy P. 1989. "Winners, Losers, and Also-Rans: Toward a Comparative Sociology of Latin American Guerrilla Movements." In *Power and Popular Protest: Latin American Social Movements*, ed. Susan Eckstein, pp. 132–81. Berkeley: University of California Press.

Wildavsky, Aaron B. 1984. *The Nursing Father: Moses as a Political Leader*. University, Al.: University of Alabama Press.

———. 1992. "Indispensable Framework or Just Another Ideology? Prisoner's Dilemma as an Antihierarchical Game." *Rationality and Society* 4 (January): 8–23.

Wilkinson, Paul. 1979. "Terrorist Movements." In *Terrorism: Theory and Practice*, ed. Yonah Alexander, David Carlton, and Paul Wilkinson, pp. 99–117. Boulder, Colo.: Westview.

———. 1986. *Terrorism and the Liberal State*. New York: New York University Press.

Willer, David, and George K. Zollschan. 1964. "Prolegomenon to a Theory of Revolutions." In *Explorations in Social Change*, ed. George K. Zollschan and Walter Hirsch, pp. 125–51. Boston: Houghton Mifflin.

Williams, John T. 1990. "The Political Manipulation of Macroeconomic Policy." *American Political Science Review* 84 (September): 767–95.

Wills, Garry. 1970. *Nixon Agonistes: The Crisis of the Self-Made Man*. New York: Signet.

Wilson, James Q. 1961. "The Strategy of Protest: Problems of Negro Civic Action." *Journal of Conflict Resolution* 5 (September): 291–303.

———. 1973. *Political Organizations*. New York: Basic Books.

Wilson, Kenneth L., and Anthony M. Orum. 1976. "Mobilizing People for Collective Political Action." *Journal of Political and Military Sociology* 4 (Fall): 187–202.

Wintrobe, Ronald. 1990. "The Tinpot and Totalitarian: An Economic Theory of Dictatorship." *American Political Science Review* 84 (September): 849–72.

Wolf, Eric R. 1969. *Peasant Wars of the Twentieth Century.* New York: Harper Torchbooks.

Wolfsfeld, Gadi. 1988. *The Politics of Provocation: Participation and Protest in Israel.* Albany, N.Y.: State University of New York Press.

Woolf, S. J. 1968. "Discussion—Fascism and Society." In *The Nature of Fascism,* ed. S. J. Woolf, pp. 104–15. New York: Random House.

Wrong, Dennis H. 1988. *Power: Its Forms, Bases, and Uses.* Chicago: University of Chicago Press.

Zagorin, Perez. 1982a. *Rebels and Rulers, 1500–1660. Volume I: Society, States, and Early Modern Revolution, Agrarian and Urban Rebellions.* Cambridge: Cambridge University Press.

———. 1982b. *Rebels and Rulers, 1500–1660. Volume II: Provincial Rebellion: Revolutionary Civil Wars, 1560–1660 .* Cambridge: Cambridge University Press.

Zald, Mayer N. 1979. "Macro Issues in the Theory of Social Movements: SMO Interaction, The Role of Counter-Movements and Cross-National Determinants of the Social Movement Sector." Center for Research on Social Organization, University of Michigan: CRSO Working Paper No. 204.

———. 1980. "Issues in the Theory of Social Movements." *Current Perspectives in Social Theory* 1: 61–72.

———. 1988. "The Trajectory of Social Movements in America." *Research in Social Movements, Conflicts and Change* 10: 19–41.

———. 1992. "Looking Backward to Look Forward: Reflections on the Past and Future of the Resource Mobilization Research Program." In *Frontiers in Social Movement Theory,* ed. Aldon D. Morris and Carol McClurg Mueller, pp. 326–48. New Haven, Conn.: Yale University Press.

Zald, Mayer N., and Roberta Ash. 1966. "Social Movement Organizations: Growth, Decay and Change." *Social Forces* 44 (March): 327–41.

Zald, Mayer N., and Michael A. Berger. 1978. "Social Movements in Organizations: Coup d'Etat, Insurgency, and Mass Movements." *American Journal of Sociology* 83 (January): 823–61.

Zald, Mayer N., and John D. McCarthy. 1979a. "Social Movement Industries: Competition and Cooperation Among Movement Organizations." CRSO Working Paper No. 201. Center for Research on Social Organization: University of Michigan.

———. 1979b. "Introduction." In *The Dynamics of Social Movements: Resource Mobilization, Social Control and Tactics,* ed. Mayer N. Zald and John D. McCarthy, pp. 1–5. Cambridge, Mass.: Winthrop.

———. 1979c. "Epilogue: An Agenda for Research." In *The Dynamics of Social Movements: Resource Mobilization, Social Control and Tactics*, ed. Mayer N. Zald and John D. McCarthy, pp. 238–345. Cambridge, Mass.: Winthrop.

———. 1980. "Social Movement Industries: Competition and Cooperation Among Movement Organizations." *Research in Social Movements, Conflicts and Change* 3: 1–20.

———. 1990. *Social Movements in an Organizational Society: Collected Essays*. New Brunswick, N.J.: Transaction Books.

Zimmermann, Ekkart. 1983. *Political Violence, Crises, and Revolutions: Theories and Research*. Cambridge, Mass.: Schenkman.

Zolberg, Aristide R. 1972. "Moments of Madness." *Politics and Society* 2 (Winter): 183–207.

———. 1986. "How Many Exceptionalisms?" In *Working-Class Formation: Nineteenth-Century Patterns in Western Europe and the United States*, ed. Ira Katznelson and Aristide R. Zolberg, pp. 397–455. Princeton, N.J.: Princeton University Press.

Zuckerman, Alan S. 1975. "Political Cleavage: A Conceptual and Theoretical Analysis." *British Journal of Political Science* 5 (April): 231–48.

———. 1989. "The Bases of Political Cohesion: Apply and Reconstructing Crumbling Theories." *Comparative Politics* 21 (July): 473–95.

Zurcher, Louis A. and Russell L. Curtis. 1973. "A Comparative Analysis of Propositions Describing Social Movement Organizations." *Sociological Quarterly* 14 (Spring): 175–88.

# Author Index

# Subject Index